THE LONDON CUSTOMS ACCOUNTS

24 Henry VI (1445/46)

Edited by

STUART JENKS

2018

BÖHLAU VERLAG KÖLN WEIMAR WIEN

Gedruckt mit freundlicher Unterstützung der Possehl-Stiftung Lübeck.

Bibliografische Information der Deutschen Nationalbibliothek:
Die Deutsche Nationalbibliothek verzeichnet diese Publikation in der
Deutschen Nationalbibliografie; detaillierte bibliografische Daten
sind im Internet über http://dnb.d-nb.de abrufbar.

Umschlagabbildung:
Umschlagabbildung: © The British Library Board: MS Julius E IV art. 6, f. 5r
The text, showing Richard Beauchamp, earl of Warwick, supervising the loading of
cloth prior to his pilgrimage to Jerusalem (1408), reads:
Here shewes howe good provisioun made of Englissh clothe and other thynges necessary and licence hadde of the kyng, erle Richard sailed towards the holy londe and specially to the holy cite of Jherusalem, where our lorde Jhesu Criste wilfully suffered his bitter passioun for the redempcioun of al man kynde.

Lindenstraße 14, D-50674 Köln, www.boehlau-verlag.com

Druck und Bindung: Hubert & Co., Göttingen
Gedruckt auf chlor- und säurefreiem Papier
Printed in the EU

ISBN 978-3-412-50708-4

QUELLEN UND DARSTELLUNGEN ZUR HANSISCHEN GESCHICHTE

HERAUSGEGEBEN
VOM
HANSISCHEN GESCHICHTSVEREIN

NEUE FOLGE / BAND LXXIV

For convenience, the c. 45 volumes comprising the edition of the London customs accounts are sub-divided into four series, one for each of the ruling dynasties: I: Plantagenet (c. 1280–1399), II: Lancaster (1399–1461), III: York (1461–85) and IV: Tudor (1485-c. 1550). Each series is divided into several parts (1, 2, 3 etc.). For technical reasons, all of these volumes are deemed to be sub-sections of the present volume, which being the only one to appear in hard copy has been exalted to sovereign status as volume 74 of the series Quellen und Darstellungen zur hansischen Geschichte (Sources and Monographs on Hanseatic History). Its notional place in the complete edition is Series II (Lancaster), Part 9.

2018

BÖHLAU VERLAG KÖLN WEIMAR WIEN

FOREWORD

The publication of this volume marks something of a new departure for the Hansischer Geschichtsverein (Hanseatic History Association), founded in 1870 to promote scholarly research into the history of the German Hanse and its constituent towns, in particular by collecting and publishing the sources on the history of the Hanse and making them available to a larger public. Hitherto, however, the Association has only published customs accounts which have survived in the archives of towns which formerly belonged to the Hanse (Lübeck, Danzig etc.). Publishing a 'foreign' customs account might therefore be seen to exceed the Association's remit and to require some degree of justification.

However, the Hanse, which emerged in the 12th century from the informal and, as time went on, increasingly intense cooperation of towns bereft of royal protection and clinging to one another for security in a dangerous environment,[1] was never 'German' in the modern sense of the word. Indeed, the first known reference to the 'German Hanse' is in an English document (1282), and there was certainly no requirement that the merchants and towns which cooperated with one another under the aegis of the 'German Hanse' be ethnically German. Although the Diet decreed in 1366 that only full citizens of a Hanseatic town were allowed to enjoy Hanseatic rights, particularly overseas (a regulation the Kontore, particularly Bruges, did not accept), this was a far cry from restricting enjoyment of these privileges to ethnic (Low) Germans, although, as a rule, things worked out that way. However, the London Kontor counted among its members a number of merchants from Dinant, then as now a French-speaking town.

Furthermore, the Hanse's raison d'être was 'foreign' trade. Central to its commercial activities were the four overseas Kontore (London, Novgorod, Bruges, Bergen in Norway), which were flanked by numerous lesser settlements and trading posts reaching from present-day Portugal to Russia and Finland, from Scotland and Iceland to the upper reaches of the Vistula in Poland. Young boys were sent to the Kontore and trading posts to learn the local language, gain commercial experience and cultivate contacts with the local population.

Consequently, in the late medieval Hanseatic world, the line between 'domestic' and 'foreign' was much more blurred than it is today. Indeed, within the Hanse's trading area, it might be argued that it (almost) did not exist. Low German, the native language of most Hanseatic merchants, was the lingua franca of the Baltic and North Sea areas. In addition, it was not so far removed

---

[1] For an excellent introduction to the Hanse see Justyna WUBS-MROZEWICZ, 'The Hanse in Medieval and Early Modern Europe: An Introduction', Justyna WUBS-Mrozewicz, Stuart JENKS (eds.), *The Hanse in Medieval and Early Modern Europe* (The Northern World 60), Leiden: Brill, 2013, p. 1-35.

from the medieval forms of English and the Scandinavian languages that communication with the locals was particularly difficult, even without any linguistic training. In the 15th century, young men from Cologne seem to have picked up spoken and written English within a few weeks at the most. And Hanseatic merchants had been treated as free of London since the late 13th century, enjoying a higher status than non-Londoners. To put it another way, a young merchant from Hamburg or Danzig was – literally and figuratively – far less 'foreign' in London than a chapman from Norwich or York.

Therefore, nothing precludes the Association from following the merchants it studies wherever their overseas trade led them. Indeed, it would seem to be incumbent upon the Association to publish any and all customs accounts which throw light on their commercial activities, even if these records are 'foreign'. This applies particularly to England, which was of abiding, indeed paramount importance to the Hanse, and most particularly to London, which in the 15th century was rapidly overshadowing all other English towns and achieving the mighty preeminence which it has never since relinquished.

This volume, covering the London customs accounts for 1445/46 and the sources relevant to the accounting of the customers at the Exchequer, is only the first of many volumes which the Association will publish.[2] For technical reasons, all following books are deemed to be sub-sections of volume 74 of the Association's series Quellen und Darstellungen zur hansischen Geschichte (Sources and Monographs on Hanseatic History). For convenience, they are sub-divided into four series, one for each of the ruling dynasties: I: Plantagenet (c. 1280-1399), II: Lancaster (1399-1461), III: York (1461-85) and IV: Tudor (1485-c. 1550). Each series is divided into several parts (1, 2, 3 etc.). Thus, the first volume of the York series, covering the London customs accounts surviving from the first four regnal years of Edward IV, is designated as 'vol. 74 III 1', the first volume of the Tudor series, covering the accounts surviving from the first five regnal years of Henry VII, as 'vol. 74 IV 1' and so forth. In the end, all extant London customs accounts accounts between 1280 and 1560 will be edited in their entirety.

Rolf Hammel-Kiesow, Vorsitzender des Hansischen Geschichtsvereins
President, Hanseatic History Association

[2] *Subsequent volumes will appear in open access on the Association's website: www.hansischergeschichtsverein.de.*

CONTENTS

List of illustrations

List of Tables

List of maps

List of diagrams

List of graphs

ACKNOWLEDGEMENTS

It is my great pleasure to thank all those who over the years patiently answered my many queries on such matters ranging from Latin palaeography to editorial technique and overall editorial strategy, in particular Amanda Bevan, Paul Brand, Margaret Condon, David Crook, Sean Cunningham, Christopher Dyer, Carolyn Fenwick, Evan Jones, Maryanne Kowaleski, Malcolm Mercer, Stephen O'Connor, Mark Ormrod, James Ross, Christopher Whittick and Margaret Yates. In addition, I am grateful to the Public Record Office (as it then was) for appointing me a temporary editor in the summers of 1992 to 1996. I hasten to add that I am equally indebted to the staff behind the counter in Chancery Lane and Kew, who repeated kept out my documents although I had forgotten to reserve them. In addition, I am obliged to the British Academy for a grant-in-aid for the completion of this volume.

The astute reader will have noticed that this volume is being published not by the British Academy in Oxford University Press, but by the Hanseatic History Association in Böhlau (Cologne). Taking over the task, Böhlau was understandably nervous about its legal position. As the *quid pro quo* for its quitclaim in respect of any rights it might have possessed in regard to the present volume, the British Academy required the following statement to be published verbatim.

> This volume was originally (2008) accepted by the British Academy as Volume 45 in its Records of Social and Economic History, New Series, and accordingly announced as forthcoming by Oxford University Press and cited as such in the scholarly literature. It has subsequently been agreed by all parties that it would be more appropriate for the Hansischer Geschichtsverein to take over the publication. I am therefore doubly grateful to the Hansischer Geschichtsverein for agreeing to do this. The text published here is, barring the correction of minor errors and the odd update on the scholarly literature in the footnotes, identical to that submitted to the British Academy.

Finally, I am grateful to the Possehl Foundation (Lübeck) for its financial assistance in publishing this volume.

Fürth, 27 March 2017

A GUIDE TO THE PERPLEXED[1]

In the thirteenth century, the kings of England realized that a good deal of money could be made by imposing duties on merchants trading overseas.[2] Largely, if not universally, the monarch relied on locals to collect these duties, and in turn, required these customers to appear at the Exchequer and account for the income they had collected in his name. Of course, given the amount of money involved, the king didn't just take the customers' word for this. They had to prove that they had taken in every farthing the crown was owed, and they did so by drawing up customs accounts,[3] listing all dutiable imports and exports ship by ship and merchant by merchant, with the duties charged entered into the right margin. Let's look at a typical entry.[4]

> *[3]* Out of the ship of Lam van Passe called 'George of Antwerp' on the same day *[27 Jan. 1446]*

From Goyken van Lente for 500 lb. of hemp. Value 66s 8d............customs 10d
From the said skipper for 60 measures of woad. Value 30s............customs 4½d
From Henry Nase for 2 bales of Toulouse madder, 1 fat with 4 dozen knives, 6 dozen belts, 40 dozen shears and haberdashery of various kinds. Value £6 10s ....customs 19½d

The Exchequer clerks worked through these accounts, checking the customers' calculations line by line – entering a dot over the customs charge if everything was correct and a cross in the left margin if there was any irregularity – and summing up the crown's income page by page. It must have been stultifying work, and it is difficult to avoid the conclusion that the customs accounts are among the most spectacularly dull administrative documents the English

---

[1] If you have already worked with customs accounts, you should skip to the introduction.

[2] In the fifteenth century, the income from such duties formed a large part of the royal income: Stuart Jenks, 'Die Effizienz des englischen Exchequers zur Zeit des Hundertjährigen Krieges' *Archiv für Diplomatik* 33, 1987, p. 337.

[3] These are called the 'particulars of customs accounts' (TNA: PRO, E122) to distinguish them from the enrolled accounts (TNA: PRO, E356), which contain summaries of customs income in a particular port during a particular time under various headings, together with the customers' disbursements of royal customs income.

[4] *infra*, p. 72.

monarchy produced in the middle ages.

However, it is precisely the mindnumbing detail which makes the medieval customs accounts so important. They put flesh on the bare bones of England's trade statistics.[5] The enrolled account for 1445/46 tells us that foreign merchants imported and exported merchandise worth a total of £18,409 6s,[6] but only the customs account tells us about the ship of Lam van Passe and the details of the merchandise Goyken van Lent, Lam van Passe, Henry Nase and all the others shipped in and out of London in 1445/46. With the information the customs accounts provide on shipping, merchants and merchandise, economic historians can ask all sorts of questions. Since foreign trade was largely, if now wholly the province of wealthy merchants who left their footprints all over the urban and national records, particularly because they governed the towns in England and abroad, one can trace the careers of individual merchants, follow the trade of groups of merchants, be they members of one London company like the mercers, citizens of one town like Bristol or foreign nationals like Hansards or Florentines, Genoese and Venetians. In much the same way, the information in the customs accounts on products and prices allows one to focus on one product or another, be it the English cloth, salt, furs and so forth, asking who controlled the trade, how trade volume and prices developed and so forth. Finally, the information the customs accounts provide on shipping can be analyzed to uncover shipping routes and the range as well as the patterns of shipping (in convoy or alone, seasonal variations). One can also characterize individual skippers' mode of operation (plying a regular route or trying one's luck as a tramp steamer) and even piece together a biography or two.[7]

As important as the customs accounts are, they are a comparatively recent addition to the historian's arsenal of sources. They were rediscovered not quite a hundred years ago, in 1911,[8] and not much was made of them before Gras

[5] These are transmitted in the Enrolled Customs Accounts, which survive from 1279/80. As of even date, the first seven volumes of the calendar for the medieval period have appeared under the auspices of the List and Index Society: Stuart Jenks (ed.), *The Enrolled Customs Accounts (PRO, E356, E372, E364) 1279/80-1508/09 (1523/24)* (List and Index Society 303, 306-7, 313-4, 319, 324), London 2004-8. The remaining five volumes will appear more or less yearly.

[6] The enrolled account for petty customs in 1445/46 is edited *infra*, p. 206-14. The figure for miscellaneous alien merchandise is contained in § 2, p. 206.

[7] For a thumbnail biography of Lam (or Lambrecht) van Passe see Gustaaf Asaert, *De Antwerpse scheepvaart in de XVe eeuw (1394-1480). Bijdrage tot de ekonomische geschiedenis van de stad Antwerpen* (Verhandelingen van de Koninklijke Academie voor Wetenschappen, Letteren en Schone Kunsten van België, Klasse der Letteren 72), Brussels 1973, p. 338-41.

[8] Susan Flavin, Evan Jones (eds.), *Bristol's trade with Ireland and the Continent, 1503-1601. The evidence of the Exchequer customs accounts*, Dublin 2009, p. xi, citing *Royal commission on public records, first report*, appendix I, part 1, p. 45 and 47.

stumbled across them quite fortuitously when investigating the English corn trade.[9] In the 1920s, a group of scholars working under the direction of Eileen Power at the London School of Economics studied them intensely, in the hope of demonstrating their value as evidence. Whether the customs accounts recorded real ships, real merchants and the goods they in fact shipped was open to doubt, since one of the group, Eleanor Carus Wilson, was rightly sceptical about another class of royal records, the aulnage accounts.[10] The fruit of their labours was a seminal volume of essays, published in 1933, entitled *Studies in English Trade in the Fifteenth Century*,[11] which marked out the lines of inquiry which have been followed ever since. Five of the seven articles utilized the customs accounts to great effect to discuss trade, and each of them was followed by a host of similar enquiries.

Eileen Power's analysis of the wool trade (p. 39-90) not only spawned a much more detailed study of English wool exports,[12] but also other studies of individual products like salt,[13] furs,[14] wine[15] and lead,[16] all of which made meticulous and systematic use of the customs accounts to ask who was involved in trading a particular product, what different types of wool, salt, furs etc. were traded, the bottoms in which they were shipped (occasionally also the sailing season), prices, the total value or volume of the trade and the share the English and their foreign competitors had in the trade in question.

M.M. Postan's contribution on the economic and political relations between England and the Hanse (p. 91-153) was followed by two more detailed studies of the Hansards in England[17] and of other groups of foreigners

---

[9] Norman Scott Brien Gras, *The Early English Customs System. A documentary study of the institutional and economic history of the customs from the thirteenth to the sixteenth century*, Cambridge/Mass. 1918, p. vii. Gras, p. 3-12, deals with the literature on the customs up to his time.

[10] Eleanor Carus-Wilson, 'The Aulnage accounts: A criticism', *Economic History Review*, 1st Ser., 2, 1929, p. 114-23, repr. E.M. Carus-Wilson, *Medieval Merchant Venturers. Collected Studies*, London 1954, p. 279-91.

[11] Eileen Power, M.M. Postan (eds.), *Studies in English Trade in the Fifteenth Century*, London 1933.

[12] T.H. Lloyd, *The English Wool Trade in the Middle Ages*, Cambridge 1977.

[13] A.R. Bridbury, *England and the Salt Trade in the Later Middle Ages*, Oxford 1955.

[14] Elspeth M. Veale, *The English Fur Trade in the Later Middle Ages*, Oxford 1966, second revised edition London 2003; Robert Delort, *Le commerce des fourrures en occident à la fin du moyen âge (vers 1300-vers 1450)* (Bibliothèque des Écoles Françaises d'Athènes et de Rome fasc. 236), 2 vols., Rome 1978

[15] Margery Kirkbride James, *Studies in the Medieval Wine Trade*, Oxford 1971.

[16] Ian Blanchard, *International Lead production and Trade in the "Age of the Saigerprozess" 1460-1560* (Zeitschrift für Unternehmensgeschichte Beiheft 85), Stuttgart 1995.

[17] Stuart Jenks, *England, die Hanse und Preußen. Handel und Diplomatie, 1377-1474* (Quellen und Darstellungen zur hansischen Geschichte NF 38), 3 vols., Cologne 1992;

trading with England, namely the inhabitants of the Low Countries,[18] Castilians,[19] Irish,[20] Portuguese,[21] Norwegians[22] and Italians.[23] The salient feature of these works is that their authors have systematically tracked down every relevant foreigner in the customs accounts and have used them to build up a typology of the merchandise which was traded back and forth. Some, too, have used the customs accounts to analyze shipping, detailing the provinence of the vessells, their routes and seasonal variations in shipping.

Carus Wilson's article on the English trade with Iceland (p. 155-82) inspired analyses of English trade with Castile[24] and the Mediterranean,[25] while the immense literature on the merchant adventurers[26] and the English trading companies of the sixteenth century[27] lies beyond the scope of this essay.

Finally, Carus Wilson's article on the Overseas Trade of Bristol (p. 183-246) and Thrupp's on the London Grocers (p. 247-92) inaugurated a series of studies of the foreign trade of the urban elites of Bristol,[28] Exeter[29]

John D. Fudge, *Cargoes, Embargoes and Emissaries. The Commercial and Political Interaction of England and the German Hanse, 1450-1510*, Toronto 1995.

[18] N.J.M. Kerling, *Commercial relations of Holland and Zealand with England from the late thirteenth century to the close of the middle ages*, Leiden 1954; Jean de Sturler, *Les relations politiques et les échanges commerciaux entre le ducé de Brabant et l'Angleterre au moyen âge*, Paris 1936; Marie-Rose Thielemans, *Bourgogne et Angleterre: Relations politiques et économiques entre les Pays-Bas bourguignons et l'Angleterre, 1435-1467* (Université Libre de Bruxelles, Travaux de la Faculté de Philosophie et Lettres 30), Brussels 1966.

[19] Wendy R. Childs, *Anglo-Castilian trade in the later Middle Ages*, Manchester 1978.

[20] Wendy R. Childs, 'Ireland's trade with England in the later Middle Ages' *Irish Economic and Social History* 9, 1982, p. 5-33.

[21] Wendy R. Childs, 'Anglo-Portuguese Relations in the Fourteenth Century', James L. Gillespie (ed.), *The Age of Richard II*, Stroud 1997, p. 27-49.

[22] Arnved Nedkvitne, 'Handelssjøfarten mellom Norge og England i høymiddelalderen', *Sjøfartshistorisk Årbok*, 1976, p. 7-252.

[23] A.A. Ruddock, *Italian Merchants and Shipping at Southampton, 1270-1600* (Southampton Records Series 1), Southampton 1951.

[24] Childs, *Anglo-Castilian trade*, covers both English trading to Castile and Castilians trading to England.

[25] Stuart Jenks, *Robert Sturmy's commercial expedition to the Mediterranean (1457/8)* (Bristol Record Society Publications 58), Bristol 2006.

[26] This was inaugurated by an article by Eleanor Carus Wilson, 'The Origins and Early Deveopment of the Merchant Adventurers' Organization in London', *Economic History Review* 1st Ser. 4, 1932/3, p. 147-76, repr. Carus Wilson, *Merchant Adventurers*, p. 143-82.

[27] For a rough overview of the monographic literature on the English companies see Jenks, *Robert Sturmy's commercial expedition*, p. 28-48.

[28] Eleanor Carus Wilson (ed.), *The Overseas Trade of Bristol in the later Middle Ages*

and York, Beverley and Hull.[30] In addition, these articles inspired an interest in the foreign trade of the members of the greater London companies such as the mercers[31] and grocers.[32] Common to all these studies is that the authors have trawled through the customs accounts, looking for the members of the group on which their studies are focussed and identifying the products they imported and exported. This, in turn, prompted them to determine the relative weight of individual merchants within the group and of the entire group in relation to its competitors.

If this survey has conveyed the impression that no stone has been left unturned, that would be false. While much remains to be discovered, it must be emphasized that it is essential to understand the customs accounts in the proper context. They are fiscal documents, forming one part of the procedure imposed on the customers when accounting for the crown's customs income before the Exchequer. That is the reason why all the other accounting documents relating to the London accounts for 1445/46 are published in this edition. More importantly, it is the reason for the highly technical introduction to the volume, which explains the customs system and the Exchequer's accounting procedures.

(Bristol Record Society Publication 7), Bristol 1937.

[29] Maryanne Kowaleski, *Local markets and regional trade in medieval Exeter*, Cambridge 1995.

[30] Jenny Kermode, *Medieval Merchants. York, Beverley and Hull in the Later Middle Ages* (Cambridge Studies in Medieval Life and Thought 38), Cambridge 1998.

[31] Anne Sutton, *The Mercery of London: Trade, Goods and People, 1130-1578*, Aldershot 2005.

[32] Pamela Nightingale, *A Medieval Mercantile Community. The Grocers' Company & the Politics & Trade of London 1000-1485*, New Haven 1995.

INTRODUCTION

An edition of the London customs accounts in the late middle ages does not really need any justification at all. After all, London was the economic centre of England during this period and generated – together with its satellite harbours Ipswich, Colchester, Sandwich and Dover – the vast bulk of the nation's trade turnover. Put very simply, London's trade is in large measure England's trade. In addition, given London's central position in international trade – a phenomenon which can be measured by the prominence of merchants from Italy, the Low Countries and the Hanse – any major development in European trade would be bound to be reflected in London. Since the customs accounts are our prime source for all these momentous regional, national and international changes, editing and publishing them must be a scholarly endeavour of central importance. Moreover, the London accounts are visibly deteriorating due to heavy use. Therefore, it is of paramount importance to transcribe every legible entry of every account, even if it is in parlous shape, before it becomes even more illegible.

This volume is part of a project which covers the period from 1280 to 1560. These years witnessed a number of pan-European economic upheavals which cannot but have left traces in London's trade. The two great bullion famines (1390-1420 and 1440-1460)[1] and the establishment of the Portuguese spice trade in Antwerp (1501/08) following the circumnavigation of Africa in 1498[2] – a development which pulled the rug out from under Venice's trade – both fall within the project's time frame. The entire edition of the London customs accounts will thus provide a unique opportunity to investigate the effects of these European developments on London's trade.

As important as illustrating the history of London's trade in this crucial period is, it is not the sole purpose of this edition. In my view, it is equally important to recognize that the customs accounts constituted the basis of the accounting of the customers at the Exchequer and that these accounting procedures are uncharted territory. Our knowledge of the most advanced financial

---

[1] John Day, 'The Great Bullion Famine of the Fifteenth Century', idem, *The Medieval Market Economy*, Oxford 1987, p. 1-54.

[2] J.H. Parry, 'Transport and Trade Routes', E.E. Rich (ed.), *Cambridge Economic History of Europe, Volume IV: The Economy of Expanding Europe in the Sixteenth and Seventeenth Centuries*, Cambridge/Engl. 1967, p. 164-5. Herman van der Wee, *The Growth of the Antwerp Market and the European Economy (fourteenth-sixteenth centuries)*, 3 vols., The Hague 1963, vol. 2, p. 124-30, 153-7.

administration in medieval Europe is based largely, if not wholly, on the analysis of the Exchequer reform ordinances (1323/26) and the reforms of the 1550s and 1560s.[3] As far as I am aware, no one has yet undertaken an empirical analysis of the accounting procedures actually utilized by the Exchequer in the later middle ages.[4] Consequently, it is the purpose of this volume to show how the accounting system of the Exchequer worked in practice, by publishing all documents relating to the accounting of the London customers at the Exchequer in 24 Henry VI (1445/46).[5]

THE ENGLISH CUSTOMS SYSTEM

Understanding the Exchequer's accounting procedures requires a preliminary description of the English customs system in the late middle ages. During our period, there were 16 customs districts, which were understood to be the stretch of coast between two towns (Map 1). In the case of London, the limits of the customs district were marked by Tilbury (Essex) in the north and Gravesend (Kent) in the south.

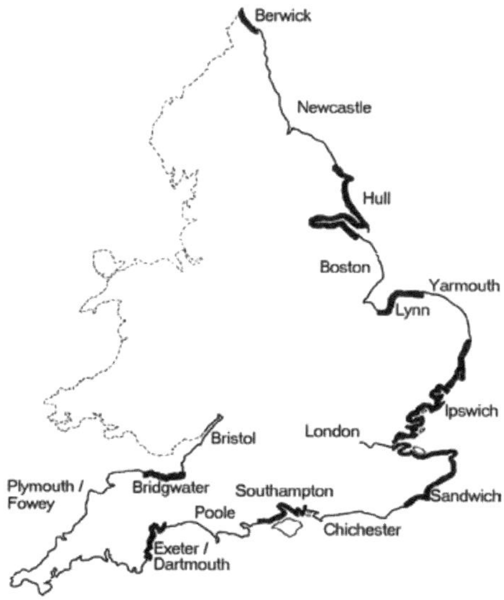

Map 1: English customs districts

[3] The reform ordinances are published in Hubert Hall (ed.), *The Red Book of the Exchequer* (Rolls Series 99), 3 vols., London 1896, vol. 3, p. 848-969 and admirably summarized by Dorothy Broome, *The Exchequer under Edward III. A Preliminary Study*, unpublished dissertation Manchester 1922, p. 14-37. See also M.C. Buck, 'The Reform of the Exchequer, 1316-1326', *English Historical Review* 98, 1983, p. 241-60. The best general study of the Exchequer in the Tudor and early Stuart period is still Frederick Charles Dietz, *English public finance, 1485-1641*, 2 vols., 2nd ed. London 1964. See J.D. Alsop, 'The structure of early Tudor finance, c. 1509-1558', Christopher Coleman, David Starky (eds.), *Revolution Reassessed. Revisions in the History of Tudor Government and Administration*, Oxford 1986, p. 135-62, here p. 135-40, for an excellent survey of the literature.

[4] Roger Schofield, *Taxation under the early Tudors 1485-1547*, Oxford 2004, p. 140-67 undertakes just such an empirical investigation regarding the Exchequer accounting procedures obtaining for collectors of parliamentary subsidies.

[5] The remaining customs accounts (for the period 1390 to 1560) and accounting documents (for the period 1390 to 1460) will be published in digital form on the Hanseatic History Association's website.

All imports and exports were subject to duties, with the following exceptions:

- Coastal, i.e. internal trade was duty-free.[6]
- Goods not intended for trade were exempt.
- Mariners were entitled to import and export small amounts of merchandise (known as 'freeboard').[7]

The duties fell into one of two distinct categories, namely customs and subsidies. From 1353, subsidies – originally extraordinary, emergency aids to the crown, but by 1390 continuously collected – had three characteristics:

- They had to be approved by parliament.
- Parliament set a time limit for the collection of a particular subsidy, after which the grant lapsed.
- Parliament set the rates of the subsidy for the period in which it would be collected.

Customs differed from subsidies in all three characteristics.

- The crown collected them by its own right.
- They were not time-limited.
- The customs rates were unchangeable.

For the sake of convenience, the various customs and subsidies were drawn together. First of all, the customs and subsidies on wool, woolfells and hides (designated collectively as 'staple merchandise'), which formed the bulk of the crown's customs income, were amalgamated (Table 1). The wool subsidy had been granted at 33s 4d/sack (indigenous) and 53s 4d/sack (aliens) for the period from 11 November 1443 to 11 November 1445 by parliament[8] and was extended by the following parliament at the same rates until 11 November 1449.[9] Despite the parliamentary grant, the king reduced the alien rates to 43s 4d/sack or 240 woolfells by a royal mandate under the privy seal to the Exchequer dated 14 July 1442,[10] but only for Italian merchants.

Table 1: Wool customs and subsidy rates in 1445/46

Customs	Indigenous	Aliens
Wool (per sack of 364 lb.)	6s 8d	10s
Woolfells (per 240 fells)	6s 8d	10s
Hides (per last of 200 hides)	13s 4d	20s

[6] Trade with Gascony and Normandy, under crown rule in 1445/46, was dutiable.

[7] The types and amounts of goods considered to be freeboard were regulated by custom. For an example see the interrogation of the mariners in Queenborough (Kent) in 1375: Travers Twiss (ed.), *The Black Book of the Admiralty* (Rolls Series 55), 4 vols., London 1871-76, vol. 1, p. 140 § 8-11. See also the discussion of portage in Robin Ward, *The World of the Medieval Shipmaster. Law, Business and the Sea, c. 1350-c.1450*, Woodbridge 2009, p. 107-13.

[8] *Rotuli parliamentorum*, vol. 5, p. 38.

[9] *Rotuli parliamentorum*, vol. 5, p. 69-70.

[10] TNA, PRO: E159/219 Brevia directa baronibus Michaelmas m 4.

Subsidy	Indigenous	Aliens
Wool (per sack of 364 lb.)	33s 4d	43s 4d/53s 4d[11]
Woolfells (per 240 fells)	33s 4d	43s 4d/53s 4d
Hides (per last of 200 hides)	33s 4d	53s 4d

Aside from staple merchandise, the customs administration collected customs and subsidies separately. The petty customs (Table 2) were an amalgamation of the customs agreed between Edward I and foreign merchants in return for the *Carta mercatoria* (1303)[12] and the cloth customs introduced in 1347.[13] Since indigenous merchants were not beneficiaries of the *Carta mercatoria*, they were not subject to the customs rates it stipulated, whereas they did have to pay the cloth customs of 1347, from which the Hansards had managed to claim exemption.[14] Consequently, only the cloth exports of indigenous merchants were subject to petty customs.

Table 2: Petty Customs rates in 1445/46

	Indigenous	Aliens	Hansards
Wax imports (per quintal=100 lb.)	exempt	1s	1s
Other imports and exports	exempt	3d/£	3d/£
pannus curtus de scarleta	2s 4d	5s 6d	2s
pannus curtus de dimidio grano	1s 9d	4s 1d	1s 6d
pannus curtus sine grano	1s 2d	2s 9d	1s
worsted simplex	1d	1½d + 3d/£	3d/£
worsted duplex	2d	3d + 3d/£	3d/£
lecti de worsted simplici	5d	7½d + 3d/£	3d/£
lecti de worsted duplici	9d	13½d + 3d/£	3d/£

The subsidies – tunnage and poundage – had been granted by parliament for the period from 1 April 1443 to 1 April 1445[15] and extended by parliament from 2 April 1445 to 2 April 1449[16] at the same rates (Table 3). Although tunnage and poundage were payable by indigenous and alien merchants alike, there were exceptions for certain kinds of merchandise and certain merchant groups. First, all imports of fresh fish and wine were exempt from poundage – the latter being covered by tunnage – as were all exports of grain, staple mer-

[11] The first rate was valid for Italian merchants, the second for all other aliens. Italians were the only aliens to have exported wool via London in 1445/46.

[12] The best edition is Konstantin Höhlbaum (ed.), *Hansisches Urkundenbuch*, vol. 2, Halle a.S. 1879, No. 31, p. 14-8.

[13] CPR 1345-48, p. 276-7. See also British Library, Additional MS 18.612, f. 93ʳ.

[14] See Stuart Jenks, 'Die Carta mercatoria: Ein "hansisches" Privileg', *Hansische Geschichtsblätter* 108, 1990, p. 45-86.

[15] *Rotuli Parliamentorum*, vol. 5, p. 39.

[16] *Rotuli Parliamentorum*, vol. 5, p. 70.

chandise[17] and victuals for Calais. Second, Hanseatic merchants were exempt from all subsidies, including tunnage and poundage, by virtue of the Treaty of London (22 March 1437).[18] Third, the grant of tunnage and poundage which took effect on 1 April 1437 exempted indigenous merchants from payment of poundage on their cloth exports.[19] Finally, alien imports of sweet Mediterranean wines had been subject to double tunnage since 1431.[20]

Table 3: Tunnage and poundage rates in 1445/46

	Indigenous	Aliens	Hansards
Tunnage: non-sweet wine	3s/tun[21]	3s/tun	exempt
Tunnage: sweet wine	3s/tun	6s/tun	exempt
Poundage	12d/£	12d/£	exempt

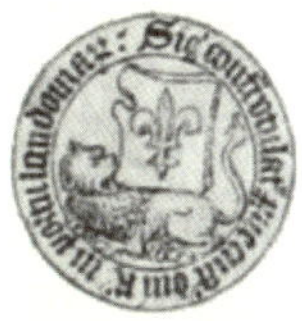

Illustration 1: Seal to be made for John Cotford, controller of the petty customs in London (TNA: PRO, E159/217 Recorda Michaelmas m 2, dated 14 Oct. 1440)

Until the last quarter of the fifteenth century, the customs administration in any given district was comprised of four officials. First and formost were the two customers themselves, who were required to collect the customs and issue the corresponding receipts (cockets) and to account before the Exchequer for all customs income and expenditures at the behest of the crown. In theory, the customers were not permitted to issue customs receipts alone, but only together with the controller, since the cocket was not valid if it was not sealed twice: on the obverse by the customers and on the reverse by the controller.[22] Clearly, any attempt to add the missing seal subsequently would damage the first seal, so that customers and controller were – in theory – forced to issue the cocket together and record the cor-

[17] These were covered by the wool subsidy.

[18] Goswin von der Ropp (ed.), *Hanserecesse*, 2nd series, vol. 2, Leipzig 1878, No. 84 § 3, p. 85.

[19] *Rotuli Parliamentorum*, vol. 4, p. 503.

[20] *Rotuli Parliamentorum*, vol. 4, p. 369.

[21] The tun of wine contained 252 gallons by statute 8 Hen. VI, St. 1, c. 14: A. Luders et al. (eds.), *Statutes of the Realm*, 11 vols., London 1810-28, vol. 2, p. 222-3.

[22] The seals of the customers and of the controller were manufactured in such a way that pins on the lower seal matrix fitted into holes on the upper seal matrix. On this form of seal matrices see Hilary Jenkinson, 'The Study of English Seals: Illustrated Chiefly From Examples in the Public Record Office', *Journal of the British Archaeological Association*, 3rd series, 1, 1937, p. 93-125, reprinted in: *Selected Writings of Sir Hilary Jenkinson*, Gloucester 1980, p. 147-185, here p. 153 (illustration). On the seals of the customs administration see Mabel H. Mills, 'The Collectors of Customs', William A. Morris, Joseph R. Strayer (eds.), *The English Government at Work, 1327-1336. Volume II: Fiscal Administration* (Publications of the Mediaeval Academy of America 48), Cambridge/Mass. 1947, p. 183.

responding imports and exports identically.[23] Finally, the fourth official, the searcher, was responsible for seizing smuggled goods and English currency, which it was illegal to export. The searcher, too, was required to account before the Exchequer for seized currency and the proceeds from the auction of smuggled merchandise.

Before appearing before the Exchequer, the customers drew up an account which listed 1) the ships which had entered or left harbour in the entire customs district with dutiable goods on board, 2) the merchants who owned the goods in question, 3) the value (or amount) of customable goods and 4) the customs or subsidy charge they had incurred. At the same time, the controller drew up a controlment roll, which included all information in the customs accounts with the exception of the charges on the merchandise in question. The difference between these two documents may be illustrated by an example, the first entry from the petty customs account and controlment roll for 24 Henry VI (Table 4).

Table 4: Customs account and controlment roll (Petty Customs, 24 Henry VI)

Customs account	Controlment roll
De navi Matelyn Pycard vocata Trinite de Cane 27° die Januarii *[27 Jan. 1446]*	De navi Matelyn Pycard vocata Trinite de Cane 27° die Januarii *[27 Jan. 1446]*
De Colyn Pavyott pro 2 pak canvas continentibus 1100 alnas, 2 barellis, 1 hoggeshede cum eneo vetere. Precii in toto £18 13s 4d .... cust' 4s 8d	De Colyn Pavyott pro 2 packes canvas continentibus 1100 alnas, 2 barellis, 1 hoggeshede cum eneo vetere. Precii in toto £18 13s 4d

The purpose of the controlment roll was, of course, comparison with the customs account in order to ferret out omissions and irregularities. If one roll omitted a ship or a merchant or recorded a differing total value (or amount) for a merchant's goods, then the customers would be called upon to explain the discrepancy. However, it did not excite suspicion if the two rolls listed the ships entering or leaving harbour on a given day, or indeed the merchants and their products in a different order. In fact, discrepancies of this sort are rather common. They occurred because the customers first recorded imports and exports on tiny strips of paper, as these goods entered or left the port in lighters (Illustration 2).

[23] In practice they delegated this task to a scribe who usually remains nameless. One exception is John Lokington: 1 Henry VI, Petty Customs, documents A 3, A 4 and A 6.

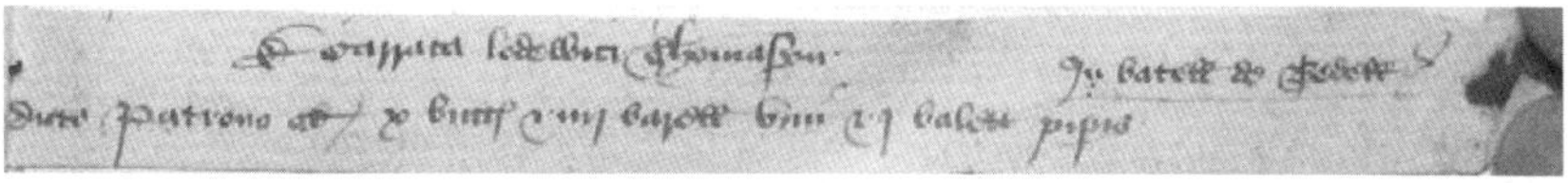

Illustration 2: Customers' first recording of imports (TNA, PRO, E122/161/7/7, probably Southampton, undated)

De carraca Lodewici Thomasyn — In batella de Bedelle

[De] dicto patrono, alienigena, [pro] 10 buttes et 4 barellis vini et 1 balett piperis [seal in red wax]

Since merchants tended to distribute their goods amongst a number of ships in order to spread risk, but wanted to be presented with a single bill for customs or subsidy payments on a given day, the customers first alphabetized these strips of paper by the name of the merchants and then produced the cockets. Consequently, the dates of entry and exit recorded in the customs accounts and controlment rolls always reflect the day on which the cocket was issued, which was not necessarily the same as the ship's date of entry or exit from harbour. Then, in order to produce the customs account, the customers classified the strips by date and ship. Since the controller worked in the same way, it is not surprising that the order of ships whose cockets were issued on a given day might vary between customs account and controlment roll, and the same is true of the order of merchants in a given ship. While, as noted above, discrepancies of this sort did not disturb the Exchequer, its officials did tend – if things got a bit confusing – to mark up the customs accounts, entering a dot in the left-hand margin for each merchant who was also recorded in the controlment roll and another dot above the total value or amount of goods, indicating agreement with the corresponding information in the controlment roll. It was then a very simple task to scan down both margins and spot omissions and discrepancies: if a dot was missing, then there was a problem.

In all customs districts other than London, one unified customs administration, consisting of the two customers and the controller, collected and accounted for wool customs and subsidy, petty customs and tunnage and poundage in a single account.[24] However, in view of the huge turnover in the London customs district, it made sense to appoint three separate groups, responsible for one of the three types of duties respectively. Table 5 shows the personnel of the customs administration in London in 1445/46.

Table 5: Customs administration in London 1445/46 (24 Henry VI)

	Customers	Controller
Wool customs and subsidy	John Poutrell[25] Thomas Pounde	William Baron[26]

[24] In both cases, there was only one search per district.

[25] Appointment 21 Nov. 1442: CFR 1437-45, p. 234 (customs), 237 (subsidy).

[26] Appointment 25 Mar. 1432: CPR 1429-36, p. 189.

Petty customs (29 Sept. 1445-26 Jan. 1446)	John Melburn[27] William de Lunes	John Cotteford[28]
Petty customs (26 Jan.-29 Sept. 1446)	John Melbourne[29] William Chattok	John Cotteford
Tunnage and poundage	Richard Quatermayns[30] Thomas Walsyngham	William Beaufitz[31]

Since London's trade was recorded by three separate groups of customers and controllers, it follows that no one account contains all information on London's trade in its entirety. Staple merchandise was not recorded in the petty customs and tunnage and poundage accounts, and indigenous cloth exports and all Hanseatic imports and exports were omitted in the tunnage and poundage acccount, whilst appearing in the petty customs account. A complete picture of London's trade can therefore only be pieced together when all three types of customs accounts (or their controlment rolls) are transmitted: wool customs and subsidy, tunnage and poundage, petty customs. Since the year 24 Henry VI (1445/46) is the first year within the period from 1390 to 1530 in which all three types of customs accounts are transmitted in fairly full form, its accounts were chosen for publication in this volume: a complete controlment roll for wool customs and subsidy (29 September 1445 to 29 September 1446), a complete customs account and controlment roll for petty customs (for the period from 26 January to 29 September 1446) and the first 24 folios of the tunnage and poundage account, containing imports from 29 September to 14 December 1445.

THE ACCOUNTING OF THE CUSTOMERS AT THE EXCHEQUER

Before entering into a detailed examination of the Exchequer's accounting practices, it is important to say a few words about methodology. Starting in 1392/93, I proceeded in ten year steps to 1462/63, examining all accounting materials of the English customers[32] in all relevant document classes in the Public Record Office (TNA)[33] for the year in question. There seemed little

[27] Appointment 21 June 1443: CFR 1437-45, p. 236.

[28] Appointment 18 Feb. 1435: CPR 1429-36, p. 450.

[29] Appointment 26 Jan. 1446: CFR 1445-52, p. 13.

[30] Appointment not enrolled in CFR, CPR.

[31] Appointment 30 Jan. 1442: CPR 1441-46, p. 33.

[32] With the exception of Berwick. The Berwick accounts tend to cover a number of years rather than only one, as is the case with all other customs districts. Clearly, they cannot be considered comparable with other customs accounts.

[33] These were the Enrolled Customs Accounts (E356), the King's Remembrancer's Memoranda Rolls (E159), the Lord Treasurer's Remembrancer's Memoranda Rolls (E368) and the Pipe Rolls (E372). In addition, I consulted the Accounts, Various (E101), the Issue Rolls (E403), the Bills (E207), the Enrolments of States of Account (E102),

point in extending the investigation to the period prior to 1392/93, since very few accounting documents were enrolled before that year. Ending the investigation in 1462/63 suggested itself because after that year very few issue rolls (TNA: PRO, E403) are transmitted. For the period 3 Edward IV (1463/64) to 19 Edward IV (1479/80) only around a third survive[34] and the series ceases altogether in 1480/81.[35] Since the issue rolls are the only source for the fees and rewards of the customers and controllers, it seemed best to limit the investigation to the period in which they are transmitted without gaps.

The accounting periods of the customers were generally determined by the rhythm of the Exchequer year, which ran from Michaelmas to Michaelmas, exceptions being made if a customer died,[36] resigned from office or was replaced. At the end of an accounting period, the customers wrote out a fair copy of the customs account and attached to it the *parcelle compoti*,[37] comprising the patent letter by which they had been appointed (omitted if they were to continue in office), all royal mandates for payment upon which they had acted, receipts of beneficiaries and so forth. They placed these documents in a parchment bag,[38] together with the tallies which had been presented to them by the recipients of crown payments and the controlment roll. With that, they travelled to Westminster to account.

The King's Remembrancer was responsible for summoning the customers and the controller to the Exchequer at the end of an accounting period. Accordingly, he kept track of who was accountable and who had accounted in his Memoranda Roll. How this was done can be seen if we look at a typical entry,

---

Exchequer Writs: Original Series (E202) and the accounting materials in the Customs Accounts (E122) when relevant.

[34] Easter term rolls have survived for 3, 4, 6-9, 11 and 18-19 Edw. IV. Michaelmas rolls have survived for 6-8 Edw. IV and 18 Edw. IV.

[35] Issue rolls continued to be produced until 1514, but they have not survived: see J.D. Alsop, 'The Exchequer in late medieval government, c 1485-1530', J.G. Rowe (ed.), *Aspects of Late Medieval Government and Society. Essays presented to J.R. Lander*, Toronto 1986, p. 179-212, here p. 188 and Schofield, *Taxation*, p. 263 n. 15.

[36] In this case, of course, the customer's executors accounted.

[37] Originally, the *parcelle compoti* were sewn onto the customs account. Normally, however, these bundles of writs and receipts were separated from the account itself and are transmitted under a different call number.

[38] Some of these bags have survived, and they customarily have an inscription on the outside with details of the account. The London petty customs account and controlment roll for the period 6 Apr. to 1 May 1466 (TNA: PRO, E122/194/17) is transmitted in a leather sack inscribed *Particule compoti Willelmi Hyde et Johannis Thomas nuper collectorum subsidii trium solidorum de dolio et 12 denariorum de libra in portu civitatis nostre London' et in singulis portubus et locis eidem portui adjacentibus, videlicet de hujusmodi subsidio regis ibidem a festo Pasche accidente sexto die Aprilis anno sexto regis nunc Edwardi iiij^{ti}* [6 Apr. 1466] *usque primum diem Maii tunc proximum sequentem* [1 May 1466]; *Contrarotulus Johannis Forster contrarotulatoris ibidem per idem tempus.*

dating from Hilary term 1433.

Suff *Memorandum, quod Johannes Godestone et Johannes Hunt collectores custume lanarum, coriorum et pellium lanutarum ac parve custume nostre necnon subsidii lanarum et pellium lanutarum ac subsidii tonagii et pondagii in portu ville Gippewici venerunt et computarunt a 14 die Marcii anno regni regis Henrici VI decimo* [14 March 1432] *usque ad festum sancti Michaelis proximum sequens* [29 September 1432]. *A quo quidem festum iidem collectores per visum et testimonium Johannis Tyndale contrarotulatoris sunt alias inde computaturi. Ideo preceptum sit vicecomiti comitatus predicti, quod predictos collectores et contrarotulatorem distringat per terras etc., ita etc., in crastino Clausi Pasche* [20 April 1433], *dictos videlicet collectores ad computandum et dictum contrarotulatorem ad testificandum in premissis.*[39]

It will be observed that the summoning of the customers to account was generated by the memorandum on the accounting of their predecessors in office. In continuation of this memorandum, the King's Remembrancer noted who the accountants' successors in office were and the fact that these were now obliged to account (*computaturi*). At a later point in time – and in another scribal hand – the entry notes that the present customers and the controller are to be summoned by a *distringas* writ to appear on a particular return day, here from 20 April 1433,[40] in order to account. When the writ was dispatched, an *'s'* was entered in the margin of the entry, so that it was simple to scan down the membrane and see which officers had been summoned and which not.

Distringas writs were returnable: The sheriff was required to enter onto the dorse of the writ (a) the names of the sureties the customers had found in order to ensure that they would appear as summoned and (b) the annual income (*exitus*) of the customers' real property in the county.[41] As soon as the endorsed writ was returned, the King's Remembrancer looked up the corresponding entry in his Memoranda Roll[42] and entered a large, long-tailed *'r'* over the *'s'*, showing that the summons (s) had been returned (r), as illustrated by the summons to William Beaufitz and Richard Bulstrode to account for the issues of tunnage and poundage in London on 29 Apr. 1454 (Illustration 3).

---

[39] TNA: PRO, E159/209 Recorda Hilary m 2.

[40] The return day was named as *crastinum Clausi Pasche*, which fell on 20 April 1433.

[41] In the case of the Southampton customers Thomas Coke and Thomas Pounde, the sheriff endorsed the writ as follows: *Mauricius Berkeley armiger vicecomes. Manucaptores Thome Pounde infrascripti: Willelmus Smythe, Rogerus West, Robertus Suthe, Ricardus Manne. Exitus terrarum 12d. Thomas Coke infrascriptus nulla habet terras neque tenementa, bona sive catalla in balliva mea, per que distringi potest.* Note that the *exitus terrarum* was net of all *reprisiones, reparaciones et onera inde exeuncia*: TNA: PRO, E159/240 fines ... et visus Michaelmas m 6d.

[42] Note that, often enough, the reference to the Memoranda Roll was entered at the foot of the writ, as the example in n. 45 shows.

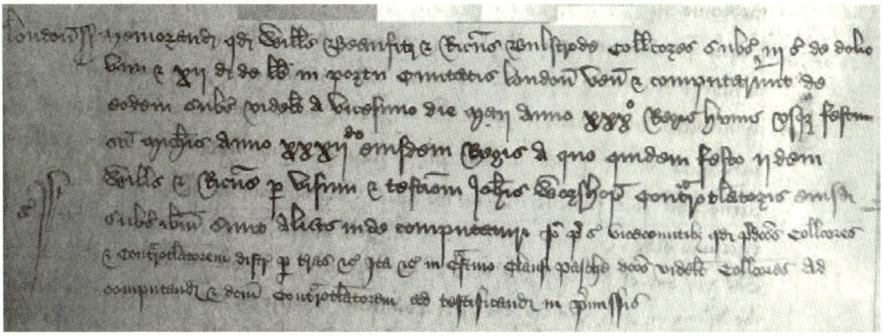

Illustration 3: Summons (*s*) and return (long-tailed *r*) of a *distringas* writ, as noted in the left hand margin[43]

Note that the sheriff had to distrain the customers' real property and chattels, ascertain the annual revenue of their real property in the county and return the writ by the return day, at which he had to produce the customers and the controller in the Exchequer.

Needless to say, problems occasionally cropped up. In the first place, the sheriff might not be able to find the customers and the controller. Moreover, they might not have any real property or chattels in the county which could be distrained. In this case the sheriff entered the appropriate memoranda (*N.N. non est inventus in balliva mea; N.N. nulla habet terras neque tenementa, bona sive catalla in ballia mea, per que distringi potest*) on the dorse of the writ and returned it into the Exchequer.[44] If the sheriff failed to return the writ at all, the King's Remembrancer noted *vicecomes non retornavit breve* in the corresponding entry. Finally, it was far from seldom that – although the customers and the controller had been distrained – they simply did not turn up on the day. This caused the King's Remembrancer to note *vocati non venerunt* in their entry in the Memoranda Roll.

If – for whatever reason – a customer did not appear on the day given to him, the *sicut alias* writ of distraint was issued for the next Exchequer term.[45]

---

[43] TNA: PRO, E159/230 Recorda Hilary m 3d. Transcription: *London' — Memorandum, quod Willelmus Beaufitz et Ricardus Bulstrode collectores subsidii 3s de dolio vini et 12d de libra in portu civitatis London' venerunt et computarunt de eodem subsidio, videlicet a vicesimo die Maii anno 30° regis hujus* [20 May 1452] *usque festum sancti Michaelis anno 32do* [29 Sept. 1453], *a quo quidem festo iidem Willelmus et Ricardus per visum et testimonium Johannis Worshop contrarotulatoris ejusdem subsidii ibidem sunt alias inde computaturi.* [Note change of scribal hand] *Ideo preceptum sit vicecomitibus, quod predictos collectores et contrarotulatorem distringant per terras etc., ita etc., in crastino Clausi Pasche* [29 Apr. 1454], *dictos videlicet collectores ad computandum et dictum contrarotulatorem ad testificandum in premissis.*

[44] Note that this did not necessarily mean that the customers and the controller did not appear at the proper time.

[45] There were three stages within the distraint writ procedure. The second and third were distinguished from the first solely by the inclusion of the words *sicut alias* and

If he once again failed to appear, a *sicut pluries* writ was issued for the following term. If the customer still did not turn up, the Exchequer issued an *attachias per corpus* writ, directing the sheriff to produce the customer, and his goods and chattels were seized into the king's hand by virtue of the writ of distraint.[46] On the basis of a writ of attachment the sheriff would normally take

---

sicut pluries after the command to the the sheriff (*Precipimus tibi*). Take, for instance, the *sicut alias* writ of distraint directed to the Southampton customers Thomas Coke and Thomas Pounde on 12 Apr. 1457 summoning them to account the return day starting on 27 June 1457 (TNA: PRO, E202/138 unnumbered): *Henricus Dei gracia rex Anglie et Francie et dominus Hibernie vicecomiti Suthamptonie salutem. Precipimus tibi sicut alias, quod non omittas propter aliquam libertatem, quin eam ingrediaris et distringas Thomam Coke et Thomam Pounde collectores custume lanarum, coriorum et pellium lanutarum ac parve custume nostre necnon subsidii lanarum et pellium lanutarum ac subsidii tonagii et pondagii in portu ville Suthamptonie per omnes terras et catalla sua in balliva tua, ita quod nec ipsi nec aliquis per ipsos ad ea manum apponeret, donec aliud inde tibi precipimus, et quod de exitibus earundem terrarum nobis respondeas et quod habeas corpora eorum coram baronibus de scaccario nostro apud Westmonasterium a die sancte Trinitatis in 15 dies* [27 June 1457] *ad reddendum nobis compotum de custumis et subsidiis predictis de tempore, quo fuerunt collectores ibidem et non computarunt. Et habeas ibi tunc hoc breve. Teste P. Arderne apud Westmonasterium, 12 die Aprilis anno regni nostri 34. Per rotulum memorandorum et eodem anno 34 regis hujus Michaelis recorda rotulo* [23d]. *Et versus Willelmum Stone contrarotulatorem eorundem custumarum et subsidiorum ibidem fit execucio per aliud breve directum vicecomiti ville Suthamptonie. Essex.* Note that Peter Arderne – who attested the writ – was the Chief Baron of the Exchequer and William Essex King's Remembrancer. This *sicut alias* writ was not recorded in the King's Remembrancer's Memoranda Roll. Rather, the cross reference to TNA: PRO, E159/232 Recorda Michaelmas m 23d leads one to the *venerunt et computarunt* entry for Coke and Pounde's predecessors in office, at the end of which the usual entry was made indicating that Coke and Pounde were now due to account, which in turn generated the first writ of distraint, as indicated by the *'s'* and *'r'* in the margin.

[46] This was the case with the Newcastle customers Thomas Bee and Alan Bird, who although *pluries districti per terras et catalla sua de veniendo hic ad plures dies preteritos et tandem ad crastinum sancti Michaelis supradictum* [30 Sept. 1454] *ad reddendum ... compotum*, had *per hujusmodi districciones seu exitus terrarum suarum forisfacturam justiciari non permiserunt, set reddicionem ejusdem compoti diffuere nituntur, in quantum potuerunt, in contemptum dicti domini regis ac compoti predicti retardacionem manifestum.* Therefore, the Exchequer ordered them to be attached *per corpora sua* to respond to the king for the contempt as well as to account. Furthermore, the Exchequer directed the sheriff to seize all their goods and chattels lands and tenements into the king's hand *nomine districcionis*: (TNA: PRO, E159/230 fines ... visus Michaelmas, unnumbered: http://aalt.law.uh.edu/AALT2/H6/E159no230/aE159no230fronts/IMG_0852.htm). The form of the *attachias* writ is: *Henricus etc. vicecomiti Suthamptonie salutem. Precipimus tibi sicut pluries, quod non omittas propter aliquam libertatem, quin eam ingrediaris et attachies N.N., ubicumque eum inveneris in balliva tua, et eum salvo et secure custodias, ita quod eum habeas coram baronibus de scaccario nostro apud Westmonasterium a die Pasche in 15 dies ad respondendum nobis de* [here followed the type of account to be rendered] *et ad ulterius re-*

sureties from the customer for this appearance, but also had the option of taking him into custody. If the customer appeared after the issuance of the *attachias* writ, he was normally imprisoned in Fleet prison until such time as he requested permission from the Exchequer to make a fine with the crown *pro contemptu regis*. However, lest the accounting procedure be delayed unduly, the Exchequer normally granted permission to find bailees[47] who had to guarantee that the customer would appear for all further stages of the accounting process and until he agreed a fine with the king.

The Exchequer seldom was forced to take such measures. The vast majority of customers and controllers appeared as directed in the first *distringas* writ, and of the few who failed to show up three or more times in a row, most were persuaded to appear in Westminster by the first *attachias* writ. Nonetheless, if a customer was not moved by these measures, then the Exchequer had no other option than to attach him *sicut alias*, and then *sicut pluries* term for term ad infinitum.[48] One Newcastle customer proved particularly recalcitrant. According to the sheriff's returns, Thomas Bee could not be found between 30 September 1454 and 14 October 1458. Furthermore, he had no distrainable property in the county. A total of fifteen *attachias* writs were sent and duly returned by the sheriff, endorsed each time with *non est inventus* and *nulla habet bona*. Finally, in Michaelmas term 1458, the Exchequer learned that Thomas Bee had died in the meantime,[49] which of course meant that there was little to be gained by dispatching further writs northwards. However, the fact that – for fifteen entire terms – the sheriff maintained that he did not have the slightest inkling of where to find Thomas Bee, but then, after almost four years, suddenly knew for certain that he was no longer amongst the living, strains the imagination. Surely, there must have been some sort of collusion. In such cases, the Exchequer was powerless.

---

cipiendum in premissis, quod curia nostra duxerit ordinandum. Et habeas ibi tunc hoc breve. Teste P. Arderne apud Westmonasterium, 12 die Februarii anno regni nostri 34. Per rotulum memorandorum de anno 32 regis hujus Pasche recorda rotulo 9. Essex (TNA: PRO, E202/138 unnumbered). The form of the sheriff's response on the dorse of an *attachias* writ is identical to that on the dorse of a *distringas* writ.

[47] For instance, when Alan Byrd finally appeared, he was incarcerated in Fleet prison. Immediately thereafter the record notes: *Et incontinenti ex gracia curie idem Alanus traditur in ballium* [four names follow], *videlicet cuilibet eorum corpus pro corpore:* TNA: PRO, E159/230 Fines ... visus Michaelmas (unnumbered): http://aalt.law.uh.edu/AALT2/H6/E159no230/aE159no230fronts/IMG_0852.htm.

[48] In the case of Nicholas Stebbyng, who had been distrained to account for the issues of customs and subsidies in Exeter/Dartmouth and then attached, the Exchequer fined one sheriff after another for untruthfully returning that the customer could not be found and under-reporting the value of his goods and chattels: TNA: PRO, E159/228 Fines ... visus m 13-14: http://aalt.law.uh.edu/AALT2/H6/E159no2228/aE159no228fronts/IMG_0592.htm, IMG_1312.htm and IMG_593.htm.

[49] TNA: PRO, E159/230 Fines ... visus Michaelmas, unnumbered.

The rhythm of the summoning of the customers to account was determined by the sessions of the Exchequer, which normally sat from 30 September (*crastinum Michaelis*) to shortly before Christmas (Michaelmas term), from the day after Hilary (14 January) to the beginning of Lent (Hilary term), from the Monday after the Sunday after Easter (*Quasimodo geniti*) until shortly before Pentecost (Easter term) and from the Monday after Trinity Sunday until around mid-July (Trinity term). While the beginnings of the Exchequer terms were fixed, the length of the sessions could vary, depending on how much work had to be done.[50] Fundamentally, the summons were issued at the end of one term for the beginning of the next, for instance at the beginning of Lent for the first day of Easter term (*crastinum Clausi Pasche*). If further summons proved necessary – because the sheriff had not returned the writ or the customers had not appeared – the customers were summoned for the beginning of the next term (*crastinum Michaelis, crastinum Hillarii* etc.). Even if the customers had appeared at the beginning of term as directed and begun to account, they normally had to be summoned repeatedly, as it was normally impossible to complete accounting on one return day. In this case, the Exchequer tended to stipulate the third week of term (*quindena Michaelis* etc.). However, this was not a hard and fast rule: later return days – in the fourth, fifth or even sixth week of term – were not unheard of.[51] All in all, it is clear that the Exchequer did not allow itself to be locked into a rigid schedule when summoning the customers, and all rules deduced from the practical, day-to-day workings of the fifteenth century Exchequer can only be considered rough-and-ready guides. Nonetheless, it is clear that the Exchequer tended to summon the customers for the first return day of term and to schedule follow-up sessions for mid-term.

In the late fourteenth century, the Exchequer customarily summoned the customers to account about a year after the end of the accounting period of their predecessors in office. Since most customs accounts ran from Michaelmas to Michaelmas, customers were normally summoned before the Exchequer on the first day of Michaelmas term,[52] which fell immediately after the

---

[50] See Appendix IV: Exchequer terms.

[51] However, the Exchequer had to take care not to summon the customers too late in term, because very late dates threatened to collide with the accounting sessions for the collectors of parliamentary subsidies (on this see J.F. Willard, *Parliamentary Taxes on Personal Property, 1290 to 1334: A Study in Mediaeval English Financial Administration* (Publications of the Mediaeval Academy of America 19), Cambridge/Mass. 1934). The Enrolments of States of Accounts (TNA: PRO, E102) show that the collectors of parliamentary subsidies were summoned for mid-term. How this worked in practice is best shown by a concrete example. In Michaelmas term 1450, the customers were summoned for one of the first four return days (*crastinum Michaelis* to *mense Michaelis*, 30 Sept. to 28 Oct.), while the collectors of the parliamentary subsidy were summoned for *crastinum Martini* (12 Nov.) and later return days.

[52] This was the case in 19 of 29 accounts in 1392/93, in 14 of 26 accounts in 1393/94 and in 14 of 23 accounts in 1403/04.

final day of the customs account.[53] However, there were exceptions, notably for customs accounts which – measured from the date on which the writ of distraint was dispatched – either had run for over a year (in these cases the customers were summoned on very short notice) or for much less than a year (in these cases the customers were given more time). In any event, it is clear that the Exchequer tended to let the accounts run for a year and only then to summon the customers to account.

THE *VISUS COMPOTI*

This did not mean that the Exchequer turned a blind eye to the customers' activities in the meantime, since the crown was chronically far too short of cash to do so. The issue rolls (TNA: PRO, E403) contain a number of entries for the expenses of messengers sent to summon the customers to Westminster for preliminary accounting. On 6 March 1383, for instance, the customers of Hull, Boston, Lynn, Yarmouth, Ipswich, Sandwich and Southampton were ordered in the middle of their (respective) accounting periods *de essendo coram domino thesaurario et baronibus de scaccario in crastino Clausi Pasche proximo futuro pro certis negociis regis.*[54] Even more common were payments to the tellers of the Exchequer who – like William Hughlot on 26 January 1385 – were dispatched to one or more customs districts *ad examinandum et diligenter inquirendum de dictis collectoribus* [in this instance: Boston and Hull] *de statu officiorum suorum* and above all to transport any and all surplus funds back to Westminster.[55] Interim accounting, of course, only made sense in districts which generated substantial customs income, namely for Southampton and the ports along the east coast. Curiously, however, there seems to be no record in the issue rolls that the London customers were ever summoned for interim accounting, although their district generated by far the most income for the crown, but one such account does in fact survive.[56]

---

[53] The form the Exchequer documents chose to designate the beginning and end of an accounting period gives rise to the impression that both the first and the last day counted. However, in practice, only the last day counted, never the first: *ultimo die computato et non primo* (TNA: PRO, E356/17 m 42). For instance, the header of the controlment roll of William Baron for the London wool customs and subsidy (TNA: PRO, E122/76/40 m 1) states that the account covers the period *a festo sancti Michaelis anno 24to regis Henrici vj^{ti}* [29 Sept. 1445] *usque festum sancti Michaelis tunc proxime sequens* [29 Sept. 1446], but in fact the account covers the period from 30 Sept. 1445 to 29 Sept. 1446.

[54] TNA: PRO, E403/487 m 20. See also E304/475 m 4 (5 Nov. 1380), E403/517 m 3 (10 May 1388) etc.

[55] TNA: PRO, E403/499 m 15 (26 Jan. 1383). See also E403/493 m 15 (25 Feb. 1384), E403/502 m 10 (5 July 1384), E403/510 m 23 (22 Jan. 1387) etc.

[56] This is the *visus compoti* of Adam Bamme and Gilbert Maghefeld for the issues of the London wool customs and subsidy between 29 Sept. 1395 and 24 June 1396 (TNA: PRO, E122/71/19). It is conceiveable that the reason for the lack of explicit issue roll entries regarding the *visus compoti* of London customers is that they are concealed in

Although at the beginning of Richard II's reign interim accounts were described rather vaguely in the issue rolls, the technical term *visus compoti* quickly established itself.[57] A *visus compoti* was comprised of a schedule detailing the customs income to date and all payments the customers had made at the king's behest, whereby income and payments from the various sources of customs income (wool customs, wool subsidy, petty customs, tunnage and poundage) were carefully kept separate. It would appear that the *visus compoti* merely served to inform the Exchequer about the state of the crown's financial resources in a particular customs district. To my knowledge, the Exchequer never ordered the customers to pay over any sums due to the crown, and often enough the customers were granted respite (*respectum*) in regard to payments which they expected to make, but had not yet made at the time of the *visus compoti*.

By 1408/09 rendering a *visus compoti* had become a normal part of the customers' duties. The Exchequer regularly summoned them to Westminster after half a year in office. At that point, a decision was made either to direct that a *visus compoti* be made or simply to summon the customers and the controller for the beginning of the following Michaelmas term.[58] If the Exchequer decided to require an interim account, its first action was to assign an auditor,[59] who examined the documents the customers had proferred and produced a schedule (*cedula*) to be presented as a bill (*billa*) to the Exchequer as a

---

the numerous entries for the tellers' journeys by river (*pro batillagio*) between London and Westminster.

[57] TNA: PRO, E403/505 m 24 (18 Mar. 1386). See also E403/510 m 27 (31 Mar. 1387), E403/515 m 3 (17 Oct. 1387) and m 22 (28 Feb. 1388) etc.

[58] If an interim account was ordered, the customers were summoned along with their colleagues from other districts for final accounting on 30 Sept. (*crastinum Michaelis*). If no *visus compoti* was required, then the customers would either be summoned for 30 Sept. or for *crastinum* or *quindena Trinitatis* (whereupon a further summons for 30 Sept. normally followed). In the handful of cases in which the previous accounting period had not ended on Michaelmas, all summonses followed with a delay of half a year (*visus compoti* at Michaelmas and final accounting from *crastinum Clausi Pasche*). It is also worth mentioning that customers who were required to render a *visus compoti* were always summoned for final accounting by a writ of distraint. With the others, it sufficed to grant them a date of continuance (*dies datus*) and distrain them only if they did not appear. Finally, one should point out that the Exchequer did not begin to record the summoning of the customers systematically (i.e. without gaps) until the beginning of Henry VI's reign (1422/23). Before that, it was common for the King's Remembrancer to record the initial summoning of the customers for 30 Sept. and final accounting in the following Trinity term without bothering to record any summonses for Hilary or Easter terms.

[59] During our period, there were five auditors in all, each earning £10 per annum: J.C. Sainty, *Officers of the Exchequer* (List & Index Society Special Series 18), London 1983, p. 105, 108.

whole.[60] To illustrate the procedure, let us take the *visus compoti* which the auditor Thomas Bennet[61] produced in Easter term 1425 for the London tunnage and poundage customers Thomas Walsingham and William Estfeld with regard to alien imports and exports.[62]

s' *Per Thomam Beneyt*

London' *Visus compoti Thome Walsingham et Willelmi Estfeld collectorum subsidii 3s de dolio et 12d de libra in portu civitatis regis London' et in singulis portubus et locis eidem portui adjacentibus per breve regis patens de magno sigillo suo datum 8 die Februarii anno primo regis nunc,*[63] *scilicet Henrici Sexti, prefatis collectoribus directum et penes ipsos remanens, videlicet de hujusmodi subsidio regis ibidem a festo sancti Michaelis anno tercio dicti regis nunc* [29 September 1424] *usque festum Pasche tunc proximum sequens* [8 April 1425], *per visum et testimonium Ricardi Quatremayns contrarotulatoris regis ibidem per idem tempus.*

Recepte *Iidem respondent de £116 15d de subsidio contingente 773 dolia, 1 pipam et 1 barellum vini diversorum mercatorum alienigenarum tam ad portus et loca predicta adducta quam ab eisdem educta et ibidem custumata infra dictum tempus hujus visus, videlicet de quolibet dolio 3s.*

Et de £1161 15s ¾d de subsidio diversarum rerum et mercandisarum consimilium mercatorum alienigenarum tam ad portus et loca predicta adductarum quam ab eisdem eductarum et ibidem custumatarum per idem tempus, que quidem res et mercandise ad £23,235 15d estimabantur juxta verum valorem earundem, videlicet de qualibet libra 12d.

Summa recepte £1277 16s 3¾d.

[Marginated] *Inde solverunt per 19 tallias £1290 12s 4d*

The auditor's task was simple: All he had to do was to calculate the total income from tunnage and poundage in London during the half-year between Michaelmas 1424 and the following Easter and draw up a corresponding schedule. Against the sum total of the issues of tunnage and poundage with which they had charged themselves (£1277 16s 3¾d), the customers are said to have 'paid' £1290 12s 4d by 19 tallies, as the margination notes.

This raises a number of questions. Clearly, the tallies by which Walsingham and Estfeld 'paid' represent assignments[64] on the issues of tunnage and pound-

---

[60] These schedules are transmitted partly in document class TNA: PRO, E207 (Bills), which is where they belong, and partly in document class E122, where they were filed by error.

[61] For Bennet as auditor see Sainty, *Officers*, p. 116.

[62] TNA: PRO, E122/73/2. I have omitted the entries on the dorse of the *visus*.

[63] CFR 1422-30, p. 37.

[64] Assignments are drafts upon anticipated crown income, which – instead of being paid into the Exchequer at the receipt – was to be disbursed at source to a crown creditor:

age. If they had paid £1290 12s 4d in cash at the receipt of the Exchequer when they appeared in Easter term 1425, they would have only been given one tally as a receipt. Our first question, therefore, is how assignments and, more generally, payments were made at the behest of the crown. Second, we must ask how the customers accounted for funds disbursed by order of the monarch at the *visus compoti*.

In our period, payments could be made by one of two methods: The Tally system and the Writ and Tally system.[65] Since Walsyngham and Estfeld 'paid' by means of 19 tallies and since the vast majority of disbursements in 24 Henry VI were effected by the Tally system (Table 6), it is best to begin with it.

Table 6: Expenditure of customs and subsidy income (nearest £), 24 Henry VI

	Income	Disbursement by		
		Tally	Patent Letter (annuities)	Expense allowances
Wool	11,636	10,238	1364	54
Tunnage & poundage	2079	450	200	0
Petty customs	1327	145	1160	22
Total	**15,041**	**11,333**	**2723**	**76**
Percent		75.35%	24.03%	2.79%

Payment by the Tally system was initiated by a warrant for issue under the privy seal directed to the treasurer and chamberlains, ordering them to pay a certain sum to a named payee, but normally leaving to them the decision of how to do so. Once it arrived in the Exchequer of Receipt, the warrant generated an entry in the issue roll recording disbursement of funds to the payee and – if the Exchequer was unable or unwilling to pay cash – the levying of a tally in assignment and corresponding entries in the tellers' roll (by the clerk of the receipt) and in the receipt roll (by the under-clerk of the receipt) recording payment[66] by the customers to whom the Exchequer had decided to assign the payment. A tally was cut in the Lower Exchequer and split into two parts – the foil and the counterfoil –, the first of which was handed over to the payee and the second deposited with the deputy chamberlains of the receipt in Westminster.[67] The payee then proceeded to present the tally to the customers whose

Anthony Steel, *The Receipt of the Exchequer 1377-1485*, Cambridge 1954, p. xxix-xxxiv.

[65] See Appendix I: How did the crown pay?

[66] On the mechanics of tally-cutting and the generation of the corresponding entries in the tellers' and receipt rolls, see Steel, *Receipt*, p. 5.

[67] The deputy chamberlains sorted the counter-tallies by county and term, strung them together in so-called *filacia* and stored them in chests. Periodically, the deputy chamberlains of the Exchequer of Account fetched the counter-tallies. On this see TNA: PRO, E159/229 Recorda Trinity m 8, transcribed in Appendix II.B.

names were inscribed on it and entered in the tellers' and receipt rolls.[68] Once the customers had paid the sum in question,[69] the payee handed over the tally – which by virtue of the inscription was a receipt of the Exchequer for a named sum of money paid in by a named individual (or named individuals)[70] and whose physical possession therefore constituted proof of payment – which the customers then presented to the Exchequer when they came in to account.

Payment by the Writ and Letter system was always warranted by a patent letter which authorized payment from a named source of crown revenue to a named individual, usually (but not exclusively) the recipient of an annuity payable half-yearly at Michaelmas and Easter. Such periodic payments required first of all a systematic method of verification within the Exchequer itself, since the patent had originally been issued by the chancery under the great seal without the Exchequer's knowledge. This problem was solved by copying the patent (in a slightly abbreviated form) onto the originalia roll[71] which the chancery sent over to the Exchequer each year. Here, the copy of the patent was transcribed in the *Recorda* section of the Lord Treasurer's Memoranda Roll, since it was the duty of the Lord Treasurer to keep track of everything of enduring importance to the crown's income, such as annuities. While this sufficed to keep the Exchequer abreast of what the crown had granted, payment had to be authorized by the chancery each half year. This involved

---

[68] Note that tallies could be forged, as the example of the tally allegedly struck on 14 Nov. 1452 shows, which purported to direct payment of £46 13s 3d out of the London wool customs and subsidy to the royal household: *London' De Johanne Poutrelle et Thoma Pounde collectoribus custume et subsidii lanarum in portu London' de eisdem custume et subsidii: Michaelis: 14 die Novembris anno regni regis Henrici VI tricesimo primo pro hospicio regis:* TNA: PRO, E159/229 Recorda Easter m 6. The forgery was so well done that it was only discovered in the Exchequer when the counterfoil could not be found. See Appendix II for a transcript of the record.

[69] Since the crown was generally strapped for cash, the customers often had to wait until enough money had been collected to pay off the tally in toto. Therefore, it is not surprising that the customers frequently paid ancient tallies, all of which were dated by the day, month and regnal year when they had been struck. However, the crown could set its own priorities. On the one hand, the king could favour certain payees by ordering the customers to pay the sum in question *de primis denariis* (see TNA: PRO, E368/216 Visus et status compotorum Michaelmas m 14d). On the other hand, the crown could hold up all other payments until the sum owing to one favoured recipient had been paid (see TNA: PRO, E403/515 m 22). On this whole question, see G.L. Harriss, 'Preference at the medieval Exchequer', *Bulletin of the Institute of Historical Research* 30, 1952, p. 17-40.

[70] According to G.L. Harriss, 'Fictitious loans', *Economic History Review* 2nd Series 8, 1955, p. 187-99, here p. 189, the inscription on a tally had to include [1] 'the name and office of the revenue collector on whom it was levied, [2] the name of the revenues which it assigned, [3] the sum for which it was cut and [4] the date in the regnal year of the king by whose authority it was issued.' (my numbering). However, the name of the payee was not inscribed on the tally, so that it could pass from hand to hand.

[71] TNA: PRO, E371.

the production of two documents by the chancery. On the one hand, the chancery ordered the customers to pay directly, without making a detour via the treasurer and chamberlains, by (1) issuing a *breve de liberate* (which summarized the patent which was the ultimate warrant for all payments and which named the source – petty customs, wool subsidy etc. – from which payment was to be made) ordering the customers to pay the sum in question to the beneficiary and (2) handing it over to him. Simultaneously, the chancery directed the Upper Exchequer to allow the customers any funds they had disbursed to the payee, by issuing a *breve de allocate* under the great seal directed to the treasurer and barons which (1) summarized the *breve de liberate*, (2) noted the fact that the king had ordered the customers to pay and (3) directed the treasurer and barons to allow the customers any funds they had demonstrably disbursed to the payee by reason of the *breve de liberate* when they came in to account. The *breve de allocate* was copied into the *Brevia directa baronibus* section of the King's Remembrancer's Memoranda Roll under the appropriate term and the original – endorsed with an entry referring to the enrolment – was filed. The payee was now in a position to obtain payment from the customers. He – or someone acting on his behest[72] – presented the *liberate* writ to the customers and requested payment, which they proceeded to do if they had enough cash on hand in the relevant customs chest (e.g. petty customs). At that point, the payee handed over the *breve de liberate* and produced one or more receipts under his own seal,[73] both of which the customers proferred when they came to account.

How did the customers account for payments effected by the Tally system? The *visus compoti* of the Poole customers in Trinity term 1453 shows how the process worked. Having been directed to appear at the beginning of Easter term,[74] Roger Ivye and Walter Payne were assigned (together with the controller John Rokes) to the auditor Richard Bedford when they came in to Westminster.[75] As the schedule he prepared shows, Ivye and Payne had received a total of £51 13s 8d between Michaelmas (29 September 1452) and Easter (1 April 1453).[76]

---

[72] This could be a creditor, a member of his retinue or a member of his household: Richard duke of York sent his receiver John Wyggemore (see the *parcelle compoti* of the wool account for 24 Henry VI, documents P 3, P 6 etc.). In all cases, the receipt recorded payment by the payee or by the hand (*per manus*) of the actual recipient.

[73] In the case of annuities, part payments – which could be documented by individual receipts – were very common.

[74] *Crastinum Clausi Pasche* (9-12 Apr. 1453): TNA: PRO, E159/229 Recorda Michaelmas m 32.

[75] TNA: PRO, E102/2 m 26 for Easter term 34 Henry VI. A different hand recorded *assignantur Bedford et fecerunt visum.* The entire entry is struck through.

[76] TNA: PRO, E207/16/5/8, m 1.

s'	*Bed[ford]*
Pole	*Visus Rogeri Ivye et Walteri Payne collectorum custumarum et subsidiorum regis in portu ville de Pole et in singulis portubus et locis eidem portui adjacentibus, videlicet a festo sancti Michaelis anno 31 regis nunc Henrici [Sexti]* [29 September 1452] *usque ad festum Pasche accidens primo die Aprilis tunc proximum sequens* [1 April 1453], *videlicet per dimidium annum et unum diem, ut inferius*
Recepta denariorum	*Iidem onerant se gratis de £51 13s 8d de parva custuma pannorum et aliarum rerum et mercandisarum ac de subsidio tonagii et pondagii tam de mercatoribus Anglicanis quam de alienigenis in portubus et locis predictis adductorum, eductorum et ibidem custumatorum per predictum tempus hujus visus*
	De aliquibus custumis seu subsidiis lanarum, coriorum aut pellium lanutarum aliquorum mercatorum indigenarum vel alienigenarum, videlicet per predictum tempus hujus visus, non respondent, eo quod nulla hujusmodi lane, coria neque pelles lanute ibidem custumata nec abinde traducta fuerunt per idem tempus, prout iidem collectores aliquo modo inquirere potuerunt
	Summa recepte *£51 13s 8d*

Sewn onto this schedule is a slip of parchment[77] – designated internally as the *declaracio* of the customers – with the following entries:

Pole	*Onus Rogeri Ivye et Walteri Payne collectorum custumarum et subsidiorum regis in portu ville de Pole et in singulis portubus et locis eidem portui adjacentibus, videlicet a festo sancti Michaelis anno 31 regis nunc* [29 September 1452] *usque festum Pasche accidens 1 die Aprilis proximum sequens* [1 April 1453], *scilicet per dimidium annum et unum diem* *£51 13s 8d*
	De quibus iidem collectores solvunt per tres tallias ad receptam scaccarii levatas super hanc declaracionem ostensas et penes ipsos collectores remanentes *£51 13s 4d*
	Et petunt pro feodo suo ad 10 marcas per annum et feodo contrarotulatoris ad 40s per annum, scilicet pro rata per tempus predictum *£4 7s 1½d*
	Et sic in superplusagio hic *£4 6s 9½d*

Against the £51 13s 8d with which the customers charged themselves, the *declaracio* states that they 'paid' by means of three tallies worth a total of £51 13s 4d and requested allowance of a further £4 7s 1½d for their fees (and those

[77] TNA: PRO, E207/16/5/8, m 2.

of the controller) on a pro rata basis for the period from Michaelmas to Easter, which left them £4 6s 9½d in credit vis-à-vis the crown.

Now, it would have been simple enough for Bedford to work out by himself whether the customers' claim for fees was justified, but he would have required assistance in order to determine whether the three tallies which the customers proferred and retained were in fact genuine. Whose assistance he sought is shown by a further bill which was drawn up by John Inwardby[78] and which dealt with the three tallies by means of which the customers had 'paid'.

Inwardeby

[1] *De Rogero Ivy et Waltero Payne collectoribus custumarum et subsidiorum regis in portu de Pole de eisdem custumis et subsidiis £5*
Michaelis: 4 die Decembris anno 31 regis Henrici Sexti [4 December 1452]*: Pro Estmerche*

[2] *De Rogero Ivy et Waltero Payne collectoribus custumarum et subsidiorum regis in portu de Pole de eisdem custumis et subsidiis £20*
pro eisdem collectoribus pro denariis mutatis pro expensis hospicii regis
Michaelis: 5 die Decembris anno 31 regis Henrici VI [5 December 1452]

[3] *De Rogero Ivy et Waltero Payne collectoribus custumarum et subsidiorum regis in portu de Pole de eisdem custumis et subsidiis £26 13s 4d*
Michaelis: 4 die Decembris anno 31 regis Henrici VI [4 December 1452] *pro eisdem collectoribus et contrarotulatori de regardo*

Now, it is very revealing that John Inwardby was consulted in regard to the tallies, since he was clerk of receipt.[79] As such he was required to (1) inscribe the tallies once they had been struck, (2) enter them in the tellers' roll and (3) file the teller's bill.[80] Therefore, Inwardby could do nothing other than inspect the tellers' bills and roll and determine whether a tally had in fact been struck. Although proving that the tally was genuine would involve matching it to the counter-tally (which was in the possession of the deputy chamberlains of the receipt), Inwardby's check against the tellers' bills and roll would suffice to determine whether there was an obvious reason to disallow the tally. Quite clearly, Inwardby supplemented the information he copied off the tallies which Ivye and Payne had proferred – the names of the officials on whom it was levied, the name of the revenues which had been assigned and the amount – with the information (indented in the transcript above) which he derived from the tellers' bill or roll, namely the term, the date the tally had been struck and the payee. Demonstrably, he could not have derived this information from the

[78] TNA: PRO, E207/16/5/49. My numbering.

[79] Sainty, *Officers of the Exchequer*, p. 205.

[80] Steel, *Receipt*, p. 5. Between the entry in the tellers' roll and the filing of the bill, the under clerk of the receipt had, of course, recorded the transaction in the receipt roll, but the clerk of the receipt had no direct access to this record.

issue rolls.[81] Had he done so, Henry Percy (or John Ogle) would have been named as the payee for the first tally, whereas Inwardby only recorded *Pro Estmerche.* Moreover, the amount would have been left off, since it was not recorded in the issue rolls.

[3] [4 December 1452] *Rogero Ivye et Waltero Payne collectoribus custumarum et subsidiorum regis in portu de Pole ac contrarotulatori eorundem ibidem in denariis eis liberatis per assignacionem isto die factam de regardo speciali pro assiduis laboribus et diligencia per ipsos habitis et sustenutis in officiis suis in anno ultimo elapso finiente ad festum sancti Michaelis ultimum preteritum per breve generale ut supra £26 13s 4d.*

[1] [4 December 1452] *Henrico Percy militi custodi ville Berewici ac Estmerche versus Scociam in denariis sibi liberatis per assignacionem isto die factam per manus Johannis Ogle armigeri de prestito super salva custodia ville ac merche predicte per breve de privato sigillo inter mandata de termino Pasche ultimo preterito* [amount omitted]. *Unde respondebit.*

[2] [5 December 1452] *Rogero Ivye et Waltero Payne collectoribus custumarum et subsidiorum regis in portu de Pole in denariis eis liberatis per assignacionem isto die factam in persolucionem £20, quas domino regi ad receptam scaccarii sui 4 die Decembris ultimo preterito* [4 Dec. 1452] *pro expensis hospicii predicti domini regis mutuo liberaverunt, ut patet in rotulo recepte de eodem die, £20.*

The fair copy of the *visus* shows some slight, but significant variations on the *declaratio.*[82]

[Marginated] *Dors'; De visu*

Facto visu compoti Rogeri Ivye et Walteri Payne collectorum custumarum et subsidiorum regis in portu ville de Pole et in singulis portubus et locis eidem portui adjacentibus, videlicet a festo sancti Michaelis anno tricesimo primo regis hujus [29 Sept. 1452] *usque festum Pasche accidens primo die Aprilis tunc proximum sequens* [1 Apr. 1453], *scilicet per dimidium annum et unum diem*

Iidem collectores onerant se gratis de £51 13s 8d receptis de parva custuma ac subsidio tonagii et pondagii ibidem, sicut continetur in quadam cedula de visu predicto facta et hic per Ricardum Bedford unum auditorum compotorum hujus scaccarii liberata, que est inter billas de hoc termino[83]

De quibus respectuatur eis pro feodis suis et contrarotulatoris ibidem per tempus predictum juxta ratam 13 marcarum per annum *£4 7s 1½d*

Et solvunt per tres tallias ad receptam hujus scaccarii levatas super hunc visum ostensas et penes ipsos collectores remanentes *£51 13s 4d*

Et habent superplusagium *£4 6s 9½d*

---

[81] TNA: PRO, E403/791 m 5. I have numbered the issue roll entries to facilitate comparison with Inwardby's bill.

[82] TNA: PRO, E159/229 Fines ... visus Trinity m [1d]: http://aalt.law.uh.edu/AALT2/H6/E159no229/bE159no229dorses/IMG_1160.htm.

[83] This is, of course, TNA: PRO, E207/16/5/8.

In the first place, the petition of the *declaracio* in regard to the fees of the customers and the controller (*Et petunt pro feodo suo ...*) was obviously approved, since the customers were granted respite for this sum until final accounting (*De quibus respectuatur eis pro feodis ...*). Second, the tallies are said to have been shown *super hunc visum* rather than *super hanc declaracionem*. Finally, the somewhat tentative conclusion of the auditor in his bill – *Et sic in superplusagio hic £4 6s 9½d* – was transformed into a positive statement: *Et habent superplusagium £4 6s 9½d*. Clearly, these were decisions which the auditor – even with the assistance of Inwardby – could not make on his own and which were reserved for a full session of the Exchequer, for which Bedford's schedule (with Inwardby's certification attached as an appendix) served as a bill.[84] Note that the Exchequer did not attempt a final validation of the tallies – which the payees had handed over to the customers and which they, in turn, had shown in the course of the *visus* –, since that would have involved comparison with the counter-tallies and retention of the tally together with its counter-foil, whereas Ivye and Payne are said to have retained the three tallies (*per tres tallias ... penes ipsos collectores remanentes*). Clearly, final validation of the tallies was postponed until Hilary, when the customers were to return to Westminster for final accounting.[85] The same was done in regard to the yearly fees[86] of the customers (10 marks per annum) and the controller (40s per annum) for the period the *visus* covered. The interim account showed that

[84] Occasionally, the date on which the auditor submitted his schedule to the Exchequer is noted on the back. Take, for example, the *visus* of the Boston customers Richard Perpoynt and William Pychard, who were also assigned to Richard Bedford. On the dorse of their *visus* – covering the period from 10 Oct. 1455 to 28 Mar. 1456 (TNA: PRO, E207/16/10 unnumbered) – is noted: *Hunc visum liberavit hic Ricardus Bedford infrascriptus 28 die Aprilis anno 34 regis Henrici Sexti* [28 Apr. 1456]. For the fair copy of the *visus* see TNA: PRO, E159/232 Fines ... visus Easter m 2d: http://aalt.law.uh.edu/AALT2/H6/E159no232/bE159no232dorses/IMG_1336.htm.

[85] There seems to have been no enrolment of the order to Ivye and Payne to appear for final accounting, but the marginated *s'* in the upper left-hand corner of Bedford's schedule shows that they were summoned, and they did account in Hilary term 1454: TNA: PRO, E159/230 Recorda Hilary m 2d, E356/20 m 45, E368/226 Visus et status compotorum Hilary m 3.

[86] Payments to the customers were of three kinds: (1) payment for expenses incurred (*pro misis et expensis* or *pro feodo*); (2) salary (*de regardo pro assiduo labore et diligencia per ipsos habitis in officiis suis*); and (3) bonus for superb work (*de regardo speciali pro continuo labore et diligencia*). With the exception of the bonuses all payments were fixed long before our period. This did not, however, mean that there were no changes at all. The London wool customers, for instance, last received an expense account for their boatsman (*stipendium batillarii*: 40s per annum) in the account for 29 Sept. to 20 Nov. 1414, and the expense account of London petty customs collectors for the costs of collecting the cloth customs (*pro misis et expensis circa colleccionem custume pannorum*) was only stabilized at 100s per annum in 1359.

the customers' credits were £4 6s 9½d higher than the total of customs and subsidies they had received.

This explains the marginated entry on the schedule of the *visus compoti* of the collectors of tunnage and poundage in London. Thomas Walsingham and William Estfeld had shown (and, undoubtedly, retained) 19 tallies totalling £1290 12s 4d. The examination of the tallies and the Exchequer's own records had shown that the tallies had in fact been struck. Therefore, the Exchequer credited Walsingham and Estfeld with the corresponding sum, as noted on the schedule, pending final accounting.

Accounting for payments by the Writ and Letter system may be illustrated by the *visus compoti* of the Sandwich customers Godwin Catesby and Thomas Medilmore for the period from 29 September 1432 to 12 April 1433. Having charged themselves with £710 2s 10¼d for wool customs and subsidy, petty customs and tunnage and poundage, they first 'paid' by showing twelve tallies dating between 30 May 1432 and 26 May 1433 worth a total of £671 18s 6½d to a plenary session of the Exchequer.[87] They were then granted respite for a payment on the annuity of Humphrey, duke of Gloucester:

> *Et respectuantur prefatis collectoribus usque alias pro tot denariis per ipsos solutis Humfrido duci Gloucestrie constabulario castri Dovorrie et custodi Quinque Portuum de illis centum marcis annuis eidem duci per dominum Henricum Quintum nuper regem Anglie per litteras suas patentes,*[88] *quas dictus dominus rex nunc confirmavit,*[89] *concessis pro constabularia ville Dovorrie percipiendis de custuma et subsidio predictis in portu predicto per manus collectorum eorundem custume et subsidii ibidem pro tempore existentes ad terminos Pasche et sancti Michaelis, videlicet pro termino Pasche dicto anno 11mo* *£33 6s 8d*
> *per breve regis de magno sigillo suo prefatis collectoribus directum ac litteras acquietancie Roberti Shiryngton generalis receptoris predicti ducis de recepta curie ostensa*

Note that the collectors presented only two documents to the Exchequer sitting in plenary session (*curie*): a writ under the great seal directed to the customers themselves – clearly the *breve de liberate* – and a receipt from Robert Shirington, duke Humphrey's receiver general. No mention was made of the *breve de allocate*. Note also that the Exchequer did not undertake to verify the writ by directing the King's Remembrancer to search out the *breve de allocate* and comparing it with the *breve de liberate* and Shirington's receipt. Nor was a final decision reached on whether to allow the customers the disbursement: they were simply granted respite *usque alias*. What was meant by that is revealed at the end of the *visus*, where the Exchequer granted the customers respite *usque compotum suum* for the remaining 17s 7¾d still owing to the

[87] TNA: PRO, E159/209 Fines ... visus Easter m [4d]: http://aalt.law.uh.edu/AALT1/H6/E159no209/bE159no209dorses/IMG_0945.htm.
[88] CPR 1413-16, p. 374 dated 27 Nov. 1415.
[89] CPR 1422-29, p. 82-3 dated 20 Dec. 1422.

crown. Immediately thereafter, a different hand recorded the order to the sheriff of Kent to distrain Catesby and Medilmore for final accounting on 30 September 1433.

Therefore, we can see that the *visus compoti* was just an interim account, designed to inform the Exchequer about the state of the crown's financial resources in a particular customs district. No final decision was reached on any claims advanced by the customers for allowance for payments by tally (which were shown to the Exchequer and retained by the customers) or by writ and letter (which were also shown to the Exchequer and retained). Nor indeed was a final decision reached regarding the fees of the customers and controller. In all cases, the Exchequer, sitting in full session, merely granted respite until final accounting.

After completion of the *visus compoti*, the schedule prepared by the auditor and the documents the *visus* had generated within the Exchequer were handed over to the King's Remembrancer, who entered a fair copy of the *visus compoti* in the section of his Memoranda Roll called *Fines, manucapciones, dies datus, respectus et visus* under the term in which the interim accounting had taken place.[90] Initially, however, the King's Remembrancer spiked the *visus compoti* until he had distrained the customers to appear for final accounting. Once the distraint writ had been sent out, the King's Remembrancer entered an *s'* on the schedule and filed it under the other bills of that term.[91]

This bi-annual rhythm of interim and final accounting apparently proved to be very effective, and the Exchequer retained it for the rest of our period. At the beginning of Michaelmas term 1407 at the very latest – and probably earlier[92] – the King's Remembrancer drew up a list of the *Status et visus custuma-*

---

[90] Ivye and Payne's *visus compoti* was conducted in Trinity term 1453. Consequently, the documents it generated were filed under the bills for this term (TNA: PRO, E207/16/6). The fair copy of the *visus compoti* was entered in the section *fines ... visus* of the King's Remembrancer's Memoranda Rolls under Trinity term (TNA: PRO, E159/229 fines ... visus m 1).

[91] The schedules are transmitted partly in the document classes TNA: PRO, E207 (Bills) and E122, as noted above. The *distringas* writs were sorted by term and county and are transmitted in the series Exchequer Writs: Original Series (TNA: PRO, E202).

[92] Entries in the first extant Enrolment of States of Accounts (TNA: PRO, E102/1) prove that m 2 of this document, which listed the customers who were to be summoned for *crastinum Clausi Pasche* 1408, was based on the entries in the *Recorda* section of the King's Remembrancer's Memoranda Roll for Michaelmas term 1407 (TNA: PRO, E159/183 Recorda Michaelmas). In order to illustrate this point, I quote the entries for the Southampton customers in both documents.

TNA: PRO, E102/1 m 2

Michaelis 8, rotulo 4.

Suth' *Thomas Barton et Thomas Midlyngton collectores tam magne quam parve custume regis in portu predicto sunt computaturi a festo sancti Michaelis anno 7* [29 Sept. 1406]. *Ideo preceptum sit etc. in crastino Clausi Pasche* [4 Apr.

rum in singulis portubus Anglie for the relevant half year (Michaelmas or Easter). These lists of customers who were to account were clearly working documents, since a number of distinct scribal hands entered all further measures, for instance the assignment of an auditor or the completion of accounting. Once final accounting had taken place, the King's Remembrancer's duties came to an end. Consequently, the last entry in these lists is normally *comp[utarunt]*. The entry in the *Status et visus custumarum* was then struck through from top to bottom, making it simple for the King's Remembrancer to cast an eye down the membrane and see which customers had not yet appeared to account and summon them anew.

It is important to note that the half-yearly list of customers to be called to account in the *Status et visus custumarum* was the basis for the dispatch of writs of distraint to the sheriffs of the counties in question.[93] At the end of term, these writs – together with all other writs the Exchequer sent out – were

---

1407]. *Ad quem diem vicecomes retornavit breve. Et iidem collectores veniunt et assignantur Hesylle. Postea* [Margination: *Non possunt computare sine contrarotulatore*].

TNA: PRO, E159/183 Recorda Michaelmas m 4 (8 Hen. IV)

Suth' *Memorandum, quod Thomas Burton et Thomas Midlyngton nuper collectores parve custume regis in portu ville Suthamptonie venerunt et computarunt de eadem custuma, videlicet a 18 die Decembris anno regni regis Henrici IV sexto usque festum sancti Michaelis sequens. A quo festo iidem collectores inde computarunt usque festum sancti Michaelis proximum sequens. A quo quidem festo iidem collectores sunt alias inde computaturi. Et quia amoti sunt ab officio predicto, preceptum sit vicecomiti, quod ipsos distringeret per terras etc., ita etc., in crastino Clausi Pasche ad computandum in premissis* [Margination: *s'; r'*]

The fact that the scribe who wrote the entry in E102/1 m 2 used the information in the Recorda section of the King's Remembrancer's Memoranda Roll up to the point where he noted that the customers were to be summoned for *crastinum Clausi Pasche* leaps to the eye. Once the sheriff returned the distraint writ, the King's Remembrancer entered a long-tailed 'r' in his Memoranda Roll and *Ad quem diem vicecomes retornavit breve* in E102/1 m 2. A second scribal hand then noted the appearance of the customers before the Exchequer in E102/1 m 2, the assignment of William Hesylle as their auditor and the reason for adjournment (the absence of the controller). Even if E102/1 m 2 does not contain any cross-reference to the King's Remembrancer's Memoranda Roll, the relationship between the two documents is plain.

[93] See TNA: PRO, E207/12/8/7 for a list, drawn up at the end of Hilary term 1414 (1 Hen. V), of the customers to be summoned for *crastinum Clausi Pasche*. Under the heading *Fiunt brevia directa vicecomitibus ad distringendum collectores in portubus subscriptis retornabilia crastino Clausi Pasche* the King's Remembrancer's clerk listed the chief ports of the customs districts in one column and the counties in a second column. As the writs were dispatched, the clerk entered a dot just to the left of the name of the chief port. Note that this list was alphabetized in precisely the same order as the entries in E102, namely by the name of the county (and not the chief port). To my mind, this proves that E207/12/8/7 and similar lists were drawn up on the basis of the entries in E102.

bundled by county and return day (*crastinum Michaelis, octabas Michaelis, quindena Michaelis* etc.) and counted. This was the basis for the table of the *Brevia emanencia de scaccario*, which the Exchequer drew up each term and which showed how many writs for each return day had been sent to the sheriffs of which counties. Only after the writs had been counted and the *Brevia emanencia de scaccario* – normally the last piece in the bundle of bills for the term – drawn up could the bundles be given to the Exchequer's messengers for delivery to the sheriffs, who had to certify receipt of each bundle separately.[94]

Once the sheriffs returned the writs – bundle by bundle – the Exchequer entered a long-tailed *'r'* beside the name of the county, provided the writs arrived on time. If this was not the case, then the clerk entered a cross beside the name of the county. If the writs were subsequently returned, then the clerk entered a long-tailed *'r'* beside the name of the county and the date of receipt next to the number of writs in the corresponding column. This procedure may be illustrated by an excerpt from one such table, for Trinity term 1453.[95]

Numerus brevium emanencium de scaccario de termino sancte Trinitatis, videlicet 15 die Julii anno 31 regis Henrici VI [15 July 1453] *retornabilium ad dies subscriptos, videlicet*

	[County]	*cras' Mich'*	*8 Mich'*	*15 Mich'*
r'	*Dovorr'*[96]	*13*		
r' +	*Bed' Buk'*	*10 (9 Octobris)*		
r' r' +	*Bristoll'*	*10 (3 Octobris)*	*7*	
r'	*Cant' Hunt'*	*10*		
r'	*Cornub'*		*24*	

From 1408/09 to the end of our period, the Exchequer's practice remained unchanged. After a half year in office, the customers were summoned to Westminster, where the Exchequer decided whether to conduct a *visus compoti* or simply summon them for final accounting. However, the form of words in which the King's Remembrancer captured these administrative actions did change. In 31 Henry VI (1452/53) the King's Remembrancer began to break off the fair copy of the *visus compoti* after determining whether the customers were indebted to the crown or in credit. In complete contrast to earlier years, the *visus* no longer ends with an entry noting that a writ of distraint had been sent out to summon the customers to the final accounting in Westminster.

---

[94] Cf. TNA: PRO, E207/16/5/45: *Presens indentura testatur, quod Johannes Baxtere vicecomes ville Novi Castri Super Tynam recepit de Johanne Dene uno nunciorum currencium de scaccario domini regis 2 die Junii anno regni regis Henrici VI post conquestum Anglie 31* [2 June 1453] *13 brevia domini regis in duobus filaciis retornabilia coram baronibus domini regis de eodem scaccario in crastino sancti Johannis Baptiste proximo futuro.* The sheriff's seal is impressed on the indenture.

[95] All in all, 759 writs were sent out by the King's Remembrancer in Trinity term 1453.

[96] Dover was, of course, not a county. The writs were sent to the Warden of the Cinque Ports in recognition of their immunities: K.M.E. Murray, *The Constitutional History of the Cinque Ports*, Manchester 1935, p. 84-8.

Reading the King's Remembrancer's Memoranda Rolls in isolation, one could gain the impression that the *visus compoti* no longer constituted the basis for the King's Remembrancer's summoning of the customers to final accounting. However, this was not the case, as the surviving *visus compoti* (TNA: PRO, E122 and E207) continue to contain a marginated *'s'*, showing that they did indeed serve as the basis for the customers' summons to final accounting and that the older practice had survived without a break. The second change in the form of the *visus compoti* occured in 2/3 Edward IV (1462/63). Up to 1462/63 the sum of the issues of customs and subsidies was always followed by the statement, *sicut continetur in quadam cedula de visu per N.N. auditorem liberata, que est inter billas de hoc termino*. From 1462/63 its place was taken by the entry, *sicut continetur in X rotulis ipsorum collectorum de particulis super hunc visum ostensis et examinatis ac per sacramentum ipsorum collectorum.*[97] However, the impression that the auditor no longer drew up a schedule in the course of the *visus compoti* would be false. Precisely for 1462/63 a number of schedules have survived in document class E207 which are identical in form to those of earlier years.

FINAL ACCOUNTING

At the end of the accounting period, the customers and the controller were summoned to Westminster for final accounting. Since this could be a long drawn out procedure, it is scarcely surprising that the customers often nominated deputies to act in their place. This was permissible, so long as one of the barons of the Exchequer had given his approval, as the following example – from Trinity term 1453 – shows.

Norff' Thomas Fenne unus collectorum custumarum et subsidiorum in portu ville de Magna Jernemuthe posuit loco suo Thomam Edmond alterum collectorum ad reddendum pro eo domino regi compotum de custumis et subsidiis predictis de tempore, quo inde fuerunt collectores ibidem et non computarunt, et ad omnia alia etc.

Per J. Durem[98]

This slip of parchment served as a bill for the Exchequer, and a number of similar approvals are transmitted in the Exchequer bills (TNA: PRO, E207). The King's Remembrancer was responsible for transcribing such deputizations, which were entered in the section *Presentaciones, attornati, dies datus et respectus* in the Memoranda Roll.

---

[97] Of course, the reference to *rotuli* was replaced by *in quodam libro de particulis* when the customers had used a codex provided by the Exchequer for the fair copy of their account. On this, see TNA, PRO, E159/209 Recorda Michaelmas m 5 and the mandate in E159/205 Recorda Michaelmas m 18.

[98] TNA: PRO, E207/16/5/92. John Durem was one of the barons of the Exchequer. The approval of a deputy could also be given by a full session of the Exchequer, e.g. in TNA: PRO, E207/16/5/83.

Irrespective of whether a customer had named a deputy or appeared in person, someone had to turn up on the return day. The summons for a particular return day – *crastinum Michaelis*, for instance – seems to have been a pure formality, since I know of no case in which the Exchequer began work precisely on 30 September. Presumably, the customers turned up and waited until being called up to take the oath to account faithfully[99] and hand in their account and the *parcelle*, whereupon the Exchequer assigned them an auditor. It would appear that the customers had to be prepared to be patient, since it could take a long time before they were called up. The Bristol customers Thomas Russell and Makelin Waleyn, who were summoned to Westminster as of 30 September 1434 to account for the period 19 October 1433 to 5 July 1434, had to wait until 9 October 1434 to be sworn in.[100] Entries in the *Status et visus custumarum in singulis portubus Anglie* suggest that other customers had to wait even longer. For instance, the Exchequer only assigned auditors to the customers summoned to Westminster for 30 September 1452 on 24 and 30 October, 7, 8, 14, 17 and 21 November 1452.[101]

Having taken the oath to account, handed in their documentation and been assigned an auditor, the customers again had to wait around until the auditor had calculated the sum of the issues of the customs and subsidies, the *summa recepte,* for which the customers had to answer to the crown. The auditor's task was to compare the customs account (*particule compoti*) with the controlment roll and determine if these two records of the entry and exit of ships and goods corresponded materially in every particular.[102] If this was not the case, then the official was in deep trouble. The minute the auditor had reason to suspect that a customs official had winked at smuggling – and consequently withheld crown income – he was required to report this to the Exchequer in full session. The example of the Bristol customers Thomas

[99] The statute 4 Hen. IV, St. 1, c. 20 (Luders et al. (eds.), *Statutes of the Realm*, vol. 2, p. 139), gives us an idea about what the form of the oath must have been: *et qe chescun custumer desore enavaunt sur son accompt rendre en lescheqer soit jurrez par son serement de respondre loialmont a mesme nostre seignur le roy sanz fraude ou male engine des toutz maners proitz et commiditees pur paiement dascun assignement, soit il par taill ou autrement, par lui ou aucun autre resceuz ou a resceivers pur achate dascun taille ou en autre manere qeconque.* For the corresponding oath of the controller see TNA: PRO, E159/210 Recorda Michaelmas m 18.

[100] TNA: PRO, E159/210 Recorda Michaelmas m 18.

[101] TNA: PRO, E102/2 m 25.

[102] It is often stated that the chief weakness of the English customs system was the Exchequer's inability to discover peculation if the customers and the controller had colluded to hide it and made sure that the customs account and the controlment roll were identical (if false). While one can find numerous examples of collusion in the Recorda of the King's Remembrancer's Memoranda Rolls (e.g. TNA: PRO, E159/167 Recorda Hilary m 17), I am not convinced that such malfeasance could be kept hidden forever. See Stuart Jenks, 'Zollamt, Häfen und Außenhandel in England: ca. 1377-1470', *Vierteljahrschrift für Sozial- und Wirtschaftsgeschichte* 75, 1988, p. 305-38.

Russell and Makelin Walewyn demonstrates this in full detail. The auditor, Roger Appelton, noticed a number of discrepancies between their customs account and the controlment roll of John Sistern, which had been handed over to him on 9 October 1434. Consequently, he appeared before the Exchequer on 15 November 1434 and stated,

> *qualiter ipse super examinacionem particularum dictorum collectorum in eorum libro supradicto contentarum facta cum particulis in dictis rotulis dicti contrarotulatoris contentis invenit, quod 36 naves in eisdem rotulis separatim plenius specificate onerate cum diversis mercandisis infra portum predictum per tempus predictum ... separatim applicantes et extra eundem portum per idem tempus exeuntes ac diverse mercandise in eisdem navibus contente necnon custume et subsidia domino regi de eisdem mercandisis debita, que quidem custume et subsidia inter se attingunt ad summam £76 13s 9¼d, videlicet custume inde ad £15 6s 3½d et subsidia ad £61 7s 5¾d, extra dictum librum collectorum predictorum ommittuntur et concelantur.*[103]

In the vast majority of cases, the customs account and the controlment roll did not diverge materially from one another,[104] and the auditor could proceed to calculate the *summa recepte*, the raw total of the crown's income from customs and subsidies. This was a straightforward, if time-consuming task. The rates of customs and subsidies were common knowledge, and the auditor simply had to identify which of the many categories of customs and/or subsidies the entries related to and multiply the total units (in the case of goods like wine, wool, cloth and wax which were customed by unit, e.g. tun, sack etc.) or the total value (for the goods which were customed ad valorem) to arrive at a sub-total for the particular category (e.g. tunnage). Then he had to add up the crown's income category by category to arrive at the total amount of crown income, for which the customers had to answer at the Exchequer. These calculations, which the Exchequer designated as the *determinatio*, were first entered as a table at the end of the customs account. In order to illustrate this procedure, let us look at the auditor's calculations (in Michaelmas term 1436) for the customs account of John Bedford and John Tamworth for the issues of the customs and subsidies in Hull between Michaelmas 1435 and Michaelmas 1436.

---

[103] TNA: PRO, E159/210 Recorda Michaelmas m 18.

[104] As noted above, the order of ships on a given day could vary between one roll and the other, as could the order of merchants in a given ship and the order of products a given merchant had imported or exported, without giving rise to suspicion.

Table 7: Customs receipts in Hull, 29 September 1435-29 September 1436[105]

Receipts	Calculation
I: Staple merchandise	
a) £229 9s 4¾d	Wool customs on 638 sacks (@ 364 lb., 2 stone (@ 14 lb.) and 1 clove (@ 7 lb.) of wool exported to Calais and on 2235 woolfells (240 woolfells = 1 sack) @ 6s 8d per sack
b) £1112 6s 11¼d	Wool subsidy on the exports of wool and woolfells to Calais @ 33s 4d per sack
c) 9s 2d	Cocket fees for 55 cockets @ 2d per cocket
II. Tunnage and Poundage	
d) £208 2s 6d	Tunnage on 1387½ tuns (@ 252 gallons @ 3s per tun
e) £180 10s 11d	Poundage on indigenous and alien imports and exports worth £3610 17s 8d @ 12d/£
III. Petty Customs	
f) £56 19s ½d	Cloth customs on 827½ *panni curti sine grano*[106]

[105] Source: TNA, PRO, E356/18 m 25d (calendared Stuart Jenks (ed.), *The Enrolled Customs Accounts (PRO, E356, E372, E364) 1279/80-1508/09 (1523/24) Volume 7: E356/17, E356/18* (List and Index Society 324), London 2008, E356/18, No. 140) and E368/209 Visus et status compotorum Michaelmas m 8. The figures given in Power and Postan, *Studies in English Trade*, p. 331 for this account do not agree with the source in regard to the number of tuns of wine and woolfells.

[106] English broadcloths had a standard dimension of 24 x 1½ yards: St. 7 Hen. IV, c. 10 (*Statutes of the Realm*, vol. 2, p. 154). Cloths of non-standard dimensions were reckoned as fractions of whole cloths, as the Lynn petty customs account for 24 May to 29 Sept. 1398 (TNA, PRO, E122/159/7) shows. The account itself shows Hanseatic exports of 36 broadcloths *sine grano* and 58 narrow cloths *sine grano*. The auditor's *determinatio* shows Hanseatic exports of 32½ broadcloths. If we calculate (36 ÷ 2) + (58 ÷ 4) = 18 + 14½ = 32½, then we can conclude that the auditor's calculations were correct and that the question of whether a particular piece of cloth had the exact length and breadth required by the Assize of Cloth posed no great difficulties for the customers or the Exchequer: Whatever did not match, was simply treated as a half cloth, quarter cloth (or whatever the appropriate fraction might be). Therefore, in regard to the English customs administration, the comments of A.R. Bridbury, *English Clothmaking in the Middle Ages*, London 1983, p. 106-11, are wide of the mark. For customs purposes, the English customs administration distinguished three kinds of cloth, depending upon the extent to which the most expensive dye (*kermes*, also called *granum*) had been used in their manufacture. Those dyed completely with *granum* (*pannus curtus cum grano* or *de scarleta*) were charged most heavily, those partially dyed with *granum* (*pannus curtus cum dimidio grano*) less and those dyed altogether without *granum* (*pannus curtus sine grano*) least of all: See Table 2 for the rates (On scarlets see John Munro, 'The Medieval Scarlet and the Economics of Sartorial Splendour', N.B. Harte, K.G. Ponting (eds.), *Cloth and clothing in Medieval Europe. Essays in Memory of Professor E.M. Carus-Wilson* (Pasold Studies in Textile History 2), London 1983, p. 13-70). The actual colour of the cloth in question was immaterial,

exported by indigenous merchants @ 14d per cloth and on 19½ *panni curti sine grano* exported by alien merchants @ 2s 9d per cloth

g) £4 10½d — Petty customs on alien imports and exports worth £323 7s 6d @ 3d/£

Summa recepte
£1778 18s 10d

First of all, note that Bedford and Tamworth's auditor omitted a number of categories of crown income from customs and subsidies, simply because no corresponding goods had been shipped via Hull during the accounting period. Moreover, it is to be emphasized that the *determinatio* was entered in the customs account only – and not in the controlment roll – because only Bedford and Tamworth were fiscally responsible vis-à-vis the crown. Even if the first membrane of an account is missing, the presence of a *determinatio* on the last membrane is always incontrovertable proof that it is a customs account and not a controlment roll. Customs accounts can also usually be identified by the fact that interim sums are entered at the foot of the membrane (or page). Occasionally, this takes the form of the notation of the counters on the board (Illustration 4).[107]

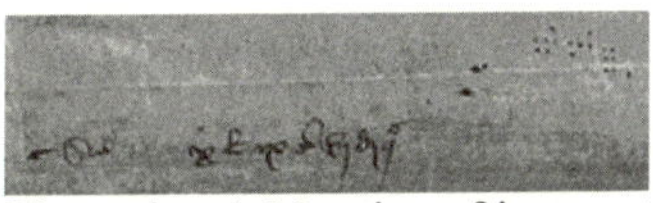

Summa £10 9s 6¼d

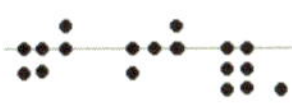

£	s	d	¼d
5	5	11	
111	111	11	
11	1	111	1

Illustration 4: Notation of issues at the foot of the membrane as text and as position of the counters on the board, with resolution of the 'pen and ink dots' (TNA: PRO, E122/76/48 m 1d)

Following the completion of the *determinatio*, the auditor transferred the information (which he had entered at the end of the customs account) to a second piece of parchment. This copy of the *determinatio*, which displayed the crown's income from the customs district in question, divided up according to the various categories of customs and subsidy revenue, was entered into the Enrolled Customs Accounts (TNA: PRO, E356). The Enrolled Customs Accounts constituted one part of the Pipe Rolls (TNA: PRO, E372), even if they had been bound separately in accordance with § 8 of the Cowick Ordinances[108]

as the example of the Danzig merchant Johann Swart demonstrates. On 30 Oct. 1447 Swart had customed 20½ *panni curti sine grano* in Ipswich. However, on 12 June 1448, an investigation ordered by thc Exchequer showed that of these cloths 11 were dyed blue, 3½ light blue and 6 medly (i.e. with different coloured warp and woof): TNA: PRO, E159/224 Recorda Easter m 11.

[107] The placement of counters on the board is derived from the abacus: Charles Johnson (ed.), *De Necessariis Observantiis Scaccarii Dialogus qui vulgo dicitur Dialogus de Scaccario*, London 1950, p. xxxv-xxxvii.

[108] Hall, *Red Book*, vol. 3, p. 860.

because by 1323 the Pipe Roll had grown to such dimensions as to be unwieldy. Consequently, all entries recording sums owing to the crown for which the sheriff did not have to answer were entered onto rolls which were physically separate for convenience's sake.[109] Since the Enrolled Customs Accounts were part of the Pipe Rolls, they were drawn up by the clerks in the Pipe Roll Office. That meant that the auditor had to send the copy of the *determinatio* over to the Pipe Roll Office for transcription. Once this had been taken care of, the clerks in the Pipe Roll Office entered *Irrotulatur rotulo compotorum de subsidio 3s de dolio et 12d de libra*[110] onto the dorse of the copy of the *determinatio* and sent it back to the auditor.

In the meantime, the auditor had to report back to the Exchequer on the state of the account. In order to do so, he produced yet another bill for the Exchequer with the heading *Nomina computancium coram N.N.*, entering his name as well as the term and indicating – in general, if not always – which of the two remembrancers was responsible for summoning those royal officials (i.e. not only the customers) who were required to account. In the case of the customers, this was always the King's Remembrancer, which the auditor indicated by entering *Ex parte remembratoris regis* in the upper left-hand corner of the *Nomina computacium* bill.[111]

While the purpose of the accounting procedure up to this point was to determine the crown's total income from customs and subsidies in the individual customs district during the accounting period in question, it was now necessary to determine the customers' net liability vis-à-vis the crown. It is imperative to emphasize that no final decision had been reached in the course of the *visus compoti* on the validity of payments effected by the customers (whether they had been made by tally or by writ and letter). Everything had to be checked again and validated in a full session of the Exchequer.[112] Let us demonstrate this by returning to the *visus compoti* of the Sandwich customers Godwin Catesby and Thomas Medilmore and comparing it to their final account. For the period from 29 September 1432 to 12 April 1433, they declared that they had received a total of £710 2s 10¼d. Against this sum they reckoned a total of

---

[109] From the early 1220s, these 'foreign accounts' had been excised from the sheriffs' accounts in the Pipe Roll and entered onto separate membranes, which were sewn onto the Pipe Roll at the end.

[110] TNA: PRO, E122/73/3, relating to the tunnage and poundage account for the period from 4 Apr. to 29 Sept. 1429. Needless to say, only the words *Irrotulatur rotulo compotorum* were common to all dorsal entries: in other cases, the appropriate name (*de magna custuma* etc.) was entered.

[111] One should bear in mind that *Nomina computancium* lists are not transmitted with any regularity in the Exchequer bills (TNA: PRO, 207), so that my conclusions must be taken with a grain of salt.

[112] This was mandated by § 1 of the Westminster ordinance of 1326: *Et les allowances a faire par brefs et tailles a la fyn de tieux acomptes se facent en plein Escheqier:* Hall, *Red Book*, vol. 3, p. 932.

£709 5s 2½d (Table 8), which was comprised of twelve payments by tally, one payment by writ and letter and respites for their and the controller's fees.

Table 8: Payments by tally and respites of Godwin Catesby and Thomas Medilmore, Sandwich, 29 September 1432-12 April 1433 (text slightly shortened)[113]

[1] *de custuma lanarum 14mo die Maii dicto anno 11mo* [14 May 1433] *pro garderoba regis continet £16 13s 4d*

[2] *de dicto subsidio lanarum 26 die Maii anno decimo regis hujus* [26 May 1432] *pro duce Norff' continet £33 6s 8d*

[3] *de eodem subsidio 30mo die Maii eodem anno decimo* [30 May 1432] *pro Henrico Brounflet continet £100, inde solverunt in partem solucionis ejusdem £81*

[4] *de eodem subsidio secundo die Maii dicto anno 11mo* [2 May 1433] *pro Calesia continet £114 17s 2½d*

[5] *de dictis custuma et subsidio 10mo die Julii dicto anno 10mo* [10 July 1432] *pro Johanne Tyrelle thesaurario hospicii regis continet £66 13s 4d*

[6] *de eisdem custuma et subsidio 20mo die Novembris dicto anno 11mo* [20 November 1432] *pro Johanne Martyn continet £26 16d*

[7] *de eisdem custuma et subsidio provenientibus de bonis Aufreomi Spinela de Janua 19mo die Februarii eodem anno 11mo* [19 February 1433] *continet £66 13s 4d*

[8] *de eisdem custuma et subsidio eodem die* [19 February 1433] *pro Victore Capello continet £66 13s 4d*

[9] *de eisdem custuma et subsidio eodem die* [19 February 1433] *continet £66 13s 4d*

[10] *de parva custuma ac subsidio 3s de dolio et 12d de libra 23 die Februarii dicto anno 11mo* [23 February 1433] *continet £13 6s 8d*

[11] *per 1 talliam ibidem levatam de subsidio 3s de dolio et^a^ 12d de libra 14mo die Maii dicto anno 11mo* [14 May 1433] *continet £120*

[12] *Et respectuantur prefatis collectoribus usque alias pro tot denariis per ipsos solutis Humfrido duci Gloucestrie constabulario castri Dovorrie et custodi Quinque Portuum ... pro termino Pasche dicto anno 11mo £33 6s 8d*

[13] *Et respectuantur eisdem collectoribus usque alias pro feodo suo ac feodo contrarotulatoris predicti ..., videlicet per tempus visus predicti £4*

When Catesby and Medilmore came in to the Exchequer in Michaelmas term 1433 for final accounting for the entire period from 29 September 1432 to 17 August 1433, they declared receipts of £1080 14s 3¼d, against which they reckoned the payments which they had effected. Since both the *visus* and the final account give fairly detailed information about the tallies and receipts the customers presented, we can see that every single item which had been res-

[113] TNA: PRO, E159/209 Fines ... visus Easter m [4d]: http://aalt.law.uh.edu/AALT1/H6/E159no209/bE159no209dorses/IMG_0945.htm. I have shortened the text slightly.

pited in the *visus compoti* in Easter term was verified anew (Table 9), although some tallies were summed up together (c). The final accounting also included payments and credits from the time after 12 April 1433 (b, c, i).

Table 9: Disbursements by the Sandwich customers, 29 September 1432-17 August 1433 (the number of item in the *visus* is given in square brackets at the end of the line)[114]

[a] *In thesauro £16 13s 4d 14mo die Maii anno 11mo* [14 May 1433] *de custuma lanarum* [1]

[b] *Et in thesauro £25 2s 8° die Decembris anno 12°* [8 December 1433] *de parva custuma*

[c] *Et in thesauro £441 5s 2d in 6 talliis de custumis et subsidiis* [3, 5, 6, 8, 9 = £307 20d]

[d] *Et in thesauro £148 3s 10½d in 2 talliis de subsidio lanarum* [2, 4]

[e] *Et in thesauro £120 14° die Maii anno 11°* [14 May 1433] *de subsidio 3s de dolio vini et 12d de libra* [11]

[f] *Et in thesauro £13 6s 8d 23^cio^ die Februarii anno 11°* [23 February 1433] *de parva custuma ac subsidio 3s de dolio vini et 12d de libra* [10]

[g] *Et in thesauro £66 13s 4d 19° die Februarii anno 11°* [19 February 1433] *de custumis et subsidiis provenientibus de bonis et mercandisis Aufreomi Spynela et sociorum suorum mercatorum de Janua* [7]

[h] *Et eisdem collectoribus pro misis et expensis suis per tempus predictum 117s 4¼d de rata 10 marcarum per annum* [13]

[i] *Et prefato contrarotulatori pro vadiis suis per idem tempus 35s 1¼d de rata 40s per annum* [13]

[j] *Et in superplusagio, quod iidem collectores habent in alio compoto suo de custuma lanarum a secundo die Aprilis anno 10mo usque festum sancti Michaelis tunc proximum sequens* [2 April-29 September 1432] *rotulo compotorum de hujusmodi custuma*[115] *7s 6d*

[k] *Et Humfrido duci Gloucestrie ... 50 marce de termino Pasche anno 11mo* [12]

Since the decisions regarding the tallies and the customers' petitions for allocation (i.e. allowance of sums paid out at the crown's behest) and exoneration (i.e. for sums which the auditor had wrongly charged the customers) – all of which, if approved, would reduce the customers' liability – were reserved for the Exchequer sitting in full session, the preparation had to be meticulous. Therefore, the auditor directed the customers to submit their *parcelle compoti*, which were comprised of the tallies they had received as proof of payment and their petitions for allocation and exoneration together with all supporting

[114] TNA: PRO, E356/18 m 44.

[115] TNA: PRO, E356/18 m 43d, calendared Jenks, *Enrolled Customs Accounts, vol. 7*, E356/18, No. 257.

documents.[116] At the same time, the auditor sent the copy of the *determinatio* (which had been copied into the Enrolled Customs Accounts and returned with the appropriate endorsement) to the baron who was responsible for guiding the customers through final accounting.[117] In addition, the customers were given a date for final accounting before a full session of the Exchequer. Finally, the Lord Treasurer's Remembrancer – who would assume responsibility for all further summons once the customers had presented their petitions to the full Exchequer (which would deal with the petitions and make a preliminary determination of the customers' net liability to the crown) – entered a brief summary of the copy of the auditor's *determinatio* in his Memoranda Roll (TNA: PRO, E368) in the section entitled *Visus et status compotorum* under the appropriate term. Take, for instance, the first lines of the Lord Treasurer's Remembrancer's entry for the final accounting of John Bokenham and John Bukworth for the issues of wool customs and subsidies and petty customs in Lynn between 29 September 1416 and 29 September 1417:

Lenne Audito compoto Johannis Bokenham et Johannis Bukworth collectorum custumarum et subsidiorum lanarum, coriorum et pellium lanutarum ac parve custume in portu ville de Lenne et in singulis portubus et locis eidem portui adjacentibus per breve regis patens datum 13 die Marcii anno regis nunc secundo prefatis collectoribus directum et annotatum in compoto eorundem collectorum de eodem anno, videlicet de hujusmodi custumis et subsidiis regis ibidem a festo sancti Michaelis anno quarto usque ad festum sancti Michaelis proximum sequens
Debent £996 17s 6¼d

Lenne Audito compoto Johannis Bokenham et Johannis Bukworth collectorum subsidii trium solidorum et dolio et duodecim denariorum de libra in portu et locis predictis per tempus predictum
Debent £369 8s 8¼d[118]

At some point before the full session of the Exchequer which would deal with the customers' petitions for allocation and exoneration, the auditor had to examine the petitions and their supporting documents. The *examinatio* of the *parcelle compoti* was a long drawn out procedure, which is best understood if one takes a concrete example. At final accounting, Thomas Chynnore and John

---

[116] It would appear that this occurred in the term following the assignment of the auditor and the drawing up of the *determinatio*, a conclusion which proceeds from the comparison between the *Nomina computancium* lists and the entries regarding the summoning of the customers in the *recorda* of the King's Remembrancer's Memoranda Roll. However, one is bound to note that auditors' reports on the state of accounting are rare for the customers represented in my ten year steps, simply because the transmission of *Nomina computancium* lists has so many gaps.

[117] With this, the names of the baron and the auditor were entered at the head of the copy of the *determinatio*.

[118] TNA: PRO, E368/190 Visus et status compotorum Michaelmas m 14. Usually, a second scribal hand continues the entry following the *Debent* clause.

Norman, who had collected the petty customs in London from 29 September 1435 to 29 September 1436, handed in not only seven tallies, but also a petition for allowance of the customary expenses of collectors of the petty customs in London[119] and a twelve point petition for allowance of payments of various annuities. The auditor whose task it was to evaluate these *parcelle* could set the tallies aside for the moment, since the Exchequer – sitting in full session – would consider them valid if they matched up to the counterfoils which were in the possession of the deputy chamberlains of the Exchequer of Account.[120] The auditor's first task, then, was to determine whether the customary expenses Chynnore and Norman claimed had in fact been allowed to earlier customers.[121] Then he had to reach a preliminary decision as to whether the sums which the customers had paid out by virtue of the Writ and Letter system were actually allowable. After all, the customers' *parcelle compoti* only contained the *brevia de liberate* (which they had received from the payees) and the indentures or receipts (which certified payment). In each individual case, the auditor had to determine whether there was a corresponding *breve de allocate*, that is to say he had to direct the King's Remembracer's clerks to search out the corresponding document. If the *brevia de allocate* could be found in the King's Remembracer's Memoranda Roll, an entry to this effect was made on the dorse of each individual *breve de allocate*[122] and the originals were tied up in a bundle together with the *brevia de liberate* and the receipts (or indentures).[123] Assuming the auditor found no forgeries amongst the *parcelle compoti*, his next step was to draw up a bill for the full session of the Exchequer which would deal with the customers' petition. Take, for the sake

---

[119] These were: (1) 23 marks (£15 6s 8d) for general expenses (*pro misis et expensis*); (2) 33s 4d for the rent of a house for the collection of customs (*pro quadam domo conducta*); and (3) 100s for expenses incurred in collecting the cloth custom (*pro misis et expensis circa colleccionem custume pannorum*). The sum was £22.

[120] On the whereabouts of the tallies prior to and during accounting, see Appendix II.C.

[121] At least one certification that this was indeed the case has survived among the documentation of the accounting of Chynnore and Norman for the issues of the petty customs in London during the period from 27 Aug. to 29 Sept. 1434: TNA: PRO, E207/14/10 (unnumbered).

[122] See, for instance, TNA: PRO, E122/75/22/4. This is a *breve de allocate* dated 7 Oct. 1436 for Christina Houchon, who had been granted 4d per diem from the London petty customs. The *breve de allocate* was directed to the treasurer and barons of the Exchequer and ordered them to allow the customers all sums which they had demonstrably paid to Houchon. On the dorse of the document was entered *Irrotulatur termino sancti Michaelis anno 14, rotulo 24* (= TNA: PRO, E159/212 Brevia directa baronibus Michaelmas m 24).

[123] This sounds complicated, but is in fact very simple. If the bundle (tied together with a parchment thong in the upper left-hand corner) has not come asunder, the *parcelle compoti* are in good order: payment No. 1 is documented by *breve de allocate* No. 1, *breve de liberate* No. 1, receipt(s) No. 1; payment 2 by *breve de allocate* No. 2, *breve de liberate* No. 2, receipt(s) No. 2 and so forth.

of illustration, the bill the auditor drew up for the petition of Chynnore and Norman (and which he attached to the bundle of *brevia* and receipts).[124]

Thomas Chynnore et Johannes Norman a festo sancti Michaelis anno 13 usque idem festum extunc proximum sequens reddunt compotum de £1675 8s 5¾d

Inde solverunt in thesauro £710 in 5 talliis

Item £133 6s 8d in 2 talliis

Et pro misis et expensis suis per tempus predictum 23 marce. Et eisdem collectoribus pro quadam domo conducta 33s 4d. Et eisdem collectoribus pro misis et expensis suis circa colleccionem custume pannorum 100s

Item Christine Houchon de 4d per diem a festo Michaelis anno 13 usque idem festum proximum sequens £6 20d

Item Johanni Cornewaylle militi pro terminis sancti Michaelis et Pasche anno 13 £218 15s 8d

Item Simoni Campe pro termino Pasche anno 13 £20

Item Johanne regine Anglie pro termino Pasche anno 13 £70 18s 4¼d

Item Johanni comiti Somerset' de £333 6s 8d per annum £300, inde £20 15s 8½d in plenam solucionem de termino sancti Michaelis anno 12 et £166 13s 4d pro termino Pasche anno 12 et £112 10s 11½d in partem solucionis £166 13s 4d pro termino sancti Michaelis anno 13 £300

Item Isabelle Fynbarughe de £10 per annum £11 2s 5¾d, videlicet inde 22s 5¾d in plenam solucionem pro termino sancti Michaelis anno 13 et 100s pro termino Pasche anno 13 et 100s pro termino sancti Michaelis anno 14 £11 2s 5¾d

Item Johanni Pauntone de 6d per diem £13 6s 6d, videlicet a 14 die Aprilis anno 12 usque festum sancti Michaelis anno 14 per 533 dies £13 6s 8d

Item Johanni Yerde armigero de £20 per annum £20 pro terminis sancti Michaelis et Pasche anno 13 £20

Item Johanni Seyntlo de £20 per annum £10 pro termino sancti Michaelis anno 13 £10

Item Philippe Waldyff de £10 per annum £15, videlicet £10 pro terminis sancti Michaelis et Pasche anno 13 et 100s pro termino sancti Michaelis anno 14 £15

Item dicti collectores petunt allocari pro Marko Markadelli, prout irrotulatur termino Michaelis anno 14, rotulo 21 £4 8s 7½d

Item Margarete ducisse Clarencie de £166 13s 4d per annum £100, videlicet inde £83 6s 8d pro termino Pasche anno 12 et £16 13s 4d in partem solucionis de termino sancti Michaelis anno 13 £100

124 TNA: PRO, E122/72/22. The bill is the last piece in the bundle.

Item dictis collectoribus in 1 talliam levatam pro regardo collectorum etc.[125] *£20*

Summa *£1674 19s 11½d*

Once the auditor had drawn up this bill, sewn it to the bundle containing the *brevia* and the receipts and sent it – together with the tallies – off to the baron of the Exchequer whose task it was to guide the customers through final accounting, his job was done. Given the amount of checking that had to be done to evaluate the *parcelle compoti* and prepare the bill, it is scarcely surprising that the auditors were frequently forced to report to the Exchequer that final accounting would have to be delayed for a term because they had been unable to complete the *examinacio* on time.[126]

The full session of the Exchequer had two tasks: verifying payments by tally and dealing with the petitions of the customers. The first task was simple. The customers proferred the tallies they had received from various payees, and the deputy chamberlains of the Exchequer of Account were directed to search out the corresponding counter-tallies for verification. In case of doubt, a check might also be made in the tellers' rolls and/or the receipt rolls, in order to determine if a tally had in fact been levied for the stated amount.[127] If everything matched up, the Exchequer accepted the tallies as proof of payment and a corresponding entry was made in the Enrolled Customs Account.

If the Exchequer approved the customers' petitions for allocation for payment at the behest of the crown, then a corresponding entry was made on the dorse of the relevant *breve de allocate* beneath the *Irrotulatur* entry which recorded where it had been copied onto the King's Remembrancer's Memoranda Roll. In Chynnore and Norman's case, this entry was as follows.

Allocatur in compoto Thome Chynnore et Johannis Norman collectorum parve custume in portu civitatis London' a festo sancti Michaelis anno 13 regis Henrici VI^ti^ usque idem festum tunc proximum sequens rotulo compotorum de eadem custuma[128]

---

[125] This last entry represented the customers' salary. See TNA, PRO, E403/723 m 7 for the issue of £20 to the customers and 20 marks for the controller on 17 June 1437.

[126] See, for example, the *Nomina computancium* list which the auditor William Proctour drew up at the end of Michaelmas term 1462: *Kyngeston super Hull: Johannes Fereby et Johannes Grene collectores custumarum et subsidiorum regis ibidem assignabantur ad computandum in medio hujus termini et parcelle compoti sunt in examinando* [to which a second scribal hand added] *et habent diem per curiam usque proximum terminum:* TNA, PRO, E207/18/4 unnumbered. It is self-evident that the second scribal hand recorded the decision of a full session of the Exchequer (on the basis of a corresponding bill), that the petitions of the Hull customers could not be dealt with in the present term and that this would have to be adjourned to Hilary term, simply because the auditor had not been able to complete the *examinacio* by mid-term.

[127] See Appendix II.B.

[128] TNA: PRO, E122/75/22/1 dorse. The reference to the *rotulus compotorum de eadem custuma* indicated the account in the Enrolled Customs Accounts: TNA: PRO, E356/18 m 20, calendared Jenks, *Enrolled Customs Accounts, vol. 7*, E356/18, No. 118.

In the case of Chynnore and Norman, all petitions for allocation were approved. Therefore, the Exchequer scribe bracketed *allocatur* against all entries on the auditor's bill quoted above. As the entry on the dorse of the individual *brevia de allocate* shows, the Exchequer's decision was also entered in the Enrolled Customs Accounts. Finally, the Lord Treasurer's Remembrancer – who had taken over the task of summoning the customers from the King's Remembrancer[129] – recorded the decisions of the full session of the Exchequer in the section of his Memoranda Roll entitled *Visus et status compotorum* (TNA: PRO, E368) in the appropriate term. The bill which the auditor had prepared and the customers' petition were cancelled by being struck through from top to bottom and were then delivered – together with the customs account and the *parcelle compoti* – to the King's Remembrancer for archiving.[130]

Verification of tallies and allocation of payments at the behest of the crown was the easy part of final accounting. Dealing with the customers' petitions for exoneration was more difficult, since the Exchequer had to determine if the auditor had charged the customers with sums which they did not, in fact, owe to the crown and hence were not liable to pay. In order to understand this decision-making process, it is well to look closely at a specific example. Let us therefore return to the account of the Lynn customers John Bokenham and John Bukworth for the period from 29 September 1416 to 29 September 1417. After reaching a decision on the customers' petitions, the Exchequer determined that they were still liable to the crown for £10 4s 6½d (for wool customs and subsidy and petty customs) and £9 13s 4d (for tunnage and poundage), which the Lord Treasurer's Remembrancer recorded in his Memoranda Roll.[131] At this point Bokenham and Bukworth presented a petition for exoneration with regard to the goods in two ships, explaining that the merchandise had already been customed in other ports.[132] In support of their petition, Bokenham and Bukworth attached the cocket which the customers in Blakeney (in the

---

[129] The King's Remembrancer's responsibility for summoning the customers ended at the moment the first full session of the Exchequer came together to deal with the customers' petitions. Once this session was over, the full Exchequer sent the King's Remembrancer a notice that the customers had 'come and accounted' and that their successors in office were now required to account. Some of these notices were obviously scribbled in great haste: See TNA: PRO, E207/15/13 unnumbered, referring to the Sandwich customers Richard Veer and Ralph Toke. The notices were transcribed verbatim in the recorda of the King's Remembrancer's Memoranda Roll and formed the basis for summoning the customers' successors in office.

[130] On this see TNA: PRO, E368/189 Visus et status compotorum Michaelmas m 22 and *A Guide to the Contents of the Public Record Office*, 3 vols., 2nd edition, London 1963-6, vol. 1, p. 49.

[131] TNA: PRO, E368/190 Visus et status compotorum Michaelmas m 14 (m 189 stamped).

[132] The original petition is transmitted under TNA: PRO, E122/95/31. For the transcription by the Lord Treasurer's Remembrancer see E368/190 Visus et status compotorum Michaelmas m 14 (m 190 stamped).

Yarmouth customs district) had issued on 14 March 1417 when the merchandise had been imported by the alien merchants Carl Henrykson, Arnold Petirson and Peter Johanson in *La Seynte Marye shippe* of the Dordrecht skipper Peter Johanson. In the same petition, the customers also sought exoneration for certain cloth exports by the indigenous merchants William Style and William Ingold 'in a certain ship' (*in aliqua navi*), explaining that customs and subsidy had already been paid in Ipswich. In this case, the customers were unable to attach a cocket and were reduced to swearing an oath that their statements were true and requesting the Exchequer to examine the Ipswich customs account of John Godeston and John Hawe. Pending investigation, the Exchequer granted Bokenham and Bukworth respite (*respectum*) for one term and set a date – *quindena Hillarii* (28 January 1418) – for the continuation of accounting. At the same time, the Exchequer directed the sheriff of Norfolk to ascertain by inquisition whether the goods allegedly customed in Blakeney were the same as those named in the cocket, as Bokenham and Bukworth had claimed.[133] Judging from the delays, it would appear that the sheriff had difficulties in conducting this inquisition, and Bokenham and Bukworth were summoned each term from Hilary 1418 to Michaelmas 1422, only to hear that the matter had been adjourned for yet another term. Finally, in 1430/31, the Exchequer found that the customers only owed 18s, and the Pipe Roll recorded payment of this sum on 9 November 1431.[134] In short, it had taken the Exchequer over 13 years to complete accounting on one customs account.

The Lord Treasurer's Remembrancer was responsible for summoning the customers from the first full session of the Exchequer in which the treasurer and barons dealt with the account for the first time until accounting was completed, at which point the Lord Treasurer's Remembrancer entered *Ideo non fiat hic ulterius execucio* (no further action is necessary) in his Memoranda Roll at the end of the entry for the account. However, the Exchequer did not always wait until the customers had paid the last farthing owing to the crown before declaring accounting complete. It was fairly common to break off the accounting procedure although the customers still owed money or indeed were in surplus (*habent superplusagium*) vis-à-vis the crown.

If accounting procedure was declared complete with the customers in arrears to the crown, the Exchequer directed them to pay up. There were a number of methods of doing so. If the customers were still in office, it was simple enough to charge the sum in question to their current account. For instance, at the end of the entry in the Enrolled Customs Accounts for the account of John Godestone and William Warner for the issues of the wool customs and subsidy and of petty customs in Ipswich in the period from 12 April to 29 September 1413, the Exchequer recorded a net liability of £43 19s 5½d and directed that Gode-

---

[133] TNA: PRO, E122/95/31 in the margin: *Respectum et inquire, si sunt eadem bona seu diversa vicecomiti Norff' per breve directum.*

[134] TNA: PRO, E372/275 Item Kanc'.

stone and Warner *respondent in rotulo sequenti post aliud compotum suum de hujusmodi custumis et subsidiis a festo sancti Michaelis anno 1* [29 Sept. 1413] *usque festum sancti Michaelis proximum sequens* [29 Sept. 1414],[135] that is to say in the following account. It was also possible to transfer surplusses from one account to balance out deficits in another, provided all parties were agreed and the transfer was approved by a full session of the Exchequer on the basis of a corresponding bill. The Boston customer John Belle, for instance, petitioned the Exchequer on 14 November 1403 to transfer £40 14s 10½d of the total surplus of £76 5s 3d from his and John Cok's account for wool customs and subsidy and petty customs in Boston from 2 October to 6 November 1403 to the immediately following account of Richard Aylward and himself for wool customs and subsidy and petty customs in Boston from 6 November 1402 to 19 May 1403.[136]

However, the Exchequer employed these methods of collecting the residue of an account comparatively rarely. It was far more common simply to transfer the debt onto the Pipe Roll and collect it from the sheriff of the appropriate county. This method appears to have impressed itself upon the Exchequer with ever-increasing force for the very reasons which the case of the 18s debt of the Lynn customers Bokenham and Bukworth makes apparent. It was difficult and time-consuming to summon customers (who were not always cooperative or easy to find) to the Exchequer term after term in order to pay small sums. By contrast, it was simplicity itself to make the sheriff responsible for the payment, since he was required to come to Westminster at least yearly to account anyway, so that no special summons was necessary. Moreover, each sheriff was responsible for the debts his predecessors had not discharged, whereas only the customers themselves – and not their successors in office – were liable for debts to the crown arising from their period in office. Once the customers' debt had been transferred to the Pipe Roll, the Exchequer could dispense with summoning them and collect the debt from the sheriff. How he recovered the money from the customers was, to put it briefly, his problem.

As soon as the customers' debt had been transferred to the Pipe Roll, the Clerk of the Pipe (*clericus magni rotuli*) entered a cross-reference to the relevant section of the correct year's Pipe Roll[137] at the end of the record of ac-

---

[135] TNA: PRO, E356/17 m 42d.

[136] TNA: PRO, E368/176 Recorda Michaelmas m 12d and E356/17 m 5d. It is clear that this was a favourite method of the Exchequer for balancing out the customers' surplusses. However, there is at least one case of transferral of a surplus onto the Pipe Roll in order to cancel out a customs account debit: TNA: PRO, E356/19 m 6d and E372/289 Bristoll'.

[137] It is perhaps not altogether otiose to point out that the membranes of the Pipe Roll were bound in the alphabetical order of the county names in Latin. If more than one membrane was required for the county (this was usually the case in our period), then they were designated (at the foot of the dorse) as *London'* (m 1), *Item London'* (m 2), *Adhuc Item London'* (m 3), *Item Adhuc Item London'* (m 4), *Residuum London'* (m 5),

counting contained in the Enrolled Customs Accounts. With this entry the accounting record in the Enrolled Customs Accounts came to an end, since the customers' debt (or surplus) had been transferred from one of the supplementary Pipe Rolls (which was what, in the end, the Enrolled Customs Accounts were) onto the Pipe Roll itself. It was superfluous to keep a redundant second record of the remainder of the accounting procedure.

Nonetheless, the Exchequer still had to see to it that the customers paid their debts to the crown. With the transfer of the debt to the Pipe Rolls, the responsibility for summoning passed from the Lord Treasurer's Remembrancer to the Clerk of the Estreats (*clericus ad extractas in magno scaccario transcribendas*), since it was no longer the customers, but the sheriff who had to be summoned.[138] If the sheriff was unable to obtain payment from the customers the first time around, then responsibility for issuing all further writs – called Summons of the Pipe (*summoniciones pipe*) – passed to the Controller of the Pipe Roll (*contrarotulator magni rotuli*). Irrespective of who was responsible for issuing the writs, the Exchequer's procedure was unvarying. The moment the customers or the sheriff paid over any money at all, the entire procedure of checking tallies against counter-tallies and/or of dealing with petitions for allocation and exoneration was set in motion once again. In the end, when the entire debt was paid off, the Clerk of the Pipe issued a *breve de quieto*, which freed the customers from all further action by the Exchequer. With that, the accounting procedure was truly completed.

Item Residuum London' (m 6), *Adhuc Item Residuum London'* (m 7) etc.

[138] These summons were called 'Summons of the Green Wax' (*summoniciones cere viride*), since they were sealed with green wax. They were issued exclusively for new debts and then handed over by the Clerk of the Estreats to the *summonitor* of the Exchequer (whom the sources occasionally designate as a clerk of the Chancellor of the Exchequer). The *summonitor* passed them on to the Usher of the Upper Exchequer (*hostiarius magni scaccarii*), who sealed them and handed them over to the individual sheriffs or to the Exchequer's messengers for delivery to the sheriffs. On this see TNA: PRO, E207/18/4 unnumbered. At the end of each term, the usher (*hostiarius*) was reimbursed for the costs of sealing and delivering the writs: TNA: PRO, E403, where on the last membrane of each term these costs are totalled under the heading *Liberaciones camerariorum et aliorum ministeriorum tam de magno scaccario quam de recepta scaccarii*. For the sealing and delivery fees see Hall, *Red Book*, vol. 3, p. 835-8.

DIPLOMATIC NOTES ON THE FORM OF THE EDITION

The transcriptions of Latin documents in this edition observe the conventions of the Monumenta Germaniae Historica. The source texts (and all variants) are reproduced in normal type, whilst editorial intrusions are printed without exception in italics (e.g. mardre *L3, in error*). Unambiguous abbreviations are expanded silently (i.e. without use of square brackets or italics to indicate missing letters). u/v and i/j have been regularized silently to accord with pronunciation: thus *vniuersalis* in the source text is rendered *universalis*, whilst 'i' is transcribed if the letter is pronounced as a vowel (*imperii*), and 'j' if the letter is pronounced as a consonant, i.e. like the 'y' in 'you' (*majestas*), even if the source writes *imperij* and *maiestas*.

Personal names and place names are transcribed exactly as written and only regularized in the Index of People and Places.

Roman numerals are reproduced as Arabic numerals, except for the sovereign's ordinal (*Henrici vj*^{ti}). Arabic numerals which occur in the source texts are indicated by bold type. *ob'* is given as ½d, *q'* as ¼d and *ob' q'* as ¾d.

When transcribing the customs accounts, I have numbered the ships consecutively in italics in square brackets. The individual paragraphs of longer texts have also been numbered in the same way. The reason for this is that the digital version of the accounts has no pagination, since the amount of text displayed on the screen depends on the size of the monitor and its resolution. Consequently, cross references – whether within a single document, from one document to another or in the indices – to 'page thus-and-such' are meaningless, and some internal sub-division of the text which can be linked in is unavoidable. Since some scholars will want to use the printed version of the edition and others the digital edition, it is necessary to provide a common basis. Thus, if one scholar refers to ship No. 24 in the digital version of a particular account, those using the printed version will be able to find the vessel in question.

All dates and cross references in the source texts have been resolved in italics in square brackets in the text of the edition, rather than in footnotes.

Note that in resolving return days, I have noted the first date only, relying upon the reader to be aware of the fact that a given return day covers more than one day.[1]

---

[1] C.R. Cheney, Michael Jones (eds.), *A Handbook of Dates for Students of British History* (Royal Historical Society Guides and Handbooks 4), 2nd ed., Cambridge 2000, p. 99, 105-6.

If both the particulars of account and the controlment roll survive, certain variants have been supressed to avoid inflating the text-critical apparatus. Thus, neither the substitution of 'y' in one text for 'i' in the other (e.g. Willyamson, Williamson) nor middle English plural variants (-es, -is, -ys etc.) have been noted in the apparatus criticus. In general, I have limited the notation of textual variants to those cases in which the variant spelling of a word changes the pronunciation. Thus, the variant *federbeds* will be noted against *fetherbeds*, but not *fedderbeds* or *federbeddes* against *federbeds*.

Punctuation is artificial and ignores all medieval full stops, commas and so forth. Since Latin is a syntactic language (like German), the eminently useful MGH convention – namely to employ punctuation (according to the pre-reform German rules) to mark up the grammatical structure of the sentence – has been employed here. I have also broken up the stylistically elegant, but utterly incomprehensible run-on Latin sentences of the source texts into manageable units.

The reader will note that all documents in the *parcelle compoti* of the three accounts and some documents in the subsidiary documents are calendared in English. The reason for this is that, as Hunnisett states, documents embodying routine administrative matters should not be transcribed in full.[2] There can be no doubt that this is the case with the *parcelle compoti*. For instance, the entire story of Henry IV's grant of 4d per diem in alms to Christine Houchon is told in two writs issued to the customers, ordering them to pay Houchon for the half year in question (P 6, P 7, p. 197-8), again in two writs issued to the Exchequer, ordering it to exonerate the customers on proof of payment (P 4, P 5, p. 196-7), in both receipts Houchon issued (P 8, P 9, p. 198) and in the enrolled account (A 4, § 12, p. 210).[3] Nor is there anything to be learned from the full Latin text of 21 receipts issued by John Wygmore in the name of Richard, duke of York, acknowledging payments on York's annuity, since these receipts are identical but for the date and the amount. Such routine administrative matters may be confidently calendared. However, I have adhered to certain rules, reproducing portions of the original Latin text for the following categories of information in the documents: 1) the date and the information about the seal (in diplomatics: the *corroboratio*); 2) all annotations at the foot and on the dorse of the document; 3) proper names; 4) anything particularly significant (especially if it gives an indication of Exchequer procedures), ambiguous or obscure.

Since we are dealing with late medieval administrative Latin, there are some cases which call for local by-laws.

---

[2] R.H. Hunnisett, *Editing Records for Publication* (British Records Association: Archives and the User 4), London 1977, p. 15.

[3] It is as well to note that the Exchequer ran through this entire procedure every year of Christine Houchon's life and that consequently all petty customs accounts for which the *parcelle* survive (in the original or in copy) contain mutatis mutandis identical instructions to the customers and the Exchequer.

First of all, there are a number of middle English words embedded in the Latin texts which have to be assigned a gender, since they are often modified by an abbreviated adjective (e.g. *pro 1 parv' fetherbed*). Since the adjectives are written out in a number of instances (*pro 1 parvo fetherbed*), I have treated middle English words as masculine rather than litter the edition with apostophes.

Second, the sources themselves are in a muddle as to whether the words *custuma* and *subsidium* are singular or plural, and usually avoid the problem by writing *cust'* and *subs'*. If a scribe does write out the one or the other word, it is almost inevitable that he will contradict himself, writing *custuma* in one line and *custume* a few lines later. This muddle is not merely the result of scribal carelessness or the contemporaneous low standard of Latinity. In the fifteenth century, it was possible to differentiate between the collective noun (in the singular) denoting the charges to be paid and the individual sums (in the plural) which each merchant rendered. Even bearing this in mind, however, scribes are simply not consistent. Taking each individual text as a whole, I have done my best to reproduce what the scribe seemed to be thinking.

WOOL CUSTOMS AND SUBSIDY CONTROLMENT ROLL 29 SEPT. 1445-29 SEPT. 1446

Controlment roll of William Baron *for the issues of the wool customs and subsidy in London during the period from 29 Sept. 1445 to 29 Sept. 1446*

L TNA: PRO, E122/76/40. Original controlment roll bound in Exchequer style (7 membranes; contemporaneous numbering of the membranes in the apex: Rotuli Willelmi Baron contrarotulatoris *(beneath that)* rotulo primo *(m 1);* rotulo 2 *(m 2);* rotulo 3 *(m 3);* rotulo 4 *(m 4);* rotulo 5 *(m 5);* rotulo 6 *(m 6);* rotulo 7 *(m 7)). Parchment. Unsealed. Transmitted in a leather bag inscribed* Particule compoti Johannis Poutrell et Thome Pounde collectorum custumarum et subsidiorum lanarum et pellium lanutarum ac custume coriorum in portu civitatis London' et in omnibus aliis portubus et locis eidem portui adjacentibus, videlicet a festo sancti Michaelis anno 24to regis Henrici vj^{ti} *[29 Sept. 1445]* usque festum sancti Michaelis tunc proximum sequens *[29 Sept. 1446]*, scilicet per unum annum integrum, ut infra. *[beneath that there follows a further inscription (possibly relating to the controlment roll) which is illegible but for the words]* custum' et subs'; *[at the bottom]* London'.

m 1
[Marginated] London'

Rotuli Willelmi Baron contrarotulatoris custume et subsidii lanarum et pellium lanutarum ac custume coriorum in portu civitatis London' et in singulis portubus et locis eidem portui adjacentibus, videlicet a festo sancti Michaelis anno 24to regis Henrici vj^{ti} *[29 Sept. 1445]* usque festum sancti Michaelis tunc proxime sequens *[29 Sept. 1446]*, scilicet per unum annum integrum, tempore Johannis Poutrell et Thome Pounde collectorum custume et subsidii predictorum ibidem per idem tempus.

[1] In navi Petre[a] Adreansson vocata Mariknyαt de Ernemouthe exeunte 12[mo] die Octobris anno 24° regis Henrici vj[ti] *[12 Oct. 1445]*

[b]De Angelo Donati [c]de Alledobrando[c], mercatore de Florencia, alienigena, 25 sacci, 9 clavi lane in 24 pokes

[a] *Sic L.* [b] *+ [cross] marginated against this entry and struck through L. Cf. variant c.* [c–c] *Entered by a different hand L.*

[2] In navi Johannis Blomard vocata Holigost de Andewarp exeunte eodem die *[12 Oct. 1445]*

[a]De Angelo Donati [b]de Alledobrando[b], mercator de Florencia, alienigena, 12½ sacci, 7½ clavi lane in 12 pokes

[a] *+ [cross] marginated against this entry and struck through L. Cf. variant b.* [b-b] *Entered by a different hand L.*

[3] In navi Willelmi Johansson vocata Jacobus de Ernemouth exeunte 15° die Novembris *[15 Nov. 1445]*

[a]De [b]Geraso[b] de Pillei et Belizardo de Bardes [c]mercatoribus de Florencia[c], alienigenis, 12½ sacci, 5½ clavi lane in 12 pokes

[a] *+ [cross] marginated against this entry and struck through L. Cf. variant c.* [b–b] *Interlined above* Georgeo, *struck through L.* [c–c] *Entered by a different hand L.*

[4] [a]In navi Johannis Pay vocata Goddysknyαt de le Castelle [b]de Calesia[b] exeunte 12° die Februarii *[12 Feb. 1446]*

De Henre[c] Draper indigena 6 dacre coriorum

[a] *+ [cross] marginated against this entry and struck through L. Cf. variant b.* [b–b] *Interlined L.* [c] *Sic L.*

[5] In navi Johannis Colvylle vocata Maria de London' exeunte 13° die Marcii *[13 Mar. 1446]*

De Willelmo de la Pole, marchione Suff', indigena, 35½ sacci, 11 clavi lane in 15 sarrpellariis, 2 pokes
De Willelmo Holte, indigena, 13½ sacci, 15 clavi lane in 6 sarrpellariis
De eodem Willelmo Holt, indigena, 2700 pelles lanute in 6 fardellis
De Johanne Felde, indigena, 800 pelles lanute in 2 fardellis

[6] In navi Laurencii Shyrett vocata Gabrielle de Suthamptonia exeunte eodem die *[13 Mar. 1446]*

De Thoma Chalton, indigena, 14½ sacci, 11 clavi lane in 6 sarrpellariis
De Willelmo Cantelowe, indigena, 30 sacci, 13 clavi lane in 12 sarrpellariis
De Willelmo Holte, indigena, 9½ sacci, 8 clavi lane in 4 sarrpellariis

[7] In navi Johannis Martyn vocata James de London' exeunte eodem die *[13 Mar. 1446]*

De Willelmo Holte, indigena, 13½ sacci, 11 clavi lane in 6 sarrpellariis
De eodem Willelmo Holte, indigena, 2700 pelles lanute in 6 fardellis
De Willelmo de la Pole, marchione Suff', indigena, 9 sacci, 21 clavi lane in 4 sarrpellariis
De Johanne Felde, indigena, 1600 pelles lanute in 4 fardellis
De Johanne Walden, indigena, 22 sacci, 8 clavi lane in 9 sarrpellariis

[8] [a]In navi Thome [b]Roger[b] vocata Trenyte de [c]Suthamptonia[c] exeunte eodem die *[13 Mar. 1446]*

De Willelmo Holte, indigena, 14 sacci, 10 clavi lane in 6 sarrpellariis
De eodem Willelmo Holte, indigena, 2700 pelles lanute in 6 fardellis
De Willelmo Cantelowe, indigena, 9½ sacci, 12 clavi lane in 4 sarrpellariis
De Johanne Felde, indigena, 1200 pelles lanute in 3 fardellis

[a] + *[cross] marginated against this entry and struck through L. Cf. variants b and c.* [b-b] *Interlined above* Rocher, *struck through L.* [c–c] *Interlined above* Hamton, *struck through L.*

m 1d
m 1d is blank
m 2

[9] In navi Jurdan Mary vocata Johan de Sandewico exeunte 24[to] die Marcii anno 24° *[24 Mar. 1446]*

De Johanne Walden, indigena, 12½ sacci, 15 clavi lane in 5 sarrpellariis
De eodem Johanne Walden, indigena, 350[a] pelles lanute in 1 fardello
De Thoma Chalton, indigena, 11½ sacci, 17 clavi [lane] in 5 sarrpellariis
De Johanne Tate, indigena, 11 sacci, 3 clavi lane in 5 sarrpellariis
De Willelmo Combes, indigena, 11 sacci, 5 clavi lane in 5 sarrpellariis
De Thoma Shrubbe, indigena, 5 sacci, 1 clavus lane in 2 sarrpellariis
De dicto Johanne Walden, indigena, 1 saccus, 13 clavi lane in 1 poke

[a] *Corrected in L from* 352.

[10] In navi Janyn Gylottys vocata le George de Harflete exeunte eodem die *[24 Mar. 1446]*

De Willelmo Cantelowe, indigena, 13 sacci, 8 clavi lane in 5 sarrpellariis, 1 poke
De Thoma Chalton, indigena, 12 sacci, 4 clavi [lane] in 5 sarrpellariis
De Johanne Walden, indigena, 9½ sacci, 7 clavi [lane] in 4 sarrpellariis
De Johanne Pygott, indigena, 10 sacci, 14 clavi lane in 4 sarrpellariis

[11] In navi Willelmi Gaunse vocata Katerine de Grymesby exeunte eodem die *[24 Mar. 1446]*

De Thoma Chalton, indigena, 23 sacci, 24 clavi lane in 10 sarrpellariis
De Willelmo Combes, indigena, 13 sacci, 11 clavi lane in 6 sarrpellariis
De Johanne Walden, indigena, 34 sacci, 23 clavi [lane] in 14 sarrpellariis
De eodem Johanne Walden, indigena, 2550 pelles lanute in 6 fardellis
De Johanne Felde, indigena, 14½ sacci lane in 6 sarrpellariis
De Roberto Horne, indigena, 9 sacci, 15 clavi lane in 4 sarrpellariis
De eodem Roberto Horne, indigena, 4400 pelles lanute in 11 fardellos
De Johanne Tate, indigena, 15½ sacci, 7 clavi lane in 7 sarrpellariis
De Willelmo Holte, indigena, 13½ sacci, 17 clavi lane in 6 sarrpellariis

[12] In navi Thome Hogon vocata James de London' exeunte eodem die *[24 Mar. 1446]*

De Thoma Chalton, indigena, 11½ sacci, 25 clavi lane in 5 sarrpellariis
De Willelmo Holte, indigena, 18 sacci lane in 8 sarrpellariis
De eodem Willelmo Holte, indigena, 4400 pelles lanute in 11 fardellis
De Johanne Pygotte, indigena, 12½ sacci, 20 clavi [lane] in 5 sarrpellariis
De Johanne Felde, indigena, 12½ sacci, 11 clavi lane in 5 sarrpellariis
De eodem Johanne Felde, indigena, 1200 pelles lanute in 3 fardellis
De Thoma Shrubbe, indigena, 9½ sacci, 22 clavi lane in 4 sarrpellariis
[a]De [b]Johanne[b] Walden, indigena, 11 sacci lane in 5 sarrpellariis
De Roberto Horne, indigena, 1200 pelles lanute in 3 fardellis

[a] *+ [cross] marginated against this entry and struck through L. Cf. variant b.*
[b-b] *Interlined above* Willelmo, *struck through L.*

[13] In navi Rogeri Asshecombe vocata Michaell de Dertford exeunte eodem die *[24 Mar. 1446]*

De Willelmo Holte, indigena, 13 sacci, 11 clavi lane in 6 sarrpellariis
De eodem Willelmo Holte, indigena, 2800 pelles lanute in 7 fardellis
De Thoma Shrubbe, indigena, 7½ sacci lane in 3 sarrpellariis
De Johanne Walden, indigena, 4½ sacci, 15 clavi lane in 2 sarrpellariis
De Johanne Pygott, indigena, 9½ sacci, 16 clavi lane in 4 sarrpellariis
De Roberto Horne, indigena, 800 pelles lanute in 2 fardellis
De Johanne Felde, indigena, 1600 pelles lanute in 4 fardellis

[14] In navi Petri Alisaundre vocata Christofore de Rouchestre exeunte eodem die *[24 Mar. 1446]*

De Willelmo Holte, indigena, 14 sacci lane in 6 sarrpellariis
De eodem Willelmo, indigena, 2400 pelles lanute in 6 fardellis
De Thoma Shrubbe, indigena, 9½ sacci, 23 clavi lane in 4 sarrpellariis
De Johanne Tate, indigena, 2 sacci, 12 clavi lane in 1 sarrpellario

De Johanne Mynne et dicto Johanne Tate, indigenis, 1200 pelles lanute in 3 fardellis
De Willelmo Combes, indigena, 2 sacci, 8 clavi lane in 1 sarrpellario
De Roberto Horne, indigena, 1200 pelles lanute in 3 fardellis

[15] In navi Johannis Benslee vocata Trynite de Rochestre exeunte eodem die *[24 Mar. 1446]*

De Willelmo Holte, indigena, 13 sacci, 24 clavi lane in 6 sarrpellariis
De eodem Willelmo Holte, indigena, 3200 pelles lanute in 8 fardellis
De Thoma Shrubbe, indigena, 7 sacci, 23 clavi lane in 3 sarrpellariis
De Johanne Pygott, indigena, 7½ sacci, 7 clavi lane in 3 sarrpellariis
De Willelmo Combes, indigena, 4 sacci, 18 clavi lane in 2 sarrpellariis
De Johanne Mynne et Johanne Tate, indigenis, 2950 pelles lanute in 7 fardellis
m 2d

[16] In navi Ricardi Scotte vocata Cristofore de London' exeunte eodem die *[24 Mar. 1446]*

De Johanne Walden, indigena, 5 sacci, 9 clavi lane in 2 sarrpellariis
De Johanne Felde, indigena, 4½ sacci, 21 clavi lane in 2 sarrpellariis
De eodem Johanne Felde, indigena, 2000 pelles lanute in 5 fardellis
De Willelmo Holte, indigena, 7 sacci, 9 clavi lane in 3 sarrpellariis

[17] In navi Jakett le Gase vocata Maria de Caudebek exeunte eodem die *[24 Mar. 1446]*

De Willelmo Cantelowe, indigena, 25½ sacci lane in 10 sarrpellariis
De Johanne Walden, indigena, 19½ sacci, 5 clavi lane in 8 sarrpellariis
De Thoma Chalton, indigena, 7 sacci, 23 clavi lane in 3 sarrpellariis
De Willelmo Holte, indigena, 22 sacci, 2 clavi lane in 10 sarrpellariis
De eodem Willelmo Holte, indigena, 2600 pelles lanute in 6 fardellis
De Alano Johnson, indigena, 1200 pelles lanute in 3 fardellis

[18] In navi Johannis Frere vocata Thomas de Rochestre exeunte eodem die *[24 Mar. 1446]*

De Johanne Felde, indigena, 800 pelles lanute in 2 fardellis
De Johanne Mynne, indigena, et Johanne Tate, indigena, 1600 pelles lanute in 4 fardellis
De eodem Johanne Tate, indigena, 2 sacci, 9 clavi lane in 1 sarrpellario
De Roberto Horne, indigena, 800 pelles lanute in 2 fardellis
De eodem Roberto Horne indigena, 7 sacci, 4 clavi lane in 3 sarrpellariis
De Willelmo Holte, indigena, 8 sacci, 18 clavi lane in 4 sarrpellariis
De Johanne Pygott, indigena, 13 sacci, 5 clavi lane in 5 sarrpellariis
De Johanne Walden, indigena, 7½ sacci, 22 clavi lane in 3 sarrpellariis
De Willelmo Combes, indigena, 2 sacci, 13 clavi lane in 1 sarrpellario
De Thoma Chalton, indigena, 2 sacci, 24 clavi lane in 1 sarrpellario

De Willelmo Bere, indigena, 2000 pelles lanute in 5 fardellis
De Alano Johnson, indigena, 1200 pelles lanute in 3 fardellis

[19] In navi Davy Boteler vocata Maria de Wynchelsse exeunte primo die Aprilis *[1 Apr. 1446]*

De Willelmo Combes, indigena, 15½ sacci, 17 clavi lane in 7 sarrpellariis
De Johanne Tate, indigena, 18 sacci, 8 clavi lane in 8 sarrpellariis
De Thoma Shrubbe, indigena, 10 sacci, 5 clavi lane in 4 sarrpellariis
De Roberto Horne, indigena, 17 sacci, 20 clavi lane in 7 sarrpellariis
De eodem Roberto Horne, indigena, 2800 pelles lanute in 7 fardellis
De Johanne Walden, indigena, 16½ sacci, 18 clavi lane in 7 sarrpellariis
De Willelmo Holte, indigena, 15 sacci, 12 clavi lane in 6 sarrpellariis, 2 pokes
[a]De Johanne Mynne et [b]dicto[b] Johanne Tate, indigenis, 2600 pelles lanute in 9 fardellis

[a] + *[cross] marginated against this entry and struck through L. Cf. variant b.*
[b-b] *Interlined L.*

[20] In navi Alexandri Stone vocata Margareta de London' exeunte eodem die *[1 Apr. 1446]*

De Willelmo Cantelowe, indigena, 39 sacci, 23 clavi lane in 16 sarrpellariis
De Johanne Walden, indigena, 21½ sacci, 9 clavi lane in 9 sarrpellariis
De Willelmo Holte, indigena, 12½ sacci, 19 clavi lane in 5 sarrpellariis
De Willelmo Combes, indigena, 2 sacci, 13 clavi lane in 1 sarrpellario
De Johanne Tate, indigena, 2 sacci, 10 clavi lane in 1 sarrpellario
De Thoma Chalton, indigena, 4½ sacci, 9 clavi lane in 2 sarrpellariis
De Alano Johnson, indigena, 2000 pelles lanute in 5 fardellis

[21] In navi Willelmi Bunhawe vocata Julyan de Rothomago exeunte eodem die *[1 Apr. 1446]*

De Willelmo Cantelowe, indigena, 21½ sacci lane in 9 sarrpellariis
De Willelmo Holte, indigena, 6½ sacci, 24 clavi lane in 3 sarrpellariis
De Willelmo Combes, indigena, 4½ sacci, 10 clavi lane in 2 sarrpellariis
De Alano Johnson, indigena, 800 pelles lanute in 2 fardellis

[22] In galea Marco de Priole patroni galee de Venisia exeunte 9° die Aprilis *[9 Apr. 1446]*

De Foresto de Robat, mercatore de Florencia, alienigena, 46½ sacci, 13 clavi lane in 40 pokes
De Marco Barbarigo de Venisia, alienigena, 14½ sacci, 13 clavi lane in 13 pokes
De dicto Marco Priole patrono, alienigena, et novem marionariorum[a] suorum 38 coria

[a] *Sic L.*

[23] [a]In galea Johannis Capelle [b]patroni unius galee de Venisia[b] exeunte eodem die *[9 Apr. 1446]*

De eodem Johanne Capelle patrono et 8 marionariis[c] suis, alienigenis, 35 coria

[a] + *[cross] marginated against this entry and struck through L. Cf. variant b.*
[b-b] *Interlined L.* [c] *Sic L.*

[24] In navi Willelmi Cristian vocata Thomas de Sandewico exeunte 14° die Aprilis *[14 Apr. 1446]*

De Johanne Bolle, indigena, 7½ sacci, 17 clavi lane in 3 sarrpellariis
De Johanne Pygott, indigena, 5 sacci, 1 clavus lane in 2 sarrpellariis
De Roberto Horne, indigena, 4½ sacci, 3 clavi lane in 2 sarrpellariis
De eodem Roberto, indigena, 800 pelles lanute in 2 fardellis
De Willelmo Holte, indigena, 4½ sacci, 8 clavi lane in 2 sarrpellariis
De Johanne Tate, indigena, 4 sacci[a], 24 clavi lane in 2 sarrpellariis
De Willelmo Combes, indigena, 2 sacci, 15 clavi lane in 1 sarrpellario
De Johanne Polter, indigena, 1600 pelles lanute in 4 fardellis
De Johanne Mynne et dicto Johanne Tate, indigenis, 600 pelles lanute in 2 fardellis

[a] saccr' *L, in error.*

m 3

[25] In navi Willelmi Taunte vocata Julian de Sandewico exeunte 14° die Aprilis *[14 Apr. 1446]*

De Johanne Bolle, indigena, 10½ sacci, 4 clavi lane in 4 sarrpellariis
De Johanne Pygott, indigena, 5 sacci, 6 clavi lane in 2 sarrpellariis
De Johanne Walden, indigena, 9 sacci, 20 clavi lane in 4 sarrpellariis
De Johanne Tate, indigena, 6½ sacci, 17 clavi lane in 3 sarrpellariis
De Roberto Horne, indigena, 4½ sacci, 10 clavi [lane] in 2 sarrpellariis
De Willelmo Holte, indigena, 8½ sacci, 24 clavi lane in 4 sarrpellariis
De Thoma Wandesford, indigena, 7 sacci, 12 clavi lane in 3 sarrpellariis
De Willelmo Cantelowe, indigena, 4 sacci, 2 clavi lane in 2 sarrpellariis
De Alano Johnson, indigena, 800 pelles lanute in 2 fardellis
De Willelmo Combes, indigena, 4 sacci, 16 clavi lane in 2 sarrpellariis

[26] In navi Roberti Fynneux vocata John de Sandewico exeunte eodem die *[14 Apr. 1446]*

De Johanne Bolle, indigena, 12½ sacci, 18 clavi lane in 5 sarrpellariis
De Roberto Horne, indigena, 4 sacci, 25 clavi lane in 2 sarrpellariis
De Johanne Pygott, indigena, 4½ sacci, 12 clavi lane in 2 sarrpellariis
De Johanne Walden, indigena, 9½ sacci, 6 clavi lane in 4 sarrpellariis
De Willelmo Cantelowe, indigena, 11½ sacci, 12 clavi lane in 5 sarrpellariis
De Willelmo Holte, indigena, 7 sacci, 21 clavi lane[a] in 3 sarrpellariis
De Alano Johnson, indigena, 1200 pelles lanute in 3 fardellis

De Johanne Tate, indigena, 5 sacci, 1 clavus lane in 2 sarrpellariis
De Willelmo Combes, indigena, 2 sacci, 17 clavi lane in 1 sarrpellario

[a] lane *follows, struck through L.*

[27] In navi Johannis Colvyle vocata Maria de London' [a]exeunte[a] eodem die *[14 Apr. 1446]*

De Roberto Horne, indigena, 5 sacci, 6 clavi lane in 2 sarrpellariis
De Johanne Pygott, indigena, 4½ sacci, 20 clavi lane in 2 sarrpellariis
De Willelmo Holte, indigena, 7 sacci, 14 clavi lane in 3 sarrpellariis
De Johanne Tate, indigena, 4½ sacci, 2 clavi lane in 2 sarrpellariis
De Johanne Walden, indigena, 7 sacci lane in 3 sarrpellariis
De Thoma Wandesford, indigena, 6½ sacci, 14 clavi lane in 3 sarrpellariis
De Johanne Pulter, indigena, 3200 pelles lanute in 8 fardellis
De dicto Roberto Horne, indigena, 2800 pelles lanute in 7 fardellis

[a-a] *Interlined L.*

[28] In navi Johannis Pastor vocata Trinite de Dele exeunte eodem die *[14 Apr. 1446]*

De Willelmo Combes, indigena, 4½ sacci, 24 clavi lane in 2 sarrpellariis
De Johanne Bolle, indigena, 7 sacci, 20 clavi lane in 3 sarrpellariis
De Johanne Tate, indigena, 4 sacci, 24 clavi lane in 2 sarrpellariis
De Willelmo Cantelowe, indigena, 6½ sacci, 2 clavi lane in 3 sarrpellariis
De Johanne Waldon, indigena, 7½ sacci, 6 clavi lane in 3 sarrpellariis
De Willelmo Holte, indigena, 2250 pelles lanute in 5 fardellis
De Johanne Felde, indigena, 800 pelles lanute in 2 fardellis
De Roberto Horne, indigena, 350 pelles lanute in 1 fardello

[29] In navi Johannis Breton vocata Thomas de Sandewico exeunte eodem die *[14 Apr. 1446]*

De Johanne Pygott, indigena, 7 sacci, 21 clavi lane in 3 sarrpellariis
De Willelmo Cantelowe, indigena, 2 sacci, 2 clavi lane in 1 sarrpellario
De Johanne Tate, indigena, 2 sacci, 22 clavi lane in 1 sarrpellario
De Johanne Mynne et dicto Johanne Tate, indigenis, 900 pelles lanute in 3 fardellis
De Willelmo Combes, indigena, 6 sacci, 15 clavi lane in 3 sarrpellariis
De Johanne Bolle, indigena, 5 sacci, 10 clavi lane in 2 sarrpellariis
De Johanne Walden, indigena, 4 sacci, 24 clavi lane in 2 sarrpellariis
[a]De Johanne Pulter, indigena, [b]400[b] pelles lanute in 1 fardello
De Johanne Felde, indigena, 800 pelles lanute in 2 fardellis
De Roberto Horne, indigena, 3600 pelles lanute in 9 fardellis

[a] *+ [cross] marginated against this entry and struck through L. Cf. variant b.*
[b-b] *Written over erasure L.*

[30] In navi Edwardi Stone vocata Petrus de London' exeunte eodem die *[14 Apr. 1446]*

De Willelmo Cantelowe, indigena, 6½ sacci, 18 clavi lane in 3 sarrpellariis
De Johanne Felde, indigena, 10 sacci, 12 clavi lane in 4 sarrpellariis
De Roberto White, indigena, 2½ sacci lane in 1 sarrpellario
De Thoma Wymarke, indigena, 7½ sacci, 10 clavi lane in 3 sarrpellariis
De Roberto Horne, indigena, 7 sacci, 10 clavi lane in 3 sarrpellariis
De Johanne Walden, indigena, 2 sacci, 11 clavi lane in 1 sarrpellario
De Johanne Tate, indigena, 6½ sacci, 24 clavi lane in 3 sarrpellariis
[a]De [b]dicto Johanne Felde[b], indigena, 1200 pelles lanute in 3 fardellis
[c-d]De Willelmo Combes, indigena, 6½ sacci, 25 clavi lane in 3 sarrpellariis[d]

[a] b *marginated against this entry L, in order to correct the order of entries which had been disturbed by the fact that William* Combes' *wool exports were added subsequently between the lines. Cf. variant c* [b-b] *Written over erasure by a different hand L.* [c] a *marginated against this entry L, in order to correct the order of entries. Cf. variant a.* [d-d] *Entered subsequently between the lines by a different hand L.*

[31] In navi Thome Boder vocata Johan de Kyngesdon exeunte eodem die *[14 Apr. 1446]*

De Willelmo Combes, indigena, 4½ sacci, 11 clavi lane in 2 sarrpellariis
De Johanne Bolle, indigena, 10½ sacci, 10 clavi lane in 4 sarrpellariis
De Willelmo Holte, indigena, 7 sacci, 10 clavi lane in 3 sarrpellariis
De eodem Willelmo Holte, indigena, 1700 pelles lanute in 4 fardellis
De Johanne Walden, indigena, 6½ sacci, 20 clavi lane in 3 sarrpellariis
De Roberto Horne, indigena, 700 pelles lanute in 2 fardellis
De Johanne Felde, indigena, 1200 pelles lanute in 3 fardellis

[32] In navi Willelmi Brode vocata Maria de Walmere exeunte eodem die *[14 Apr. 1446]*

De Willelmo Holte, indigena, 7½ sacci, 1 clavus lane in 3 sarrpellariis
De Johanne Bolle, indigena, 11½ sacci, 9 clavi lane in 4 sarrpellariis, 1 poke
De Thoma Wymarke, indigena, 12½ sacci, 25 clavi lane in 5 sarrpellariis
De Johanne Walden, indigena, 6½ sacci, 7 clavi lane in 3 sarrpellariis
De Roberto Horne, indigena, 4½ sacci, 2 clavi lane in 2 sarrpellariis
De Johanne Tate, indigena, 4 sacci, 24 clavi lane in 2 sarrpellariis
De dicto Roberto Horne, indigena, 900 pelles lanute in 3 fardellis
De Johanne Bolle juniore, indigena, 400 pelles lanute in 1 fardello
m 3d

[33] In navi Willelmi Popley vocata Maria de Sandewico exeunte eodem die *[14 Apr. 1446]*

De Roberto Horne, indigena, 7 sacci, 25 clavi lane in 3 sarrpellariis
De eodem Roberto Horne, indigena, 1050 pelles lanute in 3 fardellis

De Thoma Wandesford, indigena, 6½ sacci, 20 clavi lane in 3 sarrpellariis
De Johanne Pygott, indigena, 7 sacci, 4 clavi lane in 3 sarrpellariis
De Thoma Wymarke, indigena, 7½ sacci, 12 clavi lane in 3 sarrpellariis
De Johanne Felde, indigena, 12 sacci, 18 clavi lane in 5 sarrpellariis
De dicto Roberto Horne, indigena, 400 pelles lanute in 1 fardello

[34] In navi Johannis Garner vocata Maria Eborum exeunte eodem die *[14 Apr. 1446]*

De Roberto Horne, indigena, 7 sacci, 6 clavi lane in 3 sarrpellariis
De eodem Roberto Horne, indigena, 2500 pelles lanute in 7 fardellis
De Willelmo Combes, indigena, 11½ sacci, 12 clavi lane in 5 sarrpellariis
De Johanne Tate, indigena, 6½ sacci, 9 clavi lane in 3 sarrpellariis
De Johanne Pygott, indigena, 4½ sacci, 19 clavi lane in 2 sarrpellariis
De Thoma Wandesford, indigena, 4 sacci, 24 clavi lane in 2 sarrpellariis
De Thoma Wymarke, indigena, 7½ sacci, 6 clavi lane in 3 sarrpellariis
De Johanne Felde, indigena, 1600 pelles lanute in 4 fardellis
De Willelmo Holte, indigena, 900 pelles lanute in 2 fardellis

[35] In navi Thome Fyneux vocata Peter de Dele exeunte eodem die *[14 Apr. 1446]*

De Johanne Bolle, indigena, 10 sacci, 12 clavi lane in 4 sarrpellariis
De Willelmo Holte, indigena, 7 sacci, 22 clavi lane in 3 sarrpellariis
De Johanne Walden, indigena, 6½ sacci, 20 clavi lane in 3 sarrpellariis
De Thoma Wymarke, indigena, 5 sacci, 4 clavi lane in 2 sarrpellariis
De Johanne Felde, indigena, 1600 pelles lanute in 4 fardellis

[36] In navi Stephani Charles vocata George de Dele exeunte eodem die *[14 Apr. 1446]*

De Johanne Bolle, indigena, 10½ sacci, 6 clavi lane in 4 sarrpellariis
De Roberto Horne, indigena, 5 sacci lane in 2 sarrpellariis
De Thoma Wandesford, indigena, 4½ sacci, 16 clavi lane in 2 sarrpellariis
De Willelmo Holte, indigena, 6½ sacci, 19 clavi lane in 3 sarrpellariis
De Roberto Whyte, indigena, 9½ sacci, 12 clavi lane in 4 sarrpellariis
De Alano Johnson, indigena, 1600 pelles lanute in 4 fardellis

[37] In navi Henrici Godyng vocata Trenyte de Castelond exeunte eodem die *[14 Apr. 1446]*

De Roberto Horne, indigena, 9 sacci, 22 clavi lane in 4 sarrpellariis
De Roberto Whyte, indigena, 7 sacci, 18[a] clavi lane in 3 sarrpellariis
De Johanne Felde, indigena, 9 sacci, 11 clavi lane in 4 sarrpellariis
De Alano Johnson, indigena, 2000 pelles lanute in 5 fardellis

[a] Corrected in L from *17*.

[38] In navi Johannis Mellar vocata Maria de Lynne exeunte eodem die *[14 Apr. 1446]*

De Roberto White, indigena, 9½ sacci, 10 clavi lane in 4 sarrpellariis
De Johanne Feld, indigena, 9½ sacci, 4 clavi lane in 4 sarrpellariis
De eodem Johanne Felde, indigena, 2000 pelles lanute in 5 fardellis
De Johanne Pulter, indigena, 4½ sacci, 22 clavi lane in 2 sarrpellariis
De Johanne Pygott, indigena, 5 sacci, 2 clavi lane in 2 sarrpellariis
De Roberto Horne, indigena, 7½ sacci, 16 clavi lane in 3 sarrpellariis
De Willelmo Turke, indigena, 1350 pelles lanute in 3 fardellis
De dicto Roberto Horne, indigena, 800 pelles lanute in 2 fardellis

[39] In navi Ricardi Brere vocata Valentyne de Doncastre exeunte eodem die *[14 Apr. 1446]*

De Roberto Whyte, indigena, 15 sacci, 1 clavus lane in 6 sarrpellariis
De Willelmo Holte, indigena, 7 sacci, 15 clavi lane in 3 sarrpellariis
De Roberto Horne, indigena, 9½ sacci, 24 clavi lane in 4 sarrpellariis
De Johanne Pygott, indigena, 9½ sacci, 16 clavi [lane] in 4 sarrpellariis
De Johanne Felde, indigena, 7½ sacci, 1 clavus [lane] in 3 sarrpellariis
De Thoma Wandesford, indigena, 2 sacci, 10 clavi lane in 1 sarrpellario
De dicto Roberto Horne, indigena, 600 pelles lanute in 2 fardellis
De Johanne Pulter, indigena, 3200 pelles lanute in 8 fardellis

[40] In navi Johannis Fyrmyn vocata George de Cane exeunte eodem die *[14 Apr. 1446]*

De Roberto Horne, indigena, 14 sacci, 3 clavi lane in 6 sarrpellariis
De Roberto Whyte, indigena, 9½ sacci, 16 clavi lane in 4 sarrpellariis
De Willelmo Holte, indigena, 19½ sacci, 23 clavi [lane] in 8 sarrpellariis
De Johanne Pulter, indigena, 9½ sacci, 12 clavi lane in 4 sarrpellariis
De Thoma Wymarke, indigena, 5 sacci, 14 clavi lane in 2 sarrpellariis
De Ricardo Cely et Ricardo Bowell, indigenis, 6½ sacci, 17 clavi lane in 3 sarrpellariis
De dicto Roberto Horne, indigena, 1600 pelles lanute in 4 fardellis
De dicto Willelmo Holte, indigena, 3200 pelles lanute in 8 fardellis
De Willelmo Cantelow, indigena, 6½ sacci, 4 clavi lane in 3 sarrpellariis
m 4

[41] In navi Rogeri Vytemylle vocata Julian de Hareflete exeunte eodem die *[14 Apr. 1446]*

De Willelmo Holte, indigena, 17½ sacci, 21 clavi lane in 8 sarrpellariis
De Roberto Horne, indigena, 12 sacci, 5 clavi lane in 5 sarrpellariis
De Johanne Pulter, indigena, 4½ sacci, 6 clavi lane in 2 sarrpellariis
De Willelmo Cantelowe, indigena, 7 sacci, 8 clavi lane in 3 sarrpellariis
De Johanne Felde, indigena, 2000 pelles lanute in 5 fardellis

De dicto Roberto Horne, indigena, 3000 pelles lanute in 8 fardellis
De dicto Willelmo Holte, indigena, 7 sacci, 10 clavi lane in 3 sarrpellariis
De Ricardo Cely et Ricardo Bowell, indigenis, 7 sacci, 18 clavi lane in 3 sarrpellariis

[42] In navi Roberti Michell vocata Margareta de Thorphith exeunte eodem die *[14 Apr. 1446]*

De Johanne Pulter, indigena, 4½ sacci, 21 clavi lane in 2 sarrpellariis
De Johanne Tate, indigena, 2 sacci, 16 clavi lane in 1 sarrpellario
De Ricardo Cely et Ricardo Bowell, indigenis, 6½ sacci, 21 clavi lane in 3 sarrpellariis
De Roberto Horne, indigena, 7 sacci, 6 clavi lane in 3 sarrpellariis
De Roberto Whyte, indigena, 7 sacci, 23 clavi lane in 3 sarrpellariis
De Johanne Mynne et dicto Johanne Tate, indigenis, 650 pelles lanute in 2 fardellis
[a]De dicto Johanne Pulter, indigena, 3100 pelles lanute in 8[b] fardellis

[a] *+ [cross] marginated against this entry and struck through L. Cf. variant b.*
[b] *Corrected in L from* 7.

[43] In navi Nicholai Baron vocata Plente de Calesia exeunte 11° die Junii *[11 June 1446]*

De Johanne Pygott, indigena, 15 sacci, 11 clavi lane in 6 sarrpellariis
De Roberto White, indigena, 33½ sacci, 4 clavi lane in 13 sarrpellariis
De Johanne Wymark, indigena, 5 sacci lane in 2 sarrpellariis
De Johanne Pulter, indigena, 19 sacci, 6 clavi lane in 8 sarrpellariis
De Johanne Felde, indigena, 12½ sacci, 20 clavi lane in 6 sarrpellariis
De eodem Johanne Felde, indigena, 800 pelles lanute in 2 fardellis
De Roberto Horne, indigena, 9½ sacci, 23 clavi lane in 5 sarrpellariis
De Alano Johnson, indigena, 14 sacci, 16 clavi lane in 5 sarrpellariis, 2 pokes
De Johanne Walden, indigena, 9 sacci, 17 clavi lane in 4 sarrpellariis

[44] [a]In navi Willelmi Henryson vocata Mychell de Sneythe[b] exeunte eodem die *[11 June 1446]*

De Alano Johnson, indigena, 15 sacci, 11 clavi lane in 6 sarrpellariis
De Roberto Horne, indigena, 7½ sacci, 14 clavi lane in 4 sarrpellariis
De Johanne Walden, indigena, 12 sacci, 11 clavi lane in 5 sarrpellariis
De Johanne Felde, indigena, 8 sacci, 24 clavi lane in 4 sarrpellariis
De Roberto White, indigena, 5 sacci lane in 2 sarrpellariis
De Thoma Shrubbe, indigena, 1200 pelles lanute in 3 fardellis
De Willelmo Combes, indigena, 2400 pelles lanute in 6 fardellis
De Johanne Mynne, indigena, 352 pelles lanute in 1 fardello

[a] *+ [cross] marginated against this entry and struck through L. Cf. variant b.*
[b] *Corrected in L from* Snethe.

[45] In navi Roberti Bridsall vocata Nicholaus de Hull exeunte eodem die *[11 June 1446]*

De Alano Johnson, indigena, 13 sacci, 7 clavi lane in 5 sarrpellariis
De Johanne Walden, indigena, 13½ sacci, 6 clavi lane in 6 sarrpellariis
De Roberto White, indigena, 9 sacci, 22 clavi lane in 4 sarrpellariis
De Roberto Horne, indigena, 7½ sacci, 19 clavi lane in 4 sarrpellariis
De Johanne Felde, indigena, 8 sacci, 25 clavi lane in 4 sarrpellariis
De eodem Johanne Felde, indigena, 400 pelles lanute in 1 fardello
De Roberto Danvers, indigena, 6 sacci, 22 clavi lane in 3 sarrpellariis
De Johanne Tate, indigena, 487 pelles lanute in 1 fardello
De Willelmo Combes, indigena, 3600 pelles lanute in 9 fardellis

[46] In navi Johannis Pay vocata Goddesknyght de Calesia exeunte eodem die *[11 June 1446]*

De Johanne Felde, indigena, 4 sacci, 1 clavus lane in 2 sarrpellariis
De eodem Johanne Felde, indigena, 760 pelles lanute in 2 fardellis
De Johanne Pygott, indigena, 6 sacci, 16 clavi lane in 2 sarrpellariis, 1 poke
De Roberto Whyte, indigena, 5 sacci lane in 2 sarrpellariis
De Roberto Horne, indigena, 3½ sacci, 18 clavi lane in 2 sarrpellariis
De Johanne Pulter, indigena, 7 sacci, 14 clavi lane in 3 sarrpellariis
De Johanne Levyng, indigena, 4 sacci, 22 clavi lane in 2 sarrpellariis
De Thoma Shrubbe, indigena, 1600 pelles lanute in 4 fardellis
De dicto Roberto Whyte, indigena, 2½ sacci, 5 clavi lane in 2 pokes
De Thoma Wymark, indigena, 1½ sacci, 13 clavi lane in 2 pokes
De Alano Johnson, indigena, 760 pelles lanute in 2 fardellis
De Willelmo Combes, indigena, 400 pelles lanute in 1 fardello
De Willelmo Holte, indigena, 1200 pelles lanute in 3 fardellis
De Willelmo Bere, indigena, 6½ sacci, 21 clavi lane in 2 sarrpellariis, 2 pokes
De dicto Johanne Felde, indigena, 400 pelles lanute in 1 fardello
m 4d

[47] In navi Johannis Clynke vocata Nyghtynghale de Calesia exeunte eodem die *[11 June 1446]*

De Johanne Pygott, indigena, 7 sacci, 9 clavi lane in 3 sarrpellariis
De Roberto Whyte, indigena, 4½ sacci, 8 clavi lane in 2 sarrpellariis
De Alano Johnson, indigena, 5 sacci, 16 clavi lane in 2 sarrpellariis
De Roberto Horne, indigena, 2½ sacci, 5 clavi lane in 2 pokes
De Willelmo Hychecok, indigena, 4 sacci, 25 clavi lane in 2 sarrpellariis
De Willelmo Combes, indigena, 2 sacci, 12 clavi lane in 1 sarrpellario
De Johanne Pulter, indigena, 2 sacci, 20 clavi lane in 1 sarrpellario
De Thoma Shrubbe, indigena, 800[a] pelles lanute in 2 fardellis
De Johanne Felde, indigena, 800 pelles lanute in 2 fardellis
De Willelmo Holte, indigena, 800 pelles lanute in 2 fardellis

[a] *Corrected in L from* 700.

[48] In navi Johannis Covy vocata Margareta de Dunwych exeunte eodem die *[11 June 1446]*

De Johanne Felde, indigena, 6 sacci, 23 clavi lane in 3 sarrpellariis
De Johanne Pulter, indigena, 8½ sacci, 21 clavi lane in 4 sarrpellariis
De Johanne Pygott, indigena, 4½ sacci, 25 clavi lane in 2 sarrpellariis
De Roberto Whyte, indigena, 10½ sacci lane in 4 sarrpellariis
De Willelmo Holte, indigena, 5½ sacci, 4 clavi lane in 2 sarrpellariis, 1 poke
De Johanne Levyng, indigena, 4 sacci, 21 clavi lane in 2 sarrpellariis
De Johanne Tate, indigena, 1600 pelles lanute in 4 fardellis
De Thoma Wymark, indigena, 400 pelles lanute in 1 fardello
De dicto Roberto Whyte, indigena, 21 clavi lane in 1 poke
De Willelmo Combes, indigena, 2800 pelles lanute in 7 fardellis
De dicto Johanne Felde, indigena, 400 pelles lanute in 1 fardello

[49] In navi Johannis Hadham vocata Antonius Magnus de London' exeunte eodem die *[11 June 1446]*

De Roberto Danvers, indigena, 21 sacci, 23 clavi lane in 10 sarrpellariis
De Roberto Whyte, indigena, 39½ sacci, 15 clavi lane in 15 sarrpellariis
De Willelmo Hychecok, indigena, 4½ sacci, 18 clavi lane in 2 sarrpellariis
De Willelmo Combes, indigena, 20½ sacci, 17 clavi lane in 9 sarrpellariis
De Willelmo Cantelow, indigena, 74 sacci, 16 clavi lane in 30 sarrpellariis
De Johanne Pygott, indigena, 7 sacci, 4 clavi lane in 3 sarrpellariis
De Johanne Harowe, indigena, 13 sacci, 15 clavi lane in 6 sarrpellariis
De Johanne Walden, indigena, 30½ sacci, 13 clavi lane in 13 sarrpellariis
De Alano Johnson, indigena, 5 sacci, 5 clavi lane in 2 sarrpellariis
De eodem Alano Johnson, indigena, 4000 pelles lanute in 10 fardellis
De Johanne Felde, indigena, 11 sacci, 4 clavi lane in 5 sarrpellariis
De Roberto Horne, indigena, 12½ sacci lane in 6 sarrpellariis
De Willelmo Holte, indigena, 71½ sacci, 22 clavi lane in 30 sarrpellariis
De Thoma Chalton, indigena, 11 sacci, 12 clavi lane in 5 sarrpellariis
De Johanne Haryngton, indigena, 4 sacci, 19 clavi lane in 2 sarrpellariis
De Johanne Pulter, indigena, 23 sacci, 21 clavi lane in 10 sarrpellariis
De Johanne Levyng, indigena, 4½ sacci, 14 clavi lane in 2 sarrpellariis
De Ricardo Sharpe, indigena, 22½ sacci, 17 clavi lane in 10 sarrpellariis

[50] In navi Willelmi Edrich vocata Elena de London' exeunte eodem die *[11 June 1446]*

De Roberto Horne, indigena, 12½ sacci, 3 clavi lane in 6 sarrpellariis
De Johanne Pygott, indigena, 12 sacci, 10 clavi lane in 5 sarrpellariis
De Roberto Danvers, indigena, 22 sacci, 5 clavi lane in 10 sarrpellariis, 1 poke
De Willelmo Cantelowe, indigena, 57 sacci, 4 clavi lane in 23 sarrpellariis
De Johanne Harowe, indigena, 11½ sacci, 25 clavi lane in 6 sarrpellariis

De Roberto Whyte, indigena, 21 sacci, 21 clavi lane in 8 sarrpellariis
De Willelmo Holte, indigena, 46½ sacci, 25 clavi lane in 20 sarrpellariis
De Johanne Haryngton, indigena, 17½ sacci, 15 clavi lane in 8 sarrpellariis
De Johanne Walden, indigena, 27 sacci, 22 clavi lane in 12 sarrpellariis
De Johanne Pulter, indigena, 6½ sacci, 14 clavi lane in 3 sarrpellariis
De Alano Johnson, indigena, 2½ sacci, 8 clavi lane in 2 pokes
De Johanne Levyng, indigena, 2 sacci, 10 clavi lane in 1 sarrpellario
De Willelmo Combes, indigena, 24½[a] sacci, 25 clavi lane in 10 sarrpellariis
De Ricardo Sharpe, indigena, 6½ sacci, 15 clavi lane in 3 sarrpellariis
De Willelmo Hychecok, indigena, 2 sacci, 14 clavi lane in 1 sarrpellario
De dicto Alano Johnson, indigena, 3764 pelles lanute in 9 fardellis

[a] *Corrected in L from* 23½.

m 5

[51] In navi Willelmi Cruce vocata Anna de London' exeunte eodem die *[11 June 1446]*

De Johanne Walden, indigena, 30 sacci, 3 clavi lane in 13 sarrpellariis
De Roberto Horne, indigena, 20½ sacci, 22 clavi lane in 9 sarrpellariis
De Roberto Danvers, indigena, 23 sacci, 23 clavi lane in 10 sarrpellariis, 1 poke
De Johanne Pulter, indigena, 30 sacci lane in 13 sarrpellariis
De Roberto Whyte, indigena, 26 sacci, 3 clavi lane in 10 sarrpellariis
De Johanne Harowe, indigena, 12½ sacci, 5 clavi lane in 6 sarrpellariis
De Willelmo Combes, indigena, 21 sacci, 18 clavi lane in 9 sarrpellariis
De Willelmo Cantelowe, indigena, 29½ sacci, 3 clavi lane in 12 sarrpellariis
De Alano Johnson, indigena, 15 sacci, 25 clavi lane in 6 sarrpellariis
De Johanne Pygott, indigena, 5 sacci, 4 clavi lane in 2 sarrpellariis
De Johanne Felde, indigena, 6½ sacci, 16 clavi lane in 3 sarrpellariis
De Willelmo Holte, indigena, 40 sacci, 3 clavi lane in 17 sarrpellariis
De Thoma Chalton, indigena, 5 sacci, 1 clavus lane in 2 sarrpellariis, 1 poke
De Johanne Levyng, indigena, 6 sacci, 19 clavi lane in 3 sarrpellariis
De Johanne Haryngton, indigena, 2 sacci, 12 clavi lane in 1 sarrpellario
De Thoma Shrubbe, indigena, 2800 pelles lanute in 7 fardellis
De Willelmo Fallan, clerico, indigena, 4½ sacci, 14 clavi lane in 1 sarrpellario, 2 pokes
De Ricardo Sharpe, indigena, 2 sacci, 14 clavi lane in 1 sarrpellario
De dicto Willelmo Combes, indigena, 800 pelles lanute in 2 fardellis

[52] In navi Edwardi Stone vocata Peter de London' exeunte eodem die *[11 June 1446]*

De Roberto Horne, indigena, 9 sacci, 1 clavus lane in 4 sarrpellariis
De Roberto Whyte, indigena, 18 sacci, 25 clavi lane in 7 sarrpellariis
De Johanne Felde, indigena, 7½ sacci, 1 clavus lane in 3 sarrpellariis
De Johanne Levyng, indigena, 16 sacci, 2 clavi lane in 7 sarrpellariis

De dicto Johanne Felde, indigena, 1600 pelles lanute in 4 fardellis

[53] In navi Thome Broun vocata James de London' exeunte eodem die *[11 June 1446]*

De Roberto Whyte, indigena, 20½ sacci, 10 clavi lane in 8 sarrpellariis
De Roberto Danvers, indigena, 15 sacci, 24 clavi lane in 7 sarrpellariis
De Willelmo Hychecok, indigena, 2 sacci, 15 clavi lane in 1 sarrpellario
De Willelmo Holte, indigena, 18½ sacci, 15 clavi lane in 8 sarrpellariis
De Johanne Harowe, indigena, 8 sacci, 24 clavi lane in 4 sarrpellariis
De Johanne Tate, indigena, 1600 pelles lanute in 4 fardellis
De Ricardo Sharpe, indigena, 9 sacci, 16 clavi lane in 4 sarrpellariis
De Johanne Haryngton, indigena, 4½ sacci, 23 clavi lane in 2 sarrpellariis
De Johanne Walden, indigena, 2½ sacci lane in 1 sarrpellario
De Johanne Pulter, indigena, 4½ sacci, 14 clavi lane in 2 sarrpellariis
De Johanne Levyng, indigena, 2 sacci, 8 clavi lane in 1 sarrpellario
De Willelmo Combes, indigena, 4000 pelles lanute in 10 fardellis
De Johanne Felde, indigena, 2000 pelles lanute in 5 fardellis
De Katerina Felde, indigena, 400 pelles lanute in 1 fardello

[54] In navi Colyn Geryn vocata le Jonet de Roen exeunte eodem die *[11 June 1446]*

De Willelmo Combes, indigena, 9 sacci, 4 clavi lane in 4 sarrpellariis
De Johanne Harowe, indigena, 10½ sacci, 21 clavi lane in 5 sarrpellariis
De Willelmo Cantelow, indigena, 27½ sacci, 2 clavi lane in 11 sarrpellariis
De Johanne Levyng, indigena, 4½ sacci, 16 clavi lane in 2 sarrpellariis
De Alano Johnson, indigena, 800 pelles lanute in 2 fardellis

[55] In navi Henrici Geduke vocata Katerine de Dunwych exeunte eodem die *[11 June 1446]*

De Ricardo Sharpe, indigena, 9 sacci lane in 4 sarrpellariis
De Willelmo Combes, indigena, 4½ sacci, 2 clavi lane in 2 sarrpellariis
Dc Johanne Pulter, indigena, 20 sacci, 4 clavi lane in 9 sarrpellariis
De Roberto White, indigena, 5 sacci, 10 clavi lane in 2 sarrpellariis
De Johanne Levyng, indigena, 4½ sacci, 14 clavi lane in 2 sarrpellariis
De Willelmo Holte, indigena, 4½ sacci, 21 clavi lane in 2 sarrpellariis
De Johanne Levyng juniore et Roberto Levyng, indigenis, 1 saccus, 11 clavi lane in 1 poke
De Willelmo Bere, indigena, 800 pelles lanute in 2 fardellis
De Johanne Pygott, indigena, 231 pelles lanute in 1 fardello

[56] In navi Johannis Sutton vocata Margareta de London' exeunte eodem die *[11 June 1446]*

De Willelmo Holte, indigena, 12 sacci, 13 clavi lane in 5 sarrpellariis
De Willelmo Hychecok, indigena, 2 sacci, 14 clavi lane in 1 sarrpellario

De Ricardo Sharpe, indigena, 4½ sacci, 4 clavi lane in 2 sarrpellariis
De Roberto Danvers, indigena, 9 sacci, 1 clavus lane in 4 sarrpellariis
De Willelmo Cantelowe, indigena, 16 sacci, 7 clavi lane in 6 sarrpellariis, 1 poke
De Johanne Har[o]we, indigena, 7 sacci, 9 clavi lane in 3 sarrpellariis
De Johanne Tate, indigena, 2000 pelles lanute in 5 fardellis
De Johanne Walden, indigena, 5½ sacci, 15 clavi lane in 2 sarrpellariis, 1 poke
De Thoma Chalton, indigena, 5 sacci, 21 clavi lane in 2 sarrpellariis, 1 poke
De Johanne Pulter, indigena, 4½ sacci, 8 clavi lane in 2 sarrpellariis
De Willelmo Combes, indigena, 3200 pelles lanute in 8 fardellis
De eodem Willelmo Combes, indigena, ½ [saccus], 13 clavi lane in 1 poke
De dicto Ricardo Sharpe, indigena, 1166 pelles lanute in 3 fardellis
m 5d

[57] In navi Rogeri Asshecombe vocata Michell de Dertford exeunte eodem die *[11 June 1446]*

De Johanne Levyng, indigena, 4½ sacci, 8 clavi lane in 2 sarrpellariis
De Johanne Pulter, indigena, 4½ sacci, 2 clavi lane in 2 sarrpellariis
De Willelmo Bere, indigena, 8 sacci, 9 clavi lane in 3 sarrpellariis, 1 poke
De Roberto Whyte, indigena, 5 sacci, 25 clavi lane in 2 sarrpellariis
De Willelmo Cantelowe, indigena, 7½ sacci, 5 clavi lane in 3 sarrpellariis
De Willelmo Combes, indigena, 6½ sacci, 15 clavi lane in 3 sarrpellariis
De Thoma Shrubbe, indigena, 1600 pelles lanute in 4 fardellis
De Johanne Mynne, indigena, 2000 pelles lanute in 7 fardellis
De dicto Willelmo Bere, indigena, 1700 pelles lanute in 4 fardellis

[58] In navi Ricardi Bryre vocata Valentyn de Dancastre exeunte eodem die *[11 June 1446]*

De Roberto Whyte, indigena, 17 sacci, 23 clavi lane in 7 sarrpellariis
De Willelmo Cantelowe, indigena, 4½ sacci, 25 clavi lane in 2 sarrpellariis
De Roberto Danvers, indigena, 2 sacci lane in 1 sarrpellario
De Willelmo Holte, indigena, 16 sacci, 21 clavi lane in 7 sarrpellariis
De Ricardo Sharpe, indigena, 4 sacci, 19 clavi lane in 2 sarrpellariis
De Johanne Haryngton, indigena, 4 sacci, 21 clavi lane in 2 sarrpellariis
De Willelmo Combes, indigena, 4½ sacci, 4 clavi lane in 2 sarrpellariis
De Johanne Pulter, indigena, 4½ sacci, 14 clavi lane in 2 sarrpellariis
De Thoma Shrubbe, indigena, 2150 pelles lanute in 5 fardellis
De Ricardo Cely et Ricardo Bowell, indigenis, 3152 pelles lanute in 8 fardellis

[59] In navi Johannis Frere vocata Thomas de Rochestre exeunte eodem die *[11 June 1446]*

De Willelmo Combes, indigena, 9½ sacci, 2 clavi lane in 4 sarrpellariis
De Johanne Mynne, indigena, 4 sacci, 16 clavi lane in 2 sarrpellariis
De Johanne Pulter, indigena, 16 sacci, 25 clavi lane in 7 sarrpellariis

De Johanne Pygott, indigena, 2½ sacci lane in 1 sarrpellario
De Roberto Whyte, indigena, 4½ sacci, 16 clavi lane in 2 sarrpellariis
De Ricardo Sharp, indigena, 4½ sacci, 3 clavi lane in 2 sarrpellariis
De Thoma Shrubbe, indigena, 2400 pelles lanute in 6 fardellis
De dicto Johanne Mynne, indigena, 1000 pelles lanute in 4 fardellis
De dicto Johanne Pulter, indigena, 1600 pelles lanute in 4 fardellis
De Ricardo Cely et Ricardo Bowell, indigenis, 1600 pelles lanute in 4 fardellis

[60] In navi Henrici Vyde vocata Christoforus de Colchestre exeunte eodem die *[11 June 1446]*

De Johanne Levyng, indigena, 9 sacci, 23 clavi lane in 4 sarrpellariis
De Willelmo Combes, indigena, 14½ sacci, 2 clavi lane in 6 sarrpellariis
De Johanne Felde, indigena, 4½ sacci, 15 clavi lane in 2 sarrpellariis
De Roberto Whyte, indigena, 9½ sacci, 15 clavi lane in 4 sarrpellariis
De Ricardo Sharpe, indigena, 4 sacci, 15 clavi lane in 2 sarrpellariis
De Johanne Har[o]we, indigena, 4 sacci, 2 clavi lane in 2 sarrpellariis
De Willelmo Cantelowe, indigena, 2 sacci, 22 clavi lane in 1 sarrpellario
De Thoma Wymark, indigena, 1000 pelles lanute in 3 fardellis
De Roberto Danvers, indigena, ½ [saccus], 12 clavi lane in 1 poke

[61] In navi Johannis Eston vocata Leonard de Eborum exeunte eodem die *[11 June 1446]*

De Roberto Whyte, indigena, 14 sacci, 25 clavi lane in 6 sarrpellariis
De Johanne Harowe, indigena, 11½ sacci, 19 clavi lane in 5 sarrpellariis
De Johanne Levyng, indigena, 8½ sacci, 6 clavi lane in 4 sarrpellariis
De Willelmo Cantelowe, indigena, 12½ sacci, 7 clavi lane in 5 sarrpellariis
De Willelmo Combes, indigena, 9 sacci lane in 4 sarrpellariis
De Thoma Wandesford, indigena, 4½ sacci, 8 clavi lane in 2 sarrpellariis
De Johanne Pygott, indigena, 7 sacci, 25 clavi lane in 3 sarrpellariis
De Ricardo Cely et Ricardo Bowell, indigenis, 9 sacci, 16 clavi lane in 4 sarrpellariis
De Ricardo Sharpe, indigena, 2 sacci, 20 clavi lane in 1 sarrpellario
De Roberto Danvers, indigena, 4½ sacci, 1 clavus lane in 2 sarrpellariis
De Alano Johnson, indigena, 190 pelles lanute in 1 fardello
De Johanne Felde, indigena, 1200 pelles lanute in 3 fardellis

[62] In navi Willelmi Henrikson vocata George van Scluse exeunte eodem die *[11 June 1446]*

De Johanne Pulter, indigena, 7½ sacci, 3 clavi lane in 3 sarrpellariis
De Johanne Harowe, indigena, 7 sacci, 9 clavi lane in 3 sarrpellariis
De Thoma Wandesford, indigena, 6½ sacci, 16 clavi lane in 3 sarrpellariis
De Ricardo Sharpe, indigena, 4 sacci, 19 clavi lane in 2 sarrpellariis
De Roberto Danvers, indigena, 9 sacci lane in 4 sarrpellariis
De Johanne Penne, indigena, 1900 pelles lanute in 5 fardellis

De Johanne Tate, indigena, 1200 pelles lanute in 3 fardellis
De Willelmo Combes, indigena, 3200 pelles lanute in 8 fardellis

[63] In navi Laurencii de Lyle vocata Nycholaus de Roone exeunte eodem die *[11 June 1446]*

De Willelmo Cantelowe, indigena, 9½ sacci, 21 clavi lane in 4 sarrpellariis
De Johanne Harowe, indigena, 2 sacci, 16 clavi lane in 1 sarrpellario
De Willelmo Combes, indigena, 7 sacci, 10 clavi lane in 3 sarrpellariis
De Roberto Danvers, indigena, 6½ sacci, 2 clavi lane in 3 sarrpellariis
De Roberto Whyte, indigena, 8 sacci, 6 clavi lane in 3 sarrpellariis
De Johanne Pulter, indigena, 6½ sacci, 18 clavi lane in 3 sarrpellariis
De Ricardo Sharpe, indigena, 800 pelles lanute in 2 fardellis
m 6

[64] In navi Petri Alexander vocata Christofore de Rochestre exeunte eodem die *[11 June 1446]*

De Johanne Pulter, indigena, 5 sacci, 4 clavi lane in 2 sarrpellariis
De Johanne Harowe, indigena, 7 sacci, 2 clavi lane in 3 sarrpellariis
De Johanne Levyng, indigena, 2 sacci, 6 clavi lane in 1 sarrpellario
De Johanne Penne, indigena, 400 pelles lanute in 1 fardello
De Johanne Tate, indigena, 800 pelles lanute in 2 fardellis
De Willelmo Holte, indigena, 8½ sacci, 22 clavi lane in 4 sarrpellariis
De Roberto Danvers, indigena, 2 sacci, 2 clavi lane in 1 sarrpellario
De Ricardo Sharpe, indigena, 2 sacci, 22 clavi lane in 1 sarrpellario
De Ricardo Cely et Ricardo Bowell, indigenis, 1 saccus, 4 clavi lane in 1 poke
De Willelmo Combes, indigena, ½ saccus, 12 clavi lane in 1 poke
De dicto Willelmo Holte, indigena, 2200 pelles lanute in 5 fardellis
De Ricardo Cely et Ricardo Bowell, indigenis, 1750 pelles lanute in 4 fardellis

[65] In navi Johannis Hochon vocata Alyson de Newhithe exeunte eodem die *[11 June 1446]*

De Thoma Wandesford, indigena, 7 sacci lane in 3 sarrpellariis
De Johanne Pulter, indigena, 6½ sacci, 13 clavi lane in 3 sarrpellariis
De Roberto Whyte, indigena, 8 sacci, 12 clavi lane in 3 sarrpellariis
De Willelmo Combes, indigena, 2½ sacci, 4 clavi lane in 1 sarrpellario
De Thoma Chalton, indigena, 2 sacci, 24 clavi lane in 1 sarrpellario
De Thoma Wymark, indigena, 400 pelles lanute in 1 fardello
De dicto Willelmo Combes, indigena, 400 pelles lanute in 1 fardello
De Johanne Felde, indigena, 2800 pelles lanute in 7 fardellis
De Roberto Horne, indigena, 350 pelles lanute in 1 fardello

[66] [a]In navi Johannis Garner vocata [b]Maria[b] de Eborum exeunte eodem die *[11 June 1446]*

De Johanne Pygott, indigena, 4½ sacci, 20 clavi lane in 2 sarrpellariis

De Johanne Walden, indigena, 14 sacci, 3 clavi lane in 6 sarrpellariis
De Johanne Haryngton, indigena, 2 sacci, 18 clavi lane in 1 sarrpellario
De Willelmo Holte, indigena, 9½ sacci, 14 clavi lane in 3 sarrpellariis
De Thoma Shrubbe, indigena, 2000 pelles lanute in 5 fardellis
De Willelmo Combes, indigena, 9½ sacci, 20 clavi lane in 4 sarrpellariis
De Thoma Wymark, indigena, 400 pelles lanute in 1 fardello
De Thoma Wandesford, indigena, 4½ sacci, 8 clavi lane in 2 sarrpellariis
De Johanne Harowe, indigena, 4½ sacci, 10 clavi lane in 2 sarrpellariis
De Johanne Felde, indigena, 1600 pelles lanute in 4 fardellis
De dicto Thoma Shrubbe, indigena, 850 pelles lanute in 2 fardellis
De Ricardo Cely et Ricardo Bowell, indigenis, 700 pelles lanute in 2 fardellis

[a] *+ [cross] marginated against this entry and struck through L. Cf. variant b.*
[b-b] *The letters* ia *of the word* Maria *written over erasure L.*

[67] In navi Johannis Bensley vocata Trynite de Rouchestre exeunte eodem die *[11 June 1446]*

De Willelmo Cantelowe, indigena, 7½ sacci, 20 clavi lane in 3 sarrpellariis
De Johanne Penne, indigena, 1049 pelles lanute in 3 fardellis
De Willelmo Holte, indigena, 14 sacci, 19 clavi lane in 6 sarrpellariis
De Johanne Harowe, indigena, 4½ sacci, 8 clavi lane in 2 sarrpellariis
De Ricardo Cely et Ricardo Bowell, indigenis, 4½ sacci, 2 clavi lane in 2 sarrpellariis
De Roberto Danvers, indigena, 7 sacci, 25 clavi lane in 3 sarrpellariis
De Johanne Felde, indigena, 3½ sacci, 21 clavi lane in 2 sarrpellariis
De Johanne Tate, indigena, 1180 pelles lanute in 3 fardellis
De dicto Willelmo Holte, indigena, 2850 pelles lanute in 7 fardellis
De Johanne Levyng, indigena, 25 clavi lane in 1 poke
De Willelmo Turke, indigena, 328 pelles lanute in 1 fardello
De dictis Ricardo Cely et Ricardo Bowell, indigenis, 450 pelles lanute in 1 fardello
De Willelmo Levyng, indigena, 350 pelles lanute in 1 fardello
De Ricardo Levyng, indigena, 350 pelles lanute in 1 fardello

[68] In navi Ricardi Harry vocata Christoforus de Calesia exeunte eodem die *[11 June 1446]*

De Johanne Harowe, indigena, 1½ sacci, 2 clavi lane in 2 pokes
De Nicholao Mattok, indigena, 1½ sacci, 11 clavi lane in 1 sarrpellario
De Roberto Danvers, indigena, ½ saccus, 14 clavi lane in 1 poke
De Johanne Walden, indigena, 1½ sacci lane in 1 poke
De Thoma Wandesford, indigena, 1 saccus lane in 1 poke
De Thoma Wymarke, indigena, 400 pelles lanute in 1 fardello
De Willelmo Combes, indigena, 2000 pelles lanute in 5 fardellis
De Ricardo Hardbene, indigena, 1 saccus, 24 clavi lane in 1 poke
De Roberto Horne, indigena, 400 pelles lanute in 1 fardello

De Johanne Stratton, indigena, 1 saccus lane in 1 poke

[69] In navi Johannis Myller vocata Christoforus de Southwald exeunte eodem die *[11 June 1446]*

De Willelmo Cantelow, indigena, 12 sacci, 19 clavi lane in 5 sarrpellariis
De Johanne Mynne, indigena, 5 sacci, 9 clavi lane in 2 sarrpellariis, 1 poke
De Johanne Pulter, indigena, 4 sacci, 14 clavi lane in 2 sarrpellariis
De Johanne Levyng, indigena, 6½ sacci, 12 clavi lane in 3 sarrpellariis
De Johanne Walden, indigena, 4½ sacci, 6 clavi lane in 2 sarrpellariis
De dicto Johanne Mynne, indigena, 801 pelles lanute in 3 fardellis
m 6d
De Willelmo Bere, indigena, 700 pelles lanute in 2 fardellis
De Nicholao Mattok, indigena, 360 pelles lanute in 1 fardello
De Ricardo Cely et Ricardo Bowell, indigenis, 700 pelles lanute in 2 fardellis
De dicto Johanne Pulter, indigena, 400 pelles lanute in 1 fardello

[70] In navi Johannis Lawson vocata le Goost de Wynchelse exeunte eodem die *[11 June 1446]*

De Willelmo Cantelowe, indigena, 22 sacci, 22 clavi lane in 9 sarrpellariis
De Johanne Levyng, indigena, 4 sacci, 24 clavi lane in 2 sarrpellariis
De Thoma Chalton, indigena, 6 sacci, 21 clavi lane in 3 sarrpellariis
De Johanne Haryngton, indigena, 13 sacci, 11 clavi lane in 6 sarrpellariis
De Johanne Walden, indigena, 6½ sacci, 8 clavi lane in 3 sarrpellariis
De Johanne Harowe, indigena, 3 sacci, 24 clavi lane in 1 sarrpellario, 1 poke
De Johanne Tate, indigena, 489 pelles lanute in 1 fardello
De Ricardo Cely et Ricardo Bowell, indigenis, 6½ sacci, 21 clavi lane in 3 sarrpellariis
De Johanne Felde, indigena, 400 pelles lanute in 1 fardello
De Thoma Wandesford, indigena, 6½ sacci, 22 clavi lane in 3 sarrpellariis
De Johanne Pulter, indigena, 6½ sacci, 16 clavi lane in 3 sarrpellariis
De Roberto Danvers, indigena, 2 sacci, 15 clavi lane in 1 sarrpellario
De Thoma Cantelowe, indigena, 4½ sacci, 20 clavi lane in 2 sarrpellariis
De Willelmo Combes, indigena, 5600 pelles lanute in 15 fardellis

[71] In navi Johannis Tymeott vocata Margareta de London' exeunte eodem die *[11 June 1446]*

De Willelmo Holte, indigena, 21 sacci, 2 clavi lane in 8 sarrpellariis, 1 poke
De eodem Willelmo Holte, indigena, 3200 pelles lanute in 8 fardellis
De Willelmo Cantelowe, indigena, 17[a] sacci, 4 clavi lane in 7 sarrpellariis
De Thoma Cantelowe, indigena, 10 sacci, 3 clavi lane in 4 sarrpellariis
De Thoma Wandesford, indigena, 6 sacci, 8 clavi lane in 3 sarrpellariis
De Ricardo Cely et Ricardo Bowell, indigenis, 1988 pelles lanute in 5 fardellis
[b-c]De dicto Willelmo Holt, indigena, 400 pelles lanute in 1 fardello[c]

[a] *Corrected in L from* 16. [b] + *[cross]* deficiunt 400 pelles *marginated against this entry and struck through L. Cf. variant c.* [c–c] *Entered subsequently between the lines by a different hand L.*

[72] In navi Willelmi Bey vocata Marieknyght de le Scluse exeunte eodem die *[11 June 1446]*

De Willelmo Holte, indigena, 7½ sacci, 4 clavi lane in 3 sarrpellariis
De Willelmo Cantelowe, indigena, 7 sacci, 14[a] clavi lane in 3 sarrpellariis
De Ricardo Cely et Ricardo Bowell, indigenis, 2 sacci, 22 clavi lane in 1 sarrpellario
De Ricardo Danvers, indigena, 4½ sacci, 20 clavi lane in 2 sarrpellariis
De Ricardo Sharpe, indigena, 2 sacci, 14 clavi lane in 1 sarrpellario
De Thoma Wandesford, indigena, 4 sacci, 22 clavi lane in 2 sarrpellariis
De Johanne Pulter, indigena, 4½ sacci, 3 clavi lane in 2 sarrpellariis
De Willelmo Bere, indigena, 3674 pelles lanute in 9 fardellis
De eodem Willelmo Bere, indigena, 4½ sacci, 14 clavi lane in 2 sarrpellariis
De Nicholao Levyng, indigena, 1 saccus, 24 clavi lane in 1 poke
De Johanne Levyng, indigena, 2½ sacci, 4 clavi lane in 1 sarrpellario
De dicto Willelmo Bere, indigena, 8 sacci, 9 clavi lane in 3 sarrpellariis, 1 poke

[a] *Corrected in L from* 13.

[73] In navi Willelmi Daniell vocata Christoforus de London' exeunte eodem die *[11 June 1446]*

De Thoma Cantelowe, indigena, 9½ sacci, 13 clavi lane in 4 sarrpellariis
De Willelmo Cantelowe, indigena, 12 sacci, 2 clavi lane in 5 sarrpellariis
De Thoma Wandesford, indigena, 4½ sacci, 17 clavi lane in 2 sarrpellariis
De Willelmo Holte, indigena, 17½[a] sacci, 15 clavi lane in 7 sarrpellariis
De Willelmo Combes, indigena, 4½ sacci, 6 clavi lane in 2 sarrpellariis
De Roberto Danvers, indigena, 2 sacci, 18 clavi lane in 1 sarrpellario
De dicto Willelmo Cantelowe, indigena, 116 pelles lanute in 1 fardello
De Willelmo Bere, indigena, 3½ sacci, 7 clavi lane in 2 sarrpellariis
De Willelmo Turke, indigena, 426 pelles lanute in 1 fardello
De dicto Willelmo Holte, indigena, 800 pelles lanute in 2 fardellis

[a] *Corrected in L from* 16½.

[74] [a]In navi Petri [b]Leman[b] vocata Petrus de Calesia exeunte eodem die *[11 June 1446]*

De Willelmo Combes, indigena, 5½ sacci, 2 clavi lane in 2 sarrpellariis
De Johanne Walden, indigena, 13 sacci, 14[c] clavi lane in 6 sarrpellariis
De Johanne Felde, indigena, 3 sacci, 24 clavi lane in 1 sarrpellario, 1 poke
De Johanne Haryngton, indigena, 2 sacci, 4 clavi lane in 1 sarrpellario
De Thoma Cantelowe, indigena, 4½ sacci, 18 clavi lane in 2 sarrpellariis
De Thoma Wandesford, indigena, 4½ sacci, 23 clavi lane in 2 sarrpellariis

De Willelmo Cantelowe, indigena, 4½ sacci, 23 clavi lane in 2 sarrpellariis
De Willelmo Holte, indigena, 5 sacci, 14 clavi lane in 2 sarrpellariis
De Thoma Shrubbe, indigena, 360 pelles lanute in 1 fardello
De dicto Johanne Walden, indigena, 423 pelles lanute in 1 fardello
[d]De dicto Willelmo Combes, indigena, 1008[e] pelles lanute in 3 fardellis
De dicto Willelmo Holte, indigena, 2000 pelles lanute in 5 fardellis
De dicto Johanne Felde, indigena, 1500 pelles lanute in 4 fardellis
De Johanne Stratton, indigena, 400 pelles lanute in 1 fardello

[a] *+ [cross] marginated against this entry and struck through L. Cf. variant b.* [b–b] *Interlined above* le Man, *struck through L.* [c] *Corrected in L from* 13. [d] *+ [cross] marginated against this entry and struck through L. Cf. variant e.* [e] *The number* 8 *of* 1008 (M[l] viij) *written over erasure L.*

m 7

[75] In navi Johannis Pouderham vocata George Heron de London' exeunte eodem die *[11 June 1446]*

De Willelmo Cantelowe, indigena, 88½ sacci, 25 clavi lane in 37 sarrpellariis
De Johanne Pulter, indigena, 35½ sacci, 11 clavi lane in 16 sarrpellariis
De Willelmo Holte, indigena, 82 sacci, 10 clavi lane in 34 sarrpellariis
De Roberto Danvers, indigena, 4½ sacci, 8 clavi lane in 2 sarrpellariis
De Johanne Walden, indigena, 8½ sacci, 18 clavi lane in 4 sarrpellariis
De Johanne Haryngton, indigena, 6 sacci, 18 clavi lane in 3 sarrpellariis
De dicto Johanne Pulter, indigena, 1600 pelles lanute in 4 fardellis

[76] In navi Willelmi Cote vocata Christofore de Gowe exeunte eodem die *[11 June 1446]*

De Willelmo Combes, indigena, 1½ sacci, 2 clavi lane in 1 sarrpellario
De Ricardo Sharpe, indigena, 4 sacci, 25 clavi lane in 2 sarrpellariis
De Willelmo Cantelowe, indigena, 30½ sacci, 23 clavi lane in 13 sarrpellariis
De Ricardo Cely et Ricardo Bowell, indigenis, 9 sacci, 3 clavi lane in 4 sarrpellariis
De Willelmo Cantelowe juniore, indigena, 1½ sacci, 4 clavi lane in 1 sarrpellario
De Johanne Haryngton, indigena, 2 sacci, 5 clavi lane in 1 sarrpellario
De Willelmo Holte, indigena, 7 sacci, 4 clavi lane in 3 sarrpellariis
De Johanne Felde, indigena, 327 pelles lanute in 1 fardello
De Johanne Pulter, indigena, 1156 pelles lanute in 3 fardellis
De dictis Ricardo Cely et Ricardo Bowell, indigenis, 800 pelles lanute in 2 fardellis
De Willelmo Bere, indigena, 1½ sacci, 22 clavi lane in 1 sarrpellario
De Willelmo Holte, indigena, 1112 pelles lanute in 3 fardellis
De dicto Johanne Felde, indigena, 579 pelles lante in 1 fardello
De Johanne Felde juniore, indigena, 400 pelles lanute in 1 fardello
De Johanne Walden, indigena, 269 pelles lanute in 1 fardello

De Roberto Manfeld, indigena, 2 sacci, 4 clavi lane in 1 sarrpellario

[77] In navi Cornelii Haynesson vocata Maria de London' exeunte eodem die *[11 June 1446]*

De Willelmo Cantelowe, indigena, 27½ sacci, 19 clavi lane in 11 sarrpellariis
De Ricardo Cely et Ricardo Bowell, indigenis, 6½ sacci, 22 clavi lane in 3 sarrpellariis
De Laurencio Cantelowe, indigena, 1 saccus, 23 clavi lane in 1 poke
De Alano Johnson, indigena, 450 pelles lanute in 1 fardello
De Willelmo Holte, indigena, 7 sacci, 12 clavi lane in 3 sarrpellariis
De Roberto Danvers, indigena, 4½ sacci, 10 clavi lane in 2 sarrpellariis
De Johanne Walden, indigena, 1420 pelles lanute in 3 fardellis
De dicto Willelmo Holte, indigena, 754 pelles lanute in 2 fardellis
De Roberto Manfeld, indigena, 6½ sacci, 9 clavi lane in 3 sarrpellariis

[78] In navi Roberti Blytturswyke vocata Jocob de Colonia exeunte eodem die *[11 June 1446]*

De Angelo Donati de Aldebrando, mercatore de Florence[a], alienigena, 18[b] sacci, 19 clavi lane in 20 pokes

[a] *Sic L.* [b] *Corrected in L from* 17.

[79] In navi Hayn Bulschamp vocata Andrewe de Ermoth exeunte 8° die Augusti *[8 Aug. 1446]*

De Benedicto Boromey de Florencia, mercatore, alienigena, 15½ sacci, 25½ clavi lane in 16 pokettes

[80] In navi Lambe Johan Williamson vocata Marikneght de Middilburgh exeunte eodem die *[8 Aug. 1446]*

De Benedicto Boromey de Florencia, mercatore, alienigena, 14½ sacci, 24½ clavi lane in 15 pokettes

[81] In navi Coppyn Lambe vocata Martinkneght de Ermoth exeunte 7° die Septembris anno 25[to] *[7 Sept. 1446]*

De Angelo Donati de Alledobrando, mercatore de Florencia, alienigena, 10 sacci, 16½ clavi lane in 10 pokettes

[82] In navi Willelmi Johansson vocata James de Ermoth exeunte eodem die *[8 Aug. 1446]*

De Angelo Donati de Alledobrando, mercatore de Florencia, alienigena, 31 sacci, 12 clavi lane in 29 pokettes

[a]Examinatur cum libro collectorum[a]

[a-a] *Auditor's entry L.*

m 7d is blank

PARCELLE COMPOTI

[P 1] *Henry VI to the treasurer and barons of the Exchequer: since Henry V* (pater noster) *by patent confirmed by the present king*[1] *appointed his brother Humphrey, duke of Gloucester, as constable of Dover and warden of the Cinque Ports for life, granting him the same £300 yearly for his own maintenance and that of the chaplains, servants, watchmen and a carpenter* (unius carpentarii) *dwelling in the castle of Dover as Henry V himself had had as constable and warden, of which £146 was payable from the wards pertaining to the castle of Dover* (de wardis ad predictum castrum pertinentibus), *100 marks from the issues of the customs in Sandwich and the remaining £87 6s 8d from the issues of the wool customs and subsidy in London at Easter and Michaelmas in equal portions; and since the present king has ordered [untraceable] the collectors of the wool customs and subsidy in London to pay the duke all arrears of the said £87 6s 8d; the king orders the Exchequer to allow* (debite allocetis) *the customers all payments made in this regard when they account, provided they produce the said mandate for payment directed to them and the duke's receipts* (litteras acquietancie). — *1446 Oct. 8* (Teste me ipso apud Westmonasterium, 8 die Octobris anno regni nostri vicesimo quinto. *[signed by the scribe]* [a]'Haseley'[a]).[2] *Westminster.*

L1 TNA: PRO, E122/75/39/1. Original. Parchment. Seal on tongue torn away. Severely damaged by damp; in addition, the ink used for the second entry on the dorse has eaten through the parchment. On the dorse: (at the top) Irrotulatur termino sancti Michaelis anno 25[to] rotulo secundo *[TNA: PRO, E159/223 Brevia directa baronibus Michaelmas m 2d = L2]*; *(beneath that)* Allocatur in compoto Johannis Poutrell et Thome Pounde collectorum custumarum et subsidiorum regis in portu London' computancium a festo sancti Michaelis anno 24[to] regis hujus *[29 Sept .1445]* usque idem festum tunc proximum sequens *[29 Sept. 1446]* inde rotulo compotorum de antiqua custuma *[TNA: PRO, E356/19 m 3-3d; No. A 3, § 15].*

---

[1] *Henry V's patent dated from 27 Nov. 1415 (CPR 1413-16, p. 374) and Henry VI's confirmation from 20 Dec. 1422 (CPR 1422-29, p. 82-3).*

[2] *Thomas Haseley, kt., was a chancery clerk: CPR 1441-46, p. 461.*

L2 TNA: PRO, E159/223 Brevia directa baronibus Michaelmas m 2d. Contemporaneous official copy. Parchment. Unsealed. Marginated: Pro collectoribus custume et subsidii in portu London'.

[a-a] *Omitted L2.*

[P 2] *Richard, duke of York, acknowledges receipt of 100s by the hand of John* Knyght, *esq. (*per manus Johannis Knyght armigeri) *owing to him by virtue of the annuity of £289 6s 8d yearly granted by Ricard II [cf. No. S 2], payable from the issues of the wool customs and subsidy in London, from the collectors of the wool customs and subsidy in London John* Poutrell *and Thomas* Pounde. — *1445 Oct. 5* (per presentes sigillo nostro signatas. Datum quinto die Octobris anno regni regis Henrici Sexti post conquestum vicesimo quarto). *[London].*

L TNA: PRO, E122/75/39/2. Original. Parchment. Seal on tongue slightly damaged.

[P 3] *John* Wyggemore, *receiver of Richard, duke of York* (receptor Ricardi ducis Eborum), *acknowledges receipt of 100s by the hand of John* Knyght, *esq.* (per manus Johannis Knyght armigeri) *owing to the duke by virtue of the annuity of £289 6s 8d yearly granted by Ricard II [cf. No. S 2], payable from the issues of the wool customs and subsidy in London, from the collectors of the wool customs and subsidy in London John* Poutrell *and Thomas* Pounde. — *1446 Apr. 20* (per presentes sigillo meo per me signatas. Datum vicesimo die Aprilis anno regni regis Henrici Sexti vicesimo quarto). *[London].*

L TNA: PRO, E122/75/39/3. Original. Parchment. Traces of seal on tongue.

[P 4] *Henry VI to the collectors of the wool customs and subsidy in London: since Henry V* (pater noster) *by patent confirmed by the present king*[3] *appointed his brother Humphrey, duke of Gloucester, as constable of Dover and warden of the Cinque Ports for life, granting him the same £300 yearly for his own maintenance and that of the chaplains, servants, watchmen and a carpenter* (unius carpentarii) *dwelling in the castle of Dover as Henry V himself had had as constable and warden, of which £146 was payable from the wards pertaining to the castle of Dover* (de wardis ad predictum castrum pertinentibus), *100 marks from the issues of the customs in Sandwich and the remaining £87 6s 8d from the issues of the wool customs and subsidy in London at Easter and Michaelmas in equal portions; the king orders the customers to pay the duke all arrears, accepting in turn his receipts* (litteras suas acquietancie), *which together with this mandate for payment shall suffice for the allowance* (debitam allocacionem) *of all payments made in this regard*

---

[3] *Henry V's patent dated from 27 Nov. 1415 (CPR 1413-16, p. 374) and Henry VI's confirmation from 20 Dec. 1422 (CPR 1422-29, p. 82-3).*

when the customers account at the Exchequer. — 1446 Oct. 8 (Teste me ipso apud Westmonasterium, 8° die Octobris anno regni nostri vicesimo [quinto]. *[signed by the scribe]* 'Haseley'). *Westminster.*

L TNA: PRO, E122/75/39/4. Original. Parchment. Seal on tongue torn away. Severely damaged (script worn away in places, damaged by reagents).

[P 5] *Humphrey, duke of Gloucester, acknowledges receipt by the hand of the treasurer of his household, master Clement* Denston (per manus magistri Clementis Denston thesaurarii hospicii nostri) *of £43 13s 4d owing to him by virtue of the grant of £87 6s 8d by Henry V*[4] *in regard to his office as constable of Dover, from the collectors of the wool customs and subsidy in London John* Poutrell *and Thomas* Pounde. — *1445 Oct. 2* (per presentes sigillo nostro signatas. Datum secundo die Octobris anno regni domini mei regis Henrici Sexti vicesimo quarto). *[London].*

L TNA: PRO, E122/75/39/5. Original. Parchment. Seal on tongue lost.

[P 6] *John* Wyggemore, *receiver of Richard, duke of York* (receptor Ricardi ducis Eborum), *acknowledges receipt of £10 by the hand of John* Erneis, *esq.* (per manus Johannis Erneis armigeri) *owing to the duke by virtue of the annuity of £289 6s 8d yearly granted by Ricard II [cf. No. S 2], payable from the issues of the wool customs and subsidy in London, from the collectors of the wool customs and subsidy in London John* Poutrell *and Thomas* Pounde. — *1446 Apr. 23* (per presentes sigillo meo per me signatas. Datum vicesimo tercio die Aprilis anno regni regis Henrici Sexti vicesimo quarto). *[London].*

L TNA: PRO, E122/75/39/6. Original. Parchment. Seal on tongue intact. Some damage from damp. On the tongue: [acquiet]acio pro Johanne Erneis de £10.

[P 7] *Humphrey, duke of Gloucester, acknowledges receipt of £43 13s 4d owing to him by virtue of the grant of £87 6s 8d yearly by Henry V, which was confirmed by Henry VI,*[5] *in regard to his office as constable of Dover, to wit for Easter term last* (pro termino Pasche ultimo preterito), *from the collectors of the wool customs and subsidy in London John* Poutrell *and Thomas* Pounde. — *1446 Apr. 24* (Datum sub signeto nostro mensis Aprilis die vicesimo quarto anno regni [domini mei regis] Henrici Sexti post conquestum Anglie vicesimo quarto). *[London].*

---

[4] *Henry V's patent dated from 27 Nov. 1415 (CPR 1413-16, p. 374) and Henry VI's confirmation from 20 Dec. 1422 (CPR 1422-29, p. 82-3).*

[5] *Henry V's patent dated from 27 Nov. 1415 (CPR 1413-16, p. 374) and Henry VI's confirmation from 20 Dec. 1422 (CPR 1422-29, p. 82-3).*

L TNA: PRO, E122/75/39/7. Original. Parchment. Signet on tongue slightly damaged. Some damage from damp on the right side of the document.

[P 8] *John* Wyggemore, *receiver of Richard, duke of York* (receptor Ricardi ducis Eborum), *acknowledges receipt of 149 marks 2s 2d by the hand of Edward* George, *esq.* (per manus [a]Edwardi George armigeri[a]) *owing to the duke by virtue of the annuity of £289 6s 8d yearly granted by Ricard II [cf. No. S 2], payable from the issues of the wool customs and subsidy in London, from the collectors of the wool customs and subsidy in London John* Poutrell *and Thomas* Pounde. — *1446 Feb. 20* (per presentes sigillo meo per me signatas. Datum vicesimo die Februarii anno regni regis Henrici Sexti vicesimo quarto). *[London].*

L TNA: PRO, E122/75/39/8. Original. Parchment. Seal on tongue intact. Some damage from damp on the right side of the document.

[a–a] *Reading uncertain owing to damage from damp L.*

[P 9] *John* Wyggemore, *receiver of Richard, duke of York* (receptor Ricardi ducis Eborum), *acknowledges receipt of £100 by the hand of Andrew* Ogard, *kt.* (per manus Andree Ogard militis) *owing to the duke by virtue of the annuity of £289 6s 8d yearly granted by Ricard II [cf. No. S 2], payable from the issues of the wool customs and subsidy in London, from the collectors of the wool customs and subsidy in London John* Poutrell *and Thomas* Pounde. — *1446 Apr. 2* (per presentes sigillo meo per me signatas. Datum secundo die Aprilis anno regni regis Henrici Sexti vicesimo quarto). *[London].*

L TNA: PRO, E122/75/39/9. Original. Parchment. Seal on tongue slightly damaged. Receipt severely damaged (reagents applied in the upper middle portion of the text; the upper right-hand portion has rotted away).

[P 10] *John* Wyggemore, *receiver of Richard, duke of York* (receptor Ricardi ducis Eborum), *acknowledges receipt of £10 by the hand of John* Ernaiz, *esq.* (per manus Johannis Ernaiz armigeri) *owing to the duke by virtue of the annuity of £289 6s 8d yearly granted by Ricard II [cf. No. S 2], payable from the issues of the wool customs and subsidy in London, to wit for Easter term 23 Hen. VI and Michaelmas term 24 Hen. VI* (pro terminis Pasche anno vicesimo tercio [et] sancti Michaelis anno vicesimo quarto*), from the collectors of the wool customs and subsidy in London John* Poutrell *and Thomas* Pounde. — *1446 Apr. 7* (per presentes sigillo meo per me signatas. Datum septimo die Aprilis anno regni re[g]is Henrici Sexti vicesimo quarto). *[London].*

L TNA: PRO, E122/75/39/10. Original. Parchment. Seal on tongue severely damaged. Receipt slightly damaged by damp; script worn away in places on the right-hand margin.

[P 11] John Wyggemore, *receiver of Richard, duke of York* (receptor Ricardi ducis Eborum), *acknowledges receipt of £10 by the hand of Thomas* Dunkan (per manus Thome Dunkan) *owing to the duke by virtue of the annuity of £289 6s 8d yearly granted by Ricard II [cf. No. S 2], payable from the issues of the wool customs and subsidy in London, from the collectors of the wool customs and subsidy in London John* Poutrell *and Thomas* Pounde. — *1446 May 1* (per presentes sigillo meo per me signatas. Datum primo die Maii anno regni regis Henrici Sexti vicesimo quarto). *[London].*

L TNA: PRO, E122/75/39/11. Original. Parchment. Traces of seal on tongue. On the tongue: De Johanne Wyggemore pro, *followed by four illegible words on the next line). Receipt slightly damaged by damp; script worn away in places.*

[P 12] Richard, duke of York, acknowledges receipt of 100 marks owing to him by virtue of the annuity of £289 6s 8d yearly granted by Ricard II [cf. No. S 2], payable from the issues of the wool customs and subsidy in London, from the collectors of the wool customs and subsidy in London John Poutrell *and Thomas* Pounde. — *144[6] June 4* ([In cujus rei testimonio sigillum nostrum] presentibus apposuimus. Datum quarto die Junii anno regni regis Henrici Sexti post conquestum Anglie vicesimo [quarto]). *[London].*

L TNA: PRO, E122/75/39/12. Original. Parchment. Traces of seal on tongue. Severely damaged (the right-hand side of the receipt has rotted away; the seal has left a shadow on the parchment).

[P 13] John Wyggemore, *receiver of Richard, duke of York* (receptor Ricardi ducis Eborum), *acknowledges receipt of £20 by the hand of John* Clay, *esq.* (per manus Johannis Clay armigeri), *owing to the duke by virtue of the annuity of £289 6s 8d yearly granted by Ricard II [cf. No. S 2], payable from the issues of the wool customs and subsidy in London, from the collectors of the wool customs and subsidy in London John* Poutrell *and Thomas* Pounde. — *1446 May 17* (per presentes sigillo meo per me signatas. Datum decimo septimo die Maii anno regni regis Henrici Sexti vicesimo quarto). *[London].*

L TNA: PRO, E122/75/39/13. Original. Parchment. Traces of seal on tongue. On the dorse: Clay. *Slightly damaged by damp; script worn away in places.*

[P 14] John Wyggemore, *receiver of Richard, duke of York* (receptor Ricardi ducis Eborum), *acknowledges receipt of 20 marks by the hand of Richard* Wodevyle, *kt.* (per manus Ricardi Wodevyle militis) *owing to the duke by virtue of the annuity of £289 6s 8d yearly granted by Ricard II [cf. No. S 2], payable from the issues of the wool customs and subsidy in London, to wit for Michaelmas term last* (ut pro termino sancti Michaelis ultimo preterito), *from the collectors of the wool customs and*

subsidy in London John Poutrell *and Thomas* Pounde. — *1445 Nov. 15* (per presentes sigillo meo per me signatas. Datum quintodecimo die Novembris anno regni regis Henrici Sexti vicesimo quarto). *[London].*

L TNA: PRO, E122/75/39/14. Original. Parchment. Seal on tongue intact. Slightly damaged by damp; script worn away in places.

[P 15] Richard, duke of York, acknowledges receipt of 50 marks by the hand of his councillor Andrew Ogard, *kt.* (per manus Andree Ogard militis consiliarii nostri), *owing to the duke by virtue of the annuity of £289 6s 8d yearly granted by Ricard II [cf. No. S 2], payable from the issues of the wool customs and subsidy in London, from the collectors of the wool customs and subsidy in London John* Poutrell *and Thomas* Pounde. — *1446 June 16* (per presentes sigillo nostro signatas. Datum sextodecimo die mensis Junii anno regni dicti domini mei regis Henrici Sexti post conquestum Anglie vicesimo quarto). *[London].*

L TNA: PRO, E122/75/39/15. Original. Parchment. Remnants of seal on tongue. Sign manual (R. York) *beneath the text. Severely damaged by damp; in addition, the ink has eaten through the parchment on the right-hand side of the receipt.*

[P 16] John Wyggemore, *receiver of Richard, duke of York* (receptor Ricardi ducis Eborum), *acknowledges receipt of 40 marks by the hand of Thomas* Wilde, *esq,. executor of † John* Cressy, *kt.* (per manus Thome Wilde armigeri executoris testamenti Johannis Cressy militis defuncti), *owing to the duke by virtue of the annuity of £289 6s 8d yearly granted by Ricard II [cf. No. S 2], payable from the issues of the wool customs and subsidy in London, from the collectors of the wool customs and subsidy in London John* Poutrell *and Thomas* Pounde. — *1446 Mar. 20* (per presentes sigillo meo per me signatas. Datum vicesimo die Marcii anno regni regis Henrici Sexti vicesimo quarto). *[London].*

L TNA: PRO, E122/75/39/16. Original. Parchment. Seal on tongue slightly damaged.

[P 17] Robert Roos, *kt.* (miles), *acknowledges receipt of £90 owing to him and his wife Anne by virtue of the annuity of £60 yearly granted by Henry VI,*[6] *payable from the issues of the wool customs and subsidy in London, to wit £30 for Easter term 23 Hen. VI* (pro termino Pasche anno 23^{cio}) *and the remaining £60 for Michaelmas and Easter terms 24 Hen. VI* (pro terminis Michaelis et Pasche anno 24to), *from the collectors of the wool customs and subsidy in London John* Poutrell *and Thomas* Pounde. — *1446 Oct. 3* (per presentes sigillo meo signatas. Datum tercio die Octobris anno regni regis Henrici Sexti vicesimo quinto). *[London].*

L TNA: PRO, E122/75/39/17. Original. Parchment. Seal on tongue lost.

---

[6] *CPR 1441-46, p. 365 dated 26 Mar. 1445.*

[P 18] John Wyggemore, *receiver of Richard, duke of York* (receptor Ricardi ducis Eborum), *acknowledges receipt of £20 by the hand of John* Fastolf, *kt.* (per manus Johannis Fastolf militis), *owing to the duke by virtue of the annuity of £289 6s 8d yearly granted by Ricard II [cf. No. S 2], payable from the issues of the wool customs and subsidy in London, to wit for Michaelmas and Easter terms last* (pro terminis sancti Michaelis et Pasche ultimo preteritis), *from the collectors of the wool customs and subsidy in London John* Poutrell *and Thomas* Pounde. — *1445 Aug. 30* (per presentes sigillo meo signatas. Datum London' penultimo die Augusti anno regni regis Henrici Sexti vicesimo tercio). *London.*

L TNA: PRO, E122/75/39/18. Original. Parchment. Seal on tongue slightly damaged. Slightly damaged by damp; some holes in the parchment on the right-hand side.

[P 19] The king's secretary Richard Andrewe *acknowledges receipt of £60 owing to him by virtue of the annuity of £40 yearly granted by Henry VI at pleasure* (quamdiu regi placuerit),[7] *payable from the issues of the wool customs and subsidy in London, to wit £20 for Easter term 23 Hen. VI* (pro termino Pasche anno 23^{cio}) *and the remaining £40 for Michaelmas and Easter terms 24 Hen. VI* (pro terminis Michaelis et Pasche anno 24to), *from the collectors of the wool customs and subsidy in London John* Poutrell *and Thomas* Pounde. — *1446 June 21* (per presentes sigillo meo signatas. Datum vicesimo primo die Junii anno regni regis Henrici Sexti vicesimo quarto). *[London].*

L TNA: PRO, E122/75/39/19. Original. Parchment. Seal on tongue severely damaged. Receipt slightly damaged by damp; script worn away in places; shadow of seal on parchment. On the dorse: Allocatur in compoto Johannis Poutrell et Thome Pounde collectorum custumarum in portu regis London' de anno 24to inde rotulo compotorum de antiqua custuma *[TNA: PRO, E356/19 m 3-3d; No. A 3, § 17].*

[P 20] John [Wyggemore], *receiver of Richard, duke of York* (receptor Ricardi ducis Eborum), *acknowledges receipt of [amount is illegible]*[8] *by the hand of Henry* Marchall (per manus Henrici Marchall), *owing to the duke by virtue of the annuity of £289 6s 8d yearly granted by Ricard II [cf. No. S 2], payable from the issues of the wool customs and subsidy in London, to wit for Easter and Michaelmas terms last* ([de] terminis Pasche et sancti Michaelis ultimo preteritis), *from the collectors of the wool customs and subsidy in London John* Poutrell *and Thomas*

[7] *CPR 1441-46, p. 354.*

[8] *The amount cannot be calculated by summing up the receipts and subtracting the known payments from the total given in No. P 26, since only 24 of the original 25 receipts have survived. However, since they record payments totalling £596 2s 2d, the sum paid in No. P. 20 cannot be greater than £11 13s 4d.*

Pounde. — *144[6] Mar. 9* (per presentes sigillo meo per me signatas. Datum nono die Marcii anno regni [regis Henrici Sexti vicesimo quarto]). *[London].*

L TNA: PRO, E122/75/39/20. Original. Parchment. Seal on tongue lost. Severely damaged by damp (the right-hand side of the receipt has rotted away).

[P 21] John Wyggemore, *receiver of Richard, duke of York* (receptor Ricardi ducis Eborum), *acknowledges receipt of £40 by the hand of Thomas, lord Scales* (per manus Thome domini de Scalis), *owing to the duke by virtue of the annuity of £289 6s 8d yearly granted by Ricard II [cf. No. S 2], payable from the issues of the wool customs and subsidy in London, from the collectors of the wool customs and subsidy in London John* Poutrell *and Thomas* Pounde. — *1446 Mar. 10* (per presentes sigillo meo per me signatas. Datum quinto decimo die Marcii anno regni regis Henrici Sexti post conquestum vicesimo quarto). *[London].*

L TNA: PRO, E122/75/39/21. Original. Parchment. Seal on tongue severely damaged. On the tongue: Scales. *Receipt slightly damaged by damp.*

[P 22] John Wygmore, *receiver of Richard, duke of York* (receptor Ricardi ducis Eborum), *acknowledges receipt in the duke's name of 10 marks by the hand of John* Steward, *kt.* (per me nomine dicti ducis per manus Johannis Steward militis), *owing to the duke by virtue of the annuity of £289 6s 8d yearly granted by Ricard II [cf. No. S 2], payable from the issues of the wool customs and subsidy in London, from the collectors of the wool customs and subsidy in London John* Poutrell *and Thomas* Pounde. — *1446 May [..]* (per presentes sigillo meo signatas. Datum qu..[a] die mensis Maii anno regni regis Henrici Sexti post conquestum Anglie vicesimo quarto). *[London].*

L TNA: PRO, E122/75/39/22. Original. Parchment. Seal on tongue lost. Severely damaged by damp.

[a] *Only the letters* qu *are clearly legible L.*

[P 23] John Wyggemore, *receiver of Richard, duke of York* (receptor Ricardi ducis Eborum), *acknowledges receipt of 20*[a] *marks, owing to the duke by virtue of the annuity of £289 6s 8d yearly granted by Ricard II [cf. No. S 2], payable from the issues of the wool customs and subsidy in London, from the collectors of the wool customs and subsidy in London John* Poutrell *and Thomas* Pounde. — *1445 Oct. 15* (per presentes sigillo meo per me signatas. Datum quintodecimo die Octobris anno regni regis Henrici Sexti vicesimo quarto). *[London].*

L TNA: PRO, E122/75/39/23. Original. Parchment. Seal on tongue slightly damaged. Receipt slightly damaged by damp (there are some holes in the parchment where it has rotted away). Sign manual (Wyggemore) *beneath the text.*

[a] *The word* viginti *is written in the same hand and with ink of the same colour as the sign manual at the end of the writ L. This leads one to conclude that it was entered by* Wyggemore *himself, the rest of the receipt having been written in advance.*

[P 24] Richard, duke of York, acknowledges receipt of £20 by the hand of John Fastolf, *kt.* (per manus Johannis Fastolf militis), *owing to the duke by virtue of the annuity of £289 6s 8d yearly granted by Ricard II [cf. No. S 2], payable from the issues of the wool customs and subsidy in London, to wit for Michaelmas and Easter terms last* (pro terminis sancti Michaelis et Pasche ultimo preteritis), *from the collectors of the wool customs and subsidy in London John* Poutrell *and Thomas* Pounde. — *1446 Apr. 22* (per presentes sigillo nostro signatas. Datum London', vicesimo secundo die mensis Aprilis anno regni regis Henrici Sexti post conquestum vicesimo quarto). *London.*

L TNA: PRO, E122/75/39/24. Original. Parchment. Seal on tongue lost. Sign manual (R. York) *beneath the text.*

[P 25] John Wyggemore, *receiver of Richard, duke of York* (receptor Ricardi ducis Eborum), *acknowledges receipt of £40 by the hand of Richard* Wodevyle, *kt.* (per manus Ricardi Wodevyle militis), *owing to the duke by virtue of the annuity of £289 6s 8d yearly granted by Ricard II [cf. No. S 2], payable from the issues of the wool customs and subsidy in London, from the collectors of the wool customs and subsidy in London John* Poutrell *and Thomas* Pounde. — *1445 June 25* (per presentes sigillo meo per me signatas. Datum London', vicesimo quinto die mensis Junii anno regni regis Henrici Sexti post conquestum vicesimo tercio). *London.*

L TNA: PRO, E122/75/39/25. Original. Parchment. Traces of seal on tongue. Sign manual (Wyggemore) beneath the text. *Entry on the tongue illegible.*

[P 26] John Harleston, *esq.* (armiger), *receiver general of Richard, duke of York* (receptor generalis illustris et prepotentis principis Ricardi ducis Eborum), *acknowledges receipt of £20 , owing to the duke by virtue of the annuity of £289 6s 8d yearly granted by Ricard II [cf. No. S 2], payable from the issues of the wool customs and subsidy in London, from the collectors of the wool customs and subsidy in London, John* Poutrell *and Thomas* Pounde. — *1446 July 8* (In cujus rei testimonium sigillum meum [presentibus] apposui. Datum octavo die Julii anno regni regis Henrici Sexti post conquestum vicesimo quarto). *[London].*

L TNA: PRO, E122/75/39/26. Original. Parchment. Seal on tongue severely damaged. Sign manual (Harleston) beneath the text. *On the dorse: (at the top)* Summa harum 25 acquietanciarum £607 15s 6d; *(beneath that)* Allocatur in compoto Johannis Poutrell et Thome Pounde collectorum custumarum et subsidiorum regis in portu London' de anno 24[to] inde rotulo compotorum de antiqua custuma *[TNA: PRO, E356/19 m 3-3d; No. A 3, § 16]*.

[P 27] John Wyggemore, *receiver of Richard, duke of York* (receptor Ricardi ducis Eborum), *acknowledges receipt of 20 marks by the hand of Richard* Wydevyle, *kt.* (per manus Ricardi Wydevyle militis), *owing to the duke by virtue of the annuity of £289 6s 8d yearly granted by Ricard II [cf. No. S 2], payable from the issues of the wool customs and subsidy in London, from the collectors of the wool customs and subsidy in London John* Poutrell *and Thomas* Pounde. — *1446 May 20* (per presentes sigillo meo per me signatas. Datum vicesimo die Maii anno regni regis Henrici Sexti vicesimo quarto). *[London]*.

L TNA: PRO, E122/75/39/27. Original. Parchment. Traces of seal on tongue. Slightly damaged by damp; script illegible in places.

[P 28] John Wyggemore, *receiver of Richard, duke of York* (receptor Ricardi ducis Eborum), *acknowledges receipt of 100s by the hand of John* Malpas (per manus Johannis Malpas[a]), *owing to the duke by virtue of the annuity of £289 6s 8d yearly granted by Ricard II [cf. No. S 2], payable from the issues of the wool customs and subsidy in London, from the collectors of the wool customs and subsidy in London John* Poutrell *and Thomas* Pounde. — *1446 Apr. 15* ([per presentes] sigillo meo per me signatas. Datum quintodecimo die Aprilis anno regni regis Henrici Sexti post conquestum vicesimo quarto). *[London]*.

L TNA: PRO, E122/75/39/28. Original. Parchment. Remnants of seal on tongue. Severely damaged by damp; the right-hand side has rotted away.

[a] *Only the letters* M lpa *are clearly legible L.*

[P 29] Henry VI to the treasurer and barons of the Exchequer: since the king by patent[9] *issued on 25 Aug. 1444* (vicesimo quinto die Augusti anno regni nostri vicesimo secundo) *appointed Robert* Danvers *as justice of assizes* (unus justiciariorum nostrorum ad assisas in diversis comitatibus regni nostri Anglie arramandas capiendas); *and since the king had ordered [No. P 47] the collectors of the wool customs in London in view of the act of the parliament*[10] *meeting in Westminster in 18 Hen. VI regarding such judges' fees and rewards* (de feodis et regardis) *(a copy of which was sent to the customers) to pay* Danvers, *who has a right to a fee of £20 yearly for this office, all arrears owing from the date of his appointment; the king orders the Exchequer to allow* (debite allocetis) *the customers all payments made in this regard when they account, provided they produce the said mandate of payment directed to them and* Danvers' *receipts* (litteras acquietancie). — *1446 June 10* (Teste me

---

[9] *CPR 1441-46, p. 280.*

[10] *Rotuli Parliamentorum, vol. 5, p. 13-4.*

ipso apud Westmonasterium, 10 die Junii anno regni nostri vicesimo quarto). *Westminster.*

L1 TNA: PRO, E122/75/39/29. Original. Parchment. Seal on tongue torn away. Severely damaged by damp; script worn away in places. On the dorse: (at the top) Irrotulatur termino sancti Michaelis anno vicesimo quinto rotulo primo [*TNA: PRO, E159/223 Brevia directa baronibus Michaelmas m 1d = L2*]; *(beneath that)* Allocatur in compoto Johannis Poutrell et Thome Pounde collectorum custumarum regis in portu London' de anno 24to regis Henrici vj^{ti} *[TNA: PRO, E356/19 m 3-3d; No. A 3, § 23].*

L2 TNA: PRO, E159/223 Brevia directa baronibus Michaelmas m 1d. Contemporaneous official copy. Parchment. Unsealed. Marginated: Pro Roberto Danvers.

[P 30] Henry VI to the treasurer and barons of the Exchequer: since the king by patent[11] *issued on 26 Mar. 1445* (vicesimo sexto die Marcii anno regni nostri vicesimo tercio) *granted Robert* Roos, *kt.* (miles), *in recompense for past and future service to the crown, together with his wife Anne £110 yearly, payable from 29 Sept. 1444* (a festo sancti Michaelis dicto anno vicesimo tercio) *onwards at Easter and Michaelmas in equal portions from the issues of the wool customs in London (£60) and Southampton (£50) for life, whichever of them shall live longest* (pro termino vite eorum et alterius eorum diucius viventis), *until the king or his successor should provide them with lands* (de terris et tenementis sibi aggreabilibus) *for life* (pro termino vite eorum et alterius eorum diucius viventis) *producing the same income; and since the king has ordered [No. P 31] the collectors of the wool customs in London to pay Robert and Anne all arrears of the said £60 yearly owing from the said 29 Sept. 1444* (a predicto festo sancti Michaelis dicto anno vicesimo tercio)*; the king orders the Exchequer to allow* (debite allocetis) *the London customers all payments made in this regard when they account, provided they produce the said mandate for payment directed to them and the receipts* (litteras acquietancie) *of the beneficiaries. — 1446 Oct. 1* (Teste me ipso apud Westmonasterium, primo die Octobris anno regni nostri vicesimo quinto). *Westminster.*

L1 TNA: PRO, E122/75/39/30. Original. Parchment. Seal on tongue torn away. Severely damaged by damp (holes in the parchment; script worn away in places; shadow of the seal on the parchment). On the dorse: (at the top) Irrotulatur termino sancti Michaelis anno 25° rotulo tercio [*TNA: PRO, E159/223 Brevia directa baronibus Michaelmas m 3 = L2*]; *(beneath that)* Allocatur in compoto Thome Pounde et Johannis Poutrell collectorum custumarum regis in portu London' de anno 24to inde rotulo compotorum de antiqua custuma *[TNA: PRO, E356/19 m 3-3d; No. A 3, § 18].*

---

[11] *CPR 1441-46, p. 365.*

L2 TNA: PRO, E159/223 Brevia directa baronibus Michaelmas m 3. Contemporaneous official copy. Parchment. Unsealed. Marginated: Pro Roberto Roos milite.

[P 31] Henry VI to the collectors of the wool customs and subsidy in London: since the king by patent[12] *issued on 26 Mar. 1445* (vicesimo sexto die Marcii anno regni nostri [a]vicesimo tercio[a]) *granted Robert* Roos, *kt.* (miles), *in recompense for past and future service to the crown, together with his wife Anne £110 yearly, payable from 29 Sept. 1444* (a festo sancti Michaelis dicto anno vicesimo tercio) *onwards at Easter and Michaelmas in equal portions from the issues of the wool customs in London (£60) and Southampton (£50) for life, whichever of them shall live longest* (pro termino vite eorum Roberti et Anne et eorum alterius diucius viventis), *until the king or his successor should provide them with lands producing the same income in England* (quousque prefatis Roberto et Anne de terris et tenementis sibi aggreabilibus clari valoris centum et decem librarum per annum infra dictum regnum nostrum Anglie) *for life, whichever of them shall live longest* (pro termino vite eorum et alterius eorum diucius viventis); *the king orders the customers to pay* Roos *all arrears of the said £60 from 29 Sept. 1444* (a predicto festo sancti Michaelis dicto anno vicesimo tercio), *accepting in turn* Roos' *receipts* (litteras suas acquietancie), *which together with this mandate for payment shall suffice for the allowance* (debitam allocacionem) *of all payments made in this regard when the customers account at the Exchequer. — 144[6] Sept. 30* (Teste me ipso apud Westmonasterium, 30 die Septembris anno regni nostri vicesimo quinto. *[signed by the scribe]* 'Mouter'). [13] *Westminster.*

L TNA: PRO, E122/75/39/31. Original. Parchment. Seal on tongue lost. Slightly damaged by damp (the parchment has rotted away in places).

[a-a] *Interlined L.*

[P 32] John Wyggemore, *receiver of Richard, duke of York* (receptor Ricardi ducis Eborum), *acknowledges receipt of £11 13s 4d, owing to the duke by virtue of the annuity of £289 6s 8d yearly granted by Ricard II [cf. No. S 2], payable from the issues of the wool customs and subsidy in London, from the collectors of the wool customs and subsidy in London John* Poutrell *and Thomas* Pounde. *— 144[6] [month and year illegible]* (per presentes sigillo meo per [me signatas. Datum ...] vicesimo quarto). *[London].*

L TNA: PRO, E122/75/39/32. Original. Parchment. Traces of seal on tongue. On the tongue: [...] Wyggemore £11 13s 4d. *Receipt severely damaged by damp (the right-hand side has rotted away).*

---

[12] *CPR 1441-46, p. 365.*

[13] *Ralph Mouter was a chancery clerk: CCR 1441-47, p. 384.*

[P 33] John, duke of Exeter, son and heir of John, earl of Huntingdon, and his wife Elizabeth, acknowledges receipt of £60 owing to him by virtue of the grant of £60 yearly by Henry VI,[14] *payable from the issues of the wool customs and subsidy in London, to wit for Michaelmas and Easter terms last* (pro terminis sancti Michaelis et Pasche ultimo preteritis), *from the collectors of the wool customs and subsidy in London John* Poutrell *and Thomas* Pounde. — *1446 June 24* (per presentes sigillo nostro signatas. Datum 24 die Junii anno regni regis Henrici Sexti vicesimo quarto). *[London].*

L TNA: PRO, E122/75/39/33. Original. Parchment. Seal on tongue severely damaged. Receipt slightly damaged by damp.

[P 34] John Wygmore, *receiver of Richard, duke of York* (receptor Ricardi ducis Eborum), *acknowledges receipt in the duke's name of 10 marks by the hand of John [...] (*nomine dicti ducis per manus Johannis [...]*), owing to the duke by virtue of the annuity of £289 6s 8d yearly granted by Ricard II [cf. No. S 2], payable from the issues of the wool customs and subsidy in London, from the collectors of the wool customs and subsidy in London John* Poutrell *and Thomas* Pounde. — *144[6] Oct.* ([...] die Octobris anno regni regis Henrici Sexti post conquestum [vicesimo quinto]). *[London].*

L TNA: PRO, E122/75/39/34. Original. Parchment. Traces of seal on tongue. Severely damaged by damp (the right-hand side has rotted away).

[P 35] John, earl of Shrewsbury (Salop'), *lord Talbot and Furnivale* (de Furnyvale) *acknowledges receipt of 300 marks owing to him by virtue of the grant of 300 marks yearly by Henry VI,*[15] *payable from the issues of the wool customs and subsidy in London, to wit for Michaelmas and Easter terms last* (ut pro terminis sancti Michaelis et Pasche ultimo preteritis), *from the collectors of the wool customs and subsidy in London John* Poutrell *and Thomas* Pounde. — *144[6]* (In cujus rei testimonium presentibus sigillum nostrum apposuimus. Datum [...] anno vicesimo quarto). *[London].*

L TNA: PRO, E122/75/39/35. Original. Parchment. Seal on tongue severely damaged. On the dorse: Allocatur in co[mpoto Johannis] Poutrell [et Thome] Pounde [collectorum custumarum] regis Hen[rici vj^ti^ in portu] London' de [anno 24to] *[TNA: PRO, E356/19 m 3-3d; No. A 3, § 19].*

---

[14] *CPR 1441-46, p. 242.*

[15] *CPR 1441-46, p. 227-8.*

[P 36] Nicholas Ayssheton, *justice in the Common Bench* (de communi banco)[16] *and of assizes* (ad assisas in diversis comitatibus Anglie capiendas assignatorum)[17] *acknowledges receipt of £17 15s 1d in part payment of his fees and rewards (40 marks fee and 110 marks reward yearly as justice in the Common Bench and £20 fee yearly as judge of assizes, both payable from the issues of the wool customs and subsidy in London) for Michaelmas term last* (pro termino sancti Michaelis ultimo preterito), *from the collectors of the wool customs and subsidy in London John* Poutrell *and Thomas* Pounde. — *1446 Oct. 6* (per presentes sigillo meo signatas. Datum sexto die Octobris anno regni regis Henrici Sexti post conquestum Anglie vicesimo quinto). *[London].*

L TNA: PRO, E122/75/39/36. Original. Parchment. Seal on tongue severely damaged. Receipt slightly damaged (script worn away in the middle in places). On the dorse: Allocatur in[a] compoto Johannis Poutrell et Thome Pounde collectorum custumarum et subsidiorum regis in portu London' de anno 24[to] regis Henrici vj[ti] *[TNA: PRO, E356/19 m 3-3d; No. A 3, § 21].*

[a] rotulo *follows, struck through L.*

[P 37] This document is a fragment no larger than a postage stamp, on which only the name [Thomas] Pounde *can be deciphered. Consequently it must be a receipt of some sort.*

L TNA: PRO, E122/75/39/36A. Original (fragment). Parchment. Seal lost.

[P 38] William Baron, *esq.* (armiger), *acknowedges receipt of £50, owing to him by virtue of the annuity of £20 yearly granted by Henry VI,*[18] *payable from the issues of the wool customs in London, to wit for Easter term 22 Hen. VI, Michaelmas and Easter terms 23 Hen. VI and Michaelmas and Easter terms 24 Hen. VI* (videlicet pro termino Pasche anno 22[do], terminis Michaelis et Pasche [anno 23[cio] et Michaelis et] Pasche anno 24[to]), *from the collectors of the wool customs and subsidy in London John* Poutrell *and Thomas* Pounde. — *144[6]* (per presentes sigillo [meo signatas. Datum...] anno regni regis Henrici Sexti vicesimo quarto). *[London].*

L TNA: PRO, E122/75/39/37. Original. Parchment. Seal on tongue severely damaged. Receipt severely damaged (right-hand side torn away; script worn away in places). On the dorse: (at the top) London'; *(beneath that)* Pro Johanne Poutrell et Thoma Pounde collec-

---

[16] *John H. Baker, The Order of Serjeants at Law. A Chronicle of Creations, with related texts and a historical introduction (Selden Society Supplementary Series 5), London 1984, p. 497.*

[17] *CPR 1441-46, p. 171.*

[18] *CPR 1441-46, p. 71.*

torum custumarum lanarum in portu regis London' de anno 24[to] regis Henrici vj[ti].

[P 39] John, duke of Exeter, son and heir of John, earl of Huntingdon, and his wife Elizabeth, acknowledges receipt of £7 6s 8d owing to him by virtue of the grant of £60 yearly by Henry VI,[19] *payable from the issues of the wool customs and subsidy in London, from the collectors of the wool customs and subsidy in London John* Poutrell *and Thomas* Pounde. — *1446 Mar. 25* (Datum vicesimo quinto die Marcii anno regni regis Henrici Sexti post conquestum vicesimo quarto). *[London].*

L TNA: PRO, E122/75/39/38. Original. Parchment. Seal on tongue lost. Severely damaged by damp (the parchment has rotted away in places on the right-hand side of the receipt).

[P 40] Nicholas Ayssheton, *justice in the Common Bench* (de communi banco)[20] *and of assizes* (ad assisas in diversis comitatibus Anglie capiendas assignatorum)[21] *acknowledges receipt of £120 in part payment of his fees and rewards (40 marks fee and 110 marks reward yearly as justice in the Common Bench and £20 fee yearly as judge of assizes, both payable from the issues of the wool customs and subsidy in London) for Michaelmas and Easter terms last* (pro terminis sancti Michaelis et Pasche ultimo preteritis), *from the collectors of the wool customs and subsidy in London John* Poutrell *and Thomas* Pounde. — (per presentes sigillo meo signatas ... [Henrici] Sexti post conquestum Anglie vicesimo ..). *[London].*

L TNA: PRO, E122/75/39/39. Original. Parchment. Seal on tongue lost. Severely damaged by damp (the lower right-hand corner has rotted away; script elsewhere scarcely legible). On the dorse: Allocatur in compoto Johannis [Poutrell] et Thome Pounde collectorum [custumarum] regis in portu London' de anno 24[to] regis Henrici vj[ti] *[TNA: PRO, E356/19 m 3-3d; No. A 3, § 20].*

[P 41] Henry VI to the treasurer and barons of the Exchequer: since the king by patent issued on 22 Nov. 1443 (vicesimo secundo die Novembris anno regni nostri vicesimo secundo)[22] *granted John, duke of Exeter – under the name John, earl of Huntingdon, son and heir of John, formerly earl of Huntingdon, and his wife Elizabeth* (per nomen Johannis comitis Huntyngdonie filii et heredis Johannis nuper comitis Huntyngdonie et Elizabethe nuper uxoris ejus), *and their legitimate heirs* (sibi et heredibus suis de corpore suo exeuntibus) – *500 marks yearly, payable from 29 Sept. 1443* (a festo sancti Michaelis Archangeli anno regni

[19] *CPR 1441-46, p. 242.*

[20] *Baker, Sergeants at Law, p. 497.*

[21] *CPR 1441-46, p. 171.*

[22] *CPR 1441-46, S. 242.*

nostri vicesimo secundo) *at Michaelmas and Easter in equal portions from the issues of the customs in London, Southampton, Bristol and Hull, in particular £60 from the issues of the wool customs and subsidy in London and £40 from the issues of the petty customs in London; and since the king has ordered [mandate untraceable] the customers to pay John all arrears of the said £60 owing from Michaelmas term last* (pro festo sancti Michaelis ultimo preterito) *and all sums which shall fall due thereafter; the king orders the Exchequer to allow* (debite allocetis) *the customers all payments made in this regard when they account, provided they produce the said mandate for payment directed to them and the duke's receipts* (litteras acquietancie). — *1445 Oct. 13* (Teste me ipso apud Westmonasterium, 13° die Octobris anno regni nostri vicesimo quarto. *[signed by the scribe]* [a]'Hill'[a]).[23] *Westminster.*

L1 TNA: PRO, E122/75/39/40. Original. Parchment. Seal on tongue torn away. On the dorse: (at the top) Irrotulatur termino sancti Michaelis anno 24to rotulo 10mo *[TNA: PRO, E159/222 Brevia directa baronibus Michaelmas m 10 = L2]*; *(beneath that)* Allocatur in compoto Johannis Poutrell et Thome Pounde collectorum custumarum lanarum in portu regis London' de anno 24to regis Henrici vj^ti^ *[TNA: PRO, E356/19 m 3-3d; No. A 3, § 24].*

L2 TNA: PRO, E159/222 Brevia directa baronibus Michaelmas m 10. Contemporaneous official copy. Parchment. Unsealed. Marginated: Pro collectoribus magne custume in portu civitatis London'.

[a-a] *Omitted L2.*

[P 42] Henry VI to the treasurer and barons of the Exchequer: since the king by patent issued on 22 Nov. 1443 (vicesimo secundo die Novembris anno regni nostri vicesimo secundo)[24] *granted John, duke of Exeter – under the name John, earl of Huntingdon, son and heir of John, formerly earl of Huntingdon, and his wife Elizabeth* (per nomen Johannis comitis Huntyngdonie filii et heredis Johannis nuper comitis Huntyngdonie et Elizabethe nuper uxoris ejus) – *and his legitimate heirs* (sibi et heredibus suis de corpore suo exeuntibus) *500 marks yearly, payable from 29 Sept. 1443* (a festo sancti Michaelis Archangeli anno regni nostri vicesimo secundo) *at Michaelmas and Easter in equal portions from the issues of the customs in London, Southampton, Bristol and Hull, in particular £60 from the issues of the wool customs and subsidy in London and £40 from the issues of the petty customs in London; and since the king has ordered [mandate untraceable] the customers to pay John all arrears of the said £60 owing from Easter term last* (pro festo Pasche ultimo preterito); *the king orders the Exchequer to allow* (debite allocetis) *the customers all payments made in this regard when they account, provided they produce the said mandate for payment directed to*

[23] *William Hill was a chancery clerk: CCR 1441-47, p. 368 et passim.*

[24] *CPR 1441-46, S. 242.*

them and the duke's receipts (litteras acquietancie). — *1445 Apr. 13* (Teste me ipso apud Westmonasterium, 13 die Aprilis anno regni nostri vicesimo tercio. *[signed by the scribe]* [a]"Hill"[a]). *Westminster.*

L1 TNA: PRO, E122/75/39/41. Original. Parchment. Seal on tongue torn away. On the dorse: (at the top) Irrotulatur termino Pasche anno 23[cio] rotulo 10[mo] *[TNA: PRO, E159/221 Brevia directa baronibus Easter m 10Bd = L2]; (beneath that)* Allocatur in compoto Johannis Poutrell et Thome Pounde collectorum custumarum regis in portu London' de anno 24[to] *[TNA: PRO, E356/19 m 3-3d; No. A 3, § 24]*; *(beneath that)* Pro Johanne duce Exon'.

L2 TNA: PRO, E159/221 Brevia directa baronibus Easter m 10Bd. Contemporaneous official copy. Parchment. Unsealed. Marginated: Pro collectoribus magne custume in portu London'.

[a-a] *Omitted L2.*

[P 43] Robert Danvers, *justice of assizes* (unus justiciariorum ad assisas in diversis comitatibus regni nostri Anglie capiendas assignatorum),[25] *acknowledges receipt of £31 17s 7d, owing to him for his fees by virtue of the act of the parliament*[26] *meeting in Westminster in 18 Hen. VI, to wit for Easter term last and before that* (ad festum Pasche ultimo preteritum et antea pro feodo meo pro officio meo), *from the collectors of the wool customs and subsidy in London John* Poutrell *and Thomas* Pound. — *1446 July 2* (In cujus rei testimonium presentibus sigillum meum apposui. Datum secundo die Julii anno regni regis Henrici Sexti post conquestum vicesimo quarto). *[London].*

L TNA: PRO, E122/75/39/42. Original. Parchment. Traces of seal on tongue. On the dorse: Allocatur in compoto Johannis Poutrell et Thome Pounde collectorum custumarum regis in portu London' de anno 24[to] *[TNA: PRO, E356/19 m 3-3d; No. A 3, § 23].*

[P 44] Nicholas Ayssheton, *justice in the Common Bench* (de communi banco)[27] *acknowledges receipt of £11 13s 11¼d owing to him yearly as justice in the Common Bench for robes, payable from the issues of the wool customs and subsidy in London, to wit 63s 6d for robes due at Pentecost 1445, 63s 6d for robes due at Pentecost 1446 and 106s 11¼d for robes due at Christmas 1445, from the collectors of the wool customs and subsidy in London John* Poutrell *and Thomas* Pounde. — Datum [...] anno regni regis Henrici Sexti post conquestum Anglie vicesimo quarto. *[London].*

L TNA: PRO, E122/75/39/43. Original. Parchment. Remnants of seal on tongue. Severely damaged by damp (the lower right-hand corner has rotted away); elsewhere, the script has largely worn away.

---

[25] *CPR 1441-46, p. 280.*

[26] *Rotuli Parliamentorum, vol. 5, p. 13-4.*

[27] *Baker, Sergeants at Law, p. 497.*

[P 45] Henry VI to the treasurer and barons of the Exchequer: since the king by patent[28] *issued on 28 Apr. 1442* (vicesimo octavo die Aprilis anno regni nostri vicesimo) *granted William* Malbon *and William* Baron, *esq.* (armiger), *£20 yearly for life, whichever of them shall live longest* (durante vita eorum et alterius eorum, qui supervixerit), *payable from the issues of the wool customs in London at Easter and Michaelmas in equal portions; and since the king ordered [No. P 46] the collectors of the wool customs in London to pay the arrears owing from Easter and Michaelmas terms last* (pro terminis Pasche et sancti Michaelis ultimo preteritis)*; the king orders the Exchequer to allow* (debite allocetis) *the customers all payments made in this regard when they account, providing they produce this mandate for payment and the receipts* (litteras acquietancie) *of the beneficiaries. — 1444 Oct. 9* (Teste me ipso apud Westmonasterium, 9 die Octobris anno regni nostri vicesimo tercio. *[signed by the scribe]* [a]'Pemberton'[a]).[29] *Westminster.*

L1 TNA: PRO, E122/75/39/44. Original. Parchment. Seal on tongue torn away. On the dorse: (at the top) London'; antiqua custuma; *(beneath that)* Irrotulatur termino sancti Michaelis anno 24to rotulo quarto*; [TNA: PRO, E159/222 Brevia directa baronibus Michaelmas m 4d = L2] (beneath that)* Allocatur in compoto Johannis Poutrell et Thome Pounde collectorum custumarum regis lanarum in portu London' regis computancium a festo sancti Michaelis anno 24to regis hujus *[29 Sept. 1445]* usque idem festum tunc proximum sequens *[29 Sept. 1446]* inde rotulo compotorum de antiqua custuma *[TNA: PRO, E356/19 m 3-3d; No. A 3, § 25]*.

L2, TNA: PRO, E159/222 Brevia directa baronibus Michaelmas m 4d. Contemporaneous official copy. Parchment. Unsealed. Marginated: Pro collectoribus magne custume in portu London'.

a-a *Omitted L2.*

[P 46] Henry VI to the collectors of the wool customs and subsidy in London: since the king by patent[30] *issued on 28 Apr. 1442* (vicesimo octavo die Aprilis anno regni nostri vicesimo) *granted William* Malbon *and William* Baron, *esq.* (armiger), *£20 yearly for life, whichever of them shall live longest* (durante vita eorum et alterius eorum, qui supervixerit), *payable from the issues of the wool customs in London at Easter and Michaelmas in equal portions; the king orders the customers to pay the beneficiaries all arrears owing from Easter and Michaelmas terms last* (pro terminis Pasche et sancti Michaelis ultimo preteritis), *accepting in turn the beneficiaries' receipts* (litteras suas acquietancie), *which together with this mandate for payment shall suffice for the allowance* (debitam allocacionem) *of all payments made in this regard when they*

---

[28] *CPR 1441-46, p. 71.*

[29] *John Pemberton was a chancery clerk: CCR 1441-47, p. 319.*

[30] *CPR 1441-46, p. 71.*

account. — 1444 Oct. 8 (Teste me ipso apud Westmonasterium, 8 die Octobris anno regni nostri vicesimo tercio. *[signed by the scribe]* 'Pemberton'). *Westminster.*

L TNA: PRO, E122/75/39/45. Original. Parchment. Seal on tongue torn away.

[P 47] Henry VI to the collectors of the wool customs and subsidy in London: since the king by patent[31] *issued on 25 Aug. 1444* (vicesimo quinto die Augusti anno regni nostri vicesimo secundo) *appointed Robert* Danvers *as justice of assizes* (unus justiciariorum nostrorum ad assisas in diversis comitatibus regni nostri Anglie arramandas capiendas)*; the king orders the collectors of the wool customs in London in view of the act of the parliament*[32] *meeting in Westminster in 18 Hen. VI regarding such judges' fees and rewards* (de feodis et regardis justiciariis solvendis) *(a copy of which was sent to the customers) to pay* Danvers, *who has a right to a fee of £20 yearly for this office, all arrears of his fee* (de feodo suo) *of £20 per annum owing from the date of his appointment on 25 Aug. 1444* (a predicto vicesimo quinto die Augusti), *accepting in turn his receipts* (litteras suas acquietancie), *which together with this mandate for payment shall suffice for the allowance* (debitam allocacionem) *of all payments made in this regard when the customers account at the Exchequer. — 1446 June 9* (Teste me ipso apud Westmonasterium, 9 die Junii anno regni nostri vicesimo quarto. *[signed by the scribe]* 'Bate').[33] *Westminster.*

L TNA: PRO, E122/75/39/46. Original. Parchment. Seal on tongue torn away. On the dorse: Allocatur in compoto Johannis Poutrell et Thome Pounde collectorum custumarum regis in portu London' de anno 24[to] regis Henrici vj[ti] *[TNA: PRO, E356/19 m 3-3d; No. A 3, § 23].*

[P 48] Henry VI to the treasurer and barons of the Exchequer: since the king by patent[34] *issued on 28 Apr. 1442* (vicesimo octavo die Aprilis anno regni nostri vicesimo) *granted William* Malbon *and William* Baron, *esq.* (armiger), *£20 yearly for life, whichever of them shall live longest* (durante vita eorum et alterius eorum, qui supervixerit), *payable from the issues of the wool customs in London at Easter and Michaelmas in equal portions; and since the king ordered [mandate untraceable] the collectors of the wool customs in London to pay the arrears owing from Michaelmas term last* (a festo sancti Michaelis ultimo preterito) *and all sums which shall fall due in the future; the king orders the Exchequer to allow* (debitc allocetis) *the customers all payments made in this regard*

---

31 *CPR 1441-46, p. 280.*

32 *Rotuli Parliamentorum, vol. 5, p. 13-4.*

33 *John Bate was a chancery clerk: CCR 1441-47, p. 384.*

34 *CPR 1441-46, p. 71.*

when they account, providing they produce this mandate for payment and the receipts (litteras acquietancie) *of the beneficiaries. — 1445 Mar. 2* (Teste me ipso apud Westmonasterium, secundo die Marcii anno regni nostri vicesimo tercio. *[signed by the scribe]* [a]'Pemberton'[a]). *Westminster.*

L1 TNA: PRO, E122/75/39/47. Original. Parchment. Seal on tongue torn away. On the dorse: (at the top) London'; antiqua custuma; *(beneath that)* Irrotulatur termino Pasche anno 23[cio] rotulo secundo *[TNA: PRO, E159/221 Brevia directa baronibus Easter m 2 = L2]*; *(beneath that)* Allocatur in compoto Johannis Poutrell et Thome Pounde collectorum custumarum regis lanarum in portu London' computancium a festo sancti Michaelis anno 24[to] regis hujus *[29 Sept. 1445]* usque idem festum tunc proximum sequens *[29 Sept. 1446]* inde rotulo compotorum de antiqua custuma *[TNA: PRO, E356/19 m 3-3d; No. A 3, § 25]*.

L2 TNA: PRO, E159/221 Brevia directa baronibus Easter m 2. Contemporaneous official copy. Parchment. Unsealed. Marginated: Pro Willelmo Malbon et Willelmo Baron armigero.

[a-a] *Omitted L2.*

ACCOUNTING DOCUMENTS

[A 1] Having distrained John Poutrell *and Thomas* Pounde *to appear together with the controller William* Baroun *on 25 Apr. 1446,*[1] *the Exchequer continues their case until 27 June 1446, when they appear, take the oath to account faithfully and are assigned William* Proctour *as their auditor. Since accounting could not be completed in Trinity term, the case was continued until 30 Sept. 1446.*

L TNA: PRO, E159/222 Fines, manucapciones, dies datus, attornati, respectus et visus Easter m 2d. Contemporaneous official fair copy of the Exchequer proceedings. Parchment. Unsealed.

[Marginated] London'; De die dato

[1] Datus est dies hic per thesaurarium et barones Johanni Poutrell et Thome Pounde collectoribus custume et subsidii lanarum et pellium lanutarum ac custume coriorum in portu civitatis London' ac Willelmo Baroun contrarotulatori eorundem custumarum et subsidii ibidem usque quindenam sancte Trinitatis *[27 June 1446]*, dictis videlicet collectoribus ad reddendum regi compotum de custumis et subsidio predictis de tempore, quo inde fuerunt collectores et non computarunt, et dicto contrarotulatori ad faciendum, quod ad officium contrarotulatoris pertinet in hac parte, quem diem admiserunt periculo, quod etc.

[2] [a]Ad quem diem iidem collectores et contrarotulator venierunt [b]in propriis personis suis[b], et dicti collectores et contrarotulator prestiterunt sacramentum, dicti videlicet collectores ad fideliter computandum etc. et dictus contrarotulator ad fideliter testificandum etc. in premissis. Et super hoc Willelmus Proctour unus auditorum compotorum hujus scaccarii assignatur ad compotum illum audiendum etc. Et quia iidem collectores non possunt percomputare durante termino etc., datus est dies hic eisdem collectoribus usque crastinum sancti Michaelis *[30 Sept. 1446]* ad percomputandum in premissis.

[3] Ad quem diem iidem collectores venierunt et computarunt de custumis et subsidio predictis, sicut continetur in memorandis anni sequentis, videlicet inter recorda de termino sancti Michaelis *[TNA: PRO, E159/223 Recorda Michaelmas m 2; No. A 2]*. Ideo non fiat hic ulterius execucio. *[The 'finished' sign follows].*

[a] *The remainder of the document was written by a different hand L.*
[b-b] *Interlined L.*

---

[1] *TNA: PRO, E159/222 Recorda Michaelmas m 10d. No view of account was taken.*

[A 2] *John* Poutrell *and Thomas* Pounde *appear before the Exchequer in Michaelmas term 1446 to account for the issues of the wool customs and subsidy in London in the period from 29 Sept. 1445 to 29 Sept. 1446. Since they and the controller William* Baron *continue in office, the London sheriffs are ordered to distrain them to appear before the Exchequer on 17 Apr. 1447 [for a view of account]. Before that, however, they appear in Hilary term 1447 and account for the following period [29 Sept.-31 Dec. 1446].*

L TNA: PRO, E159/223 Recorda Michaelmas m 2. Contemporaneous official fair copy of the Exchequer proceedings. Parchment. Unsealed.

[Marginated] London'

[1] Memorandum, quod Johannes Poutrell et Thomas Pounde collectores custume [a]lanarum, coriorum et pellium lanutarum[a] ac subsidii lanarum et pellium lanutarum in portu civitatis London' venerunt et computarunt de eisdem custuma et subsidio ibidem, videlicet a festo sancti Michaelis anno vicesimo quarto regis hujus *[29 Sept. 1445]* usque idem festum proximum sequens *[29 Sept. 1446]*, a quo quidem festo iidem collectores per visum et testimonium Willelmi Baron contrarotulatoris eorundem custume et subsidii ibidem sunt alias inde computa[tu]ri. [b]Ideo preceptum sit vicecomitibus, quod ipsos collectores et contrarotulatorem distringant per terras etc., ita etc. in crastino Clausi [Pasche] *[17 Apr. 1447]*, dictos videlicet collectores ad reddendum regi compotum et dictum contrarotulatorem ad testificandum in premissis.

[2] Ante quem diem predicti collectores venerunt et computarunt de custuma et subsidio predictis, sicut continetur alibi in hiis memorandis, videlicet inter recorda de termino sancti Hillarii rotulo[c] [2] *[TNA: PRO, E159/223 Recorda Hilary m 2]*. Ideo non fiat hic ulterius execucio. *[The 'finished' sign follows].*

[a–a] *Interlined L.* [b] *The remainder of the document was written by a different hand L.* s' *marginated against this line.* [c] *1 cm room left for completion of the entry L.*

[A 3] *John* Poutrell *and Thomas* Pounde *appear before the Exchequer in Michaelmas term 1446 and account for the issues of the wool customs and subsidy in London in the period from 29 Sept. 1445 to 29 Sept. 1446.*

L TNA: PRO, E356/19 m 3-3d. Contemporaneous official fair copy of the Exchequer proceedings. Parchment. Unsealed. In the upper left-hand margin: • s' •; termino sancti Michaelis anno 25[to] regis Henrici vj[ti]. *In the 5 cm left free by the indentation of the first line* – Auditores: W. Fallon baro, W. Proctour clericus.

[Marginated] London'

[1] Compotus Johannis Poutrell et Thome Pounde collectorum custumarum et subsidiorum lanarum et pellium lanutarum ac custume coriorum in portu civitatis London' et in singulis portubus et locis eidem portui adjacentibus per

duo brevia regis nunc Henrici vj^ti de magno sigillo suo patencia[2] data 21mo die Novembris anno regni sui 21mo *[21 Nov. 1442]* prefatis collectoribus directa, super hunc compotum ostensa et penes ipsos remanencia aliasque in compoto suo de eodem anno *[TNA: PRO, E356/19 m 2-2d]*[3] plenius annotata, videlicet de hujusmodi custumis et subsidiis regis ibidem a festo sancti Michaelis anno regis predicti 24to *[29 Sept. 1445]*, ante quod festum iidem collectores inde computarunt rotulo compotorum de custuma *[TNA: PRO, E356/19 m 3]*,[4] usque festum sancti Michaelis tunc proximum sequens *[29 Sept. 1446]*, scilicet per unum annum integrum, per visum et testimonium Willelmi Baron contrarotulatoris custumarum et subsidiorum regis predictorum ibidem per idem tempus, a quo quidem festo sancti Michaelis anno 25to *[29 Sept. 1446]* iidem collectores per visum et testimonium contrarotulatoris predicti sunt alias inde computaturi.

[Marginated] Recepta denariorum

[2] Iidem reddunt compotum de £1847 5s 9¾d de custuma contingente tam 4465 saccos, 11 clavos lane quam 258,131 pelles lanutas facientes 1075½ saccos, 11 pelles diversorum mercatorum indigenarum in portu et locis predictis custumata et abinde versus stapulam regis Calesie traducta infra predictum tempus hujus compoti, videlicet de quolibet hujusmodi sacco lane 6s 8d et de quibuslibet 240 pellibus lanutis 6s 8d, per unum breve predictorum duorum brevium supra in titulo hujus compoti annotatorum, sicut continetur tam in quodam libro ipsorum collectorum quam in 7 rotulis predicti contrarotulatoris de particulis inde hic in thesauro liberatis.

[3] Et de £9234 19s 7¾d de subsidio contingente tam dictos 4465 saccos, 11 clavos lane quam dictas 258,131 pelles dictorum mercatorum indigenarum in portu et locis predictis custumata et abinde versus dictam stapulam regis Calesie traducta infra tempus predictum, videlicet de quolibet hujusmodi sacco 33s 4d et de quibuslibet 240 pellibus lanutis 33s 4d, per unum aliud breve predictorum duorum brevium supra in titulo hujus compoti annotatorum, sicut continetur ibidem.

[4] Et de £101 8s 3¼d de custuma contingente 202½ saccos, 15½ clavos lane diversorum mercatorum alienigenarum in portu et locis predictis custumatos et abinde versus partes exteras de licencia regis infra tempus predictum traductos, videlicet de quolibet hujusmodi sacco 10s, per predictum breve supra in tercia particula precedenti annotatum, sicut continetur ibidem.

[5] Et de £439 7s 11d de subsidio contingente dictos 202½ saccos, 15½ clavos lane diversorum mercatorum alienigenarum in portu et locis predictis

---

[2] *CFR 1437-45, p. 234.*

[3] *Stuart Jenks (ed.), The Enrolled Customs Accounts (PRO, E356, E372, E364) 1279/80-1508/09 (1523/24) Volume 8: E356/19, E356/20 (List and Index Society) [in press], E356/19, No. 6.*

[4] *Stuart Jenks (ed.), The Enrolled Customs Accounts (PRO, E356, E372, E364) 1279/80-1508/09 (1523/24) Volume 8: E356/19, E356/20 (List and Index Society) [in press], E356/19, No. 8.*

custumatos et abinde versus dictas partes exteras de licencia regis, ut predicitur, traductos infra tempus predictum, videlicet de quolibet hujusmodi sacco 43s 4d, per breve predictum supra in tercia particula precedenti annotatum, sicut continetur ibidem.

[6] De 10s domino regi debitis de subsidio cujuslibet sacci lane predictorum mercatorum alienigenarum in proxima particula precedenti annotati ultra dictos 43s 4d superius oneratos juxta tenorem brevis predicti non respondent per breve regis de privato sigillo suo datum 14 die Julii anno regni sui 20mo *[14 July 1442]* thesaurario et baronibus de scaccario suo directum et irrotulatum in memorandis inter brevia directa baronibus de termino sancti Michaelis anno ejusdem regis 21mo rotulo 4to ex parte remembratoris regis *[TNA: PRO, E159/219 Brevia directa baronibus Michaelmas m 4; No. S 1]*.

[7] Set respondent de 10s 7¾d de custuma contingente tam 5 dacras coriorum diversorum mercatorum indigenarum quam 7 dacras, 3 coria diversorum mercatorum alienigenarum in portu et locis predictis custumata et abinde educta infra tempus predictum, videlicet de dictis 5 dacris corriorum indigenarum juxta afferenciam 13s 4d pro 1 lasto coriorum de indigenis et de dictis 7 dacris, 3 corriis alienigenarum juxta afferenciam 20s pro 1 lasto corriorum de alienigenis, per breve predictum supra in 6ta particula precedenti annotatum, sicut continetur ibidem.

[8] Et de £6 15s 5¼d de deveriis Calesie provenientibus tam de dictis 202½ saccis, 15½ clavis lane quam de dictis 7 dacris, 3 corriis diversorum mercatorum alienigenarum in portu et locis predictis custumatis et abinde versus dictas partes exteras in forma predicta traductis infra tempus predictum, videlicet de quolibet hujusmodi sacco lane 8d et de dictis 7 dacris, 3 corriis juxta afferenciam 16d pro 1 lasto corriorum de alienigenis per idem breve, sicut continetur ibidem.

[9] Et de 102s 6d de exitibus sigilli regis, quod dicitur cokettus, provenientibus de 615 mercatoribus lanas, pelles lanutas et corria predicta extra portum predictum in forma predicta traducentibus infra tempus predictum, videlicet de quolibet mercatore 2d per idem breve, sicut continetur ibidem.

[10] De aliqua custuma seu subsidio pellium lanutarum aliquorum mercatorum alienigenarum in portubus et locis predictis, videlicet per predictum tempus hujus compoti, non respondent, eo quod nulle hujusmodi pelles lanute ibidem custumate seu traducte fuerunt infra idem tempus, ut dicunt super sacramentum suum, sicut continetur ibidem.

[11] Nec respondent de aliquibus proficuis sive commoditatibus per ipsos collectores vel aliquem alium eorum nomine pro solucione alicujus assignamenti per talliam vel aliter pro empcione alicujus tallie aut alio modo quocumque receptis juxta formam statuti in parliamento domini Henrici iiij^{ti} nuper regis Anglie apud Westmonasterium in crastino sancti Michaelis anno regni sui 4to *[30 Sept. 1402]* tento editi,[5] videlicet per tempus predictum, eo quod

[5] *St. 4 Hen. IV, c. 20: Statutes of the Realm, vol. 2, p. 139; cf. Rotuli Parliamentorum,*

nulla hujusmodi proficua sive commoditates pro hujusmodi solucione sive empcione perceperunt vel habuerunt per idem tempus, ut dicunt super sacramentum suum.
[Marginated] Examinatur

Summa totalis recepte: £11,635 10s 9¼d, unde custuma lanarum, pellium lanutarum et corriorum cum deveriis Calesie et exitibus coketti £1961 3s 2½d; subsidium lanarum et pellium lanutarum £9674 7s 6¾d

[12] In thesauro £973 14s 6½d in 21 talliis de custuma et subsidio. Et in thesauro £3681 5s 3d in 64 talliis de subsidio lanarum. Et in thesauro £5471 10s 8d in 6 talliis de subsidio lanarum. Et in thesauro £67 10s in 2 talliis de custuma et subsidio lanarum.
[13] Et eisdem collectoribus pro feodo suo per tempus predictum £40, sicut allocatum est in compotis precedentibus. Et prefato contrarotulatori pro vadiis suis per idem tempus £10, sicut allocatum est ibidem. Et eisdem collectoribus pro quadam domo conducta ad tronagium regis lanarum in portu predicto tronandarum ponderandum necnon diversis aliis cameris cum uno solario, aisiamento custumariorum, contrarotulatoris et clericorum suorum ibidem pro tempore existencium solvendo ad terminos Pasche et sancti Michaelis £4 de termino Pasche anno 24to et termino Michaelis anno 25to, sicut allocatum est in compotis precedentibus.
[14] Et in superplusagium, quod iidem collectores habent in rotulo 23^{cio} *[TNA: PRO, E372/290]* in Item Adhuc Item London', 16s 2d *[No. S 7]*.
[15] Et Humfrido duci Gloucestrie, cui dominus Henricus nuper rex Anglie Quintus per litteras suas patentes, quas rex nunc confirmavit,[6] concessit constabulariam castri Dovorrie ac custodiam Quinque Portuum regis habendas ad totam vitam suam percipiendo in officio illo per annum pro sustentacione sua necnon capellanorum, servientum et vigilum ac unius carpentarii in dicto castro morancium, quantum idem nuper rex percepit in officio supradicto, et quod idem dux haberet et perciperet occasione premissa in specie, prout moris tunc fuerit, trescentas libras, videlicet de wardis ad dictum castrum pertinentibus centum, quadraginta et sex libras, de exitibus custume regis in portu ville de Sandewico centum marcas et residuas quaterviginti et septem libras, sex solidos et octo denarios de custuma et subsidio in portu civitatis regis London' per manus collectorum eorundem custumarum et subsidiorum in eisdem portubus, qui pro tempore fuerint, ad festa Pasche et sancti Michaelis per equales porciones, £87 6s 8d de terminis Michaelis et Pasche anno 24to per breve regis irrotulatum in memorandis de anno 25to regis hujus termino sancti Michaelis

vol. 3, p. 506.
[6] *Henry V's patent was issued on 17 Nov. 1415 (CPR 1413-6, p. 374), then surrendered and re-issued on 23 June 1416 (CPR 1416-22, p.34), while Henry VI's confirmation was issued on 20 Dec. 1422 (CPR 1422-9, p. 82-3).*

rotulo secundo *[TNA: PRO, E159/223 Brevia directa baronibus Michaelmas m 2d; No. P 1]* et duas litteras acquietancie ipsius ducis *[No. P 5 and P 7]* de recepta.

[16] Et Ricardo nunc duci Eborum consanguineo et heredi masculo Edmundi nuper ducis Eborum defuncti, cui quidem Edmundo nuper duci Eborum et heredibus suis masculis de corpore suo exeuntibus dominus Ricardus nuper rex Anglie Secundus concessit[7] quendam annuum redditum sive annuitatem ducentarum, quaterviginti et novem librarum, sex solidorum et octo denariorum percipiendorum annuatim tam de antiquis custumis ipsius nuper regis Ricardi et heredum suorum lanarum, coriorum et pellium lanutarum quam de subsidio lanarum, coriorum et pellium lanutarum dicti nuper regis Ricardi concesso de omni hujusmodi subsidio prefato nuper regi Ricardo vel heredibus suis extunc imposterum concedendo in portu civitatis London' per manus custumariorum, collectorum, firmariorum, receptorum seu occupatorum hujusmodi custumarum et subsidiorum in portu predicto pro tempore existencium habendum dicto Edmundo et heredibus suis masculis de corpore suo exeuntibus quodque prefatus Ricardus nunc dux Eborum filius Ricardi fratris Edwardi nuper ducis Eborum filii et heredis predicti Edmundi est consanguineus et propinquior heres predicti nuper ducis et habuit liberacionem dictorum £289 6s 8d annuorum, sicut plenius continetur in rotulo 20mo regis hujus *[TNA: PRO, E372/287]* in Adhuc Res' London' *[No. S 8]*, £607 15s 6d, videlicet £171 6s 10d inde in plenam solucionem £289 6s 8d a festo sancti Michaelis anno 22do regis hujus *[29 Sept. 1443]* usque idem festum tunc proximum sequens *[29 Sept. 1444]*, et £289 6s 8d a festo sancti Michaelis anno 23^{cio} regis hujus *[29 Sept. 1444]* usque idem festum tunc proximum sequens *[29 Sept. 1445]* et £147 2s residua in partem solucionis £289 6s 8d a festo sancti Michaelis anno 24to regis hujus *[29 Sept. 1445]* usque idem festum tunc proximum sequens *[29 Sept. 1446]*, per breve regis, quod est inter communia de anno 19no regis hujus termino sancti Hillarii rotulo 11mo *[TNA: PRO, E159/217 Brevia directa baronibus Hilary m 11; No. S 2]*, et 25 litteras acquietancie, videlicet tres sub nomine dicti ducis *[No. P 2, P 12, P 15 and P 24]* et 21 sub nomine Johannis Wygmore receptoris dicti ducis *[No. P 3, P 6, P 8, P 9, P 10, P 11, P 13, P 14, P 16, P 18, P 20, P 21, P 22, P 23, P 25, P 27, P 28, P 32, P 34, P 37]* et 1 sub nomine Johannis Harleston armigeri receptoris generalis ipsius ducis *[No. P 26]*, de recepta, sicut continetur in memorandis ex parte remembratoris regis de anno 24to regis hujus, videlicet inter recorda de termino sancte Trinitatis rotulo [4] *[TNA: PRO, E159/222 Recorda Trinity m 4d; No. S 3]*.

[17] [a]Et Ricardo Andrewe secretario regis, cui rex quintodecimo die Maii anno 23^{cio} *[15 May 1445]* concessit[8] centum libras percipiendas singulis annis a festo sancti Michaelis tunc ultimo preterito *[29 Sept. 1444]*, quamdiu regi placuerit, videlicet quadraginta libras inde de custumis regis lanarum, coriorum

---

[7] *CPR 1385-89, p. 62. Cf. No. S 2 for the complex history of this annuity.*

[8] *CPR 1441-46, p. 354.*

et pellium lanutarum in portu regis London' per manus collectorum earundem custumarum in eodem portu London' pro tempore existencium ad terminos Pasche et sancti Michaelis per equales porciones, £60 de termino Pasche anno 23[cio] et terminis Michaelis et Pasche anno 24[to] per breve regis irrotulatum in memorandis de anno 23[cio] regis hujus termino sancte Trinitatis rotulo tercio *[TNA: PRO, E159/221 Brevia directa baronibus Trinity m 3; No. S 4]*, [b]quod est inter communia de eodem anno[b], et litteras acquietancie ipsius Ricardi de recepta *[No. P 19]* [b]et per peticionem dictorum collectorum[b].

[18] Et Roberto Roos militi et Anne uxori ejus, quibus rex 26[to] die Marcii anno 23[cio] *[26 Mar. 1445]* concessit[9] centum et decem libras percipiendas singulis annis a festo sancti Michaelis dicto anno 23[cio] *[29 Sept. 1444]* pro termino vite ipsorum Roberti et Anne et eorum alterius diucius viventis, videlicet sexaginta libras inde per annum de custumis lanarum et pellium lanutarum in portu civitatis London' per manus collectorum earum custumarum pro tempore existencium ad festa Pasche et sancti Michaelis per equales porciones, quousque prefatis Roberto et Anne de terris et tenementis sibi aggreabilibus clari valoris centum et decem librarum per annum infra regnum regis Anglie habendis pro termino vite eorum et alterius eorum diucius viventis per regem seu heredes suos provisum foret et concessum, £90 de termino Pasche anno 23[cio] et terminis Michaelis et Pasche anno 24[to] per breve regis irrotulatum in memorandis de anno 25[to] regis hujus termino sancti Michaelis rotulo tercio *[TNA: PRO, E159/223 Brevia directa baronibus Michaelmas m 3; No. P 30]* et litteras acquietancie ipsius Roberti de recepta *[No. P 17]* [b]ac per peticionem dictorum collectorum[b].

[19] Et eisdem collectoribus pro denariis per ipsos solutis Johanni comiti Salopie, domino[c] Talbot et de Furnyvale, cui rex tercio die Decembris anno 22[do] *[3 Dec. 1443]* inter alia concessit[10] 300 marcas per annum de omnimodis subsidiis lanarum et pellium lanutarum extra portum London' exeuncium per manus custumariorum sive collectorum eorundem subsidiorum in portu illo pro tempore existencium ad terminos Pasche et sancti Michaelis per equales porciones, quousque eidem comiti de summa £10,426[d] 4¼d plenarie solutum fuerit et contentatum, in portu predicto et in aliis diversis locis 300 marce de termino Pasche anno 23[cio] et termino Michaelis anno 24[to] ultra £733 6s 8d prius allocata de summa predicta, sicut continetur in rotulo 23[cio] *[TNA: PRO, E372/290]* in Adhuc Res' London' *[No. S 3, in the tunnage and poundage account, 24 Hen. VI]* in debito Johannis Melbourne et Willelmi de Lwnes collectorum parve custume regis in portu civitatis London', per breve regis irrotulatum in memorandis de anno 23[cio] regis hujus termino sancte Trinitatis rotulo 22[do] *[TNA: PRO, E159/221 Brevia directa baronibus Trinity m 22d; No. S 5]*, quod est inter communia de eodem anno, et litteras acquietancie ipsius comitis de recepta *[No. P 35]*.

---

[9] *CPR 1441-46, p. 365.*

[10] *CPR 1441-46, p. 227-8.*

[20] Et eisdem collectoribus pro denariis per ipsos solutis Nicholao Ayssheton uni justiciariorum regis de communi banco[11] ac uni justiciariorum regis ad assisas in diversis comitatibus Anglie capiendas assignatorum[12] tam pro feodo suo ad 40 marcas per annum et pro regardo suo ad 110 marcas per annum pro dicto officio unius justiciariorum de communi banco quam pro feodo suo ad £20 per annum pro dicto officio unius justiciariorum regis ad assisas sibi per dominum regem nunc concessas solvendas annuatim ad terminos sancti Michaelis et Pasche per equales porciones, videlicet in plenam solucionem eorundem feodorum et regardorum suorum pro utroque officiorum predictorum pro terminis sancti Michaelis et Pasche anno 24to, £120 per breve regis irrotulatum in memorandis de anno 24to regis hujus termino sancti Hillarii rotulo 14° *[TNA: PRO, E159/222 Brevia directa baronibus Hilary m 14; No. S 6]*, quod est inter communia de eodem anno, et prout hujusmodi feoda allocantur Roberto Mouter clerico custode hanaperii cancellarie regis in compoto suo computanti a primo die Septembris anno 23^{cio} *[1 Sept. 1444]* usque primum diem Septembris tunc proximum sequentem *[1 Sept. 1445]* inde rotulo 23^{cio} rotulo compotorum G *[TNA: PRO, E364/79 m G]*, et per litteras acquietancie ipsius Nicholai de recepta *[No. P 40]*.
[21] Et eisdem collectoribus pro denariis per ipsos solutis prefato Nicholao Ayssheton, videlicet in partem solucionis feodorum et regardorum suorum predictorum sibi debitorum pro officiis suis predictis pro termino sancti Michaelis anno 25to, £17 15s 1d per breve predictum et litteras acquietancie ipsius Nicholai de recepta *[No. P 36]*.
[22] Et eisdem collectoribus pro denariis per ipsos solutis prefato Nicholao Ayssheton pro valore robarum suarum cum linura[e] et furrura pro eisdem sibi per dominum regem debitarum causa dicti officii sui unius justiciariorum de communi banco tam pro festo Pentecostes anno 23^{cio} quam pro festis Natalis Domini et Pentecostes anno 24to, videlicet pro utraque dictarum robarum cum linura pro dictis duobus festis Pentecostes [f]63s 6d[f] et pro dicta roba cum furrura pro dicto festo Natalis Domini 106s 11¼d, £11 13s 11¼d per breve predictum et prout allocatur prefato Roberto Mouter clerico custode hanaperii[g] cancellarie regis in compoto suo annotato supra, et litteras acquietancie ipsius Nicholai de recepta *[No. P 44]* ac sicut plenius continetur in peticione eorundem collectorum.
[23] Et eisdem collectoribus pro denariis per ipsos solutis Roberto Danvers uni justiciariorum regis ad assisas in diversis comitatibus Anglie capiendas assignatorum[13] in persolucionem feodi sui ad £20 per annum sibi per dominum regem debiti pro officio suo predicto, videlicet tam juxta ratam dictarum £20 per annum a 25to die Augusti anno 22do regis hujus *[25 Aug. 1444]*, quo die rex

[11] *Baker, Serjeants at Law, p. 497.*
[12] *CPR 1441-46, p. 171.*
[13] *CPR 1441-46, p. 280.*

per litteras suas patentes[14] constituit prefatum Robertum Danvers unum justiciariorum suorum ad assisas in diversis comitatibus Anglie, usque festum sancti Michaelis tunc proximum sequens *[29 Sept. 1444]* quam pro termino Pasche anno 23^cio^ et terminis Michaelis et Pasche anno 24to, £31 17s 7d per breve regis irrotulatum in memorandis de anno 25to regis hujus termino sancti Michaelis rotulo primo *[TNA: PRO, E159/223 Brevia directa baronibus Michaelmas m 1d; No. P 29]* et litteras acquietancie ipsius Roberti de recepta *[No. P 43]* et sicut plenius continetur in peticionibus eorundem collectorum.

[24] Et Johanni duci Exonie, cui rex 22do die Novembris anno 22do *[22 Nov. 1443]* concessit[15] per nomen Johannis comitis Huntyngdonie filii et heredis Johannis nuper comitis Huntyngdonie et Elizabethe nuper uxoris ejus quingentas marcas [b]annuatim[b] habendas, percipiendas et levandas sibi et heredibus suis de corpore suo exeuntibus a festo sancti Michaelis Archangeli anno 22do *[29 Sept. 1443]* de custumis regis in portubus London', Suthamptonie, Bristollie ac Kyngeston super Hull per manus collectorum earundem pro tempore existencium ad festa sancti Michaelis et Pasche per equales porciones, videlicet £60 inde de magna custuma regis in predicto portu London' per manus collectorum earundem custumarum ibidem pro tempore existencium ad festa predicta, £87 6s 8d, videlicet £27 6s 8d inde in plenam solucionem £30 pro termino Pasche anno 23^cio^ et £60 residue pro terminis sancti Michaelis et Pasche anno 24to, per duo brevia regis irrotulata in memorandis, unum videlicet termino[h] Pasche anno 23^cio^ rotulo 10mo *[TNA: PRO, E159/221 Brevia directa baronibus Easter m 10Bd; No. P 42]* et aliud termino Michaelis anno 24to rotulo 10mo *[TNA: PRO, E159/222 Brevia directa baronibus Michaelmas m 10; No. P 41]*, quod est inter communia de eodem anno, et duas litteras acquietancie ipsius ducis de recepta *[No. P 33 and P 39]*.

[25] Et Willelmo Baron armigero, cui ac Willelmo Malbon jam defuncto rex 28vo die Aprilis anno 20mo *[28 Apr. 1442]* concessit[16] viginti libras percipiendas annuatim durante vita eorum et alterius eorum, qui superviveret, de magna custuma lanarum in portu London' per manus collectorum ejusdem custume pro tempore existencium ad terminos sancti Michaelis et Pasche per equales porciones, £50 de termino Pasche anno 22do, terminis Michaelis et Pasche anno 23^cio^ et terminis Michaelis et Pasche anno 24to per [i]duo brevia[i] regis irrotulata in memorandis[c], [b]unum videlicet termino Michaelis anno 24to rotulo 4to *[TNA: PRO, E159/222 Brevia directa baronibus Michaelmas m 4d; No. P 45]* et aliud[b] anno 23^cio^ regis hujus termino Pasche rotulo secundo *[TNA: PRO, E159/221 Brevia directa baronibus Easter m 2; No. P 48]*, quod est inter communia de eodem anno, et sicut allocatum est in compoto dictorum collectorum de hujusmodi custuma *[TNA: PRO, E356/19 m 2d]*[17] computancium ab

---

[14] *CPR 1441-46, p. 280.*

[15] *CPR 1441-46, p. 242.*

[16] *CPR 1441-46, p. 71.*

[17] *Stuart Jenks (ed.), The Enrolled Customs Accounts (PRO, E356, E372, E364) 1279/80-1508/09 (1523/24) Volume 8: E356/19, E356/20 (List and Index Society) [in*

8[vo] die Julii anno 21[mo] regis hujus *[8 July 1443]* usque festum sancti Michaelis anno 23[cio] *[29 Sept. 1444]* et litteras acquietancie ipsius Willelmi de recepta *[No. P 38]* [b]et sicut allocatum est prefatis collectoribus in alio compoto suo de anno 22[do] regis hujus[b].

[26] Et in thesauro £44 5s in 2 talliis de custumis et subsidiis.

[Marginated] Examinatur

[27] Et habent superplusagium £21 6s 3½d, qui allocantur prefatis collectoribus in alio compoto suo de hujusmodi custumis et subsidis inmediate infra *[TNA: PRO, E356/19 m 3d]*.[18]

[a] Non fiat hic ulterius allocacio per hoc breve de dormant, quia quamdiu domino regi placeret *marginated against this entry L.* [b–b] *Interlined L.* [c] de *follows, underlined for the purpose of cancellation L.* [d] £10,526 *L, in error.* [e] linir[a] *L, apparently in error.* [f–f] *Interlined above* 66s 8d, *underlined for the purpose of cancellation L.* [g] regis *follows, underlined for the purpose of cancellation L.* [h] Michaelis *follows, underlined for the purpose of cancellation L.* [i–i] *Interlined above* breve, *underlined for the purpose of cancellation L.*

[A 4] *Audit (in Michaelmas term 1446) of the account of John* Poutrell *and Thomas* Pounde *for the issues of the wool customs and subsidy in London in the period from 29 Sept. 1445 to 29 Sept. 1446.*

L TNA: PRO, E368/219 Visus et status compotorum Michaelmas m 7 (m 274 stamped). Contemporaneous official fair copy of the Exchequer proceedings. Parchment. Unsealed.

[Marginated] London'

[1] Audito compoto Johannis Poutrell et Thome Pounde collectorum custume et subsidii lanarum et pellium lanutarum ac custume coriorum in portu civitatis London' et in singulis portubus et locis eidem portui adjacentibus, videlicet de hujusmodi custumis et subsidio regis ibidem a festo sancti Michaelis anno 24[to] regis nunc *[29 Sept. 1445]* usque festum sancti Michaelis tunc proximum sequens *[29 Sept. 1446]*, per visum et testimonium Willelmi Baron contrarotulatoris custume et subsidii regis predictorum ibidem per idem tempus.

[2] Debent £11,635 10s 9¼d.

[3] Et factis allocacionibus in dicto compoto ingrossato quieti sunt ibidem. *[The 'finished' sign follows]*.

---

press], E356/19, No. 7. Cf. TNA: PRO, E368/217 Visus et status compotorum Michaelmas m 16d (m 191d stamped).

[18] *Stuart Jenks (ed.), The Enrolled Customs Accounts (PRO, E356, E372, E364) 1279/80-1508/09 (1523/24) Volume 8: E356/19, E356/20 (List and Index Society) [in press], E356/19, No. 10.*

SUBSIDIARY DOCUMENTS

[S 1] Henry VI to the treasurer and barons of the Exchequer: having freed the Italian merchants from the alien rate of wool subsidy (viz. 53s 4d per sack), so that they are only obliged to pay a lower rate (43s 4d per sack), he orders the Exchequer to exonerate the Italians and the customers accordingly. — 1442 Juli 14. Fulham.

L TNA: PRO, E159/219 Brevia directa baronibus Michaelmas m 4. Contemporaneous official copy. Parchment. unsealed.

[Marginated] Pro Victore Capello et aliis mercatoribus de Italia

Henri par la grace de Dieu roy etc. as tresorer et barons de nostre eschequier saluz. Monstrez ount a nous noz bien amez Victor Capello, Jacob Cornerio, Leonard Contaryn, Laurence Marcanovo, John Maunche, Jerom Dandalo, Marc Justignian, John Consonane, Benedict Boromeis, Giroce de Pylly, Bernard Dalzate, Philip Boromei, John Michell, Forece de Rabata, Beligard de Bardys, Lowys Dalza, Thomas Albertis marchauntz Italians et toutz autres marchauntz Italians en ycelle nostre royaulme esteantz et repairantz, comment en la parlement tenuz a Westmonstre lendemayn de saint Martyn lan de nostre reigne 18^e^ *[12 Nov. 1439]* a nous fuit grauntez par auctoritee de ycelle une subsidie[1] pur estre a nous paie en la manere et fourme, que ensuyt, cestassavoir de chascun sakk de layne et de chascuns 240 peaulx lanutz de chascun marchaunt alien issant hors de nostre reaulme dEngleterre de la feste de saint Martyn en ivern adonques prouchain ensuant *[11 Nov. 1440]* par trois ans adonques prochain ensuantz 53s 4d destre paies et leves en la manier et fourme, come ils furent adonques paiables et levables, si come en lacte de mesme le parlement est contenuz plus au plain, et que nient obstant diverses grauntes de tils subsidies faictes a nous avant ces heures par les communes de nostre dit reaulme en noz parlementz assembles unquore pur eschuer le importable charge des ditz merchauntes Italians de paiement du dit subsidie, nous de nostre bon faveur avons a eux ottroye de paier a nous 43s 4d solement pur chascun sakk de layne et 240 peaulx lanutz par eux hors de nostre dit reaulme caries, nous considerantz le bons et aggreables naturesses et services par les ditz marchans aliens a nous tressouvent foitz faitz et monstrees et les graundez notable sommes dargent par yceulx marchauntz a nous paiez annuellement pur le subsidie de lour laynes et autres marchaundises, de nostre grace especiall volons et vous mandons et chargeons, que vous facez deschargier les ditz mar-

[1] *Rotuli Parliamentorum, vol. 5, p. 5-6.*

chauntz Italians et chascun de eulx de les surplusages sur eulx en celle partie grauntez oultre les ditz 43s 4d et de toutz deniers et surplusages par force del dit graunte ou de aschun autre graunte a nous dues oultre les ditz 43s 4d et que vous facez discharger et acquitier envers nous et noz heirs pur toutz iours de les surplusages suisditz oultre les ditz 43s 4d et de les ditz deniers a nous duez par force del dicte graunte ou daschun aultre graunte des subsidies des laynes et peaulx lanutz oultre les ditz 43s 4d, sibien les ditz marchauntes Italians et chascun de eux come toutz les collectours del dit subsidie, qi ore sont ou qui avaunt ceulx heures ount este ou qi en apres serront collectours de ycelle subsidie en queconque port de nostre dit reaulme en lour accomptz, que ils devaunt ceux hoeures ount fait ou en apres ferront devant vous de ycelle subsidie ou de aschun autre subsidie, le dite graunte de subsidie fait en nostre dit parlement ou aschun autre graunte de subsidie des laynes et peaulx lanutz a nous avant ceux hoeures fait en aschun autre parlement nient obstant. Doune soubz nostre prive seal a Fulham, le 14^e^ jour de Juyl lan de nostre regne vintisme.

[S 2] Henry VI to the treasurer and barons of the Exchequer: since Richard II – at the request of the commons and with the assent of the lords and the council in the parliament meeting in Westminster on 12 Nov. 1390[2] *– raised his uncle Edmund [of Langley] to be duke of York, he promised to provide him with lands and rents worth £1000 yearly heritable in tail male (over and above all earlier grants made by Edward III) in order to maintain his station, and granted him various annuities – £400 yearly, payable from the issues of the wool customs and subsidy in Hull, and £289 6s 8d yearly, payable from the issues of the wool customs and subsidy in London at Easter and Michaelmas in equal portions, with the remainder of the said £1000 being payable at the Exchequer – until such time as lands yielding the said £1000 yearly could be assigned to him; and since an inquisition*[3] *held before Nicholas* Wotton, *formerly*

---

[2] *The duchy had been created on 6 Aug. 1385 (CChR 1341-1417, p. 300), at which time Edmund had been granted a total of £1000 (with the remainder to his heirs male) to maintain his station (£100 from the issues of Yorkshire, £400 from the issues of the wool customs and subsidy in Hull and £500 from the issues of the wool customs and subsidy in London: CPR 1385-89, p. 62). Since Edmund had been unable to obtain payment of these annuities, as he stated in his petition to parliament, Richard II ordered the issue of a new charter on 12 Nov. 1390 (CChR 1341-1417, p. 323, with incorrect date '1391'), to which parliament assented (Rotuli Parliamentorum, vol. 3, p. 278).*

[3] *Nicholas* Wotton *was mayor and ex officio escheator of London in 1415/16: Alfred B. Beaven (ed.),The Aldermen of the City of London, temp. Henry III-1908, vol. 2, London 1913, p. 2. The writ* diem clausit extremum *was issued on 30 Oct. 1415, and the corresponding inquisition was held in London on 20 Jan. 1416: John L. Kirby (ed.), Calendar of inquisitions post mortem and other analogous documents preserved in the Public Record Office, vol. 20: 1-5 Henry V (1413-1418), London 1995, No. 391, p. 118-*

mayor and escheator of London, found that Edmund had possessed the said annuity on the day of his death [1 Aug. 1402] and that it had passed to his son Edward, whereby Edmund's widow Joan had been assigned one third (£96 8s 10½d) of the annuity in dower, and that Richard, the present duke of York, as the son of Edward's brother Richard was the next heir; and since an inquisition[4] *held before John* Perneys, *formerly mayor and escheator of London,*[5] *had found that Edward's widow Philippa had possessed one third (£64 5s 11d) of Edward's portion of the said annuity in dower on the day of her death and that the reversion of the said portion of the annuity (together with the other properties which Edward had possessed on the day of his death [25 Oct. 1415]) belonged to the present duke of York as the next heir; and the said inquisition also found that † Edmund, earl of March, had possessed various lands – in part as tenant in chief – on the day of his death [18 Jan. 1415] and that the reversion of these lands belonged to the present duke of York, who was the son of Edmund's sister; moreover, while various inquisitions*[6] *had proved that the present duke of York had reached his majority, this did not hold true of the inquisitions held upon the death of the earl of March [in 1425] and duke Edward [in 1415]; since, however, the inquisitions held upon the death of duke Edward and of his widow Philippa were not fully taken or returned into the chancery, the present duke cannot sue and have his livery of the properties in the king's hand by reason of his minority without the king's special favour; therefore the king – in view of the fact that the present duke has reached his majority, the fact that the said lands had become waste during the time they were in the king's hands and of the loyal service of the present duke in England and France – on 12 May*

---

9. The assignment of £96 8s 10½d to Edmund's widow Joan had been effected on 12 Dec. 1403: John L. Kirby (ed.), Calendar of inquisitions post mortem and other analogous documents preserved in the Public Record Office, vol. 18: 1-6 Henry IV (1399-1405), London 1987, No. 861, p. 296. The inquisition post mortem for Edmund had been ordered by writ diem clausit extremum *issued on 4 Aug. 1402, and the corresponding inquisition held in Westminster on 19 Sept. 1402: Kirby, Calendar of inquisitions post mortem, vol. 18, No. 626, p. 206.*

[4] *The writ* diem clausit extremum *was issued on 31 Oct. 1432 and the London inquisition was held in the Guildhall on 14 Nov. 1432: Claire Noble (ed.), Calendar of inquisitions post mortem and other anaogous documents preserved in the Public Record Office, vol. 23: 6 to 10 Henry VI (1427-1432), Woodbridge 2004, No. 700, p. 366.*

[5] *John Perneys was mayor and escheator of London in 1432/33: Beavan, Aldermen, vol. 2, p. 5.*

[6] *Kate Parkin (ed.), Calendar of inquisitions post mortem and other anaogous documents preserved in the Public Record Office, vol. 22: 1 to 5 Henry VI (1422-1427), Woodbridge 2003, No. 467-512, p. 409-86.*

1432 granted[7] *livery of the inheritance of the house of York (including the properties Philippa held in dower) – fealty and homage being respited – and ordered the mayor and escheator of London to release those portions of the inheritance in London to the present duke; and since a later inquisition*[8] *held before John* Brokley, *formerly mayor and escheator of London, found that Edmund's widow Joan had possessed one third (£96 8s 10½d) of the said annuity on the day of her death and that the reversion of this potion belonged to the present duke, the king granted livery of this portion of the inheritance on 25 June 1434*[9] *and directed the escheator of London to release to the present duke the portion of the inheritance which Joan had possessed in dower and which had come into the king's hands by reason of Joan's death, homage and fealty being respited; and since the king has ordered [mandate untraceable] the collectors of the wool customs and subsidy in London to pay the present duke all arrears of Edward's portion of the said annuity (£192 17s 9½d yearly) owing from 12 May 1432 and all arrears of Joan's portion of the said annuity (£96 8s 10½d yearly) owing since 25 June 1434 and all sums which shall fall due in the future by reason of the whole annuity (£289 6s 8d yearly); the king orders the Exchequer to allow the customers all payments made in this regard when they account, provided they produce the mandate for payment directed to them and the receipts of the present duke; should, however, the issues of the wool customs and subsidy in London not suffice for the said payments, the Exchequer is ordered to make up the difference. — 1439 Dec. 26. Windsor.*

L TNA: PRO, E159/217 Brevia directa baronibus Hilary m 11. Contemporaneous official copy. Parchment. Unsealed.

[Marginated] Pro custumariis civitatis London'

Rex thesaurario et baronibus suis ac camerariis de scaccario salutem. Cum dominus Ricardus nuper rex Anglie Secundus post conquestum de communi assensu et consilio omnium prelatorum, magnatorum et procerum regni sui Anglie ac aliorum de consilio suo in parliamento suo apud Westmonasterium in crastino sancti Martini anno regni sui quartodecimo *[12 Nov. 1390]* tento existencium necnon ad specialem requisicionem et de assensu tocius communitatis ejusdem regni in eodem parliamento similiter existentis ex habundanti voluntate et gracia sua speciali et ex certa sciencia et mero motu suis dederit, concesserit et carta sua confirmaverit pro se et heredibus suis carissimo avunculo suo Edmundo nomen, statum, titulum et honorem ducis Eborum habenda

---

[7] *CCR 1429-35, p. 150-1. Cf. CPR 1429-36, p. 207-8.*

[8] *The writ* diem clausit extremum *was issued on 15 Apr. 1434: CFR 1430-37, p, 166-7. No return of an inquisition in London has survived (TNA: PRO, C139/67/63 is the Middlesex return); cf. Kirby (ed.), Calendar of inquisitions post mortem, vol. 20, No. 476, p. 149.*

[9] *CFR 1430-37, p. 207.*

et tenenda sibi et heredibus suis masculis de corpore suo exeuntibus imperpetuum ac eciam de gracia sua speciali et de assensu predicto et ad requisicionem predictam eidem duci ac dictis heredibus suis masculis de corpore suo exeuntibus pro dicto statu ducali decencius manutenendo et sustentando terras, tenementa, possessiones et redditus infra dictum regnum Anglie usque ad valorem mille librarum sterlingorum per annum pro se et heredibus suis dare, concedere, assignare et liberare promiserit, que cum effectu idem nuper rex vel heredes sui prefato duci et heredibus suis masculis predictis tradi, dari, liberari et assignari realiter facerent habenda et tenenda eidem duci et dictis heredibus suis masculis imperpetuum preter et ultra omnes et singulas promissiones, donaciones, concessiones et assignaciones per predictum nuper regem aut per dominum Edwardum [III] nuper regem Anglie avum suum dicto duci ad vitam suam aut sibi et heredibus suis vel sibi et heredibus suis de corpore suo exeuntibus seu sibi et heredibus suis masculis de corpore suo exeuntibus aut sibi et Isabelle uxori sue seu sibi et dicte Isabelle uxori sue et Edwardo filio ipsorum ducis et Isabelle factas et qualitercumque per ipsum nuper regem Ricardum vel heredes suos faciendas alias quam promissiones, donaciones, concessiones et assignaciones, quas eidem duci et dictis heredibus suis masculis pro dicto statu suo ducali, ut premittitur, fecerat seu predictus nuper rex Ricardus vel heredes sui sibi et eisdem heredibus suis masculis pro dicto statu ducali extunc facerent; et voluerit ulterius et concesserit et carta sua confirmaverit pro se et heredibus suis de assensu predicto et ad requisicionem predictam prefato duci, quod ipse et heredes sui masculi predicti imperpetuum haberent, tenerent et perciperent predictas mille libras per annum sibi pro predicto statu ducali decencius manutenendo concessas ad scaccarium suum et heredum suorum et alibi infra dictum regnum suum Anglie in locis prefato duci et dictis heredibus suis masculis assignatis in forma subsequenti, videlicet tam de antiquis custumis ipsius nuper regis Ricardi et heredum suorum lanarum, coriorum et pellium lanutarum quam de subsidio lanarum, coriorum et pellium lanutarum eidem nuper regi Ricardo concesso et de omni hujusmodi subsidio sibi vel heredibus suis extunc concedendo in portubus regni predicti subscriptis pro toto tempore, quo hujusmodi custume seu subsidia ibidem forent, videlicet in portu de Kyngeston super Hull quadringentas libras, in portu civitatis London' ducentas, quaterviginti et novem libras, sex solidos et octo denarios per manus custumariorum, collectorum, firmariorum, receptorum seu occupatorum hujusmodi custumarum et subsidiorum in portubus predictis, qui pro tempore forent, aliquibus ordinacionibus, concessionibus seu assignacionibus super custumis vel subsidiis predictis factis vel faciendis non obstantibus, habenda et tenenda in partem satisfaccionis dictarum mille librarum annuarum eidem duci et heredibus suis masculis predictis pro dicto statu ducali decencius sustinendo per prefatum nuper regem Ricardum concessarum in forma predicta ad terminos Pasche et sancti Michaelis per equales porciones, ita semper quod, quocienscumque et quandocumque summe predicte in portubus predictis in forma predicta percipiendo seu aliqua parcella earundem in aliquo dictorum portuum de custumis et subsidiis predictis levari, percipi et haberi non possent, tunc idem dux et dicti heredes sui masculi omne illud, quod inde pro tempore deforet, ad scaccarium predicti nuper regis Ricardi et heredum suorum haberent et perciperent imperpetuum in forma predicta, quousque prefato duci vel heredibus suis masculis predictis de terris, tenementis, possessionibus et redditibus infra dictum regnum Anglie ad valorem earundem mille librarum per annum pro dicto statu ducali sustinendo et manutenendo per prefatum nuper regem Ricardum vel heredes suos provisum foret, datum et assignatum in forma predicta, habendarum et tenendarum eidem duci et heredibus suis masculis predictis in forma predicta imperpetuum; ac nuper comperto per quandam inquisicionem coram Nicholao Wotton nuper majore civitatis London' et escaetore domini Henrici [V] nuper regis Anglie patris nostri in civitate predicta de mandato ejusdem patris nostri captam et in cancellaria sua retornatam, quod Edmundus nuper dux Eborum fuit seisitus in dominico suo ut de feodo talliato sibi et heredibus masculis de corpore suo exeuntibus de quodam annuo redditu sive annuitate ducentarum, quaterviginti et novem librarum, sex solidorum et octo denariorum ex concessione et dono domini Ricardi nuper regis Anglie Secundi post conquestum prefato Edmundo nuper factis percipiendorum annuatim tam de antiquis custumis ipsius nuper regis Ricardi et heredum suorum lanarum, coriorum et pellium lanutarum quam de subsidio lanarum, coriorum et pellium lanutarum dicto nuper regi Ricardo concesso et de omni subsidio hujusmodi predicto nuper regi Ricardo vel heredibus suis extunc imposterum concedendo in dicto portu civitatis London' per manus custumariorum, collectorum, firmariorum, receptorum seu occupatorum hujusmodi custumarum et subsidiorum in eodem portu pro tempore existencium habendarum dicto Edmundo et heredibus suis masculis de corpore suo exeuntibus in partem satisfaccionis mille librarum annuarum eidem nuper duci et heredibus suis masculis de corpore suo exeuntibus pro statu suo ducali decencius sustinendo per prefatum nuper regem Ricardum concessarum, qui quidem Edmundus de tali statu de predictis ducentis, quaterviginti et novem libris, sex solidis et octo denariis annuis obiit seisitus; post cujus mortem iidem ducente, quaterviginti et novem libre, sex solidi et octo denarii annui descendebant Edwardo nuper duci Eborum ut filio et heredi dicti Edmundi; et postea quaterviginti et sexdecim libre, octo solidi, decem denarii et obolus annui ut tercia pars predictorum ducentarum, quaterviginti et novem librarum, sex solidorum et octo denariorum assignati fuerunt Johanne, que fuit uxor predicti Edmundi, jam defuncte habendi in dotem suam post mortem dicti Edmundi ipsam de predictis ducentis, quaterviginti et novem libris, sex solidis et octo denariis contingentem; et quod predictus Edwardus obiit seisitus de statu suo predicto de centum, quaterviginti et duodecim libris, decem et septem solidis, novem denariis et obolo residuis de predicto annuo redditu sive annuitate ducentarum, quaterviginti et novem librarum, sex solidorum et octo denariorum ultra predictas quaterviginti et sexdecim libras, octo solidos, decem denarios et obolum annuos predicte Johanne in dotem suam, ut predicitur, assignatos quodque

Ricardus nunc dux Eborum filius Ricardi fratris predicti Edwardi nuper ducis est consanguineus et propinquior heres ejusdem nuper ducis; ac postmodum per quandam aliam inquisicionem coram Johanne Perneys majore civitatis predicte et escaetore nostro in eadem civitate de mandato nostro captam et in cancellaria nostra retornatam similiter sit compertum, quod Philippa, que fuit uxor predicti Edwardi, defuncta tenuit in dotem die, quo obiit, in balliva sua *[viz. the mayor's]* post mortem dicti Edwardi quondam viri sui de hereditate dicti nunc ducis consanguinei et heredis predicti Edwardi nuper ducis, videlicet filii Ricardi fratris ejusdem Edwardi, sexaginta et quatuor libras, quinque solidos et undecim denarios percipiendos annuatim tam de antiquis custumis quam de subsidiis lanarum, coriorum et pellium lanutarum in portu dicte civitatis per manus custumariorum, collectorum, receptorum aut aliorum occupatorum eorundem custume et subsidii pro tempore existencium ad terminos Pasche et sancti Michaelis per equales porciones, que quidem sexaginta [et] quatuor libre, quinque solidi et undecim denarii sunt parcella ducentarum, quaterviginti et novem librarum, sex solidorum et octo denariorum, quos dictus nuper rex per litteras suas patentes concessit predicto Edmundo patri dicti Edwardi nuper ducis et heredibus masculis de corpore ipsius Edmundi legitime procreatis, percipiendarum annuatim tam de predictis antiquis custumis quam de dicto subsidio lanarum, coriorum et pellium lanutarum in portu civitatis predicte per manus custumariorum, collectorum, receptorum aut aliorum occupatorum predictorum eorundem custumarum et subsidiorum pro tempore existencium; ac cum prefatus Edwardus nuper dux seisitus fuisset de diversis terris et tenementis in dominico suo ut de feodo talliato, cui prefatus nunc dux virtute tallie predicte est heres, videlicet filius Ricardi fratris predicti Edwardi nuper ducis, qui quidem nuper dux parcellam eorundem terrarum et tenementorum tenuit in capite die, quo obiit, de dicto patre nostro, ac consanguineus et heres Edmundi nuper comitis Marchie, videlicet filius Anne sororis predicti nuper comitis Marchie, qui quidem comes diversa alia terras et tenementa tenuit de nobis in capite die, quo obiit; ac idem nunc dux secundum etatem suam per plures inquisiciones captas post mortem predicti nuper comitis Marchie virtute brevium nostrorum de diem clausit extremum et aliorum mandatorum coram pluribus escaetoribus nostris in quampluribus comitatibus Anglie et Marchie Wallie compertam nuper pervenerit ad suam plenam etatem ac secundum etatem suam tam per diversas alias inquisiciones post mortem predicti nuper comitis Marchie quam per diversas inquisiciones post mortem predicti Edwardi nuper ducis in diversis comitatibus Anglie et Marchie Wallie ac villa Calesie captas compertam ad plenam etatem suam non pervenisset aceciam quedam inquisiciones capte post mortem predictorum Edwardi nuper ducis et comitis et eciam post mortem prefate Philippe, que diversa terras et tenementa tenuit de nobis in capite die, quo obiit, in dotem et aliter post mortem ejusdem nuper ducis de hereditate predicti nunc ducis non fuerint plenarie et sufficienter capte, facte et inquisite neque retornate, pro quibus causis idem nunc dux secundum cursum cancellarie nostre liberacionem suam terrarum et tenementorum predictorum sine gracia nostra speciali in ea parte prosequi et haberi non potuit; et nos considerantes, quod predictus nunc dux per diversas inquisiciones predictas inventus fuit plene etatis et qualiter predicta terre et tenementa racione minoris etatis ejusdem nunc ducis tam in manibus nostris quam in manibus prefati patris nostri longo tempore extiterunt, infra quod quidem tempus grandia vasta, exilia et destrucciones in terris et tenementis predictis facta extiterunt in ipsius nunc ducis grave dampnum, deperditum et detrimentum, attendentes eciam bonum et gratuitum servicium, quod idem nunc dux per magnum tempus tam in regno nostro Francie de mandato nostro quam in Anglia pro posse suo impendit ad sua gravia custus et onera, volentesque proinde eidem nunc duci graciam in ea parte facere specialem duodecimo die Maii anno regni nostri decimo *[12 May 1432]* auctoritate parliamenti nostri apud Westmonasterium tunc ultimo tenti ordinaverimus et concesserimus, quod cancellarius Anglie pro tempore existens plenam haberet potestatem et auctoritatem faciendi predicto nunc duci liberacionem omnium castrorum, dominiorum, maneriorum, terrarum, tenementorum, feodi firmarum, annuitatum, reddituum, serviciorum, feodorum militum, patronatuum abbatiarum, prioratuum, advocacionum ecclesiarum, vicariarum, cantariarum, capellarum, hospitalium et aliorum beneficiorum ecclesiasticorum quorumcumque, visuum franciplegii, curiarum, hundredorum, commotorum, cantredorum, officiorum, franchesiarum, libertatum et aliorum possessionum et hereditamentorum cum pertinenciis quibuscumque in aliquibus inquisicionibus post mortem alicujus antecessorum suorum predictorum aut prefate Philippe captis, contentorum et specificatorum et in manus nostras racione minoris etatis predicti nunc ducis seisitorum aut aliter per mortem alicujus eorundem absque officio inde capto in manibus nostris tunc seisitorum sive retentorum racione minoris etatis prefati nunc ducis in Anglia, Wallia, Marchia Wallie, Hibernia et villa Calesie vel que post mortem predicte Philippe reverterunt, devenerunt et contigerunt et in manibus nostris racione minoris etatis prefati nunc ducis seisita extiterunt, adeo plene et integre ac, si omnia inquisiciones et officia capta tam post mortem alicujus antecessorum suorum predictorum vel predicte Philippe plenarie et sufficienter inquisita, capta, facta et in cancellaria nostra absque aliquo defectu in eisdem retornata extitissent aceciam sicut ipse plene etatis adtunc in qualibet inquisicione predicta compertus et etas sua debite probata fuissent, et quod ipse haberet liberacionem ac tanta brevia, quanta sibi forent necessaria in ea parte, prout in litteris nostris patentibus inde confectis plenius continetur; ac predicto duodecimo die Maii *[12 May 1432]* pro quodam fine nobis soluto in hanaperio nostro homagium et fidelitatem ipsius nunc ducis nobis in ea parta debita usque ad certum diem jam preteritum respectuaverimus et preceperimus tunc majori civitatis predicte et escaetori nostro in eadem civitate, quod eidem nunc duci castra, dominia, maneria, terras, tenementa, feodi firmas, annuitates, redditus, servicia, feoda militum, patronatus abbatiarum, prioratuum, advocaciones ecclesiarum, vicariarum, cantariarum, capellarum, hospitalium et aliorum beneficiorum ecclesiasticorum quorumcumque, visus franciplegii, curias, hundreda, commota, cantreda, officia, franchesias, libertates et alia possessiones et hereditamenta predicta cum pertinenciis in balliva sua liberaret juxta tenorem litterarum nostrarum predictarum, sicut per inspeccionem rotulorum cancellarie nostre predicte nobis constat; subsequenterque comperto per quandam aliam inquisicionem coram Johanne Brokley nuper majore civitatis predicte et escaetore nostro in eadem civitate de mandato nostro captam et in cancellariam nostram retornatam, quod Johanna, que fuit uxor Henrici Brounflete militis, nuper ducissa Eborum, defuncta tenuit in dotem die, quo obiit, ex dotacione Edmundi nuper ducis Eborum quondam viri sui de hereditate Ricardi nunc ducis Eborum consanguinei et heredis ejusdem Edmundi, videlicet filii Ricardi filii ejusdem Edmundi, quaterviginti et sexdecim libras, octo solidos, decem denarios et obolum annuos percipiendos singulis annis ad festa Pasche et sancti Michaelis per equales porciones tam de antiquis custumis quam de subsidiis lanarum, coriorum et pellium lanutarum in portu predicto per manus firmariorum, custumariorum, collectorum aut aliorum occupatorum quorumcumque hujusmodi custume et subsidii in eodem portu London' pro tempore existencium ut racionabilem dotem suam ipsam contingentem de ducentis, quaterviginti et novem libris, sex solidis et octo denariis annuis, quos dictus Edmundus percepit annuatim ad terminos predictos per equales porciones per manus firmariorum, custumariorum, collectorum aut aliorum occupatorum quorumcumque custume et subsidii eorundem in dicto portu London' pro tempore existencium; et nos vicesimo quinto die Junii anno regni nostri duodecimo *[25 June 1434]* pro quodam fine nobis soluto in hanaperio nostro homagium et fidelitatem ipsius nunc ducis nobis pro omnibus terris et tenementis, que prefata ducissa tenuit in dotem post mortem predicti nuper ducis quondam viri sui de hereditate predicti nunc ducis de nobis in capite die, quo obiit, debita usque certum diem jam preteritum respectuaverimus et ei terras et tenementa illa cum pertinenciis reddiderimus et preceperimus tunc escaetori nostro in civitate predicta, quod eidem nunc duci de omnibus terris et tenementis, que prefata nuper ducissa tenuit in dotem post mortem prefati nuper ducis de hereditate predicta cum pertinenciis in balliva sua et que per mortem ipsius nuper ducisse capta fuerunt in manum nostram plenam seisinam habere faceret, sicut per inspeccionem rotulorum ejusdem cancellarie nostre similiter nobis constat; ac per breve nostrum preceperimus custumariis, collectoribus, firmariis, receptoribus et aliis occupatoribus tam antique custume quam subsidii lanarum, coriorum et pellium lanutarum in dicto portu civitatis London', qui nunc sunt vel qui pro tempore fuerint, quod eidem nunc duci id, quod ei aretro est tam de predictis centum, quaterviginti et duodecim libris, decem et septem solidis, novem denariis et obolo annuis parcella predictorum ducentarum, quaterviginti et novem librarum, sex solidorum et octo denariorum annuorum a predicto duodecimo die Maii *[12 May 1432]* quam de predictis quaterviginti et sexdecim libris, octo solidis, decem denariis et obolo annuis residuis eorundem ducentarum, quaterviginti et novem librarum, sex solidorum et octo denariorum annuorum a predicto vicesimo quinto die Junii

[25 June 1434] et eosdem ducentas, quaterviginti et novem libras, sex solidos et octo denarios annuos exnunc singulis annis durante vita sua de custumis et subsidiis predictis in portu illo ad festa predicta de tempore in tempus solverent juxta tenorem carte, litterarum et liberacionum predictarum; vobis — vos prefati thesaurarie et barones — mandamus, quod viso mandato nostro predicto id, quod vobis constare poterit ipsos custumarios, collectores, firmarios, receptores et alios occupatores eidem nunc duci pretextu mandati nostri predicti racionabiliter solvisse et exnunc solvere, prefatis custumariis, collectoribus, firmariis, receptoribus et aliis occupatoribus in compoto suo ad scaccarium predictum de tempore in tempus debite allocetis, recipientes ab eisdem custumariis, collectoribus, firmariis, receptoribus et aliis occupatoribus de tempore in tempus litteras acquietancie ipsius nunc ducis singulas soluciones, quas ei sic fecerint, testificantes, que pro nobis sufficientes fuerint in hac parte, vosque — prefati thesaurarie et camerarii — eidem nunc duci, si dicte ducente, quaterviginti et novem libre, sex solidi et octo denarii annui de custumis et subsidiis predictis in dicto portu London' in forma predicta levari, percipi et haberi non possint, tunc eidem nunc duci omne illud, quod inde deest seu exnunc deesse continget, ad scaccarium predictum ad festa predicta de tempore in tempus de thesauro nostro solvatis juxta tenorem carte, litterarum et liberacionum predictarum. Teste me ipso apud castrum nostrum de Wyndesore, 27 die Decembris anno regni nostri decimo octavo.

Per breve de privato sigillo

[S 3] *On 7 July [1446], John* Harleston*, esq., presents the Exchequer a certification dated 2 June [1446] and a patent dated 1 June [1446] of Richard, duke of York, by which York serves notice that he has discharged his previous* receyvour generall*, John* Wyggemore*, and appointed* Harleston *in his place to receive his annuities in London, Hull and Yorkshire.*

L TNA: PRO, E159/222 Recorda Trinity m 4d. Contemporaneous official fair copy of the Exchequer proceedings. Parchment. Unsealed.

[Marginated] London'; Littere patentes Ricardi ducis Eborum facte Johanni Harleston armigero de recepcione omnium annuitatum suarum in portubus London', Hull et civitatis Eborum irrotulate etc.

[1] Memorandum, quod Johannes Harleston armiger presens hic in curia in propria persona sua septimo die Julii hoc termino *[7 July 1446]* exhibuit curie hic quandam litteram sub signeto Ricardi ducis Eborum sigillatam [a]baronibus hujus scaccarii directam[a], que est in custodia hujus remembratoris, cujus tenor sequitur in hec verba:

[2] Be the duk of York, erle of Marche and Ulvestre, lord of Wyggemore and of Clare. Welbeloved! We grete yow welle, certefying yow for divers causes that hath mevehed us and for the grete charge that longeth unto oure generall atturneyship we have discharged oure trusty and welbeloved servaunt John Wyggemore as of receite of oure annuite, whiche is due unto us yerely to be resceived als welle out of the receite

of the kynges eschequer as of the custumes in the poortes of London' and Kyngeston upon Hulle and be the handes of the shereve of Yorkshire for the tyme beyng. Wherfor we pray yow to accept and admitte oure right trusty and welbeloved servaunt John Harleston squyer oure receyvour generall to be oure receyvour of oure seid annuite in manere and fourme as the seid John Wyggemore occupied and in oure behalve resceyved afore this tyme, noghtwithstondyng ony graunt made be us to the seid John Wyggemore contrary, whyche more pleynly and effectually appereth by oure lettres patentes graunted unto oure seid resceivour severall with hym remaynyng, and that ye wille fulfille thees premisses att oure reveraunce as we may doo for yow in tyme commyng, with the grace of Jhesu whiche preserve yow. Wryten in our lochyng att London', the 2[de] day of Jun' *[1446]*.

[3] Que quidem [a]littera cum manu ipsius ducis subscribitur sic "R. York"[a]. Et tenor litterarum patencium, de quibus superius fit mencio, sequitur in hec verba:

[4] Ricardus dux Eborum, comes Marchie et Ultonie, dominus de Wyggemore et de Clare omnibus, ad quos presentes littere pervenerint, salutem. Sciatis [nos] — in fidelitate, circumspeccione et diligencia dilecti nobis Johannis Harleston armigeri plenius confidentes — ipsum Johannem commisisse, constituisse et ordinasse receptorem omnium annuitatum nostrarum, quas jure hereditario percipimus de domino nostro rege super custumis lanarum et pellium lanutarum in portubus civitatis London' et in portu ville de Kyngeston super Hulle ac in scaccario domini nostri regis et per manus vicecomitis civitatis Eborum pro tempore existentis, dantes et concedentes eidem Johanni plenam tenore presencium potestatem et auctoritatem ad omnes denarios nobis debitos de annuitatibus nostris predictis recipiendos, colligendos et levandos ac de recepta acquietancias et generaliter omnia alia et singula facere, que dicto officio pertinent quovismodo, percipiendo de nobis annuatim vadia, feoda et regarda dicto officio antiquitus debita et consueta. In cujus rei testimonium has litteras nostras fieri fecimus patentes ad voluntatem nostram duraturas. Datum sub sigillo nostro London', primo die mensis Junii anno regni supradicti nostri regis Henrici Sexti post conquestum Anglie vicesimo quarto.

[a–a] *Interlined L.*

[S 4] *Henry VI to the treasurer and barons of the Exchequer: Having – by patent*[10] *dated 15 May 1445* (quintodecimo die Maii ultimo preterito) – *granted his secretary Richard* Andrewe *in view of his* grandes custus, labores et expensas, in particular circa attendenciam carissime consortis notre in partibus regni nostri Francie et in adventu suo ad presenciam nostram, *and in view of his past and future service to the crown £100*

[10] *CPR 1441-46, p. 354.*

per annum from 29 Sept. 1444 (a festo sancti Michaelis ultimo preterito), *at pleasure* (quamdiu nobis placeret), *payable from the wool customs in Southampton (£60) and London (£40) at Easter and Michaelmas in equal portions, and having already directed the London wool customers to pay* Andrewe *all sums which are due for Easter term last* (pro termino Pasche ultimo preterito) *and which shall fall due in the future, the king directs the Exchequer to allow* (debite allocetis) *the London wool customers all payments to Andrewe in this regard, provided they present this mandate and the corresponding receipts* (litteras acquietancie) *when they account. — 1445 Mai 26* (Teste me ipso apud Westmonasterium, 26 die Maii anno regni nostri vicesimo tercio). *Westminster.*

L TNA: PRO, E159/221 Brevia directa baronibus Trinity m 3. Contemporaneous official copy. Parchment. Unsealed. Marginated: Pro Ricardo Andrew secretario regis.

[S 5] *Henry VI to the treasurer and barons of the Exchequer: Desiring to repay his debt of £10,426*[a] *4¼d to John, earl of Shrewsbury* (Salopie), *lord Talbot and de Furnyvale, and having granted him by patent*[11] *dated 3 Dec. 1443* (tercio die Decembris anno regni nostri vicesimo secundo) *300 marks yearly payable from the wool subsidy in London at Easter and Michaelmas in equal portions until the said debt is repaid – the said grant, however, being payable only after the king's debt of £21,000 owing to his uncle Henry, cardinal of England and bishop of Winchester, has been repaid – and understanding now that this has transpired and having therefore directed the London wool customers to pay the said earl of Salisbury all sums which are due from Easter term last* (pro termino Pasche ultimo preterito) *and which shall fall due thereafter, the king directs the Exchequer to allow* (debite allocetis) *the London wool customers all payments to the earl of Shrewsbury in this regard, provided they present this mandate and the corresponding receipts* (litteras acquietancie) *when they account. — 1445 Apr. 3* (Teste me ipso apud Westmonasterium, tercio die Aprilis anno regni nostri vicesimo tercio). *Westminster.*

L TNA: PRO, E159/221 Brevia directa baronibus Trinity m 22d. Contemporaneous official copy. Parchment. Unsealed. Marginated: Pro comite Salopie.

[a] £10,526 *L, in error.*

[S 6] *Henry VI to the treasurer and barons of the Exchequer: Having – by patent*[12] *dated 13 May 1443* (terciodecimo die Maii anno regni nostri vicesimo primo) *– appointed Nicholas* Ayssheton *as justice of assizes* (ad assisas in diversis comitatibus regni nostri Anglie arramandas capi-

[11] *CPR 1441-46, p. 227-8.*

[12] *CPR 1441-46, p. 171.*

endas) *and having – by a later patent dated 9 Oct. 1444* (nono die Octobris anno regni nostri vicesimo tercio) – *appointed him as justice of Common Pleas* (de banco) *at pleasure* (quamdiu nobis placeret) *with the customary emoluments* (feodum consuetum) *and an additional 110 marks sterling per annum to maintain his status* (ut idem Nicholaus statum suum decencius manutenere [et] expensas, quas ipsum in officio predicto facere oporteret, sustinere valeret) – *the said 110 marks being payable at Michaelmas and Easter in equal portions (in accordance with the act*[13] *of the parliament at Westminster in 18 Hen. VI) from the hanaper* (per manus clerici sive custodis hanaperii nostri) *or from the customs in London, Bristol and Hull – and having granted him an additional 106s 11¼d* et sextam partem unius oboli *yearly at Christmas for a robe and lining* (pro una roba et linura pro eadem) *[and 66s 6d yearly at Whitsuntide for a robe and lining], also payable from the hanaper or the said customs, and having already directed the London wool customers to pay the said justice (in view of the act of parliament communicated to them in copy) to pay* Ayssheton *all sums which are due to him since the said appointments and which shall fall due in the future, the king directs the Exchequer to allow* (debite allocetis) *the London wool customers all payments to* Ayssheton *in this regard, provided they present this mandate and the corresponding receipts* (litteras acquietancie) *when they account. — 1446 Jan. 7* (Teste me ipso apud Westmonasterium, 7° die Januarii anno regni nostri vicesimo quarto). *Westminster.*

> *L TNA: PRO, E159/222 Brevia directa baronibus Hilary m 14. Contemporaneous official copy. Parchment. Unsealed. Marginated:* Pro custode hanaperii aut pro custumariis in portubus London', Bristollie et ville de Kyngeston super Hull.

[S 7] *Extract from the continuation of the account of John* Poutrell *and Thomas* Pounde *for the issues of wool customs and subsidy in London in the period from 29 Sept. 1444 to 29 Sept. 1445.*

> *L TNA: PRO, E372/290 Item Adhuc Item London' (dorse). Contemporaneous official fair copy of the Exchequer proceedings. Parchment. Unsealed.*

Et habent superplusagium 16s 2d. Qui allocantur prefatis collectoribus in compoto suo de custumis et subsidiis computantibus a festo sancti Michaelis anno 24to regis hujus *[29 Sept. 1445]* usque idem festum tunc proximum sequens *[29 Sept. 1446]* inde rotulo compotorum de antiqua custuma.

[S 8] *Extract from the continuation of the account of John* Poutrell *and Thomas* Pounde *for the issues of wool customs and subsidy in London in the period from 22 Nov. 1442 to 8 July 1443.*

---

[13] *Rotuli Parliamentorum, vol. 5, p. 13-4.*

L TNA: PRO, E372/287 Adhuc Res' London'. Contemporaneous official fair copy of the Exchequer proceedings. Parchment. Unsealed.

Et Ricardo nunc duci Eborum consanguineo et heredi masculo Edmundi nuper ducis Eborum defuncti, cui quidem Edmundo nuper duci Eborum et heredibus suis masculis de corpore suo exeuntibus dominus Ricardus nuper rex Anglie Secundus concessit quendam annuum redditum sive annuitatem ducentarum, quaterviginti et novem librarum, sex solidorum et octo denariorum percipiendum annuatim tam de antiquis custumis ipsius nuper regis Ricardi et heredum suorum lanarum, coriorum et pellium lanutarum quam de subsidiis lanarum, coriorum et pellium lanutarum dicti nuper regis Ricardi concessis de omnibus hujusmodi subsidiis prefato nuper regi Ricardo vel heredibus suis extunc imposterum concedendis in portu civitatis London' per manus custumariorum, collectorum, firmariorum, receptorum seu occupatorum hujusmodi custumarum et subsidiorum in portu predicto pro tempore existencium, habendum dicto Edmundo et heredibus suis masculis de corpore suo exeuntibus in partem satisfaccionis mille librarum annuarum eidem nuper duci et herdibus suis masculis de corpore suo exeuntibus[a] pro statu suo ducali decencius sustinendo per prefatum nuper regem Ricardum concessum, qui quidem Edmundus de tali statu de predictis ducentis, quaterviginti et novem libris, sex solidis et octo denariis annuis obiit seisitus. Post cujus mortem iidem ducente, quaterviginti et [b]novem[b] libre, octo solidi [c]et octo[c] denarii[d] annui[e] descendebant Edwardo nuper duci Eborum ut filio et heredi predicti Edmundi. Et postea quaterviginti et sexdecim libre, octo solidi, decem denarii et obolus annui ut tercia pars predictarum ducentarum, quaterviginti, novem librarum, sex solidorum et octo denariorum assignati fuerunt Johanne, que fuit uxor predicti Edmundi, habendi in dotem suam post mortem predicti Edmundi ipsam de predictis ducentis, quaterviginti et novem libris, sex solidis et octo denariis contingentem et quod predictus Edwardus obiit seisitus de statu suo predicto de centum, quaterviginti et duodecim libris, decem et septem solidis, novem denariis et obolo residuis de predicto annuo redditu sive annuitate ducentarum, quaterviginti et novem librarum, sex solidorum et octo denariorum[f] ultra predictas quaterviginti sexdecim libras, octo solidos, [g]decem[g] denarios et obolum annuos predicte Johanne in dotem suam, ut predicitur, assignatos quodque Ricardus nunc dux Eborum filius Ricardi fratris predicti Edwardi nuper ducis est consanguineus et propinquior heres ejusdem nuper ducis et 12[mo] die Maii anno 10[mo] regis hujus *[12 May 1432]* habuit liberacionem de £192 17s 9½d ut pro duabus partibus predictorum £289 6s 8d annuorum dicto Edmundo et heredibus suis masculis concessorum; et idem Ricardus 25[to] die Junii anno 12[mo] regis [g]hujus[g] *[25 June 1434]* habuit liberacionem de £96 8s 10½d residuis post mortem prefate Johanne nuper ducisse Eborum ut pro tercia parte predictorum £289 6s 8d[h] annuorum prefate Johanne nuper ducisse Eborum assignatorum nomine dotis sue: £335 13s 6½d, videlicet £39 3s 8½d in plenam solucionem £289 6s 8d tam de duabus partibus quam de tercia parte supradictis a festo sancti Michaelis anno 19[no] regis hujus *[29 Sept. 1440]* usque idem festum tunc proximum sequens *[29 Sept. 1441]* et £289 6s 8d a festo sancti Michaelis anno 20[mo] *[29 Sept. 1441]* usque idem festum tunc proximum sequens anno 21[mo] *[29 Sept. 1442]* et £7 3s 2d residua in partem solucionis £289 6s 8d tam de duabus partibus quam de tercia parte supradictis a festo sancti Michaelis anno 21[mo] regis hujus *[29 Sept. 1442]* usque idem festum tunc proximum sequens *[29 Sept. 1443]*, per breve regis, quod est inter communia de anno 19[no] regis hujus termino sancti Hillarii rotulo 11[mo] *[TNA: PRO, E159/217 Recorda Hilary m 11]*, et quinque litteras acquietancie Johannis Wygmore generalis receptoris ipsius ducis in eodem portu de recepta.

[a] in partem satisfaccionis *follows, underlined for the purpose of cancellation L.* [b-b] *Interlined above* sexdecim, *underlined for the purpose of cancellation L.* [c-c] *Interlined above* decem, *underlined for the purpose of cancellation L.* [d] et obolus *follows, underlined for the purpose of cancellation L.* [e] ut tercia pars predictarum ducentarum, quaterviginti novem *follows, underlined for the purpose of cancellation L.* [f] ultra predictorum quaterviginti sex solidorum et octo denariorum *follows L, apparently in error.* [g-g] *Interlined L.* [h] pro *follows, underscored with dots for the purpose of cancellation L.*

PETTY CUSTOMS PARTICULARS OF ACCOUNT AND CONTROLMENT ROLL 26 JAN.–29 SEPT. 1446

Particulars of account of John Melbourne *and William* Chattok *and the controlment rolls of John* Cotteford *for the issues of the petty customs in London in the period from 26 Jan. to 29. Sept. 1446*

L1 *TNA: PRO, E122/73/20A. Original particulars of account (imports) bound as a codex (quire structure* $VI^{12} + X^{[32]}$*. f. [25-27] have been cut away. Only f. 1-23 were numbered contemporaneously in Roman numerals in the lower right-hand corner of the recto side of the folio). Parchment. Unsealed (the hole for the Exchquer seal is visible in the upper left-hand corner of the recto side of the folios and cover). On the inside of the front cover* 38s 5d; *on the inside of the back cover* £186 14s 10¼d *(this is the sum total of this part of the account). The back cover of L1 is sewn to the front cover of the export codex L2 by a parchment tag. The auditor has entered a dot (a) over each merchant's customs charge, (b) over the sum total of the issues on the page and (c) over each figure in the summing up of the crown's income (f.* 23^{v}*)*

L2 *TNA: PRO, E122/73/20B. Original particulars of account (exports) bound as a codex (quire structure* $X^{20} + X^{[40]}$*. f. [34] has been cut away. Only f. 1-32, onto which the customers entered their account, were numbered contemporaneously in Roman numerals in the lower left-hand corner of the recto side of the folio). Parchment. Unsealed (the hole for Exchequer seal is visible in the lower right-hand corner of the recto side of the folios and the cover). The front cover of L2 is sewn together with the back cover of the import codex L1 by a parchment tag. The auditor has entered a dot (a) over each merchant's customs charge, (b) over the sum total of the issues on the page and (c) over each figure in the summing up of the crown's income (f.* 33^{r}*)*

L3 *TNA: PRO, E122/73/20 "Pt. I", m 2-12. (imports).*[1] *Original controlment roll bound in Exchequer style. Parchment. Unsealed. At the top of m 2:* Post obitum Willelmi de Lunes. *The customs charges were (as is usual with controlment rolls) omitted here. Originally bound separately from the exports. Some membranes were contemporaneously numbered in Roman nu-*

---

[1] *The modern stamped numeration of the membranes begins with 2. There is no m 1.*

merals in the top right-hand corner of the membrane: rotulus prima *(m 2)*, rotulus secunda *(m 3)*, rotulo 5ta *(m 9)*, rotulo 7 *(m 11)*.

L3 TNA: PRO, E122/73/20 "Pt. I", m 13-25. Original controlment roll bound in Exchequer style. Parchment. Unsealed. The customs charges were (as is usual with controlment rolls) omitted here. Most membranes were contemporaneously numbered in the top right-hand corner of the membrane: rotulus prima *(m 13)*, rotulus 2^{a} *(m 14)*, rotulus 3^{a} *(m 15)*, rotulus 4ta *(m 16)*, rotulus prima *(m 18, after Easter)*, rotulus 2^{a} *(m 19)*, rotulus 3^{a} *(m 20)*, rotulus 4^{a} *(m 21)*, rotulus 6ta *(m 23)*, rotulus 7^{a} *(m 24)*, rotulus 8^{a} *(m 25)*

E122/73/20A [f. 1^{r}]

[Marginated] London'

L1

Particule compoti Johannis Melbourne et Willelmi Chattok collectorum parve custume regis in portu civitatis London' et in singulis portubus et locis eidem portui adjacentibus, videlicet de hujusmodi custuma regis ibidem a 26to die Januarii anno regni regis Henrici Sexti 24to *[26 Jan. 1446]* usque festum sancti Michaelis tunc proximum sequens anno ejusdem regis 25to *[29 Sept. 1449]*, scilicet per dimidium annum et 64 dies, per visum et testimonium Johannis Cotford contrarotulatoris ejusdem custume regis ibidem per idem tempus.

L3

Contrarotulum Johannis Cotteford contrarotulatoris parve custume regis in portu civitatis London', videlicet de hujusmodi custuma regis ibidem a 26to die Januarii anno 24to regis nunc Henrici Sexti *[26 Jan. 1446]* usque festum sancti Michaelis tunc[a] proximum sequens *[29 Sept. 1449]*, scilicet dimidum annum et 64 dies, de tempore Johannis Melbourne et Willelmi Chattok collectorum ejusdem custume regis ibidem per idem tempus.

[a] tunnc *L3*.

[1] De navi Matelyn Pycard vocata Trinite de Cane 27° die Januarii *[27 Jan. 1446]*

De Colyn Pavyott pro 2 pak canvas continentibus 1100 alnas, 2 barellis, 1 hoggeshede cum eneo vetere. Precii in toto £18 13s 4d .... cust' 4s 8d

De Martyno Morley pro 2 dossenis dublettes de fustian. Precii 40s ....cust' 6d

<1> *Auditor's marginated entry L1:* cera.

[2] De navi Jacobi Faste vocata Jacob de Dunkirk eodem die *[27 Jan. 1446]*

De eodem pro 2 barellis allecis albi. Precii 13s 4d....................................cust' 2d

[3] De navi Lam van Passe vocata Georg dAnwarp eodem die *[27 Jan. 1446]*

De Goyken van Lente pro 500 lb. canabis. Precii 66s 8d........................cust' 10d
De dicto magistro pro 60 puntellis wolde. Precii 30s............................cust' 4½d
De Henrico Nase pro 2 balis madre[a] Tollouse, 1 fatto cum 4 duodenis cultellorum, 6 duodenis zonarum, 20 marc sheres et diverso haberdashe. Precii £6 10s...cust' 19½d
De Johanne Dasse pro 5 balis madre[a] Zelandie. Precii £10.................cust' 2s 6d
De Willelmo van Ende pro 1 sacco hoppes continente 2 hodes hoppes. Precii 10s...cust' 1½d

<aa>10s 9½d<aa>

E122/73/20A f. 1v

De Giles Braynford pro 7 barellis olei, 6 barellis saponis, [b]2 dossenis felt hattes. Precii £9 6s 8d ....cust' 2s 4d[b]
De Cristyan[c] van Bleken pro 4 balis madre[a] Zelandie. Precii £8..............cust' 2s
De Henrico Hode pro 8 hodes hoppes, 4 baggis nucum magnarum. Precii 66s 8d ....cust' 10d
De Luca Fideler pro 1 barello cum 15 lb. gete bedes, 10 dossenis cultellorum, 20 dossenis mirrours et diverso haberdashe. Precii £6 ....cust' 18d
De Otte van Dorne pro 1 hoggeshede[d] cum 6 dossenis spowtes, 300 pectinibus de ligno et diverso haberdashe. Precii 33s 4d ....cust' 5d
De Hans Rynge pro 2 lastis, 5 barellis saponis. Precii £14 10s........cust' 3s 7½d
De Johanne Woutersson pro 9 barellis rape olei. Precii £6....................cust' 18d
De Petro Petirsson pro 1 pipa, 1 cista, 1 corffe[e], 4 parvis barellis cum 6 duodenis zonarum, 10 duodenis quaterspelles, 4 duodenis parvorum forcers, 20 duodenis pawteners et diverso haberdashe. Precii in toto 100s ....cust' 15d

[a] mader *L3.* [b-b] *Entered subsequently by a different hand in darker ink L1.* [c] Cristean *L3.* [d] pro *follows, struck through L1.* [e] cum *follows, struck through L1.*

[4] De navi Poppe Gilesson vocata Gastehous de Middilburgh eodem die *[27 Jan. 1446]*

De Henrico Brewer pro 2 balis madre[a] Zelandie. Precii £4....................cust' 12d
De Petro Persson pro 1 maunda cum 6 duodenis felthattes. Precii 40s....cust' 6d
De Goyken van Lente pro 3 lastis saponis Brabancie, ½ lasto rape olei, 250 lb. canabi[s]. Precii in toto £23 13s 4d...cust' 5s 11d
De Casper Justynean pro 100 peciis figes et resins. Precii £6 13s 4d....cust' 20d

<aa>-<aa> *Auditor's entry L1: Sum of the issues on the page.*

De Cristyan[b] van Bleken pro 2 balis madre[a] Zelandie, 500 lb. canabis, 1 barello clavorum, 1 barello plate albe, 1 barello cum 18 lb. fili de cotono. Precii £10 9s .... cust' 2s 7½d

De Otte van Dorne pro 1 hoggeshede cum 12 gros cultellorum, 2 gros laces et diverso haberdashe. Precii in toto 40s .... cust' 6d

De Petro Petirsson pro 3 pipis cum 20 marc sheres, 7 dossenis daggers, 12 gros spectacles, 4 gros spurres, 12 gros cultellorum et diverso haberdashe. Precii £8 16s 8d .... cust' 2s 2½d

De dicto magistro pro 1000 pavyngtille magnis. Precii 13s 4d .... cust' 2d

[a] mader *L3.* [b] Cristean *L3.*

<aa>25s 8½d<aa> [a]Item 2s 4d[a]

[a-a] *Auditor's supplement necessitated by the correction of the customs charges for Giles* Braynford's *goods L1.*

E122/73/20A f. 2[r]

[5] De navi Johannis Curterok vocata Leonard de Bergh eodem die *[27 Jan. 1446]*

De Johanne Hatheltak pro 1 bala madre[a] Tollouse, 190 skyve tasilles. [Precii] £6 10s .... cust' 19½d

De dicto magistro pro 2500 pavyngtille, 200 warp ollarum et patellarum terre, 1000 bakstone. Precii in toto 48s 4d .... cust' 7¼d

De Willelmo van Ende pro 4 saccis hoppes continentibus 8 hodes [b]hoppes[b]. Precii 40s .... cust' 6d

De Cristyan[c] van Bleken pro 1 tabula[d] pro altare. Precii 20s .... cust' 3d

De Johanne van Synard pro 1 barello olei. Precii 13s 4d .... cust' 2d

[a] mader *L3.* [b] *Omitted L3.* [c] Cristean *L3.* [d] tabille *L3.*

[6] De navi Petri Adreansson vocata Marikneght de Ermoth eodem die *[27 Jan. 1446]*

De Johanne Rolmyswerd[a] pro 3 parvis forcers cum uno cipho de jasper garnisato cum auro et cum 20 saphiris, 17 balacez, 122 perles, 9 parvis dyamantis. Precii £133 6s 8d .... cust' 33s 4d

De Petro Persson pro 1 maunda cum 6 duodenis felthattes. Precii 40s .... cust' 6d

De Henrico Nase pro 9 barellis olei. Precii £6 .... cust' 18d

De Cristyan[b] van Bleken pro 3 balis madre Zelandie, 600 lb. canabis. Precii £10 .... cust' 2s 6d

De Leonardo van Brusille pro 2 maundis cum 18 dossenis felthattes, [c]8 lb. bristilles, 100 alnis tele lini. Precii £6 .... cust' 18d[c]

De Imbright van Sassonhouson pro 1 barello cum 2500 bokillis ferri pro zonis, 6 bundellis[d] paternoster de bone, 1 mantello de shankes[e]. Precii 30s .... cust' 4½d

<z> *Auditor's marginated entry L1:* cera.

De Otte van Dorne pro 1 pipa, 1 parvo barello cum 8 gros cultellorum, 6 gros rasours, 6 duodenis pawtener rynges et diverso haberdashe. Precii 66s 8d ....cust' 10d

[a] Rolinxswerd *L3.* [b] Cristean *L3.* [c-c] *Entered subsequently by a different hand in darker ink L1.* [d] cum *follows, struck through L1.* [e] scanches *L1.*

[7] De navi Clays Gileman vocata Hors de Middilburgh eodem die *[27 Jan. 1446]*

De Roberto Blitterswyk[a] pro 4 balis madre[b] Zelandie, 3 parvis barellis plate albe. Precii £10 .... cust' 2s 6d

De Bertram Questenbargh pro 4 balis madre[b] Zelandie. Precii £8........... cust' 2s

[a] Blittersweke *L3.* [b] mader *L3.*

<aa>46s 8¼d<aa> [a]Item 18d[a]

[a-a] *Auditor's supplement necessitated by the correction of the customs charges for Leonard van Brusille's goods L1.*

E122/73/20A f. 2v

[8] De navi Poppe Johansson vocata Molle de Middilburgh eodem die *[27 Jan. 1446]*

De Goyken van Lente pro 10 hodes hoppes. Precii 50s........................cust' 7½d

De Jacobo Blokke pro 5 coppebord[a], 1 countour, 1 tabula. Precii 33s 4d ....cust' 5d

De [b]Paulo Phelippes[b] pro 1 pipa vine[c] egre. Precii 13s 4d ....cust' 2d

[a] cupebord *L3.* [b-b] Poulo Philippes *L3.* [c] vini *L3.*

[9] De navi Willelmi Henriksson vocata Marikneght de Lescluse eodem die *[27 Jan. 1446]*

De eodem pro 1 lasto allecis albi, 5 skyve tasilles, 20 barellis ceparum[a]. Precii £4 13s 4d...cust' 14d

De Cristyan[b] van Bleken pro 100 hodes salis de Berfflete. Precii £12..... cust' 3s

[a] cepparum *L3.* [b] Crystean *L3.*

[10] De navi Coppin Lambe vocata Martinkneght de Ermoth[a] eodem die *[27 Jan. 1446]*

De Casper[b] Justynean pro 100 peciis figes et resins. Precii £6 13s 4d...cust' 20d

[a] Ermouth *L3.* [b] Gasper *L3.*

[11] De navi Petri Hughsson vocata Friday de Middilburgh eodem die *[27 Jan. 1446]*

De Casper[a] Justynean pro 400 peciis figes et resins. Precii £26 13s 4d .... cust' 6s 8d

[a] Gasper *L3.*

<aa>-<aa> *Auditor's entry L1: Sum of the issues on the page.*

[12] De navi Johannis Blomard vocata Holigost de Andwarp[a] eodem die *[27 Jan. 1446]*

De Henrico Nase pro 10 barellis olei. Precii £6 13s 4d.......cust' 20d

De Otte van Dorne pro 1 pipa cum 6 dossenis tabellarum, 1000 thymbilles, 4 gros lokes et diverso haberdashe. Precii 33s 4d.......cust' 5d

De Adreano Matisson pro 50 warp ollarum et patellarum terre. Precii 3s 4d ....cust' ½d

De dicto magistro pro 1000 pavyngtille magnis. Precii 13s 4d.......cust' 2d

[a] Andewarpp *L3.*

<aa>16s<aa>

E122/73/20A f. 3r

[13] De navi Simonis Allardsson vocata Marikneght de Holandia eodem die *[27 Jan. 1446]*

De Henrico Nase pro[a] 1 sacco cum 60 alnis tele lini Holandie. Precii 20s ....cust' 3d

De Johanne Hatheltak pro 10 skyve tasilles. Precii 5s.......cust' ¾d

De Johanne in den Hoffe pro 1 parvo basketto cum 5 dikeris[b] cultellorum, 8 dossenis zonarum de corio et diverso haberdashe. Precii 10s.......cust' 1½d

De Matis van Seint Trude pro 5 parvis mantellis peltrie debilis. Precii 11s ....cust' 1¾d

[a] pro *repeated L1, in error.* [b] deker *L3.*

[14] De navi Hayn Ole vocata James de Colonia eodem die *[27 Jan. 1446]*

De Imbright van Sassonhouson pro 1 bagga cum 3 duodenis felthattes. Precii 20s.......cust' 3d

De Hermanno Wesill pro 4 balis fustian. Precii £40.......cust' 10s

De Petro Cangheter pro 3 balis fustian, 2 pak fili Colonie continentibus 50 dossenas lb. Precii £46 13s 4d.......cust' 11s 8d

De Henrico Nase pro 100 lb. hatt heer, 8 balis madre[a] Zelandie, 1 fatto cum 24 dossenis cultellorum, 16 dossenis mirrours et diverso haberdashe. Precii £19 10s.......cust' 4s 10½d

De Otte van Dorn pro 1 cista cum 15 quayers papiri depicti. Precii 26s 8d ....cust' 4d

De Johanne Laurence pro 4 balis madre[a] Zelandie. Precii £8.......cust' 2s

De Johanne Hatheltak pro 16 barellis saponis, 4 barellis aluminis. Precii £16 ....cust' 4s

De Henrico Brewer[b] pro 1 barello cum 10 dossenis swerde bladys. Precii £4 ....cust' 12d

<z> *Auditor's marginated entry L1:* cera.

De Gerwyn Potte pro 3 dimidiis balis bokram, 4 pak fili Colonie continentibus 100 dossenas lb., 3 balis fustian. Precii in toto £103 6s 8d.......... cust' 25s 10d
De Clays Swarte pro 2 balis fustian. Precii £20 .... cust' 5s
De Johanne Blitterswyk pro 4 pak fili Colonie continentibus 100 dossenas lb., 6 dimidiis barellis calabis, 7 dimidiis balis carde, 11 ferthkyns plate albe, 11 balis madre[a] Zelandie, 10 scok duplariorum, 3 barellis plate. Precii in toto £150 .... cust' 37s 6d
De Matis Shonebagh pro 6 balis madre[a] Zelandie. Precii £12 .... cust' 3s
De Johanne Harderode pro 4 pak fili Colonie continentibus 100 dossenas lb., 4 balis fustian. Precii in toto £73 6s 8d.. cust' 18s 4d

<aa>£6 4s 4½d<aa>

E122/73/20A f. 3[v]

De Hans Rynge pro 4 balis madre Zelandie, 1 lasto saponis, 1 bundello cum 800 lb. latone plate, 1 maunda cum 18 sherman[c] sheres. Precii £26 .... cust' 6s 6d
De Bertram Questenbergh pro 12 balis madre[a] Zelandie, 2 saccis[d] seminis ceparum. Precii £26 10s... cust' 6s 7½d
De Arnaldo[e] van Pynxstyn pro 1 barello cum 16,000 pellibus [f]et[f] 23 tymbre pellium ruskin, 8 balis madre[a] Zelandie, 6 barellis aluminis. Precii £48 .... cust' 12s
De Cristyan[g] van Bleken pro 23 barellis saponis, 6 saccis cum 1600 lb. canabis. Precii £19 .... cust' 4s 9d
De Johanne Dasse pro 10 balis madre Zelandie. Precii £20..................... cust' 5s
De Hans Hope pro 1 rolla cum 600 alnis Westfale. Precii £8 .... cust' 2s
De Gerloff van Berkenrade[h] pro 1 pak fili Colonie continente 25 dossenas lb., 4 balis fustian. Precii £48 6s 8d .... cust' 12s 1d
De Henrico Overbagh pro 7 balis fustian, 4 balis madre Zelandie, ½ bala madre[i] ungerofed. Precii in toto £77 .... cust' 19s 3d
De Johanne van Synard pro 2 pipis wode debilis. Precii 66s 8d............cust' 10d
De Petro Persson pro 1 pipa cum 4 dossenis banquer[j] clothes, 12 gros cultellorum, 500 mirrours et diverso haberdashe. Precii in toto 66s 8d..........cust' 10d
De Ricardo Williamsson pro 400 lb. hatt heer. Precii 53s 4d ....cust' 8d
De Petro Persson[k] pro 1 corffe cum 18 dossenis felthattes. Precii 100s ....cust' 15d
De Dancard Johansson pro 1 barello cum 6 dossenis pawteners[l] parvorum, 10 dossenis cultellorum, 12 dossenis zonarum et diverso haberdashe. Precii 100s..cust' 15d
De dicto magistro pro 1000 pavyngtille magnis. Precii 13s 4d................cust' 2d
De Arnaldo[e] Williamsson pro 1 hod hoppes. Precii 5s............................cust' ¾d

[a] mader *L3.* [b] Brwer *L3.* [c] sharman *L3.* [d] cum *follows L3.* [e] Arnoldo *L3.* [f–f] *Omitted L3.* [g] Crystean *L3.* [h] Berkenrode *L3.* [i] mardre *L3, in error.* [j] banker *L3.* [k] Peersson *L3.* [l] pawtenerys *L3.*

<aa>-<aa> *Auditor's entry L1: Sum of the issues on the page.*

<aa>73s 3¼d<aa>

E122/73/20A f. 4r

[15] De navi Gunsalvus[a] de la Mace vocata Katerin de Hispania 28 die Januarii *[28 Jan. 1446]*

De eodem pro 3 hoggeshedes poys ferri. Precii 37s 6d........................cust' 5¾d

[16] De navi Petri Georgesson[a] vocata Cristofre de Lescluse eodem die *[28 Jan. 1446]*

[b]De eodem pro 1000 bakstone. Precii 3s 4d..cust' ½d

[a] Georsson *L1.* [b] Deficit *marginated against this entry L1.*

[17] De navi Clays Sibotsson vocata Jamesknegh t de Holandia eodem die *[28 Jan. 1446]*

De eodem pro 1500 shafteell, 200 stobill eell, 16,000 pympernelle, 10 barellis anguillarum salsarum [a]middle elle[a], 4 barellis anguillarum salsarum pympernelle. Precii in toto £31 10s ....cust' 7s 10½d

[a–a] midd' *L1.* midd' eell' *L3.*

[18] De navi Bertoldi Berntsson vocata Gabriell de Holandia eodem die *[28 Jan. 1446]*

De eodem pro 14,000 pympernelle, 1100 shafteell, 150 stobill eell recent. Precii £20..cust' 5s

[19] De navi Willelmi Martinsson vocata Cristofre de Holandia eodem die *[28 Jan. 1446]*

De eodem pro 13,000 pympernelle, 1000 shafteell, 50 stobill eell, 4 barellis anguillarum salsarum midd[ell], 4 barellis pympernelle salsorum. Precii £20 ....cust' 5s

[20] De navi Gilberti Jamesson vocata George de Holandia eodem die *[28 Jan. 1446]*

De eodem pro 12,000 pympernelle, 1200 shafteell, 100 stobill eell. Precii £13 ....cust' 3s 3d

[21] De navi Gilberti Jacobsson vocata Mogell de Holandia eodem die *[28 Jan. 1446]*

De eodem pro 10,000 pympernelle, 900 shafteell, 100 stobill eell, 9 barellis anguillarum salsarum midd[ell], 3 barellis kyve eell salsorum, 3 barellis pympernelle salsorum, 1 barello anguillarum rubearum salsarum, 20 alnis tele lini, 1 fetherbed. Precii in toto £24..cust' 6s

<z> *Auditor's marginated entry L1:* cera.

<aa>27s 7¾d<aa>

E122/73/20A f. 4v

[22] De navi Pauli[a] Haynsson vocata Holigost de Holandia eodem die *[28 Jan. 1446]*

De eodem pro 16,000 pympernelle, 1500 middell eell, 150 stobill eell, 18 barellis anguillarum salsarum midd[ell] eell, 3 barellis pympernelle salsorum, 4 barellis anguillarum rubearum salsarum, 16 eghtendelle anguillarum rubearum salsarum continentibus 2 barellos. Precii in toto £38 10s .... cust' 9s 7½d

[a] Pouli *L3.*

[23] De navi Ilbrand van Wolde vocata Reynald de Dansk eodem die *[28 Jan. 1446]*

De Gerwyn Potte pro 12 pak fili Colonie continentibus 300 dossenas lb., 6 balis fustian, 2 saccis seminis ceparum, 2 dimidiis barellis calibis. Precii in toto £170 .... cust' 42s 6d

De Clays Swarte pro 1 bala fustian, 28 balis madre[a] Zelandie, 1 barello cum 11 timbre martrins, 23 timbre herewark. Precii in toto £84 10s ...... cust' 21s 1½d

De Henrico Nase pro 8 balis madre Zelandie, 1 fatto, 1 hoggeshede cum 700 alnis tele lini Holandie, 10 dossenis spectacle cases, 6 dossenis penners et hi[n]khorns[b]. Precii £17 10s .... cust' 4s 4½d

De Johanne Harderode pro 6 balis madre Zelandie. Precii £12 .... cust' 3s

De Matis Shonebagh pro 10 balis madre [c]Zelandie[c]. Precii £20 .... cust' 5s

De Hans Rynge pro 8 balis madre, 4 dimidiis barellis calabis, 1 maunda cum 18 sherman sheres. Precii £35 10s .... cust' 8s 10½d

De Johanne Salmer pro 8 fraillis, 2 bashrunez, 1 pipa batrie, 1 baletto basins, 1 maunda cum 2 rippes cacaborum. Precii £98 .... cust' 24s 6d

De Lambert Joses pro 6 fraillis, 2 meys copre plate. Precii £56 .... cust' 14s

De Bertram Questenbergh pro 13 balis madre Zelandie. Precii £26 ... cust' 6s 6d

De Bertram Sleghter pro 2 saccis hatt heer ponderantibus 200 lb. Precii in toto 20s .... cust' 3d

De Cristyan[d] van Bleken pro 8 balis madre Zelandie, 5 lastis [e]et[e] 1 barello saponis, 1 barello calabis, 1 cista cum 6 lb. serici fini, 3½ dossenis [lb.] cottoni fili, 12 lb. fili. Precii in toto £52 10s .... cust' 13s 1½d

De Johanne Dasse pro 2 lastis saponis, 9 balis fustian, 2 barellis cum gladiis, 20 balis madre, 32 dossenis swerd blades[f]. Precii in toto £153 ...... cust' 38s 3d

De Hans Hope pro 3 lastis bowstaves[g] wrak, 1 barello cum 6 timbre martrins, 1 timbre ficheux[h]. Precii in toto £22 .... cust' 5s 6d

<aa>£9 16s 7½d<aa>

E122/73/20A f. 5r

<aa>-<aa> *Auditor's entry L1: Sum of the issues on the page.*

De Johanne Hatheltak pro 6 balis madre Zelandie, 3 lastis saponis. Precii £30 .... cust' 7s 6d

De Arnaldo[i] van Pynxstyn pro 10 balis madre Zelandie, 17 barellis aluminis, 1 barello cum 5 timbre bever, 12 pellibus bever, 3000 pellibus pople, 1000 pellibus ruskin, 2 timbre martrins, 2 timbre lettuse, ½ [e]timbre[e] ficcheux[j], 5000 pellibus herewark[k]. Precii in toto £77 .... cust' 19s 3d

De Gerloff van Berkenrade[l] pro 3 pak fili Colonie continentibus 90 dossenas [m]lb.[m], 4 balis fustian. Precii in toto £70 .... cust' 17s 6d

De Imbright van Sassonhouson pro 2 dimidiis barellis calibis, 1 cista, 1 barello plate et[n] 16 sherman sheres. Precii in toto £11 .... cust' 2s 9d

De Johanne Warenthorp pro 5 lastis saponis, 12 barellis aluminis, 2 dimidiis barellis calibis, 3 balis madre Zelandie. Precii £68 .... cust' 17s

De Petro Cangheter pro 2 pak fili Colonie continentibus 50 dossenas lb., 2 dimidiis balis carde. Precii in toto £30 13s 4d .... cust' 7s 8d

De Henrico Overbagh pro 8 pak fili Colonie continentibus 200 dossenas lb., 4 balis fustian, dimidio barello calibis. Precii in toto £110 13s 4d ... cust' 27s 8d

De Johanne Dasse pro 4 balis madre Zelandie. Precii £8 .... cust' 2s

De Johanne Harderode pro 1 fatto cum 24 parvis mantellis de water myse. Precii £3 .... cust' 9d

De Nicholao Naghell pro 7 balis madre Zelandie. Precii £14 .... cust' 3s 6d

De Henrico Brewer pro 4 balis madre Zelandie, dimidio barello calibis, 1 cista, 1 corff, 1 fatto cum 10 dossenis hamours et diversis mercandisis. Precii £16 .... cust' 4s

De Roberto Blitterswyk[o] pro 1 pak fili Colonie continente 25 dossenas [m]lb.[m], dimidio barello calibis, 400 latone plate, 10 balis madre Zelandie, 1 corffe, 1 pakk cum 1000 lb. canabis. Precii £44 6s 8d .... cust' 11s 1d

[p]De Johanne Blitterswyk[o] pro 2 pak fili Colonie continentibus 50 dossenas lb., 3 dimidiis balis carde, 9 balis madre Zelandie. Precii in toto £55 13s 4d .... cust' 13s 11d[p]

De Paulo[q] Rode pro 1 pak cum 1000 alnis tele stricte bolte. Precii £10 .... cust' 2s 6d

De Willelmo Spyker pro 1 pipa olei [e]rape[e]. Precii 40s .... cust' 6d

De Arnaldo[i] van Langfeld pro 2 lastis allecis albi, 1 barello cum 20 papir poyntes, 8 duodenis calcarium, 4 duodenis styrop yrens. Precii £10 10s .... cust' 2s 7½d

De Cristyan[d] Edilkynd pro 8 dimidiis barellis calibis, 2 balis fustian, 1 pak fili Colonie continente 25 dossenas lb. Precii in toto £60 6s 8d .... cust' 15s 1d

<aa>£7 15s 3½d<aa>

[a] mader *L3.* [b] hynghorns *L3.* [c] *Omitted L3.* [d] Crystean *L3.* [e–e] *Interlined L1.* [f] bladys *L3.* [g] wark *follows, struck through L3.* [h] fechaux *L3.* [i] Arnoldo *L3.* [j] fecheux *L3.* [k] heerwarke *L3.* [l] Berkenrode *L3.* [mm] *Omitted L1.* [n] cum *L3.* [o] Blittersweke *L3.* [p-p] *Johann* Blitterswyk*'s imports entered at the end of the ship (after those of Cristyan* Edilkynd*) L3.* [q] Poulo *L3.*

<z> *Auditor's marginated entry L1:* cera.

E122/73/20A f. 5[v]

[24] De navi Lambe Johan Williamsson vocata [a]Marikneght de Ermoth[a] eodem die *[28 Jan. 1446]*

De Gerwyn Potte pro 10 balis fustian. Precii £100 ... cust' 25s

De Johanne Hardrod pro 7 pack fili Colonie continentibus 155 dossenas lb., 4 balis fustian. Precii £91 13s 4d ... cust' 22s 11d

De Hans Rynge pro 10 [b]dimidiis[b] barellis calibis, 6 balis fustian, 8 parvis barellis plate albe, 2 maundis, 1 barello cum 125 petris wyre ferri. Precii £103 5s ... cust' 25s 9¾d

De Johanne Warenthorp pro 2 lastis saponis. Precii £12 ... cust' 3s

De Johanne Salmer pro 3 fraillis, 1 bashrune, 1 pipa, 5 maundis cum 10 rippes cacaborum, 5 barellis gray cupri. Precii £76 ... cust' 19s

De Lambert Joses pro 1 fraillo, 5 basshrunez, 3 maundis cum 6 rippes cacaborum, 1 meis cupri plate [c]albi[c]. Precii £70 ... cust' 17s 6d

De Bertram Questenbergh pro 9 balis fustian, 2 pack fili Colonie continentibus 50 dossenas lb. Precii £106 13s 4d ... cust' 26s 8d

De Johanne van Sibright[d] pro 5 pack fili Colonie [b]continentibus 50 dossenas lb.[b], 4 balis fustian. Precii £90 ... cust' 22s 6d

De Cristyan van Bleken pro 4 barellis alume. Precii £8 ... cust' 2s

De Johanne Dasse pro 8 balis fustian, 1 corf cum 200 alnis tele lini, 2 saccis cum semine ceparum. Precii £68 ... cust' 17s

De Arnaldo[e] van Pynxsten pro 2 balis fustian. Precii £20 ... cust' 5s

De Henrico Overbagh pro 5 pack fili Colonie [b]continentibus 130 dossenas lb.[b], 4 balis fustian, 2 dimidiis barellis calibis. Precii £91 6s 8d ... cust' 22s 10d

De Petro Cangheter pro 13 balis fustian, 4 pack fili Colonie continentibus 75 dossenas lb. Precii £155 ... cust' 38 9d

De Tilman Crome pro 1 bala fustian, [f]3 pack fili Colonie[f] continentibus 100 dossenas [c]lb.[c] Precii £44 10s ... cust' [g]11s 1½d[g]

De Henrico Brewer pro 2 balis fustian, 1 barello aluminis, 4 dimidiis barellis calibis, 1 maunda cum 10 dossenis felt hattes. Precii £50 ... cust' 12s 6d

De Johanne Blitterswyk[h] pro 2 balis fustian, 1 fatto[i], 1 barello, 1 maunda cum 300 lb. fili albi, 400 [j]lb.[j] canabis[k]. Precii £27 ... cust' 6s 9d

De Gerardo[l] Johansson pro 4 barellis wyre continentibus 80 petra, 1 baskett [c]cum[c] 5 dossenis felt hattes. Precii £5 ... cust' 15d

[m]De [n]Hermano Wesille[n] pro 2 pack cum 4 balis fustian. Precii £40 ... cust' 10s[m]

De Willelmo Gerrard[o] pro 1 maunda cum 4 peciis tele lini Holandie, 1 pecia fustian, 6 dossenis qwyshene[p] clothes, 2 pack cum downe. Precii £8 ... cust' 2s

[q]De Gerlof van Berkenrode[r] pro 2 balis fustian. Precii £20 ... cust' 5s[q]

[q]De [s]dicto magistro[s] pro 800 pavyngtile. Precii 11s 4d ... cust' 2d[q]

<aa>£14 16s 6¼d<aa> [t]Item 3d[t]

E122/73/20A f. 6[r]

<aa>-<aa> *Auditor's entry L1: Sum of the issues on the page.*

De Cristyan Edilkynd pro 1 bala fustian, 1 pack fili [c]Colonie[c] continente 26 dossenas lb. Precii £18 13s 4d .... cust' 4s 2d

[a–a] Mariknyght de Ermouth *L3.* [b-b] *Interlined L1.* [c-c] *Omitted L1.* [d] Sibrygh *L3.* [d–d] *Interlined L1.* [e] Arnoldo *L3.* [f–f] *Interlined L3.* [g–g] *Interlined above* 10s 10½d, *struck through L1.* [h] Blittersweke *L3.* [i] fatte *L3.* [j] *Omitted L3.* [k] canebis *L1.* [l] Gerrardo *L3.* [m–m] *Herman* Wesille*'s exports were entered at the end of the ship (i.e. after those of Cristian* Edilkynd*) L3.* [n–n] Harmano Wesell *L3.* [o] Garred *L3.* [p] quysson *L3.* [q–q] *Order of entries for the exports of Gerlof* van Berkenrode *and the skipper reversed L3.* [r] Bleken *L1, surely in error.* [s–s] *Interlined above* Hermanno Wesille, *struck through L1.* [t–t] *Auditor's supplement necessitated by the correction of the customs charges on* Tilman Crome*'s goods L1.*

[25] De navi Hayn Bulscamp[a] vocata Andreas de Ermoth[b] eodem die *[28 Jan. 1446]*

De Gerwyn Potte pro [c]2 dimidiis[c] barellis calibis. Precii £8 .... cust' 2s

De Clays Swart pro 4 balis madir[d], 1 barello cum 12,000 pellibus ruskyn. Precii £20 .... cust' 5s

De Henrico Nase pro 2 barellis, 1 fatto[e] cum 600 alnis tele lini, 10 dossenis hamourz[f], 6 dossenis musk balles et diverso haberdashe. Precii in toto £14 .... cust' 3s 6d

De Matis Shonebagh pro 2 balis fustian, 4 balis madir[d]. Precii £28........ cust' 7s

De Johanne Hardrod pro 6 balis madir[d]. Precii £12 .... cust' 3s

De Hans Rynge pro 6 balis madir[d]. Precii £12........ cust' 3s

De Imbright van Sassonhousen[g] pro 4 dimidiis barellis calibis, 1 fardello cum 150 dyker[h] cultellorum, 1 fardello cum 100 alnis tele lini, 16 dossenis felt hattes. Precii £29 13s 4d .... cust' 7s 5d

De Petro Cangheter pro [i]1 pack fili Colonie continente 25 dossenas lb., 2 dimidiis balis carde[i]. Precii £22 6s 8d .... cust' 5s 7d

De Johanne Salmer pro 5 fraillis, 2 bashrunez, 1 pipa, 2 maundis cum 4 rippes cacaborum. Precii £76 .... cust' 19s

De Lambert Joses pro 5 fraillis, 3 maundis cum 5 rippes[j] cacaborum, 1 meis cupri [k]plate[k]. Precii £59........ cust' 14s 9d

De Bertram Questenbergh pro 2 pack fili Colonie continentibus 60 dossenas lb., 1 bala fustian, 6 saccis seminis[l] ceparum. Precii £36........ cust' 9s

De Johanne van Sibright[m] pro 3 pack fili Colonie continentibus 90 dossenas lb. Precii £30........ cust' 7s 6d

De Rogero Russe pro 2 balis fustian. Precii £20........ cust' 5s

De Johanne Hatiltak pro 1 fatto[e] cum 300 alnis tele lini. Precii £6 10s .... cust' 19½d

De Arnaldo[n] van Pynxsten pro 1 barello cum 8000 [et] 21 timbre pellium ruskin. Precii £9........ cust' 2s 3d

De Henrico Overbagh pro 6 balis madir[d], dimidio barello calibis. Precii £16 .... cust' 4s

<z> *Auditor's marginated entry L1:* cera.

De Johanne Blitterswyk[o] pro 5 saccis seminis[l] ceparum, 2 barellis, 4 dimidiis barellis plate nigre, 8 parvis barellis plate albe, dimidio barello calibis. Precii £17 .... cust' 4s 3d
[p]De Roberto Blitterswyk[o] pro 2 balis fustian. Precii £20 .... cust' 5s[p]
De Henrico Brewer pro 2 balis fustian, 9 balis madir[d]. Precii £38 ...... cust' 9s 6d
De Jasper[q] Ofman pro 1 barello cum 4 dossenis mirrourz, 8 parvis bundellis latone [r]wyre[r]. Precii 40s .... cust' 6d

<aa>£6 3s [s]6½d[s•]<aa>

E122/73/20A f. 6[v]

De Petro Petersson[t] pro 3 pipis cum 12 gros paternosters, [r]60 lb. paternosters[r] nigrorum, 12 gros cultellorum, 12 gros keybandes[u], 8 [k]lb.[k] fili blodii et diverso haberdashe. Precii £11 6s 8d .... cust' 2s 10d
De Johanne van Synard pro 1 balla madir, 800 lb. ferri. Precii £3 .... cust' 9d
De Henrico Hode pro 2 fardellis, 1 sacco [v]canebis [k]continentibus 250 lb.[k•v], 100 lb. seminis ceparum, 6 dossenis coverlyttes, 7 dossenis bankers. Precii £22 .... cust' 5s 6d

[a] Bulschamp *L3.* [b] Ermouth *L3.* [c-c] *Corrected in L1 from* 2. 2 *L3.* [d] mader *L3.* [e] fatte *L3.* [f] hamers *L3.* [g] Sassenhowson *L3.* [h] deker *L3.* [i-i] 2 dimidiis balis carde, 1 pack fili Colonie continente 25 dossenas lb. *L3.* [j] reppes *L3.* [k-k] *Interlined L1.* [l] semine *L3, in error.* [m] Sibrygh *L3.* [n] Arnoldo *L3.* [o] Blittersweke *L3.* [p-p] *Robert* Blitterswyk*'s exports recorded above, between those of* van Pynxsten *and* Overbagh *L3.* [q] Gasper *L3.* [r-r] *Omitted L3.* [s-s] *Interlined above* ½d, *struck through L1 (correction necessary because* Jasper Ofman*'s goods were initially omitted from the calculation).* [t] Peersson *L3.* [u] keybondys *L3.* [v-v] cum 250 lb. canebis *L3.*

[26] De navi Johannis de Ceta vocata Seint John de Gatall' ultimo die Januarii *[31 Jan. 1446]*

De dicto[a] magistro pro 50,000 clavis, 3 barellis piscium salsorum, 2000 orenges. Precii £4 13s 4d .... cust' 14d

[a] eodem *L3.*

[27] De navi Clays Martynsson vocata Kateryn de Ermoth 9 die Februarii *[9 Feb. 1446]*

De Alwyn Verger pro [a]7 hodes hoppes[a]. Precii 35s .... cust' 5¼d
De Henrico Nase pro 60 skyve tasilles. Precii 30s .... cust' 4½d
De dicto magistro pro 800 pavyngtile. Precii 11s 8d .... cust' 1¾d

[a-a] 4 saccis hoppes continentibus 7 hodes *L3.*

[28] De navi Johannis Chawdebett vocata Katerin de Cane 11. die Februarii *[11 Feb. 1446]*

De Gillam John pro 80 quarteriis frumenti. Precii £4 19s .... cust' 15d

<aa>-<aa> *Auditor's entry L1: Sum of the issues on the page.*

[29] De navi Johannis Bernard de Firmyn vocata George de Cane 18 die Februarii *[18 Feb. 1446]*

De Rawlyn[a] le Graunt pro 1 pipa, [b]1 barello[b] cum 800 [c]lb.[c] enei veteris. Precii 53s 4d..cust' 8d

De dicto Rawlyn le Graunt et Johanne Huet pro 260 quarteriis frumenti. Precii £16 5s..cust' 4s ¾d

[a] Radulpho *L3.* [b-b] *Omitted L3.* [c] *Omitted L1.*

[30] De navi Adreani Johansson vocata [a]Fynknest de Flyshing[a] 2 die Marcii *[2 Mar. 1446]*

De eodem [b]magistro[b] pro 4 lastis, 10½ barellis allecis albi, 5 dimidiis barellis salmonis [c]debilis[c], 4 peciis figes, 3 peciis resins, 2 barellis sope, 1 warp ollarum et patellarum terre, 7 stoppis saponis. Precii £22 10s.........cust' 5s 7½d

[a-a] Fenkeneste de Fluschyng *L3.* [b] *Omitted L1.* [c-c] *Omitted L3.*

<aa>22s 9¾d<aa>

E122/73/20A f. 7r

[31] De navi Willelmi Clement vocata [a]Trinite de Gravesend[a] 3° die Marcii *[3 Mar. 1446]*

De Clays[b] Hattmaker pro 2 baggis cum 400 lb. hatt heere, 100 lb. gotes here, 1 fethirbed vetere. Precii 30s..cust' 4½d

[c]De H[c]

[a-a] Trenite de Gravisende *L3.* [b] Johanne *L3.* [c-c] *Obviously erroneous entry L1 (error occasioned by confusion with the next entry, viz. for the ship of* Hermann Yanson*).*

[32] De navi Hermanni Yanson vocata Mariknyght de Westscowe[a] 5 die Marcii *[5 Mar. 1446]*

De eodem pro 20 barellis ceparum, 4 balis cours madir[b], 2 barellis allecis albi, 4 parvis peciis tele lini Zelandie continentibus 28 alnas. Precii £6 16s 8d ....cust' 20½d

De Johanne Petersson pro 14 balis cours madir, 8 skyve tasiles. Precii £18 17s 4d..cust' 4s 8¾d

[a] Westowe *L3.* [b] madre *L3.*

[33] De navi Clays van Yffen vocata James de London' eodem die *[5 Mar. 1446]*

De Lowys Stroys pro 44 balis almundes. Precii £58 13s 4d.............cust' 14s 8d

<z> *Auditor's marginated entry L1:* cera.

[34] De navi Derik Baysson vocata Magdalen[a] de Ermoth 7 die Marcii *[7 Mar. 1446]*

De eodem pro 120 barellis ceparum, 50 bunchis allei, 100 bowstaves, 100 spere shaftes. Precii £4 11s 8d .... cust' 13¾d

[a] Madelen *L3.*

[35] De navi Gylmyn Bassyn vocata Nicholaus de Roon[a] eodem die *[7 Mar. 1446]*

[b]De Johanne Florey pro 30 quarteriis frumenti, 11 pipis pomorum[b]

De Johanne Wessell[c] pro 2 barellis cum 600 lb. enei veteris. Precii 40s .cust' 6d

[a] Roan *L3.* [b-b] *Entry struck through L1, L3, with* nichil de custuma, quia marcator de Rotomago *(L1),* nichil de custuma, quia mercator de Roon *(L3) marginated against it.* [c] Wesill *L3.*

[36] De navi Mattalyn Pychard[a] vocata Kateryn de Kane eodem die *[7 Mar. 1446]*

De Colyn Pavyott pro 4 pack canvas continentibus 2600 alnas, 4 fardellis[b], 1 barello cum 400 lb. enei veteris. Precii £36 .... cust' 9s

[a] Pycar *L3.* [b] cum eneo po[nderante] *follows L1, in error.*

[37] De navi Peryn Obard vocata Jonet de Cane eodem die *[7 Mar. 1446]*

De Colyn Folonya pro 1 cabille, 1 roppe, 4 bundellis rope yerne, 2 pack canvas [a]continentibus[a] 800 alnas. Precii £11 13s 4d .... cust' 2s 11d

De Robyn Rosay pro 2 pack canvas continentibus 800 alnas. Precii £10 13s 4d .... cust' 2s 8d

De dicto magistro pro 6 dossenis carde veteris. Precii 20s .... cust' 3d

[a] *Omitted L1.*

<aa>37s 11½d<aa>

E122/73/20A f. 7[v]

[38] De navi Bowdyn Henriksson vocata Margaret de London' 8 die Marcii *[8 Mar. 1446]*

De Johanne Dasse pro 12 balis madir Zelandie. Precii £24 .... cust' 6s

De Henrico Brewer pro 4 balis madir Zelandie. Precii £8 .... cust' 2s

De Tilman Crome pro 14 balis madir Zelandie. Precii £28...................... cust' 7s

[39] De navi Willelmi Danyell vocata Cristofre de London' eodem die *[8 Mar. 1446]*

De Johanne Dasse pro 18 balis madir Zelandie. Precii £36 .... cust' 9s

<aa>-<aa> *Auditor's entry L1: Sum of the issues on the page.*

De Henrico Brewer pro 4 doliis, 2 pipis olei, 4 balis madir[a], 2½ lastis sope. Precii £48 .... cust' 12s
De Alwyn Verger pro ½ lasto saponis, 3 barellis olei. Precii £5 .... cust' 15d
De Tilman Crome pro 16 balis madir. Precii £32 .... cust' 8s

[a] madre *L3.*

[40] De navi Petri George vocata Cristofre de Scluse eodem die *[8 Mar. 1446]*

De Remond Vydale pro 500 bowstaves, 4 balis aunes. Precii £10 ..... cust' 2s 6d

[41] De navi Jakett de Gares vocata Maria de Caudebek eodem die *[8 Mar. 1446]*

De Johanne Dukeyne[a] pro 1 pipa pomorum. Precii 3s 4d .... cust' ½d

[a] Dukeny *L3.*

[42] De navi Hugonis Petersson vocata George de Fever-sham eodem die *[8 Mar. 1446]*

De Nicholao Bonevyle pro 1 fetherbed[a], 1 bolster, 1 coverlytt, 1 baskett cum 1 candi[l]stik[b] de latone pendenti, [c]1 lavour et 1 pelvi[c] de latone. Precii 20s .... cust' 3d

[a] federbed *L3.* [b] candelebrio *L3.* [c] 1 pelvi, 1 lavour *L3.*

[43] De navi Michaelis[a] Henriksson vocata Wilbord de Flysh[yng][b] 9 die Marcii *[9 Mar. 1446]*

De eodem pro 5 lastis allecis albi, 3 barellis sope[c]. Precii £21 10s .. cust' 5s 4½d
De Adreano Hughsson pro 3 lastis allecis albi. Precii £12 .... cust' 3s

[a] Michaellis *L1.* [b] Flyssyng *L3.* [c] saponis *L3.*

[44] De navi Arnaldi Cotte[a] vocata Kateryn de Newport eodem die *[9 Mar. 1446]*

De eodem pro 1 fatto wode debilis, 1 barello saponis, 2 sortes figes et ressins[b], 300 pavyngtile magnis[c] crude. Precii £3 3s 4d .... cust' 9½d

[a] Cote *L3.* [b] resyns *L3.* [c] et *follows L3.*

<aa>57s 2½d<aa>

E122/73/20A f. 8r

[45] De navi Peryn Paryvyn vocata Gillam de Hunflett eodem die *[9 Mar. 1446]*

De Andrea Gerard pro 50 alnis canvas. Precii 13s 4d .... cust' 2d

<z> *Auditor's marginated entry L1:* cera.

[46] De navi Clays Brewer vocata Kateryn de Dunkirk eodem die *[9 Mar. 1446]*

De eodem pro 2 barellis, 1 corf cum gulles salsis. Precii 20s ....cust' 3d
De Clays Claysson pro 1 corf, 2 barellis [cum] gulles salsis. Precii 20s..cust' 3d

[47] De navi Clays Petersson vocata Holygost de Hardwik [a]11°[a] die Marcii *[11 Mar. 1446]*

De Henrico Nase pro 7 barellis allecis albi, 12 dimidiis barellis anguillarum salsarum, 150 bunchis allei, 50 sparres. Precii £7 6s 8d.....................cust' 22d

[a-a] *Interlined above* eodem, *struck through L1.*

[48] De navi Ilbrand Davys vocata Albright[a] de Dunkirk eodem die *[11 Mar. 1446]*

De Gerardo Bars pro 2 lastis codling in barellis, 2 lastis piscium salsorum, 11 barellis nucum magnarum, 20 ferthkins allecis albi. Precii £23 6s 8d ....cust' 5s 10d

[a] Albrygh' *L3.*

[49] De navi Johannis Garettson vocata Goodewill de Ermouth eodem die *[11 Mar. 1446]*

De Jacobo Claysson pro 2 corfes, 6 barellis piscium salsorum. Precii 40s ....cust' 6d

[50] De navi Rogeri Vyntmyle vocata Julian de Roon 21 die Marcii *[21 Mar. 1446]*

De Johanne Varlett[a] pro 40 mewes[b] frumenti. Precii £30 ....cust' 7s 6d

[a] Barlett *L3.* [b] mewe *L1.*

[51] De navi Jakett le Garse vocata Marie de Cawldebek[a] eodem die *[21 Mar. 1446]*

De Johanne Varlett[b] pro 40 mewes[c] frumenti. Precii £30 ....cust' 7s 6d

[a] Caldebek *L3.* [b] Barlett *L3.* [c] mews *L1.*

[52] De navi Willelmi Malpasse vocata Trinite de London' 22° die Marcii *[22 Mar. 1446]*

De Petro Treguran et [a]Remond de[a] Michaell pro 43 pipis wode. Precii £120 ....cust' 30s

[a-a] *Interlined L1.*

<aa>-<aa> *Auditor's entry L1: Sum of the issues on the page.*

[53] De navi Colyn Page vocata Gabrell de Cane 26 die Marcii *[26 Mar. 1446]*

De Gillam de Lane pro 120 quarteriis frumenti, 1 hoggeshede nucum. Precii £7 10s..cust' 22½d

<aa>55s 8½d<aa>

E122/73/20A f. 8v

[54] De navi Johannis Osgard vocata [a]Kateryn[a] de Dunkirk eodem die *[26 Mar. 1446]*

De Danyello Petersson pro 125 bunchis ceparum. Precii 10s ....cust' 1½d

[a-a] *Interlined above* Margarete, *struck through L3.*

[55] De navi Arnaldi[a] Claysson vocata Swanne de Harlow eodem die *[26 Mar. 1446]*

De Johanne Hede pro 2 saccis hoppes continentibus 6 hodes. Precii 30s ....cust' 4½d

De dicto magistro pro 1 lasto dogstonz, 2000 pavyngtile, 2 vagis vitri, 60 skyve tasilles, 4 saccis hoppes continentibus 12 hodes, 100 warp ollarum et patellarum terre, 300 crusys terre, 1 barello sope, 1 barello cabelows. Precii £10 .... cust' 2s 6d

[a] Arnoldi *L3.*

[56] De navi Copyn Lamb vocata Seynt Martynknyght[a] eodem die *[26 Mar. 1446]*

De Arnaldo[b] Adreansson pro 1 sacco hoppes continente 3 hodes. Precii 15s ....cust' 2½d

De Everardo Johansson pro 1 parvo forcerio, 1 parvo basketto cum 15 parvis peciis tele lini. Precii £6 13s 4d ....cust' 20d

[c]De Curte Spyse pro 2 parvis barellis cum 22 dossenis zonarum Colonie[d], 40 paribus calopodiorum. Precii 26s 8d..cust' 4d

De Henrico Brewer pro 5 barellis saponis. Precii 50s..........................cust' 7½d

De dicto magistro pro 100 warp ollarum et patellarum terre, 2000 pavyngtile rubeis. Precii 20s..cust' 3d

De Edmundo[e] Bowdynsson pro 18 barellis gulles. Precii 53s 4d............cust' 8d

[a] Martynknygh *L3.* [b] Arnoldo *L3.* [c] + *[cross] marginated against this entry and struck through L1.* [d] de Colonia *L3.* [e] eodem *L3, in error.*

[57] De navi Johannis Bernard vocata George de Kane[a] ultimo die Marcii *[31 Mar. 1446]*

De Rawlyn Graund pro 120 quarteriis frumenti. [b]Precii[b] £7 10s.........cust' 22½d

<z> *Auditor's marginated entry L1:* cera.

De Johanne Huet pro 120 quarteriis frumenti, 1 dolio nucum magnarum. Precii £7 16s 8d..cust' 23½d

[a] Cane *L3.* [b] *Omitted L1.*

[58] De navi Naunt[a] Rikworth vocata Flyer de Flandria primo die Aprillis *[1 Apr. 1446]*

De eodem pro 1 sacco cum 1 hod hoppes. Precii 5s ....cust' ¾d

[a] Nawnt *L3.*

[59] De navi Adreani Mone vocata Come Well to Howse[a] 4to die Aprilis *[4 Apr. 1446]*

De eodem pro 1 barello rape ole[b], 6 barellis allecis albi, 1000 bakstone, 1 sort figes and resins[c]. Precii 46s 8d...cust' 7d

[a] Hose *L1.* [b] oyle *L3.* [c] reysins *L3.*

<aa>10s 10¾d<aa> [a]Item 4d[a]

[a-a] *Auditor's supplement necessitated L1, because* Curte Spyse*'s goods (marked above with an asterisk: ship of* Copyn Lamb *(No. 56), variant c) were initially omitted from the calculation.*

E122/73/20A f. 9r

[60] De navi Jacobi Male vocata George de Newport eodem die *[4 Apr. 1446]*

De eodem pro 7000 bakstone albis, 2 peciis figes and resins. Precii 16s 8d ....cust' 2½d

[61] De navi Ricardi Walshe vocata [a]Trynyte de Gravesend[a] 7e die Aprilis *[7 Apr. 1446]*

De Cristian van Bleken pro 6 balis madir[b]. Precii £12............................ cust' 3s

[a-a] Trenite de Gravyssende *L3.* [b] mader *L3.*

[62] De navi Willelmi Henriksson vocata George de Flyshing[a] 16 die Aprilis *[16 Apr. 1446]*

De eodem pro 4 saccis hoppes continentibus 13 hodes. Precii £3 5s....cust' 9¾d

[b]De Cristian van Bleken pro 100 hodes salis de Berflette, 3 [c]saccis[c] ca[na]bis continentibus 1500 lb., 6[d] barellis saponis. Precii £21.................... cust' 5s 3d

De Elys Wynter pro 1 barello cum 20 timbre trones, 18½ timbre herwerk debilis, 7 tymbre skevens. Precii £9 .... cust' 2s 3d

De Johanne Hede pro 1 hoggeshede cum 7 dossenis cordwayn, 1 dossena pellium rubearum. Precii 40s..cust' 6d

[a] Fluscheyng *L3.* [b] cot *(L1),* cal' canabis *(L3) marginated against this entry.* [c-c] *Interlined L1.* [d] continentibus *follows, struck through L1.*

<aa>-<aa> *Auditor's entry L1: Sum of the issues on the page.*

[63] De navi Lambe Henriksson vocata Mariknyght de London' eodem die *[16 Apr. 1446]*

De eodem magistro pro 13 hodes hoppes, 50 warp ollarum et patellarum terre, 9 skyve tasilles, 5 fedirbedes[a], 125 sparres, 9 barellis beere. Precii £7 6s 8d ....cust' 22d

De Bowden Hughsson pro 3 fedirbedz[b], 50 sparres. Precii 26s 8d ....cust' 4d

De Geretrud Damys pro 10 hodes hoppes, 50 werp[c] ollarum et patellarum terre. Precii £3 13s 4d ....cust' 11d

[a] fetherbeddes *L3.* [b] fedirbeddes *L3.* [c] warp *L3.*

[64] De navi Naunt Rikworth vocata le [a]Flygher de Dunkirk[a] eodem die *[16 Apr. 1446]*

De eodem pro 5 hodes hoppes, 1000 bakstone. Precii 33s 4d..................cust' 5d

De [b]Augustyn Doloretto[b] pro 2 caleptris. Precii 6s 8d ....cust' 1d

[a] Fleer van Dunkerk *L3.* [b-b] Austyn de la Recto *L3.*

[65] De navi Clays Martynsson vocata Kateryn de Ermoth[a] 11 die Maii *[11 May 1446]*

De Henrico Mighell pro 1 barello cum 40 parvis mooldes veteribus, 8 gros broches. Precii 13s 4d ....cust' 2d

De Gasper Ofman pro 6 parvis barellis cum plat[a] alb[a]. Precii £8 ...... cust' 2s

[a] Ermouth *L3.*

[66] De navi Johannis de Carris vocata Trinite[a] de Naunte 16 die Maii *[16 May 1446]*

De eodem pro 2½ chargiis[b] salis de Bay. Precii 20s ....cust' 3d

[a] Trenite *L3.* [b] charge *L3.*

<aa>18s ¼d<aa>

E122/73/20A f. 9v

[67] De navi Peryn Obard vocata Jonett[a] de Cane 23 die Maii *[23 May 1446]*

De Michaele de Boys pro 2850 alnis canvas. Precii £38 .... cust' 9s 6d

De Colyn Foloyn[b] pro 1800 alnis canvas. Precii £24..............................cust' 6s

De Robyn Arnawd pro 1000 alnis canvas. Precii £13 6s 8d .... cust' 3s 4d

De dicto magistro pro 2 fardellis canvas continentibus 700 alnas. Precii £9 6s 8d .... cust' 2s 4d

[a] Jenott *L3.* [b] Folyn *L3.*

<z> *Auditor's marginated entry L1:* cera.

[68] De navi Johannis Affons vocata Salvator de[a] London' eodem die *[23 May 1446]*

De eodem magistro et sociis suis pro 3000 orenges. Precii 10s ....cust' 1½d
De Johanne Cutery pro 1 pipa olei. Precii 40s ....cust' 6d

[a] Bayn *follows, struck through L3.*

[69] De navi Totyn Gobyn vocata John de Cane eodem die *[23 May 1446]*

De Colyn Trenchaunt pro 2000 alnis canvas [a]et[a] in uno fardello 70 alnis canvas. Precii £26 8s 4d ....cust' 6s 7¼d

[a] *Omitted L3.*

[70] De navi Willelmi Bey vocata Mariknight[a] de Scluse 25 die Maii *[25 May 1446]*

De Siprian Spynola pro 10 balis madir[b]. Precii £20 ....cust' 5s
De Alexandro van Feld pro 2 parvis barellis saponis, 3 barellis vini agri, 3 barellis cum cyrupo[c], 1 barello coperose. Precii £4 10s...................cust' 13½d

[a] Mariknygh *L3.* [b] mader *L3.* [c] cyripo *L3.*

[71] De navi Johannis Askew vocata Nicholaus de Dunkirk primo [a]die[a] Junii *[1 June 1446]*

De Johanne de Vyle pro 30 balis lycorys[b]. Precii £5..............................cust' 15d

[a] *Omitted L1.* [b] lecorys *L3.*

[72] De navi Alberti Blytterswyk vocata James de Colayn[a] eodem die *[1 June 1446]*

De Johanne Salmar pro 2 fraillis batrie, 2 bashrunez, 2 pipis, 3 basketes cum 6 rippes cacaborum. Precii £70...cust' 17s 6d
De Johanne Dasse pro 2 balis fustian, ½ bala bukrams[b], 2 fardellis, 1 rolla continentibus 3000 [alnas] canvas. Precii £64 ....cust' 16s
De Johanne Hope pro 3 balis fustian, 2 lastis saponis, ½ bala fustian. Precii £48 ....cust' 12s
De Cristian van Bleken pro 2 balis fustian, 1 lasto saponis. Precii £28 ... cust' 7s
De Henrico Brewer pro 33 peciis tele lini Minystre continentibus 936 alnas, 360 alnis tele lini Holandie, 850 lb. canebis. Precii £42 18s 4d.. cust' 10s 8¾d

<aa>£4 19s<aa>

E122/73/20A f. 10r

De Henrico Nase pro 8 balis madir[c], 800 alnis tele lini. Precii £36 ....cust' 9s
De Tilman Crome pro 2 balis fustian, 6 dimidiis balis carde. Precii £68 ....cust' 17s

<aa>-<aa> *Auditor's entry L1: Sum of the issues on the page.*

De Roberto Blitterswyk pro 2 barellis cum 80 petris wyre ferri. Precii £6 13s 4d .... cust' 20d

De Johanne Blytterswyk pro 5 dimidiis balis carde, 2 dimidiis balis bukram[b-d], 260 [e]lb. petris[e] wyre ferri, 3 dimidiis barellis calibis, 7 scok delys[f], 1 lasto saponis. Precii £98 .... cust' 24s 6d

De Hermano Wesill pro 2 lastis saponis, 8 balis fustian, 5 balis madir[g]. Precii £66 .... cust' 16s 6d

De Bertram Questenbergh pro 7 balis fustian, ½ bala carde, ½ bala bukram[b], [h]74 dossenis lb. fili Colonie[h]. Precii £113 6s 8d .... cust' 28s 4d

De Matis Shonebagh pro 15 balis madir[i]. Precii £30 .... cust' 7s 6d

De Johanne van Dorne pro 5 balis fustian, 9 barellis saponis. Precii £54 10s .... cust' 13s 7½d

De Johanne van Sybright pro 6 balis fustian, [j]224 dossenis lb. fili Colonie[j], 2 dimidiis balis carde. Precii £150 13s 4d .... cust' 37s 8d

De Cristian Edilkynd[k] pro 3 balis fustian, 1 pack fili Colonie continente 36 dossenas lb. Precii £42 .... cust' 10s 6d

De Petro Cangheter[l] pro 11 balis fustian, [m]120 dossenis lb. fili Colonie[m], 2 lastis saponis. Precii £162 .... cust' 40s 6d

De Johanne Hathiltak[n] pro 3½ lastis saponis, 1 cista cum 4 dossenis candilstiks, 6 dossenis sheres, 3 dossenis rasourz[o] et diverso haberdashe. Precii £40 .... cust' 10s

De [p]Imbright van Sassonhossen[p] pro 1 parvo barello cum 8 basins, 2 dossenis parvorum balancez[q], 1½ gros lokkes. Precii £3 .... cust' 9d

De Johanne Lufort pro [r]52 dossenis lb. fili Colonie[r], [s]3 corffes, 2 barellis cum[s] 30 bundellis wyre, 100 [t]frieng pannes[t], 250 key bondes, 20 gros zonarum, 1 bundello latone, 7 rynges [u]de latone[u] et diverso haberdashe. Precii £22 6s 8d .... cust' 5s 7d

De Johanne Stokde[v] pro 10 balis fustian, 2 pack fili Colonie continentibus 72 dossenas lb., ½ bala bukram[b]. Precii £138 .... cust' 34s 6d

De Gerlof van Berkenrode pro 3 balis bukrams[b], 1 bala carde. Precii £50 .... cust' 12s 6d

De Johanne Rynge pro 6 dimidiis barellis calibis, 18 balis fustian, 8 balis madir[i], 7 ferthkins[w] plate albe. Precii £122 .... cust' 30s 6d

De Gerwyn Potte pro [x]175 dossenis lb. fili Colonie[x], 5 dimidiis barellis calibis. Precii in toto £78 6s 8d .... cust' 19s 7d

De Petro Persson pro [s]1 parvo basketto[s], 12 dossenis rough hattes. Precii £3 .... cust' 9d

<aa>£16 11½d<aa>

E122/73/20A f. 10[v]

De Leonardo van Brusill pro 5 parvis corfes cum 70 dossenis felt hattes et rough hattes. Precii £16 13s 4d .... cust' 4s 2d

De Hayn Ole pro 2 saccis hoppes continentibus 8 hodes. Precii 40s .... cust' 6d

<z> *Auditor's marginated entry L1:* cera.

De Johanne van Ae[y] pro 1 corf, 1 cista cum 8 dossenis rough hattes. Precii 50s ....cust' 7½d

De Lambert Joses[z] pro 2 fraillis batrie, 1 bashrune batrie, 1 pipa, 2 maundis [aa]cum 3 rippis cacaborum[aa], 1 meise plate. Precii £48 .... cust' 12s

[a] Colonia *L3.* [b] bokerams *L3.* [c] mader *L3.* [d] 4 barellis cum *follows L3.* [e-e] *Sic L1, L3.* [f] doll' *L3.* [g] madre *L3.* 1 parvo barello *follows, struck through L1.* [h-h] 2 pak fili Colonie continentibus 64 *[sic]* dossenas lb. fili Colonie *L3.* [i] madre *L3.* [j-j] 6 pak fili Colonie continentibus 224 dossenas lb. *L3.* [k] Edilkyng *L3.* [l] Cangether *L3.* [m-m] 3 pak fili Colonie continentibus 120 dossenas lb. *L3.* [n] Hatiltake *L3.* [o] rasours *L3.* [p-p] Ingilbright van Sassonhouson *L3.* [q] balons *L3.* [r-r] 2 pak fili Colonie continentibus 52 dossenas lb. *L3.* [s-s] *Omitted L1.* [t-t] frying panis *L3.* [u-u] wyre laton *L3.* [v] Stokede *L3.* [w] ferthekenes de *L3.* [x-x] 5 pak fili Colonie continentibus 175 dossenas lb. *L3.* [y] Ha *L3.* [z] Josse *L3.* [aa-aa] *Omitted L1. Interlined L3.*

[73] De navi Willelmi Cote vocata Cristofor de[a] Gowe eodem die *[1 June 1446]*

De eodem pro 3000 pavingtile magnis, 6000 brekestone, 100 werp[b] ollarum et patellarum terre. Precii 53s 4d ....cust' 8d

De Willelmo Spyker pro 1 sacco hoppes continente 9 hodes, 2 baskettis, 1 parvo basketto [c]cum[c] 1 parvo barello cum 2 dossenis [d]glase botelles[d], 20 face[e] vitri, 23 gros lasing poyntes[f], 45 drynkyng[g] glasses. Precii £6 6s 8d ....cust' 19d

De Nicholao Rychardesson pro 4 barellis saponis, 40 skyve tasilles. Precii £3 13s 4d..cust' 11d

De Leonardo van Brussill pro 4 baskettis cum 400 glasse botelles, 30 face[c] virres vitri. Precii £3[h] 6s 8d...cust' 10d

De Henrico Johansson pro 8 saccis hoppes continentibus 16 hodes. Precii £4 ....cust' 12d

De Arnaldo[i] van Langfeld pro 6 saccis hoppes continentibus 30 hodes, 2 cistis cum 200 papir poyntes[f]. Precii £14... cust' 3s 6d

De Ricardo Mighell pro 1 barello cum 2 peciis tele lini Holandie. Precii 20s ....cust' 3d

De Petro[j] Fraunk[k] pro 2 saccis hoppes continentibus 8 hodes. Precii 40s ....cust' 6d

[a] van der *L3.* [b] warp *L3.* [c] *Omitted L3.* [d-d] glasse botelles vitri *L3.* [e] fasse *L3.* [f] poyentes *L3.* [g] dryngkyn *L3.* [h] *Corrected in L1 from £6. Written over erasure L3.* [i] Arnoldo *L3.* [j] Ptro *L1, in error.* [k] Franke *L3.*

[74] De navi Johannis Stold vocata Cristofor de[a] Dansk 8 die Junii *[8 June 1446]*

De eodem pro 15 lastis cinerum, 1300 waynscottes, 4 scok delys, 3½ lastis clapholt[b], 150 treys, 4 parvis mastes, 2 pak lini, 4 [c]bundellis candilyarn con-

<aa>-<aa> *Auditor's entry L1: Sum of the issues on the page.*

tinentibus[c] 80 lb., 5 scok trenchours, 100 ores, 1000 swerd scales, ½ lasto beere, 50 waynscottes, 6 bundellis[d] lini. Precii £48 15s .... cust' 12s 2¼d

<aa>38s 8¾d<aa>

E122/73/20A f. 11[r]

De Henrico Brewer pro 2 lastis lini, 1 pack, 1 cista [e]cum[e] 100 alnis [e]tele[e] hinderlond. Precii £14 13s 4d .... cust' 3s 8d

<z>•[f]Et pro 1 parva rolla cere ponderante[g] 2 quintallos[f] .... cust' 2s

De Elys Wynter pro 3000 wrake bowstaves, 11 barellis coperos. Precii £22 6s 8d .... cust' 5s 7d

De Vincent Doryng pro 2 pack lini, 37 balis lini, 20[h] barellis beere, 9 cistis cum 4 tymbre skevenes[i], 300 lb. fili Prucie, 1 fatto[j] sturgeon, 3 fardellis vernysh[k], 3 countours, 5 scok sebuttes[l], 2 lastis cinerum, ½ lasto tarre, 200 lb. candilgarn, 18 bundellis wyndyng, 1 scok merlyng, 2 peciis tele lini continentibus 80 alnas gros[sis]. Precii £30 10s .... cust' 7s 7½d

De Jacobo Swarte pro 2 pack lini, 1 pack candilyarn[m] continente 400 lb., 36 lb. twyne, 150 [alnis] canvas. Precii £11 10s .... cust' 2s 10½d

De Helmych[n] Nybur pro 3 pack lini, 8 barellis pictis, 1 cista cum 80 lb. fili Prucie, 40 alnis canvas. Precii £10 .... cust' 2s 6d

De Matis[o] Spryghorne pro 5 lastis lini, 4 barellis beere, 2 cistis cum 6 scok trenchours, 6 peciis wyndyng. Precii £21 13s 4d........................... cust' 5s 5d

De Bertram Sleighter[p] pro 6 lastis cinerum, 1000 waynscottes. Precii £16 .... cust' 4s

De Hans Fox pro 4 lastis lini, 6 barellis [q]cupri gray[q]. Precii £28 .... cust' 7s

De Johanne Dasse pro 6 pack lini. Precii £12 .... cust' 3s

[a] van *L3.* [b] clapholtt *L1.* [c-c] bondels candilgarn continente *L3.* [d] bondels *L3.* [e-e] *Omitted L3.* [f-f] *Entered at the end of the membrane, after Jacob Swarte's goods, and preceded by* De dicto Henrico Brewer *L3.* [g] continente *L3.* [h] 22 *L3.* [i] skevenys *L3.* [j] fatte *L3.* [k] vernych *L3.* [l] sepboxis *L3.* [m] candilgarn *L3.* [n] Helnych *L1.* [o] Mattis *L3.* [p] Slygheter *L3.* [q-q] copre grey *L3.*

[75] De navi Ilbrand[a] van the Wold vocata Reynald[b] de Dansk eodem die *[8 June 1446]*

De Henrico Brewer pro 1 pack lini, 3 barellis, 1 cista cum 4½ tymbre herwark, 1 timbre ermyns, 11 pellibus mink, 1 scok trenchourz[c], 140 alnis canvas. Precii £5[d] .... cust' 15d

De Poull[e] Rode pro 2 barellis [f]cupri rubei[f], 1 pack cum 1200 alnis canvas, 2 cistis cum 300 lb. fili Prucie[g]. Precii £18 10s .... cust' 4s 7½d

[h]Et pro 2 strawe cere ponderantibus 13 quintallos[h]

De Hans Howold pro 3 barellis beere, 1½ lastis pictis et tarre, 15 bundellis[i] lini, 6 bundel[l]is[i] fili continentibus 200 lb., 10 scok trenchours, 6 parvis treis, 3 cistis cum 200 lb. fili Prucie. Precii £6 .... cust' 18d

<z>Et pro 2 parvis peciis cere ponderantibus[j] 1 quintallum .... cust' 12d

<z> *Auditor's marginated entry L1:* cera.

De Nicholao Bee pro 5 bundellis[i] fili continentibus 33 lb., 5 timbre skevenes, 5 paribus[k] tabillarum[l], 1 dossena cerotecarum[m], 5 bursis. Precii 26s 8d..cust' 4d

<z>Et pro 2 parvis peciis cere ponderantibus[j] 1 quintallum ....cust' 12d

<aa>53s 4½d<aa>

E122/73/20A f. 11[v]

De Bernardo Swether pro 8 barellis osmond, 4 barellis beer, 9 bundellis[i] candilgarn continentibus 600 lb., 4 bundellis[i] fili Prucie continentibus 300 lb., 2 scok trenchours, 1 cista cum 2 peciis [n]canvas continentibus 80 alnas stricti[n]. Precii £10.. cust' 2s 6d

De Alloff Lye pro 3 pack lini, 18 peciis candi[l]yarn[o], 20 bundellis lini, 2 cistis cum 400 lb. fili Prucie[g], 24 alnis canvas, 4 scok trenchourz[c]. Precii £13 10s ....cust' 3s 4½d

De Elys Wynter pro 2700 bowstaves wrak[p], 9 bundellis[i] ferri, 2 barellis[q] [r]cupri gray[r]. Precii £19 16s 8d..cust' 4s 11½d

De Nicholao Noyghell pro 4 lastis cinerum, 3 lastis lini, 1 parvo barello cum 200 lb. fili Prucie[g], 2000 [et] 5 tymbre letowark[s], 1 chessmeyny[t]. Precii £20 6s 8d.. cust' 5s 1d

De Matys[u] Sprynghorn pro 1 lasto lini, 1 parvo pack continente 150 [h]alnas[h] canvas, 10 balis lini, 6 barellis [r]cupri gray[r]. Precii £16.........................cust' 4s

De Henrico Egard[v] pro 2 pack [w]cum 2000 alnis canvas stricti[w], 1 cista cum 30 alnis tele lini, 20 lb. seminis ceparum. Precii £10 15s................cust' 2s [x]8¼d[x]

De Bertram Sleighter pro 5 barellis cupri [h]gray[h], 5 meis cupri rubei, 6 lastis cinerum, 400 clapholtt, 1100 waynscottes, 15 barellis selsmolt[y], ½ lasto tarre, ½ lasto piccis, 3 pack lini, 4 barellis, 2 cistis cum 200 alnis canvas, 6 scok trenchourz[c], 30 tymbre [z]pellium[z] popillorum, 11 tymbre pellium ruskyn. Precii £67... cust' 16s 9d

<z>Et pro 7 strawe cere ponderantibus 41 quintallos .... cust' 41s

De Derik Nayle pro 2 lastis lini, 2 cistis cum 6 peciis candilyarn[o]. Precii £10 13s 4d.. cust' 2s 8d

De Clement Greve pro 2 pack candilyarn[o], 1 lasto piccis, 4 barellis tarre, 1 scok treis, 15 scok trenchours, 10 bundellis bastes, 2 cistis, 1 fatto[aa] cum 2000 pellibus skevens, 1000 pellibus helsing, 9 pellibus bever, 100 lb. fili Prucie[g], 9 pellibus martrinz, 30 pellibus fecheux, 30 scok trenchourz[c]. Precii £11 .... cust' 2s 9d

De Cristian van Bleken[ab] pro 2 lastis cinerum. Precii 40s........................cust' 6d

De Hans Rynge pro 8 lastis et 4 barellis cinerum, 100 clapholt, 200 waynscottes, 18 barellis gray cupri[ac], 4 lastis osmond, 2 pack lini, 1 pack cum 700 alnis canvas grossi. Precii £62 13s 4d... cust' 15s 8d

<z>Et pro 1 straw cere ponderante 6 quintallos.................................. cust' 6s

<aa>107s 11¼d<aa>

E122/73/20A f. 12[r]

<aa>-<aa> *Auditor's entry L1: Sum of the issues on the page.*

De Hans Fox pro 2 pack candilyarn[o], 1 cista cum 100 lb. fili Prucie[g]. Precii £5 ....cust' 15d

De Everardo Stumell pro 1 pack canvas continente 900 alnas. Precii £9 ....cust' 2s 3d

<z>De Johanne Warenthorp pro 2 strawe cere ponderantibus 13 quintallos ....cust' 13s

De Johanne Dasse pro 4 barellis cupri gray, [ad]1000 alnis canvas[ad]. Precii £16 ....cust' 4s

[a] Ibbrand *L1.* [b] Rynold *L3.* [c] trenchours *L3.* [d] 13s 4d *follows, struck through L3.* [e] Powll *L3.* [f-f] *Interlined L1, L3.* [g] Prus *L3.* [h-h] *Omitted L1.* [i] bondelles *L3.* [j] continentibus *L3.* [k] pare *L3.* [l] tabules *L3.* [m] precii *follows, struck through L1.* [n-n] tele lini continentibus 80 alnas canvas stricti *L3.* [o] candilgarn *L3.* [p] warke *L3, in error.* [q] copre *follows, struck through L3.* [r-r] cupre grey *L3.* [s] lettowe warke *L3.* [t] chessemayny *L3.* [u] Mattis *L3.* [v] Eggard *L3.* [w-w] tele lini continentibus 2000 alnas canvas stricti *L3.* [x-x] *Interlined above* 7¾d, *struck through L1.* [y] selfsmolt *L3.* [z] *Omitted L3.* [aa] fatte *L3.* [ab] Bleyken *L3.* [ac] copre *L3.* [ac-ac] 1 packe canvas continente 1000 alnas *L3.*

[76] De navi Clays Rodman[a] vocata Marikneght[b] van Kuonybergh eodem die *[8 June 1446]*

De eodem pro 5 lastis cinerum, 450 waynscottes, 300 clapholt, 400 treis, 36 ores [c]evens[c], 50 bolles, 10 barellis beer, 3 lastis piccis, 4 scok trenchourz[d], 4 bundellis lini, [e]100 lb. fili Prucie[e]. Precii £20 17s 8d....................cust' 5s 2¾d

<z>Et pro 1 parva pecia cere ponderante 20 lb....................cust' 2½d[f]

De Hans Meire pro 1 lasto cinerum, ½ lasto piccis, 3 scok tabularum pro sutoribus, 24 bundellis[g] lini, 1 cista cum 8 scok trenchourz[d], 3 pellibus martrinz, 2 pellibus ermynz. Precii £3 13s 4d....................cust' 11d

De Tydman Hugh pro 7 lastis piccis, 3 lastis tarre[h], 3 lastis cinerum, 4 barellis selsmolt, 20 tabilis pro sutoribus, 2 cistis cum 300 lb. fili Prucie[i], 3 tymbre trunes[j] debilium, 12 balis lini. Precii £20 3s 8d....................cust' 5s ¾d

<z>Et pro 1 quintallo cere ....cust' 12d

De Laurencio Synner pro 3 barellis beere, 3 cistis cum 25 timbre pellium skevens, 4 tymbre swethis[k] debilium, 30 pellibus martrinz, 200 lb. fili Prucie[i]. Precii £7 6s....................cust' 22d

De Jacobo Bardman[l] pro 6 barellis beere, 6 barellis cinerum, 14 barellis piccis, 3 cistis, 1 forcerio cum 400 lb. fili Prucie[i], 4½ timbre skevens, 11 pellibus martrinz. Precii £8 19s 4d....................cust' 2s 3d

De Jacobo Cale pro 15 barellis piccis, 8 barellis cinerum, 1 scok sebuttes[m], 2 barellis, 3 cistis cum 2000 pellibus lettowark[n], 6 timbre pellium ermyns, 4 pellibus bever, 3 timbre fechcux. Precii £11 10s 6d....................cust' 2s 10¾d

<z>Et pro 4 parvis peciis cere ponderantibus[o] 1½ quintallos ....cust' 18d

<aa>41s 4¾d[p]•<aa>

<z> *Auditor's marginated entry L1:* cera.

[a] Rodeman *L3.* [b] Mariknygh *L3.* [c-c] *Omitted L3.* [d] trenchours *L3.* [e-e] 4 bundellis fili Prus continentibus 100 lb. *L3.* [f] *Corrected in L1 from* 2¼d. [g] bondelles *L3.* [h] terre *L3.* [i] Prus *L3.* [j] trowyns *L3.* [k] swthes *L1.* [l] Bardeman *L3.* [m] sepbox *L3.* [n] lettowerk *L3.* [o] continentibus *L3.* [p] *Corrected in L1 from* 4¼d.

E122/73/20A f. 12[v]

[77] De navi Godkyn[a] Moys vocata Mariknight van Dansk eodem die *[8 June 1446]*

De eodem pro 3 lastis, 4 barellis cinerum, 1 lasto piccis et tarre, 375 waynscottes, 1 scok delys, 400 clapholt, 3 tabilis[b] pro sutoribus. Precii £13 2s 2d .... cust' 3s 3½d[c]

De Henrico Wydilburse[d] pro 2 pack candilyarn et lini, 8 barellis beer, 4 barellis tarre[e], 1 lasto cinerum, 1 countour, 3 nest cofers, 24 scok trenchourz[f], 2 scok treis, [g]17 lb. fili Prucie[g], 6 platterz[h] depictis, 4 cistis cum 5 tymbre pellium redewerk[i], ½ timbre fecheux, 300 lb. fili Prucie, 5 pawteners[j], 6 [k]Prus[k] bursis. Precii £18 13s 4d .... cust' 4s 8d

De Matis[l] Springhorn pro 1 lasto lini. Precii £4 .... cust' 12d

De Hans Smyth pro 1 pack lini, 9 barellis cinerum, 2 barellis beer, 6 parvis forceriis, 4 bundellis[m] candilyarn[n] continentibus 100 lb., 1 scok treis, 1 scok sebuttes[o], 12 paribus[p] tabillarum[q], 30 scok trenchours, 17 platterz[h], 2 scok parvorum platterz[h], 1 trow [r]cum[r] 27 lb. saponis albi, 2 cistis cum 100 lb. fili Prucie, 4 dossenis bursarum, 3 pellibus martrinz, 3 pellibus fecheux, 45 peciis wyndyng. Precii £8 7s 6d .... cust' 2s 1¼d

De Bertram Sleighter[s] pro 12 lastis cinerum, 12 barellis selsmoltt, 200 ores, 10 barellis cupri rubei, 19 pack lini. Precii £82 .... cust' 20s 6d

<z>Et pro 2 parvis strawe cere ponderantibus[t] 10 quintallos .... cust' 10s

De Andrea van Groten[u] pro 4 pack candilyarn, 1 barello, 20 cofires triplicatis, 1 cista, 3 fattis [k]cum[k] 6 tymbre helsing, 50 lb. fili Prucie. Precii £14 2s 8d .... cust' 3s 6½d[v]

De Henrico Egard[w] pro 2 pack candilyarn, 10 barellis selsmolt, 100 ores, 7 pack lini, 3 barellis coperos, 4 parvis peciis cupri. Precii £30 14s .... cust' 7s 8¼d

De Hans Bukke pro 8 barellis selsmoltt, 1 pack candilyarn[x], 2 scok treis, 2 pellibus martrins, 20 pellibus fecheux stage. Precii £7 15s .... cust' [y]23¼d[y]

De Derik Nayll pro 1 pack lini, 7 barellis selsmolt. Precii £6 13s 4d .... cust' 20d

<z>De Andrea Rogynthorp[z] pro 2 strawe cere ponderantibus[t] 12 quintallos .... cust' 12s

<z>De Cristian van Bleken[aa] pro 1 strawe cere ponderante[ab] 6 quintallos .. cust' 6s

<z>De Hans Rynge pro 1 strawe cere ponderante[ab] 7 quintallos .... cust' 7s

<aa>£4 16¾d[ac]•<aa>

[a] Goydken *L3.* [b] bordes *L3.* [c] *Corrected in L1 from* 3¼d. [d] Wydilbur *L3.* [e] terre *L3.* [f] trenchours *L3.* [g-g] 1 pecia fili Pruce continente 17 lb.

<aa>-<aa> *Auditor's entry L1: Sum of the issues on the page.*

L3. [h] platerys *L3.* [i] redewarke *L3.* [j] pawtenerys *L3.* [k] *Omitted L3.* [l] Mattis *L3.* [m] bondelles *L3.* [n] candilliarn *L3.* [o] sepbuttes *L3.* [p] payr *L3.* [q] tabellarum *L3.* [r-r] *Interlined L1.* [s] Slyghter *L3.* [t] continentibus *L3.* [u] Gruten *L3.* [v] *Corrected in L1 from* 6¼d. [w] Eggard *L3.* [x] candeliarn *L3.* [y-y] *Interlined above* 22¾d, *struck through L1.* [z] Roygynthorp *L3.* [aa] Bleyken *L3.* [ab] continente *L3.* [ac] *Corrected in L1 from 16¼d (in consequence of the correction of the customs charges on* Hans Bukke*'s goods).*

E122/73/20A f. 13r

[78] De navi Jacobi Moys vocata Mariknyght de Dansk eodem die *[8 June 1446]*

De eodem pro 150 clapholtt, 100 ores, 1 lasto cinerum, 1 lasto piccis, 4 bundellis[a] candilyarn[b] continentibus 100 lb., 6 dimidiis barellis sturgeon, 4 barellis selsmoltt, 4 bundellis[a] fili Prucie continentibus 50 lb., 100 waynscottes. Precii £11 .... cust' 2s 9d

<z>Et pro 2 peciis cere ponderantibus[c] 1 quintallum.......... cust' 12d

De Jacobo Swarte pro 1 pack candilyarn[d], ½ lasto osmond, ½ lasto piccis, 100 clapholtt, 1 lasto beere, 1½ scok treis, 4 barellis tarre[e], ½ scok bastes, 6 bundellis[a] candilyarn[d], 1 barello candilyarn[b] continente 100 lb., 1 dossena parium tabullarum[f], 3 cistis, 15 balis lini, 150 alnis tele canvas, 30 lb. twyne. Precii £15 13s 4d .... cust' 3s 11d

De Nicholao Noyell[g] pro 4 pack lini, 100 ores, 4 cistis cum 10 scok trenchours. Precii £11 5s .... cust' 2s 9¾d

De Clays Stopp pro 8 barellis beere, 16 balis lini, 200 lb. fili Prucie[h], 100 alnis tele lini. Precii £5 19s 4d .... cust' 18d

<z>Et pro 2 parvis peciis cere ponderantibus[c] ½ quintallum[i] .... cust' 6d

De Martyno Drews pro 2 pack candilyarn[b], 8 bundellis[j] fili Prucie[h] continentibus 200 lb., ½ timbre fecheux, 6 pellibus martrinz, 2 pellibus ermyns, 4 neste cofres[k], 1 parva pecia tele lini continente 20 alnas. Precii £8 9s 4d .... cust' 2s 1½d

De Petro Rekewyn pro 7 pack lini, 1 barello cum 25 timbre pellium skevens, 6 timbre letwes[l], 1 timbre ermyns, 1 cista cum 40 lb. fili Prucie, 100 alnis tele[m] canvas. Precii £19 12s.......... cust' [n]4s 11d[n]

<z>Et pro 1 pecia cere continente 1½ quintallos .... cust' 18d

De Poullo[o] Crympyn pro 12 barellis beere, 11 bundellis[a] fili Prucie[h] continentibus 200 lb., 16 tymbre pellium herewerk[p], 8 scok trenchours, 6 peper[q] querens, 6 dossenis lasing poyntes[r], 2 cistis cum 2 elky[s] skynz, 6 buk skynez, 3 parvis forceriis, 12 bursis, 20 alnis tele lini. Precii £8 .... cust' 2s

De Bertram Sleighter pro 6 lastis cinerum, 2 barellis [t]gray cupri[t], 1 cista cum 3 barellis cupri rubei, 6 barellis selsmoltt, 700 waynscottes, 3 pack lini. Precii £31 6s 8d.......... cust' 7s 10d

<z>Et pro 2 strawe cere ponderantibus[c] 13 quintallos .... cust' 13s

<aa>41s 9¾d<aa> [u]Item 2s ½d[u]

<z> *Auditor's marginated entry L1:* cera.

E122/73/20A f. 13ᵛ

De Henrico[v] Brewer pro 10 barellis cupri gray[w]. Precii £20 .... cust' 5s

De Hans Buk pro 2 pack lini, 10 bundellis[a] fili Prucie[h] continentibus 200 lb., 1 cista cum 3 timbre pellium trones[x], 3 scok trenchours. Precii £8 .... cust' 2s

De Andrea Rakenthorp pro 2 barellis cupri rubei. Precii £4 .... cust' 12d

De Michaele[y] Swarte pro 2 pak candilyarn[z], 2 cistis[aa] cum 5 scok trenchours, 2 peciis tele lini continentibus 20 alnas, 120 lb. fili Prucie. Precii £10 7s 2d .... cust' 2s 7¼d

<z>Et pro 1 parvo strawe cere ponderante 4 quintallos .... cust' 4s

De Hans Rynge pro 10 pack lini. Precii £20 .... cust' 5s

De Johanne Dasse pro 8 pack lini, 2 pack canvas continentibus 2000 alnas, 2 barellis cupri[ab] rubei, 80 tabillis[ac] pro sutoribus, 1 barello cum 20 bundellis fili Prucie continentibus 100 lb., 4 timbre skevens, 2 pellibus bevere. Precii £42 3s 2d .... cust' 10s 6½d

[a] bondelles *L3.* [b] candilgarn *L3.* [c] continentibus *L3.* [d] candelgarn *L3.* [e] terre *L3.* [f] tabillarum *L3.* [g] Noyghell *L3.* [h] Prus *L3.* [i] *cere follows L3.* [j] boundelles *L3.* [k] ceffers *L3.* [l] letewis *L3.* [m] *lini follows L3.* [n-n] *Interlined above 2s 10½d, struck through L1.* [o] Pulo *L3.* [p] herwarke *L3.* [q] piper *L1.* [r] poyentes *L3.* [s] helk *L3.* [t-t] grey copre *L3.* [u-u] *Auditor's supplement necessitated by the correction of the customs charges on Peter* Rekewyn*'s goods L1.* [v] Hurie *L3, in error.* [w] rubei *L3.* [x] trownys *L3.* [y] Mychall' *L3.* [z] candelyarn *L3.* [aa] cestes *L3.* [ab] copre *L3.* [ac] tabellis *L3.*

[79] De navi Matis[a] Niendank vocata Cristofor de Dansk eodem die *[8 June 1446]*

De eodem pro 4000 waynscottes, 20 lastis cinerum, 300 clapholtt, 100 bothom holt, 400 ores, 3 scok delys, 1200 [b]bowstaves wrak[b]. Precii £82 ... cust' 20s 6d

De Jacobo van Bury pro 2 pack lini, 1 lasto osmond, 2 countourz[c], 4 barellis beere, 5 peciis canvas continentibus 100 alnas, 1 [d]buketto cum glase[d], 2 cistis cum 3 dossenis bukk skynnez[e], 10 scok trenchourz[f]. Precii £12 14s 8d .... cust' 3s 2¼d

De Hans Wynter pro 4 barellis cupri rubei, 6 barellis cupri gray[g], 3000 [b]bowstaves wrak[b], 1 barello, 1 fe[r]thkyn[h] cum 10½ tymbre skevens, 10 timbre fecheux, 15 bever wombz[i]. Precii £48 7s 8d .... cust' 12s 1¼d

De Baltazer[j] Styper pro 2 pack lini, 14 barellis piccis, 21 barellis tarre. Precii £7 18s 4d .... cust' 23¾d

De Bertram Questenbergh pro 14 lastis cinerum. Precii £14 .... cust' 3s 6d

De Matis Sprynghorn pro 3½ lastis lini, 6 barellis cupri rubei, 2 pack canvas continentibus 1800 alnas. Precii £44 .... cust' 11s

<aa>£4 2s 5d<aa>

E122/73/20A f. 14ʳ

<aa>-<aa> *Auditor's entry L1: Sum of the issues on the page.*

De Bernardo Swether pro 3 pack lini, 1 lasto cinerum, 1 countour, 1 chist[k] cum 30 lb. fili Prucie[l], 18 paribus cerotecarum[m], 4 dossenis bursarum. Precii £8 .... cust' 2s

De Derik Hunter pro 3 pack lini, 2 lastis cinerum, 8 neste forceriorum[n], 6 parvis countours, 12 scok trenchourz[f], 4 scok sebuttes[o], 6 cistis cum 400 lb. fili Prucie[l], 17 scok merlyng, 2 dossenis tabilarum, 3 dossenis key bondes. Precii £18 13s 4d.. cust' 4s 8d

<z>Et pro 1 [p]parva[p] pecia cere ponderante[q] 1 quintallum..................cust' 12d

De Bertram Sleighter pro 2 lastis osmond, 1 fatto[r] cum 6 timbre bever wombz[i], 3 timbre fech[e]ux, 1 timbre mynkes, 3½ timbre martrinz, 7 timbre ermyns, 1500 pellibus lettowark[s]. Precii £29 8s 4d.................................. cust' 7s 4¼d

De Hans Rynge pro 1 pack canvas continente 1000 alnas. Precii £10 .... cust' 2s 6d

De Nicholao Noyell pro 50 ore evyns[t]. Precii 20s ....cust' 3d

De Michaelle Swarte pro 1 pack lini, 1 pack candilyarn[u]. Precii £4 ......cust' 12d

De Johanne Wolf pro 100 lb. candilyarn[u], 40 bundellis[v] wyndynge, 12 lb. saille yarn, 10 pellibus fecheux, 2 pellibus otter[w], 2 pellibus Prucie[l], 5 neste cofres, 1 countour, 12 bursis, 1 pecia tele lini continente 40 alnas, 1 lasto tarre, ½ scok treis, 7 scok trenchourz[f], 15 pellibus fech[e]ux. Precii £4 14s 5d ....cust' 14¼d

<z>Et pro 1 parva pecia cere ponderante[q] ½ quintallum ....cust' 6d

De Tilman Wydbury pro 2 bundellis[v] candilyarn[u] continentibus 100 lb., 12 ores, 6 tabillis pro sutoribus, 4 barellis piccis, 12 bursis, 2 pack cum 600 lb. candilyarn[u], 200 alnis canvas stricti, 2 cistis cum 18 lb. fili Prucie[l], 18 lb. candilyarn, 26 alnis tele lini stricte. Precii £6 4s 3d........................cust' 18½d

<z>De Rymer Skepill pro [x]1[x] pecia cere ponderante 4 quintallos .... cust' 4s

<z>De Johanne[y] Warenthorp pro 2 straw cere ponderantibus 10 quintallos .... cust' 10s

[a] Mattis *L3.* [b-b] bowstavys wark *L3, in error.* [c] countours *L3.* [d-d] bokett' cum glos' *L3.* [e] skynnys *L3.* [f] trenchours *L3.* [g] grey *L3.* [h] ferdekent *L3, in error.* [i] wombes *L3.* [j] Batezer *L3, in error.* [k] cista *L3.* [l] Prus *L3.* [m] sirotecarum *L3.* [n] forsers *L3.* [o] sopbottes *L3.* [p-p] *Omitted L1.* [q] continente *L3.* [r] fatte *L1, L3.* [s] lettowe *L3.* [t] evens *L3.* [u] candilgarn *L3.* [v] bondelles *L3.* [w] otterys *L3.* [x-x] *Omitted L3.* [y] Johanne *follows, struck through L1.*

[80] De navi Johannis Sandow vocata Cristofor de Dansk eodem die *[8 June 1446]*

De eodem pro 5 lastis cinerum, 5 pack lini, 400 clapholtt, [a]100[a] ores [b]evens[b], 2 saccis hoppes [c]continentibus[c] 4 hodes, 1 scok bastes, ½ lasto sclsmolt, 1 lasto tarre, 5 barellis piccis. Precii £27 13s 4d .... cust' 6s 11d

<aa>42s 11¼d<aa>

E122/73/20A f. 14[v]

<z> *Auditor's marginated entry L1:* cera.

De Johanne Dasse pro 3 pack canvas [b]grossi[b] continentibus 3000 alnas. Precii £36 ... cust' 9s
<z>Et pro 1 strawe cere ponderante 7 quintallos ... cust' 7s
De Jacobo van Bury pro 100 tabillis[d] pro sutoribus, 3 rollis tylde here, 1 barello wod. Precii 58s 4d ... cust' 8½d
<z>Et pro 1[e] rolla cere ponderante 11 quintallos ... cust' 11s
<z>De Cristian van Bleken[f] pro 1 strawe cere ponderante 6 quintallos ... cust' 6s
[g]De Bernardo Skymer pro 2 countourz[h] cum 6 scok trenchourz[i], 6 platterz[j], 2 pack lini. Precii £4 15s ... cust' 14¼d[g]
De Henrico Northehous pro 1 barello cupri rubei. Precii 40s ... cust' 6d
De Clays Bulkyn pro 1 lasto cinerum, 1 lasto piccis, 300 alnis canvas cours, 9 cofirres, 1 dossena treis, 1 scok sebuttes[k], 6 bukskynes[l], 1 dossena bursarum, 1 barello, 2 cistis cum 6 scok trenchourz[i], 300 lb. candilyarn[m]. Precii £7 7s ... cust' 22¼d
<z>Et pro 1 parva pecia cere ponderante 12 lb. ... cust' 1½d
De Andrea Rakenthorp[n] pro 1 pack lini. Precii 40s ... cust' 6d
De [o]Bartholomeo Grono[o] pro 4 pack lini, 3 barellis tarre, 2 barellis piccis, 2 scok treis, 2 bundellis[p] candilyarn[m] [q]continentibus 30 lb.[q], 9 cistis cum 4 neste cofres, 4 dossenis bursarum, 10 scok trenchours, 10 balis lini, 20 alnis canvas [b]stricti[b], 200 lb. fili Prucie[r]. Precii £16 2s 10d ... cust' 4s ½d
De Derik Nayle pro ½ lasto selsmolt, [s]1 pack [q]cum[q] 15 peciis candilyarn [q]continentibus 1 lastum[q], 1 pack canvas continente 800 alnas[s]. Precii £18 ... cust' 4s 6d
De Derik Hunter pro 5 pack lini, 15 barellis selsmolt, 1 pack canvas continente 650 [b]alnas canvas[b]. Precii £26 10s ... cust' 6s 7½d
De [t]Andrea van Groten[t] pro 8 pack lini, 1 pack candilyarn[m], 2 barellis gray cupri, 1 cista cum 40 alnis canvas, 1 neste parvorum forceriorum[u], 30 lb. fili Prucie[r]. Precii £22 10s 10d ... cust' 5s 7¾d
De Henrico Brewer pro 6 barellis cupri[v] rubei. Precii £10 ... cust' 2s 6d
De Bertram Sleighter pro 4 barellis cupri rubei. Precii £8 ... cust' 2s
<z>Et pro 4 strawe cere ponderantibus 25 quintallos ... cust' 25s
De Hans Rynge pro 2 pack lini. Precii £4 ... cust' 12d
<z>Et pro 1 strawe cere ponderante 6 quintallos ... cust' 6s
De Henrico Egard[w] pro 1 pack candilyarn[m], 1 pack canvas continente 600 alnas [b]stricti[b], 8 timbre letwes[x], 1 timbre martrinz, 2 tymbre ermyns, 2 tymbre fecheux, 1 cista. Precii £9 11s 8d ... cust' 2s 4¾d
De Nicholao Nayell[y] pro 4 pack lini, 2 barellis cupri rubei, 1[e] scok bastes, 8 parvis cistis cum 12 scok trenchours, 100 lb. fili Prucie[r]. Precii £20 4s ... cust' 5s ¾d

<aa>102s 7¾d<aa>

E122/73/20A f. 15[r]

<aa>-<aa> *Auditor's entry L1: Sum of the issues on the page.*

De Johanne Warenthorp pro 1 lasto selsmolt, 1 pack [z]cum 500 alnis canvas[z]. Precii £13 .... cust' 3s 3d

[a-a] *Interlined L3.* [b-b] *Omitted L1.* [c-c] *Omitted L3.* [d] bordes *L3.* [e] 2 *L3.* [f] Bleyken *L3.* [g-g] *Entered lower down, after the goods of Andreas* Rakenthorp *L3.* [h] countours *L3.* [i] trenchours *L3.* [j] platerys *L3.* [k] sepbottes *L3.* [l] bukskynnys *L3.* [m] candilgarn *L3.* [n] Rokenthorp *L3.* [o-o] Bernardo Gronehow *L1.* [p] bondelles *L3.* [q-q] *Interlined L1.* [r] Prus *L3.* [s-s] 1 pack canvas continente 800 alnas, 1 packe candilgarn [cum] 15 peciis candilgarn continentibus 1 lastum *L3.* [t-t] Andre van Gruten *L3.* [u] cofferres *L3.* [v] gray *follows, struck through L1, L3.* [w] Eggard *L3.* [x] letewes *L3.* [y] Noyell *L3.* [z-z] tele lini continente 500 alnas canvas Prus *L3.*

[81] De navi Hankyn Thomas vocata Holigost de Dansk eodem die *[8 June 1446]*

De eodem pro 900 waynscottes, 100 ore evyns, 2 lastis piccis, 4 barellis beere, 1 fardello cum 80 lb. candilyarn[a]. Precii £13 .... cust' 3s 3d

De Bertram Sleighter pro 2 pack lini, 1 pack candilyarn[a]. Precii £6 ...... cust' 18d

<z>Et pro 2 strawe cere ponderantibus 12 quintallos .... cust' 12s

De Nicholao Noyell pro ½ lasto tarre, 3 scok sebuttes[b]. Precii 16s 8d.. cust' 2½d

De Hans Bukke pro 300 clapholt, 2 lastis cinerum, 1300 bowstaves, 3 cistis cum 16 tableres, 5 scok trenchours. Precii £6 2s 2d .... cust' 18½d

De dicto Nicholao Noyell pro 100 clapholt, 2 lastis cinerum. Precii £3[c] . cust' 9d

De Clays Sculte pro 3 pack lini, 2½ lastis piccis, 3 barellis tarre, ½ scok bastes, 15 peciis tele lini continentibus 200 alnas canvas, 1 cista cum 50 lb. fili Prucie[d], 20 alnis canvas, 1 bala lini. Precii £13 15s 2d .... cust' 3s 5½d

De Henrico Northouse pro 2 lastis cinerum, 100 clapholtt. Precii £3 6s 8d .... cust' 10d

De Hans Rynge pro 13 lastis cinerum, 3 pak lini, 1 countour, 5 barellis cupri rubei, 8 bordes. Precii £30 13s 4d .... cust' 7s 8d

<z>Et pro 1 strawe cere ponderante 5 quintallos .... cust' 5s

De Johanne [e]Sandow[e] pro 2 lastis cinerum, 3 parvis mastis, 2 cistis cum 100 lb. fili Prucie[d], 3 scok trenchours, 40 alnis tele lini, 40 alnis canvas. Precii £5 16s 8d .... cust' 17½d

[a] candilgarn *L3.* [b] sepbuttes *L3.* [c] 60s *L3. 8d follows, struck through L3.* [d] Prus *L3.* [e-e] *InterlinedL1.*

[82] De navi Derik Johansson vocata Wilbord de Flysshing[a] 17 die Junii *[17 June 1446]*

De eodem pro 50 piscibus[b] salsis. Precii 13s 4d .... cust' 2d

De Willelmo Johansson pro 1200 piscibus[b] salsis. Precii £15 .... cust' 3s 9d

[a] Flyschyn *L3.* [b] pissibus *L3.*

<z> *Auditor's marginated entry L1:* cera.

[83] De navi Bowden[a] Hughsson vocata[b] Holigost van Midilburgh[c] eodem die *[17 June 1446]*

De eodem pro 3000 pavyngtile, 400 ollis terre, 5 dossenis parvorum basketto-rum. Precii £4 16s 8d .... cust' 14½d

De Nicholao Cristiansson pro 2½ dossenis scabellorum, 1 corfe cum 4 doss-enis pannorum depictorum, 8000 bokellis ferri, [d]100 alnis tele lini[d]. Precii £11 .... cust' 2s 9d

De Goss[on] Braynten pro 6 saccis hoppes continentibus 24 hodes. Precii £6 .... cust' 18d

De Petro Fraunk[e] pro 1 sacco hoppes continente 4 hodes. Precii 20s ...... cust' 3d

[a] Bawyn *L3.* [b] wr *follows, struck through L1.* [c] Midilborgh *L3.* [d-d] 3 peciis tele lini continentibus 100 alnas *L3.* [e] Frankes *L3.*

<aa>50s 6½d<aa>

E122/73/20A f. 15[v]

[84] De navi Gerardi[a] Johansson vocata Holigast[b] de And-warp eodem die *[17 June 1446]*

De Clays Lyndman pro 3 fattis cum 280 petris[c] wyre ferri. Precii £21 .... cust' 5s 3d

De eodem magistro pro 400 pavyngstone albis. Precii 6s 8d .... cust' 1d

De Ambilbright Cornelys[d] pro 2 barellis saponis, 5 dossenis besoms[e]. Precii 24s .... cust' 3¾d

De Johanne Dasse pro 1 basketto cum 15 dossenis [f]felt et thrum hattes[f]. Precii £5 .... cust' 15d

De Tilman Crome pro 2 balis fustian, ½ bala bukram[g]. Precii £24 .... cust' 6s

De Henrico Nase pro 2 balis madir[h], 2 saccis canabis[i] continentibus 600 lb.[j], 3 saccis hoppes continentibus 10 hodes. Precii £10 10s .... cust' 2s 7½d

De Petro Cangheter pro 8 balis madir[k]. Precii £16.................................. cust' 4s

De Johanne Stokde pro 8 balis madir[k]. Precii £16 .... cust' 4s

De Henrico Overbagh pro 4 dimidiis barellis calibis. Precii £16............ cust' 4s

De Imbright[l] van Sassonhowsen pro 1 barello calibis, 3 dimidiis barellis plate albe. Precii £8 .... cust' 2s

[a] Gerradi *L3.* [b] Holygost *L3.* [c] stone *L3.* [d] Cornell *L3.* [e] besomnys *L3.* [f-f] thrumez et felt hattes *L3.* [g] bokerams *L3.* [h] madre *L3.* [i] canebis *L1.* [j] *Omitted L3.* [k] mader *L3.* [l] Ingilbryght *L3.*

[85] De navi Petri Adreansson vocata Mariknyght[a] de Lon-don' 21 die Junii *[21 June 1446]*

De Bertram Questenbergh pro 3 balis fustian. Precii £30 .... cust' 7s 6d

De Petro Fraunk pro 2 saccis hoppes continentibus 8 hodes. Precii 40s..cust' 6d

De Henrico Nase pro 3 saccis canabis[b] continentibus 700 lb. Precii £5 .... cust' 15d

<aa>-<aa> *Auditor's entry L1: Sum of the issues on the page.*

De Henrico Brewer pro 9 barellis aluminis. Precii £9 .... cust' 2s 3d
De Johanne Blitterswyk[c] pro 3 dimidiis barellis calibis. Precii £12 .... cust' 3s
De Willelmo Damesson pro 1 barello cum 18 felt hattes, 40 alnis tele lini crude. Precii 20s .... cust' 3d
De Otte van Dorne pro 1 parvo barello, 1 [d]parvo[d] basketto cum 6 gros lasyng poyentes, 12 lb. counters, 2 grossis calcarium[e], 2 dossenis bagpypes[f] et diverso haberdashe. Precii £3 10s .... cust' 10½d

[a] Mariknygh *L3.* [b] canebis *L1.* [c] Blitersweke *L3.* [d] *Omitted L1.* [e] spores *L3.* [f] bagge pipis *L3.*

[86] De navi Poppe Gylesson vocata [a]Gasthows de Midilburgh[a] eodem die *[21 June 1446]*

De Gerrardo Broke pro 1 maunda cum 4 sadill[b] treis. Precii 3s 4d .... cust' ½d

[a-a] Gastehous de Middilborgh *L3.* [b] sadell *L3.*

<aa>45s 2¼d<aa>

E122/73/20A f. 16[r]

[87] De navi Johannis Curtroke vocata Leonard van Bergh eodem die *[21 June 1446]*

De Adreano Matisson pro 200 werp[a] ollarum et patellarum terre. Precii 13s 4d .... cust' 2d
De Henrico Nase pro 3 balis madir[b], 2 saccis hoppes continentibus 7½ hodes, 60 skyve[c] tasilles, 1 parvo basketto cum 1000 wymbill[d] yrens. Precii £17 10s .... cust' 4s 4½d

[a] warp *L3.* [b] mader *L3.* [c] skewe *L3.* [d] whymbell *L3.*

[88] De navi Hayn Dankard vocata Cristofor van Bury eodem die *[21 June 1446]*

De Clays Lyndman[a] pro 1 bala madir[b], 3 saccis hoppes continentibus 16 hodes. Precii £6 .... cust' 18d
De Johanne Dankard[c] pro 3 saccis hoppes continentibus 12 hodes. Precii £3 .... cust' 9d
De Arnaldo van Langfeld pro 2 saccis hoppes continentibus 6 hodes. Precii 30s .... cust' 4½d
De Martyno Hartisson pro 4 saccis hoppes continentibus 12 hodes. Precii £3 .... cust' 9d

[a] Lyndeman *L3.* [b] madre *L3.* [c] Dankert *L3.*

[89] De navi Hayn Bulscamp vocata Andreas van Ermoth eodem die *[21 June 1446]*

De Henrico Nase pro 6 balis madir[a] Selandie. Precii £12 .... cust' 3s
De Henrico Brewer pro 4 balis fustian. Precii £40 .... cust' 10s

<z> *Auditor's marginated entry L1:* cera.

De Bertram Questenbergh pro 3 pack fili Colonie continentibus 80 dossenas lb., 3 balis fustian, 1 corf cum 10 dossenis thrume hattes. Precii £60 cust' 15s

De Johanne Ery pro 1 parvo fardello cum 300 alnis tele lini bolte. Precii £4 10s ....cust' 13½d

De [b]Everardo Stomell[b] pro [c]4 cistis cum[c] 11 balis canebis ponderantibus 100[d] lb., 1½ timbre ermyns[e], 8 lb. fili Prucie, 3 [f]mantellis[f] pellium gray, 2 mantellis pellium calibrorum wombz. [Precii] £8 18s 8d..............cust' 2s [g]3d[g]

De Gerwyn Potte pro 1 pack fili Colonie continente 30 dossenas lb., 12 balis madir[a]. Precii £34.. cust' 8s 6d

De Hans Hixsten pro 2 saccis canebis ponderantibus[h] 500[i] [c]lb. canebis[c]. Precii £3 6s 8d...cust' 10d

De Hans Hatiltak pro 1 barello, 1 corf cum 13 dossenis felt hattes, 3000 [et] 21 timbre pellium popilorum[j], 11 timbre trones. Precii £8 13s 4d........ cust' 2s 2d

De Johanne van Sibright pro 3 pack fili Colonie continentibus 112 dossenas lb. Precii £37 6s 8d ....cust' [k]9s 4d[k]

De Cristian Edilkynd pro 2 dimidiis barellis calibis[l], 2 balis fustian, 1 pack fili Colonie continente 31 dossenas lb. Precii £38 6s 8d .... cust' 9s 7d

De Gerardo[m] Johansson pro 2 maundis cum 15 dossenis felt hattes, 4 peciis tele lini continentibus 40 alnas, 1 barello cum 20 petris wyre ferri. Precii £6 13s 4d...cust' 20d

De Lambert Joses pro 5 bashrunez, 2 fraillis, 5 baskettis baterie[n]. Precii £81 .... cust' 20s 3d

De Johanne Salmer pro 5 fraillis, 5 bashrunez, 5 baskettis [c]batrie[c]. Precii £105 .... cust' 26s 3d

<aa>117s [o]10½d[o]·<aa>

E122/73/20A f. 16v

De Hans Rynge pro 3½ pack fili Colonie continentibus 60 dossenas lb., 1 maunda cum 3 dossenis [et] 3 [p]sherman sheres[p]. Precii £33 6s 8d .cust'[q] 8s 4d

De Clays Lyndman[r] pro 2 pack fili Colonie continentibus 120 dossenas [et] 10 lb. Precii £40... cust' 10s

De Roberto Blitterswyk pro 1 barello cum 40 petris wyre ferri. Precii £3 6s 8d ....cust' 10d

De Johanne Blitterswyk pro 7 barellis calibis[l], 7 dimidiis barellis plate albe, 5 dimidiis balis bukram[s], 6 dimidiis balis carde, 5 dimidiis balis carde cours[t], 2 pack fili Colonie continentibus 72 dossenas lb. Precii £209 6s 8d .... cust' 52s 4d

De Tilman Crome pro 6 balis fustian, 1 pack fili Colonie continente 30 dossenas lb. Precii £70... cust' 17s 6d

De Johanne Stokde pro 7 balis fustian, 2 pack fili Colonie continentibus 60 dossenas lb. Precii £90... cust' 22s 6d

De Henrico Hode pro 1 sacco canebis continente 250 [lb.], 1 parvo fardello cum 4 coverlittes Flandrie, 1 banker. Precii £3....................................cust' 9d

<aa>-<aa> *Auditor's entry L1: Sum of the issues on the page.*

De Derik van Camp pro 1 cista, 1 barello cum 6 parvis pannis depictis, 80 alnis tele lini, 40 lb. cupri[u] rubei, 50 lb. argulle. Precii £3 ....cust' 9d
De Johanne de Vyle pro 1 bala aunes. Precii 26s 8d...............................cust' 4d
De Otte van Dorne pro 1 barello cum 9 somes brak[v] nailles, 1½ gros paternoster vitri, 3 gros lokkes, 3 dossenis bodkyns[w] et diverso haberdashe. Precii £3 10s...cust' 10½d
De Cristian Edilkynd pro 2 dimidiis barellis calibis. Precii £8 ....cust' 2s
De Petro Person[x] pro 2 parvis corfes cum 24 dossenis [y]thrume hattes et felt[y]. Precii £5...cust' 15d

[a] madre *L3.* [b-b] Everas Stumell *L3.* [c-c] *Omitted L3.* [d] 150 *L3.* [e] armyns *L3.* [f-f] *Interlined L1.* [g-g] *Interlined above* 2¾d, *struck through L1.* [h] continentibus *L3.* [i] 1 fatto, 1 barello *follows, struck through L3.* [j] poplorum *L3.* [k-k] *Interlined above* 8s 10d, *struck through L1.* [l] calebis *L3.* [m] Gerrardo *L3.* [n] batri *L3.* [o-o] *Interlined above* 4½d, *struck through L1 (auditor's correction necessitated by the correction of the customs charges on the goods of Everard* Stommell *and Johann* van Sibright*).* [p-p] cherman cheres *L3.* [q] 7s 10d *follows, struck through L1.* [r] Lyndeman *L3.* [s] bokrams *L3.* [t] cors *L3.* [u] copr *L1.* [v] brakett *L3.* [w] bodkens *L3.* [x] Persson *L3.* [y-y] thrummz et felthattes debilium *L3.*

[90] De navi Bowden Adreansson[a] vocata [b]Marikneght de Ermoth[b] eodem die *[21 June 1446]*

De Henrico Brewer pro 3 barellis aluminis, 2 lastis osmond. Precii £19 ....cust' 4s 9d
De Johanne Dasse pro 39 balis madir[c]. Precii £78 ....cust' 19s 6d
De Cristian Edilkynd pro 8 dimidiis barellis calibis. Precii £32 ....cust' 8s
De Bertram Questenbergh pro 7 balis madir[d], 1 pack fili Colonie continente 30 dossenas lb. Precii £24..cust'[e] 6s
De Gerwyn Pott[f] pro 4 baskettis cum 2 balis bukram[g], 8 balis carde. Precii £92 ....cust' 23s

<aa>£8 17s 2½d<aa> [h]Item 18d[h]

E122/73/20A f. 17[r]

De Petro Fraunk[i] pro 1 corfe cum 14 sellis[j]. Precii 46s 8d.......................cust' 7d
De Petro Cangheter pro dimidio pack cum 4 balis fustian. Precii £40...cust' 10s
De Cristian van Bleken[k] pro 12 balis madir[c], 3 lastis saponis. Precii £42 ....cust' 10s 6d
De Petro Mews[l] pro 200 bowstaves. Precii 40s.......................................cust' 6d
De Arnaldo[m] Adreansson pro 6 ketilles. Precii 6s 8d.............................cust' 1d
De Petro Person pro 1 corfe cum 4 dossenis rough[n] hattes. Precii 26s 8d ....cust' 4d
De Johanne Salmer pro 6 bashrunez, 2 baskettis cum 4 rippes cacaborum. Precii £58...cust' 14s 6d

<z> *Auditor's marginated entry L1:* cera.

De Lambert Joses pro 5 bashrunez, 3 maundis cum 6 rippes cacaborum. Precii £55 .... cust' 13s 9d[o]
De Gerardo[p] Broun pro 3 barellis cum 36 alnis tele lini Holandie, 3 bankers, 9 papir poyntes[q], 80 lb. bristilles. Precii £3 10s .... cust' 10½d
De Hans Rynge pro 10 parvis barellis plate [r]albe[r], 3 maundis cum 270 [s]lb.[s] wyre ferri, 1 pipa cum 1500 lb. [t]wyre de latone[t], 2 barellis cum 900 lb. latone plate. Precii £74 9s 2d .... cust' 18s 7½d
De Gerardo[p] Johansson pro 2 barellis, 1 hoggeshede cum 80 petris wyre ferri. Precii £4 .... cust' 12d
De Johanne Hede pro 9 saccis hoppes continentibus 18 hodes, 3 barellis saponis, 1 hoggeshede cum 200 lb. bristilles, 1 maunda cum 2 fedirbedes[u], 11 pannis depictis. Precii £8 .... cust' 2s
De Gerardo[p] Petersson[v] pro 500 ollis terre, 6 [w]parvis peciis[w] tele lini continentibus 40 alnas. Precii 40s .... cust' 6d
De Derik van Cappell pro 4 saccis hoppes continentibus 15 hodes, 1 parvo barello, 1 corfe cum 15 dossenis [x]hattes[x] straminis, 6 forceriis vacuis, 80 [x]lb.[x] fili pro arblastis[y]. Precii £5 6s 8d .... cust' 16d
De Johanne Blitterswyk[z] pro 4 pack fili Colonie continentibus 120 dossenas lb., 3 hoggeshedes cum 4000 lb. latone wyre, 8 balis madir[c], 12 parvis barellis plate albe. Precii £114 .... cust' 28s 6d
De Roberto Blitterswyk[aa] pro 6 balis madir[d], 2 pack fili Colonie continentibus 52 dossenas lb., 1 parvo barello cum 25 lb. latone wyre, 18 bundellis twyne albi ponderantibus[ab] 100 lb. Precii £34 16s 10d .... cust' 8s 8¾d
[ac]De Johanne Stokde pro 3 balis fustian, 3 pack fili Colonie continentibus 80 dossenas lb. Precii [ad]£56[ad] 13s 4d .... cust' 14s 2d
De Jacobo Peryman[ae] pro 2 pok canebis[af] continentibus 400 lb. Precii 40s .... cust' 6d
De [s]dicto[s] magistro pro 2 balis madir[c], 2 barellis sope, 1 sacco canebis[af] continente 250 [lb.], 1 maunda cum 300 piscibus[ag] salsis. Precii £7 6s 8d .... cust' 22d
De Nicholao Eglemoure[ah] pro 1 sacco hoppes continente 3 hodes, 1 corfe cum 14 dossenis felt hates[ai]. Precii £5 8s 8d .... cust' 16¼d
De Johanne Chirchyerde[aj] pro 1 sacco hoppes continente 2 hodes. Precii 10s .... cust' 1½d

<aa>£6 9s 9½d<aa>

E122/73/20A f. 17v

De Imbright van Sassonhousen[ak] pro 2 barellis calibis. Precii £8 .... cust' 2s
De Willelmo Damsson pro 1 parvo basketto cum 40 ollis terre, 50 whyskeres[al]. Precii 3s 4d .... cust' ½d
De Matis van [am]Akyn[am] pro 2 saccis canebis[an] ponderantibus 500 lb. Precii £3 6s 8d .... cust' 10d

<aa>-<aa> *Auditor's entry L1: Sum of the issues on the page.*

De Alexandro Palestrell pro 1 parvo fardello cum 9 peciis badekyns[ao] broched cum auro de Luke, 8 peciis brokkettorum[ap] de auro, 12 peciis siclaton[aq]. Precii £44 .... cust' 11s

De Arnaldo[ar] Williamsson pro 2 querenstones. Precii 6s 8d .... cust' 1d[as]

[at]De [au]Galeaco Negro[au] [x]pro[x] 3 balis madir[d] Zelandie, 1 fardello cum sirpis[av]. Precii £6 .... cust' 18s[at]

[a] Adreanson *L3.* [b-b] Maryknyght de Ermouth *L3.* [c] mader *L3.* [d] madre *L3.* [e] 5s *follows, struck through L1.* [f] Potte *L3.* [g] bokerams *L3.* [h-h] *Auditor's supplement necessitated by the correction of the customs charges on the goods of* Hans Rynge *and* Bertram Questenbergh *L1.* [i] Frankes *L3.* [j] sadilles *L3.* treeys *follows, struck through.* [k] Blekyn *L3.* [l] Mewes *L3.* [m] Arnado *L1, in error.* [n] routh *L3, in error.* [o] *On the next line, the entry for the goods of* Cristian van Bleken *is repeated (in error), with* nichil, quia supra in eadem navi, *marginated against it L3.* [p] Gerrardo *L3.* [q] poyentes *L3.* [r-r] *Interlined L1. Omitted L3.* [s-s] *Interlined L1.* [t-t] latone wyre *L3.* [u] fetherbeddes *L3.* [v] Peterson *L3.* [w-w] peciis remanentibus *L3.* [x] *Omitted L1.* [y] alblastris *L1.* [z] Bletersweke *L3.* [aa] Blitersweke *L3.* [ab] continentibus *L3.* [ac] pro rasura nota *marginated against this entry L1 (cf. variant ad).* [ad-ad] *Written over erasure L1.* [ae] Puryman *L3.* [af] canabis *L3.* [ag] pissibus *L3.* [ah] Eggelemore *L3.* [ai] hates *L1.* [aj] Chircheyarde *L3.* [ak] Sassonhowson *L3.* [al] sweskeres *L3.* [am-am] Aken *L3, interlined.* [an] candil *L3, in error.* [ao] bodekens *L3.* [ap] brokettorum *L3.* [aq] seclaton *L3.* [ar] Arnoldo *L3.* [as] *On the next line* De Humfrido Justinean pro 1 parvo fardello, 1 cista *follows, struck through L3, with* nichil, quia pro stauro *marginated against it.* [at-at] *The goods of* Galeaco Negro *are entered between those of William* Damsson *and* Matis van Aken *L3.* [au-au] Galeas de Negro *L3.* [av] cirpis *L3.*

[91] De navi Copyn Lamb vocata [a]Seint[a] [b]Martinknyght de Ermoth[b] eodem die *[21 June 1446]*

De Arnaldo[c] [a]van[a] Langfeld pro 6 saccis hoppes continentibus 12 hodes. Precii £3 .... cust' 9d

[a-a] *Omitted L3.* [b-b] Martynknygh de Ermouth *L3.* [c] Arnoldo *L3.*

[92] De navi Peryn Obard vocata Jonett de Cane eodem die *[21 June 1446]*

De eodem pro 1 parvo fardello canvas continente 150 alnas, 1 hoggeshede cum 6 dossenis carde veteris, 2 dossenis carde novi. Precii £3 10s .... cust' 10½d

[93] De navi Johannis de la Lownd vocata Nicholaus de Cane eodem die *[21 June 1446]*

De eodem pro 12 mews[a] frumenti, 1 pipa cum 10 dossenis carde [b]veteris[b]. Precii £11 13s 4d .... cust' 2s 11d

De Roberto Maryn pro 12 mews[a] frumenti. Precii £9 .... cust' 2s 3d

De [c]Ada Cornell[c] pro 6 meus[a] frumenti. Precii [d]£4 17s 6d[d] .... cust' [e]14¾d[e]

<z> *Auditor's marginated entry L1:* cera.

De Johanne Former[f] pro 1 pack canvas continente 500 alnas. Precii £6 13s 4d ....cust' 20d

De Johanne Huett pro 2 pack fili pro retibus[g] ponderantibus[h] 400 lb. Precii £4 ....cust' 12d

[a] mewes *L3.* [b-b] *Interlined L1, L3.* [c-c] Adam Cornell *L1,* Adam Cornel *L3.* [d-d] *Corrected in L1 from* £4 10s *(cf. variant e).* [e-e] *Interlined above* 13½d *(this would have been the correct charge for goods worth £4 10s: cf. variant d), struck through L1.* [f] Forner *L3.* [g] rethibus *L3.* [h] continentibus *L3.*

[94] De navi Johannis Pyssott vocata[a] 27 die Junii *[27 June 1446]*

De Ricardo Pychard pro 7 mews[b] frumenti. Precii £5 5s ....cust' 15¾d

[a] *5 cm (L1) and 8cm (L3) room left for completion of the entry.* [b] mewes *L3.*

[95] De navi Thome Walsheworth[a] vocata Thomas de Cosyche[b] 29 die Junii *[29 June 1446]*

De Jacobo Styward[c] pro 5 lastis samonis salsi. Precii £20 ....cust' 5s

[a] Wyscheworth *L3.* [b] Cosive *L3.* [c] Stuard milite *L3.*

[96] De navi Roberti[a] Cankerell vocata Maria[b] de Cane 5 die Julii *[5 July 1446]*

De Robyn Rosay pro 6½ mews[c] frumenti. Precii £4 [d]17s 6d[d] .... cust' [e]14¾d[e]

[a] Robyn *L3.* [b] Mari *L3.* [c] mewes *L3.* [d-d] *Interlined above* 10s, *struck through L1 (cf. variant e).* [e-e] *Interlined above* 13½d *(which would have been the correct customs charge for goods worth £4 10s: cf. variant d), struck through L1.*

<aa>33s 5d<aa> [a]Item 3¼d[a]

[a-a] *Auditor's supplement necessitated by the correction of the customs charges on the goods of Adam* Cornell *and* Robyn Rosay *and by the erroneous addition of the original figures L1.*

*E122/73/20A f. 18^r^*

[97] De navi Cornelii[a] Johansson vocata James de Flaundres 11 die Julii *[11 July 1446]*

De Johanne van Feld[b] pro 2 barellis saponis albi ponderantibus 1100 [c]lb.[c], 2 barellis saltpetre, dimidio barello gunne powdir[d], 1 barello drugery[e], 6 barellis saponis nigri, 12 barellis viniegre[f], 2 fattis de diversis druggery[g], 1 barello brymstone, 1 maunda, 1 parvo basketto vermylon, 1 barello plumbi rubei, 1 barello chalk nigri, 1 barello blew chalk[h], 1 fatto[i] bolles, 1 baletto[j] commyn[k], 4 balis madir[l], 80 lb. coperos[m], 12 lb. mastyk, 10 lb. spyknard[n]. Precii £46 13s 4d ....cust' 11s 8d

[a] Cornellii *L3.* [b] Veld *L3.* [c-c] *Omitted L3.* [d] pouder *L3.* [e] druggery *L3.* [f] vinegre *L3.* [g] drugery *L3.* [h] blwe chalke *L3.* [i] fatte *L3.* [j] balet *L3.* [k] comyn *L3.* [l] mader *L3.* [m] coporos *L3.* [n] spykenale *L3.*

<aa>-<aa> *Auditor's entry L1: Sum of the issues on the page.*

[98] De navi Johannis de la Flowre vocata Cristofor de Cane eodem die *[11 July 1446]*

De Colyn Inglesh[a] pro 160 quarteriis frumenti. Precii £10 2s 6d..... cust' 2s 6½d

[a] Ingeles *L3.*

[99] De navi [a]Roberti Saumson[a] vocata Katerin de Roone[b] 23 die Julii *[23 July 1446]*

De Nicholao Vavasour[c] pro 1 maunda cum 500 lb. enei[d] veteris. Precii £3 6s 8d ....cust' 10d

De Clement Basyn pro 120 quarteriis frumenti. Precii £20 .... cust' 5s

[a] Robyn Sawmson *L3.* [b] Rone *L1.* [c] Vasyner *L3.* [d] enen' *L3, in error.*

[100] De navi Gosson Petersson vocata Cristofor de Flyssyng[a] 28° die Julii *[28 July 1446]*

De eodem pro 100 cabelows[b], 150 sparres. Precii 40s ....cust' 6d

De Remond Vydale pro 9 balis alyminis[c]. Precii £12 .... cust' 3s

De Raphaelle de Ponsola[d] pro 4 buttes cum[e] pulvere pro pellibus. Precii 26s 8d ....cust' 4d

De Johanne Chircheyerd[f] pro 1 lasto saponis, 1 fatte, 1 pipa wod. Precii £17 .... cust' 4s 3d

De Adreano Scaper pro 10 wey salis de Berflete, 80 baskettis [g]vacuis[g]. Precii £10 6s 8d... cust' 2s 7d

[h]De Petro George pro 1000 pavyngtile magnis. Precii 20s .... cust' 3d[h]

De Johanne Armerer pro 1 bundello[i] gladiorum[j] veterum, 4 gladiis novis. Precii 26s 8d..cust' 4d

De Henrico Bett pro 4 balis madir[k]. Precii £8 .... cust' 2s

[a] Scluse *L3.* [b] pissibus salsis cabillons *L3.* [c] alm' *L3.* [d] Pounceter *L1.* [e] de *L3.* [f] Chercheyard *L3.* [g-g] *Omitted L3.* [h-h] *Peter* George*'s goods entered after those of John* Armerer *L3.* [i] bondell *L3.* [j] gladiys *L3.* [k] mader *L3.*

[101] De navi Deryk Baysson vocata [a]Magdalena de Ermoth[a] 28° die Julii *[28 July 1446]*

De eodem pro 1000 pavyngtile [b]magnis[b]. Precii 20s...............................cust' 3d

De Henrico Nase pro 100 skyve[c] tasilles. Precii 50s............................cust' 7½d

De Petro[d] Symon pro 1000 pavyngtile. Precii 20s ....cust' 3d

[a-a] Magdale van Ermouth *L3.* [b-b] *Omitted L1.* [c] skeve *L3.* [d] Ptro *L1, in error.*

<aa>34s 5d<aa>

E122/73/20A f. 18[v]

<z> *Auditor's marginated entry L1:* cera.

[102] De navi Clays Martynsson vocata Kateryn de Ermouth eodem die *[28 July 1446]*

[a]De Gerardo Bursse pro 3 cistis cum[a]

De Arnaldo[b] Adreanson[c] pro 2 saccis hoppes continentibus 6½ hodes, 1 copbord[d]. Precii 37s 6d....cust' 5¾d

De Willelmo Dames pro 100 puntellis[e] wold, 50 tasilles, 1 sacco canebis[f] ponderante[g] 250 [lb.], 100 warpp ollarum et patellarum terre, 1 basketto cum 50 distaves, 50 relles[h], 3 sadillz[i], 4 ketylles[j], 100 alnis tele lini grosse, 48 pelvys[k] et diverso haberdashe. Precii £8 .... cust' 2s

De eodem [l]magistro[l] pro 2000 pavyngtile, 4 pokes hoppes continentibus 8 hodes. Precii £4....cust' 12d

De Gyles Puchyn[m] pro 1 parvo basketto cum 12 dossenis cordwayne. Precii £3 10s....cust' 10½d

De Henrico van Oye pro 2 maundis, 1 parvo basketto, 1 barello, 1500 pectinibus[n] de ligno, 11 papir poyntes[o], 8 gros lasyng poyntes[o], 20 dyker[p] cultellorum, 8 dossenis felt hattes et diverso haberdashe. Precii £10 .... cust' 2s 6d

De Nicholao Petersson pro 1 hoggeshede cum 12 dossenis sporres, 16 dossenis pectinum[n] de ligno, 4 gros lasing poyntes[o] et diverso haberdashe. Precii £3 6s 8d....cust' 10d

De Arnaldo[b] van Bell pro 2 barellis cum 300 spyse cakys[q]. Precii 26s 8d ....cust' 4d

De Johanne Reyner pro 2 saccis hoppes continentibus 8 hodes. Precii 40s ....cust' 6d

De Johanne Henriksson pro 3 polaxes, 1 barello, 1 pipa cum 30 alnis tele lini Holandie, 2 fedir[r] beddes, 3 bolsterys[s], 12 ketilles[j], 1 mantello [t]de[t] gray. Precii £5 6s 8d....cust' 16d

De Gilys Braynford pro 3 saccis canebis[f] ponderantibus[u] 750 [lb.]. Precii £4 13s 4d....cust' 14d

De Johanne Plakker pro 2 saccis canebis[f] ponderantibus[u] 500 lb., 1 pipa cum 1[v] some [w]patyn nailles[w], 12 papir poyntes[o], 1 tabille[x] clothe, 150 alnis tele lini Holandie[y]. Precii £9 6s 8d.... cust' 2s 4d

De Petro Persson pro 2 corffes cum 24 dossenis thromme[z] hattes debilium. Precii £4....cust' 12d

[a-a] *Entry struck through L1, with* nichil, quia pro stauro *marginated against it.* [b] Arnoldo *L3.* [c] Adreansson *L3.* [d] cupbord *L3.* [e] pontellis *L3.* [f] canabis *L3.* [g] continente *L3.* [h] relic' *L1, in error.* [i] sadelles *L3.* [j] ketelles *L3.* [k] pelwis *L1.* [l] *Omitted L3.* [m] Powchyn *L3.* [n] pec' *L1.* [o] poyentes *L3.* [p] deker *L3.* [q] kakes *L3.* [r] fether *L3.* [s] bolstez *L1, surely in error.* [t-t] *Omitted L1.* [u] continentibus *L3.* [v] 1½ *L3.* [w-w] paten nayelles *L3.* [x] borde *L3.* [y] et diverso haberdashe *follows L3.* [z] thrummz *L3.*

<aa>-<aa> *Auditor's entry L1: Sum of the issues on the page.*

[103] De navi Lambe Johan Williamsson vocata Mariknygh de Ernemoth eodem die *[28 July 1446]*

De Imbright van Sassonhowsen pro 3 balis bokerams, 1 bala carde, 2 balis fustian, dimidio barello calibis, [a]2 barellis[a], 4 corffes cum 33 peciis tele lini [b]Holandie[b] continentibus 500 alnas, 4 gros knyvys, 12 bever hattes, 30 sherman sherys, 4 dossenis byttes, 8 somes clavorum, 40 dossenis hattes. Precii £98 13s 4d .... cust' 24s 8d

De Tilman Crome pro 1 pack fili Colonie continente 36 dossenas lb., 8 balis fustian. Precii £92 .... cust'[c] 23s

De Cristian Edilkynd[d] pro 3 barellis calibis. Precii £12 .... cust' 3s

De Lambert Gruter pro 2 balis fustian, 1 pack fili Colonie continente 30 dossenas lb. Precii £30 .... cust' 7s 6d

<aa>70s 6¼d<aa> [e]Item 2s[e]

E122/73/20A f. 19r

De[f] Johanne Chircheyard pro 5 fattis wod. Precii £10 .... cust' 2s 6d

De Johanne Hatiltak pro 8 balis madir[g], 1 corfe cum 18 peciis tele lini Busk continentibus 300 alnas. Precii £23 10s .... cust' 5s 10½d

De Gerlof van Berkenrode pro 2 balis madir[g], 7 pack fili Colonie continentibus 200 dossenas lb., 1 parvo barello cum 42 dossenis lb. fili Colonie. Precii £84 13s 4d .... cust' 21s 2d

De Lambert Joses pro 6 bashrunez, 2 fraillis, 1 pipa baterie[h], 5 baskettis cum 10 rippes cacaborum, 1 barello calamyne. Precii £97 10s .... cust' 24s 4½d

De Cristian van Bleken[i] pro 8 balis madir[g], 1 bala fustian, 33 saccis canebis[j] ponderantibus[k] 9600 [a]lb.[a], ½ rolla tele lini continente 200 alnas [b]Sultwyche[b], 1 corfe, 1 cista cum 23 dossenis felt hattes, 6 mantellis pellium popillorum, 160 alnis canvas grossi. Precii £96 6s 8d .... cust' 24s 1d

De Henrico Nase pro 3 maundis cum 16 dossenis felt hattes, 72 peciis tele lini [b]Holandie grosse[b]. Precii £80 .... cust' 20s

De Felice Favyan[l] pro 1 fardello cum 60 alnis[m] tele lini Holandie. Precii 33s 4d .... cust' 5d

De Willelmo Garedsson[n] pro 1 parvo corf, 2 balis madir[g] et 4 tykes[o], 60 alnis tele lini stricte, 400 lb. downe[p]. Precii £11 .... cust' 2s 9d

De Petro Cangheter pro ½ bala carde, 5 balis fustian, 3 pack fili Colonie continentibus 90 dossenas lb., [q]26 balis madir[g], dimidio pack cum 6 dimidiis balis carde[q]. Precii £188 .... cust' 47s

De Henrico Overbagh pro [r]8 balis madir[g], 6 pack fili Colonie continentibus 162 dossenas lb., 5 balis fustian[r]. Precii £120 .... cust' 30s

De dicto magistro pro 11 parvis mastis. Precii £3 6s 8d .... cust' 10d

De Henrico Brewer pro 3 lastis saponis, 4 balis fustian, 12 balis madir[g], 3 corfes, 1 barello, 1 parvo fardello cum 26 peciis tele lini continentibus 300 alnas Holandie, [s]20 dossenis parium linthiaminum[s], 500 alnis tele lini Brounswyke stricte, 5 peciis tele lini stricte continentibus 200 alnas, 34 peciis tele lini

<z> *Auditor's marginated entry L1:* cera.

Busk continentibus 1240 alnas, 12 dossenis gladiorum[t] et diverso haberdashe. Precii £153 13s 4d .... cust' 38s 5d
De Johanne Blitterswyk[u] pro 1 pack fili Colonie continente 28 dossenas lb., 1 bala carde, 1 parvo barello cum [a]100 alnis tele lini [v]et aliis[a] diversis mercandisis[v]. Precii £20 .... cust' 5s
De Matis Shonebagh pro 8 balis madir[g]. Precii £16 .... cust' 4s
De Johanne van Sibright[w] pro 3 pak fili Colonie continentibus 80 dossenas lb., ½ bala carde. Precii £34 13s 4d .... cust' 8s 8d

<aa>£11 15s 1d<aa>

E122/73/20A f. 19[v]

De Cornelio[x] Williamsson pro 40 ollis terre. Precii 3s 4d .... cust' ½d
De [y]Arnaldo van Pynxsten[y] pro 18 balis madir[g], 1 bala fustian. Precii £46 .... cust' 11s 6d
De Gerwyn Potte pro 9 pack fili Colonie continentibus 280[z] dossenas lb., 12 balis fustian, 9 dimidiis barellis calibis. Precii £246 .... cust' 61s 6d
De Bertram Questenbergh pro 10 balis madir[g], 2 pack fili Colonie continentibus 90 dossenas lb. Precii £43 6s 8d .... cust' 10s 10d
De Nicholao Swarte pro 8 balis fustian, 6 balis madir[g]. Precii £92 .... cust' 23s
De Hans Rynge pro 2 balis fustian. Precii £20 .... cust' 5s
De Hans Hope pro 8 balis madir[g], 7 balis fustian. Precii £86 .... cust' 21s 6d
De Godscalke[aa] Trente pro 1 bala fustian, 1 barello cum 3 dossenis palettes, 5 gardebras[ab], 2½ dossenis gloves et diverso haberdashe. Precii £13 . cust' 3s 3d
De Arnoldo Ofman[ac] pro 1 corfe cum 2 fedirbedes[ad] veteribus, 2 tykes[o], 1 dossena qwysshons[ae]. Precii 26s 8d .... cust' 4d
De Clement Symondsdoughter[af] pro 1 corfe cum 4 fedirbedes[ad], 1 bolster. Precii 53s 4d[ag] .... cust' 8d
De Johanne Salmer pro 3 fraillis, 7 bashrunez, 2 baskettis [a]batrie[a], 1 barello cupri[ah] rubei. Precii £98 .... cust' 24s 6d
De Frederigo Paradys pro 1 fatto, 1 barello cum 60 peciis tele lini Holandie cours continentibus 1200 alnas. Precii £36 .... cust' 9s
[ai]De Bowden[aj] Frende pro 6 pipis, 1 fatto wod, 1 pipa cum 2 basyns, 2 lavourz[ak], 24 alnis tele lini [b]brode[b], 2 fedirbedes[ad]. Precii £15 .... cust' 3s 9d
De Henrico van Asper pro 2 barellis cum 2 gros sporres, 1 gros lokes, 100 shepes[al] belles, 3 dossenis hamers et diverso haberdashe. Precii £4 10s .... cust' [am]13½d[am]
De Otte van Dorne pro 3 barellis cum 5 habirgeons[an], 20 merke[ao] sherys, 500 thymbylles et diverso haberdashe. Precii £7 18s 5d .... cust' [ap]2s[ap]
De Johanne Blitterswyk[u] pro 1 barello cum 2000 pellibus [b]et[b] 16 timbre fecheux, 2 timbre martrins[aq]. Precii £54 .... cust' 13s 6d
De Johanne Warenthorp pro 1 barello[ar] cum 80 alnis tele lini. Precii 50s .... cust' 7½d

<aa>£9 8s 4½d<aa> [as]Item 3s 9d[as]

<aa>-<aa> *Auditor's entry L1: Sum of the issues on the page.*

E122/73/20A f. 20[r]

De Jacobo Fermarysson[at] pro 1 hoggeshede cum 2 pelvibus, 1 qwylt[au], 1 panno depicto, 12 rollis pro capis[av]. Precii 20s ....cust' 3d

De Gilys Braynford pro 1 pipa cum 12 peciis tele lini Busk continentibus 260 alnas, 22[aw] salettes[ax], 1 gros lasyng poyntes[ay] et diverso haberdashe. Precii £4 ....cust' 12d

De Johanne Dasse pro 15 balis madir[g], 5 balis fustian, 1 barello, 2 parvis baskettis, 1 parvo fardello fili Colonie continentibus 48 dossenas lb. [a]et[a] 29 peciis tele lini continentibus 500 alnas, 15 dossenis gladiorum[t]. Precii £118 10s.. cust' 29s 7½d

[az]De Johanne van Sybright[ba] pro 3 pack fili Colonie continentibus 90 dossenas lb. Precii £30..cust' 7s 6d[az]

De Johanne Stokde pro 20 balis madir[g], 2 balis fustian, 2 pack fili [a]Colonie[a] continentibus 60 dossenas lb. Precii £80 ....cust' 20s

[a-a] *Omitted L3.* [b] *Omitted L1.* [c] 21s *follows, struck through L1.* [d] Edilkynt *L3.* [e-e] *Auditor's supplement necessitated by the correction of the customs charge for the goods of* Tilman Crome *L1.* [f] Lambe *follows, struck through L1.* [g] mader *L3.* [h] batrie *L1,* batry *L3.* [i] Bleyken *L3.* [j] canabis *L3.* [k] continentibus *L3.* [l] Fauvean *L3.* [m] alnis *repeated L1, in error.* [n] Gareddesson *L3.* [o] tekes *L3.* [p] doune *L1.* [q-q] ½ pack cum 6 dimidiis balis carde, 26 balis madir *L3.* [r-r] 6 pack fili Colonie continentibus 162 dossenas lb., 5 balis fustian, 8 balis madir *L3.* [s-s] 10 dossenis payr shetes *L3.* [t] swerdes *L3.* [u] Blitersweke *L3.* [v-v] *Interlined L1.* [w] Sybrygh *L3.* [x] Cornellio *L3.* [y-y] Arnoldo van Pxnxsten *L3, surname in error.* [z] 290 *L3.* [aa] Godys Scalke *L3.* [ab] gardbras *L1.* [ac] Offman *L3.* [ad] fetherbeddes *L3.* [ae] quyssons *L3.* [af] Simondysdofter *L3.* [ag] 8d *L3.* [ah] copre *L3.* [ai] pro precio + *[cross] marginated against this entry and struck through L1.* [aj] Bowdewyn *L3.* [ak] lavours *L3.* [al] shepys *L3.* [am-am] *Interlined above* 12¾d, *struck through L1.* [an] habergeynys *L3.* [ao] marke *L3.* [ap-ap] *Interlined above* 23¾d, *struck through L1.* [aq] marterons *L3.* [ar] parvo fardello *L3.* [as-as] *Auditor's supplement necessitated by the fact that the goods of* Bowden Frende *were initially overlooked in the calculations L1.* [at] Firmarysson *L3.* [au] quylt *L3.* [av] capus' *L1.* [aw] sadill *follows, struck through L1.* [ax] sadelles *L3.* [ay] poyentes *L3.* [az-az] *Johann* van Sybright*'s goods were entered between those of* Hans Hope *and* Godscalke Trente *L3.* [ba] Sibrygh *L3.*

[104] De navi Johannis Henriksson vocata le [a]Swanne de Ermoth[a] eodem die *[28 July 1446]*

De Arnaldo[b] Claysson pro 1½ lastis dogstones[c], 2000 pavyngstone, 1000 crusys[d], 40 skyve[e] tasilles, 100 sparres, 3 saccis hoppes continentibus 7 hodes, 1 barello cum 10 dossenis compayse[f]. Precii £6 13s 4d ....cust' 20d

[g]De Petro Johansson pro 2 barellis beere. Precii [h]6s 8d[h] ....cust' 1d

[g]De Johanne Grene pro 1 basketto cum 4 dossenis [i]strawe hattes[i]. Precii 10s ....cust' 1½d

<z> *Auditor's marginated entry L1:* cera.

[g]De Johanne Reyner pro 1 cista cum 130 alnis tele lini Ostred[j]. Precii 50s ....cust' 7½d

[a-a] Swan de Ermouth *L3.* [b] Arnoldo *L3.* [c] doggestone *L3.* [d] cruses *L3.* [e] skeve *L3.* [f] compas *L3.* [g] *These three entries in the order* Grene, Reyner, Johansson *L3.* [h-h] *Struck through L3.* stet *interlined above.* [i-i] hattes straminis debilibus *L3.* [j] Austrett' *L3.*

[105] De navi Johannis Cole vocata Cristofor de Andwarp[a] eodem die *[28 July 1446]*

De eodem pro 2500 pavyngstone, 100 ollis et patellis terre. Precii 45s ....cust' 6¾d

De Willelmo Spyker pro 3 maundis cum 38 fase[b] vitri[c]. Precii 40s ....cust' 6d

De Henrico Hode pro[d] 2 saccis canebis ponderantibus[e] 500 lb., [f]1 pack cum[f] 58 coverlettes Flandrie, 8 dossenis qwyshen[g] clothes, 3 bankers. Precii £18 13s 4d ....cust' 4s 8d

De Johanne van Dyke pro 4 saccis hoppes continentibus 10 hodes, 3 saccis canebis[h] continentibus 300 [i]lb.[i]. Precii £8 10s..............................cust' 2s 1½d

<aa>68s 8¾d<aa>

E122/73/20A f. 20[v]

De Johanne Dasse pro 100 skyve[j] tasilles, 1 cupbord, 1 roundtabil[k], 1 baga[l] cum[m] plumis. Precii 40s ....cust' 6d

De Johanne Hatiltak pro 3 balis madir[n], 1 fardello plumarum, 14 cistis vitri. Precii £12 ....cust' 3s

De Hans Hope pro 5 barellis saponis. Precii £3 6s 8d...........................cust' 10d

De Giles Braynford pro 3 saccis hoppes continentibus 9 hodes, 3 saccis canebis[h] continentibus 750 [lb.], 1 bundello cum 18 polaxes, 1 bundello cum 12 sarris[o], 21 skyve[j] tasilles. Precii £8 3s 4d....................................... cust' 2s ½d

De [p]Imbright van Sassonhowssen[p] pro 3 tabulis[q] pro altare. Precii 40s ...cust' 6d

De Henrico van Openhayn[r] pro 1 barello, 1 parvo barello cum 1 sadille[s], 3 dossenis calendres[t], 16 clowte nedilles, 1 gros spectacles[u], 9 dossenis lokkes, 2 dossenis hamers, 12 gros alle yrens, 8 lb. gete, 1 dossena pawteners[v] et diverso haberdashe. Precii £6 13s 4d ....cust' 20d

De Henrico van Assper[w] pro 1 basketto cum 3 kettiles[x], 2 dossenis rough[y] hattes[z]. Precii 33s 4d ....cust' 5d

De Willelmo Bokham[aa] pro 1 basketto cum 2 fedirbedes[ab], 5[ac] hebergeonz[ad] debilibus, 18 swerdes debilibus, [i]2 dossenis hamers[i] et diverso haberdashe. Precii £3 .... cust'[ae] 9d

De Johanne Henriksson pro 2 barellis saponis, 1 maunda cum 6 dossenis felt hattes. Precii[af] 53s 4d ....cust' 8d

De Otte van Dorne pro 2 barellis cum 8 lb. nailles, 3 gros sporres, 2 dossenis merkyng[ag] yrens, 7 dossenis tabillarum[q] et diverso haberdashe. Precii £5 10s ....cust' 16½d

<aa>-<aa> *Auditor's entry L1: Sum of the issues on the page.*

De Francisco Henriksson pro 1 bala pectinum[ah] de ligno, 1 pipa, 1 maunda cum 24 dossenis sporres, 12 dossenis daggers, 2 [ai]paribus balaunces[ai], 18 [aj]parvis saccis belles[aj], 15 dossenis felt hattes et diverso haberdashe. Precii £14 .... cust' 3s 6d

[a] Andewarp *L3.* [b] fasse *L3.* [c] et botelles *follows L3.* [d] 1 packe *follows L3.* [e] continentibus *L3.* [f-f] *Omitted L3.* [g] cosseyn *L3.* [h] canabis *L3.* [i-i] *Omitted L1.* [j] skeve *L3.* [k] roundtabelle *L3.* [l] bagge *L3.* [m] cum *repeated L1, in error.* [n] mader *L3.* [o] sawes *L3.* [p-p] Ingilbrygh van Sassonhowson *L3.* [q] tabell' *L3.* [r] Uppon Hayn *L3, in error.* [s] sadelle cum *L3.* [t] calenders *L3.* [u] spectakelles *L3.* [v] pawteneris *L3.* [w] Asper *L3.* [x] ketelles *L3.* [y] roug *L1.* [z] et diverso haberdashe *follows L3.* [aa] Bokeham *L3.* [ab] fetherbeddes *L3.* [ac] heberieg *follows, struck through L1.* [ad] habergeynys *L3.* [ae] 3 *follows, struck through L1.* [af] 30 *follows, struck through L1.* [ag] merkyn *L3.* [ah] cum pectinibus *L3.* [ai-ai] payr balons *L3.* [aj-aj] saccis parv' ketelles *L3.*

[106] De navi Johannis Cole [a]senioris[a] vocata [b]Crokenbrowe de Andwerp[b] 29 die Julii *[29 July 1446]*

De Otte van Dorne pro 2 barellis cum 7 gros paternosters[c], 200 alle haftes, 2 gros lokkes, 4 dossenis compases[d] et diverso haberdashe. Precii £6 11s 8d .... cust' 19¾d

De Johanne Hatiltak pro 2 lastis saponis, 3 balis madir[e]. Precii £22... cust' 5s 6d

<aa>22s 4¾d<aa>

E122/73/20A f. 21r

De Henrico van Asper pro 40 lb. bristilles, 8 [f]lb.[f] gete bedes, 1 gros rasourz[g], 3 dossenis tabillarum[h] et diverso haberdashe. Precii £3 16s 8d .... cust' 11½d

De Georgio Johansson pro 1 barello cum 200 thymbilles, 12 lb. here, 6 dossenis lokkes, 1 dossena pennes[i] et diverso haberdashe. Precii 26s 8d.... cust' 4d

De Godscalk[j] Trente pro 1 scok dowbill[k], 1 bundello[l] [f]cum[f] 18 swerd blades, 1 barello cum 2 paribus[m] coras, 1 dossena palettes, 6 vyser[n], 8 paribus[m] vambrase, 7 gardebrase, 4 paribus[m] legharnes[o] et diverso haberdashe. Precii £8 .... cust' 2s

De [p]Matys Shonebagh[p] pro 1 lasto saponis, 5 balis madir[e], 1 parvo basketto cum 50 alnis tele lini Holandie, 1 federbed[q]. Precii 40s .... cust' 6d

De Henrico Brewer pro 11 bundellis[r] dobille[s]. Precii £3 6s 8d .... cust' 10d

De Gyles Braynford pro 3 bundellis[r] [f]cum[f] 3 dossenis swerd blades, 18 pollaxes, 12 sarris[t], [u]3 saccis canebis continentibus 500 [lb.], 3 saccis hoppes continentibus 9 hodes[u]. Precii £3 .... cust' 9d

De Gerlof van Berkenrode pro 6 balis madir[e]. Precii £12 .... cust' 3s

De Johanne van Dorne pro 6 balis madir[e]. Precii £12 .... cust' 3s

De Johanne Henriksson pro 600 pavyngstone, 200 ollis et patellis terre, 1 barello cum 4 mantellis[v] fecheux, 1 mantello bevere, 2 mantellis boge[w]. Precii £5 .... cust' 15d

<z> *Auditor's marginated entry L1:* cera.

De Johanne van Dyke pro 5 saccis hoppes continentibus 15 hodes. Precii £4 ....cust' 12d

[x]De Bowdyn[y] Spynall pro[z] 2 fardellis cum 1200 alnis canvas albi. Precii £12 ....cust' 3s

[a] *Omitted L1.* [b-b] Kronebrowe de Andewarp *L3.* [c] p[a]p *L1,* p[a]pis *L3.* [d] compas *L3.* [e] mader *L3.* [f-f] *Omitted L3.* [g] rasours *L3.* [h] tabell' *L3.* [i] pennys *L3.* [j] Godis Skalk *L3.* [k] duble *L3.* [l] bondelle *L3.* [m] peyre *L3.* [n] fesor *L3.* [o] lagharneys *L3.* [p-p] Mattis Shonebawgh *L3.* [q] fetherbedd *L3.* [r] boundelles *L3.* [s] doll' *L3.* [t] sawys *L3.* [u-u] 3 saccis hoppes continentibus 9 hodes, 3 saccis canabis continentibus 500 [lb.] *L3.* [v] matellis *L1, in error.* [w] boche *L3.* [x] * *[cross] marginated against this entry and struck through L1.* [y] Bowdewyn *L3.* [z] parvis *follows L3.*

[107] De navi Lambe Haynsson vocata Mariknyght[a] de[b] London' primo die Augusti *[1 Aug. 1446]*

De eodem pro 12,000 brekestone[c]. Precii 25s ....cust' 3¾d

[a] Mariknyth *L3.* [b] de *repeated L1, in error.* [c] brekstone *L3.*

[108] De navi [a]Jacobi Ernest[a] vocata Holigost de Dansk 6° die Augusti *[6 Aug. 1446]*

De eodem pro 350 clapholt, 1 parvo pack cum 14 tymbre skevens[b]. Precii £4 ....cust' 12d

<aa>17s 11¼d<aa>

E122/73/20A f. 21[v]

De Jacobo Clotte[c] pro 1 lasto candilyarn[d], ½ lasto lini, 1 lasto osmond, 11 barellis tarre, 4 barellis piccis, 4 ferthkynz[e] sturgeon, 1 scok treis, 1 [f]scok parvorum[f] treis, 1 dossena tabillarum pro sutoribus, 1 quarterio lini, 3 scok sebuttes, 1 [g]lanterna magna[g], 1 scok bastes, 2 barellis beere, 2 countourz, 8 cistis cum 120 lb. fili Prucie, 50 alnis tele lini stricte, 10 balis lini, ½ scok syphis[h], 1 scok trenchours, 6 bursis, 13 pellibus Prucie, 48 wyndyng, 6 paribus[i] cerotecarum[j], 8 scok trenchours, 8 Pruce[k] coffirres[l], 16 balis lini, 10 alnis[m] canvas, 50 alnis tele lini, 4 peciis wyndyng, 24 [n]fyshyng lynes[n]. Precii £15 5s 2d..cust' 3s 9¾d

<z>Et pro [o]40 lb. cere[o] ....cust' 3¾d

De [p]Poulo Neyman[p] pro 7 pack lini, 7 barellis piccis, 2½ scok treis, 15 cistis, 1 barello cum 600 lb. fili Prucie, 7 timbre skevens, 1 pelle martrin, 2 scok sebuttes[q]. Precii £25 18s 4d...cust' 6s 5¾d

<z>Et pro [r]3 quintallis cere[r] ....cust' 3s

De Fyk Cleyvyng pro 1 lasto tarre, 20 bundellis[s] fili Prucie, ½ scok treis, 2½ dossenis tabillarum pro sutoribus, 22 balis lini, 21 scok trenchourz[t], 21 alnis tele lini, 1 dossena lutes[u], 12 ores, 1½ scok merlyng, 2 countourz[v], 6 cistis. Precii £10 3s 4d ....cust' 2s 6½d

<aa>-<aa> *Auditor's entry L1: Sum of the issues on the page.*

De Michaelle[w] Routhe pro 1 lasto lini, 4 barellis tarre, 3 cistis cum 15 balis lini, 200 lb. fili Prucie, 160 alnis canvas stricti, 3 scok trenchours, 7 piperquerens[x]. Precii £6 .... cust' 18d

De Benedicto Howsank pro ½ lasto lini, 7 barellis tarre, 4 barellis beere, 1 countour, 3 cistis [y]cum[y] 5 timbre letowes[z], ½ timbre ermyns, 40 piperquerens[x], 100 lb. fili Prucie, 7 scok trenchours, 6 Prucie forceriis. Precii £12 2s 10d .... cust' 3s ½d

De Hans Dorhem[aa] pro 3 pack [y]cum[y] 10 scok trenchours, 1 cista cum 17 tymbre skevens, 8 pellibus fecheux, 1 pelle martrin, 600 lb. fili Prucie, 500 alnis canvas stricti, ½ lasto candilyarn[d], ½ lasto lini. Precii £17 13s 4d .. cust' 4s 5d

De Hans Froskill[ab] pro 1½ lastis lini, 1 pack candilyarn[d], 1[ac] scok tabillarum pro sutoribus, 2 scok treis, 2½ scok sebuttes[q], 8 nest cofres, 1 barello[ad], 4 cistis cum 2 pellibus bever, 14 pellibus martrins, 6 pellibus fecheux, 3 timbre skevens, 700 lb. fili Prucie, 22 alnis tele [ae]lini[ae] canvas. Precii £21 6s 8d .... cust' 5s 4d

<aa>30s 5¼d<aa>

E122/73/20A f. 22r

De Nicholao Fosse pro 10 lastis cinerum, 1000 waynscottes, 1 lasto piccis, 1 lasto tarre, 100 clapholt, 100 ores, 2½ lastis lini, 1 pack candilyarn[d], 3½ barellis sturgeon, 1 barello samonis, 3 pack [af]canvas continentibus 3000 alnas[af], 2 barellis, 6 cistis cum 2 bundellis[s] fili Prucie ponderantibus[ag] 20 lb.[ad], 60 lb. lini. Precii £81 5s .... cust' 20s 3¾d

De Bertram Questenbergh[ah] pro 7 lastis lini, 9 barellis cupri rubei. Precii £46 .... cust' 11s 6d

De Elys Wynter pro 600 bowstaves wrak[ai], 9 barellis copros[aj]. Precii £9 .... cust' 2s 3d

De Bertram Sleighter[ak] pro 13 balis lini, 12 barellis cupri rubei, 1 cista cum 3 timbre trones[al], 7 balis lini, 1 barello cum 21½[am] timbre pellium martrin. Precii £41 15s .... cust' 10s [an]5¼d[an]

<z>Et pro 1 rolla cere ponderante 5 quintallos .... cust' 5s

De Cristian van Bleken pro 200 ores, 15 barellis cinerum, [ao]2 cistis[ao]. Precii £3 5s .... cust' 9¾d

De Hans Scoyte pro 1 lasto tarre, 50 ores, 1 lasto cinerum, 2 cistis cum 10 balis lini, 1 bundello[ap] fili Prucie ponderante[aq] 12 lb., 4 platterz depictis, 5 scok trenchours. Precii £3 12s 6d .... cust' 10¾d

De Hans Rynge pro 1 pack canvas continente 800 alnas, 5 peciis cupri rubei ponderantibus[ar] 150 lb., 1 barello cum 7 timbre bever wombz, 9 timbre pellium martrin, 1000 [et] 3 tymbre pellium calabrorum. Precii £29 ... cust' 7s 3d

De Matys[as] Sprynghorn pro 3½ lastis lini, 1 lasto candilyarn[d], 2 pack [at]cum 2000 alnis canvas grossi[at]. Precii £38 .... cust' 9s 6d

<z>Et pro 2 strawe cere ponderantibus[ar] 12 quintallos .... cust' 12s

<z>De Johanne Warenthorp[au] pro 1 strawe cere ponderante 6 quintallos .. cust' 6s

<z> *Auditor's marginated entry L1:* cera.

De Johanne Dasse pro 2 pack canvas continentibus 1800 alnas. Precii £18 .... cust' 4s 6d

De Michaele[av] Clawe pro 2 cistis cum 100 alnis canvas, 2 balis lini. Precii 40s ....cust' 6d

[a-a] James Ernyst *L3.* [b] skevewenys *L3.* [c] Clote *L3.* [d] candilgarn *L3.* [e] ferdekyns *L3.* [f-f] parvorum scoke *L3.* [g-g] magna lanterna *L3.* [h] chiphis *L3.* [i] payre *L3.* [j] ceros *L3.* [k] Prus *L3.* [l] cofferes *L3.* [m] tele lini *follows L3.* [n-n] fyssyng lynys *L3.* [o] cere precii *[sic]* 40 lb. *L3.* [p-p] Poullo Nyenman *L1.* [q] sepbuttes *L3.* [r-r] cere 3 quintallos *L3.* [s] boundelles *L3.* [t] trenchours *L3.* [u] luttes *L3.* [v] cuntours *L3.* [w] Mychelle *L3.* [x] peper quernys *L3.* [y] *Omitted L3.* [z] letowys *L3.* [aa] Dorn Heyn *L3.* [ab] Froskell *L3.* [ac] ½ *L3.* [ad] cum *follows L3.* [ae] *Omitted L1.* [af-af] continentibus 3000 alnas canvas *L3.* [ag] continentibus *L3.* [ah] Questenberght *L3.* [ai] warke *L3, in error.* [aj] cuper ros *L3.* [ak] Slegheter *L3.* [al] trownes *L3.* [am] 11½ *L3.* [an-an] *Interlined above* 4¾d, *struck through L1.* [ao-ao] *Interlined L1.* [ap] boundelle *L3.* [aq] continente *L3.* [ar] continentibus *L3.* [as] Mattis *L3.* [at-at] tele lini continentibus 2000 alnas [canva]s grossi *L3.* [au] Warynthorp *L3.* [av] Michelle *L3.*

[109] De navi Johannis[a] de Castello vocata Seint John de Sabastian[b] sexto die Augusti *[6 Aug. 1446]*

De Johanne de Vermell pro 6 doliis ponderis ferri. Precii £15 .... cust' 3s 9d

<aa>£4 14s [c]8½d[c]<aa>

E122/73/20A f. 22[v]

De Cristian Bartilmewe[d] pro 2 doliis ponderis ferri. Precii £5 6s 8d .....cust' 16d

De Domingo Dago pro 1 dolio, [e]3 hoggeshedes[e] ponderis ferri. Precii £4 10s ....cust' 13½d

De Martyn Dayo pro 3 hoggeshedes ponderis ferri. Precii 37s 6d........cust' 5¾d

De Lopp de Ryale[f] pro 8 barellis clavorum. Precii £3 6s 8d ....cust' 10d

De Johanne de Getaria pro 7 doliis [e]ponderis[e] ferri. Precii £17 10s. cust' 4s 4½d

De Roderigo [e]de[e] Vermewe pro 1 dolio [e]ponderis[e] ferri. Precii 50s ......cust' 7½d

[a] Johanne *L3, in error.* [b] Cebastyan *L3.* [c-c] *Interlined above 7¾d, struck through L1 (change necessitated by the correction of the customs charges on the goods of* Bertram Sleighter*)..* [d] Bertilmewe *L3.* [e-e] *Omitted L3.* [f] Riolo *L3.*

[110] De navi Johannis Scopp vocata George de London' 6 die Augusti *[6 Aug. 1446]*

De Bertram Sleighter[a] pro 200 ores, 3 pack lini, 1 barello cum 1000 pellibus popillorum, 1000 pellibus lettowark[b], 1½ timbre bever wombz. Precii £15 .... cust' 3s 9d

<z>Et pro 4 strawe cere ponderantibus[c] 28 quintallos .... cust' 28s

De Matys[d] Sprynghorn pro 1 barello cum 1000 [e]pellibus[e] lettowark[f], 1000 pellibus popillorum. Precii 40s ....cust' 6d

<aa>-<aa> *Auditor's entry L1: Sum of the issues on the page.*

<z>De Johanne Warenthorp[g] pro 1 strawe cere ponderante[h] 6 quintallos .. cust' 6s

[a] Sleghter *L3.* [b] letow *L3.* [c] continentibus *L3.* [d] Mattis *L3.* [e] *Omitted L3.* [f] letowe werke *L3.* [g] Waryngthorp *L3.* [h] continente *L3.*

[111] De navi Clement Edward[a] vocata Margaret[b] de Newport 9 die Augusti *[9 Aug. 1446]*

De eodem pro 14,000 brekstone[c]. Precii 26s 8d..cust' 4d

[a] Everard *L3.* [b] Margerete *L3.* [c] albis *follows L3.*

[112] De navi Peryn Obard[a] vocata Jonett de Cane 16 die Augusti *[16 Aug. 1446]*

De Johanne Pycard[b] pro 14 mews[c] frumenti. Precii £10 10s............cust' 2s 7½d

De dicto magistro pro 2 saccis carde continentibus[d] 10[e] dossenas [carde] veteris[f], 1 pipa cum 12 dossenis carde veteris, 1 fardello [g]cum 200 alnis canvas[g], 1 parva pecia tele lini continente 15 alnas. Precii £6 8s 4d..............cust' 19¼d

[a] Oberd *L3.* [b] Pecard *L3.* [c] mewes *L3.* [d] cum *L3.* [e] *Corrected in L1 from* 15 *by erasure.* [f] parium *L1, surely in error.* [g-g] parvo canvas continente 200 alnas *L3.*

[113] De navi Robyn Martynvyle vocata Katerin[a] de Cane eodem die *[16 Aug. 1446]*

De Ricardo Pycard pro 12 mews[b] frumenti, 1 fardello [c]cum 450 alnis canvas[c], 4 barellis brasse veteris, 1 fardello [d]cum 9 dossenis cordewayn[d]. Precii £12 11s 8d..cust' 3s [e]1½d[e]

<aa>54s [f]8½d[f]<aa>

[a] Catelyn *L3.* [b] mewes *L3.* [c-c] canvas 450 aln' *L3.* [d-d] cordewayn continente 9 dossenas *L3.* [e-e] *Interlined above* 1¼d, *struck through L1.* [f-f] *Corrected in L1 from* 3½d *(correction necessitated initially by errors in adding up the (incorrect) figures and then by the correction of the customs charge for the goods of Richard* Pycard*).*

E122/73/20A f. 23r

[114] De navi Clays Rutersson[a] vocata [b]Mariknight de Scluse[b] 29 die Augusti *[29 Aug. 1446]*

[c]De Remond Vydale pro 8 barellis sugre, 6 balis almundes[d]. Precii £46 13s 4d ....cust' 11s 8d

De Raphaelle de Aurea pro 30 balis madir[e]. Precii £60 ....cust' 15s

De Johanne Warenthorp pro 2 lastis saponis. Precii £16 ....cust' 4s

[a] Rotkerson *L3.* [b-b] Mariknyth de Skluce *L3.* [c] pro precio + *[cross] marginated against this entry and struck through L1.* [d] almondes *L3.* [e] mader *L3.*

<z> *Auditor's marginated entry L1:* cera.

[115] De navi Johannis Hartilby[a] vocata [b]Maryknyght de Danske[b] eodem die *[29 Aug. 1446]*

De Hans Rynge pro 1400 fungiis. Precii £5 12s ....cust' 17d
De [c]Godard van[c] Aspen pro 400 fungiis. Precii 33s 4d............................cust' 5d

[a] Hartilly *L3.* [b] Mariknygh van Danske *L3.* [c] Goderd gan *L3, in error.*

[116] De navi Jacobi Gerrardsson[a] vocata [b]Plak Rose de Holandia[b] eodem die *[29 Aug. 1446]*

De eodem pro 6000 breke [c]stone[c] rubeis[d], 150 warp ollarum et patellarum terre[c-e]. Precii 25s ....cust' 3¾d
De Leonardo van Werde pro [f]2 barellis cum 2 dossenis[g] thrume[h] hattis, 2 dossenis[g] shetylles, 24 alnis tele lini, 5 dossenis[g] zonarum de coreo et diverso haberdashe. Precii 66s 8d ....cust' 10d[f]
De [i]Michaelle Wyssell[i] pro 1 fatto wod. Precii [f]60s................................cust' 9d[f]
De Martyno van de Crosse pro 3 saccis canebis[j] continentibus 800 [k]lb.[k], 5 skyve[l] tasilles, 1 sacco cum 20 lb. packfili[m]. Precii £5 10s ....cust' 16½d
De Willelmo Dames pro 2 saccis hoppes continentibus 10½ hodes, 1 copbord[d], 1 barello cum 18 Yperlyng. Precii £3 6s 8d.......................................cust' 10d
De Hans van Guluk pro dimidio barello cum 5 peciis tele lini Holandie continentibus 80 alnas. Precii £3 ....cust' 9d
De Henrico van Calker pro 1 cista cum 8 alnis tele lini. Precii 6s 8d ......cust' 1d

[a] Gerrardesson *L3.* [b-b] Plokke Rose de Holon' *L3.* [c] *Omitted L1.* [d] et *follows L3.* [e] 6000 brekstone *follows L1.* [f-f] *Entered by a different hand L1.* [g] dussenis *L1.* [h] thrummz *L3.* [i-i] Marcell Wyswyll *L3.* [j] canabis *L3.* [k] *Omitted L3.* [l] skeve *L3.* [m] yarn pack *L3.*

[117] De navi Cornelii[a] Floresson vocata Mariknyght[b] de Stanby eodem die *[29 Aug. 1446]*

De Jacobo Gerrardsson[c] pro 18,500 brekestone. Precii 35s ....cust' 5¼d

[a] Cornellii *L3.* [b] Mariknyth *L3.* [c] Garrardesson *L3.*

<aa>37s 10½d<aa>

[a]Examinatur cum particulis contrarotulatoris[a]

[a-a] *Auditor's entry, marginated L1. Auditor's entry* Examinatur cum particulis custumariorum *L3.*

E122/73/20A f. 23[v]

Summa totalis hujus libri	Valor mercandisarum alienigenarum, unde 3d de libra	£13,858 19s 8d	cust' £173 5s 2½d
	Quintallorum cere	269 quintalli 68 lb.	cust' £13 9s 7¾d

Summa totalis recepte hujus libri conjuncta £186 14s 10¼d

<aa>-<aa> *Auditor's entry L1: Sum of the issues on the page.*

EXPORTS

E122/73/20B f. 1^{r}
[Marginated] London'

L2

[a]Adhuc particule compoti Johannis Melbourne et Willelmi Chattok collectorum parve custume regis in portu civitatis London' etc., videlicet de hujusmodi custuma regis ibidem a 26to die Januarii anno 24to regis nunc Henrici vj^{ti} *[26 Jan. 1446]* usque festum sancti Michaelis proximum sequens etc. *[29 Sept. 1446]*.

L3

Adhuc contrarotulum Johannis Cotford contrarotulatoris parve custume domini regis in portu London', videlicet a 26° die Januarii anno 24° Henrici vj^{ti} *[26 Jan. 1446]* usque festum sancti Michaelis archangeli anno Henrici Sexti 25to *[29 Sept. 1446]*.

[a] *Preceded by* Tempore Johannis Melborne et Willelmi Chattok collectorum parve custume anno Henrici 24°, *entered in the upper right-hand corner of the page L2.*

[118] In navi Francisci de Bercus[a] vocata Seynt Spirit de Bajona 27 die Januarii *[27 Jan. 1446]*

<a>De Thoma Countys pro 2 fardellis cum [b]36 peciis kersey continentibus 12 pannos, 6 dossenis caparum de kendal de diverso colore continencium 1 pannum curtum sine grano
Et pro 9 ulnis panni largi sine grano[b] .... Ind' cust' 15s 7¼d
<a>De Bonefacio[c] Burnell pro 1 [d]parvo[d] fardello cum 2 pannis, 22 ulnis curtis sine grano .... Ind' cust' 3s 5d
<a>De Thoma Coke pro 1 bala cum 23 pannis, 18 ulnis curtis sine grano .... Ind' cust' 27s 8½d

[a] Barcus *L3.* [b-b] 13 pannis, 9 ulnis curtis sine grano *L2.* [c] Bonefaco *L3.* [d] *Omitted L2.*

<aa>46s 8¾d<aa>

E122/73/20B f. 1^{v}

[119] In navi Arnoldi de Nawte vocata Julyan de Bajona eodem die *[27 Jan. 1446]*

<a>De Willelmo Overey pro 1 bala cum [a]21 peciis kersey, 18 dossenis [panni] stricti continentibus 11½ pannos curtos[a] sine grano .... Ind' cust' 13s 5d

<a>De Willelmo Kerver pro 2 fardellis cum 16 pannis curtis sine grano .... Ind' cust' 18s 8d

<b>Et pro 15 ulnis panni largi de dimidio grano .... Ind' cust' 13d

<a>De Johanne Reynkyn[b] pro 1 bala cum 12 pannis, 6 ulnis curtis sine grano .... Ind' cust' 14s 3½d

[a-a] 11½ pannis curtis *L2.* [b] Reynken *L3.*

[120] In navi Johannis Clynke vocata Maria[a] de Calesia [b]exeunte[b] eodem die *[27 Jan. 1446]*

<a>De Willelmo Holand pro 1 fardello cum 2 pannis, 18 ulnis curtis sine grano .... Ind' cust' 3s 2½d

<b>Et pro 3 quarteriis ulne panni largi de dimidio grano .... Ind' cust' ¾d

<c>Et pro dimidia ulna panni largi de scarlet .... Ind' cust' ¾d

[a] de *follows, struck through L2.* [b] *Omitted L2.*

[121] In navi Nicholai Wander vocata Nicholaus de Asshe [a]versus Plumouth carcata 29° die Januarii[a] et ibidem ad recarcandum in quadam vas[a][b] exeunte versus Portugaliam *[29 Jan. 1446]*

<d>De Johanne Alfouns[c] pro 1 fardello cum 10 pannis curtis sine grano .... Al' cust' 27s 6d

<a>De Petro Alfold[d] pro 1 fardello cum 5 pannis curtis sine grano .... Ind' cust' 5s 10d

[a-a] 29° die Januarii versus Plumouth carcata *L3.* [b] navi *L3.* [c] Alfons *L3.* [d] Alffold *L3.*

<aa>£4 4s 1½d<aa>

E122/73/20B f. 2^{r}

[122] In navi Willelmi Bawdewyn[a] vocata Jesus de London' [b]exeunte[b] ultimo die Januarii *[31 Jan. 1446]*

<a>De Bertram de la Greyra[c] pro 1 fardello cum 4 pannis, 8 ulnis curtis sine grano .... Ind' cust' 5s ¾d

<b>Et pro 2½ ulnis panni largi de dimidio grano .... Ind' cust' 2¼d

<c>Et pro 1 ulna panni largi de scarlet[d] .... Ind' cust' 1¼d

Auditor's marginated entries L2: <a> pannus indigenus <b> pannus de dimidio grano indigenus <c> scarleta indigena <d> pannus alienigenus <e> pannus de dimidio grano alienigenus <f> scarleta alienigena <g> pannus hanse <h> pannus de dimidio grano hanse <i> scarleta hanse

<a>De Ricardo Perepount[e] pro 1 bala cum 20 pannis curtis sine grano ... Ind' cust' 23s 4d

<a>De Petro Mapertuce pro 1 fardello cum 1 panno, 11 ulnis curtis sine grano ... Ind' cust' 20½d

<a>De Johanne Steell pro 2 fardellis, 1 pipa cum 14 pannis, 20 ulnis curtis sine grano ... Ind' cust' 17s 3¾d

<a>De [b]dicto[b] Ricardo Perepount pro 1 fardello cum 3 pannis, 16 ulnis curtis sine grano ... Ind' cust' 4s 3½d

<a>De Willelmo Bodvyle[f] pro 1 fardello cum 3 pannis, 8 ulnis curtis sine grano ... Ind' cust' 3s 10¾d

<a>De Johanne Carpenter pro 1 fardello cum 6 pannis, 16 ulnis curtis sine grano ... Ind' cust' 7s 9½d[g]

<a>De Roberto Edolfe pro 1 fardello cum 2½ pannis curtis sine grano ... Ind' cust' 2s 11d

[a] Baudewyn *L3.* [b] *Omitted L3.* [c] Crayra *L3.* [d] scharlett *L3.* [e] Perpount *L3.* [f] Bodevyle *L3.* [g] Require postea in principio secundi rotuli sequentis *marginated beneath the entry for John* Carpenter *L3. There (m 14), under the heading* Adhuc in navi Willelmi Bawdewyn, *the exports of* Perpoynt, Bodevyle *and* Edolfe *are entered.*

[123] In navi Petri Georgesson vocata Cristofor de Scluce 5° die Februarii *[5 Feb. 1446]*

De Johanne de Jake pro 30 balis licoricie. Precii £5 ... cust' 15d

[124] In navi Johannis Corteroke[a] vocata Leonard de Bergh[b] 15° die Februarii *[15 Feb. 1446]*

[c]De Gerardo[d] Johansson pro 2 fodris, 228 lb. plumbi, 30 deker [e]de[e] parvis peciis scissis de ventribus vaccarum tannatis, 4 dossenis pellium vitulorum, 110 quarteriis siliginis[f]. Precii £26 6s 8d ... cust' 6s 7d

[a] Courteroke *L3.* [b] Berght *L3.* [c] *Auditor's entry + [cross]* mercandise stapule, *marginated L2.* [d] Gerrardo *L3.* [e] *Omitted L3.* [f] sigalli *L3, in error.*

<aa>£3 14s 5¼d<aa>

E122/73/20B f. 2v

[125] In navi Willelmi Henrykesson[a] vocata [b]Marikneght de Scluce[b] 17[e] die Februarii *[17 Feb. 1446]*

De Philippo Lomelyn[c] pro 12 pipis cum 20 balis alum Foille. Precii £25 10s ... cust' 6s 4½d

De Lowis[d] Bernard pro 2 hoggeshedes, 1 barello cum carne et linguis bovium salsis. Precii 33s 4d ... cust' 5d

Auditor's marginated entries L2: <k> worsted simplex indigene <l> worsted simplex alienigene <m> worsted duplex indigene <n> worsted duplex alienigene <o> lectus de worsted simplex indigene <p> lectus worsted simplex alienigene <aa>-<aa> *Auditor's entry: Sum of the issues of the page L2.*

Et pro 1 barello cum 12 dossenis lb. candellarum de sepo[e]. Precii 13s 4d ....cust' 2d

De Andrea Furnario[f] pro 1 bala paper. Precii [g]33s 4d[g] .... cust'[h] 5d

De [i]Cristean van Bleyken[i] pro 1 barello cum [j]4 centenis, 56[j] [k]lb.[k] vasorum stanni, 16 barellis cum 19 vagis [l]sepi multonis[l]. Precii in toto £13 12s cust' 3s 5d

De Egard Yong pro 30 cadis sprottes. Precii 40s ....cust' 6d

[a] Henriksson *L3.* [b-b] Mariknyght de Sluce *L3.* [c] Lumlyn *L3.* [d] Lowes *L3.* [e] cepo *L3.* [f] de Fornario *L3.* [g-g] *Interlined above* 13s 4d, *struck through L2 (cf. variant h).* [h] 2d *(this would have been the appropriate customs charge for goods worth 13s 4d: cf. variant g) follows, struck through L2.* [i-i] Cristian van Bleken *L3.* [j] 4½ centenis *L3.* [k] *Omitted L3.* [l-l] cepi moltonis *L3.*

[126] In navi Lambe van Passe vocata George de Andewarp [a]exeunte[a] 19° die Februarii *[19 Feb. 1446]*

De Johanne Wouterson[b] pro 36 quarteriis ordei. Precii £5 8s ....cust' 16¼d

<a>De Ricardo Burgh[c] pro 1 fardello cum 2 pannis, 8 ulnis curtis sine grano .... Ind' cust' 2s 8¾d

<g>De Gerloff[d] van Berkenrode pro 1 bala cum 19 pannis curtis sine grano ....Hans cust' 19s

<g>De Gerwin Potte pro 1 bala cum 20 pannis curtis sine grano....Hans cust' 20s

Et pro 1 barello cum 13 cadis sprottes, 2 caseis. Precii 16s 8d ......cust' 2½d

<g>De Johanne van Sybryght pro 1 bala cum 16½ pannis curtis sine grano ....Hans cust' 16s 6d

<g>Et pro 11 ulnis panni motle[e] continentibus 11 ulnas panni largi sine grano .... Hans cust' 5½d

Et pro ½ [a]rolla[a] frisii Wallie. Precii 10s..cust' 1½d

<g>De Hans Dasse pro [a]1 bala[a] cum 21 pannis curtis sine grano....Hans cust' 21s

Et pro 1 barello cum 4 cadis sprottes. Precii 5s...............................cust' ¾d

<g>De Johanne[f] Ryng pro 1 bala cum 15 pannis curtis sine grano .Hans cust' 15s

Et pro 1 basket[g] cum 10 cadis sprottes, 12 caseis. Precii 21s 4d....cust' 3¼d

<g>De Hermano Wesyll pro 1 bala cum 32 pannis curtis sine grano ....Hans cust' 32s

Et pro 1 [a]parvo[a] basket[g] cum 3 cadis sprottes. Precii 4s ....cust' ¾d

<aa>£6 19s 9¾d<aa> [h]Item 3d[h]

E122/73/20B f. 3[r]

<g>De Bertram Questenbergh[i] pro 1 bala cum 25½ pannis curtis sine grano ....Hans cust' 25s 6d

Et pro 1 basket[g] cum 6 cadis sprottes, 50 stockefisch[j]. Precii 20s .....cust' 3d

Auditor's marginated entries L2: <a> pannus indigenus <b> pannus de dimidio grano indigenus <c> scarleta indigena <d> pannus alienigenus <e> pannus de dimidio grano alienigenus <f> scarleta alienigena <g> pannus hanse <h> pannus de dimidio grano hanse <i> scarleta hanse

<g>De Matys Schonebagh[k] pro 1 bala cum 10 pannis curtis sine grano .... Hans cust' 10s
<a>De Waltero Chandeler[l] pro 1 [a]parvo[a] fardello cum 1 panno curto sine grano .... Ind' cust' 14d
<g>De Henrico Overbagh pro 1 bala cum 26 pannis curtis sine grano .... Hans cust' 26s
<g>De Tilman Crome pro 1 bala cum 20 pannis curtis sine grano . Hans cust' 20s
Et pro ½ [a]rolla[a] frisii Wallie. Precii 10s 1½d
De Hans Roo pro 1 barello cum [m]4 centenis, 56[m] [a]lb.[a] vasorum stanni. Precii £6 .... cust' 18d
<a>De Bartholomeo Stratton pro 1 bala cum 11 pannis curtis sine grano .... Ind' cust' 12s 10d

[a-a] *Omitted L3.* [b] Woutersson *L3.* [c] Brugh *L3.* [d] Gerlof *L3.* [e] motele *L3.* [f] Hans *L3.* [g] basketto *L3.* [h-h] *Auditor's supplement necessitated by the correction of the customs charges for the goods of* Andreas Furnario *L2.* [i] Questenberght *L3.* [j] fungiis *L3.* [k] Shonebaght *L3.* [l] Chaundeler *L3.* [m-m] *4½* centenis *L3.*

[127] In navi Petri Johansson vocata Maria de London' 1° die Marcii *[1 Mar. 1446]*

<a>De Johanne Stocker[a] pro 1 bala cum 15 pannis curtis sine grano .... Ind' cust' 17s 6d

[a] Stokker *L3.*

[128] In navi Hylbrand[a] van Wold vocata Reynold de Danske 3° die Marcii *[3 Mar. 1446]*

De Matheo[b] Bogys pro 1 barello cum 2¾ centenis [lb.] vasorum stanni. Precii £3 13s 4d .... cust' 11d
<g>De Bertram Sleyghter pro 5 balis cum 88 pannis, 23 ulnis curtis sine grano .... Hans cust' £4 8s 11½d
Et pro 1 gros poyntes[c], 14 godis panni stricti Wallie. Precii 13s 4d .. cust' 2d
<d>De Martino Sabyll pro 1 cista cum [d]1 pecia kersey cont[in]ente 8 ulnas curtas[d] sine grano .... Al' cust' 11d
Et pro 1 centena lb. vasorum stanni. Precii 26s 8d .... cust' 4d
<g>De Lambert Houne[e] pro 1 cista cum 2 pannis curtis sine grano .. Hans cust' 2s
<g>De Nicholao Noell pro 1 bala cum 19 pannis, 8 ulnis curtis sine grano .... Hans cust' 19s 4d
Et pro 2 coverlettes Wyntonie, 2½ ulnis worsted duplicis. Precii 20s .... cust' 3d

<aa>£11 7s 9d<aa>

Auditor's marginated entries L2: <k> worsted simplex indigene <l> worsted simplex alienigene <m> worsted duplex indigene <n> worsted duplex alienigene <o> lectus de worsted simplex indigene <p> lectus worsted simplex alienigene <aa>-<aa> *Auditor's entry: Sum of the issues of the page L2.*

E122/73/20B f. 3[v]

<a>De Willelmo Canyngges pro 1 cista cum 1 panno curto sine grano ....Ind' cust' 14d

<g>De Johanne Warenthorp[f] pro 1 bala cum 21 pannis curtis sine grano ....Hans cust' 21s

<g>De Matheo Sprynghorn pro 4 balis, 1 fardello, 2 cistis cum 78 pannis, 21½[g] ulnis curtis sine grano ....Hans cust' £3 17s 10¾d

Et pro 600 godis panni stricti Wallie, 4 gros poyntes[c], 1 toga[h] vetera enbroudata[i] cum argento, 1 cado allecis rubei. Precii in toto £16 13s 4d ....cust' 4s 2d

<g>De Tym Gyse pro 7 balis, 1 fardello, 1 cista, 2 barellis cum 138 pannis, 11½ ulnis curtis sine grano ....Hans cust' £6 18s 5¾d

Et pro 60 peciis [et] 2¼ ulnis de worsted duplicis cours, 21 godis panni stricti Wallie, 2 parvis coverlettes, 2 centenis, 59 lb. vasorum stanni, 1 carpetto, 2 dossenis pellium agnorum tawed[j], 13 quayr papir, 2 pannis tele lini depictis, 6 candelabris de latone, 4 cadis sprottes. Precii in toto £66 13s 4d ....cust' 16s 8d

<a>De Jacobo[k] Wryght pro 1 bala cum 20 pannis, 16 ulnis curtis sine grano ....Ind' cust' 24s 1½d

<a>De Johanne Hyne pro 1 bala cum 20 pannis, 20 ulnis curtis sine grano ....Ind' cust' 24s 3¾d

<a>De Willelmo Overey pro 2 fardellis cum 48 pannis, 14 ulnis curtis sine grano ....Ind' cust' 56s 8¼d

<a>De Stephano Barry pro 1 bala cum 23½ pannis curtis sine grano ....Ind' cust' 27s 5d

<a>De Johanne Brampton pro 1 bala cum 20½ pannis curtis sine grano ....Ind' cust' 23s 11d

<a>De Thoma Whatton pro 1 bala cum 20 pannis curtis sine grano ....Ind' cust' 23s 4d

<g>•[l]De Matys Sprynghorn pro 2 balis cum 38½ pannis curtis sine grano ....Hans cust' 38s 6d[l]

[l]Et extra pro 2 caseis, 1 cado[m] sprottes. Precii 3s 4d ....cust' ½d[l]

<a>•[n]De Stephano Stychemerssh[o] pro 2 fardellis cum 13 pannis, 19 ulnis curtis sine grano ....Ind' cust' 16s 1d[n]

<a>De [p]dicto[p] Jacobo Wryght pro 1 bala[q] cum 14 pannis, 8 ulnis curtis sine grano ....Ind' cust' 16s 8¾d

[a] Ilbrand *L3.* [b] Michaele *L3.* [c] poyentes *L3.* [d-d] 8 ulnis panni largi *L2.* [e] Howne *L3.* [f] Warenthorpp *L3.* [g] *Corrected in L2 from* 21. [h] taga *L2, apparently in error.* [i] enbrodata *L3.* [j] albarum *follows L3.* [k] James *L3.* [l-l] Sprynghorn*'s goods entered after* De dicto Jacobo Wryght *L3.* [m] cade

Auditor's marginated entries L2: <a> pannus indigenus <b> pannus de dimidio grano indigenus <c> scarleta indigena <d> pannus alienigenus <e> pannus de dimidio grano alienigenus <f> scarleta alienigena <g> pannus hanse <h> pannus de dimidio grano hanse <i> scarleta hanse

L3. [n-n] *The entry for Stephan* Stychemerssh*'s goods is the first in the ship L3.* [o] Stychemersch *L3.* [p-p] *Interlined L2.* [q] terlyng *L3.*

<aa>£25 11s 6¼d<aa>

E122/73/20B f. 4r

[129] In navi Hayn Bulscamp[a] vocata Andreas de Ermoth 11° die Marcii *[11 Mar. 1446]*

De Petro Petersson pro 1 barello cum 6 centenis lb. vasorum stanni. Precii £8 .... cust' 2s

Et pro 1 maunda cum 150 godis panni [b]Wallie stricti[b]. Precii £4....cust' 12d

De Johanne van Synder pro 2 maundis cum 3700 pellibus cuniculorum crude sesone, 2200 pellibus cuniculorum[c] stage, 1 barello cum 12 dossenis lb. candellarum de sepo, 2 pipis cum carne[d] bovium salsa. Precii in toto £15 .... cust' 3s 9d

De Godyscalke[e] Smedyng pro 2 cistis cum 80 dossenis lb. candellarum de sepo. Precii £4 13s 4d .... cust' 14d

De Johanne Ere pro 25 barellis cum 29 vagis sepi multonis, 1 barello cum 6 centenis lb. vasorum stanni. Precii £19 13s 4d .... cust' 4s 11d

<g>De Lambert Jose pro 1 bala cum 18 panni curtis sine grano.....Hans cust' 18s

Et pro 1 rolla[f] frisii Wallie. Precii 20s .... cust' 3d

<g>De Johanne Salmer pro 1 bala cum 12½ pannis curtis sine grano .... Hans cust' 12s 6d

Et pro 2 peciis worsted duplicis, 1½ gros poyntes, 1 rolla frisii Wallie. Precii in toto £4 5s 6d .... cust' 13d[g]

Et pro 10 barellis cum 6 miliariis lb. vasorum stanni. Precii £75 .... cust' 18s 9d

<g>De Johanne Blyterswyke[h] pro 3 balis cum 49 pannis curtis sine grano .... Hans cust' 49s

Et pro 15½ peciis worsted [i]duplicis[i], ½ rolla frisii Wallie. Precii £18 11s 8d .... cust' 4s 7¾d

<d>De Johanne de Vyle pro 1 bala cum 11 pannis curtis sine grano .... Al' cust' 30s 3d

<g>De Hans Harderode pro 1 bala cum 18½ pannis curtis sine grano .... Hans cust' 18s 6d

<d>De Petro Symson pro 1 maunda cum 1 panno curto sine grano .... Al' cust' 2s 9d

Et pro 1200 pellibus cuniculorum crude, unde [j]600 pelles stage[j]. Precii 45s .... cust' 6¾d

<g>De Gerwyn Potte pro 5 balis cum 97 pannis, 6 ulnis curtis sine grano .... Hans cust' £4 17s 3d

Auditor's marginated entries L2: <k> worsted simplex indigene <l> worsted simplex alienigene <m> worsted duplex indigene <n> worsted duplex alienigene <o> lectus de worsted simplex indigene <p> lectus worsted simplex alienigene <aa>-<aa> *Auditor's entry: Sum of the issues of the page L2.*

<g>De Arnoldo[k] Stakelhowson[l] pro 1 bala cum 17 pannis[m] curtis sine grano .... Hans cust' 17s
Et pro ½ rolla frisii Wallie. Precii 10s .... cust' 1½d
De Matheo Feller pro 1 poke cum 10 vagis thrummes[n]. Precii £7 10s .... cust' 22½d
<aa>£14 5s 4½d[o]•<aa>

E122/73/20B f. 4[v]
De Gyles Braynford pro 1 poke cum 8½[p] vagis thrummes. Precii £6 7s 6d .... cust' 19¼d
De Henrico Hode[q] pro 1 poke cum 9 vagis, 4 petris thrummes[n]. Precii £6 17s 6d .... cust' 20¾d
<a>De Thoma Dey pro 1 bala cum 12½ pannis curtis sine grano .... Ind' cust' 14s 7d
De Clays Sybotson[r] pro 4 barellis cum 2 miliariis, 4 centenis lb. vasorum stanni. Precii £32 .... cust' 8s
De Gylbert Jacobesson[s] pro 4 barellis cum 2 miliariis, 4 centenis lb. vasorum stanni. Precii £32 .... cust' 8s
De [t]Bertolt Berntson[t] pro 3 barellis cum 1 miliario, 8 centenis lb. vasorum stanni. Precii £24 .... cust' 6s
De [u]Poulo Heyn[u] pro 3 barellis cum 1 miliario, 8 centenis lb. vasorum stanni. Precii £24 .... cust' 6s
<g>•[v]De Bertram Questenbergh pro 3 balis cum 52 pannis curtis sine grano .... Hans cust' 52s[v]
<a>De Johanne Wortys[w] pro 1 fardello cum 4 pannis curtis sine grano .... Ind' cust' 4s 8d
<g>De Clays Swart[x] pro 2 balis cum 35 pannis, 2 ulnis curtis sine grano .... Hans cust' 35s 1d
Et pro 1 rolla frisii Wallie. Precii 20s .... cust' 3d
<d>De Arnoldo[k] Massane pro 2 balis cum 31 pannis curtis sine grano .... Al' cust' £4 5s 3d
<g>De Henrico Bruer[y] pro 2 balis cum 41 pannis curtis sine grano .... Hans cust' 41s
<g>De Johanne Ryng pro 2 balis cum 55 pannis curtis sine grano .... Hans cust' 55s
<g>De dicto Hans Harderode pro 1 bala cum 22½ pannis curtis sine grano .... Hans cust' 22s 6d
De [z]Deryk van Capell[z] pro 1 pipa cum 2200 pellibus cuniculorum [i]crude[i], unde stage 800 pelles. Precii £4 16s .... cust' 14½d
Et pro 1 parvo barello cum parvis pectinibus de ligno box. Precii 4s .... cust' ¾d

Auditor's marginated entries L2: <a> pannus indigenus <b> pannus de dimidio grano indigenus <c> scarleta indigena <d> pannus alienigenus <e> pannus de dimidio grano alienigenus <f> scarleta alienigena <g> pannus hanse <h> pannus de dimidio grano hanse <i> scarleta hanse

<g>De Tilman Crome pro 3 balis cum 69½ pannis curtis sine grano .... Hans cust' £3 9s 6d
Et pro 1½ rollis frisii Wallie. Precii 30s .... cust' 4½d
<g>De Arnoldo[k] van Pynxsten pro 1 bala cum 16 pannis, 8 ulnis curtis sine grano .... Hans cust' 16s 4d
Et pro ½ rolla frisii Wallie[aa], 8 gros poyntes. Precii 26s 8d .... cust' 4d
De Nicholao Ewayns pro 1 maunda cum 1700 pellibus cuniculorum crude sesone [i]et[i] 1500 pellibus cuniculorum[c] stage, 7 pellibus vitulorum crude. Precii in toto £5 3s 4d .... cust' 15½d
<aa>£21 10s 9¼d<aa>

E122/73/20B f. 5[r]

<g>De Petro Cangheter pro 2 balis cum 50 pannis, 16 ulnis curtis sine grano .... Hans cust' 50s 8d
Et pro 152 godis panni stricti Wallie. Precii £3 16s .... cust' 11½d
<a>De Johanne Malvern pro 1 cista cum 1 panno, 8 ulnis curtis sine grano .... Ind' cust' 18¾d
<a>De Johanne Lok[ab] pro 1 bala cum 51½ pannis curtis sine grano .... Ind' cust' £3 1d
<a>De Willelmo Gronde pro 1 bala cum 27 pannis curtis sine grano .... Ind' cust' 31s 6d
<g>De Johanne van Sybryght pro 3 balis cum 61½ pannis curtis sine grano .... Hans cust' £3 18d
Et pro [ac]1½ rollis frisii Wallie. Precii 30s[ac] .... cust' 4½d
De Arnoldo[k] van Langfeld pro 1 cista cum 350 pellibus cuniculorum crude, unde stage 100 pelles. Precii 15s .... cust' 2¼d
<a>De Rogero Mydylmore[ad] pro 3 balis cum 149 pannis, 4 ulnis curtis sine grano .... Ind' cust' £8 14s ½d
<a>De Johanne Okeherst[ae] pro 1 fardello cum 6 pannis, 16 ulnis curtis sine grano .... Ind' cust' 7s 9½d
<g>De Cristean Edylkynt[af] pro 1 bala cum 16 pannis curtis sine grano .... Hans cust' 16s
Et pro ½ [ag]rolla[ag] frisii Wallie. Precii 10s .... cust' 1½d
<g>De Cristean van Bleyken[ah] pro 1 bala cum 23 pannis, 16 ulnis curtis sine grano .... Hans cust' 23s 8d
Et pro 39 godis panni stricti Wallie. Precii 19s 3d[ai] .... cust' 3d
<g>De Johanne Hathyltak[aj] pro 1 bala cum 44 pannis curtis sine grano .... Hans cust' 44s
<g>De Hans Hope pro 2 balis cum 44 pannis curtis sine grano ...... Hans cust' 44s
<g>De Henrico Overbagh pro 3 balis cum 56 pannis curtis sine grano .... Hans cust' 56s

Auditor's marginated entries L2: <k> worsted simplex indigene <l> worsted simplex alienigene <m> worsted duplex indigene <n> worsted duplex alienigene <o> lectus de worsted simplex indigene <p> lectus worsted simplex alienigene <aa>-<aa> *Auditor's entry: Sum of the issues of the page L2.*

<g>De Johanne Dasse pro 2 balis cum 61 pannis curtis sine grano .... Hans cust' £3 12d

<a>De Johanne Malvern pro 1 bala cum 40 pannis, 8 ulnis curtis sine grano .... Ind' cust' 47s ¾d

De Johanne van Dyke pro 1 parvo barello cum 2 centenis, 56 lb. vasorum stanni. Precii £3 6s 8d .... cust' 10d

De Willelmo van Spyker pro 2 pokes et 3½ pokes cum 32 vagis thrummes[n], 60 pellibus cuniculorum crude sesone. Precii £24 2s 6d .... cust' 6s ½d

<g>De Petro Cangheter pro 1 bala cum 17 pannis, 16 ulnis curtis sine grano .... Hans cust' 17s 8d

Et pro 14 godis panni stricti Wallie. Precii 6s 8d .... cust' 1d

<aa>£35 5s 4¾d<aa>

E122/73/20B f. 5^v

<g>De Enghebryght Sassynhowsyn[ak] pro 1 bala cum 25 pannis curtis sine grano .... Hans cust' 25s

<g>De Gerloff van Berkenrode pro 1 bala cum 30 pannis, 4 ulnis curtis sine grano .... Hans cust' 30s 2d

<g>Et pro 1 rolla frisii London' continente 1 pannum, 4 ulnas curta sine grano .... Hans cust' 14d

<g>De Johanne van Dorne pro 1 bala cum 32[al] pannis curtis sine grano .... Hans cust' 32s

De Hans Rynge pro 1 maunda[am] cum 1060 godis panni stricti Wallie. Precii £35 6s 8d .... cust' 8s 10d

[a] Bulschamp *L3.* [b-b] stricti Wallie *L3.* [c] crude *follows L3.* [d] carnibus *L3.* [e] Godysscalke *L3.* [f] cum *follows, struck through L2.* [g] *Corrected in L2 from* 12¾d. [h] Blitterswyk *L3.* [i-i] *Omitted L3.* [j-j] stage 600 pelles *L3.* [k] Arnaldo *L3.* [l] Stakilhowson *L3.* [m] 6 ulnis *follows L3, in error.* [n] thrummez *L3.* [o] *Corrected in L2 from 4¼d (necessitated by the correction of the customs charges on the goods of* Johann Salmer*).* [p] *Corrected in L2 from* 8. [q] Hed *L3.* [r] Sybottsson *L3.* [s] Jacobson *L3.* [t-t] Bernt Berntsson *L3.* [u-u] Poullo Hayn *L3.* [v-v] Questenbergh*'s goods were entered subsequently by another hand in lighter ink at the end of the ship (after the exports of* Hans Rynge*) L3.* [w] Worste *L3.* [x] Swerte *L3.* [y] Brewer *L3.* [z-z] Dederik van Cappell *L3.* [aa] precii *follows, struck through L2.* [ab] Lokk *L3.* [ac-ac] *Entered subsequently by a different hand in lighter ink L3.* [ad] Middilmore *L3.* [ae] Okerste *L3.* [af] Edilkynd *L3.* [ag-ag] *Omitted L2.* [ah] Bleken *L3.* [ai] 4d *L3.* [aj] Hatiltake *L3.* [ak] Sassonhoson *L3.* [al] *Corrected in L2 from* 22. [am] maunde *L3.*

Auditor's marginated entries L2: <a> pannus indigenus <b> pannus de dimidio grano indigenus <c> scarleta indigena <d> pannus alienigenus <e> pannus de dimidio grano alienigenus <f> scarleta alienigena <g> pannus hanse <h> pannus de dimidio grano hanse <i> scarleta hanse

[130] In navi Hayn Ole vocata James de Colonia [a]exeunte[a] eodem die *[11 Mar. 1446]*

<g>De Lambert Jose pro 1 bala cum 6 pannis, ¾ ulna curtis sine grano .... Hans cust' 6s ½d

Et pro 4 rollis frisii Wallie, 9½ peciis worsted duplicis, 3 gros poyntes, 3 dossenis lasyng poyntes. Precii £17 4s 4d .... cust' 4s 3¾d

Et pro 9 barellis cum 5 miliariis, 4 centenis lb. vasorum stanni, 1 bala[b] cum 12 caseis, 1 matte cum 3 Pruce forcer[i]is. Precii in toto £68 8s 4d .... cust' 17s 1¼d

<g>De Johanne Salmer pro 1 fardello cum 2 pannis, 8 ulnis curtis sine grano .... Hans cust' 2s 4d

Et pro 8½ rollis frisii Wallie, 1 pipa, 1 barello cum 2 vagis thrummes[c], 2 dossenis[d] candelabris de latone, 6 hures sengylle[e] sine grano. Precii in toto £11 5s 8d .... cust' 2s 10d

<g>De Johanne Blyterswyke[f] pro [a]4 balis cum[a] 82½ pannis curtis sine grano .... Hans cust' £4 2s 6d

Et pro 1 rolla frisii Wallie, 1 barello cum 4 centenis, 19 lb. vasorum stanni, 1 basket[g] cum 8 cadis sprottes. Precii in toto £7 .... cust' 22d

<g>De Hans Harderode[h] pro 1 bala cum 18 pannis curtis sine grano .... Hans cust' 18s

Et pro ½ rolla frisii Wallie. Precii 10s .... cust' 1½d

<aa>£11 12s 2d<aa>

E122/73/20B f. 6r

<g>De Gerwyn Potte pro 3 balis cum 64 pannis, 8 ulnis curtis sine grano .... Hans cust' £3 4s 4d

Et pro 1 barello cum 33 dossenis lb. candellarum de sepo[i]. Precii 40s .... cust' 6d

De [j]Arnoldo Stakelhowson[j] pro 1 barello cum 6¼ centenis, 14 lb. vasorum stanni. Precii £8 .... cust' 2s

De Matheo Feller pro 2 pokes, 1 sacco cum 26 vagis thrummes[c]. Precii £19 10s .... cust' 4s 10½d

De Gyles Braynford pro 2 pokes[k] cum 12 vagis thrummes[c]. Precii £9 .... cust' 2s 3d

De Leonardo van Werd pro [a]2[a] pokes cum 8 vagis thrummes[c]. Precii £6 .... cust' 18d

<g>De Roberto Blyterswyke[l] pro 1 bala cum 16½ pannis curtis sine grano .... Hans cust' 16s 6d

<g>De [m]Bertram Questenbergh[m] pro 2 balis cum 51½ pannis curtis sine grano .... Hans cust' 51s 6d

Auditor's marginated entries L2: <k> worsted simplex indigene <l> worsted simplex alienigene <m> worsted duplex indigene <n> worsted duplex alienigene <o> lectus de worsted simplex indigene <p> lectus worsted simplex alienigene <aa>-<aa> *Auditor's entry: Sum of the issues of the page L2.*

<a>De Thoma Niche pro 1 bala cum 28 pannis, 8 ulnis curtis sine grano .... Ind' cust' 33s ¾d
<g>De Henrico Brewer pro 1 bala cum 31 pannis curtis sine grano .... Hans cust' 31s
Et pro 2 parvis barellis cum 7 centenis, 56 lb. vasorum stanni. Precii £9 7s 6d .... cust' 2s 4¼d
<g>De Johanne Rynge pro 2 balis cum 54 pannis curtis sine grano .... Hans cust' 54s
Et pro 1 rolla frisii Wallie. Precii 20s .... cust' 3d
<g>De Tilman Crome pro 1 bala cum 20 pannis curtis sine grano . Hans cust' 20s
<g>De [n]Gerardo Gastorp[n] pro 1 bala cum 13 pannis, 6 ulnis curtis sine grano .... Hans cust' 13s 3d
Et pro 26 ulnis frisii Wallie. Precii 16s 8d .... cust' 2½d
<g>De Enghebryght[o] Sassynhowson pro 1 bala cum 15½ pannis curtis sine grano .... Hans cust' 15s 6d
<g>De Arnoldo Stakelhowsen pro 1 bala cum 17 pannis, 23 ulnis curtis sine grano .... Hans cust' 17s 11½d
Et pro 1 gros poyntes, ½ rolla frisii Wallie. Precii in toto 12s 6d ..... cust' 2d
De Leonardo van Brusill pro 1 corfe, 1 maunda cum 1 rolla frisii Wallie, 54 godis [p]Walssh kendal[p] stricti, 1100 [a]pellibus[a] cuniculorum crude, unde stage 600 pelles, 1900 pellibus ovium tawed, 3 cadis sprottes. Precii in toto £12 .... cust' 3s
<aa>£16 14s 2½d<aa>

E122/73/20B f. 6[v]

<g>De Petro Cangheter pro 3 balis cum 68 pannis, 4 ulnis curtis sine grano .... Hans cust' £3 8s 2d
Et pro 14 peciis worsted duplicis [q]et[q] cours[r], 99 godis panni stricti Wallie. Precii in toto £16 9s 6d .... cust' 4s 1½d
<g>De Cristean[s] Edilkynt pro 1 bala cum 14 pannis curtis sine grano .... Hans cust' 14s
Et pro ½ rolla frisii Wallie. Precii 10s .... cust' 1½d
<a>De Johanne Smith pro 1 maunda cum 2 pannis, 14 ulnis curtis sine grano .... Ind' cust' 3s ¼d
De dicto magistro pro 1 fodra[t] plumbi. Precii £4 13s [u]4d[u] .... cust' 14d
<g>De Johanne Warenthorp pro 1 bala cum 45 pannis curtis sine grano .... Hans cust' 45s
<g>De Hans Hope pro 1 bala cum 30 pannis curtis sine grano .... Hans cust' 30s
<g>De Henrico Overbagh pro 3 balis cum 74 pannis curtis sine grano .... Hans cust' £3 14s
Et pro 14½ peciis worsted duplicis. Precii £18 .... cust' 4s 6d

Auditor's marginated entries L2: <a> pannus indigenus <b> pannus de dimidio grano indigenus <c> scarleta indigena <d> pannus alienigenus <e> pannus de dimidio grano alienigenus <f> scarleta alienigena <g> pannus hanse <h> pannus de dimidio grano hanse <i> scarleta hanse

Et pro 1 parvo barello cum 4 centenis, 10 lb. vasorum stanni. Precii £5 6s 8d ....cust' 16d

De Peryn Bayle pro 1 maunda cum 2300 pellibus cuniculorum crude sesone, 700 pellibus cuniculorum stage, 20 pellibus vitulorum crude. Precii in toto £6 15s........cust' 20¼d

<g>De Johanne Dasse pro 3 balis cum 69[v] [w]pannis, 8 ulnis curtis sine grano[w] ....Hans cust' £3 9s 4d

<g>De Tilman Crome pro 2 balis cum 37 pannis curtis sine grano. Hans cust' 37s

Et pro 3 gros poyntes[x]. Precii 6s 8d........cust' 1d

<g>De Johanne Sybryght pro 1 bala cum 22 pannis, 8 ulnis curtis sine grano ....Hans cust' 22s 4d

Et pro ½ rolla frisii Wallie. Precii 10s........cust' 1½d

<g>De Johanne van Dorne pro 1 bala cum 29½ pannis curtis sine grano ....Hans cust' 29s 6d

Et pro 2 gros poyntes[x], 4 pellibus cheverellorum, 1 ulna worsted [q]duplicis[q], 1 cappe de scarlet[y] et 3 hures duple de dimidio grano. Precii in toto 18s ....cust' 2¾d

<g>De Cristean[s] van Bleyken pro 1 bala cum 11 pannis, 8 ulnis curtis sine grano ....Hans cust' 11s 4d

Et pro 100 godis panni stricti Wallie. Precii £3 6s 8d ....cust' 10d

<aa>£20 17s 10¾d<aa>

[a-a] *Omitted L2.* [b] barello *L3.* [c] thrummez *L3.* [d] lb. *follows, struck through L2.* [e] sengle *L3.* [f] Blitterswyk *L3.* [g] basketto *L3.* [h] Hardrode *L3.* [i] cepo *L3.* [j-j] Arnaldo Stakilhowsen *L3.* [k] 1 sacco *follows L3.* [l] Blitersweke *L3.* [m-m] Berteram Questenberght *L3.* [n-n] Gerrardo Gastorpp *L3.* [o] Enbright *L3.* [p-p] Walsch kendall *L3.* [q] *Omitted L3.* [r] cource *L2.* [s] Cristian *L3.* [t] foder *L3.* [u-u] *Interlined L2.* [v] lb. *follows L3, in error.* [w-w] *Entered subsequently by a different hand in lighter ink L3.* [x] poyentes *L3.* [y] scarlett *L3.*

E122/73/20B f. 7[r]

[131] In navi Bertolt Berntson[a] vocata Gabriell de Holandia 11° die Marcii *[11 Mar. 1446]*

De eodem pro 20 [b]dossenis[b] pellium vitulorum tannatarum. Precii £3 ....cust' 9d

[a] Berntisson *L3.* [b-b] *Interlined L2.*

[132] In navi Arnoldi Cotys vocata Katerin de Newport [a]exeunte[a] eodem die *[11 Mar. 1446]*

<a>De Willelmo Hulyn pro 1 fardello cum 2 pannis curtis sine grano ....Ind' cust' 2s 4d

[a] *Omitted L3.*

Auditor's marginated entries L2: <k> worsted simplex indigene <l> worsted simplex alienigene <m> worsted duplex indigene <n> worsted duplex alienigene <o> lectus de worsted simplex indigene <p> lectus worsted simplex alienigene <aa>-<aa> *Auditor's entry: Sum of the issues of the page L2.*

[133] In navi Willelmi Pegge vocata George de London' 11° die Marcii *[11 Mar. 1446]*

<a>De Roberto Stocker[a] pro 1 bala, 2 fardellis cum 31 pannis, 18 ulnis curtis sine grano........................Ind' cust' 37s ½d
<a>De Johanne Stocker[a] pro 2 balis, 3 fardellis cum 54 pannis, 2 ulnis curtis sine grano........................Ind' cust' £3 3s 1¼d
<g>De Nicholao Noell[b] pro 1 bala cum 22 pannis curtis sine grano........................Hans cust' 22s
<g>De Hereberd[c] Sternbergh pro 1 bala cum 17 pannis, 8 ulnis curtis sine grano........................Hans cust' 17s 4d
<a>De Johanne Bromer pro 1 bala cum 13 pannis, 14 ulnis curtis sine grano........................Ind' cust' 15s 10¼d
<g>De Tym Gyse pro 6 balis cum 126 pannis, 4 ulnis curtis sine grano........................Hans cust' £6 6s 2d
Et pro 1 rolla frisii Wallie. Precii 20s........................cust' 3d
<a>•[d]De Johanne Iche pro 1 bala cum 13 pannis, 16 ulnis curtis sine grano........................Ind' cust' 15s 11½d[d]
<a>•[e]De Stephano Stychemerssh[f] pro 1 fardello cum 2 pannis curtis sine grano........................Ind' cust' 2s 4d[e]
<g>De Matys Sprynghorn pro 5 balis cum 90½ pannis curtis sine grano........................Hans cust' £4 10s 6d
<g>Et pro 1 cista cum 2 ulnis panni largi sine grano................ Hans cust' 1d
Et pro 1 centena lb. vasorum stanni, 3 furruris de pellibus cuniculorum. Precii in toto 41s 8d........................cust' 6¼d

[a] Stoker *L3.* [b] Noeell *L3.* [c] Herberd *L3.* [d-d] *Entered between the goods of* Nicholaus Noeell *and* Herberd Sternbergh *L3.* [e-e] *Entered between the goods of Robert* Stoker *and John* Stoker *L3.* [f] Stychemersch *L3.*

<aa>£19 14s 2¾d<aa>

E122/73/20B f. 7v

[134] In navi Johannis Powdram[a] vocata George Heron de London' 13° die Marcii *[13 Mar. 1446]*

<a>De Willelmo Bodvyle pro 1 fardello cum 6 pannis, 16 ulnis curtis sine grano........................Ind' cust' 7s 9½d
<a>De Ricardo Selby [b]pro 1 panno, 16 ulnis curtis sine grano .... Ind' cust' 23½d[b]
<a>De Thoma West[c] pro 1 bala cum 10 pannis, 8 ulnis curtis sine grano........................Ind' cust' 12s ¾d[d]
<a>De Thoma Moughton pro 16 ulnis panni largi sine grano..........Ind' cust' 9½d

Auditor's marginated entries L2: <a> pannus indigenus <b> pannus de dimidio grano indigenus <c> scarleta indigena <d> pannus alienigenus <e> pannus de dimidio grano alienigenus <f> scarleta alienigena <g> pannus hanse <h> pannus de dimidio grano hanse <i> scarleta hanse

<a>De Ricardo Malte pro 1 fardello cum 7 pannis, 16 ulnis curtis sine grano .... Ind' cust' 8s 11½d

<m>•[e]De dicto Thoma West pro 3 peciis worsted duplicis continentibus 4½ pecias .... Ind' cust' 9d[e]

[a] Powderam *L3.* [b-b] *Entered subsequently by a different hand in lighter ink L3.* [c] Weste *L3.* [d] *On the next line* Et pro 3 peciis worsted duplicis continentibus 4½ pecias Ind' *follows L3 (cf. variant e).* [e-e] *Omitted L3 (cf. variant d).*

[135] In navi Willelmi Martynsson vocata Cristofor de Holandia eodem die *[13 Mar. 1446]*

De eodem pro 4 barellis cum 2 miliariis, 4 centenis lb. vasorum stanni. Precii £32 .... cust' 8s

[136] In navi Petri George vocata Cristofor de Scluse[a] eodem die *[13 Mar. 1446]*

De Rogero Russe pro 5 cistis cum 165 dossenis lb. candellarum de sepo[b], 7 baskettis cum 9 vagis sepi multonis. Precii £14 16s .... cust' 3s 8½d

[a] Selandia *L2.* [b] ceppo *L3.*

[137] In batella Willelmi Tabard versus portum Gippewici carcata 15° die Marcii et ibidem ad recarcandum in navi vocata George de London', unde Willelmus Pegge est magister *[15 Mar. 1446]*

<a>De Thoma Whatton pro 1 fardello cum 6 pannis, 16 ulnis curtis sine grano .... Ind' cust' 7s 9½d

[138] In navi Clays Sybotson[a] vocata Jameskneyght[b] de Holandia 19° die Marcii *[19 Mar. 1446]*

De eodem pro 2 barellis cum 12 centenis lb. vasorum stanni. Precii £16 cust' 4s
Et pro 10 quarteriis ordei[c]. Precii 21s 8d .... cust' 3¼d

[a] Sybottysson *L3.* [b] Seynt James Kneght *L3.* [c] ordii *L3.*

<aa>56s 1d<aa>

E122/73/20B f. 8[r]

[139] In navi Gilberti Jacobesson[a] vocata George[b] de Holandia eodem die *[19 Mar. 1446]*

De eodem pro 4 barellis cum 24 centenis lb. vasorum stanni. Precii £32 cust' 8s
Et pro 10 quarteriis ordei[c]. Precii 21s 8d .... cust' 3¼d

Auditor's marginated entries L2: <k> worsted simplex indigene <l> worsted simplex alienigene <m> worsted duplex indigene <n> worsted duplex alienigene <o> lectus de worsted simplex indigene <p> lectus worsted simplex alienigene <aa>-<aa> *Auditor's entry: Sum of the issues of the page L2.*

[a] Jacobsson *L3.* [b] Seynt George *L3.* [c] ordii *L3.*

[140] In navi Pouli Heynsson vocata Holygost de Holandia eodem die *[19 Mar. 1446]*

De eodem pro 3 barellis cum 18 centenis lb. vasorum stanni. Precii £24 cust' 6s
Et pro 8 quarteriis ordei[a]. Precii 17s 4d ....cust' 2¾d
[a] ordii *L3.*

[141] In navi Gilmyn[a] Basyn vocata Nicholaus de Roan[b] 23° die Marcii *[23 Mar. 1446]*

De Johanne [c]de[c] Flor pro 4 grindestones[d], 1 chaldra carbonum, 1 hoggeshede, 1 barello cum 825 [lb.] aluminis Foille. Precii in toto £7 6s 8d[e]............cust' 22d
[a] Gilman *L3.* [b] Roon *L3.* [c-c] *Omitted L3.* [d] grindstones *L3.* [e] 2d *L2, in error (the customs charge (22d) corresponds to goods worth a total of £7 6s 8d).*

[142] In [a]batella[a] Johannis [b]Gant de Feveresham[b] carcata versus Sandewicum 24° die Marcii et ibidem ad recarcandum in navi vocata Goost[c] de London', unde Johannes Heyborn[d] est magister *[24 Mar. 1446]*

<a>De Johanne Dolond pro 1 bala cum 14½ pannis curtis sine grano ....Ind' cust' 16s 11d
[a-a] *Interlined above* navi, *struck through L3.* [b] Gaunte de Feversham *L3.* [c] Gost *L3.* [d] Haybourn *L3.*

[143] In navi Johannis de Ceta vocata Seynt John de Gytar 26° die Marcii *[26 Mar. 1446]*

<a>De Simone Weston pro 6 balis, 4 fardellis cum 109 pannis, 15 ulnis curtis sine grano..Ind' cust' £6 7s 10¾d
<c>Et pro 16 ulnis panni largi de scarlet[a] ....Ind' cust' 18¾d
<m>Et pro 4 peciis worsted duplicis continentibus 6 pecias.......Ind' cust' 12d
<d>De dicto magistro pro 1 fardello cum 2½ pannis curtis sine grano .... Al' cust' 6s 10¾d
<d>De Sam Sebastean[c] pro 1 fardello cum 1 panno, 20 ulnis curtis sine grano .... Al' cust' 5s ½d
Et pro 1 pecia worsted duplicis, 4 ulnis frisii Wallie. Precii 28s 4d ....cust' 4¼d
<n>Et pro predicta 1 pecia worsted duplicis.................................Al' cust' 3d

<aa>£8 16s 3d[c]•<aa>

E122/73/20B f. 8[v]

Auditor's marginated entries L2: <a> pannus indigenus <b> pannus de dimidio grano indigenus <c> scarleta indigena <d> pannus alienigenus <e> pannus de dimidio grano alienigenus <f> scarleta alienigena <g> pannus hanse <h> pannus de dimidio grano hanse <i> scarleta hanse

<d>De Johanne de Loyn de Getary pro 15 ulnis panni largi sine grano .... Al' cust' 20¾d

Et pro 1 laver[d] de latone. Precii 5s........ cust' ¾d

<d>De Innygo de Somayo pro 12 ulnis panni largi sine grano........ Al' cust' 16½d

[a] scarlett *L3.* [b] Bastyan *L3.* [c] *Corrected in L2 from* 2¾d. [d] lavour *L3.*

[144] In navi Dederici Baysson vocata Magdalen Ernemoth[a] eodem die *[26 Mar. 1446]*

<g>De Hans Dasse pro 1 bala cum 38 pannis, 18 ulnis curtis sine grano .... Hans cust' 38 9d

Et pro 4 gros[b] poyntes[c]. Precii 10s........ cust' 1½d

<g>De Matys Shonebagh[d] pro 1 bala cum 21 pannis curtis sine grano .... Hans cust' 21s

<g>De Henrico Bruer[e] pro 2 balis cum 15 pannis curtis sine grano .... Hans cust' 15s

Et pro 180 godis frisii [f]Wallie[f]. Precii £16 18s 4d........ cust' 4s 2¾d

<g>De Henrico Overbagh pro 2 balis cum 49 pannis curtis sine grano .... Hans cust' 49s

Et pro 2 gros poyntes[c], 3 paribus serotecarum[g] de cheverello. Precii 6s 8d .... cust' 1d

<g>De Henrico Nase pro 2 balis, 1 fardello[h], 1 cista cum 36 pannis curtis sine grano........ Hans cust' 36s

<i>Et pro 6 ulnis panni largi de scarlet........ Hans cust' 6d

Et pro 4 gros poyntes[c]. Precii 10s........ cust' 1½d

[a] Ermouth *L3.* [b] groc' *L2, apparently in error.* [c] poyentes *L3.* [d] Sshonebagh *L2, in error.* [e] Brewer *L3.* [f-f] *Omitted L3.* [g] seretecarum *L2.* [h] cum *follows, struck through L2.*

[145] In navi Gunsalvus de la Mase vocata Katerin de Seynt Vincent[a] 26° die Marcii *[26 Mar. 1446]*

<d>De eodem pro 1 bala cum 11 pannis, 19 ulnis curtis sine grano .... Al' cust' 32s 5¼d

De [b]Garsye de Berete[b] pro 8 dossenis zonarum de coreo, 2 dossenis parium cultellorum, 3 bursis de coreo. Precii in toto 6s 8d........ cust' 1d

[a] in Calec[ia] exeunte *follows L3.* [b-b] Garsey de Barett *L3.*

Auditor's marginated entries L2: <k> worsted simplex indigene <l> worsted simplex alienigene <m> worsted duplex indigene <n> worsted duplex alienigene <o> lectus de worsted simplex indigene <p> lectus worsted simplex alienigene <aa>-<aa> *Auditor's entry: Sum of the issues of the page L2.*

[146] In batella Johannis Simon[a] carcata versus Sandewicum 28° die Marcii et ibidem ad recarcandum in quadam vas[a] exeunte versus partes exteras *[28 Mar. 1446]*

<a>De Stephano Forster pro 20 parvis fardellis cum 65 pannis curtis sine grano .... Ind' cust' £3 15s 10d

[a] Simond *L3.*

<aa>£13 16s 4d<aa>

E122/73/20B f. 9r

[147] In navi Nicholai Bruer vocata Katerin de Dunkirk 29° die Marcii *[29 Mar. 1446]*

<a>De Johanne Sygar[a] pro 1 fardello cum 4 pannis curtis sine grano .... Ind' cust' 4s 8d

[a] Segar *L3.*

[148] In navi Johannis Clerk vocata Bartholomeus de London' 1° die Aprilis[a] *[1 Apr. 1446]*

<a>De Bawdewyn[b] Boteler pro 1 pipa cum 3 pannis curtis sine grano .... Ind' cust' 3s 6d

[a] custuma *follows, struck through L2.* [b] Baudewyn *L3.*

[149] In navi Polento[a] de Raparatso vocata Trinite[b] de Bajona 4° die Aprilis *[4 Apr. 1446]*

<a>De Janycott de Garr pro 3 fardellis cum 6 pannis, 18 ulnis curtis sine grano .... Ind' cust' 7s 10½d

<a>Et pro 1 dossena [et] 10 paribus caligarum et extra 6 paribus caligarum [c]et[c] 8 ulnis panni largi continentibus in toto 22 ulnas panni largi sine grano .... Ind' cust' 13d

<a>De Stephano de Rege pro 1 fardello cum 2 pannis, 10 ulnis curtis sine grano .... Ind' cust' 2s 10d

[a] Palento *L3.* [b] Tren[e]te *L3.* [c-c] *Omitted L3.*

[150] In navi Johannis Gerardesson[a] vocata Jamesknegh de Wyke 8° die Aprilis *[8 Apr. 1446]*

<a>De Johanne Howgate pro 8 ulnis panni largi sine grano .... Ind' cust' 4¾d

[a] Gerrardesson *L3.*

Auditor's marginated entries L2: <a> pannus indigenus <b> pannus de dimidio grano indigenus <c> scarleta indigena <d> pannus alienigenus <e> pannus de dimidio grano alienigenus <f> scarleta alienigena <g> pannus hanse <h> pannus de dimidio grano hanse <i> scarleta hanse

[151] In navi Johannis Swan vocata Trinite[a] de London' 8° die Aprilis *[8 Apr. 1446]*

<a>De Thoma Croxston pro 3 balis cum 53½ pannis curtis sine grano .... Ind' cust' £3 2s 5d

<a>Et pro 1 cista cum 1 rolla frisii London' continente 1 pannum, 4 ulnas curtis sine grano .... Ind' cust' 16½d

<a>De Thoma Couper pro 1 bala cum 16½ pannis curtis sine grano .... Ind' cust' 19s 3d

<a>Et pro 1 cista cum 3 ulnis panni largi sine grano .... Ind' cust' 1¾d

<a>De Johanne Okeherst[b] pro 1 fardello cum 5 pannis curtis sine grano .... Ind' cust' 5s 10d

<a>De Johanne Swan pro 1 bala cum 12 pannis, 18 ulnis curtis sine grano .... Ind' cust' 14s 10½d

<a>De Alano Johnson[c] pro 1 bala cum 10 pannis curtis sine grano .... Ind' cust' 11s 8d

<aa>£6 15s 11d<aa>

E122/73/20B f. 9[v]

<a>De Pers[d] Alfold pro 1 fardello cum 5 pannis, 17 ulnis curtis sine grano .... Ind' cust' 6s 8d

<a>De Johanne Tregaran[e] pro 1 fardello cum 5 pannis, 18 ulnis curtis sine grano .... Ind' cust' 6s 8½d

<a>De Simone[f] Horn pro 6 fardellis cum 69 pannis, 18 ulnis curtis sine grano .... Ind' cust' £4 16½d

<a>De Roberto Horn pro 2 balis cum 29 pannis curtis sine grano .... Ind' cust' 33s 10d

<a>Et pro 1 cista cum 7 ulnis panni largi sine grano .... Ind' cust' 4d

<a>De Bartholomeo Couper pro 7 balis cum 119 pannis, 4 ulnis curtis sine grano .... Ind' cust' £6 19s ½d

<c>Et pro 1 panno curto scarlet[g] .... Ind' cust' 2s 4d

<a>De Willelmo Bodevyle pro 4 fardellis cum 33 pannis, 2 ulnis curtis sine grano .... Ind' cust' 38s 7¼d

<a>De Johanne Chyrche pro 2 fardellis cum 25 pannis, 17 ulnis curtis sine grano .... Ind' cust' 30s

<a>De Johanne Brampton pro 4 fardellis cum 42½ pannis curtis sine grano .... Ind' cust' 49s 7d

<a>De dicto Willelmo Bodvyle pro 1 fardello cum 2 pannis, 21 ulnis curtis sine grano .... Ind' cust' 3s 4¼d

<a>De Willelmo Corbet[h] pro 1 fardello cum 8 pannis, 8 ulnis curtis sine grano .... Ind' cust' 9s 8¾d

Auditor's marginated entries L2: <k> worsted simplex indigene <l> worsted simplex alienigene <m> worsted duplex indigene <n> worsted duplex alienigene <o> lectus de worsted simplex indigene <p> lectus worsted simplex alienigene <aa>-<aa> *Auditor's entry: Sum of the issues of the page L2.*

<a>De Johanne Granesden pro 1 bala, 1 fardello cum 22 pannis curtis sine grano ... Ind' cust' 25s 8d

<a>De Ricardo Perepount[i] pro 6 fardellis cum 46 pannis, [j]18 ulnis[j] curtis sine grano ... Ind' cust' 54s 6½d

<a>De Willelmo Havelok pro 1 fardello cum 5½ pannis curtis sine grano ... Ind' cust' 6s 5d

<a>De Henrico Logan pro 2 fardellis cum 4 pannis, 20 ulnis curtis sine grano ... Ind' cust' 5s 7¾d

<a>De Thoma Twyg[k] pro 2 fardellis cum 18 pannis curtis sine grano ... Ind' cust' 21s

<a>De Willelmo Haydok pro 1 fardello cum 6 pannis, 20 ulnis curtis sine grano ... Ind' cust' 7s 11¾d

<a>De Willelmo Grond pro 1 bala cum 14 pannis, 16 ulnis curtis sine grano ... Ind' cust' 17s 1½d

<m>Et pro 2 peciis worsted duplicis, 3 peciis worsted simplicis continentibus 6 pecias [j]worsted duplicis[j] ... Ind' cust' 12d

<m>Et pro 1 cista cum 1 pecia worsted duplicis ... Ind' cust' 2d

<a>De Ricardo Orgar pro 1 fardello cum 7½ pannis curtis sine grano ... Ind' cust' 8s 9d

De Alfounce Dyes pro 1 fardello cum 18 gros poyntes[l], 25 lb. fili Colonie. Precii 23s 4d ... cust' 3½d

<aa>£27 10s 1¾d<aa>

[a] Trenite *L3.* [b] Okerste *L3.* [c] Johnsson *L3.* [d] Petro *L3.* [e] Treguran *L3.* [f] Symound *L3.* [g] scarlett *L3.* [h] Corbett *L3.* [i] Perpoynt *L3.* [j-j] *Interlined L2.* [k] Twygg *L3.* [l] poyentes *L3.*

E122/73/20B f. 10r

[152] In navi Thome Adam vocata Grace Dieu de London' 11° die Aprilis *[11 Apr. 1446]*

<a>De Simone Horn pro 1 fardello cum 9 pannis, 6 ulnis curtis sine grano ... Ind' cust' 10s 9½d

<a>De Willelmo Swan pro 3 fardellis cum 52 pannis curtis sine grano ... Ind' cust' £3 8d

<a>De Thoma Ery[a] pro 1 bala cum 15½ pannis curtis sine grano ... Ind' cust' 18s 1d

<a>De Willelmo Pychard pro 2 fardellis cum 22 pannis curtis sine grano ... Ind' cust' 25s 8d

<a>De Johanne Brampton pro 1 bala cum 20 pannis curtis sine grano ... Ind' cust' 23s 4d

Auditor's marginated entries L2: <a> pannus indigenus <b> pannus de dimidio grano indigenus <c> scarleta indigena <d> pannus alienigenus <e> pannus de dimidio grano alienigenus <f> scarleta alienigena <g> pannus hanse <h> pannus de dimidio grano hanse <i> scarleta hanse

<a>De Johanne Chipnal pro 2 fardellis cum 22 pannis, 16 ulnis curtis sine grano .... Ind' cust' 26s 5½d

<a>De Thoma Fulborn[b] pro 5 fardellis cum 57 pannis curtis sine grano .... Ind' cust' £3 6s 6d

<a>De Alexandro Haysand[c] pro 3 fardellis, 2 pipis, 1 cista cum 48 pannis, 18 ulnis curtis sine grano .... Ind' cust' 56s 10½d

<c>Et pro 9 ulnis panni largi de scarlet[d] .... Ind' cust' 10½d

<a>De Roberto Edolfe pro 1 fardello cum 8 pannis, 6 ulnis curtis sine grano .... Ind' cust' 9s 7½d

[a] Eyr *L2*. [b] Fulbourn *L3*. [c] Haysaund *L3*. [d] scarlett *L3*.

[153] In galea Johannis Capell patroni [a]exeunte[a] eodem die *[11 Apr. 1446]*

<d>De Johanne Martyn pyloto[b] pro 1 cista cum 6 ulnis panni largi sine grano .... Al' cust' 8¼d

Et pro 12 lb. vasorum stanni. Precii 3s 4d .... cust' ½d

<d>De Nicholao de Napyll pro 3 cistis, 1 male[c] cum 10½[d] pannis curtis sine grano .... Al' cust' 28s 10½d

<d>Et pro [a]12 paribus caligarum continentibus[a] 6 ulnas panni largi sine grano .... Al' cust' 8¼d

Et pro 9 ulnis frisii [e]Wallie[e], 3 platers [f]de stanno[f]. Precii 6s .... cust' 1d

<d>De Marco Malipero pro 3 cistis cum 4 pannis, 8 ulnis curtis sine grano .... Al' cust' 11s 11d

Et pro 2 peciis worsted duplicis, 4 ulnis panni frisii Wallie. Precii 56s .... cust' 8½d

<n>Et pro predictis 2 peciis worsted duplicis .... Al' cust' 6d

<d>De Johanne de Curfu pro 1 cista cum 1 panno, 18 ulnis curtis sine grano .... Al' cust' 4s 10¾d

<d>De Danyelo[g] Clement pro 1 cista cum 10 pannis, 14 ulnis curtis sine grano .... Al' cust' 29s 1¼d

<aa>£18 16s 3½d<aa>

E122/73/20B f. 10[v]

<d>De Martino de Squytere[h] pro 1 cista cum 18 ulnis panni largi sine grano .... Al' cust' 2s ¾d

<d>De Johanne Mowbele[i] pro 1 cista cum 4 pannis curtis sine grano .... Al' cust' 11s

Et pro 1 centena, 56 lb. vasorum stanni. Precii 40s .... cust' 6d

<d>De Johanne de Dulcenyo pro 3 cistis cum 10 pannis, 5 ulnis curtis sine grano .... Al' cust' 28s 1d

Auditor's marginated entries L2: <k> worsted simplex indigene <l> worsted simplex alienigene <m> worsted duplex indigene <n> worsted duplex alienigene <o> lectus de worsted simplex indigene <p> lectus worsted simplex alienigene <aa>-<aa> *Auditor's entry: Sum of the issues of the page L2.*

<d>Et pro [a]4 dossenis [et] 10 paribus caligarum continentibus[a] 1 pannum, 5 ulnas curta sine grano.. Al' cust' 3s 4d

Et pro 1 barello cum 2 centenis lb. vasorum stanni. Precii 53s 4d....cust' 8d

<d>De Johanne de Nicholao pro 1 cista cum 1 panno, 10 ulnis curtis sine grano .... Al' cust' 3s 10¾d

<d>De Poulo de Squytere[h] pro 1 cista cum 14 ulnis panni largi sine grano .... Al' cust' 19¼d

<d>De Dominico [a]de[a] Suaso[j] pro 1 cista cum 21 ulnis panni largi sine grano .... Al' cust' 2s 5d

Et pro [a]2 paribus caligarum continentibus[a] 1 ulnam panni largi sine grano .... Al' cust' 1¼d

<d>De Jacomo Ryche [et] Peron Juratt[k] pro 1 cista cum 7 pannis, 10 ulnis curtis sine grano.. Al' cust' 20s 4¾d

Et pro [e]2[e] peciis [a]worsted[a] motle simplicis. Precii 30s....................cust' 4½d

<l>Et pro predictis 2 peciis [a]worsted[a] motle simplicis..................Al' cust' 3d

<d>De Nicholao de Napolo pro 1 fardello cum 3 pannis, 11 ulnis curtis sine grano .... Al' cust' 9s 6¼d

<d>De Alegreto de Bodna pro 1 cista cum [a]1 pecia kersey, 2 paribus caligarum continentibus in toto[a] 9 ulnas panni largi sine grano................ Al' cust' 12¾d[l]

Et pro 16 discis [f]de stanno[f]. Precii 3s 4d ....cust' ½d

<d>De Johanne de Jane pro 1 cista, 1 sacco, 1 barello cum 4 pannis curtis sine grano .... Al' cust' 11s

<d>Et pro [a]20 paribus caligarum continentibus[a] 10 ulnas panni largi sine grano .... Al' cust' 13¾d

Et pro 5 candelabris, 1 parva pelvi[m] [a]et[a] 1 lavour de latone, 18 lb. vasorum stanni. Precii in toto 13s 4d..cust' 2d

<d>De Alegreto de Catero[n] pro 1 cista cum [a]6 paribus caligarum, 1 mantello continentibus in toto[a] 6 ulnas panni largi sine grano...................Al' cust' 8¼d

De Dederico [a]de[a] Almayn pro 1 cista cum 200 pellibus agnorum mesan[is]. Precii 26s 8d ....cust' 4d

<d>De Johanne de Medyco pro 1 fardello cum 11 ulnis panni largi sine grano .... Al' cust' 15¼d

Et pro 1 pecia worsted duplicis. Precii 26s 8d.................................cust' 4d

<n>Et pro predicta 1 pecia worsted duplicis.................................Al' cust' 3d

<d>De Matheo[o] Flor pro 1 cista cum 1 panno, 8 ulnis curtis sine grano .... Al' cust' 3s 8d

<d>De Lazaro de Boyan pro 1 cista cum 8 ulnis panni largi sine grano .... Al' cust' 11d

<d>Et pro [a]6 paribus caligarum continentibus[a] 3 ulnas panni largi sine grano .... Al' cust' 4d

Auditor's marginated entries L2: <a> pannus indigenus <b> pannus de dimidio grano indigenus <c> scarleta indigena <d> pannus alienigenus <e> pannus de dimidio grano alienigenus <f> scarleta alienigena <g> pannus hanse <h> pannus de dimidio grano hanse <i> scarleta hanse

<d>De Julio Georg[io] Caraldo[p] pro 3 cistis cum 20½ pannis curtis sine grano .... Al' cust' 56s 4½d
<aa>£8 21½d<aa>

E122/73/20B f. 11[r]

<d>De Bernardo Barber pro 1 cista, 1 barello et 1 sacco cum 3 pannis, 17 ulnis curtis sine grano .... Al' cust' 10s 2½d
Et pro 6 coverlettes Northfolke[q], 2 centenis lb. vasorum stanni. Precii in toto £3 12s 10d[r] .... cust' 11d
<d>De Andrea Conterin pro 2 fardellis cum 9 pannis, 13 ulnis curtis sine grano .... Al' cust' 26s 3d
<e>Et pro 14 ulnis panni largi de dimidio grano .... Al' cust' 2s 5d
Et pro 1 pecia sarge duple, 1 pecia fustian. Precii in toto 46s 8d ...... cust' 7d
<n>Et pro predicta 1 pecia sarge duple .... Al' cust' 3d
<d>De Nicholao Maryn pro 1 cista cum 3 pannis curtis sine grano .... Al' cust' 8s 3d
<d>De Bertuche[s] Dodo pro 1 cista cum 16 ulnis panni largi sine grano .... Al' cust' 22d
<d>De Andrea Russo pro 1 sacco cum 12 ulnis panni largi sine grano .... Al' cust' 16½d
[t]•<d>De Johanne Capell patrono pro 7 balis cum 204 pannis curtis sine grano .... Al' cust' £28 12d
[t]•<d>•[u]Et[v] pro 1 bala cum 48 pannis curtis sine grano .... Al' cust' £6 12s
[t]•[u]Et pro [w]55 peciis stanni ponderantibus 15 miliaria lb.[w] Precii £150 .... cust' 37s 6d
[t]De Lowes Bernard[x] pro [y]69 peciis stanni ponderantibus 17 miliaria, 3 centenis, 16 lb.[y] Precii £173 .... cust' 43s 3d
[t]De Marco Priole patrono [z]pro 122 peciis stanni ponderantibus 31 miliaria, 4 centenas, 6 lb.[z] Precii £314 .... cust' £3 18s 6d
[t]Et pro [aa]48 peciis stanni ponderantibus 12 miliaria, 3 centenas, 17 lb.[aa] Precii £123 .... cust' 30s 9d
[t]•<d>Et pro 2 balis cum 85 pannis curtis sine grano .... Al' cust' £11 13s 9d
[t]De Marco Barbarigo pro [ab]32 peciis stanni ponderantibus 8 miliaria lb.[ab] Precii £81 .... cust' 20s 3d
<a>De Johanne Maunche pro 5 balis cum 160 pannis curtis sine grano .... Ind' cust' £9 6s 8d
[t]De Jacomo Dodo [ac]factori Juliani Contarin[ac] [ad]pro 11 peciis stanni ponderantibus 3 miliaria, 2¾ centenas [lb.][ad] Precii £32 15s .... cust' 8s 2¼d
[t]•<d>De Humfrido Justynean pro 2 balis cum 52 pannis curtis sine grano .... Al' cust' £7 3s

Auditor's marginated entries L2: <k> worsted simplex indigene <l> worsted simplex alienigene <m> worsted duplex indigene <n> worsted duplex alienigene <o> lectus de worsted simplex indigene <p> lectus worsted simplex alienigene <aa>-<aa> *Auditor's entry: Sum of the issues of the page L2.*

[a-a] *Omitted L3.* [b] pylote *L3.* [c] male *L3.* [d] 10 *L3.* [e-e] *Omitted L2.* [f-f] stanni *L3.* [g] Danyello *L3.* [h] Squetery *L3.* [i] Moubele *L3.* [j] Swaso *L3.* [k] Jur' *L2.* [l] *Corrected in L2 from* 12¼d. [m] pelle *L3, in error.* [n] Cator *L2.* [o] de *follows L3.* [p] Caroldo *L2.* [q] Norffolke *L3.* [r] 6d *L3.* [s] Bertuse *L3.* [t] mercator de Venisia *marginated against this entry L2, L3.* [u-u] *These two lines in reverse order L3.* [v] dicto patrono *follows L3.* [w-w] 15 miliariis lb. stanni *L3.* [x] Bernardo *L3.* [y-y] 17 miliariis, 3 centenis [et] 16 lb. stanni *L3.* [z-z] cum *(in error)* 31 miliariis, 7 centenis, 6 lb. stanni *L3.* [aa-aa] 12 miliariis, 3 centenis, 17 lb. stanni *L3.* [ab-ab] 8 miliariis lb. stanni *L3.* [ac-ac] *Interlined L2, L3.* [ad-ad] cum *(in error)* 3 miliariis, 2¾ centenis [lb.] stanni *L3.*

[154] In galea Marci Priole patroni exeunte eodem die *[11 Apr. 1446]*

<d>De Nicholao Belvyder pro 1 cista cum 3 pannis, 10 ulnis curtis sine grano .... Al' cust' 9s 4¾d

<d>De Nicholao Custaunce pro 1 cista cum 5½ pannis curtis sine grano .... Al' cust' 15s 1½d

<aa>£77 11s 5½d[a•]<aa>

E122/73/20B f. 11v

<d>De Anthonio de Tragura pro 1 cista cum 2 pannis curtis sine grano .... Al' cust' 5s 6d

<d>De Dominico de Dulcenio pro 1 cista cum 12 ulnis panni largi sine grano .... Al' cust' 16½d

<d>De Pero Som pro 1 cista cum 20 ulnis panni largi sine grano Al' cust' 2s 3½d

<d>De Nadale de Pero pro 1 cista cum 1 panno, 16 ulnis curtis sine grano .... Al' cust' 4s 7d

Et pro 70 lb. vasorum stanni. Precii 16s 8d .... cust' 2½d

<d>De Georgio de Traho pro 1 sacco cum 18 ulnis panni largi sine grano .... Al' cust' 2s ¾d

<d>De Georgio de Tregura pro 1 cista cum 5 pannis, 21 ulnis curtis sine grano .... Al' cust' 16s 2d

Et pro 16 ulnis frisii Wallie. Precii 10s .... cust' 1½d

<d>De Johanne dAragose pro 1 cista cum 14 ulnis panni largi sine grano .... Al' cust' 19¼d

<d>De Andrea [b]de[b] Sooro pro 1 cista cum 2 pannis curtis sine grano .... Al' cust' 5s 6d

Et pro 28 lb. vasorum stanni. Precii 6s 8d .... cust' 1d

<d>De Alagreto[c] de Cursula pro 1 cista cum 14 [d]ulnis[d] panni largi sine grano .... Al' cust' 19¼d

<d>De Luca de la Tour[e] pro 1 cista cum 8 ulnis panni largi sine grano .... Al' cust' 11d

Auditor's marginated entries L2: <a> pannus indigenus <b> pannus de dimidio grano indigenus <c> scarleta indigena <d> pannus alienigenus <e> pannus de dimidio grano alienigenus <f> scarleta alienigena <g> pannus hanse <h> pannus de dimidio grano hanse <i> scarleta hanse

<d>De [f]Pero de Schoa[f] pro 1 cista cum 3 ulnis panni largi sine grano . Al' cust' 4d
Et pro 12 lb. vasorum stanni. Precii 3s 4d .... cust' ½d
<d>De Nicholao de Anthonio Counter pro 6 cistis [b]et[b] 4 parvis barellis cum 32 pannis, 10 ulnis curtis sine grano .... Al' cust' £4 9s 1¾d
Et pro 15 peciis worsted motle simplicis, 50 dossenis cappis rotundis[g], 6 centenis, 84 lb. vasorum stanni, 5 peciis stanni ponderantibus 1 miliarium, 28 lb. et extra 20 dossenis pellium vitulorum [b]tannatarum[b]. Precii in toto £37 5s .... cust' 9s 3¾d
<l>Et pro predictis 15 peciis worsted motle simplicis .... Al' cust' 22½d
<d>De Zakaria Pascalego pro 1 panno, 6 ulnis curtis sine grano . Al' cust' 3s 5¼d
<d>Et pro 1 cista cum 1 panno, 22 ulnis curtis sine grano .... Al' cust' 5s 3¼d
<d>De Bernardo Pascalego pro 1 panno, 6 ulnis curtis sine grano .... Al' cust' 3s 5¼d
<d>De Marco Malypero pro 1 cista cum 4 pannis curtis sine grano .. Al' cust' 11s
<d>De Marco Pryole [b]patrono[b] pro 2 cistis cum 7 pannis curtis sine grano .... Al' cust' 19s 3d
<d>De Bartholomeo [h]de la Indeke[h] pro 1 cista cum 3 pannis, 17 ulnis curtis sine grano .... Al' cust' 10s 2½d
Et pro 27 ulnis panni stricti Wallie. Precii 15s .... cust' 2¼d
<d>De Felice Cukaro[i] pro 1 cista cum 6 pannis, 15 ulnis curtis sine grano .... Al' cust' 18s 2½d
<aa>£10 13s 8¾d<aa>

E122/73/20B f. 12r

De Francisco Venir[j] pro 1 barello cum 77 lb. vasorum stanni. Precii 18s 4d .... cust' 2¾d
<d>De [k]Pero Gandulpho[k] pro 1 cista cum 6 pannis curtis sine grano .... Al' cust' 16s 6d
<d>De Dominico de Peruta pro 1 cista cum 8 pannis, 20 ulnis curtis sine grano .... Al' cust' 24s 3½d
<d>De Alegreto de Squytere[l] pro 1 cista cum 3 ulnis panni largi sine grano .... Al' cust' 4¼d
<d>Et pro 4 paribus caligarum continentibus 2 ulnas panni largi sine grano .... Al' cust' 2¾d
<d>De Gaspero Furyan pro 1 cista cum 8½ pannis curtis sine grano .... Al' cust' 23s 4½d
<d>De Johanne de Andrea pro 2 cistis cum 7 pannis, 6 ulnis curtis sine grano .... Al' cust' 19s 11¼d
Et pro 6 peciis stanni ponderantibus 1 miliarium, 4 centenis, 84 lb. Precii £14 15s .... cust' 3s 8¼d

Auditor's marginated entries L2: <k> worsted simplex indigene <l> worsted simplex alienigene <m> worsted duplex indigene <n> worsted duplex alienigene <o> lectus de worsted simplex indigene <p> lectus worsted simplex alienigene <aa>-<aa> *Auditor's entry: Sum of the issues of the page L2.*

<d>De Jacomo de Nicolo[m] pro 1 cista cum 12½ pannis curtis sine grano ... Al' cust' 34s 4½d
<d>De Michaelle de Todero pro 1 cista cum 5 pannis curtis sine grano ... Al' cust' 13s 9d
<d>De Jacomo de Portyngal pro 1 cista cum 15 pannis curtis sine grano ... Al' cust' 41s 3d
De Lowes Modaso pro 1 cista, 1 mala[n] cum 2 centenis, 6 lb. vasorum stanni. Precii 53s 4d ... cust' 8d
<d>Et pro 3 pannis, 4 ulnis curtis sine grano ... Al' cust' 8s 8½d
<d>De Francisco Pascalego pro 1 cista, 1 mal[a][o] cum 8 pannis, 20 ulnis curtis sine grano ... Al' cust' 24s 3½d
<d>De Pero de Curfu pro 1 cista cum 12 ulnis panni largi sine grano ... Al' cust' 16½d
<a>De Thoma Couper pro 1 parvo fardello cum 12 ulnis panni largi sine grano ... Ind' cust' 7d
<b>De magistro Willelmo Hatteclyffe[p] pro 1 fardello cum 4 ulnis panni largi de dimidio [b]grano[b] ... Ind' cust' 3½d
<c>Et pro 9 ulnis panni largi de scarlet[q] ... Ind' cust' 10½d
De[r] Dominico de Peruto pro 3 bundellis [s]cum 8 centenis, 3 lb. shotyn[t] tyn[s]. Precii £8 13s 4d ... cust' 2s 2d
<d>Et pro 1 panno curto sine grano ... Al' cust' 2s 9d
[u]De Johanne Capell patrono pro 165 peciis stanni ponderantibus 45 miliaria lb. Precii £450 ... cust' £5 12s 6d
[u]De Lowes Bernard[v] pro 54 peciis stanni ponderantibus 13 miliaria, 7 centenis, 23 lb. Precii £137 ... cust' 34s 3d
[u•<d>]De Marco Priole[w] patrono pro 3 balis cum 123 pannis curtis sine grano ... Al' cust' £16 18s 3d
[u]Et pro 86 peciis stanni ponderantibus 22 miliaria, 7 lb. Precii £220 ... cust' 55s
De Dominico de Peruto pro 3 fardellis cum 8¾ centenis, 28 lb. [x]stanni schotyn[x]. Precii £9 4s 2d ... cust' 2s 3¾d
<aa>£38 23d[y•<aa>]

E122/73/20B f. 12[v]

[u]De Marco Barbarigo[z] pro 68 peciis stanni ponderantibus 16 miliaria, 9¾ centenas, 10 lb. Precii £169 16s 8d ... cust' 42s 5½d
<a>De Johanne Maunche pro 4 balis [b]et[b] 1 fardello cum 95½ pannis curtis sine grano ... Ind' cust' £5 11s 5d
[u•<d>]De Jacomo Dodo [d]factori Juliani Contarin[d] pro 1 bala cum 36½ pannis curtis sine grano ... [aa]Al'[aa] cust' £5 4½d

Auditor's marginated entries L2: <a> pannus indigenus <b> pannus de dimidio grano indigenus <c> scarleta indigena <d> pannus alienigenus <e> pannus de dimidio grano alienigenus <f> scarleta alienigena <g> pannus hanse <h> pannus de dimidio grano hanse <i> scarleta hanse

De Augustino[ab] Priole pro 10 peciis stanni ponderantibus 2 miliaria, 4 centenas, 28 lb. Precii £24 5s .... cust' 6s ¾d

<d>Et pro 1 mal[a] cum 2 pannis, 16 ulnis curtis sine grano.... Al' cust' 7s 4d

u•<d>De dicto Marco[ac] Barbarigo pro 1 fardello cum 12 pannis curtis sine grano .... Al' cust' 33s

u•<d>De Humfrido Justynean pro 1 bala, 3 fardellis cum 35 pannis curtis sine grano .... Al' cust' £4 16s 3d

<e>Et pro[ad] 2 pannis, 23 ulnis curtis[ae] de dimidio grano ... Al' cust' [af]12s 2½d[af]

<d>Et pro 2 balis cum 47 pannis curtis sine grano .... Al' cust' £6 9s 3d

<aa>£26 17s 11½d<aa> [ag]Item 4¾d[ag]

[a] *Corrected in L2 from* 2½d. [b-b] *Omitted L3.* [c] Alegreto *L3.* [d-d] *Interlined L2.* [e] Tor *L3.* [f-f] Petro de Shoa *L3.* [g] retundis *L3, in error.* [h-h] Indeka *L3.* [i] Cucaro *L3.* [j] Vener *L3.* [k-k] Petro Candulpho *L3.* [l] Squetery *L3.* [m] Nicholao *L3.* [n] male *L3.* [o] valice *L3.* [p] Hatecleff *L3.* [q] scarlett *L3.* [r] dicto *follows L3.* [s-s] stanni shotyn ponderantibus 8 centenas, 3 lb. *L3.* [t] sshotyn *L2, apparently in error.* [u] mercator de Venisia *marginated against this entry L2, L3.* [v] Bernardo *L3.* [w] Pole *L3, in error.* [x-x] shot tyn *L3.* [y] *Corrected in L2 from* 22¾d. [z] Barbagrigo *L3, in error.* [aa-aa] *Interlined above* Ind'*, struck through L2.* [ab] Austyn *L3.* [ac] magistro *L3, in error.* [ad] *The number* 1 *follows, struck through L2.* [ae] panni largi *L2.* [af-af] *Interlined above* 11s 9¾d*, struck through L2.* [ag-ag] *Auditor's supplement necessitated by the correction of the customs charges on the goods of* Humfrid Justynean *L2.*

E122/73/20B f. 13[r]

[155] In navi Lambe Johan Williamsson vocata Marykneght[a] de Ernemoth 20° die Aprilis *[20 Apr. 1446]*

De [b]Gerardo Bart[b] pro 1 barello cum 6 centenis lb. vasorum stanni. Precii £8 .... cust' 2s

<d>De Thoma Ryse[c] pro 1 fardello cum[d] 9 pannis, 6 ulnis curtis sine grano .... Al' cust' 25s 5¼d

<f>Et pro 1 rolla cum 16 ulnis panni largi de scarlet[e] .... Al' cust' 3s 8d

<d>Et pro 3 ulnis panni stricti continentibus 1½ ulnas panni largi sine grano .... Al' cust' 2¼d

<a>De Simone Marchall pro 1 fardello cum 7 pannis, 18 ulnis curtis sine grano .... Ind' cust' 9s ½d

<a>De Johanne Malter pro 1 bala cum 10 pannis curtis sine grano .... Ind' cust' 11s 8d

[f]De Anthonio Senturyon pro 8 pipis cum 5000 lb. alum Foille. Precii £12 .... cust' 3s[f]

<a>De Johanne Smyth pro 1 cista, 1 fardello cum 1 panno, 16 ulnis curtis sine grano .... Ind' cust' 23½d

Auditor's marginated entries L2: <k> worsted simplex indigene <l> worsted simplex alienigene <m> worsted duplex indigene <n> worsted duplex alienigene <o> lectus de worsted simplex indigene <p> lectus worsted simplex alienigene <aa>-<aa> *Auditor's entry: Sum of the issues of the page L2.*

<m>Et pro 13 peciis worsted duplicis continentibus 19 pecias Ind' cust' 3s 2d

De Gylys Braynford pro 2 pokes cum 10 vagis [et] 7 petris thrummes[g], 1 corfe cum 11 dossenis pellium vitulorum tannatarum, 160 pellibus cuniculorum crude sesone. Precii £10 5s 6d ...... cust' 2s 7d

<a>De Ricardo Riche pro 2 balis cum 47 pannis curtis sine grano ...... Ind' cust' 54s 10d

<m>Et pro 9½ peciis worsted duplicis continentibus 14 pecias ...... Ind' cust' 2s 4d

<a>De Ricardo Phyppys[h] pro 1 bala cum 10 pannis curtis sine grano ...... Ind' cust' 11s 8d

<d>De Jacobo Petersson pro 1 fardello cum 7 pannis, 6 ulnis curtis sine grano ...... Al' cust' 19s 11¼d

Et extra pro 3 deker [i]parvarum[i] peciarum scissarum de ventribus vaccarum tannatarum, 6 dossenis pellium vitulorum crude. Precii 30s....... cust' 4½d

<a>De Johanne Colrede pro 1 cista cum 1 panno curto sine grano ... Ind' cust' 14d

De Matheo Feller pro 3 pokes cum 15½ vagis thrummes[g]. Precii £11 12s 6d ...... cust' 2s 11d

<a>•[j]De Johanne Lambert[k] pro 1 bala cum 12 pannis, 14 ulnis curtis sine grano ...... Ind' cust' 14s 8¼d

<a>•[j]De Henrico Smyth pro 1 fardello cum 6 pannis, 3 ulnis curtis sine grano ...... Ind' cust' 7s 1¾d

<a>De Thoma Niche pro 3 balis cum 118 pannis, 6 ulnis curtis sine grano ...... Ind' cust' £6 17s 11½d

<m>Et pro 5 peciis worsted duplicis continentibus 7 pecias....... Ind' cust' 14d

<aa>£15 16s 10¾d[l]•<aa>

E122/73/20B f. 13[v]

<a>De Johanne Okeherst[m] pro 1 bala cum 36 pannis, 6 ulnis curtis sine grano ...... Ind' cust' 42s 3½d

<a>•[n]De Johanne Lytylton pro 2 balis cum 40 pannis curtis sine grano ...... Ind' cust' 46s 8d

<a>•[n]De Johanne Dobbes pro 1 fardello cum 10 pannis, 8 ulnis curtis sine grano ...... Ind' cust' 12s ¾d

<a>De Johanne Crowe pro 1 bala, 1 fardello cum 24½ pannis curtis sine grano ...... Ind' cust' 28s 7d

[o]De Johanne Salmer pro 6 barellis cum 3 miliariis, 6 centenis lb. vasorum stanni. Precii £45 ...... cust' 11s 3d

<a>•[o]De Johanne Harwe[p] pro 1 bala cum 26 pannis, 22 ulnis curtis sine grano ...... Ind' cust' 31s 5d

<g>De Lambert Jose pro 1 bala cum 12 pannis curtis sine grano ... Hans cust' 12s

Auditor's marginated entries L2: <a> pannus indigenus <b> pannus de dimidio grano indigenus <c> scarleta indigena <d> pannus alienigenus <e> pannus de dimidio grano alienigenus <f> scarleta alienigena <g> pannus hanse <h> pannus de dimidio grano hanse <i> scarleta hanse

Et pro 5 rollis frisii Wallie, 6 barellis cum 3 miliariis, 6 centenis lb. vasorum stanni. Precii in toto £50 6s 8d ... cust' 12s 7d

<g>De [q]Gerardo Gasthorp[q] pro 1 bala cum 22 pannis, 20 ulnis curtis sine grano ... Hans cust' 22s 10d

<h>Et pro 4 ulnis panni largi de dimidio grano ... Hans cust' 3d

<i>Et pro 17 ulnis panni largi de scarlet[e] ... Hans cust' 17d

Et pro 1 pecia worsted duplicis[r], 6½ gros poyntes[s], [t]2[t] hures de dimidio grano, 13 pellibus cheverellorum, 39 godis panni stricti Wallie et ½ rolla frisii Wallie. Precii in toto £4 ... cust' 12d

<a>De Roberto Damyan pro 2 balis cum 62 pannis, 10 ulnis curtis sine grano ... Ind' cust' £3 12s 10d

<g>De Clays Swart pro 1 bala cum 26 pannis curtis sine grano ... Hans cust' 26s

Et pro 18 godis panni stricti Wallie. Precii 15s ... cust' 2¼d

<a>De Ricardo Onhond[u] pro 1 bala cum 36 pannis, 10 ulnis curtis sine grano ... Ind' cust' 42s 6d

<a>De dicto Ricardo Riche pro 6 balis cum 263 pannis, 20 ulnis curtis sine grano ... Ind' cust' £15 7s 9¾d

<m>Et pro 29 peciis worsted duplicis continentibus 43 pecias Ind' cust' 7s 2d

<g>De Johanne Dasse pro 2 balis cum 67 pannis, 8 ulnis curtis sine grano ... Hans cust' £3 7s 4d

De Johanne Petersson pro 2 barellis cum 16 coverlettes Northfolke, 17 chargeours[v] de stanno, 20 pellibus cuniculorum crude. Precii in toto £3 6s 8d ... cust' 10d

<g>De [w]Cristean van Bleyken[w] pro 5 balis cum 103 pannis, 16 ulnis curtis sine grano ... Hans cust' £5 3s 8d

<i>Et pro 1 panno, 7 ulnis curtis[x] de scarlet[e] ... Hans cust' 2s 7d

Et pro 4½ rollis frisii Wallie. Precii £4 10s ... cust' 13½d

<aa>£42 14s 4¾d<aa>

E122/73/20B f. 14[r]

<a>De Willelmo Hatter pro 1 bala[y] cum 30 pannis curtis sine grano ... Ind' cust' 35s

<a>De Johanne Lok[z] pro 1 bala cum 12 pannis, 4 ulnis curtis sine grano ... Ind' cust' 14s 2½d

<a>De Matheo Foucher pro 2 balis cum 71 pannis curtis sine grano ... Ind' cust' £4 2s 10d

De Leonardo van Werd pro 1 parvo poke cum 1 vaga thrummes[h]. Precii 15s ... cust' 2¼d

De [aa]Goykyn van Lynt[aa] pro 1 maunda [i]cum[i] 3 parvis maundis cum 12,400 pellibus cuniculorum crude, unde 10,000 pelles cuniculorum sesone[ab], 2 barellis cum butiro debili. [ac]Precii in toto £28 13s 4d[ac] ... cust' 7s 2d

Auditor's marginated entries L2: <k> worsted simplex indigene <l> worsted simplex alienigene <m> worsted duplex indigene <n> worsted duplex alienigene <o> lectus de worsted simplex indigene <p> lectus worsted simplex alienigene <aa>-<aa> *Auditor's entry: Sum of the issues of the page L2.*

<a>De Johanne Malvern pro 2 balis cum 95 pannis, 20 ulnis curtis sine grano .... Ind' cust' £5 11s 9¾d
<a>De Johanne Brod[ad] pro 1 bala cum 21 pannis curtis sine grano .... Ind' cust' 24s 6d
<m>Et pro 7 peciis worsted duplicis continentibus 10 pecias.....Ind' cust' 20d
<a>De Alexandro Orable[ae] pro 1 bala cum 32 pannis, 8 ulnis curtis sine grano .... Ind' cust' 37s 8¾d
<a>De Augustino[af] Stratton pro 1 bala cum 17 pannis, 16 ulnis curtis sine grano .... Ind' cust' 20s 7½d
<m>Et pro 71 peciis worsted duplicis continentibus 106 pecias .... Ind' cust' 17s 8d
<g>De Petro Cangheter pro 2 balis cum 34 pannis, 8 ulnis curtis sine grano .... Hans cust' 34s 4d
<a>De James Begraunt[ag] pro 1 bala cum 12 pannis, 22 ulnis curtis sine grano .... Ind' cust' 15s 1d
De Rogero van Messem[ah] pro 1 corfe cum 3000 pellibus cuniculorum crude, unde stage 800 pelles, 1 barello cum 6 centenis lb. vasorum stanni. Precii £14 10s.......... cust' 3s 7½d
<a>De Willelmo Grond pro 1 bala, 1 cista cum 49½ pannis curtis sine grano .... Ind' cust' 57s 9d
<m>Et pro 27 peciis worsted duplicis continentibus 40 pecias Ind' cust' 6s 8d
<a>De Willelmo Petyte pro 1 fardello cum 3 pannis curtis sine grano .... Ind' cust' 3s 6d
<m>Et pro 27 peciis worsted duplicis continentibus 40 pecias Ind' cust' 6s 8d
<a>De Johanne Dey pro 1 bala cum 15 pannis, octo ulnis curtis sine grano .... Ind' cust' 17s 10¾d
<a>De Matheo Leke pro 1 bala cum 25 pannis curtis sine grano. Ind' cust' 29s 2d
<g>De Johanne Hathyltak[ai] pro 1 bala cum 24 pannis curtis sine grano .... Hans cust' 24s
<g>De Tilman Crome pro 1 bala cum 27 pannis curtis sine grano . Hans cust' 27s
<aa>£28 19s 1d<aa>

E122/73/20B f. 14v

<g>De Willelmo Ketwey pro 3 balis, 1 fardello, 1 cista cum 89 pannis, 6 ulnis curtis sine grano.......... Hans cust' £4 9s 3d
Et pro 88 godis panni stricti Wallie, 3 gros pointes[s], 1 centena, 28 lb. vasorum stanni, 1 potelle potte, 2 quarte pottes et 2 pynt pottes [aj]stanni[aj]. Precii in toto £3.......... cust' 9d
<g>De Johanne Warenthorp pro 3 balis cum 75½ pannis curtis sine grano .... Hans cust' £3 15s 6d
Et pro 1 rolla frisii Wallie, 4 gros poyntes[s]. Precii 30s.......... cust' 4½d

Auditor's marginated entries L2: <a> pannus indigenus <b> pannus de dimidio grano indigenus <c> scarleta indigena <d> pannus alienigenus <e> pannus de dimidio grano alienigenus <f> scarleta alienigena <g> pannus hanse <h> pannus de dimidio grano hanse <i> scarleta hanse

<g>De Arnoldo van Pynxsten pro 3 balis cum 50 pannis, 14 ulnis curtis sine grano ... Hans cust' 50s 7d

Et pro 1½ rollis frisii [i]Wallie[i], 20 godis panni stricti Wallie[ak], 2 barellis cum 12 centenis lb. vasorum stanni. [al]Precii in toto £18 3s 4d[al] ... cust' 4s 6½d

<g>De Hans Hope pro 1 bala cum 21 pannis, 6 ulnis curtis sine grano ... Hans cust' 21s 3d

<g>De Henrico Nase pro 1 bala cum 25½ pannis curtis sine grano ... Hans cust' 25s 6d

Et pro 3 barellis cum 14 centenis, 56 lb. vasorum stanni, 10 dossenis zonarum de pergameno. Precii in toto £19 13s 4d ... cust' 4s 11d

<d>De Dominico Spyngyll pro 2 rollis cum 12 ulnis panni largi sine grano ... Al' cust' 16½d

<e>Et pro 17½ ulnis panni largi de dimidio grano ... Al' cust' 3s

<f>Et pro 8¼ ulnis panni largi de scarlet[e] ... Al' cust' 22¾d

De Arnoldo Andreasson[am] pro 2 barellis cum 12 centenis lb. vasorum stanni. Precii £16 ... cust' 4s

<d>De Henrico van Hofstatte[am] pro 1 werkefatte cum 18 ulnis panni largi sine grano ... Al' cust' 2s ¾d

Et pro 3 dossenis pellium ovium tawed, 300 pellibus cuniculorum crude, 3 gros zonarum de pergameno, 3 ulnis panni largi Wallie. Precii in toto 30s ... cust' 4½d

<a>De Willelmo Gardener pro 1 bala cum 18 pannis, 16 ulnis curtis sine grano ... Ind' cust' 21s 9½d

De Matheo Feller pro 1 poke cum 2½ vagis thrummes[g]. Precii 37s 6d. cust' 5¾d

<aa>£15 7s 7¾d<aa>

E122/73/20B f. 15[r]

<g>De Roberto Blyterswyke[ao] pro 2 balis, 1 basket[ap] cum 28 pannis, 10 ulnis curtis sine grano ... Hans cust' 28s 5d

<g>Et pro 2[aq] dossenis motle continentibus 12 ulnas panni largi sine grano ... Hans cust' 6d

Et pro 60 godis panni stricti Wallie, 2 chafowres[ar] de latone. Precii in toto 43s ... cust' 6½d

<d>De Gerardo[as] Brown pro 1 fardello cum 4 pannis curtis sine grano ... Al' cust' 11s

<a>De Johanne Lyney[at] pro 1 fardello cum 8 pannis curtis sine grano ... Ind' cust' 9s 4d

<a>De Hugone Wyche pro 1 bala, 1 fardello cum 28 pannis, 16 ulnis curtis sine grano ... Ind' cust' 33s 5½d

Auditor's marginated entries L2: <k> worsted simplex indigene <l> worsted simplex alienigene <m> worsted duplex indigene <n> worsted duplex alienigene <o> lectus de worsted simplex indigene <p> lectus worsted simplex alienigene <aa>-<aa> *Auditor's entry: Sum of the issues of the page L2.*

<a>De Johanne Brod[ad] pro 1 bala cum 25 pannis curtis sine grano .... Ind' cust' 29s 2d

<a>De Thoma Dey pro 1 bala cum 20 pannis curtis sine grano ... Ind' cust' 23s 4d

<a>De Laurencio Herd pro 1 fardello cum 8 pannis curtis sine grano .... Ind' cust' 9s 4d

De Arnoldo Henrykesson[au] pro 1 barello cum 6 centenis lb. vasorum stanni, 1 barello cum 27 gros [et] 7 dossenis zonarum de pergameno [i]et[i] 23 gros parvarum zonarum de pergameno, 100 pellibus ovium tawed. Precii in toto £12 10s .... cust' 3s 1½d

<d>De Hans Busshe[av] pro 1 fardello cum [aw]15 peciis kersey continentibus 5 pannos curtos[aw] sine grano .... Al' cust' 13s 9d[ax]

De Hans Armerer pro 1 barello cum 6 centenis lb. vasorum stanni. Precii £8 .... cust' 2s

<a>De Radulpho Verney pro 1 fardello cum [ay]22 peciis kersey continentibus 7 pannos, 8 ulnas curtos[ay] sine grano .... Ind' cust' 8s 6¾d

De Roberto Blyterswyke[ao] pro 1 bala, 1 fardello cum 917 godis panni stricti Wallie. Precii £29 10s .... cust'[az] 7s 4½d[ba]

<aa>£8 19s 10¾d<aa>

[a] Mariknygh *L3.* [b-b] Gerrardo Bard *L3.* [c] Januas' [Januense] *follows L3.* [d] pro *L2, in error.* [e] scarlett *L3.* [f-f] *The goods of* Anthonio Senturyon *are entered after those of* John Smyth *L3.* [g] thrummz *L3.* [h] Phillippus *L3.* [i-i] *Omitted L3.* [j] *Entries for the goods of John* Lambert *and Henry* Smyth *in reverse order L3.* [k] Lamberd *L3.* [l] *Corrected in L2 from* 10½d. [m] Okerste *L3.* [n] *Entries for the goods of John* Lytylton *and John* Dobbes *in reverse order L3.* [o] *Entries for the goods of John* Salmer *and John* Harwe *in reverse order L3.* [p] Harowe *L3.* [q-q] Gerrardo Gasteropp *L3.* [r] *On the next line* Et pro *follows L3.* [s] poyentes *L3.* [t-t] *Interlined L2.* [u] Honehand *L3.* [v] chargers *L3.* [w-w] Cristian van Bleken *L3.* [x] panni largi *L3.* [y] balla *L2.* [z] Lokke *L3.* [aa-aa] Goykent van Lente *L3.* [ab] Precii £28 *(then, on the next line)* Et pro *follow L3 (cf. variant ac).* [ac-ac] Precii 13s 4d *L3 (cf. variant ab).* [ad] Brodde *L3.* [ae] Orabill *L3.* [af] Austyn *L3.* [ag] Bengrant *L3.* [ah] Messen *L3.* [ai] Hatiltake *L3.* [aj-aj] de stanno *L3.* [ak] Precii 43s 4d *(then, on the next line)* Et pro *follow L3 (cf. variant al).* [al-al] Prccii £16 *L3.* [am] Adrcansson *L3.* [an] Offestat *L3.* [ao] Blitersweke *L3.* [ap] basketto *L3.* [aq] panni *follows L3.* [ar] chafours *L3.* [as] Gerrardo *L3.* [at] Lynney *L3.* [au] Henriksson *L3.* [av] Busche *L3.* [aw-aw] 5 pannis curtis *L2.* [ax] ¾d *follows, struck through L2.* [ay-ay] 7 pannis, 8 ulnis curtis *L2.* [az] cust' *repeated L2, in error.* [ba] *On the next line the entry for the goods of Henry Smyth is repeated L3, in error.*

E122/73/20B f. 15v

Auditor's marginated entries L2: <a> pannus indigenus <b> pannus de dimidio grano indigenus <c> scarleta indigena <d> pannus alienigenus <e> pannus de dimidio grano alienigenus <f> scarleta alienigena <g> pannus hanse <h> pannus de dimidio grano hanse <i> scarleta hanse

[156] In navi Copyn Lambe vocata Seynt Martynskneyght[a] eodem die *[20 Apr. 1446]*

<a>De Roberto Drope[b] pro 1 panno, 1 ulna curtis sine grano ....Ind' cust' 14¾d

<c>Et pro 6 ulnis panni largi de scarlet[c] ....Ind' cust' 7d

De Nicholao Kyrmer pro 50 deker parvarum peciarum scissarum de ventribus vaccarum tannatarum. Precii 25s ....cust' 3¾d

De Arnoldo van Langefeld[d] pro 1 corfe cum 1350 pellibus ovium tawed, 25 deker parvarum peciarum scissarum de ventribus bovium tannatarum, 340 pellibus cuniculorum crude sesone, 24 peciis sepi[e] multonis ponderantibus 10 vagas. Precii in toto £13 6s 8d .... cust' 3s 4d

<a>De Johanne Crichard pro 1 fardello cum septem pannis, 8 ulnis curtis sine grano .... Ind' cust' 8s 6¾d

De Matys van Seynt Troyne pro 1 basket[f] cum 800 pellibus cuniculorum crude, unde stage 400 pelles. Precii 35s ....cust' 5¼d

<d>Et extra [pro] 5 ulnis panni largi sine grano ....Al' cust' 7d

<a>De Willelmo Burgeis pro 1 [g]parvo[g] fardello cum 23 ulnis panni largi sine grano ....Ind' cust' 13½d

<a>De Willelmo Hatter pro 1 bala, 1 fardello cum 30 pannis, 17 ulnis curtis sine grano .... Ind' cust' 35s 10d

<a>De Matheo Foucher pro 1 bala cum 50 pannis curtis sine grano .... Ind' cust' 58s 4d

<a>De Johanne Brod[h] pro 1 bala cum 25 pannis curtis sine grano .... Ind' cust' 29s 2d

De dicto magistro pro 1 cista cum 18 dossenis lb. candellarum de sepo[i]. Precii 21s...cust' 3¼d

De Willelmo Damson pro 1 maunda cum 48 dossenis pellium ovium tawed, 50 cornibus. Precii in toto 23s 4d ....cust' 3½d

De Johanne Vette pro 1 maunda cum 400 pellibus cuniculorum sesone, 100 pellibus cuniculorum stage, 100 pellibus agnorum tawed. Precii 20s ..cust' 3d

<a>De Roberto Asseborn[j] pro 1 fardello cum 12 pannis curtis sine grano .... Ind' cust' 14s

a Martynknygh de Zelandia *L3.* b Dropp *L3.* c scarlett *L3.* d Langfeld *L3.* e seppi *L3, apparently in error.* f basketto *L3.* g-g *Omitted L2.* h Brodde *L3.* i ceppo *L3, apparently in error.* j Asschebourn *L3.*

[157] In navi Bernardi Fyrmyn[a] vocata George de Cane eodem die *[20 Apr. 1446]*

<a>De Elyas Langford armigero[b] pro 1 fardello cum 9 ulnis panni largi sine grano ....Ind' cust' 5¼d

Auditor's marginated entries L2: <k> worsted simplex indigene <l> worsted simplex alienigene <m> worsted duplex indigene <n> worsted duplex alienigene <o> lectus de worsted simplex indigene <p> lectus worsted simplex alienigene <aa>-<aa> *Auditor's entry: Sum of the issues of the page L2.*

<c>Et pro 5 ulnis panni largi de scarlet[c] ....Ind' cust' 6d

[a] Fermyn *L2.* [b] squyer *L3.* [c] scarlett *L3.*

<aa>£7 15s 3d<aa>

E122/73/20B f. 16[r]

[158] In navi Willelmi Popley vocata Maria de Sandewico 22° die Aprilis *[22 Apr. 1446]*

<a>De Johanne Parant pro 1 fardello cum 2½ pannis curtis sine grano .... Ind' cust' 2s 11d

[159] In navi Thome Hygge vocata Katerin exeunte 26° die Aprilis *[26 Apr. 1446]*

<a>De Willelmo Wodehows[a] pro 1 bala cum 13 pannis curtis sine grano .... Ind' cust' 15s 2d

[a] Wodehous *L3.*

[160] In navi Pernaton de Segewe vocata [a]Trinite de Bajona[a] eodem die *[26 Apr. 1446]*

<a>De eodem pro una cista cum 1 panno, 4 ulnis curtis sine grano ....Ind' cust' 16½d

<a>De Stephano de la Rege pro 1 fardello cum 6 pannis, 21 ulnis curtis sine grano .... Ind' cust'[b] 8s ¼d

<a>Et pro 3 dossenis parium caligarum continencium 18 ulnas panni largi sine grano ....Ind' cust' 10½d

<d>De Arnoldo Sturgeawe pro 1 fardello cum 2 pannis curtis sine grano .... Al' cust' 5s 6d

<a>De Rogero Dardeleys[c] pro 3 ulnis panni largi sine grano...........Ind' cust' 1¾d

[a] Trenite de Bayon' *L3.* [b] 7s 12½d *follows, struck through L2.* [c] Dardeles *L3.*

[161] In navi Bowdyn Hughson vocata Cristofor de Medylburgh[a] 2° die Maii *[2 May 1446]*

<d>De Clement Symondisdoughter[b] pro 1 fardello cum 3 pannis, 18 ulnis curtis sine grano.. Al' cust' 10s 3¾d

<d>Et extra [c]pro[c] 14 ulnis panni largi sine grano......................Al' cust' 19¼d

De Felice Favean pro 2 pipis cum 700 lb. sepi[d] multonis. Precii 49s....cust' 7½d

[a] Middilburgh *L3.* [b] Simondisdowghter *L3.* [c-c] *Omitted L3.* [d] seppi *L3, apparently in error.*

Auditor's marginated entries L2: <a> pannus indigenus <b> pannus de dimidio grano indigenus <c> scarleta indigena <d> pannus alienigenus <e> pannus de dimidio grano alienigenus <f> scarleta alienigena <g> pannus hanse <h> pannus de dimidio grano hanse <i> scarleta hanse

[162] In navi Willelmi Malpas vocata Trinite[a] de London' 11° die Maii *[11 May 1446]*

<g>De Hans Scult pro 1 hoggeshede cum 6 dossenis [et] 5 paribus caligarum [b]et[b] 3 ulnis panni largi continentibus in toto 1 pannum, 17½ ulnas curtis sine grano .... Hans cust' 20¾d

Et pro 4 [c]ollis quarte[c] de stanno, 12 lb. vasorum stanni. Precii 6s 8d cust' 1d

<aa>48s 4¼d<aa>

E122/73/20B f. 16v

<a>De Alexandro Haysand[d] pro 1 bala cum 21 pannis curtis sine grano .... Ind' cust' 24s 6d

<a>De Thoma Whatton pro 1 bala cum 18 pannis curtis sine grano. Ind' cust' 21s

<a>Et pro 1 cista cum 1 panno curto sine grano .... Ind' cust' 14d

<a>De Ricardo Perepount[e] pro 1 bala cum 25 pannis curtis sine grano .... Ind' cust' 29s 2d

<a>De Simone[f] Horn pro 1 fardello cum 13 pannis curtis sine grano .... Ind' cust' 15s 2d

<a>De Willelmo Bodvyle pro 1 fardello cum 6 pannis curtis sine grano .... Ind' cust' 7s

<a>De Johanne Dele pro 1 fardello cum 2 pannis, 6 ulnis curtis sine grano .... Ind' cust' 2s 7½d

<a>De Thoma Hawkyn[g] pro 1 bala cum 14 pannis, 10 ulnis curtis sine grano .... Ind' cust' 16s 10d

<g>De Cristean[h] van Bleyken pro 1 fardello cum 4 pannis, 5 ulnis curtis sine grano .... Hans cust' 4s 2½d

<a>De Willelmo Savage pro 2 balis cum 50 pannis curtis sine grano .... Ind' cust' 58s 4d

[a] Trenite *L3.* [b-b] *Omitted L3.* [c-c] quarte pottes *L3.* [d] Haysaund *L3.* [e] Perpoynte *L3.* [f] Simond *L3.* [g] Hauken *L3.* [h] Cristian *L3.*

[163] In batella Henrici Frer versus Sandewicum carcata [a]25° die Maii et ibidem ad recarcandum in quadam vas[a] exeunte versus partes exteras[a] *[25 May 1446]*

<d>De Jacobo de Layn pro 4 fangottis[b] cum 8 pannis, 4 ulnis curtis sine grano .... Al' cust' 22s 5½d

[a-a] et ibidem ad recarcandum in quadam vas[a] exeunte versus partes exteras 25[to] die Maii *L3.* [b] fangettis *L3.*

Auditor's marginated entries L2: <k> worsted simplex indigene <l> worsted simplex alienigene <m> worsted duplex indigene <n> worsted duplex alienigene <o> lectus de worsted simplex indigene <p> lectus worsted simplex alienigene <aa>-<aa> *Auditor's entry: Sum of the issues of the page L2.*

[164] In batella Henrici Bakerr[a] versus Sandewicum carcata 27° die Maii et ibidem ad recarcandum in quadam vas[a] exeunte versus partes exteras *[27 May 1446]*

De Reginaldo Salvaygo[b] pro 2 buttes, 17 parvis barellis cum 25½ vagis sepi[c] multonis. Precii £9 .... cust' 2s 3d

[a] Barker *L3.* [b] Salveygo *L3.* [c] seppi *L3, apparently in error.*

[165] In bargea Willelmi Lambe [a]de London'[a] versus Feveresham carcata 28° die Maii et deinde per terram versus portum Sandewici vel Dovorr[ie][b] et ibidem ad recarcandum in quadam navi[c] exeunte versus partes exteras *[28 May 1446]*

[d]Totalis huc: £566 8s 11d[d]

<aa>£10 4s 8½d<aa>

E122/73/20B f. 17r

<g>De Henrico Bruer[e] pro 4 balis cum 64 pannis curtis sine grano .... Hans cust' £3 4s

Et pro 223 godis panni stricti Wallie. Precii £7 [f]6s 8d[f] .... cust' 22d[g]

<g>De Cristean[h] van Bleyken pro 2 balis cum 30 pannis curtis sine grano .... Hans cust' 30s

Et pro 133 godis panni stricti Wallie. Precii £4 8s 4d .... cust' 13¼d

<g>De Clays Swart pro 3 balis cum 52 pannis curtis sine grano..... Hans cust' 52s

Et pro 96 godis panni stricti Wallie. Precii £3 4s .... cust' 9¾d

[a-a] *Omitted L3.* [b] Devor[ie] *L3.* [c] vas[a] *L3.* [d-d] *Auditor's entry L2.* 8s 11d *interlined above* 7s 7¾d, *struck through.* [e] Brewer *L3.* [f-f] *Interlined L2 (cf. variant g).* [g] *Corrected in L2 from* 21d *(this would have been the appropriate customs charge for goods worth £7: cf. variant f).* [h] Cristian *L3.*

[166] In navi Peryn Oberd vocata Jonet[a] de Cane eodem die *[28 May 1446]*

<a>De Matheo Gogh pro 1 fardello cum 8 peciis kendale[b] continentibus [c]2 pannos curtos sine grano .... Ind' cust' 2s 4d

<a>Et pro 4 pannis, 8 ulnis curtis sine grano[c] .... Ind' cust' 5s ¾d

<a>De Roberto Hewster[d] pro 1 fardello cum 10 [e]ulnis[e] panni largi sine grano .... Ind' cust' 6d

[a] Jonett *L3.* [b] kendall *L3.* [c-c] 2 pannos, 4 pannos, 8 ulnas curta sine grano continentibus in toto 6 pannos, 8 ulnas curta sine grano *L3.* [d] Howster *L3.* [e-e] *Interlined L2.*

Auditor's marginated entries L2: <a> pannus indigenus <b> pannus de dimidio grano indigenus <c> scarleta indigena <d> pannus alienigenus <e> pannus de dimidio grano alienigenus <f> scarleta alienigena <g> pannus hanse <h> pannus de dimidio grano hanse <i> scarleta hanse

[167] In navi Petri Johanson vocata Jesus de London' ultimo die Maii *[31 May 1446]*

<a>De Thoma Nyche pro 1 bala cum 28 pannis curtis sine grano Ind' cust' 32s 8d
Et extra pro 1 panno curto sine grano .... Ind' cust' 14d
<a>De Alexandro Orable[a] pro 2 balis[b] cum 49 pannis, 4 ulnis curtis sine grano .... Ind' cust' 57s 4½d
<a>De Laurencio Herd pro 1 fardello cum sex pannis, sex ulnis curtis sine grano .... Ind' cust' 7s 3½d
<a>De Johanne Brod[c] pro 1 bala cum 25 pannis, 8 ulnis curtis sine grano .... Ind' cust' 29s 6¾d
<a>•[d]De Willelmo Olyvere pro 1 bala cum 28 pannis, 16 ulnis curtis sine grano .... Ind' cust' 33s 5½d
<m>Et pro 1 pecia worsted duplicis .... Ind' cust' 2d[d]
<a>De Ricardo Ryche pro 1 bala cum 39 pannis curtis sine grano .... Ind' cust' 45s 6d
<aa>£18 4s 10d<aa>

E122/73/20B f. 17v

<a>De Johanne Dobbes pro 1 fardello cum 9 pannis, 4 ulnis curtis sine grano .... Ind' cust' 10s 8½d
<a>•[e]De Henrico Braybroke pro 2 balis cum 38 pannis curtis sine grano .... Ind' cust' 44s 4d
<a>•[e]De Willelmo Stephan[f] pro 1 bala [g]cum[g] 31 pannis curtis sine grano .... Ind' cust' 36s 2d
<a>De Thoma Stell[h] pro 1 fardello cum 3 pannis curtis sine grano Ind' cust' 3s 6d
<a>De Johanne Camvyle pro 1 fardello cum 9 pannis, 4 ulnis curtis sine grano .... Ind' cust' 10s 8½d
<a>De Johanne Spanby pro 1 fardello cum 8½ pannis curtis sine grano .... Ind' cust' 9s 11d
<c>•[i]De Thoma Onhond[j] pro 1 fardello cum 1½ pannis curtis[k] de scarlet[l] .... Ind' cust'[m] 3s 6d
<a>De Johanne Creke pro 1 bala cum 14 pannis, 8 ulnis curtis sine grano .... Ind' cust' 16s 8¾d
<a>•[b]De dicto Thoma Stell[o] pro 1 bala cum 12½ pannis curtis sine grano .... Ind' cust' 14s 7d
<b>Et pro 10 ulnis panni largi de dimidio grano .... Ind' cust' 8¾d
<a>De Willelmo Hatter pro 1 bala cum 27 pannis curtis sine grano .... Ind' cust' 31s 6d
<m>Et pro 22 peciis worsted duplicis continentibus 33 pecias Ind' cust' 5s 6d

Auditor's marginated entries L2: <k> worsted simplex indigene <l> worsted simplex alienigene <m> worsted duplex indigene <n> worsted duplex alienigene <o> lectus de worsted simplex indigene <p> lectus worsted simplex alienigene <aa>-<aa> *Auditor's entry: Sum of the issues of the page L2.*

<a>•[p]De Matheo Foucher[q] pro 1 bala cum 56 pannis curtis sine grano .... Ind' cust' £3 5s 4d

<a>•[r]De Johanne Stell[o] pro 1 bala cum 13 pannis, 8 ulnis curtis sine grano .... Ind' cust' 15s 6¾d

<a>De Johanne [s]Okeherst[s] pro 1 fardello cum 13 pannis, 13 ulnis curtis sine grano .... Ind' cust' 15s 9¾d

<b>Et pro 10 ulnis panni largi de dimidio grano .... Ind' cust' 8¾d

<a>•[t]De Johanne Crowe pro 1 fardello cum 6 pannis curtis sine grano .... Ind' cust' 7s

<a>•[t]De Johanne Grene pro[u] 1 fardello cum 1 panno, 16 ulnis curtis sine grano .... Ind' cust' 23½d

<a>De Cristoforo Percevall pro 1 bala cum 18½ pannis curtis sine grano .... Ind' cust' 21s 7d

<a>De Thoma Cryspe pro 1 fardello [v]et[v] una cista cum 4 pannis, 8 ulnis curtis sine grano .... Ind' cust' 5s ¾d

<m>Et pro 54 peciis worsted duplicis continentibus 81 pecias .... Ind' cust' 13s 6d

<a>De Johanne Penne pro 1 fardello cum 5 pannis, 8 ulnis curtis sine grano .... Ind' cust' 6s 2¾d

<a>•[v]De dicto[v] Johanne Brodde pro 1 bala cum 17 pannis curtis sine grano .... Ind' cust' 19s 10d

<a>Et pro 1 bala cum 14 pannis curtis sine grano .... Ind' cust' 16s 4d

<a>De Ricardo Ryche pro 2 balis cum 66 pannis curtis sine grano .... Ind' cust' £3 17s

<a>De Johanne Dey pro 1 fardello cum 3 pannis, 18 ulnis curtis sine grano .... Ind' cust' 4s 4½d

<d>De Luca de Negro pro 3 balis, 1 fardello cum 43 pannis, [w]1 ulna[w] curtis sine grano .... Al' cust' £5 18s 4¼d

<e>Et pro 20 ulnis panni largi de dimidio grano .... Al' cust' 3s 5½d[x]

<f>Et pro 12 ulnis panni largi de scarlet[l] .... Al' cust' 2s 9d

<aa>£29 11¾d<aa> [y]Item 21¼d[y]

E122/73/20B f. 18[r]

Et pro 12 ulnis panni Wallie, 2 [z]cappis longis[z] de scarlet[l], 2 [aa]cappis rotundis[aa] et 2 hures duple de scarlet[l]. Precii in toto 26s [g]8d[g] .... cust' 4d

<d>De Johanne de Negro pro 1 bala cum 15 pannis curtis sine grano .... Al' cust' 41s 3d

<d>De Daniello Justynean pro 3 rollis cum 1 panno, 3 ulnis curtis[ab] sine grano .... Al' cust' 3s 1¼d

<a>De Thoma Catesby pro 1 bala cum 23 pannis curtis sine grano .... Ind' cust' 26s 10d

Auditor's marginated entries L2: <a> pannus indigenus <b> pannus de dimidio grano indigenus <c> scarleta indigena <d> pannus alienigenus <e> pannus de dimidio grano alienigenus <f> scarleta alienigena <g> pannus hanse <h> pannus de dimidio grano hanse <i> scarleta hanse

<e>De Alexandro Palastrell pro 1 fangotto[ac] cum 1 panno curto de dimidio grano .... Al' cust' 4s 1½d

<d>Et pro 16 ulnis panni largi[ad] sine grano .... Al' cust' 22d

<a>De Johanne Sweteloffe[ae] pro 2 fardellis[af] cum 36 pannis, 16 ulnis curtis sine grano .... Ind' cust' 42s 9½d[ag]

<a>•[ah]De dicto Willelmo Hatter pro 1 cista cum 1½ pannis curtis sine grano .... Ind' cust' 21d

[a] Orabill *L3.* [b] pro duabus balis *follows, struck through L2.* [c] Brodde *L3.* [d-d] *The goods of William* Olyver *are entered after those of John* Dobbes *L3.* [e-e] *Entries for the goods of Henry* Braybroke *and William* Stephan *in reverse order L3.* [f] Stevens *L3.* [g-g] *Omitted L2.* [h] Stele *L3.* [i] *The goods of Thomas* Onhond *were entered after those of William* Hatter *L3.* [j] Honehand *L3.* [k] sine grano *follows, struck through L2 (cf. variant m).* [l] scarlett *L3.* [m] 21d *(this would have been the appropriate customs charge for 1½* panni sine grano*) follows, struck through L2.* [n] *These goods of Thomas* Stell *were entered before those of John* Okeherst *(below) L3.* [o] Steell *L3.* [p] *These goods of Mathew* Foucher *were entered after those of John* Creke *(above) L3.* [q] Fowcher *L3.* [r] *These goods of John Stell were entered after those of Christopher Percevall (below) L3.* [s-s] *Interlined above* Cantelowe, *struck through L2.* Okerste *L3.* [t] *The entries for the goods of John* Crowe *and John* Grene *in reverse order L3.* [u] parvo *follows L3.* [v-v] *Omitted L3.* [w-w] *Interlined L2.* [x] *Corrected in L2 from* 5¼d. [y-y] *Auditor's supplement necessitated by the correction of the customs charges on the goods of John* Creke *and* Lucas de Negro *L2.* [z-z] longe cappis *L3.* [aa-aa] round cappis *L3.* [ab] panni largi *L3.* [ac] fardello *L3.* [ad] de *follows, struck through L2.* [ae] Swetlof *L3.* [af] balis *L3.* [ag] *The second entry for Thomas* Stell *(12½* panni curti sine grano, *10 ells* panni curti de dimidio grano*) repeated here (in error) and struck through L2, with* quia supra in eadem navi, *marginated against it.* [ah] *These goods of William* Hatter *entered before those of Thomas* Cryspe *L3.*

[168] In navi Clays Martynsson vocata Katerin de Ernemoth [a]exeunte[a] eodem die *[31 May 1446]*

De Johanne Placker pro 1 fatte cum 600 pellibus cuniculorum crude sesone, 400 pellibus cuniculorum [a]crude[a] stage. Precii 40s .... cust' 6d

De Luca[b] Cremer pro 1 fatte cum 2400 pellibus cuniculorum crude sesone. Precii £6 .... cust' 18d

De Gilis Pouchen[c] pro 7 barellis cum 8 vagis sepi multonis. Precii £4 .. cust' 12d

De Johanne Brynyon[d] pro 4 fodris, 421 lb. plumbi[e]. Precii £22 6s 8d cust' 5s 7d

<d>Et pro 1 parvo fardello cum 4 ulnis panni largi sine grano... Al' cust' 5½d

Et pro 3 ulnis frisii Wallie. Precii 2s .... cust' ½d

Auditor's marginated entries L2: <k> worsted simplex indigene <l> worsted simplex alienigene <m> worsted duplex indigene <n> worsted duplex alienigene <o> lectus de worsted simplex indigene <p> lectus worsted simplex alienigene <aa>-<aa> *Auditor's entry: Sum of the issues of the page L2.*

De [f]Geretrud Damys[f] pro 1 fatte cum 1000 pellibus cuniculorum crude, unde stage 200 pelles. Precii 45s .... cust' 6¾d

<a>De Johanne Camvyle pro 1 fardello cum 2 pannis, 8 ulnis curtis sine grano .... Ind' cust' 2s 8¾d[g]

[h]<aa>£6 14s 4¾d<aa>

[a-a] *Omitted L3.* [b] Lucas *L3, in error.* [c] Pusyn *L2.* [d] Brenyon *L3.* [e] in diversis peciis *follows L3.* [f-f] Gertrud Dames *L3.* [g] *On the next line* De Johanne Lukens pro 6 pokes cum 60 wey thrummez. Precii £45 *follows, struck through L3, with* nichil *marginated against it to the left and* nichil, quia non exivit *to the right.* [h] *Preceded by* £6 7s 11½d, *struck through L2.*

E122/73/20B f. 18[v]

[169] In batella Willelmi Wodecok[a] versus Feveresham carcata 1° die Junii [b]et[b] deinde per terram versus portum Sandewici[c] et ibidem ad recarcandum in quadam vas[a] exeunte versus partes exteras *[1 June 1446]*

<g>De Johanne Dasse pro 2 balis cum 33 pannis, 6 ulnis curtis sine grano .... Hans cust' 33s 3d

Et pro 27 godis panni stricti Wallie. Precii 18s .... cust'2¾d

<g>De Johanne Hathyltak[d] pro 3 balis cum 50½ pannis curtis sine grano .... Hans cust' 50s 6d[e]

<g>De Johanne Warenthorp pro 1 bala cum 15 pannis curtis sine grano .... Hans cust' 15s

Et pro 21 godis panni stricti Wallie. Precii 13s 4d .... cust' 2d

[a] de Feversham *follows L3.* [b-b] *Omitted L3.* [c] vel Devor[ie] *follows L3.* [d] Hatiltake *L3.* [e] *On the next line* Et pro 21 godis panni stricti Wallie. Precii *follows, struck through L2 (error arose from confusion with the goods of Johann* Warenthorp*).*

[170] In navi [a]Fraunson de Dieu[a] vocata Sanctus Spiritus le balyngger de Luke 4° die Junii *[4 June 1446]*

<a>De Willelmo Corbet[b] pro 1 fardello cum 3 pannis, 8 ulnis curtis sine grano .... Ind' cust' 3s 10¾d

<a>De Johanne Reynkyn[c] pro 1 fardello cum 8 pannis curtis sine grano .... Ind' cust' 9s 4d

<a>De Willelmo Abraham pro 1 bala cum 21½ pannis curtis sine grano .... Ind' cust' 25s 1d

<a>De Stephano Forster pro 2 balis cum 26 pannis, 4 ulnis curtis sine grano .... Ind' cust' 30s 6½d

Auditor's marginated entries L2: <a> pannus indigenus <b> pannus de dimidio grano indigenus <c> scarleta indigena <d> pannus alienigenus <e> pannus de dimidio grano alienigenus <f> scarleta alienigena <g> pannus hanse <h> pannus de dimidio grano hanse <i> scarleta hanse

<a>De Thoma Countes pro [d]1 fardello cum[d] 20 ulnis panni largi sine grano ....Ind' cust' 11¾d
<a>De Arnoldo de Verges pro 1 fardello, 1 cista cum 1 panno, 16 ulnis curtis sine grano..Ind' cust' 23½d
<a>De Peryn de Lyssondo[e] pro 1 fardello cum 3 pannis, 21 ulnis curtis sine grano .... Ind' cust'[f] 4s 6¼d
<a>Et extra pro [g]1 panno, 7[g] ulnis curtis sine grano ....Ind' cust' 18d
<a>De Ponset de Solo pro 1 [d]parvo[d] fardello cum 1 panno curto sine grano ....Ind' cust' 14d
<a>De Pernton Abade pro 1 cista cum 6 paribus caligarum continentibus 3 ulnas panni largi[h] sine grano ....Ind' cust' 1¾d
<a>De [i]Janycott Lupsat[i] pro 1 fardello cum 9 pannis curtis sine grano .... Ind' cust' 10s 6d
<a>De Johanne de la Glyse pro 1 cista cum [j]2 peciis kersey [k]continentibus[j] 16 ulnas panni largi[k] sine grano ....Ind' cust' 9½d
<a>De [l]Sabotte de Madrang[l] pro 1 [d]parvo[d] fardello cum 1½ pannis curtis sine grano ....Ind' cust' 21d
<aa>£9 11s 3¾d<aa>

E122/73/20B f. 19[r]

<a>De dicto magistro pro 1 fardello cum 9 pannis, 18 ulnis curtis sine grano .... Ind' cust' 11s 4½d

[a-a] Fraunsen de Deu *L3.* [b] Corbett *L3.* [c] Reynken *L3.* [d-d] *Omitted L2.* [e] Lessondo *L3.* [f] 12¼d *follows, struck through L2.* [g-g] 31 *L3.* [h] large *L3.* [i-i] Janicot de Lupsate *L3.* [j-j] *Interlined L2.* [k-k] *Omitted L3.* [l-l] Sabaott de Madrangke *L3.*

[171] In navi Alberti Blyterswyke[a] vocata James de Colonia eodem die *[4 June 1446]*

[b]De Arnoldo Henrykesson[c] pro 5 barellis cum 3 miliariis lb. vasorum stanni. Precii £40..cust'[d] 10s
[b]De Simond Pastey[e] pro 1 barello cum 6 centenis lb. vasorum stanni. Precii £8 .... cust' 2s
<g>•[b]De Gerwyn Potte pro 1 bala cum 24½ pannis curtis sine grano .... Hans cust' 24s 6d
De Petro Howscheld pro 3 barellis cum 18 centenis lb. vasorum stanni. Precii £24 .... cust' 6s
<g>De Roberto Blyterswyke[f] pro 1 bala cum 16 pannis curtis sine grano .... Hans cust' 16s
<g>De Johanne Blyterswyke[f] pro 2 balis cum 33½ pannis curtis sine grano .... Hans cust' 33s 6d

Auditor's marginated entries L2: <k> worsted simplex indigene <l> worsted simplex alienigene <m> worsted duplex indigene <n> worsted duplex alienigene <o> lectus de worsted simplex indigene <p> lectus worsted simplex alienigene <aa>-<aa> *Auditor's entry: Sum of the issues of the page L2.*

<g>De Johanne Salmer pro 1 bala cum 18 pannis, 8 ulnis curtis sine grano .... Hans cust' 18s 4d

Et pro 3 rollis frisii Wallie, 14 godis panni stricti Wallie. Precii £3 11s 8d .... cust' 10¾d

<g>De Johanne Wynter pro 1 bala cum 21 pannis curtis sine grano .... Hans cust' 21s

<g>De Johanne Warenthorp pro 1 bala cum [g]44 peciis kersey continentibus 14 pannos, 16 ulnas curta[g] sine grano .... Hans cust' 14s 8d

Et pro 3 gros poyntes, 3 pellibus cheverellorum. Precii 6s 8d.......... cust' 1d

<g>De dicto Roberto Blyterswyke[a] pro 1 fardello cum [h]20 dossenis panni largi, 6 peciis kersey continentibus 1 pannum, 2 peciis kendall continentibus in toto 13½ pannos curtos[h] sine grano .... Hans cust' 13s 6d

<g>De [i]Matheo Schonebagh[i] pro 2 balis cum 84 pannis curtis sine grano .... Hans cust' £4 4s

<d>De Johanne de Vyle pro 2 balis cum 27½ pannis curtis sine grano .... Al' cust' £3 15s 7½d

[a] Bliterswe *L3.* [b] *These entries in the order* Pastey, Potte, Henrykesson *L3.* [c] Henriksson *L3.* [d] 6d *follows, struck through L2.* [e] Pasty *L3.* [f] Blitersweke *L3.* [g-g] 14 pannis, 16 ulnis curtis *L2.* [h-h] 13½ pannis curtis *L2.* [i-i] Matys Shonebagh *L3.*

[172] In navi [a]Hylbrand Hope vocata Raynold[a] de Danske exeunte 4° die Junii *[4 June 1446]*

<g>De Johanne Dasse pro 1 bala cum 24 pannis, 17 ulnis curtis sine grano .... Hans cust' 24s 8½d

<aa>£17 6s 7¾d<aa> [b]Item 9s 6½d[b]

E122/73/20B f. 19[v]

<g>De Bertram Questenbergh pro 1 bala cum 25 pannis curtis sine grano .... Hans cust' 25s

<g>De Henrico Breuer[c] pro 1 bala cum 11 pannis, 14 ulnis curtis sine grano .... Hans cust' 11s 7d

Et pro [d]2 peciis panni stricti Wallie continentibus 264 goda[d], 12 pellibus de roo. Precii £8 16s 8d .... cust' 2s 2½d

<g>•[e]De Hans Hope pro 2 balis cum 36 pannis curtis sine grano .... Hans cust' 36s

<g>De Hans Ryng pro 3 balis cum 52 pannis curtis sine grano ...... Hans cust' 52s

Et pro 2 rollis[f] frisii Wallie. Precii 40s .... cust' 6d

<g>De Roberto Blyterswyke[g] pro 1 bala cum 12 pannis, [h]14 ulnis[h] curtis sine grano .... Hans cust' 12s 7d

Et pro 8 godis frisii Wallie. Precii 5s .... cust' ¾d

Auditor's marginated entries L2: <a> pannus indigenus <b> pannus de dimidio grano indigenus <c> scarleta indigena <d> pannus alienigenus <e> pannus de dimidio grano alienigenus <f> scarleta alienigena <g> pannus hanse <h> pannus de dimidio grano hanse <i> scarleta hanse

[a-a] Ilbrand van Hope vocata Reynold *L3.* [b-b] *Auditor's supplement necessitated by the correction of the customs charges on the goods of Arnold* Henrykesson *L2.* [c] Brewer *L3.* [d-d] 264 godis panni stricti Wallie *L2.* [e] *These goods of* Hans Hope *entered after those of Robert* Blitersweke *L3.* [f] peciis *L3.* [g] Blitersweke *L3.* [h-h] *Interlined L2.*

[173] In navi Johannis de Skewe vocata [a]Maria de Fount Raby[a] 9° die Junii *[9 June 1446]*

<d>De Martino de Amborogh pro 1 cista cum 24 ulnis frisii London' continentibus 1 pannum curtum sine grano .... Al' cust' 2s 9d

Et pro 7 ulnis panni stricti Wallie. Precii 3s 4d ....cust' ½d

[a-a] Seint Mary de Fount Raby in Byscay *L3.*

[174] In navi Nicholai Baron vocata Plente de Calesia [a]exeunte[a] eodem die *[9 June 1446]*

<a>De Willelmo Crowcher pro 1 fardello cum 10¼ ulnis panni largi sine grano ....Ind' cust' 6d

<k>Et pro 1 pecia worsted simplicis ....Ind' cust' 1d

[a] *Omitted L3.*

<aa>£7 2s 8¾d<aa>

E122/73/20B f. 20^{r}

[175] In navi Johannis de Cayr vocata le [a]Trinite de Nauntt[a] eodem die *[9 June 1446]*

De Petro[b] Chalowe de Towr pro 3 barellis cum 1 miliario, 92 lb. vasorum stanni. Precii £14 6s 8d .... cust' 3s 7d

[a] Trenite de Naunt *L3.* [b] Pero *L3.*

[176] In navi Johannis Powdram[a] vocata George Heron[b] [c]de London'[c] 15° die Junii *[15 June 1446]*

<a>De Willelmo Bodvyle pro 1 bala cum 14 pannis, 20 ulnis curtis sine grano .... Ind' cust' 17s 3¾d

[a] Powderam *L3.* [b] Heryon *L3.* [c-c] *Omitted L3 (3 cm room left for completion of the entry).*

[177] In navi Willelmi Cruce vocata Anna[a] de London' [b]exeunte[b] eodem die *[15 June 1446]*

<a>De Johanne Judde pro 2 balis cum 24 pannis, 22 ulnis curtis sine grano .... Ind' cust' 29s 1d

[a] Anne *L3.* [b-b] *Omitted L3.*

Auditor's marginated entries L2: <k> worsted simplex indigene <l> worsted simplex alienigene <m> worsted duplex indigene <n> worsted duplex alienigene <o> lectus de worsted simplex indigene <p> lectus worsted simplex alienigene <aa>-<aa> *Auditor's entry: Sum of the issues of the page L2.*

[178] In navi Willelmi Danyell vocata[a] eodem die *[15 June 1446]*

<b>De Johanne Prout[b] pro 1 rolla cum 3 ulnis panni largi de dimidio grano .... Ind' cust' 2¾d

[a] *6½ cm (L2), 7 cm (L3) room left for completion of the entry. + [cross] marginated against the entry and struck through L2.* [b] Proute *L3.*

<aa>50s 2½d<aa>

E122/73/20B f. 20v

[179] In navi [a]Marticot de Hubiagne[a] vocata Maria de Bajona 21° die Junii *[21 June 1446]*

<a>De Willelmo Forster[b] pro 1 fardello cum 3 pannis, 8 ulnis curtis sine grano .... Ind' cust' 3s 10¾d

<a>De [c]Janicot Lupsat[c] pro 1 fardello cum 1½ pannis curtis sine grano .... Ind' cust' 21d

[a-a] Martycott de Hubeage *L3.* [b] Forstor *L2, in error.* [c-c] Janycott de Lupsate *L3.*

[180] In navi Johannis Affouns Mounter vocata Salvator [a]de Portingal[a] 22° die Junii *[22 June 1446]*

<a>De Alexandro Haysand pro 2 fardellis cum 26 pannis curtis sine grano .... Ind' cust' 30s 4d

<a>Et pro 1 cista cum 13 ulnis panni largi sine grano .... Ind' cust' 7½d

<a>De Willelmo Pychard pro 2 fardellis cum 43 pannis, 2 ulnis curtis sine grano .... Ind' cust' 50s 3¼d

<a>De Johanne Dolond pro 2 balis cum 54 pannis curtis sine grano .... Ind' cust' £3 3s

<a>•[b]De Willelmo Joy pro 1 bala cum 15 pannis curtis sine grano .... Ind' cust' 17s 6d

<d>•[b]De Petro Alverus pro 1 rolla cum 14 ulnis panni largi sine grano .... Al' cust' 19¼d

Et pro 1 barello cum 3 centenis, 28 lb. vasorum stanni. Precii £4 6s 8d .... cust' 13d

<a>De Henrico Logan pro 1 bala cum [c]40 peciis [panni] stricti continentibus 10 pannos curtos[c] sine grano .... Ind' cust' 11s 8d

<d>De Johanne Affouns pro 1 hoggeshede cum [d]1 rolla continente 1 pannum, 5 ulnas curta[d] sine grano .... Al' cust'[e] 3s 4d

Auditor's marginated entries L2: <a> pannus indigenus <b> pannus de dimidio grano indigenus <c> scarleta indigena <d> pannus alienigenus <e> pannus de dimidio grano alienigenus <f> scarleta alienigena <g> pannus hanse <h> pannus de dimidio grano hanse <i> scarleta hanse

Et pro 1 lecto [a]cum celour, testour et curt[inis][a] de worsted simplici[f], 12 discis [g]de stanno ponderantibus 12 lb.[g] et extra 4 potelle pottes stanni[h]. Precii in toto 35s .... cust' 5¼d

<p>Et pro predicto 1 lecto de worsted simplici continente 1½ lectos [a]de[a] worsted simplici .... Al' cust' 11¼d

<l>Et pro 3 peciis worsted simplicis in curt[inis] dicti lecti .... Al' cust' 4½d

<a>De Willelmo Haydok pro 1 fardello cum 4½ pannis curtis sine grano .... Ind' cust' 5s 3d

<a>De dicto Willelmo Pychard pro 1 fardello cum 16 pannis, 18 ulnis curtis sine grano .... Ind' cust' 19s 6½d

<o>Et pro 1 celour[i] et testour [j]continentibus 1 lectum de worsted simplici[j] .... Ind' cust' 5d

<d>De Raphaelle de Aurea pro 1 bala, 4 fardellis cum 32 pannis, 11 ulnis curtis sine grano .... Al' cust' £4 9s 3¼d

<f>Et pro 1 ulna panni largi de scarlet[k] .... Al' cust' 2¾d

Et pro 1 lecto [l]cum celour, testour et curt[inis] et 4 peciis pro costrez de worsted simplici[l]. Precii £3 10s .... cust' 10½d

<p>Et pro predicto 1 [m]lecto cum celour et testour de worsted simplici continente 1½ lectos de worsted simplici[m] .... Al' cust' 11¼d

<l>Et pro 3 peciis worsted simplicis in curt[inis] dicti[n] lecti [o]et dictis 4 peciis worsted simplicis pro costrez continentibus in toto 6 pecias worsted simplicis[o] .... Al' cust' 9d

<aa>£15 4s 1d<aa> [p]Item 7d[p]

E122/73/20B f. 21[r]

<d>De Affouns Gromet[q] pro 6 ulnis panni largi sine grano .... Al' cust' 8¼d

Et pro 2 potelle pottes stanni[h]. Precii 2s 8d .... cust' ½d

<a>•[r]De Willelmo Walden pro 1 fardello cum 4 pannis, 5 ulnis curtis sine grano .... Ind' cust' 4s 11d

<a>De Johanne Malter pro 1 fardello cum [s]24 dossenis [panni] stricti continentibus 6 pannos curtos[s] sine grano .... Ind' cust' 7s

<d>De Raphaelle de Ponsola pro 1 fardello cum 3 pannis curtis sine grano .... Al' cust' 8s 3d[t]

<a>•[u]De Petro Alfold pro 1 fardello, 2 cistis cum 9 pannis, 18 ulnis curtis sine grano .... Ind' cust' 11s 4½d

<o>Et pro 2 lectis de worsted simplici parve assise continentibus 3 lectos de worsted simplici .... Ind' cust' 15d

<k>Et pro 1 pecia worsted simplicis pro costrez[v] et 4 rollis worsted simplicis continentibus in toto 5 pecias worsted simplicis .... Ind' cust' 5d

<m>Et pro 6 peciis worsted simplicis in curt[inis] dictorum lectorum .... Ind' cust' 6d

Auditor's marginated entries L2: <k> worsted simplex indigene <l> worsted simplex alienigene <m> worsted duplex indigene <n> worsted duplex alienigene <o> lectus de worsted simplex indigene <p> lectus worsted simplex alienigene <aa>-<aa> *Auditor's entry: Sum of the issues of the page L2.*

<m>Et pro 1 pecia worsted duplicis .... Ind' cust' 2d

[a-a] *Omitted L3.* [b] *Entries for the goods of William* Joy *and* Petrus Alverus *in reverse order L3.* [c-c] 10 pannis curtis *L2.* [d-d] 1 panno, 5 ulnis curtis. 5 ulnis *interlined L2.* [e] 2s 9d *follows, struck through L2.* [f] dimidie assise *follows L3.* [g-g] stanni *L2.* [h] de stanno *L3.* [i] celor *L3.* [j-j] de worsted simplici continentibus 1 lectum *L3.* [k] scarlett *L3.* [l-l] de worsted simplici et 4 peciis worsted simplicis pro costeres *L3.* [m-m] pecia worsted continente 1½ lectos worsted simplicis *L3.* [n] dicte *L3, in error.* [o-o] *Entered as a sub-entry* Et pro 4 peciis worsted simplicis pro costeres continentibus 3 pecias worsted simplicis *L3.* [p-p] *Auditor's supplement necessitated by the correction of the customs charges on the goods of John* Affouns *L2.* [q] Gromett *L3.* [r] *Entries for goods of William* Walden *and John* Malter *in reverse order L3.* [s-s] 6 pannis curtis *L3.* [t] Require post in fine hujus rotuli ad hoc signum *and an insertion mark marginated to the right of this entry L3.* [u] *Heading* Adhuc in navi Johannis Affouns *L3.* [v] costerys *L3.*

[181] In navi Johannis Launson[a] vocata Gost de Wynchylse[b] 25° die Junii *[25 June 1446]*

<a>De Stephano Morys[c] pro 1 [d]parvo[d] fardello cum 5 pannis curtis sine grano .... Ind' cust' 5s 10d

[a] Lawnson *L3.* [b] Wynchilsee *L3.* [c] Mor' *L3.* [d-d] *Omitted L2.*

[182] In navi Johannis Samason vocata Cristofor de Rothomago [a]exeunte[a] eodem die *[25 June 1446]*

De Johanne de Boys pro 1 pipa cum 9 cappis, [b]2 [a]parvis[a] zonis de argento, 1 barello cum 4 dossenis lb. candellarum de cepo[b]. Precii 13s 4d .... cust' 2d

De Nicholao Bavyser pro 1 barello cum 3 centenis lb. vasorum stanni. Precii £4 .... cust' 12d

[a-a] *Omitted L3.* [b-b] 1 barello cum 4 dossenis lb. candellarum de cepo, 2 parvis zonis de argento *L3.*

[183] In navi Willelmi Cote vocata Cristofor de Gowe eodem die *[25 June 1446]*

De Leonardo van Brusyll pro 5 barellis cum 3 miliariis lb. vasorum stanni. Precii £37 10s .... cust' 9s 4½d

[a]•<aa>50s 11¾d<aa>

[a] *Preceded by* 50s ¾d, *struck through L2. Above that,* 11d *in darker ink and struck through.*

E122/73/20B f. 21[v]

Auditor's marginated entries L2: <a> pannus indigenus <b> pannus de dimidio grano indigenus <c> scarleta indigena <d> pannus alienigenus <e> pannus de dimidio grano alienigenus <f> scarleta alienigena <g> pannus hanse <h> pannus de dimidio grano hanse <i> scarleta hanse

[184] In navi Dederici[a] Johanson vocata Schypp Gode [b]exeunte[b] 28° die Junii[c] *[28 June 1446]*

<d>De Willelmo Johanson pro 1 sacco cum [d]1 pecia kersey continente 8 ulnas[d] panni largi sine grano...Al' cust' 11d

<f>Et pro 2¼ ulnis panni largi de scarlet[e]...................................Al' cust' 6¼d

Et pro 8 ulnis panni largi Wallie. Precii 6s 8d.................................cust' 1d

[a] Derike *L3.* [b] *Omitted L3.* [c] Juii *L2, in error.* [d-d] octo ulnis *L2.* [e] scarlett *L3.*

[185] In navi Bowdyn Hughson vocata Cristofore de Medilb[urgh][a] [b]exeunte[b] 5° die Julii *[5 July 1446]*

<d>De Nicholao Cristeansson[c] pro 1 barello cum [d]31 ulnis panni albi continentibus 1 pannum, 7 ulnas curta[d] sine grano................................ Al' cust' 3s 7d

Et pro 4 gryndstones[e], 300 lb. sepi multonis, 3 dossenis pectinum de ligno box. Precii in toto 41s ....cust' 6¼d

<g>De Hans Ryng pro 1 bala cum 12½ pannis curtis sine grano ....Hans cust' 12s 6d

Et pro 10 godis panni stricti Wallie. Precii 6s 8d.............................cust' 1d

<g>De Clays Lyndeman[f] pro 1 bala cum 13½ pannis curtis sine grano ....Hans cust' 13s 6d

Et pro 32 godis[g] frisii Wallie. Precii 21s 4d ....cust' 3¼d

<d>De Leonardo van Brusill pro 1 fardello cum 1½ pannis curtis sine grano .... Al' cust' 4s 1½d

[a] Middilborgh *L3.* [b] *Omitted L3.* [c] Cristiansson *L3.* [d-d] 1 panno, 7 ulnis curtis *L2.* [e] grynstones *L3.* [f] Lyndman *L3.* [g] panni *follows L3.*

[186] In navi Peryn Oberd vocata Jonet[a] de Cane 11° die Julii *[11 July 1446]*

De Colyn Trenchaunt pro 1 barello cum 300 lb. aluminis Foille. Precii 45s .... cust' 6¾d[b]

<d>De Willelmo Count pro [c]1 fardello cum[c] 18½ [d]ulnis[d] panni largi sine grano .... Al' cust' 2s 1½d

Et pro 7 ulnis [e]panni[e] frisii Wallie. Precii 5s ....cust' ¾d

[a] Jonett *L3.* [b] *Corrected in L2 from* 6¼d. [c-c] *Omitted L2.* [d-d] *Interlined above* lb.*, struck through L2.* [e] *Omitted L3.*

[187] In navi Bowdyn[a] Adreansson vocata [b]Marikneight de Ernemoth[b] 13° die Julii *[13 July 1446]*

<a>De Johanne Reynkyn[c] pro 1 bala cum 15 pannis, 4 ulnis curtis sine grano .... Ind' cust' 17s 8½d

Auditor's marginated entries L2: <k> worsted simplex indigene <l> worsted simplex alienigene <m> worsted duplex indigene <n> worsted duplex alienigene <o> lectus de worsted simplex indigene <p> lectus worsted simplex alienigene <aa>-<aa> *Auditor's entry: Sum of the issues of the page L2.*

<aa>56s[d] ¾d<aa> [e]Item 6d[e]

[a] Bouden *L3.* [b-b] Mariaknyght de Ermouth *L3.* [c] Reynken *L3.* [d] 8¼d *follows, struck through L2.* [e-e] *Auditor's supplement necessitated by initially faulty summation of customs issues L2.*

E122/73/20B f. 22r

[188] In navi Petri Adreansson vocata Marikneight[a] de London' eodem die *[13 July 1446]*

<g>De Johanne van Sybryght[b] pro 1 bala cum 14 pannis, 8 ulnis curtis sine grano .... Hans cust' 14s 4d

Et pro 10 godis frisii Willie. Precii 8s 4d .... cust' 1¼d

[a] Mariaknygh *L3.* [b] Sybrygh *L3.*

[189] In navi Clays Rodeman vocata Marikneight[a] de Danske 13° die Julii *[13 July 1446]*

<g>De eodem pro 1 bala cum 11 pannis curtis sine grano .... Hans cust' 11s

Et pro 26 vagis salis de Bay, 3 pipis vini debilis pro beverages, 1 hoggeshede olei. Precii in toto £22 6s 8d .... cust' 5s 7d

<g>De Hans Meyr pro 1 fardello cum 7 pannis, 6 ulnis curtis sine grano .... Hans cust' 7s 3d

<g>Et pro 1 barello cum 3 peciis kersey continentibus 1 pannum curtum sine grano .... Hans cust' 12d

<g>De Laurencio Syner[b] pro 1 fardello cum 6 pannis, 9 ulnis curtis sine grano .... Hans cust' 6s 4½d

Et pro 12 [c]parvis[c] coverlettes Norfolke[d]. Precii 36s .... cust' 5½d

<g>De Tideman[e] Hugh pro 1 fardello cum 10 pannis, 8 ulnis curtis sine grano .... Hans cust' 10s 4d

Et pro 2 barellis, 1 sacco cum 5 centenis lb. vasorum stanni, 7 potelle [c]pottes[c], 49 quarte [c]pottes[c], 22 pynt pottes [c]stanni[c], 2 parvis coverlettes Norfolke[d]. Precii £9 4s 6d .... cust' 2s 3¾d

<g>De Nicholao Grote pro 1 fardello cum 9 pannis, 16 ulnis curtis sine grano .... Hans cust' 9s 8d

<g>Et pro 1 cista[f], uno barello cum 1 panno curto sine grano. Hans cust' 12d

Et pro 2 parvis coverlettes Norfolke[d], 56 lb. vasorum stanni, 10 potelle pottes, 12 quarte pottes [c]stanni[c] et 37[g] lb. vasorum stanni. Precii 50s .... cust' 7½d

<g>De Henrico Byland pro 1 fardello cum 4 pannis, 16 ulnis curtis sine grano .... Hans cust' 4s 8d

<g>De Johanne Sandowe pro 1 bala cum 15 pannis, 18 ulnis curtis sine grano .... Hans cust' 15s 9d

Auditor's marginated entries L2: <a> pannus indigenus <b> pannus de dimidio grano indigenus <c> scarleta indigena <d> pannus alienigenus <e> pannus de dimidio grano alienigenus <f> scarleta alienigena <g> pannus hanse <h> pannus de dimidio grano hanse <i> scarleta hanse

<g>Et pro 1 cista cum 1 panno curto sine grano...................... Hans cust' 12d

<g>De Hermano[h] Sandebeken pro 1 bala, 1 sacco cum 7 pannis, 23 ulnis curtis sine grano...Hans cust' [i]7s[i] 11½d

<g>Et pro 1 dossena parium caligarum continencium 6 ulnas panni largi sine grano.. Hans cust' 3d

Et pro 84 lb. vasorum stanni. Precii 20s..cust' 3d

<a>De Johanne Martin pro 1 fardello cum 8 pannis, 6 ulnis curtis sine grano .... Ind' cust' 9s 7½d

[a] Maryknygh *L3.* [b] Synner *L3.* [c-c] *Omitted L3.* [d] Northfolke *L3.* [e] Tydman *L3.* [f] et *follows L3.* [g] 1 quarterio [centene] et 9 *L3.* [h] Harmano *L3.* [i-i] *Interlined L2.*

<aa>£5 9s 6½d<aa>

E122/73/20B f. 22v

[190] In navi Palento Raparatzo[a] vocata Seynt John de Bajona[b] 16° die Julii *[16 July 1446]*

<a>De eodem pro 1 fardello cum 2 pannis, 9 ulnis curtis sine grano .... Ind' cust' 2s 9¼d

<a>Et pro 4 dossenis parium caligarum continencium 1 pannum curtum sine grano ....Ind' cust' 14d

<a>De Alfouns de Seint John de Luce[c] pro 2 fardellis cum 6 pannis, 20¾ ulnis curtis sine grano... Ind' cust' 8s 1d

<c>Et pro 12 ulnis panni largi de scarlet[d]..................................Ind' cust' 14d

[a] Raparatso *L3.* [b] Bojona *L2, apparently in error.* [c] Luse *L3.* [d] scarlett *L3.*

[191] In navi Johannis de la Lounde vocata Nicholaus de Cane 18° die Julii *[18 July 1446]*

<a>De Willelmo Hering pro 1 cista cum 13 ulnis panni largi sine grano ....Ind' cust' 7½d

De Johanne Huet[a] pro 1 maunde cum 1200 lb. brasille, unde extra 2 pecii brasille. Precii £15 .... cust' 3s 9d

[a] Huett *L3.*

[192] In navi Poppe Gylysson[a] vocata [b]Gasthows de Medylb[urgh][b] 18°·[c] die Julii *[18 July 1446]*

<g>De Petro Cangheter[d] pro 1 bala cum 23 pannis curtis sine grano ....Hans cust' 23s

Et pro 1 rolla frisii Wallie. Precii 20s...cust' 3d

De dicto magistro pro 4 barellis cum 4½ vagis sepi multonis, 230 pellibus vitulorum tannatis. Precii £5 6s 8d ....cust' 16d

Auditor's marginated entries L2: <k> worsted simplex indigene <l> worsted simplex alienigene <m> worsted duplex indigene <n> worsted duplex alienigene <o> lectus de worsted simplex indigene <p> lectus worsted simplex alienigene <aa>-<aa> *Auditor's entry: Sum of the issues of the page L2.*

De Bawdewyn[e] Gromell pro 1 sacco cum 700 pellibus cuniculorum crude, unde stage 300 pelles. Precii 26s 8d ....cust' 4d

De Poulo Philipp pro 1 fardello cum 400 pellibus ovium tawed [f]debilibus[f]. Precii 26s 8d ....cust' 4d

[a] Gilesson *L3.* [b-b] Gastehows de Meddilb[urgh] *L3.* [c] *Corrected in L2 from* 28°. [d] Cangeter *L3.* [e] Boudewyn *L3.* [f-f] *Omitted L3.*

[193] In navi Goykyn[a] Moys vocata Marykneight[b] de Danske 20° die Julii *[20 July 1446]*

De Hans Fosse pro 1 barello cum 8 centenis lb. vasorum stanni[c], 1 barello cum 300 pellibus agnorum tawed. Precii [d]in toto £12[d] .... cust' 3s

<aa>45s 9¾d[e]•<aa>

E122/73/20B f. 23[r]

<g>De Vincent[f] Doring pro 1 cista cum 1 panno, 4 ulnis curtis sine grano .... Hans cust' 14d

<g>De Henrico Wydylbuske pro 1 fardello, 1 barello cum 8 pannis, 21 ulnis curtis sine grano .... Hans cust' 8s 10½d

Et pro 2 centenis, 56 lb. vasorum stanni, 2 ollis galons, 2 ollis potelle, 2 ollis quarte [g]et[g] 2 ollis pynt de stanno. Precii in toto £3 13s 4d ...cust' 11d

<g>De Hans Soredogh pro 1 cista cum 1 panno, 5 ulnis curtis sine grano .... Hans cust' 14½d

Et pro 7 parvis cornibus, 1 gros poyntes[h]. Precii 6s 8d ....cust' 1d

<g>De Dederico[i] Hunter[j] pro 2 balis cum 31 pannis, 7 ulnis curtis sine grano .... Hans cust' 31s 3½d

<g>De Hans Wynter pro 2 balis, 1 barello cum 30 pannis, 16 ulnis curtis sine grano .... Hans cust' 30s 8d

Et pro 2 gros poyntes[h], 8 centenis lb. vasorum stanni, unde extra 1 dossena trenchours et 3 platers[k] de stanno. Precii in toto £9 16s 8d.... cust' 2s 5½d

<g>De dicto magistro pro 1 fardello cum 8 pannis, 11 ulnis curtis sine grano .... Hans cust' 8s 5½d

Et pro 2 coverlettes Norfolke, 2 parvis barellis cum 2 centenis lb. vasorum stanni. Precii £3 5s 4d ....cust'[l] 10d

<g>Et extra pro 10 ulnis panni largi sine grano .... Hans cust' 5d

<g>De Bartholomeo[m] Gronehowe pro 1 fardello, 1 barello cum 4 pannis, 20 ulnis curtis sine grano .... Hans cust' 4s 10d

Et pro 3 coverlettes Norfolke[n], 5 centenis lb. vasorum stanni, 10 ollis quarte, 18 ollis pynt. Precii in toto £7 14s [o]4d[o] ....cust' 23¼d

<g>De Hermano Wetyng pro 1 fardello cum 5 pannis, 8 ulnis curtis sine grano .... Hans cust' 5s 4d

Et pro 11 coverlettes Norfolke. Precii 33s 4d..................................cust' 5d

Auditor's marginated entries L2: <a> pannus indigenus <b> pannus de dimidio grano indigenus <c> scarleta indigena <d> pannus alienigenus <e> pannus de dimidio grano alienigenus <f> scarleta alienigena <g> pannus hanse <h> pannus de dimidio grano hanse <i> scarleta hanse

<g>De Hans Wyman pro 1 bala cum 20 pannis, 6 ulnis curtis sine grano .... Hans cust' 20s 3d

<g>De Hans Bokylman[p] pro 1 bala cum 14 pannis, 10 ulnis curtis sine grano .... Hans cust' 14s 5d

<g>De Bertram Sleyghter[q] pro 2 balis cum 29 pannis curtis sine grano .... Hans cust' 29s

<g>De Andrea van Groten pro 1 bala, 1 cista, 1 barello cum 14 pannis, 3 ulnis curtis sine grano .... Hans cust' 14s 1½d

Et pro 6 centenis, 26 lb. vasorum stanni, 1 potelle potte, [r]1 quarte potte et 1 pynt potte de stanno[r]. Precii in toto £8 2s 3d .... cust' 2s ½d

<a>De Johanne Feld pro 1 fardello cum 7 pannis, 22 ulnis curtis sine grano .... Ind' cust' 9s 3d

<g>De Tym Gyse pro 3 balis cum 58 pannis curtis sine grano .... Hans cust' 58s

[a] Goyken *L3.* [b] Maryknygh *L3.* [c] precii £10 *(and on the next line)* Et pro *follow L3 (cf. variant d).* [d-d] Precii 40s *L3 (cf. variant c).* [e] *Corrected in L2 from* 9¼d. [f] Vincenc *L2.* [g-g] *Omitted L3.* [h] poyentes *L3.* [i] Dederike *L3.* [j] pro *follows, struck through L2.* [k] plateris *L3.* [l] 9¾d *follows, struck through L2.* [m] Bertholomeo *L3.* [n] Nortfolke *L3.* [o-o] *Interlined above* 2d, *struck through L2.* [p] Bukilman *L3.* [q] Sleghter *L3.* [r-r] 1 olla quarte, 1 olla pynt *L3.*

<aa>£12 5s 11¾d<aa>

E122/73/20B f. 23v

[194] In navi Jacobi Mews[a] vocata Maryknneight[b] de Danske 20° die Julii *[20 July 1446]*

<g>De Dame Wynterfeld[c] pro 1 fardello cum 1 panno, 5 ulnis curtis sine grano .... Hans cust' 14½d

<g>Et pro 3 paribus caligarum continentibus 1½ ulnas panni largi sine grano .... Hans cust' ¾d

Et pro 3 coverlettes Norfolke. Precii 24s [d]4d[d] .... cust' 3¾d

<g>De Henrico Howsank pro 1 fardello cum 1 panno, 17 ulnis curtis sine grano .... Hans cust' 20½d

Et pro 1 coverlette[e] Norfolke, 1 barello cum 6 potelle [f]pottes[f], 12 quarte [f]pottes[f], 12 pynt pottes [g]de stanno[g], 62[h] lb. vasorum stanni. Precii in toto 25s .... cust' 3¾d

<g>De Hans Wulfe[i] pro 1 fardello, 1 cista cum 5 pannis, 11 ulnis curtis sine grano .... Hans cust' 5s 5½d

Et pro 1 centena lb. vasorum stanni, 3 coverlettes Norfolke. Precii 42s .... cust' 6½d

Auditor's marginated entries L2: <k> worsted simplex indigene <l> worsted simplex alienigene <m> worsted duplex indigene <n> worsted duplex alienigene <o> lectus de worsted simplex indigene <p> lectus worsted simplex alienigene <aa>-<aa> *Auditor's entry: Sum of the issues of the page L2.*

<g>De Hans Reke pro 1 barello cum 3 pannis, 1 ulna curtis sine grano .... Hans cust' 3s ½d

<g>Et pro 2 dossenis parium caligarum continencium 12 ulnas panni largi sine grano .... Hans cust' 6d

Et pro 5 potelle pottes, 13 quarte pottes de stanno. Precii 14s 6d...cust' 2¼d

<g>De Martino Drews[j] pro 1 fardello cum 9 pannis curtis sine grano .... Hans cust' 9s

<g>Et pro 1 dossena parium caligarum continencium 6 ulnas panni largi sine grano .... Hans cust' 3d

Et pro 3 parvis coverlettes Norfolke. Precii 6s 8d .... cust' 1d

<g>De Jacobo Howholt pro 1 cista cum 1 panno, 9 ulnis curtis sine grano .... Hans cust' 16½d

Et pro 84 lb. vasorum stanni. Precii 20s .... cust' 3d

<g>De Clays Stowenbergh[k] pro 1 cista cum 2 pannis, 8 ulnis curtis sine grano .... Hans cust' 2s 4d

<g>De Clays Overbagh pro 1 fardello cum 3 pannis, 4 ulnis curtis sine grano .... Hans cust' 3s 2d

<a>De Johanne Martyn pro 1 fardello cum 8½ pannis curtis sine grano .... Ind' cust' 9s 11d

<g>De Clays Bolekyn[l] pro 1 fardello, 1 cista cum 4 pannis, 16 ulnis curtis sine grano .... Hans cust' 4s 8d

Et pro 1 coverlette[m] Sarum, 84 lb. vasorum stanni, 7 quarte pottes [f]et[f] 2 pynt pottes[n] [f]de stanno[f]. Precii 40s .... cust' 6d

<g>De Tilman Wynnebergh pro 1 fardello, 1 barello, 1 cista cum 3 pannis, 19 ulnis curtis sine grano .... Hans cust' 3s 9½d

<g>Et pro 1½ dossenis parium caligarum continencium 9 ulnas panni largi sine grano .... Hans cust' 4½d

Et pro 4 centenis, 56 lb. vasorum stanni, 1 dossena ollarum potelle, 2 dossenis ollarum quarte, 1 dossena ollarum pynt et 1 dossena ollarum[o] half-pynt de stanno [f]et[f] 2 furruris de pellibus cuniculorum. Precii in toto £8 8s 4d .... cust' 2s 1¼d

<aa>51s 1¾d[p]·<aa>

E122/73/20B f. 24[r]

<g>De Jacobo Cole pro 1 bala cum 11½ pannis curtis sine grano .... Hans cust' 11s 6d

Et pro 3 gros poyntes[q] et extra 2 dossenis ollarum quarte [f]et[f] 1 potelle potte [f]de stanno[f]. Precii in toto 21s 8d .... cust' 3¼d

<g>De Poulo Crempyn[r] pro 1 fardello cum 3 pannis, 14 ulnis curtis sine grano .... Hans cust' 3s 7d

Auditor's marginated entries L2: <a> pannus indigenus <b> pannus de dimidio grano indigenus <c> scarleta indigena <d> pannus alienigenus <e> pannus de dimidio grano alienigenus <f> scarleta alienigena <g> pannus hanse <h> pannus de dimidio grano hanse <i> scarleta hanse

<g>[s]Et pro 19 paribus caligarum pro hominibus et sex paribus caligarum pro feminis et 5 ulnis panni largi continentibus in toto 16 ulnas panni largi sine grano[s] .... Hans cust' 8d

Et pro 8 coverlettes Norfolke, 2 bankers Flandrie, 13 gros poyntes, 11 dossenis zonarum de corio[t] et extra pro 5 dossenis hures [u]alborum sengille[u], 4 platers[v], 2 [w]saltsalers de stanno[w]. [x]Precii in toto £4 12s 10d[x] .... cust' 14d

<g>Et pro 3 ulnis panni largi sine grano .... Hans cust' 1½d

<g>De Nicholao Noell pro 1 bala, 1 cista cum 22 pannis, 22 ulnis curtis sine grano .... Hans cust' 22s 11d[y]

Et pro 10 godis panni stricti Wallie. Precii 10s .... cust' 1½d

<g>De Clement Greve pro 1 bala cum 17 pannis, 6 ulnis curtis sine grano .... Hans cust' 17s 3d

<g>De Clays Scult pro 1 fardello, 1 cista cum 6 pannis, 9 ulnis curtis sine grano .... Hans cust' 6s 4½d

Et pro 2 centenis lb. vasorum stanni, 3 potelle pottes, 7 quarte pottes, 8 pynt pottes [g]de stanno[g]. Precii in toto £3 4s 10d .... cust' 9¾d

<g>De Deryk Hunter pro 3 balis, 1 pipa, 1 barello, 1 cista cum 45 pannis, 14 ulnis curtis sine grano .... Hans cust' 45s 7d

Et pro 21 parvis coverlettes Norfolke, 60 ollis potelle, 84 ollis quarte, 38 ollis pynt, 6 ollis galons de stanno, 1 pecia worsted duplicis, 4 bankers [f]Flandrie[f], 1 centena, 56 lb. vasorum stanni. Precii in toto £15 14s 8d .... cust' 3s 11¼d

<g>De Deryk Noell pro 2 balis cum 34 pannis, 7 ulnis curtis sine grano .... Hans cust' 34s 3½d

<i>Et pro 2 ulnis panni largi de scarlet[z] .... Hans cust' 2d

Et pro 3 coverlettes Norfolke, 2 barellis, 1 cista cum 5 centenis lb. vasorum stanni, 14 ollis potelle, 20 ollis quarte, 42 ollis pynt de stanno et 3 bankers Flandrie. Precii in toto £10 .... cust' 2s 6d

<g>Et pro 1 panno, 3 ulnis curtis sine grano .... Hans cust' 13½d

<g>De Henrico Brewer pro 1 bala cum 18 pannis curtis sine granoHans cust' 18s

Et pro 1 barello cum 21 parvis furruris de pellibus cuniculorum. Precii £3 10s .... cust' 10½d

<aa>£8 11s 3¼d<aa>

E122/73/20B f. 24[v]

<g>De Hans Wynter pro 2 balis cum 31 pannis, 4 ulnis curtis sine grano .... Hans cust' 31s 2d

<g>De Bernardo Syronbergh pro 1 bala, 1 fardello, 1 cista cum 28 pannis, 2 ulnis curtis sine grano .... Hans cust' 28s 1d

<g>Et extra pro 9 ulnis panni largi sine grano .... Hans cust' 4½d

Auditor's marginated entries L2: <k> worsted simplex indigene <l> worsted simplex alienigene <m> worsted duplex indigene <n> worsted duplex alienigene <o> lectus de worsted simplex indigene <p> lectus worsted simplex alienigene <aa>-<aa> *Auditor's entry: Sum of the issues of the page L2.*

Et pro 56 lb. vasorum stanni. Precii 13s 4d ... cust' 2d
<g>De Poulo Gronefeld pro 1 cista cum 1 panno, 23 ulnis curtis sine grano ... Hans cust' 23½d
<g>Et pro 2 dossenis parium caligarum continencium 12 ulnas panni largi sine grano ... Hans cust' 6d
Et pro 3 ulnis worsted duplicis. Precii 9s ... cust' 1½d
<g>De Jacobo Swart pro 5 cistis, 1 fardello, 2 barellis cum 18 pannis, 18 ulnis curtis sine grano ... Hans cust' 18s 9d
<g>Et pro 1 dossena parium caligarum continencium 6 ulnas panni largi sine grano ... Hans cust' 3d
Et pro 11 parvis coverlettes Norfolke, 2 gros poyntes[q], 2 bankers Flandrie, 3 ulnis worsted duplicis, 4 ollis galons, 25 ollis potelle, 41 ollis quarte, 36 ollis pynt [f]de stanno[f], [d]4 centenis lb. vasorum stanni[d], [aa]unde extra 2 quarte, 4 pynt pottes de stanno[aa]. Precii in toto £11 16s 8d.. cust' 2s 11½d
<g>De Hans Manelfiche pro 1 fardello, 1 cista cum 11 pannis, 23 ulnis curtis sine grano ... Hans cust' 11s 11½d
<g>De Hans Buk[ab] pro 1 bala cum 17 pannis, 4 ulnis curtis sine grano ... Hans cust' 17s 2d
<g>Et pro 1 cista cum 20½ ulnis panni largi sine grano ... Hans cust' 10¼d
Et pro 9 coverlettes Norfolke, 1 galon potte, [ac]6 ollis potelle, 10 ollis quarte, 10 ollis pynt de stanno et[ac] 2 barellis Rumney. Precii in toto £3 15s ... cust' 11¼d
De Hans Walroffe pro 1 cista cum 3 coverlettes Norfolke, 2 potelle pottes, 1 pynt potte et 2 discis de stanno. Precii in toto 11s 8d ... cust' 1¾d
<g>De Henrico van Somer pro 1 bala cum 15 pannis, 4 ulnis curtis sine grano ... Hans cust' 15s 2d
Et pro 23 ulnis frisii Wallie. Precii 13s 4d ... cust' 2d
<a>De Thoma Fulborn pro 1 fardello cum 5 pannis curtis sine grano ... Ind' cust' 5s 10d
De Nicholao Noell pro 1 barello cum 2 centenis lb. vasorum stanni, 7 furruris de pellibus cuniculorum. Precii £4 ... cust' 12d
<g>De Bertram Sleyghter pro 1 bala, 1 fardello cum 33 pannis, 16 ulnis curtis sine grano ... Hans cust' 33s 8d

<aa>£8 11s 2¾d<aa>

E122/73/20B f. 25^{r}

<a>De magistro Thoma Frank pro 1 rolla cum 5 ulnis panni largi sine grano ... Ind' cust' 3d
<g>•[f]De Andrea von Groten pro 2 balis cum 22 pannis, 16 ulnis curtis sine grano ... Hans cust' 22s 8d[f]

Auditor's marginated entries L2: <a> pannus indigenus <b> pannus de dimidio grano indigenus <c> scarleta indigena <d> pannus alienigenus <e> pannus de dimidio grano alienigenus <f> scarleta alienigena <g> pannus hanse <h> pannus de dimidio grano hanse <i> scarleta hanse

<g>De Michaelle Swart pro [ad]1 bala, 1 cista[ad] cum 17 pannis, 20 ulnis curtis sine grano .... Hans cust' 17s 10d

Et pro 56 lb. vasorum stanni, 4 ollis potelle, 13 ollis quarte de stanno. Precii 26s 8d .... cust' 4d

<g>De Henrico Tesbern pro 1 cista cum 2½ pannis curtis sine grano .... Hans cust' 2s 6d

<g>De Tym Gyse pro 5 balis, 1 fatte cum 102 pannis, 10 ulnis curtis sine grano .... Hans cust' £5 2s 5d

Et pro 194 godis panni stricti Wallie, [d]34 godis panni largi Wallie, 1 rolla frisii Wallie[d], 1 centena, 56 lb. vasorum stanni, 1 carpet[ae], 4 [w]saltsalers stanni[w], 4 corses de serico, 7 gros poyntes[q], 10 hures, 2 manicis veteribus enbroudatis[af] cum argento, 1 furrura de pellibus vulpium et 1 [ag]mantello de pellibus bever[ag] vetere, 4 ulnis bokeram[ah]. Precii in toto £13 10s .... cust' 3s 4½d

<g>De Matys Sprynghorn pro 3 balis, 2 cistis, 1 barello cum 56 pannis, 2 ulnis curtis sine grano .... Hans cust' 56s 1d

Et pro 4 paper poyntes[q], 5 coverlettes Norfolke, 10 ollis potelle, 3 dossenis [et] 6 ollis quarte, 18 ollis pynt de stanno, 1 centena lb. vasorum stanni, 1 testour Norfolke[ai], 1 celour, 3 curt[inis] bokeram[ah], 5 bonettes sengylle[aj] de scarlet[z], 4 hures duple de dimidio grano, 1 corse de serico, 2 saleres et 6 spones de argento, 8 cusshincloþes[ak] et 1 banker. Precii in toto £8 .... cust' 2s

<g>De Henrico Northows pro 1 cista cum 1 panno, 10 ulnis curtis sine grano .... Hans cust' 17d

Et pro 10 lb. vasorum stanni, 2 ollis quarte de stanno. Precii 8s 2d .... cust' 1¼d

[a] Mewes *L3.* [b] Maryknygh *L3.* [c] Wynterffeld *L3.* [d-d] *Interlined L2.* [e] lette *L3, in error.* [f-f] *Omitted L3.* [g-g] stanni *L3.* [h] ½[C] [et] 6 *L3.* [i] Wolfe *L3.* [j] Drewes *L3.* [k] Stownbergh *L3.* [l] Boleken *L3.* [m] coverlitte *L3.* [n] precii *follows, struck through L2.* [o] de *follows L3.* [p] *Corrected in L2 from* 1½d. [q] poyentes *L3.* [r] Crympyn *L3.* [s-s] Et pro 18 paribus caligarum continentibus 9 ulnas panni largi sine grano – *and, following the next line (*Et pro 8 coverlettes *...)* – Et pro 5 ulnis panni largi, 6 paribus caligarum pro feminis et 1 pari caligarum pro homine continentibus in toto 7 ulnas panni largi sine grano *L3 (i.e. the sub-entry is broken up into two sub-entries and sandwiched around the next line).* [t] coreo. Precii £4 7s 10d *followed by a line break L3 (cf. variant x).* [u-u] sengle alborum *L3.* [v] platerys *L3.* [w-w] saltselers stanni *L3.* [x-x] precii 5s *L3 (this is a consequence of the line break above: cf. variant t).* [y] ½d *follows, struck through L2.* [z] scarlett *L3.* [aa-aa] *Omitted L2.* [ab] Bukke *L3.* [ac-ac] 6 potelle pottes, 10 quarte pottes, 10 pynt pottes de stanno *L3.* [ad-ad] 1 cista, 1 bala *L3.* [ae] carpetto *L3.* [af] enbrodatis *L3.* [ag-ag] parva

Auditor's marginated entries L2: <k> worsted simplex indigene <l> worsted simplex alienigene <m> worsted duplex indigene <n> worsted duplex alienigene <o> lectus de worsted simplex indigene <p> lectus worsted simplex alienigene <aa>-<aa> *Auditor's entry: Sum of the issues of the page L2.*

furrura de beveres et *L3.* [ah] bokerams *L3.* [ai] Nortfolke *L3.* [aj] sengle *L3.* [ak] quysson clothes *L3.*

[195] In navi Matys Nyendank[a] vocata Cristofor de Danske[b] eodem die *[20 July 1446]*

<aa>£10 8s 11¾d<aa>

E122/73/20B f. 25[v]

De eodem pro 2 barellis cum 1 miliario, 2 centenis lb. vasorum stanni. Precii £16 .... cust' 4s

<g>De Henrico Eggart[c] pro 1 bala cum 23 pannis curtis sine grano .... Hans cust' 23s

<g>Et pro 1 cista cum 11 ulnis panni largi sine grano .... Hans cust' 5½d

Et pro 2 barellis cum 1 miliario lb. vasorum stanni. Precii £13 6s 8d .... cust' 3s 4d

<g>De dicto magistro[d] pro 1 fardello cum 11 pannis, 2 ulnis curtis sine grano .... Hans cust' 11s 1d

Et pro 1 testour, 1 selour et [e]3[e] curt[inis] de carde[f], 1 dossena hures. Precii 23s 4d .... cust' 3½d

[a] Nyendake *L3, in error.* [b] e[odem] d[ie] *follows, struck through L2.* [c] Eggard *L3.* [d] Matys Nyendanke *L3.* [e-e] *Interlined L2.* [f] et *follows L3.*

[196] In navi Henrici Lancassak vocata Cok John de Chereborgh 27° die Julii[a] *[27 July 1446]*

<a>De Ricardo Edward pro 2 fardellis cum 16 pannis, 16 ulnis curtis sine grano .... Ind' cust' 19s 5½d

<a>De Waltero Gylbert pro 1 fardello cum 9 pannis, 16 ulnis curtis sine grano .... Ind' cust' 11s 3½d

<a>De Ricardo Rawe pro 2 fardellis cum 8½ pannis curtis sine grano .... Ind' cust' 9s 11d

<a>De Willelmo Clerke pro 1 parvo fardello cum 20 ulnis panni largi sine grano .... Ind' cust' 11¾d[b]

<a>De Ricardo Perepount[c] pro 1 fardello, 1 hoggeshede cum 7 pannis, 21 ulnis curtis sine grano .... Ind' cust' 9s 2¼d

<a>Et pro 4 dossenis [et] 11 paribus caligarum continentibus 1 pannum, 5½ ulnas curta sine grano .... Ind' cust' 17d

<a>Et pro 1 panno, 6 ulnis curtis sine grano .... Ind' cust' 17½d

<a>De Alexandro Haysand[d] pro 1 fardello cum 19 pannis, 3 ulnis curtis sine grano .... Ind' cust' 22s 3¾d

<a>De Roberto Haysand[d] pro 1 fardello cum 6 pannis, 16 ulnis curtis sine grano .... Ind' cust' 7s 9½d

Auditor's marginated entries L2: <a> pannus indigenus <b> pannus de dimidio grano indigenus <c> scarleta indigena <d> pannus alienigenus <e> pannus de dimidio grano alienigenus <f> scarleta alienigena <g> pannus hanse <h> pannus de dimidio grano hanse <i> scarleta hanse

<a>De dicto Ricardo Perepount[e] pro 1 fardello cum 3 pannis curtis sine grano .... Ind' cust' 3s 6d

<a>De Willelmo Corbet[f] pro 1 bala cum 8 pannis, 4 ulnis curtis sine grano .... Ind' cust' 9s 6½d

<a>De Johanne Chypnall[g] pro 2 balis cum 23 pannis, 22 ulnis curtis sine grano .... Ind' cust' 27s 11d

<a>De Janycotte Lupsat[h] pro 1 fardello cum [i]28 dossenis rays Sarum continentibus 9 pannos, 8 ulnas curta[i] sine grano .... Ind' cust' 10s 10¾d

<a>De Ricardo Nedam pro 1 fardello cum 6 pannis, 6 ulnis curtis sine grano .... Ind' cust' 7s 3½d

<a>De Ricardo Smith pro 1 fardello cum 8 pannis, 11 ulnis curtis sine grano .... Ind' cust' 9s 10½d

[a] Julii *repeated L2, in error.* [b] require post ad hoc signum *and an insertion mark follow L3. The entries are continued at the bottom of the membrane, where the insertion mark is echoed.* [c] Perpoynte *L3.* [d] Haysaund *L3.* [e] Perpoyente *L3.* [f] Corbett *L3.* [g] Chipnale *L3.* [h] de Lupsate *L3.* [i-i] 9 pannis, 8 ulnis curtis *L2.*

<aa>£9 15s<aa>

E122/73/20B f. 26ʳ

[197] In navi Stephani Jawler vocata [a]Sancti Salvatoris de Bajona[a] [b]exeunte[b] eodem die *[27 July 1446]*

<a>De Alfouns de Seint John de Luce pro 1 fardello cum 6 pannis, 23 ulnis curtis sine grano .... Ind' cust' 8s 1½d[c]

<a>De dicto magistro pro 1 parvo fardello cum 9 ulnis panni largi sine grano .... Ind' cust' 5¼d

<a>De Johanne Pryse pro 3 balis cum 78 pannis, 6 ulnis curtis sine grano .... Ind' cust' £4 11s 3½d

[a-a] Sancti Salvatour de Bayon' *L3.* [b-b] *Omitted L3.* [d] *Corrected in L2 from* 2½d.

[198] In navi Cornelii[a] Johansson vocata James de Flaundres [b]exeunte[b] 29° die Julii *[29 July 1446]*

De Stephano Scapardon pro 1 barello cum garbelera alum debilis, 1 bala cum 6 remes paper, 1 parvo sacco cum garbelera grani paradisi, 74 lb. vasorum stanni, 1 pelvi et 1 lavour de latone. Precii 46s 8d .... cust' 7d

De Daniello Justynean pro 1 barello cum 92 lb. vasorum stanni, 1 cista cum 40 lb. gumme armoniac. Precii 30s .... cust' 4½d

Auditor's marginated entries L2: <k> worsted simplex indigene <l> worsted simplex alienigene <m> worsted duplex indigene <n> worsted duplex alienigene <o> lectus de worsted simplex indigene <p> lectus worsted simplex alienigene <aa>-<aa> *Auditor's entry: Sum of the issues of the page L2.*

De Johanne van de Feld pro 28 barellis cum 29 vagis sepi multonis, 5 barellis, 1 basket[c] et 2 peciis[d] ponderantibus 6 vagas sepi multonis debilis [b]et[b] 15 barellis cum 17 vagis sepi multonis. Precii in toto £20 16s .... cust' 5s 2½d

<m>De Johanne Hardeman pro 1 matte cum 7 peciis worsted duplicis continentibus 10 pecias .... Ind' cust' 20d

De Lexis[e] van de Feld pro 3 barellis cum [f]siroppe melace[f] debili. Precii 30s .... cust' 4½d

De dicto Johanne van [b]de[b] Feld pro 2 barellis salt petre, 1 parvo barello gunne pouder, 1 barello cum sulphur. Precii £8 10s .... cust' 2s 1½d

[a] Cornellii *L3.* [b] *Omitted L3.* [c] basketto *L3.* [d] sepi *follows L3.* [e] Allexis *L3.* [f-f] sirope malace *L2.*

[199] In batella Johannis Parker versus Sandewicum carcata eodem die et ibidem ad recarcandum in quadam carraca[a] versus partes Flandrie *[29 July 1446]*

<aa>£5 10s 2¼d<aa>

E122/73/20B f. 26v

<d>De Dominico Spynola pro 3 cistis cum 9 ulnis panni largi sine grano .... Al' cust' 12½d

<e>Et pro 1 ulna panni largi de dimidio grano .... Al' cust' 2¼d

Et pro 6 hures duple de scarlet[b], 3 hures duple sine grano, 1 longe cappe de scarlet[b], 14 gros poyntes[c]. Precii £4 .... cust' 12d

De Remond Vidal pro 1 fardello cum 235 pellibus murilegorum montanorum[d]. Precii 53s 4d .... cust' 8¼d

[a] caretta *L3, in error.* [b] scarlett *L3.* [c] poyentes *L3.* [d] mount' *L3.*

[200] In navi Thome Walssh[a] vocata Gabriell de London' [b]exeunte[b] 3° die Augusti *[3 Aug. 1446]*

<a>De Thoma Goldston[c] pro 1 fardello cum 1 panno, 18 ulnis curtis sine grano .... Ind' cust' 2s ½d

<a>De Ricardo Forstcr pro 1 bala cum 15 pannis curtis sine grano .... Ind' cust' 17s 6d

<a>De Thoma Eyr pro 3 balis cum 33 pannis curtis sine grano ... Ind' cust' 38s 6d

<o>Et pro 1 lecto [d]cum celour et testour de worsted simplici[d] continente 1½ lectos[e] .... Ind' cust' 7½d

<k>Et pro [f]3 [g]peciis worsted in[g] curtynes dicti lecti de worsted simplici[f] .... Ind' cust' 3d

<a>De Willelmo Wodehows[h] pro 3 fardellis cum 23 pannis, 6 ulnis curtis sine grano .... Ind' cust' 27s 1½d

Auditor's marginated entries L2: <a> pannus indigenus <b> pannus de dimidio grano indigenus <c> scarleta indigena <d> pannus alienigenus <e> pannus de dimidio grano alienigenus <f> scarleta alienigena <g> pannus hanse <h> pannus de dimidio grano hanse <i> scarleta hanse

<a>De Roberto Stocker[i] pro 1 [j]parvo[j] fardello cum 2 pannis curtis sine grano .... Ind' cust' 2s 4d

<a>De Willelmo Swan pro 1 bala cum 13 pannis, 5 ulnis curtis sine grano .... Ind' cust' 15s 5d

<a>De Thoma Estmast[k] pro 1 cista cum 12 ulnis panni largi sine grano .... Ind' cust' 7d

<a>De Thoma Grey pro [j]1[j] fardello cum 2 rollis frisii London' continentibus 2 pannos, 8 ulnas curta sine grano .... Ind' cust' 2s 8¾d

<a>De Willelmo Joy pro 2 balis, 1 fardello cum 16 pannis curtis sine grano .... Ind' cust' 18s 8d

<a>De Johanne Doland pro 1 bala cum 15 pannis, 16 ulnis curtis sine grano .... Ind' cust' 18s 3½d

[a] Walsch *L3.* [b-b] *Omitted L3.* [c] Goldeston *L3.* [d-d] de worsted simplici cum celour et testour *L3.* [e] worsted simplicis *follows L3.* [f-f] 3 curtynes de worsted simplici dicti lecti continentibus 3 pecias worsted *L3.* [g-g] *Interlined L2.* [h] Wodehous *L3.* [i] Stokker *L3.* [j-j] *Omitted L2.* [m] Estemast *L3.*

[201] In navi Dederici[a] Baysson vocata Magdalen[b] de Ernemoth[c] 8° die Augusti *[8 Aug. 1446]*

<g>De Hermano Wesyll[d] pro 2 fardellis cum 23 pannis curtis sine grano .... Hans cust' 23s

<aa>£8 9s 11¾d<aa>

E122/73/20B f. 27r

<g>De Johanne Dasse pro 1 bala cum 18 pannis curtis sine grano . Hans cust' 18s

<g>De Johanne Blyterswyk[e] pro 1 fardello cum 12½ pannis curtis sine grano .... Hans cust' 12s 6d

[a] Dederike *L3.* [b] *Corrected in L2 from* Madalen. Maudeleyn *L3.* [c] Erm[outh] *L3.* [d] Wesell *L3.* [e] Blitersweke *L3.*

[202] In navi Johannis Henrykesson[a] vocata Swan de Ernemoth[b] [c]exeunte[c] eodem die *[8 Aug. 1446]*

De Frank van Owenard pro 9 barellis cum 10 vagis sepi multonis. Precii £5 16s .... cust' 17½d

<g>De [d]Johanne[d] Lyfard pro 1 fardello cum 2 pannis, 3 ulnis curtis sine grano .... Hans cust' 2s 1½d

Et pro 2 barellis cum 56 lb. candellarum de sepo, 2 parvis barellis cum brasillo [c]debili[c]. Precii in toto £4 .... cust' 12d

De Petro Frank pro [e]2 hoggeshedes, 2 barellis, 1 basket[e], 1 corfe cum 1 miliario lb. vasorum stanni, 40 dossenis lb. candellarum de sepo[f], 200 pellibus ovium tawed. Precii £16 13s 4d .... cust' 4s 2d

Auditor's marginated entries L2: <k> worsted simplex indigene <l> worsted simplex alienigene <m> worsted duplex indigene <n> worsted duplex alienigene <o> lectus de worsted simplex indigene <p> lectus worsted simplex alienigene <aa>-<aa> *Auditor's entry: Sum of the issues of the page L2.*

De Arnoldo[g] Lunes pro 2 barellis cum 2½ vagis sepi multonis debilis et extra [c]pro[c] 337 pellibus vitulorum crude. Precii in toto £4 ....cust' 12d

De Dederico[h] van Capell pro 2 cistis cum 500 pellibus ovium tawed, 7 barellis cum 9 vagis [et] 8 lb. sepi multonis. Precii in toto £6 6s 8d ....cust' 19d

[a] Henriksson *L3.* [b] Ermouth *L3.* [c-c] *Omitted L3.* [d-d] *Interlined L2.* [e-e] 2 barellis, 2 hoggeshedes, 1 basketto et *L3.* [f] seppo *L3, apparently in error.* [g] de *follows L3.* [h] Dederike *L3.*

[203] In navi Gosson[a] Petersson vocata Cristofor de Scluce[b] eodem die *[8 Aug. 1446]*

De Andrea Scape pro 9 barellis, 2 baskettis cum 14 vagis [et] 84 lb. sepi multonis[c]. Precii £7 8s 4d..cust' 22¼d

De Arnoldo[d] van Pynxsten pro 1 barello cum 1 centena, 28 lb. vasorum stanni, 2 gros poyntes[e], 2 ollis potelle, 1 olla quarte [f]et[f] 1 olla pynt. Precii 41s ....cust' 6¼d

[a] Godson *L2.* [b] Scluse *L3.* [c] moltonis *L3.* [d] Andrea *L2, in error.* Adrea *L3, in error.* [e] poyentes *L3.* [f-f] *Omitted L3.*

<aa>44s 2½d<aa>

E122/73/20B f. 27[v]

[204] In navi Hayn Bulscamp[a] vocata Andrea de Ernemoth[b] [c]exeunte[c] 8° die Augusti *[8 Aug. 1446]*

De Dederico[d] Johanson pro 1 barello cum [e]3 centenis, 56[e] lb. vasorum stanni. Precii £4 13s 4d ....cust' 14d

De Johanne Ere pro 2½ barellis cum 15 centenis lb. vasorum stanni. Precii £20 ....cust' 5s

[f]De Johanne Johanson pro 4 barellis cum 4½ vagis sepi multonis. Precii 40s ....cust' 6d

[f]De Laurencio Poche pro 1 fardello cum 4 peciis sarge simple. Precii £4 ....cust' 12d

<i>Et pro predictis 4 peciis sarge simple.......................................Al' cust' 6d

De Lambert Jose[g] pro 14 barellis cum 8 miliariis, 4 centenis lb. vasorum stanni. Precii £105 ....cust' 26s 3d

De Johanne Salmer pro 6 barellis cum 36 centenis lb. vasorum stanni. Precii £45 ....cust' 11s 3d

<a>De Henrico Braybroke pro 1 bala cum 14 pannis, 19 ulnis curtis sine grano ....Ind' cust' 17s 3d

<d>De Thoma Rys pro 7 balis cum 88 pannis, 9¼ ulnis curtis sine grano .... Al' cust' £12 3s 1d

<e>Et pro 3 pannis, 11 ulnis curtis[h] de dimidio grano......... Al' cust' 14s 3¼d

Auditor's marginated entries L2: <a> pannus indigenus <b> pannus de dimidio grano indigenus <c> scarleta indigena <d> pannus alienigenus <e> pannus de dimidio grano alienigenus <f> scarleta alienigena <g> pannus hanse <h> pannus de dimidio grano hanse <i> scarleta hanse

<f>Et pro 3¼ ulnis [c]panni largi[c] de scarlet[i] .... Al' cust' 9d

Et pro 48 godis panni Wallie, 54 cappes de scarlet[i], 2 dossenis hures [c]duple[c] de scarlet[i]. Precii in toto £7 ....cust' 21d

De Remond Vydale pro 20 barellis sulphure debilis. Precii £6 13s 4d ..cust' 20d

De Belisardo[j] de Bardes pro 1 fardello cum 19 peciis worsted duplicis. Precii £20 .... cust' 5s

<n>·[k]Et pro predictis 19 peciis worsted duplicis .... Al' cust' 4s 9d

<d>·[k]Et pro 4 ulnis panni largi sine grano .... Al' cust' 5½d

De Arnoldo van Renson pro uno fardello cum 500 pellibus agnorum tawed, 162 pellibus vitulorum crude. Precii 53s 4d ....cust' 8d

<d>Et pro 1 maunda cum [l]2 peciis kersey continentibus 16 ulnas[l] [m]panni largi[m] sine grano .... Al' cust' 22d

Et pro 400 pellibus ovium tawed. Precii 53s 4d ....cust' 8d

<d>De Petro Tregaran[n] pro 2 fardellis cum 23 pannis, 16 ulnis curtis sine grano .... Al' cust' £3 5s 1d

Et pro 2 dossenis panni stricti Wallie. Precii 6s 8d ....cust' 1d

<a>De Johanne Tregaran[n] pro 2 fardellis cum 29½ pannis curtis sine grano .... Ind' cust' 34s 5d

<a>De Rogero Mydylmor pro 1 bala cum 17 pannis, 10 ulnis curtis sine grano .... Ind' cust' 20s 4d

<d>De Ambrosio Pynell pro 1 bala cum 8 pannis, 19 ulnis curtis sine grano .... Al' cust' 24s 2d

<e>Et pro 12 ulnis panni largi de dimidio grano .... Al' cust' 2s ¾d

<f>Et pro 22 ulnis panni largi de scarlet[i] .... Al' cust' 5s ½d

<aa>£24 9s<aa>

E122/73/20B f. 28[r]

De Gerardo[o] Johanson pro 2 fodris[p] [et] 21 lb. plumbi, 2 maundis cum 60 deker parvarum peciarum scissarum de ventribus vaccarum tannatarum, 20 dossenis pellium vitulorum tannatarum[q], 3 barellis cum 18 centenis lb. vasorum stanni. Precii in toto £35 16s 8d .... cust' 8s 11½d

<d>De Cristoforo Cataneo[r] pro 1 fardello cum 4 pannis, 7 ulnis curtis sine grano .... Al' cust' 11s 9¾d[s]

<e>Et pro 15½ ulnis panni largi de dimidio grano ....Al' cust[t] 2s 8¼d

<f>Et pro 11¾ ulnis panni largi de scarlet[i] .... Al' cust' 2s 8½d

<d>De Luca de Negro pro 2 fardellis cum 23 pannis, 21 ulnis curtis sine grano .... Al' cust' £3 5s 8d

<e>Et pro 10 ulnis panni largi de dimidio grano ....Al' cust' 20¾d

<f>Et pro 17 ulnis panni largi de scarlet[i] .... Al' cust' 3s 10¾d[u]

<a>De Willelmo Denton pro 1 bala cum [v]48 peciis kersey continentibus 16 pannos curtos[v] sine grano .... Ind' cust' 18s 8d

Auditor's marginated entries L2: <k> worsted simplex indigene <l> worsted simplex alienigene <m> worsted duplex indigene <n> worsted duplex alienigene <o> lectus de worsted simplex indigene <p> lectus worsted simplex alienigene <aa>-<aa> *Auditor's entry: Sum of the issues of the page L2.*

<a>De Thoma Whitylbery[w] pro 1 bala cum 13 pannis, 8 ulnis curtis sine grano .... Ind' cust' 15s 6¾d
<g>De Johanne Warenthorp pro 1 bala cum 16 pannis, 16 ulnis curtis sine grano .... Hans cust' 16s 8d
<g>De Hermano Wesyll[x] pro 1 bala cum 15 pannis curtis sine grano .... Hans cust' 15s
<g>De Jacobo Schrell[y] pro 1 fardello cum 14 pannis, 3 ulnis curtis sine grano .... Hans cust' 14s 1½d
<g>De Johanne Bliterswike[z] pro 3 balis, 1 fardello, 1 barello cum 109 pannis, 18 ulnis curtis sine grano .... Hans cust' £5 9s 9d
Et pro 43 godis panni [aa]stricti[aa] Wallie. Precii 32s 4d .... cust' 5d
<g>De Henrico Bruer[ab] pro 2 balis cum 46 pannis curtis sine grano .... Hans cust' 46s
<h>Et pro 1 panno, 4 ulnis curtis de dimidio grano .... Hans cust' 21d
De Roberto Blyterswyke[z] pro 2 barellis cum [ac]1 centena, 84[ac] lb. vasorum stanni, 1 olla quarte [c]et[c] 1 olla pynt [c]de stanno[c], 2 candelabris de latone, 1 furrura de martrons[ad] veteribus, 1 pecia bokram[ae], [af]2 peciis de carda, 2 ulnis worsted duplicis, 100 lb. candellarum de sepo[af]. Precii £3 6s 8d .... cust' 10d
<g>De Gerwyn Potte pro 2 balis cum 40 pannis, 15 ulnis curtis sine grano .... Hans cust' 40s 7½d
Et pro 3 pellibus cheverellorum. Precii 2s .... cust' ½d
<g>De Clays Swart pro 1 bala cum 16 pannis curtis sine grano .... Hans cust' 16s
Et pro ½ rolla frisii Wal[l]ie. Precii 10s .... cust' 1½d
<g>De Johanne Dasse pro 1 bala cum 18 pannis curtis sine grano .... Hans cust' 18s
<g>De Johanne Sybergh pro 2 balis cum 29½ pannis curtis sine grano .... Hans cust' 29s 6d
Et pro 10 godis panni stricti Wallie[ag], 1 basket[ah] cum 350 godis panni stricti Wallie. Precii [ai]in toto £12[ai] .... cust' 3s[aj]
<aa>£22 3s 6¼d<aa>

E122/73/20B f. 28[v]

<g>De Bertram Questenbergh pro 3 balis cum [ak]80 pannis, 12 ulnis[ak] curtis sine grano .... Hans cust' £4 6d
Et pro 20 godis panni [c]stricti[c] Wallie. Precii 13s 4d .... cust' 2d
<g>De Petro Cangheter pro 2 balis cum 54 pannis curtis sine grano .... Hans cust' 54s
Et pro 142 godis panni stricti Wallie. Precii £4 14s 8d .... cust' 14¼d
<g>De Johanne Stokdy pro 2 balis cum 34 pannis curtis sine grano .... Hans cust' 34s
<g>De Tilman Crome pro 3 balis cum 64½ pannis curtis sine grano .... Hans cust' £3 4s 6d

Auditor's marginated entries L2: <a> pannus indigenus <b> pannus de dimidio grano indigenus <c> scarleta indigena <d> pannus alienigenus <e> pannus de dimidio grano alienigenus <f> scarleta alienigena <g> pannus hanse <h> pannus de dimidio grano hanse <i> scarleta hanse

Et pro 85 godis panni stricti Wallie. Precii in toto [al]£3 3s 4d[al]........cust' 9½d

<g>De Hans Rynge pro 1 bala cum 16 pannis curtis sine grano .....Hans cust' 16s

Et pro 16[am] godis panni [c]stricti[c] Wallie. Precii 11s ....cust' 1¾d

<g>De Clays Lyndeman pro 1 bala cum 14 pannis curtis sine grano ....Hans cust' 14s

Et pro 68 godis panni stricti Wallie. Precii 45s 4d .... cust' 7d[an]

<g>De Henrico Nase pro 1 bala cum 20 pannis curtis sine grano ...Hans cust' 20s

Et pro 165 [ao]godis[ao] panni [c]stricti[c] Wallie. Precii £5 10s..............cust' 16½d

Et pro 1 parvo barello cum 3 centenis lb. vasorum stanni. Precii £4 ....cust' 12d

<a>De Willelmo Burgeys pro 1 fardello cum 16 pannis, 8 ulnis curtis sine grano .... Ind' cust' 19s ¾d

<g>De Cristean[ap] van Bleyken pro 2 balis cum 17 pannis, 6 ulnis curtis sine grano ....Hans cust' 17s 3d

Et pro 360 godis panni [c]stricti[c] Wallie, 2 rollis frisii Wallie. Precii £14 .... cust' 3s 6d

<g>De Henrico Overbagh pro 1 bala cum 23 pannis curtis sine grano ....Hans cust' 23s

Et pro 15 peciis worsted duplicis, ½ rolla frisii [c]Wallie[c]. Precii £20 10s .... cust' 5s 1½d

<g>De [c]dicto[c] Johanne Dasse pro 1 bala[aq] cum 17 pannis curtis sine grano ....Hans cust' 17s

<a>De Johanne Crowe pro 1 bala cum 22 pannis curtis sine grano .... Ind' cust' 25s 8d

<d>De Raphaelle de Aurea pro 1 fardello cum 1 panno, 4 ulnis curtis sine grano .... Al' cust' 3s 2½d

<f>Et pro 4 ulnis panni largi de scarlet[i]......................................Al' cust' 11d

<aa>£20 [ar]2s 11¾d[ar]•<aa>

[a] Bulschamp *L3.* [b] Erm[outh] *L3.* [c-c] *Omitted L3.* [d] Derike *L3.* [e] 3½ centenis *L3.* [f] *Entries for the goods of* Johannes Johanson *and* Laurencius Poche *in reverse order L3.* [g] Joses *L3.* [h] panni largi *L3.* [i] scarlett *L3.* [j] Belizardo *L3.* [k] *These two entries in reverse order L3.* [l-l] 16 ulnis *L2.* [m-m] curtas *L3.* [n] Tregoran *L3.* [o] Gerrardo *L3.* [p] foder *L3.* [q] precii in toto – *and, on the next line* – Et pro *follow L3 (i.e. one entry broken up into two).* [r] Catane *L2.* [s] *Corrected in L2 from* 9¼d. [t] *21d follows, struck through L2.* [u] *Corrected in L2 from* 6¾d. [v-v] 16 pannis curtis *L2.* [w] Whitilbury *L3.* [x] Wesell *L3.* [y] Sherell *L3.* [z] Blittersweke *L3.* [aa-aa] *Omitted L2.* [ab] Brewer *L3.* [ac-ac] *1¾ centenis L3.* [ad] matrons *L2.* [ae] bokerams *L3.* [af-af] 100 lb. candellarum sepi, 2 peciis carde, 2 ulnis worsted duplicis *L3.* [ag] precii 6s 8d – *and, on the next line* Et pro *follow L3 (i.e. one entry broken up into two: cf. variant ai).* [ah] basketto *L3.* [ai-ai] precii £11 13s 4d *L3*

Auditor's marginated entries L2: <k> worsted simplex indigene <l> worsted simplex alienigene <m> worsted duplex indigene <n> worsted duplex alienigene <o> lectus de worsted simplex indigene <p> lectus worsted simplex alienigene <aa>-<aa> *Auditor's entry: Sum of the issues of the page L2.*

(necessitated by the line break above: cf. variant ag). Corrected in L2 from £11 13s 4d *(*13s 4d *struck through and underscored with dots for the purpose of cancellation).* [aj] 11d *follows, struck through L2.* [ak-ak] 80½ pannis *L3.* [al-al] *Interlined above* 11s*, struck through L2 (error occasioned by confusion with the immediately following goods of* Hans Ryng*).* [am] 16 *'corrected' (apparently in error) to* 16½ *L3.* [an] *Corrected in L2 from* 6¾d. [ao-ao] *Interlined L.* [ap] Cristian *L3.* [aq] balla *L2.* [ar-ar] *Entered subsequently in darker ink L2.* 2s *written over erasure.*

*E122/73/20B f. 29^r^*

[205] In navi [a]Lambe[a] Johan Williamson[b] vocata Marykneyght[c] de Ernemoth exeunte eodem die *[8 Aug. 1446]*

<g>De Johanne Warenthorp pro 1 bala cum 24 pannis curtis sine grano .... Hans cust' 24s

<g>De Cristean[d] Edylkynt pro 1 bala cum 19 pannis, 16 ulnis curtis sine grano .... Hans cust' 19s 8d

De Matis van Ardenborgh pro 2 barellis cum 12 centenis lb. vasorum stanni. Precii £16 .... cust' 4s

<g>De Johanne Salmer pro 1 fardello cum 12 pannis, 11 ulnis curtis sine grano .... Hans cust' 12s 5½d

Et pro 2 rollis frisii Wallie, 1 gros poyntes[e] et [f]1 hure[f], 6 barellis cum 3 miliariis, 6 centenis lb. vasorum stanni. Precii in toto £47 3s 4d .... cust' 11s 9½d

<g>De Lambert Jose[g] pro 1 fardello cum 13 pannis, 9 ulnis curtis sine grano .... Hans cust' 13s 4½d

Et pro 4½ rollis frisii Wallie[h], 5 barellis cum 3 miliariis lb. vasorum stanni. [i]Precii in toto £42[i] .... cust' 10s 6d

[j]De Raphaelle de Ponsola pro 1 rolla cum 4 ulnis frisii London' de scarlet[k] continentibus 4 ulnas panni largi de scarlet[k] .... Al' cust' 11d

Et pro 1 hoggeshede, 1 barello cum 1 miliario, 8 centenis, 65 lb. vasorum stanni, 8 cassis de[l] pulvere sugre debilis. Precii in toto £31 .... cust' 7s 9d

<g>De Hermano Wcsill[m] pro 1 bala, 1 fardello cum 39 pannis curtis sine grano .... Hans cust' 39s

Et pro 40 godis panni [f]stricti[f] Wallie. Precii 26s 8d .... cust' 4d

<g>De Jacobo Schrell[n] pro 1 bala cum 19 pannis curtis sine grano Hans cust' 19s

<g>De Johanne Bliterswyke[o] pro 2 balis, 2 fardellis cum 84 pannis curtis sine grano .... Hans cust' £4 4s

Et pro 8 godis panni Wallie. Precii 6s 8d .... cust' 1d

<g>De Henrico Brewer pro 3 balis cum 73 pannis, 17 ulnis curtis sine grano .... Hans cust' £3 13s 8½d

Auditor's marginated entries L2: <a> pannus indigenus <b> pannus de dimidio grano indigenus <c> scarleta indigena <d> pannus alienigenus <e> pannus de dimidio grano alienigenus <f> scarleta alienigena <g> pannus hanse <h> pannus de dimidio grano hanse <i> scarleta hanse

Et pro 1 barello cum 6 centenis lb. vasorum stanni, 4 gros pointes[e]. Precii £7 18s .... cust' 23¾d[p]

<g>De Gerwyn Potte pro 6 balis cum 114½ pannis curtis sine grano .... Hans cust' £5 14s 6d

<g>De Clays Swart pro 1 bala cum 17 pannis curtis sine grano ..... Hans cust' 17s

Et pro ½ [q]rolla[q] frisii Wallie. Precii 10s .... cust' 1½d

<g>De Johanne Dasse pro 1 bala cum 18 pannis curtis sine grano . Hans cust' 18s

<aa>£23 12s 2¼d<aa>

E122/73/20B f. 29[v]

<g>De Johanne Sybergh pro 2 balis cum 46 pannis curtis sine grano .... Hans cust' 46s

Et pro 10 godis panni Wallie. Precii 6s 8d .... cust' 1d

<g>De Bertram Questenbergh pro 3 balis cum 87 pannis curtis sine grano .... Hans cust' £4 7s

Et pro 40 godis panni Wallie. Precii 26s 8d .... cust' 4d

<g>De Petro Cangheter pro 2 balis cum 50½ pannis curtis sine grano .... Hans cust' 50s 6d

Et pro 160 godis panni Wallie. Precii £5 6s 8d .... cust' 16d

<g>De Johanne Stokdy pro 2 balis cum 36 pannis, 10 ulnis curtis sine grano .... Hans cust' 36s 5d

Et pro 1 barello cum 84 lb. vasorum stanni, 4 pellibus cheverellorum, 1000 pynnes, 25 godis panni Wallie. Precii in toto 40s .... cust' 6d

<g>De Everard Stumbell'[r] pro 1 bala cum 12 pannis curtis sine grano .... Hans cust' 12s

<g>De Arnoldo van Pynxsten pro 1 bala cum 15 pannis, 9 ulnis curtis sine grano .... Hans cust' 15s 4½d

Et pro 17 godis panni Wallie [q]stricti[q]. Precii 11s 4d[s] .... cust' 1¾d

<g>De Gerardo[t] Growell pro 1 bala cum 21 pannis, 16 ulnis curtis sine grano .... Hans cust' 21s 8d

Et pro 216 godis panni stricti Wallie. Precii £7 .... cust' 21d

De Gerardo[t] Gastorp[u] pro 1 bala cum 620 godis panni stricti Wallie. Precii £20 13s 4d .... cust' 5s 2d

De Johanne Hathiltak[v] pro 2 barellis cum 13 centenis, 56 lb. vasorum stanni. Precii £18 .... cust' 4s 6d

<g>·[w]De Tilman Crome pro 5 balis cum 128½ pannis curtis sine grano .... Hans cust' £6 8s 6d

Et pro 44 godis panni [q]stricti[q] Wallie. Precii 32s 8d .... cust' 5d

<g>De Hans Rynge pro 2 balis cum 47 pannis, 6 ulnis curtis sine grano .... Hans cust' 47s 3d

Et pro 35 godis panni stricti Wallie. Precii 23s 4d .... cust' 3½d

Auditor's marginated entries L2: <k> worsted simplex indigene <l> worsted simplex alienigene <m> worsted duplex indigene <n> worsted duplex alienigene <o> lectus de worsted simplex indigene <p> lectus worsted simplex alienigene <aa>-<aa> *Auditor's entry: Sum of the issues of the page L2.*

<g>De Clays Lyndeman pro 2 balis cum 30 pannis curtis sine grano .... Hans cust' 30s

Et pro 61 godis panni stricti Wallie. Precii 40s .... cust' 6d

<g>De Henrico Nase pro 1 bala, 1 fardello cum 38 pannis, 6 ulnis curtis sine grano .... Hans cust' 38s 3d

<i>Et pro 1 ulna panni largi de scarlet[k] .... Hans cust' 1d

Et pro 92 godis panni[x] stricti Wallie. Precii £3 .... cust' 9d

<a>De Willelmo Burgeys pro 1 fardello cum 16 pannis, 4 ulnis curtis sine grano .... Ind' cust' 18s 10½d

<aa>£27 7s 2¼d<aa> [y]Item 6d[y]

E122/73/20B f. 30r

<g>De Cristean[d] van Bleyken[z] pro 3 balis cum 50½ pannis curtis sine grano .... Hans cust' 50s 6d

Et pro 2 rollis frisii [f]Wallie[f•aa], 80 godis panni stricti Wallie. Precii £4 13s 4d .... cust' 14d

<g>De Henrico Overbagh pro 2 balis cum 37 pannis curtis sine grano .... Hans cust' 37s

Et pro ½ rolla frisii Wallie. Precii 10s .... cust' 1½d

[a-a] *Interlined L2.* [b] Williamsson *L3.* [c] Maryknygh *L3.* [d] Cristian *L3.* [e] poyentes *L3.* [f-f] *Omitted L3.* [g] Joses *L3.* [h] precii £4 10s – *and, on the next line* – Et pro *follow L3 (i.e. one entry broken up into two: cf. variant i).* [i-i] precii £37 10s *(cf. variant h) L3.* [j] *Auditor's entry* scarlet alienigene *(corrected from* scarlet indigene*), marginated L2.* [k] scarlett *L3.* [l] cum *L3.* [m] Wesell *L3.* [n] Sherell *L3.* [o] Blittersweke *L3.* [p] *Corrected in L2 from* 2s 2¾d. [q-q] *Omitted L2.* [r] Stumell *L3.* [s] 6d *L3.* [t] Gerrardo *L3.* [u] Gasthorp *L3.* [v] Hatiltake *L3.* [w] *The goods of* Tilman Crome *entered after those of* Henricus Overbagh *(below) L3.* [x] panni *repeated L2, in error.* [y-y] *Auditor's supplement L2.* [z] Bleken *L3.* [aa] et *follows L3.*

[206] In navi Leonardi Gardotte[a] vocata Nicholaus de Roan[b] 20° die Augusti *[20 Aug. 1446]*

De Felice Favean pro 1 barello cum 12 cascis [c]de[c] Banbery et 8 caseis Suthfolke. Precii 13s 4d .... cust' 2d

[a] Cardotte *L3.* [b] Roon *L3.* [c-c] *Omitted L2.*

[207] In navi Roberti Fresier vocata Maria de Cane exeunte 25° die Augusti *[25 Aug. 1446]*

<a>De Willelmo Berkyng pro 1 parvo fardello cum 8 ulnis panni largi sine grano .... Ind' cust' 4¾d

<c>Et pro 10 ulnis panni largi de scarlet[a] .... Ind' cust' 11¾d

De Ricardo Pycatte pro 20 rollis frisii Wallie. Precii £18 10s .... cust' 4s 7½d

Auditor's marginated entries L2: <a> pannus indigenus <b> pannus de dimidio grano indigenus <c> scarleta indigena <d> pannus alienigenus <e> pannus de dimidio grano alienigenus <f> scarleta alienigena <g> pannus hanse <h> pannus de dimidio grano hanse <i> scarleta hanse

[a] scarlett *L3.*

[208] In batella Johannis Tanner[a] versus [b]portum Sandewici[b] carcata 29° die Augusti et ibidem ad recarcandum in quadam vas[a] [c]exeunte[c] versus Calesiam *[29 Aug. 1446]*

<a>De [d]Edmu[n]do Ekyney[d] pro 1 fardello cum 3 pannis, 8 ulnis curtis sine grano .... Ind' cust' 3s 10¾d
<g>De Henrico Nase pro 4 balis cum 60 pannis, 20 ulnis curtis sine grano .... Hans cust' £3 10d
Et pro 56 godis panni stricti Wallie, 2 gros pointes[e]. Precii in toto 42s 4d .... cust' 6½d
<g>De Arnoldo van Pynxsten pro 3 balis, 1 fardello cum 56 pannis, 5 ulnis curtis sine grano .... Hans cust' 56s 2½d
<h>Et pro ½ ulna panni largi de dimidio grano .... Hans cust' 1d
Et pro 2 rollis frisii Wallie, 3 gros pointes[e]. Precii 47s .... cust' 7¼d
<aa>£10 17s 1½d<aa>

E122/73/20B f. 30[v]
<g>De Johanne van Dorn pro 2 balis cum 27 pannis curtis sine grano .... Hans cust' 27s
Et pro 20 godis panni stricti Wallie. Precii 13s 4d .... cust' 2d

[a] Tannar *L2.* [b-b] Sandewicum *L3.* [c-c] *Omitted L3.* [d-d] Edmondo Ekeney *L3.* [e] poyentes *L3.*

[209] [a]In batella Willelmi Osey de Whytescapill'[b] versus Sandewicum vel Dovorriam[c] carcata eodem die et ibidem ad recarcandum in quadam vas[a][d] exeunte versus Calesiam *[29 Aug. 1446]*

<g>De Johanne Dasse pro 2 balis cum 31 pannis, 16 ulnis curtis sine grano .... Hans cust' 31s 8d
Et pro 2 rollis frisii [e]Wallie[e]. Precii 40s .... cust' 6d
<g>De Bertram Questenbergh pro 2 balis cum 29 pannis curtis sine grano .... Hans cust' 29s
Et pro 2000 pynnes. Precii 3s 4d .... cust' ½d
<g>De Johanne van Dorn pro 1 fardello cum 14 pannis curtis sine grano .... Hans cust' 14s
Et pro 36 godis panni stricti [e]Wallie[e]. Precii 20s .... cust' 3d
<g>De Cristean[f] van Bleyken pro 3 balis cum 49½ pannis curtis sine grano .... Hans cust' 49s 6d
Et pro 1 rolla frisii Wallie. Precii 20s .... cust' 3d

Auditor's marginated entries L2: <k> worsted simplex indigene <l> worsted simplex alienigene <m> worsted duplex indigene <n> worsted duplex alienigene <o> lectus de worsted simplex indigene <p> lectus worsted simplex alienigene <aa>-<aa> *Auditor's entry: Sum of the issues of the page L2.*

[a] *Entries for the* batella *of William* Osey *and the barge of William* Lambe *in reverse order L3.* [b] Whitscapell carcata *L3.* [c] Devor[iam] *L3.* [d] eo[dem die] *follows, struck through L2.* [e-e] *Omitted L3.* [f] Cristian *L3.*

[210] [a]In bargea Willelmi Lambe de London' versus Feveresham carcata [b]eodem die[b] et deinde per terram versus portum Sandewici vel Dovorrie[c] [d]et ibidem ad recarcandum in [quadam] navi exeunte versus Calesiam[d] *[29 Aug. 1446]*

<g>De Henrico Brewer pro 6 balis cum 68 pannis, 18 ulnis curtis sine grano .... Hans cust' £3 8s 9d

Et pro 138 peciis worsted duplicis. Precii £184 .... cust' 46s

<g>De Nicholao Swart pro 2 balis cum 33 pannis, 7 ulnis curtis sine grano .... Hans cust' 33s 3½d

Et pro 37 godis panni stricti Wallie, 3 gros pointes[e], 6 pellibus cheverellorum. Precii 40s .... cust' 6d

[a] *Entries for the* batella *of William* Osey *and the barge of William* Lambe *in reverse order L3.* [b-b] *Omitted L3.* [c] Devor[ie] *L3.* [d-d] 29° die Augusti *L3.* [e] poyentes *L3.*

[211] In navi Johannis Sameson[a] vocata Cristofor de Roan[b] [c]exeunte[c] 2° die Septembris *[2 Sept. 1446]*

<a>De Johanne Blundell pro 1 bala cum 6 pannis, 19 ulnis curtis sine grano .... Ind' cust' 7s 11d

<c>Et pro ¾ ulna panni largi de scarlet[d] .... Ind' cust' 1d

<aa>£15 8s 11d<aa>[e]

[a] Samason *L3.* [b] Roon *L3.* [c-c] *Omitted L3.* [d] scarlett *L3.* [e] £12 19s 2d *follows, struck through L2.*

E122/73/20B f. 31[r]

[212] In navi Clays van Owe[a] vocata Marykneyght[b] van Scluce [c]exeunte[c] eodem die *[2 Sept. 1446]*

De Lowes Bernard pro [d]1 lavour, 1 basin[d] de latone, 2 [e]saltsalers stanni[e]. Precii 8s 4d .... cust' 1¼d

[a] Ove *L3.* [b] Mariknygh *L3.* [c-c] *Omitted L2.* [d-d] 1 basin, 1 lovour *L2.* [e-e] salte selers de stanno *L3.*

[213] In navi Walteri Wymond vocata Cok John de Fowy[a] eodem die *[2 Sept. 1446]*

<a>De Willelmo Halhede pro uno fardello cum 9[b] pannis, 16 ulnis curtis sine grano .... Ind' cust' 11s 3½d

Auditor's marginated entries L2: <a> pannus indigenus <b> pannus de dimidio grano indigenus <c> scarleta indigena <d> pannus alienigenus <e> pannus de dimidio grano alienigenus <f> scarleta alienigena <g> pannus hanse <h> pannus de dimidio grano hanse <i> scarleta hanse

<a>De Willelmo Stafford pro 1 bala[c] cum 13 pannis, 20 ulnis curtis sine grano .... Ind' cust' 16s 1¾d

<c>Et pro 6 ulnis panni largi de scarlet[d] .... Ind' cust' 7d

<a>De Willelmo Bentle pro 1 bala[c] cum 14 pannis, 18 ulnis curtis sine grano .... Ind' cust' 17s 2½d

<a>De Janyn Manewe pro 1 fardello cum 2 pannis, 21½[e] ulnis curtis sine grano .... Ind' cust' 3s 4¼d

<a>De Willelmo Haydok pro 1 fardello cum 7 pannis, 18 ulnis curtis sine grano .... Ind' cust' 9s ½d

<a>De Roberto Stowell pro 1 fardello cum 11 pannis, 4 ulnis curtis sine grano .... Ind' cust' 13s ½d

<a>De Thoma Grey pro 1 fardello cum 11 pannis, 14 ulnis curtis sine grano .... Ind' cust' 13s 6¼d

<a>De Alexandro Haysand[f] pro 1 fardello cum 12 pannis, 8 ulnis curtis sine grano .... Ind' cust' 14s 4¾d

<a>De [g]Janicot Lupsat[g] pro 1 fardello cum 3 pannis, 8 ulnis curtis sine grano .... Ind' cust' 3s 10¾d

<a>De Bernardo Ape[h] pro 2 pipis cum 10 dossenis [et] 4 paribus caligarum [i]et[i] 12 ulnis panni largi continentibus in toto 3 pannos, 2 ulnas curta sine grano .... Ind' cust' 3s 7¼d

<m>Et pro 9 peciis worsted dimidii duplicis continentibus 14 pecias .... Ind' cust' 2s 4d

<a>De Andrea Body pro 1 pipa cum 17 dossenis parium caligarum continencium 4 pannos, 6 ulnas curta sine grano .... Ind' cust' 4s 11½d

<a>De Johanne Aleyn pro 1 fardello cum 4 pannis, 5 ulnis curtis sine grano .... Ind' cust' 4s 11d

<b>Et pro 2 pannis, 10 ulnis curtis de dimidio grano .... Ind' cust' 4s 2¾d

<c>Et pro 22 ulnis panni largi de [j]scarlet[j] .... Ind' cust' 2s 1¾d

[a] Fowey *L3.* [b] nono *follows, struck through L2.* [c] packe *L3.* [d] scarlett *L3.* [e] *Corrected in L2 from* 21. [f] Haysaund *L3.* [g-g] Janycott de Lupsate *L3.* [h] Appe *L3.* [i-i] *Omitted L3.* [j-j] *Interlined above* largi, *struck through L2.* scarlett *L3.*

<aa>£6 4s 9¼d<aa>

E122/73/20B f. 31[v]

[214] In navi Willelmi Bawdewyn vocata Jesus de London' exeunte 2° die[a] Septembris *[2 Sept. 1446]*

<a>De Johanne Adams[b] pro 1 fardello cum 5 pannis curtis sine grano .... Ind' cust' 5s 10d

Auditor's marginated entries L2: <k> worsted simplex indigene <l> worsted simplex alienigene <m> worsted duplex indigene <n> worsted duplex alienigene <o> lectus de worsted simplex indigene <p> lectus worsted simplex alienigene <aa>-<aa> *Auditor's entry: Sum of the issues of the page L2.*

<a>De Johanne Doland[c] pro 1 fardello cum 8 pannis curtis sine grano .... Ind' cust' 9s 4d

<a>Et pro 1 cista cum 12 ulnis frisii London' [d]et[d] sex ulnis panni largi continentibus [d]in toto[d] 18 ulnas panni largi sine grano ....Ind' cust' 10½d

<a>De Ricardo Hayll[e] pro 1 bala, 1 fardello cum 18 pannis, 18 ulnis curtis sine grano .... Ind' cust' 21s 10½d

<c>Et pro 2 celours, 2 testours[f] [g]cum curt[inis][g] de worsted simplici continentibus 2 lectos[h] .... Ind' cust' 10d

<k>Et pro 6 peciis worsted simplicis in curt[inis] [i]dictorum[i] lectorum .... Ind' cust' 6d

<a>De Willelmo Walden pro 1 fardello cum 5 pannis curtis sine grano .... Ind' cust' 5s 10d

<a>De Willelmo Swan pro 1 fardello cum 8 pannis, 6 ulnis curtis sine grano .... Ind' cust' 9s 7½d

<a>De Ricardo Perepount[j] pro 1 fardello cum 5 pannis, 20 ulnis curtis sine grano .... Ind' cust' 6s 9¾d

<a>De Johanne Stell[k] pro 2 fardellis cum 9 pannis curtis sine grano .... Ind' cust' 10s 6d

[a] de *L2, in error.* [b] Adam *L2.* [c] Dolond *L3.* [d-d] *Omitted L3.* [e] Hayle *L3.* [f] continentibus *follows, struck through L2.* [g-g] *Omitted L2.* [h] de worsted simple *follows L3.* [i-i] *Interlined above* dicti, *struck through L2.* [l] Perpoyente *L3.* [m] Steell *L3.*

[215] In navi Johannis Sylvestre vocata Maria de London' 7° die Septembris *[7 Sept. 1446]*

<a>De Roberto Edolf pro 1 fardello cum 7 pannis curtis sine grano .... Ind' cust' 8s 2d

<a>De Johanne Dolond[a] pro 1 fardello cum 9 pannis, 16 ulnis curtis sine grano .... Ind' cust' 11s 3½d

<a>De Johanne Stell[b] pro 2 fardellis cum 12 pannis, 16 ulnis curtis sine grano .... Ind' cust' 14s 9½d

<a>De Ricardo Lyon pro 1 fardello cum 10 pannis, 11 ulnis curtis sine grano .... Ind' cust' 12s 2½d

<a>De Thoma Covyntre[c] pro 1 fardello cum 4½ pannis curtis sine grano .... Ind' cust' 5s 3d

[a] Doland *L3.* [b] Steell *L3.* [c] Coventre *L3.*

Auditor's marginated entries L2: <a> pannus indigenus <b> pannus de dimidio grano indigenus <c> scarleta indigena <d> pannus alienigenus <e> pannus de dimidio grano alienigenus <f> scarleta alienigena <g> pannus hanse <h> pannus de dimidio grano hanse <i> scarleta hanse

[216] In navi Petri Persson[a] vocata Nicholaus de Vlissyng exeunte eodem die *[7 Sept. 1446]*

<a>De Willelmo Martin pro 1 fardello cum 3 pannis, 18 ulnis curtis sine grano .... Ind' cust' 4s 4½d

[a] Peersson *L3.*

<aa>£6 8s 1¼d<aa>

E122/73/20B f. 32r

[217] In navi Stephani Hawsegny vocata Nicholaus de Bajona[a] eodem die *[7 Sept. 1446]*

<a>De Stephano Forster pro 2 balis cum 33 pannis, 20 ulnis curtis sine grano .... Ind' cust' 39s 5¾d

<a>De Johanne Belyngton pro 1 fardello cum 9 pannis, 22 ulnis curtis sine grano .... Ind' cust' 11s 7d

<a>De Johanne Wykes[b] pro 1 fardello cum 13 pannis, 7 ulnis curtis sine grano .... Ind' cust' 15s 6d

<a>De Thoma Coke pro 1 [c]parvo[c] fardello cum 1 panno, 6 ulnis curtis sine grano .... Ind' cust' 17½d

[a] Bayona *L3.* [b] Wekes *L3.* [c-c] *Omitted L3.*

[218] In navi Petri Blunt vocata Maria de Ratclyffe [a]exeunte[a] eodem die *[7 Sept. 1446]*

<a>De Thoma Cooke[b] pro 1 fardello cum 7 pannis, 18 ulnis curtis sine grano .... Ind' cust' 9s ½d

<a>De Willelmo Hydeman pro 1 fardello cum 9 pannis, 9 ulnis curtis sine grano .... Ind' cust' 10s 11¼d

<a>De Pounset de Solo pro 1 cista cum 8 ulnis panni largi sine grano .... Ind' cust' 4¾d

<b>Et pro 3 ulnis panni largi de dimidio grano .... Ind' cust' 2¾d

<c>Et pro 4 ulnis panni largi de scarlet[c] .... Ind' cust' 4¾d

<a>De Gaylard Durefort[d] pro 2 cistis cum 14 ulnis panni largi sine grano .... Ind' cust' 8¼d

<a>Et pro 7 paribus caligarum[e] continentibus 3½ ulnas panni largi sine grano .... Ind' cust' 2d

<a>De domino Johanne Arnawdyn pro 1 cista cum 10 ulnis panni largi sine grano .... Ind' cust' 6d

<a>De Johanne de Selar pro 1 cista cum 8 ulnis panni largi sine grano .... Ind' cust' 4¾d

De Cristean[f] van Bleyken pro 2 mantellis bever. Precii 40s .... cust' 6d

Auditor's marginated entries L2: <k> worsted simplex indigene <l> worsted simplex alienigene <m> worsted duplex indigene <n> worsted duplex alienigene <o> lectus de worsted simplex indigene <p> lectus worsted simplex alienigene <aa>-<aa> *Auditor's entry: Sum of the issues of the page L2.*

<a>De Arnoldo Williamson[g] pro 1 fardello cum 6 pannis, 3 ulnis curtis sine grano .... Ind' cust' 7s 1¾d

<c>Et pro 6 ulnis panni largi de scarlet[c] .... Ind' cust' 7d

<a>De Willelmo Haydok pro 1 fardello cum 9½ pannis curtis sine grano .... Ind' cust' 11s 1d

<a>De Thoma Belleter pro 2 balis cum 18½ pannis curtis sine grano .... Ind' cust' 21s 7d

<b>Et pro 3 pannis, 4 ulnis curtis de dimidio grano .... Ind' cust' 5s 6¾d

<c>Et pro 14 ulnis panni largi de scarlet[c] .... Ind' cust' 16½d

<a>De Thoma Sampson pro 6 ulnis panni largi sine grano .... Ind' cust' 3½d

<aa>£6 18s 10¾d<aa>

E122/73/20B f. 32[v]

<a>De dicto Willelmo Haydok pro 1 bala cum 10 pannis curtis sine grano .... Ind' cust' 11s 8d

<a>De Willelmo Abraham pro 1 fardello cum 18 pannis, 23 ulnis curtis sine grano .... Ind' cust' 22s 1½d

<a>De Ricardo Harvy[h] pro 1 bala cum 13 pannis, 8 ulnis curtis sine grano .... Ind' cust' 15s 6¾d

Et pro 1 rolla frisii Covyntre[i] continente 1 pannum curtum sine grano .... Ind' cust' 14d

a-a *Omitted L3.* b Coke *L3.* c scarlett *L3.* d Dureford *L3.* e galig' *L2, in error.* f Cristian *L3.* g Williamsson *L3.* h Hervy *L3.* i Coventre *L3.*

[219] In navi Johannis Pay vocata Katerin [a]de[a] 25° die Septembris *[25 Sept. 1446]*

<a>De Ricardo Whetehill pro 1 fardello cum 3 pannis, 14 ulnis curtis sine grano .... Ind' cust' 4s 2¼d

<b>Et pro 12 ulnis panni largi de dimidio grano .... Ind' cust' 10½d

a-a *Omitted L3. Thereafter 4½ cm (L2), 6 cm (L3) room left for completion of the entry.*

[a]Examinatur cum rotulis contrarotulatoris[a]

a a *Auditor's entry, marginated in the lower left-hand corner of the page L2. Auditor's entry* Examinatur cum particulis custumariorum, *marginated in the lower left-hand corner of the membrane L3.*

<aa>55s 7d<aa>

[a]Summa a 16° folio £354 6s 9d Totalis £920 15s 9d[a]

a-a *Auditor's entry L2. Omitted L3.*

Auditor's marginated entries L2: <a> pannus indigenus <b> pannus de dimidio grano indigenus <c> scarleta indigena <d> pannus alienigenus <e> pannus de dimidio grano alienigenus <f> scarleta alienigena <g> pannus hanse <h> pannus de dimidio grano hanse <i> scarleta hanse

E122/73/20B f. 33ʳ

<table>
<tr><td rowspan="16">Summa totalis hujus libri</td><td colspan="3">Valor mercandisarum alienigenarum, unde 3d de libra</td><td>£4550 6s 4d</td><td>cust' £56 18s 1d</td></tr>
<tr><td colspan="2" rowspan="3">Panni de scarlet</td><td>Indigenarum</td><td>7½ panni 1¼ ulne</td><td>cust' 17s 8½d</td></tr>
<tr><td>Alienigenarum</td><td>4 panni 5¼ ulne</td><td>cust' 23s 3½d</td></tr>
<tr><td>Hans'</td><td>2 panni 9 ulne</td><td>cust' 4s 9d</td></tr>
<tr><td colspan="2" rowspan="3">Panni de dimidio grano</td><td>Indigenarum</td><td>8 panni 2¼ ulne</td><td>cust' 14s 2½d</td></tr>
<tr><td>Alienigenarum</td><td>11 panni 4 ulne</td><td>cust' 46s 4¼d</td></tr>
<tr><td>Hans</td><td>1 pannus 8½ ulne</td><td>cust' 2s 1d</td></tr>
<tr><td colspan="2" rowspan="3">Panni sine grano</td><td>Indigenarum</td><td>5500 panni 13¾ ulne</td><td>cust' £320 18s 7½d</td></tr>
<tr><td>Alienigenarum</td><td>1300 panni ¾ ulne</td><td>cust' £178 16s 6d</td></tr>
<tr><td>Hans</td><td>7085 panni 1½ ulne</td><td>cust' £354 5s ¾d</td></tr>
<tr><td rowspan="4">Panni de worsted</td><td rowspan="2">duplici</td><td>Indigenarum</td><td>436½ pecie</td><td>cust' 72s 9d</td></tr>
<tr><td>Alienigenarum</td><td>24 pecie</td><td>cust' 6s</td></tr>
<tr><td rowspan="2">simplici</td><td>Indigenarum</td><td>21 pecie</td><td>cust' 21d</td></tr>
<tr><td>Alienigenarum</td><td>30 pecie</td><td>cust' 3s 9d</td></tr>
<tr><td colspan="2" rowspan="2">Lecti de worsted simplici</td><td>Indigenarum</td><td>7½ lecti</td><td>cust' 3s 1½d</td></tr>
<tr><td>Alienigenarum</td><td>3 lecti</td><td>cust' 22½d</td></tr>
</table>

Auditor's marginated entries L2: <k> worsted simplex indigene <l> worsted simplex alienigene <m> worsted duplex indigene <n> worsted duplex alienigene <o> lectus de worsted simplex indigene <p> lectus worsted simplex alienigene <aa>-<aa> *Auditor's entry: Sum of the issues of the page L2.*

Summa totalis recepte hujus libri conjuncta	£920 15s 11d
Summa totalis recepte tam hujus libri de In navi quam alterius libri de De navi etc.	£1107 10s 9¼d

Auditor's marginated entries L2: <a> pannus indigenus <b> pannus de dimidio grano indigenus <c> scarleta indigena <d> pannus alienigenus <e> pannus de dimidio grano alienigenus <f> scarleta alienigena <g> pannus hanse <h> pannus de dimidio grano hanse <i> scarleta hanse

PARCELLE COMPOTI

[P 1] *Edmund, marquis of Dorset, acknowledges receipt of 250 marks sterling owing to him by virtue of his annuity, to wit for Michaelmas term last* (pro termino sancti Michaelis ultimo preterito), *from the collectors of the petty customs in London John* Melborne *and William* Chattok. — *1446 Nov. 20* (per presentes sigillo nostro signatas. Datum vicesimo die Novembris anno regni regis Henrici Sexti vicesimo quinto). *[London].*

L TNA: PRO, E122/75/40/2.[1] *Original. Parchment. Traces on seal on tongue. Sign manual* (Dorset E) *beneath the text. On the tongue:* Pro merchione Dercet. *On the dorse:* Summa istarum duarum aquietanciarum £333 6s 8d; *(beneath that)* Allocatur in compoto Johannis Melberne et Willelmi Chattok collectorum parve custume regis in portu civitatis London' a 26to die Januarii anno 24to regis Henrici vj^{ti} *[26 Jan. 1446]* usque festum sancti Michaelis tunc proxime sequens *[29 Sept. 1446] [TNA: PRO, E356/19 m 11-11d; No. A 4, § 10].*

[P 2] *Margaret, duchess of Somerset, acknowledges receipt of £83 6s 8d, owing to her by virtue of the £166 13s 4d due her yearly as the third of the annuity of £500 yearly assigned to her in dowry* (pro dote nostra de tercia parte quingentarum librarum), *to wit for Easter term last* (pro termino Pasche ultimo preterito), *from the collectors of the petty customs in London John* Melborne *and William* Chattok. — *1446 June 12* (per presentes sigillo nostro signatas. Datum duodecimo die Junii anno regni regis Henrici Sexti post conquestum Anglie vicesimoquarto). *[London].*

L TNA: PRO, E122/75/40/3. Original. Parchment. Seal on tongue lost.

[P 3] *Margaret, duchess of Somerset, acknowledges receipt of £80 66s*[a] *8d, owing to her by virtue of the £166 13s 4d due her yearly as the third of the annuity of £500 yearly assigned to her in dowry* (pro dote nostra de tercia parte £500), *to wit for Michaelmas term last* (pro termino Michaelis ultimo preterito), *from the collectors of the petty customs in London John* Melborne *and William* Chattok. — *1446 Nov. 1* (per presentes

[1] *One writ has been torn away. The endorsement of P 1* (Summa istarum duarum acquietanciarum £333 6s 8d) *shows that the lost writ must have been a receipt of Edmund, marquis of Dorset, for 250 marks.*

sigillo nostro signatas. Datum primo die Novembris anno regni regis Henrici Sexti post conquestum Anglie vicesimo quinto). *[London].*

L TNA: PRO, E122/75/40/4. Original. Parchment. Remnants of seal on tongue. On the tongue: Pro ducissa Somercet. *On the dorse:* Summa istarum duarum aquietanciarum £166 13s 4d; *(beneath that)* Allocatur in compoto Johannis Melberne et Willelmi Chattok collectorum parve custume regis in portu civitatis London' a 26[to] die Januarii anno 24[to] regis Henrici vj[ti] *[26 Jan. 1446]* usque festum Michaelis tunc proxime sequens *[29 Sept. 1446] [TNA: PRO, E356/19 m 11-11d; No. A 4, § 11].*

[a] *Sic L.*

[P 4] Henry VI to the treasurer and barons of the Exchequer: since Henry IV (avus noster) *by patent confirmed by Henry V* (pater noster) *and by the present king on 15 Dec. 1422* (quintodecimo die Decembris anno regni nostri primo)[2] *granted* Cristina Houchon *4d per diem in alms* (ex causa elemosine) *for life, payable from the issues of the petty customs in London; and since the king has ordered [No. P 6] the customers to pay the beneficiary all arrears of the said 4d per diem owing from 29 Sept. 1445* (a festo sancti Michaelis ultimo preterito)*; the king orders the Exchequer to allow* (debite allocetis) *the customers all payments made in this regard when they account, provided they produce the mandate for payment directed to them and the receipts* (litteras acquietancie) *of the beneficiary. — 1446 May 8* (Teste me ipso apud Westmonasterium, 8 die Maii anno regni nostri vicesimo quarto. *[signed by the scribe]* [a]'Kirkeby'[a]).[3] *Westminster.*

L1 TNA: PRO, E122/75/40/5. Original. Parchment. Seal on tongue torn away. On the dorse: Irrotulatur termino sancte Trinitatis anno 24[to] rotulo 11[mo] *[TNA: PRO, E159/222 Brevia directa baronibus Trinity m 11 = L2]*; *(beneath that)* Allocatur in compoto Johannis Melborne et Willelmi Chattok collectorum parve custume[b] London' de anno 24[to] regis Henrici vj[ti] *[TNA: PRO, E356/19 m 11-11d; No. A 4, § 12].*

L2 TNA: PRO, E159/222 Brevia directa baronibus Trinity m 11. Contemporaneous official copy. Parchment. Unsealed. Marginated: Pro Cristina Houchon.

[a–a] *Omitted L2.* [b] parve custume *repeated L1, in error.*

[P 5] Henry VI to the treasurer and barons of the Exchequer: since Henry IV (avus noster) *by patent confirmed by Henry V* (pater noster) *and by the present king on 15 Dec. 1422* (quintodecimo die Decembris anno regni

---

[2] *Henry IV's patent was issued on 16 May 1401 (CPR 1399-1401, p. 488), Henry V's confirmation on 1 Apr. 1414 (CPR 1413-16, p. 196) and Henry VI's on 15 Dec. 1422 (CPR 1422-29, p. 16).*

[3] Thomas Kirkeby was a chancery clerk: CCR 1441-47, p. 384.

nostri primo)[4] *granted* Cristina Houchoun *4d per diem in alms* (ex causa elemosine) *for life, payable from the issues of the petty customs in London; and since the king has ordered [No. P 7] the customers to pay the beneficiary all arrears of the said 4d per diem owing from 29 Sept. 1445* (a festo sancti Michaelis anno regni nostri vicesimo quarto)*; the king orders the Exchequer to allow* (debite allocetis) *the customers all payments made in this regard when they account, provided they produce the mandate for payment directed to them and the receipts* (litteras acquietancie) *of the beneficiary. — 1446 Oct. 18* (Teste me ipso apud Westmonasterium, 18 die Octobris anno regni nostri vicesimo quinto. *[signed by the scribe]* [a]'Kirkeby'[a]). *Westminster.*

L1 TNA: PRO, E122/75/40/6. Original. Parchment. Seal on tongue torn away. On the dorse: Irrotulatur termino sancti Hillarii anno 25[to] rotulo decimo *[TNA: PRO, E159/223 Brevia directa baronibus Hilary m 10 = L2]; (beneath that)* Allocatur in compoto Johannis Melborne et Willelmi Chattok collectorum parve custume London' de anno 24[to] regis Henrici vj[ti] *[TNA: PRO, E356/19 m 11-11d; No. A 4, § 12].*

L2 TNA: PRO, E159/223 Brevia directa baronibus Hilary m 10. Contemporaneous official copy. Parchment. Unsealed. Marginated: Pro Cristina Houchon.

[a–a] *Omitted L2.*

[P 6] *Henry VI to the collectors of the petty customs in London: since Henry IV* (avus noster) *by patent confirmed by Henry V* (pater noster) *and by the present king on 15 Dec. 1422* (quinto decimo die Decembris anno regni nostri primo)[5] *granted* Cristina Houchon *4d per diem in alms* (ex causa elimosine) *for life, payable from the issues of the petty customs in London; the king orders the customers to pay the beneficiary all arrears of the said 4d per diem owing from 29 Sept. 1445* (a festo sancti Michaelis ultimo preterito)*, accepting in turn her receipts* (litteras suas acquietancie)*, which together with this mandate for payment shall suffice for the allowance* (debitam allocacionem) *of all payments made in this regard when the customers account at the Exchequer. — 1446 May 7* (Teste me ipso apud Westmonasterium, 7 die Maii anno regni nostri vicesimo quarto. *[signed by the scribe]* 'Kirkeby'). *Westminster.*

L TNA: PRO, E122/75/40/7. Original. Parchment. Seal on tongue torn away.

---

[4] *Henry IV's patent was issued on 16 May 1401 (CPR 1399-1401, p. 488), Henry V's confirmation on 1 Apr. 1414 (CPR 1413-16, p. 196) and Henry VI's on 15 Dec. 1422 (CPR 1422-29, p. 16).*

[5] *Henry IV's patent was issued on 16 May 1401 (CPR 1399-1401, p. 488), Henry V's confirmation on 1 Apr. 1414 (CPR 1413-16, p. 196) and Henry VI's on 15 Dec. 1422 (CPR 1422-29, p. 16).*

[P 7] *Henry VI to the collectors of the petty customs in London: since Henry IV* (avus noster) *by patent confirmed by Henry V* (pater noster) *and by the present king on 15 Dec. 1422* (quintodecimo die Decembris anno regni nostri primo)[6] *granted* Cristina Houchon *4d per diem in alms* (ex causa elemosine) *for life, payable from the issues of the petty customs in London; the king orders the customers to pay the beneficiary all arrears of the said 4d per diem owing from 29 Sept. 1446* (a festo sancti Michaelis anno regni [a]nostri[a] vicesimo quarto), *accepting in turn her receipts* (litteras acquietancie), *which together with this mandate for payment shall suffice for the allowance* (debitam allocacionem) *of all payments made in this regard when the customers account at the Exchequer. — 1446 Oct. 17* (Teste me ipso apud Westmonasterium, 17 die Octobris anno regni nostri vicesimo quinto. *[signed by the scribe]* 'Kirkeby'). *Westminster.*

L TNA: PRO, E122/75/40/8. Original. Parchment. Seal on tongue torn away.

[a–a] *Interlined L.*

[P 8] Cristina Houchon *acknowledges receipt of 60s 10d, owing to her by virtue of the grant of 4d per diem by Henry IV,*[7] *to wit for the period from 29 Sept. 1445 to 31 Mar. 1446* (a festo sancti Michaelis anno 24[to] usque ultimum diem Marcii tunc proxime sequentem), *from one of the collectors of the petty customs in London John* Melbourne. — *1446 June 12* (per presentes sigillo meo signatas. Datum 12° die Junii anno regni regis Henrici Sexti vicesimo quarto). *[London].*

L TNA: PRO, E122/75/40/9. Original. Parchment. Traces of seal on tongue.

[P 9] Cristina Houchon *acknowledges receipt of 60s 10d, owing to her by virtue of the grant of 4d per diem by Henry IV,*[8] *to wit for the period from 29 Sept. 1445 to 29 Sept. 1446* (a festo sancti Michaelis anno 24[to] usque festum sancti Michaelis tunc proxime sequens anno 25[to] pro uno anno), *from the collectors of the petty customs in London John* Melbourne *and William* Chattok. — *1446 Nov. 22* (per presentes sigillo meo signatas. Datum 22° die Novembris anno regni regis Henrici Sexti vicesimo quinto). *[London].*

---

[6] *Henry IV's patent was issued on 16 May 1401 (CPR 1399-1401, p. 488), Henry V's confirmation on 1 Apr. 1414 (CPR 1413-16, p. 196) and Henry VI's on 15 Dec. 1422 (CPR 1422-29, p. 16).*

[7] *Henry IV's patent was issued on 16 May 1401 (CPR 1399-1401, p. 488), Henry V's confirmation on 1 Apr. 1414 (CPR 1413-16, p. 196) and Henry VI's on 15 Dec. 1422 (CPR 1422-29, p. 16).*

[8] *Henry IV's patent was issued on 16 May 1401 (CPR 1399-1401, p. 488), Henry V's confirmation on 1 Apr. 1414 (CPR 1413-16, p. 196) and Henry VI's on 15 Dec. 1422 (CPR 1422-29, p. 16).*

L TNA: PRO, E122/75/40/10. Original. Parchment. Remnants of seal on tongue.

[P 10] John Popham, *kt.* (miles), *acknowledges receipt of £10 in part payment of the £20 owing to him from Easter term last* (pro termino Pasche ultimo preterito) by virtue of his annuity of £40, *from the collectors of the petty customs in London John* Milbourn *and William* Chattok. — *1446 June 3* (per presentes sigillo meo sigillatas. Datum tercio die Junii anno regni regis Henrici Sexti post conquestum vicesimo quarto). *[London].*

L TNA: PRO, E122/75/40/11. Original. Parchment. Traces of seal on tongue. On the tongue: Poppenham. *On the dorse:* Allocatur in compoto Johannis Melberne et Willelmi Chattok collectorum parve custume London' de anno 24to regis Henrici vj^{ti} *[TNA: PRO, E356/19 m 11-11d; No. A 4, § 13].*

[P 11] John Yerde, *esq.* (armiger), *acknowledges receipt of £20 owing to him from Easter and Michaelmas terms last* (pro terminis Pasche et sancti Michaelis ultimo preteritis) *by virtue of the annuity of £20 yearly granted by Henry IV and confirmed by Henry V and Henry VI,*[9] *from the collectors of the petty customs in London John* Melborne *and William* Chattok. — *1446 Oct. 24* (per presentes sigillo meo signatas. Datum vicesimo quarto die Octobris anno regni regis Henrici Sexti vicesimo quinto). *[London].*

L TNA: PRO, E122/75/40/12. Original. Parchment. Traces of seal on tongue. On the tongue: erde. *On the dorse:* Allocatur in compoto Johannis Melborne et Willelmi Chattok collectorum parve custume London' de anno 24to regis Henrici vj^{ti} *[TNA: PRO, E356/19 m 11-11d; No. A 4, § 14].*

[P 12] Humphrey, duke of Gloucester, acknowledges receipt by the hand of the treasurer of his household, Gervase Clifton (per manus Gervasii Clifton thesaurarii hospicii nostri), *of £8 owing to him for Easter term last* (pro termino Pasche ultimo preterito) *by virtue of the grant of an annuity of* £16 yearly,[10] *from the collectors of the petty customs in London John* Melburn *and William* Chattok. — *1446 Apr. 24* (Datum sub signeto nostro 24° die Aprilis anno regni dicti domini mei regis Henrici Sexti post conquestum Anglie vicesimo quarto). *[London].*

L TNA: PRO, E122/75/40/13. Original. Parchment. Signet on tongue slightly damaged. On the tongue: Dux Gloucest[rie]. *On the dorse:* Allocatur in compoto Johannis Melborne et Willelmi Chattok collectorum parve custume London' de anno 24to regis Henrici vj^{ti} *[TNA: PRO, E356/19 m 11-11d; No. A 4, § 15].*

---

[9] *Henry IV's patent was issued on 13 Jan. 1413 (CPR 1408-13, p. 460), die Bestätigung Heinrichs V. vom 1 Oct. 1414 (CPR 1413-16, p. 272) und die Heinrichs VI. vom 20 Dec. 1422 (CPR 1422-29, p. 39).*

[10] *Henry VI's grant was made on 30 June 1441 (CPR 1436-41, p. 552). Cf. also No. S 6.*

[P 13] John Faceby, the king's physician (medicus domini nostri regis), *acknowledges receipt of £100 owing to him for Easter and Michaelmas terms last* (pro terminis Pasche et sancti Michaelis Archangeli ultimis preteritis ante datam presencium) *by virtue of the annuity of £100 yearly granted by Henry VI*[11] *for his fee* (pro feodo meo) *for life and payable from the issues of the petty customs in London at Easter and Michaelmas in equal portions, from the collectors of the petty customs in London John* Melbourne *and William* Chattok. — *1446 Nov. 24* (Per presentes sigillo meo sigillatis. Datum vicesimo quarto die Novembris anno regni regis Henrici Sexti post conquestum vicesimo quinto. *[signed by the scribe]* 'Fermory'). *[London]*

L TNA: PRO, 122/225/70/12. Original. Parchment. Traces of seal on tongue. On the tongue: Faseby. *On the dorse:* Allocatur in compoto Johannis Melbourne et Willelmi Chattok collectorum parve custume London' de anno 24to regis Henrici vj^{ti} *[TNA: PRO, E356/19 m 11-11d; No. A 4, § 16].*

[P 14] Thomas Ponsford *acknowledges receipt of £4 11s, owing to him by virtue of Henry VI's grant of 6d per diem from the issues of the petty customs in London,*[12] *to wit for the period from 29 Sept. 1445 to 31 Mar. 1446* (a festo sancti Michaelis anno vicesimo quarto regis hujus usque ultimum die Marcii tunc proxime sequentem), *from the collectors of the petty customs in London John* Melborne *and William* Chattok. — *1446 Nov. 20* (per presentes sigillo meo signatas. Datum vicesimo die Novembris anno regni regis Henrici Sexti post conquestum Anglie vicesimo quinto). *[London].*

L TNA: PRO, E122/75/40/14. Original. Parchment. Traces of seal on tongue. On the tongue: Paunsford. *On the dorse:* Allocatur in compoto Johannis Melborne et Willelmi Chattok collectorum parve custume London' de anno 24to regis Henrici vj^{ti} *[TNA: PRO, E356/19 m 11-11d; No. A 4, § 17].*

[P 15] John Seyntlo, *esq.* (armiger), *acknowledges receipt of £10 owing from Easter term last* (pro termino Pasche ultimo preterito) *by virtue of the annuity of £20 yearly, payable from the issues of the petty customs in London, granted by Henry VI*[13] *from the collectors of the petty customs in London John* Melborne *and William* Chattok. — *1446 Nov. 3* (per presentes sigillo meo signatas. Datum tercio die Novembris anno regni regis Henrici Sexti vicesimo quinto). *[London].*

L TNA: PRO, E122/75/40/15. Original. Parchment. Seal on tongue severely damaged. On the dorse: Allocatur in compoto Johannis Melborne et Willelmi Chattok collectorum parve custume London' de

---

[11] *CPR 1441-46, p. 271 dated 11 July 1444.*
[12] *CPR 1441-46, p. 164 dated 19 Feb. 1443.*
[13] *CPR 1436-41, p. 387 dated 17 Feb. 1440.*

anno 24[to] regis Henrici vj[ti] *[TNA: PRO, E356/19 m 11-11d; No. A 4, § 18].*

[P 16] John Sutton, *kt.* (miles), *lord* Duddeley, *acknowledges receipt of £10 in part payment of the £50 owing from Easter term last* (pro termino Pasche ultimo preterito) *by virtue of the annuity of £100 yearly, payable from the issues of the petty customs in London, granted by Henry VI*[14] *from the former* (nuper) *collectors of the petty customs in London John* Melborne *and William* Chattok. — *1447 Feb. 1* (per presentes sigillo meo signatas. Datum primo die Februarii anno regni regis Henrici Sexti vicesimo quinto). *[London].*

L TNA: PRO, E122/75/40/16. Original. Parchment. Remnants of seal on tongue. On the dorse: Allocatur in compoto Johannis Melborne et Willelmi Chattok collectorum parve custume London' de anno 24[to] regis Henrici vj[ti] *[TNA: PRO, E356/19 m 11-11d; No. A 4, § 19].*

[P 17] John, earl of Shrewsbury (comes Salop') *acknowledges receipt of £40 owing to him by virtue of the annuity of £40 yearly granted by Henry VI,*[15] *to wit for Easter and Michaelmas terms last* (pro terminis Pasche et sancti Michaelis ultimo preteritis), *from the collectors of the petty customs in London John* Melborne *and William* Chattok. — *1446 Dec. 8* (per presentes sigillis nostris signatas. Datum octavo die Decembris anno regni regis Henrici Sexti vicesimo quinto). *[London].*

L TNA: PRO, E122/75/40/17. Original. Parchment. Remnants of seal on tongue. On the dorse: (at the top) London' parva custuma; *(beneath that)* s'; *(beneath that)* Allocatur in compoto Johannis Melborne et Willelmi Chattok collectorum parve custume London' de anno 24[to] regis Henrici vj[ti] *[TNA: PRO, E356/19 m 11-11d; No. A 4, § 20].*

[P 18] William Yelverton, *justice in the Common Bench* (de banco) *and of assizes* (ad assisas in diversis comitatibus Anglie capiendas), *acknowledges receipt of £60 for the fees and rewards owing to him by virtue of his offices* (de feodis et regardis meis michi per dominum regem debitis causa officiorum meorum predictorum) *for Michaelmas term 24 Hen. VI* (pro termino Michaelis anno regni sui vicesimo quarto), *namely 20 marks for his fees at 40 marks yearly and 55 marks for his rewards at 110 marks yearly as justice in the Common Bench and £10 for his fees at £20 yearly as justice of assizes, from the collectors of the petty customs in London John* Melborne *and William* Chattok. — *1446 Nov. 26* (per presentes sigillo meo sigillatas. Datum vicesimo sexto die Novembris anno regni regis Henrici Sexti post conquestum vicesimo quinto). *[London].*

---

[14] *CPR 1441-46, p. 207 dated 26 Oct. 1443.*

[15] *CPR 1441-46, p. 235 dated 2 Mar. 1444.*

L TNA: PRO, E122/75/40/18. Original. Parchment. Seal on tongue lost. On the dorse: (at the bottom) Allocatur in compoto [a]Johannis[a] Melborne et Willelmi Chattok collectorum parve custume London' de anno 24[to] regis Henrici vj[ti]; *(along the side of the receipt, written in a hurried hand)* Allocatur in particulis compoti £244 7s 3d *[TNA: PRO, E356/19 m 11-11d; No. A 4, § 22].*

[a–a] *Interlined L.*

[P 19] William Ayscogh, *justice in the Common Bench* (de communi banco) *and of assizes* (ad assisas in diversis comitatibus Anglie capiendas), *acknowledges receipt of £123 3s 6d, namely £120 in full payment of the fees and rewards owing to him by virtue of his offices* (in plenam solucionem feodorum et regardorum meorum pro eisdem officiis) *for Easter term 24 Hen. VI and Michaelmas term 25 Hen. VI* (de termino Pasche anno regni domini regis nunc vicesimo quarto et sancti Michaelis Archangeli anno regni ejusdem domini regis vicesimo quinto) *and the remaining £3 3s 6d in full payment of his livery for Pentecost 24 Hen. VI* (pro vestura et linura meis erga festum Pentecostes anno vicesimo quarto supradicto), *from the collectors of the petty customs in London John* Melburne *and William* Chattoke. *— 1446 Nov. 18* (per presentes sigillo meo signatas. Datum decimo octavo die Novembris anno regni regis Henrici Sexti post conquestum Anglie vicesimo quinto). *[London].*

L TNA: PRO, E122/75/40/19. Original. Parchment. Remnants of seal on tongue. On the dorse: Allocatur in compoto Johannis Melborne et Willelmi Chattok collectorum parve custume London' de anno 24[to] regis Henrici vj[ti] *[TNA: PRO, E356/19 m 11-11d; No. A 4, § 23].*

[P 20] John Markham, *justice in the King's Bench* (ad placita coram ipso rege tenenda), *acknowledges receipt of £5 16s 10d in full payment of the fees at 40 marks yearly owing to him by virtue of his office for Michaelmas term last* (michi per dominum regem debita causa ejusdem officii mei pro termino sancti Michaelis ultimo preterito), *from the collectors of the petty customs in London John* Melborne *and William* Chattok. *— 1445 Oct. 6* (per presentes sigillo meo signatas. Datum sexto die Octobris anno regni regis Henrici Sexti post conquestum vicesimo quarto). *[London].*

L TNA: PRO, E122/75/40/20. Original. Parchment. Remnants of seal on tongue. On the dorse: (at the top) Parva custuma London'; *(beneath that)* Allocatur in compoto Johannis Melborne et Willelmi Chattok collectorum parve custume London' de anno 24[to] regis Henrici vj[ti] *[TNA: PRO, E356/19 m 11-11d; No. A 4, § 24].*

[P 21] John Markham, *justice in the King's Bench* (ad placita coram ipso rege tenenda), *acknowledges receipt of £50 in full payment of the fees and rewards owing to him by virtue of his office* (michi per dominum regem

debitas causa dicti officii mei) *for Easter term last* (pro termino Pasche ultimo preterito), *namely 20 marks for his fees at 40 marks yearly and 55 marks for his rewards at 110 marks yearly, from the collectors of the petty customs in London John* Melborne *and William* Chattok. — *1446 May 4* (per presentes sigillo meo signatas. Datum quarto die Maii anno regni regis Henrici Sexti post conquestum vicesimo quarto). *[London].*

L TNA: PRO, E122/75/40/21. Original. Parchment. Traces of seal on tongue. On the dorse: (at the top) s'; *(beneath that)* London' parva custuma; *(beneath that)* Pro Johanne Melborne et Willelmo Chattok collectoribus parve custume London' computantibus a 26to die Januarii anno 24to regis Henrici vj^{ti} *[26 Jan. 1446]* usque festum sancti Michaelis tunc proxime sequens *[29 Sept. 1446]* rotulo compotorum de custuma *[TNA: PRO, E356/19 m 11-11d; No. A 4, § 24]*; *(beneath that)* Allocatur in compoto Johannis Melborne et Willelmi Chattok collectorum parve custume London' videlicet a 26to die Januarii anno 24to regis Henrici vj^{ti} *[26 Jan. 1446]* usque festum sancti Michaelis tunc proxime sequens *[29 Sept. 1446]*.

ACCOUNTING DOCUMENTS

[A 1] The Exchequer directs the London sheriffs to distrain John Melbourne *and William* Chattok *(customers) as well as John* Cotteford *(controller) in order that they appear before the Exchequer on 30 Sept. 1446, the customers to account for the issues of the petty customs during their term of office and the controller to fulfill his office. On that date the sheriffs returned the writ, indicating that they had distrained the customers and the controller, who indeed appeared personally, swore to account faithfully and were assigned Richard* Bedford *as their auditor. Since the accounting procedure could not be completed in Michaelmas term, it was continued until 27 Jan. 1447 (in Hilary term) and completed then. — 1446 Juni 26.*

L TNA: PRO, E159/223 Communia Michaelis fines, manucapciones, dies datus, attornati, respectus et visus m 7d. Contemporaneous official memorandum of the Exchequer. Parchment. Unsealed.

[Marginated] London'; Midd'; De die dato

[1] Preceptum fuit vicecomitibus London' et Midd' per breve sub sigillo hujus scaccarii datum vicesimo sexto die Junii ultimo preterito *[26 June 1446]*, quod non omitterent etc. et distringerent [a]Johannem[a] Melbourne et Willelmum Chattok collectores parve custume regis ac Johannem Cotteford contrarotulatorem ejusdem custume ibidem per terras etc., ita etc. in crastino sancti Michaelis hoc termino *[30 Sept. 1446]*, dictos videlicet collectores ad reddendum regi compotum de custuma predicta [de] tempore, quo inde fuerunt collectores et non computarunt, et dictum contrarotulatorem ad faciendum, quod ad officium suum pertinet in hac parte.

[2] Ad quem diem vicecomites retornarunt breve et mandarunt, quod predicti Johannes, Willelmus et Johannes districti sunt, unde exitus etc., sicut continetur in indorsamento ejusdem brevis, quod est in ligula brevium de hoc anno in London' Midd'.[1] Et [a]tam[a] predicti collectores quam prefatus contrarotulator venerunt in propriis personis suis et prestiterunt sacramentum de fideliter computando et testificando in premissis. Et super hoc Ricardus Bedford unus auditorum compotorum hujus scaccarii assignatur ad compotum illum audiendum. Et quia iidem collectores non possunt percomputare in pre-

---

[1] *This refers to the repository E202 (which will at some point in the future be reclassified as E227), but no bundle survives from the year 25 Hen. VI, when this writ was issued.*

missis durante termino, datus est dies hic tam predictis collectoribus quam predicto contrarotulatori eodem statu quo nunc usque quindenam sancti Hillarii *[27 Jan. 1447]* ad percomputandum et testificandum in premissis.

[3] Ad quem diem iidem collectores venerunt in propriis personis suis et computarunt de custuma predicta, sicut continetur alibi in hiis memorandis, videlicet inter recorda de termino sancti Hillarii rotulo primo *[TNA: PRO, E159/223 Recorda Hilary m 1; No. A 3]*. Ideo versus ipsos collectores non fiat hic ulterius execucio. *[The 'finished' sign follows]*.

a–a *Interlined L.*

[A 2] In Michaelmas term 1446, William Chattok *nominates his fellow customer John* Melbourne *as his attorney to account before the Exchequer in both their names for the issues of the petty customs during their term of office [26 Jan. to 29 Sept. 1446]*

L TNA: PRO, E159/223 Communia Michaelis: Adhuc fines, manucapciones, dies datus, attornati, respectus et visus m 3. Contemporaneous official memorandum of the Exchequer. Parchment. Unsealed.

[Marginated] London'

Willelmus Chattok unus collectorum parve custume regis in portu London' ponit loco suo Johannem Melbourne alterum collectorem ejusdem custume ibidem ad reddendum pro eo domino regi una cum eodem Johanne compotum de eadem custuma et ad omnia alia dictum compotum tangencia facienda, prout idem Willelmus faceret, si personaliter interesset.

Per W. Fallan

[A 3] John Melbourne *and William* Chattok *account before the Exchequer in Hilary term 1447 for the issues of the petty customs from 24 Jan. to 29 Sept. 1446. Since they and the controller John* Cotford *continue in office, the sheriffs are (later) ordered to distrain them to appear on 17 Apr. 1447 to account for the succeeding period.*

L TNA: PRO, E159/223 Recorda Hilary m 1. Contemporaneous official fair copy of the Exchequer proceedings. Parchment. Unsealed.

[Marginated] London'

Memorandum, quod Johannes Melbourne et Willelmus Chattok collectores parve custume regis in portu civitatis London' venerunt et computarunt de eadem custuma ibidem videlicet a vicesimo sexto die Januarii anno 24[to] regis hujus *[26 Jan. 1446]* usque festum sancti Michaelis tunc proximum sequens *[29 Sept. 1446]*, a quo quidem festo iidem collectores per visum et testimonium Johannis Cotford contrarotulatoris ejusdem custume ibidem sunt alias inde computaturi. [a]Ideo preceptum sit[b] vicecomitibus, quod ipsos collectores et contrarotulatorem distringant per terras etc., ita etc. in crastino Clausi Pasche *[17 Apr. 1447]*, dictos videlicet collectores ad computandum et dictum contrarotulatorem ad testificandum in premissis *[see No. S 15]*.

a *The following lines were entered by a different hand L.* b r' *written over* s' *marginated against this line L.*

[A 4] *John* Melborne *and William* Chattok *account in Hilary term 1447 for the issues of the petty customs in London in the period from 26 Jan. to 29 Sept. 1446.*

L TNA: PRO, E356/19 m 11-11d. Original Enrolled Account. Parchment. Unsealed. Marginated against the first paragraph: • s' •; termino Hillarii anno 25[to] regis Henrici vj[ti]; • s' •. *In the 5 cm left free by the indentation of the first line: Auditores:* J. Holme baro; Ricardus Bedford clericus.

[Marginated] London'

[1] Compotus Johannis Melbourne et Willelmi Chattok collectorum parve custume regis in portu civitatis London' et in singulis portubus et locis eidem portui adjacentibus per breve[2] regis nunc Henrici Sexti de magno sigillo suo patens datum 26[to] die Januarii anno regni sui 24[to] *[26 Jan. 1446]* prefatis Johanni Melborne et Willelmo Chattok inde confectum, super hunc compotum ostensum et penes ipsos collectores remanens, per quod breve rex assignavit dictos Johannem Melbourne et Willelmum[a] Chattok ad hujusmodi custumam regis in portubus et locis predictis, quamdiu regi placuerit, levandam et colligendam et ad opus regis recipiendam ac ad sigillum regis, quod dicitur coket, ibidem custodiendum, ita quod [de] denariis inde provenientibus regi ad scaccarium suum respondeant, prout in eodem brevi regis plenius continetur, videlicet de hujusmodi custuma regis ibidem a dicto 26[to] die Januarii dicto anno 24[to] regis nunc *[26 Jan. 1446]*, ante quem diem prefatus Johannes Melbourne et Willelmus de Lwnes nuper collectores hujusmodi custume regis ibidem alias inde computarunt rotulo compotorum de hujusmodi custuma *[TNA: PRO, E356/19 m 11]*[3], usque festum sancti Michaelis tunc proximum sequens anno ejusdem regis 25[to] *[29 Sept. 1446]*, scilicet per dimidium annum et 64 dies, per visum et testimonium Johannis Cotford contrarotulatoris ejusdem custume regis ibidem per idem tempus.

[Marginated] Recepta denariorum

[2] Iidem reddunt compotum de £230 3s 3½d[b] de custuma diversarum rerum et mercandisarum diversorum mercatorum alienigenarum tam ad portus et loca predicta adductarum [c]quam ab eisdem eductarum[c] et ibidem custumatarum per predictum tempus hujus compoti, que quidem res et mercandise ad £18,409[d] 6s estimabantur juxta verum valorem earundem, videlicet de qualibet libra 3d per breve regis predictum supra in titulo hujus compoti annotatum, sicut continetur tam in duobus libris ipsorum collectorum sigillo regis hujus scaccarii sigillatis quam in 23 rotulis et una cedula predicti contrarotulatoris de particulis inde hic in thesauro liberatis.

[3] Et de £509 5s 11¼d de custuma contingente tam 7½ pannos, [c]1[c]¼ ulnas panni de assisa de scarleta, 8 pannos, 2¼ ulnas panni de assisa de dimidio

---

[2] *CFR 1445-52, p. 13.*

[3] *Stuart Jenks (ed.), The Enrolled Customs Accounts (PRO, E356, E372, E364) 1279/80-1508/09 (1523/24) Volume 8: E356/19, E356/20 (List and Index Society) [in press], E356/19 No. 44.*

grano, 5500 pannos, 13¾ ulnas panni de assisa sine grano, 436½ pecias de worsted duplici, 21 pecias et 7½ lectos de wursted simplici diversorum mercatorum indigenarum quam [e]4 pannos, 5¼ dimidium[e] ulnas panni de assisa de scarleta, 11 pannos, 4 ulnas panni de assisa de dimidio grano, 1300½ pannos et ¼ unius ulne panni de assisa sine grano, 24 pecias de wursted duplici, 30 pecias et 3 lectos de wursted simplici diversorum mercatorum alienigenarum in portubus et locis predictis custumata et abinde traducta per tempus predictum, videlicet de quolibet hujusmodi panno de scarleta de indigena 2s 4d et de alienigena 5s 6d, de dimidio grano de indigena 21d et de alienigena 4s 1½d, de assisa sine grano de indigena 14d et de alienigena 2s 9d ac de qualibet hujusmodi pecia de wursted duplici de indigena 2d et de alienigena 3d, worsted simplici de indigena 1d et de alienigena 1½d, et de quolibet hujusmodi lecto de wursted simplici de indigena 5d et de alienigena 7½d per breve regis predictum, sicut continetur ibidem.

[4] Et de £354 11s 10¾d de custuma contingente duos pannos, 9 ulnas panni de assisa de scarleta, 1 pannum, 8½ ulnas panni[f] de assisa de dimidio grano et 7085 pannos, 1½ ulnas panni de assisa sine grano diversorum mercatorum alienigenarum de Almannia vocatorum Hans' in portubus et locis predictis similiter custumata et abinde traducta per tempus predictum, videlicet de quolibet hujusmodi panno de scarleta 2s, de dimidio grano 18d et sine grano 12d per breve regis predictum ac per aliud breve dicti regis nunc de magno sigillo suo datum 8° die Novembris anno regni suo secundo *[8 Nov. 1423]* thesaurario et baronibus hujus scaccarii inde directum et irrotulatum in memorandis hujus scaccarii inter brevia directa baronibus de termino sancti Michaelis eodem anno rotulo 19[no] ex parte rememoratoris regis *[TNA: PRO, E159/200 Brevia directa baronibus Michaelmas m 19: No. S 1]*, sicut continetur ibidem.

[5] Et de £13 9s 7¾d de custuma contingente 269 quintallos, 68 lb. cere diversorum mercatorum alienigenarum ad portus et loca predicta adducta et ibidem[g] custumata per tempus predictum, videlicet de quolibet hujusmodi quintallo cere 12d per predictum breve regis patens supra in titulo hujus compoti annotatum, sicut continetur ibidem.

[6] De aliqua custuma peciarum de worsted de dimidio duplici sive lectorum de worsted duplici vel dimidio duplici aliquorum mercatorum indigenarum vel alienigenarum per predictum tempus hujus compoti non respondent, eo quod nulla hujusmodi pecie sive lecti ibidem custumata nec abinde traducta fuerit per idem tempus, ut dicti collectores dicunt super sacramentum suum, sicut continetur ibidem.

[7] Nec respondent de aliquibus proficuis sive commoditatibus per ipsos collectores seu aliquem alium eorum nomine receptis pro solucione alicujus assignamenti per talliam vel aliter pro [h]solucione[h] alicujus tallie aut alio modo quocumque receptis juxta formam statuti in parliamento regis Henrici iiij[ti]

apud Westmonasterium anno regni sui 4[to] tento inde editi,[4] videlicet per tempus predictum, eo quod nulla hujusmodi proficua sive commoditates pro hujusmodi solucione sive empcione perceperunt nec habuerunt per idem tempus, ut dicunt super sacramentum suum.
[Marginated] Examinatur

Summa recepte: £1107 10s 9¼d[i]

[8] In thesauro £33 6s 8d 15° die Novembris anno 25[to] *[15 Nov. 1446]*.

[9] Et eisdem collectoribus pro misis et expensis suis per tempus predictum £10 7s 6d de rata 23 marcarum per annum, sicut allocatum est in compotis precedentibus. Et eisdem collectoribus pro quadam domo conducta pro custuma colligenda per idem tempus 22s 10d de rata 33s 4d per annum, sicut allocatum est ibidem. Et eisdem collectoribus pro misis et expensis suis factis circa colleccionem custume pannorum predictorum per tempus predictum 67s 8½d de rata 100s per annum, sicut allocatum est in compotis precedentibus a festo sancti Michaelis anno 22[do] regis Edwardi Tercii *[29 Sept. 1348]* hucusque rotulis compotorum de custuma.

[10] Et Edmundo Beauford marchioni Dorsete fratri et heredi masculo Johannis nuper ducis Somersete filii et heredis masculi Johannis nuper comitis Somersete, cui quidem Johanni nuper comiti Somersete dominus Henricus nuper rex Anglie Quartus 12° die Novembris anno regni sui 6[to] *[12 Nov. 1404]* per litteras suas patentes[5] concessit eidem Johanni nuper comiti Somersete mille libras habendas et percipiendas annuatim eidem nuper comiti et heredibus suis masculis de corpore suo legittime procreatis pro statu comitis manutenendo et sustentando ad scaccarium ipsius nuper regis a festo sancti Michaelis [c]tunc[c] ultimo preterito *[29 Sept. 1404]* ad festa Pasche et sancti Michaelis per equales porciones, quousque idem nuper rex vel heredes sui eidem comiti vel heredibus suis masculis supradictis de terris et tenementis, que non sunt parcelle corone prefati regis, ad valorem mille librarum per annum fecisset provideri; et idem nuper rex 25[to] die Octobris anno regni [sui] 11[mo] *[25 Oct. 1409]* per alias litteras suas patentes[6] concessit prefato nuper comiti quingentas libras per annum habendas et percipiendas sibi et heredibus suis masculis de corpore suo legittime procreatis de parva custuma sua London' per manus collectorum, firmariorum aut aliorum occupatorum ejusdem pro tempore existencium ad terminos Pasche et sancti Michaelis per equales porciones in partem satisfaccionis et deduccionis mille librarum supradictarum; et prefatus nuper comes fuit seisitus in dominico suo ut de feodo talliato, videlicet sibi et heredibus suis masculis de corpore suo procreatis, de dictis quingentis libris annuis percipiendis et habendis de dicta parva custuma in

---

[4] *Statute 4 Hen. IV, c. 20 (Statutes of the Realm, vol. 2, p. 139; cf. Rotuli Parliamentorum, vol. 3, p. 506).*

[5] *CPR 1401-5, p. 477.*

[6] *CPR 1408-13, p. 142.*

portu civitatis London' ad dictos terminos Pasche et sancti Michaelis et habuit exitum prefatum Johannem nuper ducem et Edmundum Beauford marchionem Dorsete et de tali statu inde obiit seisitus, post cujus mortem dicte quingente libre prefato Johanni nuper duci ut filio et heredi prefati nuper comitis descendebant, quodque prefatus Edmundus est frater et heres masculus predicti Johannis nuper ducis propinquior et plene etatis ac rex nunc 24to die Octobris anno 23^{cio} *[24 Oct. 1444]* eidem marchioni predictas quingentas libras reddidit,[7] que per mortem predicti nuper ducis capte fuerunt in manum regis, una cum exitibus et arreragiis earundem a tempore mortis ejusdem nuper ducis et per breve suum[8] precepit Henrico Frowyk majori civitatis London' et escaetori suo in eadem civitate, quod eidem marchioni de predictis quingentis libris, que per mortem predicti nuper ducis capte fuerunt in manum regis, una cum exitibus et arreragiis earundem a tempore mortis ejusdem nuper ducis perceptis plenam seisinam habere faceret — salvo jure cujuslibet et salva Margarete, que fuit uxor predicti nuper ducis, racionabili dote sua ipsam de eisdem quingentis libris secundum legem et consuetudinem regni Anglie contingente per regem assignanda[9] — ac rex per breve suum precepit collectoribus, firmariis et aliis occupatoribus custume predicte in portu predicto, quod eidem marchioni id, quod ei aretro fuit de duabus partibus predictarum quingentarum librarum annuarum a tempore mortis predicti nuper ducis de custuma predicta, solverent, £333 6s 8d de duabus partibus predictarum £500 per annum de termino Pasche anno 24to et termino Michaelis anno 25to per breve regis, quod est inter communia de anno 24to regis hujus termino sancti Michaelis rotulo 9no *[TNA: PRO, E159/222 Brevia directa baronibus Michaelmas m 9-9d: No. S 2]*, et duas litteras acquietancie ipsius Edmundi de recepta *[No. P 1; a further receipt for 250 marks has come astray from TNA: PRO, E122/75/40]*.

[11] Et Margarete, que fuit uxor Johannis nuper ducis Somersete, cui quidem Margarete Henricus Frowyk major civitatis regis London' et escaetor in eadem civitate virtute brevis[10] domini regis eidem majori et escaetori directi assignavit prefate ducisse centum, sexaginta et sex libras, tresdecim solidos et quatuor denarios habenda in dotem suam ipsam de quadam annuitate quingentarum librarum de parva custuma regis London' per manus collectorum, firmariorum sive aliorum occupatorum ejusdem pro tempore existencium percipienda ad terminos Pasche et sancti Michaelis per equales porciones, quam idem nuper dux tenuit in balliva sua die, quo obiit, in dominico suo ut de feodo talliato sibi et heredibus suis masculis de corpore suo exeuntibus secundum legem et consuetudinem predictas contingentem, et rex per breve suum precepit collectoribus, firmariis sive aliis occupatoribus parve custume regis London', qui nunc sunt vel qui pro tempore fuerint, quod eidem ducisse id, quod ei

---

[7] *CPR 1441-46, p. 311.*
[8] *CCR 1441-47, p. 243-4.*
[9] *Cf. CPR 1441-46, p. 318.*
[10] *CCR 1441-47, p. 252.*

aretro est de predictis centum, sexaginta et sex libris, tresdecim solidis et quatuor denariis a tempore mortis predicti nuper ducis, et easdem centum, sexaginta et sex libras, tresdecim solidos et quatuor denarios exnunc singulis annis durante vita sua de parva custuma predicta ad terminos predictos de tempore in tempus solverent juxta assignacionem predictam, £166 13s 4d de tercia parte dictarum £500 per annum de termino Pasche anno 24to et termino Michaelis anno 25to per breve regis, quod est inter communia de anno 23mo regis hujus termino Pasche rotulo quarto *[TNA: PRO, E159/221 Brevia directa baronibus Easter m 4: No. S 3]*, et duas litteras acquietancie ipsius Margarete de recepta *[No. P 2 and P 3]*.

[12] Et Cristine Houchon, cui dominus Henricus nuper rex Anglie Quartus per litteras suas patentes, quas rex nunc 15° die Decembris anno primo *[15 Dec. 1422]* confirmavit,[11] concessit quatuor denarios per diem percipiendos singulis annis pro termino vite sue de parva custuma predicta in portu predicto per manus collectorum ejusdem custume pro tempore existencium, videlicet de hujusmodi quatuor denariis per diem a festo sancti Michaelis anno 24to regis hujus *[29 Sept. 1445]* usque festum sancti Michaelis tunc proximum sequens *[29 Sept. 1446]*, scilicet per 365 dies, £6 20d per duo brevia regis irrotulata in memorandis — unum videlicet termino Trinitatis anno 24to rotulo 11mo *[TNA: PRO, E159/222 Brevia directa baronibus Trinity m 11: No. P 4]* et aliud termino Hillarii anno 25to rotulo 10mo *[TNA: PRO, E159/223 Brevia directa baronibus Hilary m 10: No. P 5]* — et duas litteras acquietancie ipsius Cristine de recepta *[No. P 8 and P 9]*.

[13] Et Johanni Popham militi, cui rex 27mo die Julii anno 18vo *[27 July 1440]* de gracia sua speciali concessit[12] quadraginta libras percipiendas annuatim pro termino vite sue de exitibus, revencionibus et proficuis parve custume regis in portu civitatis regis London' provenientibus per manus custumariorum, collectorum seu receptorum ejusdem parve custume pro tempore existencium ad terminos sancti Michaelis et Pasche per equales porciones, £10 in partem solucionis £20 de termino Pasche anno 24to per breve regis, quod est inter communia de anno 19no regis hujus termino sancti Michaelis rotulo 18vo *[TNA: PRO, E159/217 Brevia directa baronibus Michaelmas m 18: No. S 4]*, et litteras acquietancie ipsius Johannis de recepta *[No. P 10]*.

[14] Et Johanni Yerde armigero, cui dominus Henricus Quartus per litteras suas patentes, quas rex nunc confirmavit,[13] concessit viginti libras percipiendas annuatim pro termino vite sue de parva custuma in portu predicto per manus custumariorum ejusdem custume pro tempore existencium ad terminos Pasche

---

[11] *Henry IV's patent was issued on 16 May 1401 (CPR 1399-1401, p. 488), Henry V's confirmation on 1 Apr. 1414 (CPR 1413-16, p. 196) and Henry VI's on 15 Dec. 1422 (CPR 1422-29, p. 16).*

[12] *CPR 1441-46, p. 432.*

[13] *Henry IV's patent was issued on 13 Jan. 1413 (CPR 1408-13, p. 460), Henry V's confirmation on 1 Oct. 1414 (CPR 1413-16, p. 272) and Henry VI's on 20 Dec. 1422 (CPR 1422-29, p. 39).*

et sancti Michaelis per equales porciones, £20 de termino Pasche anno 24to et termino Michaelis anno 25to per breve regis, quod est inter communia de anno 17° regis hujus termino sancte Trinitatis rotulo 15° *[TNA: PRO, E159/215 Brevia directa baronibus Trinity m 15: No. S 5]*, et duas litteras acquietancie ipsius Johannis de recepta *[No. P 11]*.[14]

[15] Et Humfrido duci Gloucestrie avunculo regis, cui rex 30mo die Junii anno 19no *[30 June 1441]* de gracia sua speciali concessit[15] sexdecim libras percipiendas annuatim a festo sancti Michaelis tunc ultimo preterito *[29 Sept. 1440]* pro termino vite sue de parva custuma regis in portu civitatis London' per manus collectorum ejusdem custume pro tempore existencium ad terminos Pasche et sancti Michaelis per equales porciones in recompensacionem sexdecim librarum annuarum sibi 14° die Julii anno 17mo regis hujus *[14 July 1439]* concessarum[16] de exitibus, proficuis, revencionibus et redditibus manerii de Tarent Lonston' in comitatu Dorsete *[Tarrant Launceston, Dorset]*, quod est parcella pensionum de Cadamo *[Caen]* alienigenis pertinente, £8 de termino Pasche anno 24to per breve regis, quod est inter communia de anno 19no regis hujus termino sancte Trinitatis rotulo 14mo *[TNA: PRO, E159/217 Brevia directa baronibus Trinity m 14: No. S 6]*, et litteras acquietancie ipsius ducis de recepta *[No. P 12]*.

[16] Et magistro Johanni Faceby phisico regis, cui rex 12mo die Julii anno 22do *[12 July 1444]* concessit[17] centum libras percipiendas annuatim a festo sancti Michaelis tunc ultimo preterito *[29 Sept. 1443]* pro termino vite sue de parva custuma regis in portu civitatis regis London' per manus collectorum ejusdem custume pro tempore existencium ad festa Pasche et sancti Michaelis per equales porciones, £100 de termino Pasche anno 24to et termino Michaelis anno 25to per breve regis, quod est inter communia de anno 23^cio regis hujus termino sancti Michaelis rotulo 15° *[TNA: PRO, E159/221 Brevia directa baronibus Michaelmas m 15d: No. S 7]*, et litteras acquietancie ipsius Johannis de recepta *[No. P 13]*.

[17] Et Thome Ponsford, cui ac Johanni Paunton jam defuncto rex 19no die Februarii anno 21mo *[19 Feb. 1443]* concessit[18] sex denarios per diem percipiendos pro termino vite sue et alterius eorum diucius viventis de parva custuma civitatis regis London' per manus collectorum, receptorum sive custumariorum ejusdem custume, videlicet de hujusmodi 6d per diem a festo sancti Michaelis anno 24to *[29 Sept. 1445]* usque ultimum diem Marcii tunc proximum sequentem *[31 Mar. 1446]*, £4 11s per breve regis, quod est inter communia de anno 22do regis hujus termino sancti Michaelis rotulo tercio *[TNA:*

---

[14] *The account's reference to two receipts is erroneous, since* Yerde *acknowledged receipt of the entire sum which the Exchequer allowed the customers here (£20) in one receipt dated 3 June 1446 (No. P 11).*

[15] *CPR 1436-41, p. 552.*

[16] *CPR 1436-41, p. 303-4.*

[17] *CPR 1441-46, p. 271 dated 11 July 1444.*

[18] *CPR 1441-46, p. 164.*

PRO, E159/220 Brevia directa baronibus Michaelmas m 3d: No. S 8] et prout allocatum est eisdem collectoribus in alio debito suo in rotulo 21mo regis hujus in Adhuc Item London' *[see No. S 16]*, et litteras acquietancie ipsius Thome de recepta *[No. P 14]*.

[18] Et Johanni Seyntlo armigero, cui rex 17mo die Februarii anno 18vo *[17 Feb. 1440]* concessit[19] viginti libras percipiendas annuatim a festo sancti Michaelis tunc ultimo preterito *[29 Sept. 1439]* durante vita sua de exitibus et proficuis de parva custuma regis in portu civitatis regis London' per manus custumariorum custume predicte pro tempore existencium ad terminos Pasche et sancti Michaelis per equales porciones, £10 de termino Pasche anno 24to per breve regis, quod est inter communia de anno 19no regis hujus termino sancti Hillarii rotulo 15° *[TNA: PRO, E159/217 Brevia directa baronibus Hilary m 15: No. S 9]*, et litteras acquietancie ipsius Johannis de recepta *[No. P 15]*.

[19] Et Johanni Sutton domino[j] Duddeley militi, cui rex 26to die Octobris anno 22do *[26 Oct. 1443]* de gracia sui speciali concessit[20] eidem Johanni centum libras habendas et percipiendas annuatim pro termino vite sue de exitibus, proficuis et revencionibus de parva custuma in portu regis London' provenientibus per manus custumariorum, collectorum sive receptorum ejusdem custume pro tempore existencium ad terminos Pasche et sancti Michaelis per equales porciones, £10 in partem solucionis £50 de termino Pasche anno 24to per breve regis, quod est inter communia de anno 22do regis hujus termino Pasche rotulo 7mo *[TNA: PRO, E159/220 Brevia directa baronibus Easter m 7d: No. S 10]*, et litteras acquietancie ipsius Johannis de recepta *[No. P 16]*.

[20] Et Johanni comiti Salopie, cui rex secundo die Marcii anno 22do *[2 Mar. 1444]* concessit[21] quadraginta libras habendas et percipiendas eidem comiti ad terminum vite sue annuatim ad terminos Pasche et sancti Michaelis per equales porciones de parva custuma regis et heredum suorum in portu civitatis regis London' per manus collectorum ejusdem custume pro tempore existencium, £40 de termino Pasche anno 24to et termino Michaelis anno 25to per breve regis, quod est inter communia de anno 24to regis hujus termino sancte Trinitatis rotulo 10mo *[TNA: PRO, E159/222 Brevia directa baronibus Trinity m 10: No. S 11]*, et litteras acquietancie ipsius comitis de recepta *[No. P 17]*.

[21] Et in thesauro £112 20d 11mo die Februarii anno 24to *[11 Feb. 1446]* per dictos collectores de custuma proveniente de bonis et mercandisis Julii Contaryn et sociorum suorum de Venicia, de quibus onerantur in libro de particulis compoti predicti de majori summa.

[Marginated] Pro Willelmo Yelverton

[22] Et eisdem collectoribus pro denariis per ipsos solutis Willelmo Yelverton uni justiciariorum [c]regis[c] de banco ac uni justiciariorum regis ad assisas in

---

[19] *CPR 1436-41, p. 387.*

[20] *CPR 1441-46, p. 207.*

[21] *CPR 1441-46, p. 235.*

diversis comitatibus Anglie capiendas assignatorum de feodis et regardis suis sibi per dominum regem causa eorundem officiorum suorum debitis et aretro existentibus non solutis tam hujusmodi feodi sui ad 40 marcas per annum et regardi sui ad 110 marcas per annum pro dicto officio unius justiciariorum regis de banco suo quam hujusmodi feodi sui ad £20 per annum pro dicto officio unius justiciariorum regis ad assisas percipiendas singulis annis per manus collectorum ejusdem parve custume regis in portu predicto pro tempore existencium ad terminos Pasche et sancti Michaelis per equales porciones, scilicet in plenam solucionem £60 pro termino sancti Michaelis anno 24to regis hujus, £60 per breve regis, quod est inter communia de anno 24to regis hujus termino sancti Hillarii rotulo 24to *[TNA: PRO, E159/222 Brevia directa baronibus Hilary m 24d: No. S 12]*, et prout hujusmodi vadia allocantur prefatis collectoribus in alio compoto suo *[TNA: PRO, E356/19 m 11]*[22], videlicet a festo sancti Michaelis anno 24to regis hujus *[29 Sept. 1445]* usque 26^tum^ diem Januarii tunc proximum sequentem *[26 Jan. 1446]*, et per litteras acquietancie ipsius Willelmi de recepta *[No. P 18]*.

[Marginated] Pro Willelmo Ayscogh

[23] Et eisdem collectoribus pro denariis per ipsos solutis Willelmo Ayscogh uni justiciariorum regis de banco ac uni justiciariorum domini regis ad assisas capiendas habendo, quamdiu regi placuerit, percipiendo in dicto officio unius justiciariorum de banco feodum consuetum; et insuper idem dominus nunc rex concessit[23] eidem Willelmo ad statum suum decencius manutenere et expensas, quas ipsum in officio suo predicto facere oportebit, sustinere valeat centum et decem marcas per annum ac eciam £20 pro dicto officio unius justiciariorum regis ad assisas capiendas percipiendas singulis annis ad terminos Pasche et sancti Michaelis per equales porciones per manus custodis hanaperii vel per manus collectorum parve custume regis in portu civitatis London', £120 de termino Pasche anno 24to et termino sancti Michaelis anno 25to et prout hujusmodi feoda et regarda allocantur prefatis collectoribus ibidem, per breve regis, quod est inter communia de anno 22do regis hujus termino sancte Trinitatis rotulo 14° *[TNA: PRO, E159/220 Brevia directa baronibus Trinity m 14d: No. S 13]*, et per litteras acquietancie ipsius Willelmi de recepta *[No. P 19]*.

[Marginated] Pro Johanne Markham

[24] Et eisdem collectoribus pro denariis per ipsos solutis Johanni Markham uni justiciariorum regis ad assisas in diversis comitatibus Anglie capiendas assignatorum ac uni justiciariorum regis de banco suo de feodis et regardis suis eidem Johanni per dominum regem causa eorundem officiorum suorum debitis et aretro existentibus non solutis, videlicet 116s 10d in plenam solucionem £50 de hujusmodi feodo suo ad 40 marcas per annum et regardo suo ad 110 marcas per annum pro dicto officio suo unius justiciariorum regis de banco percipien-

---

[22] *Stuart Jenks (ed.), The Enrolled Customs Accounts (PRO, E356, E372, E364) 1279/80-1508/09 (1523/24) Volume 8: E356/19, E356/20 (List and Index Society) [in press], E356/19 No. 44.*

[23] *CPR 1436-41, p. 443.*

das singulis annis per manus dictorum collectorum in forma predicta pro termino sancti Michaelis anno 24[to] regis nunc et £50 de hujusmodi feodo suo ad 40 marcas per annum et regardo suo ad 110 marcas per annum pro dicto officio suo unius justiciariorum regis de banco suo percipiendas singulis [annis] per manus dictorum collectorum in forma predicta pro termino[k] Pasche anno 24[to] regis nunc, £55 16s 10d per breve regis, quod est inter communia de anno 24[to] regis hujus termino Pasche rotulo 11[mo] *[TNA: PRO, E159/222 Brevia directa baronibus Easter m 10:*[24] *No. S 14]* et prout hujusmodi [c]feoda[c] et regarda allocantur prefatis collectoribus in alio compoto suo ex alia parte rotuli *[TNA: PRO, E356/19 m 11]*,[25] et per duas litteras acquietancie ipsius Johannis de recepta *[No. P 20 and P 21]*.

[Marginated] Pro Willelmo Ay[s]cogh

[25] Et eisdem collectoribus pro denariis per ipsos solutis Willelmo Ayscogh uni justiciariorum regis de banco suo pro valore unius robe cum linura pro eadem erga festum Pentecostes anno 24[to] regis hujus *[5 June 1446]* eidem Willelmo causa ejusdem officii [c]sui[c] ad idem festum debite: 63s 6d per breve regis, quod est inter communia de anno 22[do] regis hujus termino Trinitatis rotulo 14°[l] *[TNA: PRO, E159/220 Brevia directa baronibus Trinity m 14d: No. S 13]* et prout hujusmodi feoda et regarda allocantur prefatis collectoribus in alio compoto suo ibidem,[24] et per litteras acquietancie ipsius Willelmi de recepta *[No. P 19]*.

[Marginated] Examinatur

[26] Et habent superplusagium 8s 7¼d, qui allocantur eisdem collectoribus in alio compoto suo inmediate infra *[TNA: PRO, E356/19 m 11d]*.[26]

[a] Willelmo *L, in error.* [b] *Corrected in L from* ½d. [c–c] *Interlined L.* [d] *Corrected in L from £18,408.* [e–e] *Sic L. The account records exports of 4 scarlets and 5½ yards.* [f] panni *follows, underlined for the purpose of cancellation L.* [g] et ibidem *follows, underlined for the purpose of cancellation L.* [h–h] *Interlined above* empcione, *underlined for the purpose of cancellation L.* [i] *Corrected in L from 6¼d.* [j] de *follows, underlined for the purpose of cancellation L.* [k] sancti Michaelis anno 24[to] et £50 pro termino pro *follows, interlined and underlined for the purpose of cancellation L.* [l] 13° *L, in error.*

[24] *There, however, the membrane number 11 is corrected to 10 by erasure.*

[25] *This is the account of the customers for the immediately preceding accounting period from 29 Sept. 1445 to 26 Jan. 1446: Stuart Jenks (ed.), The Enrolled Customs Accounts (PRO, E356, E372, E364) 1279/80-1508/09 (1523/24) Volume 8: E356/19, E356/20 (List and Index Society) [in press], E356/19, No. 44.*

[26] *This is the account of the customers for the immediately succeeding accounting period from 29 Sept. 1446 to 8 Jan. 1447: Stuart Jenks (ed.), The Enrolled Customs Accounts (PRO, E356, E372, E364) 1279/80-1508/09 (1523/24) Volume 8: E356/19, E356/20 (List and Index Society) [in press], E356/19, No. 46.*

[A 5] Audit of the account of John Melbourne *and William* Chattok *for the issues of the petty customs in London during the period from 26 Jan. to 29 Sept. 1446*

L TNA: PRO, E368/219 Visus et status compotorum Hilary m 3 (m 285 stamped). Contemporaneous official fair copy of the Exchequer proceedings. Parchment. Unsealed.

[Marginated] London'

[1] Audito compoto Johannis Melbourne et Willelmi Chattok collectorum parve custume regis in portu civitatis London' et in singulis portubus et locis eidem portui adjacentibus, videlicet de hujusmodi custuma regis ibidem a 26to die Januarii anno 24to regis nunc *[26 Jan. 1446]* usque festum sancti Michaelis tunc proximum sequens *[29 Sept. 1446]*, per visum et testimonium Johannis Cotford contrarotulatoris ejusdem custume regis ibidem per idem tempus.

[2] Debent £1107 10s 9¼d.

[3] [a]Et factis allocacionibus et exoneracionibus in dicto compoto ingrossato habent superplusagium ibidem. *[The 'finished' sign follows].*

[a] *The following paragraph was entered by a different hand L.*

SUBSIDIARY DOCUMENTS

[S 1] *Henry VI to the treasurer and barons of the Exchequer: the Hanseatic merchants having claimed certain liberties and immunities by virtue of their charter of privileges which were confirmed by Henry V,*[1] *the king orders the Exchequer – provided the Hansards produce the charter – to allow them the use of the liberties granted therein. — 1423 Nov. 8. Westminster.*

L TNA: PRO, E159/200 Brevia directa baronibus Michaelmas m 19. Contemporaneous official copy. Parchment. Unsealed.

[Marginated] Pro mercatoribus de Almania

Rex thesaurario et baronibus suis de scaccario salutem. Quia mercatores regni Alemannie per cartas progenitorum nostrorum quondam regum Anglie et confirmacionem domini Henrici [V] nuper regis Anglie patris nostri clamant habere diversas libertates, quietancias et immunitates, quibus ipsi et antecessores sui mercatores Alemannie a tempore confeccionis cartarum et confirmacionis predictarum semper hactenus usi sunt et gavisi, sicut dicunt, vobis mandamus, quod visa dicta carta confirmacionis ipsos mercatores omnibus et singulis libertatibus, quietanciis et immunitatibus in dicta carta confirmacionis contentis coram vobis, quantum ad vos pertinet, uti et gaudere permittatis juxta tenorem cartarum et confirmacionis predictarum, prout eis uti debent ipsique et antecessores sui predicti libertatibus, quietanciis et immunitatibus illis a tempore predicto semper hactenus racionabiliter uti et gaudere consueverunt. Teste me ipso apud Westmonasterium, 8 die Novembris anno regni nostri secundo.

[S 2] *Henry VI to the treasurer and barons of the Exchequer: since the king has learned from the petition of Edmund, marquis of Dorset, that various possessions late of † John, duke of Somerset, have descended to*

---

[1] *The confirmation is printed in full in Thomas Rymer (ed.), Foedera, conventiones, litterae et cujuscunque generis acta publica inter reges Angliae et alios quosvis imperatores, reges, pontifices, principes vel communitates (1101-1654), London 1704-35, vol. 9, p. 72-7 (= Thomas Rymer (ed.), Foedera, conventiones, litterae et cujuscunque generis acta publica inter reges Angliae et alios quosvis imperatores, reges, pontifices, principes vel communitates (1101-1654), The Hague 1739-45, vol. 4/2, p. 54-6). Extracts of the confirmation are printed in Urkundenbuch der Stadt Lübeck (Codex diplomaticus Lubecensis 1. Abteilung), vol. 5, Lübeck 1877, No. 480, p. 520-1 and Karl Kunze (ed.), Hansisches Urkundenbuch. Fünfter Band: 1392 bis 1414, Leipzig 1899, No. 1114, p. 578-9.*

him, but that the title deeds are and will be for some time out of his possession, so that he cannot present them before inquistions post mortem held by the escheaters by virtue of writs diem clausit extremum in order to prove his title, so that he fears that he will be unable for some time to obtain release of his inheritance from the king's hand; whereupon the king by patent[2] *dated 24 Oct. 1444 granted Edmund that he may have immediate livery of the said possessions and all arrears bit by bit, as the inquisitions are held before the escheators in the various counties and are returned into chancery, with pardon of all reliefs and respite of homage for half a year to come; further since an inquisition*[3] *held before the London mayor Thomas* Catworth *found [1] that Henry IV by patent*[4] *issued on 12 Nov. 1404 had granted John, earl of Somerset, [† 16 Mar. 1410] – in order to maintain his status – an annuity of £1000 per annum in tail male which was to be paid at the Exchequer from 29 Sept. 1404 at Easter and Michaelmas in equal portions until such time as the king granted him other lands and tenements worth £1000 annually, by virtue of which patent John was seized of the said annuity in tail male; [2] that Henry IV by patent*[5] *issued on 25 Oct. 1409 granted John £500 annually (to be deducted from the annuity of £1000), payable from the issues of the petty customs in London – or, should all or part of this sum not be payable from the petty customs, at the Exchequer – at Easter and Michaelmas in equal portions, by virtue of which patent John was seized of the said £500 annually in tail male until his death; and [3] that this portion of the whole annuity descended from John [† 16 Mar 1410],*[6] *to his son John the younger [† 27 May 1444]*[7] *and thence to Edmund as John the younger's brother and next heir; consequently on 24 Oct. 1444 the king released*[8] *this portion of the whole annuity to Edmund, granting respite from homage, and ordered*[9] *the London mayor and escheator Henry* Frowyke *to release to Edmund*

---

[2] *CPR 1441-46, p. 311.*

[3] *TNA: PRO, C139/114/19, Middlesex part.* Catworth *was mayor and ex officio escheator of London in 1443/4: A.B. Beaven, The Aldermen of the City of London, temp. Henry III-1912, 2 vols., London 1908-13, vol. 2, p. 8.*

[4] *CPR 1401-5, p. 477.*

[5] *CPR 1408-13, p. 142, 147.*

[6] *The writ* diem clausit extremum *was issued on 10 Apr. 1410, and the corresponding inquisition in London held on 12 June 1410 found that † John, earl of Somerset, held among other things £500 from the petty customs in London: J.L. Kirby (ed.), Calendar of inquisitions post mortem, vol. 19 (1405-13), London 1992, No. 769, p. 275.*

[7] *TNA: PRO, C139/114/19.*

[8] *CPR 1441-46, p. 311 dated 24 Oct. 1444.*

[9] *CCR 1441-47, p. 243-4.* Frowyke *was mayor and ex officio escheator of London in 1444/5: A.B. Beaven, The Aldermen of the City of London, temp. Henry III-1912, 2 vols., London 1908-13, vol. 2, p. 7.*

this portion of the entire annuity – together with all arrears – which had been taken into the king's hand by virtue of the death of John the younger, saving the rights of John the younger's widow Margaret, who is entitled to dower amounting to a third of the annuity [£166 13s 4d per annum]; and since the king has ordered[10] *the collectors of the petty customs in London to pay Edmund all arrears of the said two thirds of the annuity and all sums which shall fall due in the future; the king orders the Exchequer to allow the customers all payments made in this regard when they account, provided they produce the mandate for payment directed to them and the receipts of the beneficiary. — 1445 Oct. 3. Westminster.*

L TNA: PRO, E159/222 Brevia directa baronibus Michaelmas m 9-9d. Contemporaneous official copy. Parchment. Unsealed.

[Marginated] Pro Edmundo marchione Dorsete

Rex thesaurario et baronibus suis de scaccario salutem. Cum nuper per quandam supplicacionem dilecti et fidelis consanguinei nostri Edmundi marchionis Dorsete nobis nuper presentatam intellexerimus, quod, ubi diversa maneria, terre, tenementa, redditus, annuitates una cum aliis possessionibus et hereditamentis sibi post mortem Johannis nuper ducis Somersete fratris sui descenderant, evidencias eorundem adtunc et per futurum tempus non modicum extra possessionem predicti consanguinei nostri fore estimabatur, sic quod ipse de sui juris titulo, qui in magna dicte hereditatis sue parte per inquisiciones coram escaetoribus nostris virtute brevium nostrorum de diem clausit extremum capiendas inveniri debuisset, nequebat insinuari, quod tempore non brevi ipsum de liberacione sua de aliqua parte dictorum hereditamentorum suorum extra manus nostras absque gracia nostra sibi in hac parte exhibita verisimiliter impedire formidabatur, ut dicebat, et nos de gracia nostra speciali et consideracione premissorum per litteras nostras patentes concesserimus dicto consanguineo nostro, quod ipse de tempore in tempus ad voluntatem suam incontinenti, postquam alique inquisiciones vigore aliquorum brevium nostrorum de diem clausit extremum vel alicujus alterius mandati nostri post mortem predicti nuper ducis capiende et in cancellariam nostram retornande absque impeticione vel impedimento nostri vel heredum nostrorum prosequi posset et habere parcellatim, particulariter et per vices separales liberacionem extra manus nostras super qualibet inquisicione sic capta et in cancellariam nostram retornata de omnibus maneriis, terris, tenementis, redditibus, serviciis, feodis militum, advocacionibus, annuitatibus, pecuniarum summis ad receptam scaccarii predicti de parva custuma portus nostri London' vel alibi solvendam franchesiis, libertatibus et omnibus aliis possessionibus et hereditamentis in aliqua tali inquisicione contentis vel specificatis, de quibus dictus consanguineus noster per dictas inquisiciones aliquo modo hereditabilis inveniretur et que sibi ut heredi masculo fratris sui predicti descenderent, remanerent, re-

[10] *This mandate is untraceable.*

verterent, pertinerent vel aliquo modo devenirent et quod ipse non[a] impediretur de aliqua liberacione extra manus nostras habenda de aliqua parcella dictorum maneriorum, terrarum, tenementorum, redituum, annuitatum cum aliis possessionibus et hereditamentis predictis, quousque omnes inquisiciones, que secundum cursum cancellarie nostre et consuetudinem regni nostri in hac parte caperentur, in cancellariam nostram retornate forent, et quod dicte particulares et separales littere parcellatim et per vices separales, ut supradictum est, fiende, prosequende et habende forent dicto consanguineo nostro, heredibus suis et assignatis talis vigoris et effectus erga nos et heredes nostros, qualis esset sibi debita et integra liberacio per ipsum de omnimodis maneriis, terris, tenementis, redditibus, annuitatibus cum aliis possessionibus et hereditamentis per cursum et consuetudinem cancellarie nostre predicte prosequenda; et ulterius de habundanti gracia nostra concesserimus dicto consanguineo nostro dictam liberacionem particularem cum omnibus exitibus, proficuis, revencionibus, redditibus et arreragiis reddituum dictorum maneriorum, terrarum, tenementorum, annuitatum, summarum denariorum cum aliis possessionibus et hereditamentis predictis a tempore mortis predicti nuper ducis habere; et insuper de gracia nostra speciali perdonaverimus predicto consanguineo nostro omnimoda relevia nobis per ipsum pro aliquo honore, dignitate vel aliquo dictorum maneriorum, terrarum, tenementorum, possessionum vel aliorum hereditamentorum sibi per vel post mortem dicti nuper ducis aliquo modo descendencium necnon et homagium nobis per ipsum debitum per spacium dimidii anni tunc proximi futuri absque fine seu feodo inde nobis solvendo restituaverimus, eo, quod expressa mencio de aliis donis vel concessionibus dicto consanguineo nostro per nos vel progenitores nostros ante ea tempora factis vel de vero valore premissorum in predictis litteris facta non existit, non obstante, prout in eisdem litteris plenius continetur; ac per quandam inquisicionem coram Thoma Catworth nuper majore et escaetore nostro in civitate predicta de mandato nostro captam et in cancellariam nostram retornatam sit compertum, quod dominus Henricus [IV] nuper rex Anglie avus noster duodecimo die Novembris anno regni sui sexto *[12 Nov. 1404]* per litteras suas patentes de gracia sua speciali et de assensu dominorum spiritualium et temporalium ac communitatum[b] regni sui Anglie in parliamento suo apud Coventre tunc tento existencium concessit Johanni nuper comiti Somersete mille libras habendas et percipiendas annuatim eidem nuper comiti et heredibus suis masculis de corpore suo legitime procreatis pro statu comitis manutenendo et sustentando ad scaccarium ipsius avi nostri a festo sancti Michaelis tunc ultimo preterito *[29 Sept. 1404]* et ad festa Pasche et sancti Michaelis per equales porciones, quousque idem nuper rex vel heredes sui eidem comiti vel heredibus suis masculis supradictis de terris et tenementis, que non sunt parcelle corone prefati regis, ad valorem mille librarum per annum fecisset provideri, prout in eisdem litteris plenius continetur, virtute cujus concessionis dictus nuper comes fuit seisitus in forma predicta de dictis mille libris annuis ad dictum scaccarium sibi et heredibus suis masculis de corpore suo procreatis, ut premittitur, percipiendis, quousque predictus nuper rex vicesimo quinto die Octobris anno regni sui undecimo *[25 Oct. 1409]* per alias litteras suas patentes recitantes in eisdem concessionem suam predictam de gracia sua speciali concesserit prefato nuper comiti per nomen carissimi fratris sui Johannis comitis Somersete quingentas libras per annum habendas et percipiendas sibi et dictis heredibus suis masculis a festo sancti Michaelis tunc ultimo preterito *[29 Sept. 1409]* de parva custuma sua London' per manus collectorum, firmariorum et aliorum occupatorum ejusdem pro tempore existencium ad terminos Pasche et sancti Michaelis per equales porciones in partem satisfaccionis et deduccionis mille librarum supradictarum, aliquibus ordinacionibus, concessionibus sive assignacionibus de dicta parva custuma incontrarium factis seu faciendis non obstantibus. Et si contingeret, quod prefatus comes vel heredes sui masculi predicti per quamcumque causam futuro tempore de dicta summa quingentarum librarum vel alicujus parcelle earundem de parva custuma predicta solvi non poterit vel poterint, tunc de omni eo, quod inde defecerit [et] recipi non poterit, satisfactum sit et solutum prefato comiti et dictis heredibus suis masculis ad scaccarium dicti nuper regis et heredum suorum imperpetuum, prout in posterioribus litteris patentibus plenius continetur, et quod prefatus nuper comes fuit seisitus in dominico suo ut de feodo talliato, videlicet sibi et heredibus suis masculis de corpore suo procreatis, de dictis quingentis libris annuis percipiendis et habendis de dicta parva custuma in portu dicte civitatis London' ad dictos terminos Pasche et sancti Michaelis juxta vim, formam et effectum dicte posterioris concessionis dicti nuper regis sibi, ut premittitur, facte et habuit exitum prefatum Johannem nuper ducem et Edmundum Beaufort marchionem Dorsete et de tali statu inde obiit seisitus, post cujus mortem dicte quingente libre prefato Johanni nuper duci ut filio et heredi prefati nuper comitis per formam concessionis predicte posteriorum litterarum patencium descendebant, qui quidem Johannes nuper dux de tali statu inde obiit seisitus sine herede masculo de corpore suo exeunte, post cujus mortem dicte quingente libre prefato Edmundo ut fratri et heredi masculo prefati Johannis nuper ducis per formam concessionis predicte posteriorum litterarum patencium descendebant quodque prefatus Edmundus est frater et heres masculus predicti Johannis nuper ducis propinquior per formam concessionis predicte posteriorum litterarum patencium et plene etatis; ac nos vicesimo quarto die Octobris ultimo preterito *[24 Oct. 1444]* homagio predicti marchionis nobis in hac parte ac pro aliis terris et tenementis, que predictus nuper dux tenuit de nobis in capite in diversis comitatibus regni nostri Anglie debite absque aliquo fine seu feodo inde nobis solvendo per certum tempus tunc futurum respectuato eidem marchioni predictas quingentas libras reddiderimus et preceperimus dilecto nobis Henrico Frowyke majori civitatis nostre London' et escaetori nostro in eadem civitate, quod eidem marchioni de predictis quingentis libris, que per mortem predicti nuper ducis capte[c] fuerunt in manum nostram una cum exitibus et arreragiis earundem a tempore mortis ejusdem nuper ducis perceptis plenam seisinam habere faceret juxta tenorem litterarum nostrarum predictarum, salvo jure cujuslibet et salva Margarete, que fuit uxor predicti nuper ducis, racionabili dote sua, ipsam de eisdem quingentis libris secundum legem et consuetudinem regni nostri Anglie contingente per nos assignanda, sicut per inspeccionem rotulorum cancellarie nostre nobis constat, et per breve nostrum preceperimus collectoribus, firmariis et aliis occupatoribus custume predicte in portu predicto, qui nunc sunt et qui pro tempore erunt, quod eidem marchioni id, quod ei aretro est de duabus partibus predictarum quingentarum librarum annuarum pro terminis Pasche et sancti Michaelis ultimo preteritis et easdem duas partes annuas exnunc singulis annis durante vita sua de custuma predicta de tempore in tempus ad terminos predictos solvant, vobis mandamus, quod viso mandato nostro predicto id, quod vobis constare poterit ipsos collectores, firmarios et alios occupatores eidem marchioni pretextu mandati nostri predicti racionabiliter solvisse et exnunc solvere, eisdem collectoribus, firmariis et aliis occupatoribus in compoto suo ad scaccarium predictum de tempore in tempus debite allocetis, recipientes a prefatis collectoribus, firmariis et aliis occupatoribus de tempore in tempus litteras acquietancie ipsius marchionis, que pro nobis sufficientes fuerint in hac parte. Teste me ipso apud Westmonasterium, tercio die Octobris anno regni nostri vicesimo quarto.

[a] nom *L, in error.* [b] communitates *L, in error.* [c] capta *L, in error.*

[S 3] Henry VI to the treasurer and barons of the Exchequer: since the king by patent[11] *issued on 19 Dec. 1444 permitted Margaret, the widow of the † king's tenant in chief John, duke of Somerset, to sue for assignment of dowry from the property of the deceased which had come into the king's hands by reason of his death, together with the arrears of the income from these properties since the deceased's date of death [27 May 1444]; and since the king had ordered*[12] *Henry* Frowyk, *mayor and escheator of London, on 1 Feb. 1445 to assign dower to Margaret – whose oath not to remarry without the king's permission had been taken by the escheator of Lincolnshire at the king's behest – from the property of her late husband in London together with the arrears from the date of his death, whereupon the mayor returned*[13] *that he had assigned Margaret one third (£166 13s 4d) of the annuity of £500 yearly, payable from the issues of the petty customs in London, which the deceased had possessed on the day of his death; and since the king has ordered*[14] *the customers to pay Margaret all arrears of the said third of the annuity owing to her and all sums which shall fall due in the future; the king orders the Exchequer to allow the customers all payments made in this regard when they account, provided they produce the*

[11] *CPR 1441-46, p. 318.*

[12] *CCR 1441-47, p. 252.*

[13] *The return has not survived in TNA: PRO, C139-C141.*

[14] *This mandate is untraceable.*

mandate for payment directed to them and the receipts of the beneficiary. — 1445 Mar. 16. Westminster.

L TNA: PRO, E159/221 Brevia directa baronibus Easter m 4. Contemporaneous official copy. Parchment. Unsealed.

[Marginated] Pro collectoribus parve custume regis in portu London'

Rex thesaurario et baronibus suis de scaccario salutem. Cum decimo nono die Decembris ultimo preterito *[19 Dec. 1444]* de gracia nostra speciali concesserimus predilecte consanguinee nostre Margarete ducisse Somersethe nuper uxori carissimi consanguinei nostri Johannis nuper ducis Somersethe defuncti, qui de nobis tenuit in capite, quod ipsa de omnibus castris, dominiis, maneriis, villis, terris, tenementis, feodis, advocacionibus, annuitatibus, franchesiis, libertatibus ac aliis possessionibus et hereditamentis cum pertinenciis quibuscumque, de quibus prefatus nuper vir suus fuit seisitus in dominico suo ut de feodo vel de feodo talliato quocumque, in manibus nostris seisitis vel seisiendis per mortem dicti nuper viri sui, sine vigore alicujus inquisicionis virtute alicujus brevis nostri vel brevium nostrorum de diem clausit extremum aut alicujus alterius mandati nostri seu aliter capte vel capiende et in cancellariam nostram retornate vel retornande vel post mortem prefati nuper viri sui nobis aliquo modo spectantibus, unde prefata Margareta per leges nostras dotabiles tunc extitit post quamcumque inquisicionem in dictam cancellariam nostram inde retornatam vel retornandam vel alio speciali modo sive generali liberacionem dotis sue sibi per et post mortem prefati nuper viri sui aliquo modo spectantis particulariter et specialiter prosequi posset et habere et quod liberacio illa separalis et specialis per ipsam in forma predicta prosequenda et habita ejusdem esset vigoris et effectus ac si integre assignacio et liberacio inde prefate ducisse per nos secundum cursum alicujus alterius legis nostre facte extitissent, habenda prefate ducisse cum omnimodis exitibus et proficuis de quibuscumque possessionibus, que sibi sic in dotem assignari deberent, provenientibus in forma predicta a tempore mortis prefati nuper viri sui, aliqua concessione prefate Margarete per nos ante predictum decimum nonum diem Decembris facta non obstante, prout in litteris nostris patentibus inde confectis plenius continetur, ac primo die Februarii ultimo preterito *[1 Feb. 1445]* per breve nostrum preceperimus dilecto nobis Henrico Frowyk majori civitatis nostre London' et escaetori nostro in eadem civitate, quod eidem ducisse, cujus sacramentum, quod se non maritaret sine licencia nostra, per escaetorem nostrum in comitatu Lincolniensi capi mandavimus, racionabilem dotem suam ipsam de omnibus castris, dominiis, maneriis, villis, terris, tenementis, feodis, advocacionibus, annuitatibus, franchesiis, libertatibus et aliis possessionibus et hereditamentis predictis cum pertinenciis quibuscumque, de quibus predictus nuper dux fuit seisitus in dominico suo ut de feodo vel de feodo talliato in balliva sua *[viz. of the London mayor]* die, quo obiit, et que per mortem predicti nuper ducis capta fuerunt in manum nostram secundum legem et consuetudinem regni nostri Anglie, contingentem juxta extentam inde factam vel aliam, si necesse foret, iterato faciendam in presencia propinquiorum amicorum Margarete filie et heredis predicti nuper ducis vel attornatorum suorum, si interesse vellent, assignari faceret habendam una cum exitibus et proficuis inde a tempore mortis predicti nuper ducis juxta tenorem litterarum nostrarum predictarum et, cum assignacionem illam sic fecisset, eam nobis sub sigillo suo mitteret, ut eam in rotulis cancellarie nostre, prout moris est, irrotulari faceremus, sicut per inspeccionem rotulorum ejusdem cancellarie nobis constat. Ac idem major nobis retornaverit, quod assignavit prefate ducisse centum, sexaginta et sex libras, tresdecim solidos et quatuor denarios habenda in dotem suam ipsam de quadam annuitate quingentarum librarum de parva custuma nostra London' per manus collectorum, firmariorum sive aliorum occupatorum ejusdem pro tempore existencium percipenda ad terminos Pasche et sancti Michaelis per equales porciones, quam idem nuper dux tenuit in dicta balliva sua die, quo obiit, in dominico suo ut de feodo talliato sibi et heredibus masculis de corpore suo exeuntibus secundum legem et consuetudinem predictas contingentem. Et per breve nostrum preceperimus collectoribus, firmariis sive aliis occupatoribus parve custume nostre London', qui nunc sunt vel qui pro tempore fuerint, quod eidem ducisse id, quod aretro est de predictis centum, sexaginta et sex libris, tresdecim solidis et quatuor denariis a tempore mortis predicti nuper ducis, et easdem centum, sexaginta et sex libras, tresdecim solidos et quatuor denarios exnunc singulis annis durante vita sua de parva custuma nostra predicta ad terminos predictos de tempore in tempus solverent juxta assignacionem predictam, vobis mandamus, quod viso mandato nostro predicto id, quod vobis constare poterit prefatos collectores, firmarios sive alios occupatores eidem ducisse pretextu mandati nostri predicti racionabiliter solvisse, eisdem collectoribus, firmariis sive aliis occupatoribus inde in compoto suo ad scaccarium predictum de tempore in tempus debite allocetis, recipientes a prefatis collectoribus, firmariis sive aliis occupatoribus de tempore in tempus litteras acquietancie ipsius ducisse, que pro nobis sufficientes fuerint in hac parte. Teste me ipso apud Westmonasterium, 16 die Marcii anno regni nostri vicesimo tercio.

[S 4] Henry VI to the treasurer and barons of the Exchequer: since the king by patent[15] *granted John Popham, kt.* (miles)*, an annuity of £40 yearly for life, payable from the issues of the petty customs in London at Michaelmas and Easter in equal portions; and since the king has ordered*[16] *the customers to pay the beneficiary all arrears of his annuity; the king orders the Exchequer to allow* (debite allocetis) *the customers all payments made in this regard when they account, provided they produce the mandates for payment directed to them and the receipts* (litteras acquietancie) *of the beneficiary. — 1440 July 27* (Teste me ipso apud castrum nostrum de Wyndesore, 27° die Julii anno regni nostri decimo octavo). *Windsor.*

---

[15] *CPR 1436-41, p. 432 and 436 dated 27 July 1440.*

[16] *This mandate is untraceable.*

L TNA: PRO, E159/217 Brevia directa baronibus Michaelmas m 18. Contemporaneous official copy. Parchment. Unsealed. Marginated: Pro custumariis London'. *Beneath the text:* Per breve de privato sigillo.

[S 5] Henry VI to the treasurer and barons of the Exchequer: since Henry IV (avus noster) *by patent confirmed Henry V* (pater noster) *and by the present king*[17] *granted † Robert* Stanley, *esq.* (armiger), *and John* Yerde, *esq.* (armiger), *an annuity of £40 yearly (£20 for each) for life, payable from the issues of the petty customs in London at Easter and Michaelmas in equal portions; and since the king has ordered*[18] *the customers to pay John all arrears of his annuity owing from Michaelmas term last* (pro termino sancti Michaelis proximo preterito) *and all sums which shall fall due in the future; the king orders the Exchequer to allow* (debite allocetis) *the customers all payments made in this regard when they account, provided they produce the mandate for payment directed to them and the receipts* (litteras acquietancie) *of the beneficiary. — 1439 May 13* (Teste me ipso apud Westmonasterium, 13 die Maii anno regni nostri decimo septimo). *Westminster.*

L TNA: PRO, E159/215 Brevia directa baronibus Trinity m 15. Contemporaneous official copy. Parchment. Unsealed. Marginated: Pro Johanne Yerde.

[S 6] Henry VI to the treasurer and barons of the Exchequer: since the king by patent[19] *issued on 14 July 1439 granted his uncle Humphrey, duke of Gloucester, among other things an annuity of £16 yearly, payable from the issues of the manor of Tarrant Launceston in Dorset, which belonged to the [abbey of St. Stephan] of Caen, from 29 Sept. 1439 onwards; and since Humphrey surrendered this patent in the expectation of a grant of a corresponding annuity, whereupon the king by patent*[20] *issued on 30 June 1441 granted him an annuity of £16 yearly, payable from the issues of the petty customs in London from 29 Sept. 1440 onwards; and since the king has ordered*[21] *the collectors of the petty customs in London to pay the beneficiary all arrears of his annuity owing from the said 29 Sept. 1440 and all sums which shall fall due in the future; the king orders the Exchequer to allow the customers all payments made in this regard when they account, provided they produce the*

[17] *Henry IV's patent was issued on 13 Jan. 1413 (CPR 1408-13, p. 460), and was confirmed by Henry V on 1 Oct. 1414 (CPR 1413-16, p. 272) and Henry VI's on 20 Dec. 1422 (CPR 1422-29, p. 39).*

[18] *This mandate is untraceable.*

[19] *CPR 1436-41, p. 303-4.*

[20] *CPR 1436-41, p. 552.*

[21] *This mandate is untraceable.*

mandate for payment directed to them and the receipts of the beneficiary. — 1441 July 19. Westminster.

L TNA: PRO, E159/217 Brevia directa baronibus Trinity m 14. Contemporaneous official copy. Parchment. Unsealed.

[Marginated] Pro Humfrido duce Gloucestrie

Rex thesaurario et baronibus suis de scaccario salutem. Cum nos quartodecimo die Julii anno regni nostri decimo septimo *[14 July 1439]* concesserimus carissimo avunculo nostro Humfrido duci Gloucestrie inter alia sexdecim libras per annum de exitibus, proficuis, revencionibus et redditibus manerii de Tarent Lounston in comitatu Dorsete *[Tarrant Launceston, Dorset]*, quod est parcella pensionum de Cadamo *[Caen]* alienigenis pertinente habendas prefato avunculo nostro ad terminum vite sue a festo sancti Michaelis tunc proximo futuro *[29 Sept. 1439]* ad festa Pasche et sancti Michaelis per equales porciones, prout in litteris nostris patentibus inde confectis plenius continetur, et nos pro eo, quod idem dux avunculus noster litteras predictas quoad easdem sexdecim libras annuas nobis in cancellaria nostra restituit vacuandas ad intencionem, quod nos sibi in recompensacionem earundem sexdecim librarum annuarum sexdecim libras percipiendas annuatim ad terminum vite sue in aliquo alio loco per nos limitando et assignando, quam quidem limitacionem sive assignacionem dictus dux avunculus noster admittere et ei agreare se vellet, graciose concedere dignaremur, tricesimo die Junii ultimo preterito *[30 June 1441]* de gracia nostra speciali premissorum intuitui concesserimus eidem duci avunculo nostro sexdecim libras percipiendas annuatim a festo sancti Michaelis ultimo preterito *[29 Sept. 1440]* pro termino vite sue de parva custuma nostra in portu civitatis London' per manus collectorum ejusdem custume pro tempore existencium ad terminos predictos per equales porciones in recompensacionem predictarum sexdecim librarum annuarum sibi dicto quartodecimo die Julii, ut premittitur, concessarum, prout in litteris nostris patentibus inde confectis plenius continetur, et per breve nostrum preceperimus collectoribus parve custume nostre in portu predicto, qui nunc sunt vel qui pro tempore erunt, quod eidem duci id, quod ei aretro est de predictis sexdecim libris annuis a dicto festo sancti Michaelis ultimo preterito et easdem sexdecim libras annuas exnunc singulis annis durante vita sua de parva custuma predicta in portu predicto de tempore in tempus ad festa predicta solvant juxta tenorem litterarum nostrarum predictarum, vobis mandamus, quod viso mandato nostro predicto id, quod vobis constare poterit ipsos collectores eidem duci pretextu mandati nostri predicti racionabiliter solvisse et exnunc solvere, eisdem collectoribus in compoto suo ad scaccarium predictum de tempore in tempus debite allocetis, recipientes a prefatis collectoribus de tempore in tempus litteras acquietancie ipsius ducis, que pro nobis sufficientes fuerint in hac parte. Teste me ipso apud Westmonasterium, 9 die Julii anno regni nostri decimo nono.

[S 7] Henry VI to the treasurer and barons of the Exchequer: since the king

by patent[22] *granted his physician* (phisicus noster), magister *John* Faceby, *an annuity of £100 yearly for life, payable from the issues of the petty customs in London at Easter and Michaelmas in equal portions from 29 Sept. 1443* (a festo sancti Michaelis ultimo preterito) *onwards; and since the king has ordered*[23] *the customers to pay the beneficiary all arrears of his annuity owing from the said 29 Sept. 1443* (a dicto festo sancti Michaelis ultimo preterito) *and all sums which shall fall due in the future; the king orders the Exchequer to allow* (debite allocetis) *the customers all payments made in this regard when they account, provided they produce the mandate for payment directed to them and the receipts* (litteras acquietancie) *of the beneficiary. — 1444 July 12* (Teste me ipso apud Westmonasterium, 12 die Julii anno regni nostri vicesimo secundo). *Westminster.*

L TNA: PRO, E159/221 Brevia directa baronibus Michaelmas m 15d. Contemporaneous official copy. Parchment. Unsealed. Marginated: Pro collectoribus parve custume regis in portu civitatis London'.

[S 8] *Henry VI to the treasurer and barons of the Exchequer: since the king by patent*[24] *granted John* Paunton *and Thomas* Ponsford *6d per diem for life, whichever of them should live longest* (pro termino vite sue et alterius eorum diucius viventis), *payable from the issues of the petty customs in London; and since the king has ordered*[25] *the collectors to pay the beneficiaries from now on all sums which shall fall due in accordance with the king's patent; the king orders the Exchequer to allow* (debite allocetis) *the customers all payments made in this regard when they account, provided they produce the mandate for payment directed to them and the receipts* (litteras acquietancie) *of the beneficiaries. — 1443 Oct. 20* (Teste me ipso apud Chesewyk, 19 die Februarii anno regni nostri vicesimo primo). *Chiswick.*

L TNA: PRO, E159/220 Brevia directa baronibus Michaelmas m 3d. Contemporaneous official copy. Parchment. Unsealed. Marginated: Pro Johanne Paunton et aliis.

[S 9] *Henry VI to the treasurer and barons of the Exchequer: since the king by patent*[26] *issued on 17 Feb. 1440* (decimo septimo die Februarii ultimo preterito) *granted John* Seintlo, *esq.* (armiger), *£20 yearly for life, payable from the issues of the petty customs in London from 29 Sept.*

---

[22] *CPR 1441-46, p. 271 dated 11 July 1444.*

[23] *This mandate is untraceable.*

[24] *CPR 1441-46, p. 164 dated 19 Feb. 1443.*

[25] *This mandate is untraceable.*

[26] *CPR 1436-41, p. 387. This grant superseded the patent issued on 11 July 1428 (CPR 1422-29, p. 480), with which Henry VI had granted* Seintlo *the annuity during pleasure* (quamdiu nobis placuerit).

1439 (a festo sancti Michaelis ultimo preterito) *onwards at Michaelmas and Easter in equal portions; and since the king has ordered*[27] *the customers to pay the beneficiary all arrears of his annuity owing from Easter term last* (pro termino Pasche ultimo preterito); *the king orders the Exchequer to allow* (debite allocetis) *the customers all payments made in this regard when they account, provided they produce the mandate for payment directed to them and the receipts* (litteras acquietancie) *of the beneficiary. — 1440 Mar. 28* (Teste me ipso apud Westmonasterium, 28 die Marcii anno regni nostri decimo octavo). *Westminster.*

L TNA: PRO, E159/217 Brevia directa baronibus Hilary m 15. Contemporaneous official copy. Parchment. Unsealed. Marginated: Pro Johanne Seintlo.

[S 10] Henry VI to the treasurer and barons of the Exchequer: since the king by patent[28] *granted John* Sutton, *kt.* (miles), *lord* Duddely, *in recognition of his service to the present king and his father* (pater noster) *in the wars in France and Normandy and in Ireland and the Mark of Calais, which occasioned great expenses* (graves labores, custus et expensas) *which he had to bear without receiving a fee* (absque aliquo feodo), *£100 yearly, payable from the issues of the petty customs in London at Easter and Michaelmas in equal portions; and since the king has ordered*[29] *the customers to pay the beneficiary all sums which shall fall due in the future by reason of his annuity; the king orders the Exchequer to allow* (debite allocetis) *the customers all payments made in this regard when they account, provided they produce the mandate for payment directed to them and the receipts* (litteras acquietancie) *of the beneficiary. — 1443 Oct. 26* (Teste me ipso apud Westmonasterium, 26 die Octobris anno regni nostri vicesimo secundo). *Westminster.*

L TNA: PRO, E159/220 Brevia directa baronibus Easter m 7d. Contemporaneous official copy. Parchment. Unsealed. Marginated: Pro collectoribus parve custume regis in portu London'.

[S 11] Henry VI to the treasurer and barons of the Exchequer: since the king by patent[30] *issued on 2 Mar. 1444* (secundo die Marcii anno regni nostri vicesimo secundo) *granted John, earl of Shrewsbury, in recognition of his service to the present king and his father* (pater noster) *in France and Normandy, £40 yearly for life, payable from the issues of the petty customs in London at Easter and Michaelmas in equal portions; and*

---

[27] *This mandate is untraceable.*
[28] *CPR 1441-46, p. 207 dated 26 Oct. 1443.*
[29] *This mandate is untraceable.*
[30] *CPR 1441-46, p. 235.*

since the king has ordered[31] *the customers to pay the beneficiary all arrears of his annuity owing from Michaelmas and Easter terms last* (pro terminis sancti Michaelis et Pasche ultimis preteritis) *and all sums which shall fall due in the future; the king orders the Exchequer to allow* (debite allocetis) *the customers all payments made in this regard when they account, provided they produce the mandate for payment directed to them and the receipts* (litteras acquietancie) *of the beneficiary. — 1445 June 6* (Teste me ipso apud Westmonasterium, 6 die Junii anno regni nostri vicesimo tercio). *Westminster.*

L TNA: PRO, E159/222 Brevia directa baronibus Trinity m 10. Contemporaneous official copy. Parchment. Unsealed. Marginated: Pro collectoribus parve custume in portu civitatis London' et Johanne comite Salop'.

[S 12] Henry VI to the treasurer and barons of the Exchequer: since the king by patent[32] *issued on 3 Nov. 1439* (tercio die Novembris anno regni nostri decimo octavo) *appointed William* Yelverton *justice of assizes* (ad assisas in diversis comitatibus regni nostri Anglie capiendas)*; and since the king later, by patent*[33] *issued on 1 July 1443* (primo die Julii anno regni nostri vicesimo primo), *appointed him justice in the King's Bench* (ad placita coram nobis tenenda) *at pleasure* (quamdiu nobis placeret), *with the customary fees* (feodum consuetum)*; and, in addition, by further patent also issued on 1 July 1443,*[34] *in order that he be able to maintain his status and bear the expenses of his office* (ut idem Willelmus statum suum decencius manutenere et expensas suas, quas ipsum in officio predicto facere operteret, sustinere valeret), *granted him 110 marks yearly, payable at Michaelmas and Easter in equal portions by the keeper or clerk of the hanaper of the chancery or by the customers in London, Bristol and Hull in accordance with the act of the parliament of 18 Hen. VI,*[35] *a further 106s 11⅓d* (106s 11¼d et sextam partem unius oboli) *yearly at Christmas for a robe with a fur lining* (pro una roba et furrura pro eadem) *and 63s 6d yearly at Pentecost for a robe with lining* (pro una roba et linura pro eadem), *also payable by the said clerk of the hanaper or the said customers in accordance with the said act of the parliament of 18 Hen. VI; and since the king has ordered*[36] *the collectors of the petty customs in London to pay the beneficiary all arrears of his annuities from the various dates of appointment in accordance with the*

---

[31] *This mandate is untraceable.*

[32] *CPR 1436-41, p. 341 (vacated) and 347.*

[33] *CPR 1441-46, p. 179.*

[34] *CPR 1441-46, p. 183.*

[35] *Rotuli Parliamentorum, vol. 5, p. 13-4.*

[36] *This mandate is untraceable.*

said act of parliament (a copy of which was sent to them) and all sums which shall fall due in the future, namely £20 for his fees as justice of assizes, 40 marks for his fees as justice in the King's Bench (coram nobis) *and 110 marks for his rewards, 106s 11⅓d* (106s 11¼d et sextam partem unius oboli) *and 63s 6d for his robes* (pro vestitura sua)*; the king orders the Exchequer to allow* (debite allocetis) *the customers all payments made in this regard when they account, provided they produce the mandate for payment directed to them and the receipts* (litteras acquietancie) *of the beneficiary. — 1446 Jan. 4* (Teste me ipso apud Westmonasterium, quarto die Januarii anno regni nostri vicesimo quarto). *Westminster.*

L TNA: PRO, E159/222 Brevia directa baronibus Hilary m 24d. Contemporaneous official copy. Parchment. Unsealed. Marginated: Pro Willelmo Yelverton.

[S 13] Henry VI to the treasurer and barons of the Exchequer: since the king by patent[37] *issued on 17 Apr. 1440* (decimo septimo die Aprilis anno regni nostri decimo octavo) *appointed William* Ayscogh *justice in the Common Bench* (de banco) *at pleasure* (quamdiu nobis placeret) *with the customary fees* (feodum consuetum)*; and by patent*[38] *also issued on 17 Apr. 1440* (eodem decimo septimo die Aprilis) *in order that he be able to maintain his status and bear the expenses of office* (de gracia nostra speciali et ut prefatus Willelmus statum suum decencius manutenere et expensas suas, quas ipsum in officio predicto facere oporteret, sustinere valeret), *granted him granted him 110 marks yearly, payable at the Exchequer* (ad scaccarium nostrum) *at Michaelmas and Easter in equal portions, and two robes per annum, one with a lining* (cum linura) *at Pentecost and the other with a fur lining at Christmas* (cum pellura)*; and since the king by patent*[39] *issued on 6 Nov. 1439* (sexto die Novembris anno predicto) *appointed him justice of assizes* (ad assisas in diversis comitatibus regni nostri Anglie arramandas capiendas)*; and since the king has ordered*[40] *the collectors of the petty customs in London to pay the beneficiary all arrears of his annuities in accordance with [1.] the act of the parliament meeting in Westminster on 12 Nov. 18 Hen. VI*[41] *(a copy of which was sent to them) in respect of the fees, rewards and clothing allowances* (pro feodis, regardis et denariorum summis pro vesturis annuis) *of royal justices, sergeants-at-law and attorneys, [2.] the copies of royal writs and certifications in the same regard, and [3.] the investigation of*

---

[37] *CPR 1436-41, p. 395.*

[38] *CPR 1436-41, p. 443.*

[39] *CPR 1436-41, p. 347.*

[40] *This mandate is untraceable.*

[41] *Rotuli Parliamentorum, vol. 5, p. 13-4.*

Robert Mouter, *warden or clerk of the hanaper of the chancery, conducted by the chancellor, archbishop John of Canterbury, on 30 Sept. 1443* (ultimo die Septembris ultimo preterito) *as to whether the issues of the hanaper sufficed for the payment of the arrears owing to the king's justices, sergeants-at-law and attorneys as mandated by parliament; the king orders the Exchequer to allow* (debite allocetis) *the collectors of the petty customs in London all payments made in this regard when they account, provided they produce the mandate for payment directed to them and the receipts* (litteras acquietancie) *of the beneficiary. — 1444 May 16* (Teste me ipso apud Westmonasterium, 16 die Maii anno regni nostri vicesimo secundo). *Westminster.*

L TNA: PRO, E159/220 Brevia directa baronibus Trinity m 14d. Contemporaneous official copy. Parchment. Unsealed. Marginated: Pro Willelmo Ayscogh.

[S 14] Henry VI to the treasurer and barons of the Exchequer: Henry VI to the treasurer and barons of the Exchequer: since the king by patent[42] *issued on 12 Dec. 1439* (duodecimo die Decembris anno regni nostri decimo octavo) *appointed John* Markham *justice of assizes* (ad assisas in diversis comitatibus regni nostri Anglie arramandas capiendas) *and later, by patent*[43] *issued on 6 Feb. 1444* (sexto die Februarii anno regni nostri vicesimo secundo), *appointed him justice in the King's Bench* (ad placita coram nobis tenenda) *at pleasure* (quamdiu nobis placeret), *with the customary fee* (feodum consuetum)*; and, in addition, by further patent*[44] *also issued on 6 Feb. 1444, in order that he be able to maintain his status and bear the expenses of his office* (ut idem Johannes statum suum decencius manutenere et expensas, quas ipsum in officio predicto facere oporteret, sustinere valeret), *granted him 110 marks yearly, payable at Michaelmas and Easter in equal portions by the keeper or clerk of the hanaper of the chancery or by the customers in London, Bristol and Hull in accordance with the act of the parliament of 18 Hen. VI,*[45] *and a further 106s 11⅓d* (106s 11¼d et sextam partem unius oboli) *yearly at Christmas for a robe with fur lining* (pro una roba et linura pro eadem) *and 63s 6d yearly at Pentecost for a robe with lining* (pro una roba et linura pro eadem), *also payable by the clerk of the hanaper or the said customers in accordance with the said act of the parliament of 18 Hen. VI; and since the king has ordered*[46] *the collectors of the petty customs in London to pay the beneficiary all arrears of his annuities in accordance with the said act of parliament (a copy of which was sent to*

[42] *CPR 1436-41, p. 355.*

[43] *CPR 1441-46, p. 232.*

[44] *CPR 1441-46, p. 250.*

[45] *Rotuli Parliamentorum, vol. 5, p. 13-4.*

[46] *This mandate is untraceable.*

them) and all sums which shall fall due in the future, namely £20 for his fees as justice of assizes from 29 Sept. 1444 onwards (a festo [a]sancti Michaelis[a] anno regni nostri vicesimo tercio), *40 marks for his fees as justice in the King's Bench* (coram nobis) *and 110 marks for his rewards, 106s 11⅓d* (106s 11¼d et sextam partem unius oboli) *and 63s 6d for his robes* (pro vestitura sua) *from the date of his appointment; the king orders the Exchequer to allow* (debite allocetis) *the collectors of the petty customs in London all payments made in this regard when they account, provided they produce the mandate for payment directed to them and the receipts* (litteras acquietancie) *of the beneficiary. — 1446 Jan. 13* (Teste me ipso apud Westmonasterium, 13 die Januarii anno regni nostri vicesimo quarto). *Westminster.*

L TNA: PRO, E159/222 Brevia directa baronibus Easter m 10. Contemporaneous official copy. Parchment. Unsealed. Marginated: Pro Johanne Markham.

[a–a] *Interlined above* Pasche, *underlined for the purpose of cancellation L.*

[S 15] The London sheriffs were ordered by writ issued by the Exchequer on 26 Jan. 1447 (26[to] die Januarii [hoc termino]) *to distrain the collectors of the petty customs in London John* Melbourne *and William* Chattok *to appear before the Exchequer on 17 Apr. 1447* (in crastino Clausi Pasche [hoc termino]) *in order to account. On the day in question the sheriffs returned the writ into the Exchequer, reporting that the customers had been distrained.* Melbourne *and* Chattok *appeared in person, swore the oath to account faithfully and were assigned Richard* Bedford *as their auditor. Since they were unable to complete accounting in Easter term, the matter was continued until 19 June 1447* (usque quindenam sancte Trinitatis), *when accounting as completed, as shown* inter recorda de termino sancte Trinitatis rotulo [2] *[TNA: PRO, E159/223 Recorda Trinity m 2: this is the account of their successors in office for the period from 29 Sept. 1446 to 8 Jan. 1447]*

L TNA: PRO, E159/223 Fines Pasche m 2d. Contemporaneous official fair copy of the Exchequer proceedings. Parchment. Unsealed. Marginated: London'; De die dato.

[S 16] William de Lunes *and John* Melborne *account before the Exchequer for the issues of the petty customs in London from 24 Jan. to 29 Sept. 1443* (a 24[to] die Januarii anno 21[mo] regis hujus usque festum sancti Michaelis tunc proximum sequens).

L TNA: PRO, E372/288 Adhuc Item London' (dorse). Original Pipe Roll. Parchment. Unsealed.

Et Johanni Paunton, cui rex Henricus Quartus per litteras suas patentes,[47] quas rex nunc 17° die Decembris anno primo *[17 Dec. 1422]* confirmavit,[48] concessit sex denarios per diem percipiendos pro termino vite sue de custuma predicta in portu predicto per manus collectorum ejusdem custume, qui pro tempore fuerint, videlicet de hujusmodi sex denariis per diem ab ultimo die Marcii anno 20mo regis hujus *[31 Mar. 1442]* usque festum sancti Michaelis tunc proximum sequens *[29 Sept. 1442]*, scilicet per 182 dies: £4 11s, per breve regis, quod est inter communia de anno 19no regis hujus termino Pasche rotulo 25to *[TNA: PRO, E159/217 Brevia directa baronibus Easter m 25]*, et litteras acquietancie ipsius Johannis de recepta.

[Further down on the same membrane] Et prefato Johanni Paunton, cui rex Henricus iiij^tus per litteras suas patentes,[49] quas rex nunc 17° die Decembris anno primo *[17 Dec. 1422]* confirmavit,[50] concessit sex denarios per diem percipiendos pro termino vite sue de custuma predicta in portu predicto[a] per manus collectorum ejusdem custume, qui pro tempore fuerint, videlicet de hujusmodi 6d per diem a festo sancti Michaelis anno 21mo regis hujus *[29 Sept. 1442]* usque 19^m diem Februarii tunc proximum sequentem *[19 Feb. 1443]*, scilicet per 142 dies: 71s, per breve regis, quod est inter communia de anno 19no regis hujus termino Pasche rotulo 25to *[TNA: PRO, E159/217 Brevia directa baronibus Easter m 25]*, et litteras acquietancie ipsius Johannis de recepta.

Et eisdem collectoribus pro denariis per ipsos solutis Johanni Paunton et Thome Ponsford, quibus rex 19no die Februarii anno 21° *[19 Feb. 1443]* concessit[51] sex denarios per diem percipiendos pro termino vite sue et alterius eorum diucius viventis de parva custuma civitatis regis London' per manus collectorum, receptorum sive custumariorum ejusdem custume, videlicet de hujusmodi 6d per diem a predicto 19no die Februarii dicto anno 21mo *[19 Feb. 1443]* usque festum sancti Michaelis tunc proximum sequens *[29 Sept. 1443]*, per 222 dies: 111s per processum inde habitum et consideracionem baronum annotata in memorandis ex parte rememoratoris thesaurarii de anno 22do regis hujus, videlicet inter status et visus compotorum de termino sancti Michaelis rotulo 14mo *[TNA: PRO, E368/216 Visus et status compotorum Michaelmas m 14d]*, ac per breve regis irrotulatum in memorandis de anno 22do regis hujus termino Michaelis rotulo 3^cio, quod est inter communia de eodem anno *[TNA: PRO, E159/220 Brevia directa baronibus Michaelmas m 3d; No. S 8]*.

[a] predicto *repeated L, in error.*

---

[47] *CPR 1399-1401, p. 63 dated 12 Nov. 1399; confirmed by Henry V on 5 Nov. 1413 (CPR 1413-16, p. 135).*

[48] *CPR 1422-29, p. 46.*

[49] *CPR 1399-1401, p. 63 dated 12 Nov. 1399; confirmed by Henry V on 5 Nov. 1413 (CPR 1413-16, p. 135).*

[50] *CPR 1422-29, p. 46.*

[51] *CPR 1441-46, p. 164.*

TUNNAGE AND POUNDAGE PARTICULARS OF ACCOUNT 29. SEPT. 1445 BIS 29. SEPT. 1446 (IMPORTS TO 14 DEC. 1445)

Particulars of account of Richard Quatermayns *and Thomas* Walsyngham *for the issues of tunnage and poundage in London during the accounting period from 29 Sept. 1445 to 29 Sept. 1446*

L TNA: PRO, E122/203/3. Original particulars of account bound as a codex (quire structure XII^{24}; only the first gathering of 24 folios – containing the imports from 29 Sept. to 14 Dec. 1445 – has survived; contemporaneous numbering of the folios from f. 1 to f. 24 in Roman numerals in the upper right-hand corner of the recto side of the leaf; damage from damp from f. 7 onwards). Parchment. Unsealed (hole for seal visible in the upper left-hand corner of the recto side of the folios). The auditor has entered a dot (a) above each merchant's subsidy charge and (b) above each item in the summation of the issues of tunnage and poundage at the foot of each page.

f. 1^{r}
[Marginated] London'

Particule compoti Ricardi Quatermayns et Thome Walsyngham collectorum subsidii tonagii et pondagii tam de mercatoribus Anglicanis quam de alienigenis in portu civitatis London' et in singulis portubus et locis eidem portui adjacentibus, videlicet de hujusmodi subsidio regis ibidem a festo sancti Michaelis anno 24to regis nunc Henrici Sexti *[29 Sept. 1445]*, ante quod festum prefati collectores inde computarunt rotulo compotorum de subsidio,[1] usque festum sancti Michaelis extunc proximum sequens *[29 Sept. 1446]*, scilicet per unum annum integrum, per visum et testimonium Willelmi Beaufitz contrarotulatoris hujusmodi subsidii regis ibidem per idem tempus, a quo quidem festo sancti

---

[1] *Stuart Jenks (ed.), The Enrolled Customs Accounts (PRO, E356, E372, E364) 1279/80-1508/09 (1523/24) Volume 6: E356/15, E356/16 (List and Index Society) [in press], E356/16, No. 245.*

Michaelis anno 25to regis predicti *[29 Sept. 1446]* prefati Ricardus et Thomas collectores ibidem per visum et testimonium contrarotulatoris predicti sunt alias inde computaturi.

[1] De navi Poppe Gilesson ultimo die Septembris *[30 Sept. 1445]*

De Bartholomeo Stratton pro 2 doliis de wode. Precii £8 .... sb' 8s
De Roberto Stowe pro 200 hode salis de Berflete. Precii £12 .... sb' 12s
De eodem magistro pro 2000 pavyngstone magnis. Precii 26s 8d .... sb' 16d

[2] De navi Roberti Walssh eodem die *[30 Sept. 1445]*

De Johanne Sturgeone pro 4 lastis fungiarum. Precii £16 .... sb' 16s
De Thoma Steele pro 3 lastis fungiarum. Precii £12 .... sb' 12s
De Johanne Doland pro 6 lastis fungiarum. Precii £24 .... sb' 24s
De eodem magistro pro 3 lastis fungiarum. Precii £12 .... sb' 12s
De Johanne Seger pro 2 lastis fungiarum. Precii £8 .... sb' 8s
De Willelmo Floure pro 6 lastis fungiarum. Precii £24 .... sb' 24s
De Johanne Teynton pro 2 lastis fungiarum. Precii £8 .... sb' 8s
De Johanne Bolle pro 9 lastis fungiarum. Precii £36 .... sb' 36s
De Thoma Clarke pro 1100 fungiis. Precii £4 8s .... sb' 4s 5d
De Johanne Chirch pro 1 lasto fungiarum. Precii £4 .... sb' 4s
De Ricardo Holmehege pro 6 lastis, 700 fungiarum. Precii £26 16s . sb' 26s 10d

[3] De navi Clays Henryksson eodem die *[30 Sept. 1445]*

De eodem magistro pro 1000 pavyngstone magnis, 3 barellis sope, 3000 bunchis allei. Precii £12 3s 4d .... sb' 12s 2d
De Reynoldo van Gose pro 1000 bunchis allei. Precii £3 6s 8d .... sb' 3s 4d

[4] De navi Lambe van Passe eodem die *[30 Sept. 1445]*

De eodem magistro pro 1000 pavyngstone magnis. Precii 13s 4d .... sb' 8d
De Henrico Andrewesson pro 3500 bunchis alei. Precii £11 13s 4d ... sb' 11s 8d

<aa>Totalis valor hujus partis — £224 7s 4d — sb' £11 4s 5d<aa>

f. 1v

[5] De navi Cornelii[a] Thonysson eodem die *[30 Sept. 1445]*

De Thoma Martesson pro 15 skyve tasilles, 3500 bunchis alei. Precii £12 .... sb' 12s

[a] Cornelius *L, in error.*

<aa>-<aa> *Auditor's marginated entry: Sum of the issues on the page L.*

[6] De navi Gosse Petersson eodem die *[30 Sept. 1445]*

De Tonys Bitter pro 14 weighes salis de Berflete, 60 caboges. Precii £9 6s 8d .... sb' 9s 4d

De Johanne Negro pro 3 pipis cum pulvere pro [a]pellibus[a]. Precii £3 .... sb' 3s

[aa] *Entered in darker ink over* vermibus, *expunged L.*

[7] De navi Coppyn Lambe eodem die *[30 Sept. 1445]*

De Ricardo Burgh pro 2500 bunchis allei, 20 barellis ceparum, 1 pipa cum swannes fedirs. Precii £9 10s .... sb' 9s 6d

[8] De navi Clays Martynsson eodem die *[30 Sept. 1445]*

De eodem magistro pro 2 barellis salmonis salsi parve bonde. Precii 20s sb' 12d

De Ricardo Burgh pro 225 hodes salis de Berflete, 1000 pavyngtile. Precii £12 13s 4d .... sb' 12s 8d

[9] De navi Willelmi Johansson eodem die *[30 Sept. 1445]*

De Johanne Wykys pro 1000 bunchis allei, 1000 pavyngstone magnis. Precii £4 .... sb' 4s

De Petro Perysson pro 1 sacco cum hattys heer. Precii 13s 4d .... sb' 8d

De Johanne Waltersson pro 700 bunchis alei. Precii £3 .... sb' 3s

[10] De navi Saundre Stone eodem die *[30 Sept. 1445]*

De Willelmo de Lunys pro 400 lb. cere. Precii £6 13s 4d .... sb' 6s 8d

De Lowes Lodewyke pro 1 lasto lini. Precii £3 6s 8d .... sb' 3s 4d

De Henrico Logan pro 200 lb. cere, 400 alnis canvas. Precii £7 6s 8d .. sb' 7s 4d

De Johanne Grene pro 350 lb. cere. Precii £5 16s 8d .... sb' 5s 10d

<aa>Totalis valor mercandisarum, unde 12d de libra — £78 6s 8d sb' — 78s 4d<aa>

f. 2[r]

De Johanne Hynde pro 400 lb. cere. Precii £6 13s 4d .... sb' 6s 8d

De Thoma Crouche pro 1 lasto lini, 11 bundellis ferri. Precii £7 .... sb' 7s

De Willelmo Bodvyle pro 3 lastis lini, 3 lastis osmound, 3 lastis cinerum, 100 waynescott, ½ lasto weyke yerne. Precii £26 13s 4d .... sb' 26s 8d

De Thoma Segryme pro ½ lasto lini, 300 lb. cere. Precii £6 13s 4d ...... sb' 6s 8d

De Ricardo Perpoynte pro 3 lastis lini, 4 lastis cinerum, ½ lasto smolt. [Precii] £16 13s 4d .... sb' 16s 8d

De Ricardo Gardener pro 300 lb. cere. Precii £5 .... sb' 5s

De Thoma Mersch pro 2 lastis cinerum, 1 lasto lini, 250 waynescott, 1 lasto osmond, 1 parvo[a] strawe cere ponderante 200 lb., 1 bundello fili. [Precii] £14 .... sb' 14s

De Roberto Horne pro 1200 lb. cere. Precii £20 .... sb' 20s

De Simond Horne pro 4 lastis lini, 4 lastis osmond, 8 lastis cinerum, 1 lasto [et] 900 clapholt, 60 delys, 30 cogbordys, 2 strawes cere ponderantibus 600 [lb.]. [Precii] £44 .... sb' 44s
De Thoma Fulburne pro 2 lastis lini, 1 lasto ferri, 2 lastis osmound, 7 lastis cinerum, 300 lb. cere. Precii £28 6s 8d .... sb' 28s 4d
De Johanne Rough pro 2 lastis lini, 1 lasto osmound. Precii £10 13s 4d .... sb' 10s 8d
De Johanne Brampton pro 2 lastis osmound, 20 barellis cinerum, 15 bundellis ferri, 1 scok delys, 5 lastis lini, 25[b] cogbord. Precii £31 10s .... sb' 31s 6d
De Johanne Hervy pro ½ lasto lini. Precii 33s 4d .... sb' 20d
De Raufe Kemp pro 12 balis lini, 5 barellis picis. Precii 20s .... sb' 12d
De Willelmo Baldry pro 2 lastis lini. Precii £6 13s 4d .... sb' 6s 8d
De Johanne Martyn pro 6 barellis osmound, ½ lasto et [1] bala lini. Precii £3 6s 8d .... sb' 3s 4d
De Johanne Bromer pro 12 bundellis ferri. Precii £4 .... sb' 4s
De Roberto Bolington pro 7 lastis cinerum. Precii £4 13s 4d .... sb' 4s 8d
De Johanne Humberston pro 50 lb. cere, 100 lb. lini. Precii 20s .... sb' 12d
De Ricardo Lee pro 1 lasto lini. Precii £3 6s 8d .... sb' 3s 4d
De Roberto Stokker pro 300 lb. cere. Precii £5 .... sb' 5s
De Thoma Bradschawe pro 2 lastis taar. Precii 40s .... sb' 2s
De Willelmo Salman pro 6 barellis taar. Precii 10s .... sb' 6d

[a] parvum *L, in error.* [b] 1 quarterio *L.*

<aa>Totalis valor mercandisarum, unde 12d— £250 6s 8d— sb' £12 10s 4d<aa>

f. 2ᵛ

[11] De navi Bernte Laurensson eodem die *[30 Sept. 1445]*

De Johanne de Negro pro 1 pipa cum 12 dossenis cordeweyne. Precii £3 . sb' 3s
De Willelmo Colyn pro 8 vagis salis de Berflete. Precii £5 6s 8d .... sb' 5s 4d
De Jose Luce pro 4 vagis salis de Berflete. Precii 53s 4d .... sb' 2s 8d

[12] De navi Cornelii[a] Bollard eodem die *[30 Sept. 1445]*

De Willelmo Henryksson pro 100 hodes salis de Berflete, 1500 bunchis allei. Precii £12 .... sb' 12s

[a] Cornelius *L, in error.*

[13] De navi Alard Johansson eodem die *[30 Sept. 1445]*

De Reynoldo Derlington pro 200 barellis ceparum, 800 pavyngstone magnis, ½ lasto sope. Precii £9 13s 4d .... sb' 9s 8d
De Johanne Wykys pro 200 bunche alei. Precii 13s 4d .... sb' 8d
De Gerrardo Naykyn pro 2 parvis fedirbeddes. Precii 13s 4d .... sb' 8d

<aa>-<aa> *Auditor's marginated entry: Sum of the issues on the page L.*

De eodem magistro pro 200 crusis terre, 50 bunchis alei, 50 barellis ceparum. Precii 10s .... sb' 6d

[14] De navi Deryk Baysson eodem die *[30 Sept. 1445]*

De Lambe Johan Williamson pro 600 bunchis allei, 4 barellis ceparum. Precii 41s 8d .... sb' 2s 1d

De eodem magistro pro 500 bunchis alei. Precii 33s 4d .... sb' 20d

De Jacobbo Andreasson pro 500 bunchis alei. Precii 33s 4d .... sb' 20d

De Hugone Wyche pro 1 dolio, 3 pipis de wode [a]debili[a], 6 barellis sope. Precii £8 .... sb' 8s

[a-a] *Interlined L.*

[15] De navi Clays Ollardesson eodem die *[30 Sept. 1445]*

De Cornelio Johansson pro 2000 bunchis allei, 500 pavyngtile magnis, 3 dossenis parvorum baskettys vacuorum. Precii £10 3s 4d .... sb' 10s 2d

[16] De navi Johannis Blomard eodem die *[30 Sept. 1445]*

De Cornelio Danyellesson pro 1000 bunchis allei. Precii £3 6s 8d .... sb' 3s 4d

De Cornelio Johansson pro 600 bunchis allei, 7 skyve tasylles. Precii 43s 4d .... sb' 2s 2d

De Willelmo Corbett pro 1200 pavyngstone magnis, 300 bakstone. Precii 16s 8d .... sb' 10d

<aa>Totalis valor mercandisarum, unde 12d — £64 8s 4d sb' — 64s 7d<aa>

f. 3[r]

De Johanne Reynekyn pro 1000 bunchis allei. Precii £3 6s 8d .... sb' 3s 4d

De Petro Piersson pro 7 dossenis thrommes et felt hattys. Precii 46s 8d .... sb' 2s 4d

De Ricardo Burgh pro 600 bunchis allei. Precii 40s .... sb' 2s

De Johanne Letyn pro 10 dossenis thrommes et felt hattys. Precii £3 6s 8d .... sb' 3s 4d

De Adrean Matysson pro 150 werpes ollarum et patellarum terre. Precii 10s .... sb' 6d

De Clays Porter pro 100 alnis tele lini Brounswyke. Precii 40s .... sb' 2s

De Thoma Bemound pro 1000 bunchis allei. Precii £3 6s 8d .... sb' 3s 4d

[17] De navi Johannis Pryme eodem die *[30 Sept. 1445]*

De eodem magistro pro 400 bunchis ceparum, 26 barellis ceparum, 150 caboges. Precii 46s 8d .... sb' 2s 4d

De Thoma Edmound pro ½ lasto allecis albi, 1 quarterio piscium salsorum. Precii 46s 8d .... sb' 2s 4d

[18] De navi Johannis Carpentere eodem die *[30 Sept. 1445]*

De eodem magistro pro 1500 pavyngtile magnis, 3000 bunchis allei, 5 cupbordys, 40 skyve tasylles, 100 werpes ollarum et patellarum terre, 100 bere cruses, 1 cista cum ymaginibus de plaster. Precii £13 6s 8d............sb' 13s 4d

[19] De navi Petri Adreansson eodem die *[30 Sept. 1445]*

De Thoma Crips pro 4500 bunchis allei. Precii £15 ....sb' 15s

De eodem magistro pro 2000 pavyngtile magnis. Precii 26s 8d .... sb' 16d

De Cornelio Bytekowe pro 13 paribus galages, 20 alnis tele lini, 13 lb. lini, 21 dossenis redlasche et blake. Precii 46s 8d ....sb' 2s 4d

[20] De navi Lambe Fysker eodem die *[30 Sept. 1445]*

De eodem magistro pro 200 bunchis ceparum, 200 cabages. Precii 16s 8d .... sb' 10d

<aa>Totalis valor mercandisarum, unde 12d — £54 6s 8d sb' — 54s 4d<aa>

f. 3[v]

[21] De navi George Georgsson[a] eodem die *[30 Sept. 1445]*

De eodem magistro pro 6 caboges, 1000 bakstone. Precii 15s.................. sb' 9d

De Willelmo Hochekyns pro 6 saccis almundes, 1 bala aunes, 1 bala yryose, 2 saccis cottoni, 1 parva casa sugre, 1 ferdkyn coperose, 1 ferdkyn arsenek. Precii £16 13s 4d ....sb' 16s 8d

[a] *Corrected in L from* Georsson.

[22] De navi Willelmi Popeley eodem die *[30 Sept. 1445]*

De dicto magistro pro 600 alnis canvas, 14 doliis ponderis petre de Caen. Precii £8 10s..sb' 8s 6d

De Peryn Russell pro 6 dossenis cordewyn, 1200 lb. de fune. Precii £5 6s 8d ....sb' 5s 4d

De Johanne Harpour pro 12 gladiis, 10 axes, 3 salettes, 3 fedirbeddes, 3 bolsters, 20 peires linthiaminum veterum. Precii £4....................................sb' 4s

De Symond Duraunt pro 700 ulnis canvas rupti. Precii £7 ....sb' 7s

De magistro Ricardo de la Toure pro 400 alnis canvas. Precii £4..............sb' 4s

[23] De navi Janyn Gelowe eodem die *[30 Sept. 1445]*

De Johanne Sharp pro 4 haberiouns, 1 parva baga cum 20 lb. croci. Precii £8 ....sb' 8s

<aa>-<aa> *Auditor's marginated entry: Sum of the issues on the page L.*

[24] De navi Myn Jon de la Masse eodem die *[30 Sept. 1445]*

De Micaew de Suharre pro 1 barello cum 10,000 clavis, 13 doliis ponderis ferri. Precii £34 3s 4d .... sb' 34s 2d
De Martyno de Ratteso pro 12 balis licorys, 13 doliis ponderis ferri. Precii £34 10s .... sb' 34s 6d
De Martyno Simean pro 8 doliis ponderis ferri, 1 barello cum 10,000 clavis. Precii £21 13s 4d .... sb' 21s 8d
De Janycott de Micaewe pro 4 doliis ponderis ferri. Precii £10 .... sb' 10s
De Micaew de la Hubeagne pro 5 doliis ponderis ferri. Precii £12 10s .... sb' 12s 6d
De Janycott de la Masse pro 3 doliis ponderis ferri. Precii £7 10s .... sb' 7s 6d
De dicto magistro pro 5 doliis ponderis ferri. Precii £12 10s .... sb' 12s 6d

[25] De navi Myn Janyn de Rattesoo eodem die *[30 Sept. 1445]*

De Sabaoth de la Hubeagne pro 56 doliis ponderis ferri. Precii £141 13s 4d .... sb' £7 20d

<aa>Totalis valor mercandisarum, unde 12d — £328 15s sb' — £16 8s 9d<aa>

f. 4^{r}

De Stephano de Solohagne pro 6 doliis, 3 hoggeshedes ponderis ferri, 1 dolio rosyn. Precii £18 10d .... sb' 18s ½d
De Johanne Smyth pro 9 doliis ponderis ferri. Precii £22 10s .... sb' 22s 6d
De Willelmo Roger pro 4 doliis ponderis ferri. Precii £10 .... sb' 10s

[26] De navi Johannis Hoberde primo die Octobris *[1 Oct. 1445]*

De eodem magistro pro 2 pipis pomorum, 1 hoggeshede pirorum. Precii 10s .... sb' 6d

[27] De navi Johannis Harlebek eodem die *[1 Oct. 1445]*

De eodem magistro pro 200 bunchis ceparum, 250 caboges. Precii 13s 4d .... sb' 8d
De Willelmo Johansson pro 1 lasto rape olei. Precii £8 .... sb' 8s
De dicto magistro pro 1 laste rape olei. Precii £8 .... sb' 8s

[28] De navi Arnoldi Petirsson 7° die Octobris *[7 Oct. 1445]*

De Ricardo Burgh pro 226 barellis ceparum. Precii £5 13s [a]4d[a] .... sb' 5s 8d

De eodem magistro pro 7000 pavyngstone, 10,000 breke, 50 werpes ollarum terre. Precii £5 10s .... sb' 5s 6d

De Johanne Lewys pro 2500 bunchis allei. Precii £8 6s 8d .... sb' 8s 4d

[a–a] *Interlined L.*

[29] De navi Clays Martynsson eodem die *[7 Oct. 1445]*

De Johanne Malter pro 200 barellis ceparum, 2000 pavyngtile. Precii £6 6s 8d .... sb' 6s 4d

De Courte Spyce pro[a] 2 parvis barellis, 1 parvo fardello cum 10 peciis bultelli, 20 lb. bristylles, 10 somes patyn nailles. Precii £5 .... sb' 5s

De Hugone Johanesson pro 10 parvis mantellis squerelle, 6 bundellis pellium agnellorum nigrorum, 10 paribus[b] peciarum de dorso fechuuz, 2 peper poyntis. Precii 46s 8d .... sb' 2s 4d

[a] cum *L, in error.* [b] parium *L, in error.*

[30] De navi Ilbrand van the Wold eodem die *[7 Oct. 1445]*

De Roberto Broke pro 600 lb. cere. Precii £10 .... sb' 10s

<aa>Totalis valor mercandisarum, unde 12d — £110 17s 6d sb' — 110s 10½d<aa>

f. 4[v]

De Thoma Fulburne pro 300 lb. cere, 4000 ruskyn. Precii £14 13s 4d sb' 14s 8d

De Johanne Felde pro 300 lb. cere. Precii £5 .... sb' 5s

De Willelmo Hyche pro 1 lasto osmond, ½ lasto parvorum barellorum smolte. Precii £7 .... sb' 7s

De Johanne Deken pro 400 lb. cere. Precii £6 13s 4d .... sb' 6s 8d

De Thoma Beverley pro 400 lb. cere, 2000 ruskyn. Precii £9 13s 4d.... sb' 9s 8d

[31] De navi Clays Gileman 9° die Octobris *[9 Oct. 1445]*

De Waryn Turpyn pro 200 parvis felt hattes debilibus. Precii 46s 8d.... sb' 2s 4d

De Johanne Brodde pro 32 dossenis rough hattes, 23 dossenis pannorum depictorum et diverso haberdashe. Precii £10 .... sb' 10s

De James Beaugraunt pro 1 bundello gladiorum, 3 dossenis rough hattes, 200 lb. packthrede. Precii 53s 4d .... sb' 2s 8d

De Johanne Malter pro 5 dimidiis barellis plate, 3 dossenis silver skynnes, 200 barellis ceparum. Precii £8 10s .... sb' 8s 6d

De Johanne Malvern pro 3 bundellis et 1 corffe cum brusshes. Precii 26s 8d .... sb' 16d

De Simond Kente pro 780 alnis tele lini crude, 450 alnis tele Brounswyke, 8 peciis bokerams et diversis mercandisis. Precii £20 .... sb' 20s

<aa>-<aa> *Auditor's marginated entry: Sum of the issues on the page L.*

[32] De navi Cornelii[a] Johansson eodem die *[9 Oct. 1445]*

De eodem magistro pro 50 barellis ceparum, 2½ barellis allecis albi, 1 barello sope, 2 dimidiis barellis samonis, 50 bunchis allei, 50 ollis et patellis terre. Precii £3 6s 8d .... sb' 3s 4d

[a] Cornelius *L, in error.*

[33] De navi Coppyn Lambe 14° die Octobris *[14 Oct. 1445]*

De Willelmo Lynsey pro 150 barellis ceparum. Precii £3 15s .... sb' 3s 9d

De Roberto Kente pro 2 barellis sope, 4 dossenis cardys, 1 dossena patens. Precii £3 .... sb' 3s

De Johanne Swetelove pro 425 alnis tele lini crude, 2 dossenis napri, 200 alnis tele pikeling. Precii £10 13s 4d .... sb' 10s 8d

De Willelmo Hatter pro 53 skyve tasylles, 25 puntellis wolde, 1 pipa swannes fethirs, 1 hoggeshede bristilles. Precii £4 18s 4d .... sb' 4s 11d

<aa>Totalis valor mercandisarum, unde 12d — £113 10s sb' — 113s 6d<aa>

f. 5r

De Clement Arbery pro 250 alnis tele lini. Precii £6 13s 4d .... sb' 6s 8d

De Hugh Gerrardesson pro 13 dossenis parvorum baskettorum vacuorum, 1 bundello roddes. Precii 13s 4d .... sb' 8d

De Johanne Baroughe pro 4 dossenis chapelettes, 4 dossenis quysson clothes, 1 gros sholaces et diverso haberdashe. Precii 46s 8d .... sb' 2s 4d

De Willelmo Mayne pro 6 barellis sope, 5 dossenis rough hattys. Precii £5 10s .... sb' 5s 6d

De Thoma Catesby pro 2398 alnis canvas, 1370 alnis tele spenall. Precii £33 6s 8d .... sb' 33s 4d

De Baudewyn van Spenall pro 400 lb. Burgoyne fili. Precii £5 .... sb' 5s

[34] De navi Johannis Osgarde 27° die Octobris *[27 Oct. 1445]*

De eodem magistro pro 350 bunchis ceparum, 200 caboges. Precii 20s.. sb' 12d

De Thoma Segrym pro 8 barellis olei, 6 barellis allecis albi. Precii £7 6s 8d .... sb' 7s 4d

De Willelmo Braybroke pro 6 barellis allecis albi. Precii 40s .... sb' 2s

De Thoma Edmound pro 6 barellis allecis albi. Precii 40s .... sb' 2s

[35] De navi Clays Rogersson eodem die *[27 Oct. 1445]*

De eodem magistro pro 80 bunchis alei debilis. Precii 3s 4d .... sb' 2d

[36] De navi Ricardi Walsh 30° die Octobris *[30 Oct. 1445]*

De Henrico Drapour pro 15 barellis olei, 2 parvis barellis anguillarum salsarum, 50 bunchis ceparum. Precii £10 13s 4d .... sb' 10s 8d

De Thoma Cokkyshede pro 23 barellis allecis albi. Precii £7 13s 4d .... sb' 7s 8d

De Johanne Bolle pro 6 barellis olei. Precii £4 .... sb' 4s

De Henrico Hofstade pro 4 dossenis pawteners, 12 dyker cultellorum, 3 dossenis rasours, 2 dossenis mirrours, 7 gros bolions de latone pro bursis, 3 dossenis pair serotecarum, 3 dossenis pair tabillarum. Precii £5 .... sb' 5s

[37] De navi Nicholai Page eodem die*[30 Oct. 1445]*

De eodem magistro pro 500 caboges. Precii 10s.. sb' 6d

<aa>Totalis valor mercandisarum, unde 12d — £93 16s 8d sb' — £4 13s 10d<aa>

f. 5^{v}

[38] De navi Johannis Herte 3° die Novembris *[3 Nov. 1445]*

De Ricardo Chaundeler pro 16 barellis allecis albi. Precii £5 6s 8d ...... sb' 5s 4d

De Thoma Gosselyn pro 2 lastis, 4 barellis allecis albi. Precii £9 6s 8d sb' 9s 4d

[39] De navi Johannis Tymeott eodem die *[3 Nov. 1445]*

De eodem magistro pro 12 barellis ceparum, 20 caboges. Precii 6s 8d ..... sb' 4d

De Johanne Malvern pro 9 gros lasyng poyntes, 12 dossenis quysson clothes et diverso haberdashe. Precii £3 .... sb' 3s

De Austyn Stratton pro 2 dossenis [et] 10 lb. fili Outenard, 200 alnis tele lini Busk crude, 4 dossenis quysson clothes et diversis mercandisis. Precii £8 10s .... sb' 8s 6d

De Bartholomeo Stratton pro 2175 alnis tele lini Busk, 3879 alnis tele Flandrie crude et albe, 4 dimidiis peciis bultelli, 16 vasis wode et diversis mercandisis. Precii £133.. sb' £6 13s

De Ricardo Mody pro 12 barellis ceparum, 40 bunchis allei. Precii 8s 4d sb' 5d

De Willelmo Hatter pro 1 pipa cum fedirs, 200 alnis canvas, 300 alnis tele spenall, 6 dossenis [lb.] cottone fili. Precii £7 13s 4d........................ sb' 7s 8d

De Roberto Tilbury pro 25 barellis ceparum. Precii 12s 6d.................... sb' 7½d

[40] De navi Willelmi Johansson eodem die *[3 Nov. 1445]*

De Thoma Dey pro 4 postis bokerams, 6 peciis bultelli, 3 peciis bustian, 600 parti gold, 1000 sylver et diversis mercandisis. Precii £10.................... sb' 10s

De James Beaugraunt pro 90 petris wire. Precii £6 10s .... sb' 6s 6d

<aa>-<aa> *Auditor's marginated entry: Sum of the issues on the page L.*

De Johanne Brodde pro 1 fedirbed, 1 bolster, 6 pelowes, 3 beddys et diverso haberdasche. Precii 53s 4d .... sb' 2s 8d

De Johanne Malvern pro 12 dossenis forcers. Precii 40s .... sb' 2s

De Edmundo Galwey pro 3 balis cours mader. Precii £6 .... sb' 6s

De Alano Corbett pro 4 dossenis, 8 sadilles, 2 quyltis. Precii £10 .... sb' 10s

De Thoma Osterich pro 2000 ballys, 8 dossenis felt hattys. Precii £4 6s 8d .... sb' 4s 4d

De Gerrardo Johansson pro 3 barellis kyve eelles. Precii 40s .... sb' 2s

De Dankard Johansson pro 4 hodes hoppes, 40 dossenis felt hattes, 24 pannes ferri. Precii £11 16s 8d .... sb' 11s 10d

De Gyles Brayneford pro 6 paper poyntes, 4 gros lasyng poyntes, 36 dyker cultellorum, 150 alnis tele Brabancie. Precii £5 10s .... sb' 5s 6d

<aa>Totalis valor mercandisarum, unde 12d — £229 10d sb' — £11 9s ½d<aa>

f. 6^{r}

De Otte van Dorne pro 6 papir poyntes, 4 gros lasyng poyntes, 36 dyker cultellorum et diverso haberdashe. Precii £3 .... sb' 3s

De Arnoldo van Langefeld pro ½ lasto mede. Precii 13s 4d .... sb' 8d

De Nicholao Giles pro 3 peciis sateyn ynde, 1 pecia sateyn crymsyn continente 2½ pecias, 1 pecia sateyn v[i]ridis continente 2 pecias, 1 pecia sigelante. Precii £16 .... sb' 16s

De Willelmo Roke pro 1 barello, 1 fardello, 1 parvo fardello cum 6 fedirbeddes et diverso haberdashe. Precii £3 6s 8d .... sb' 3s 4d

[41] De navi Poppe Gylesson eodem die *[3 Nov. 1445]*

De Bartholomeo Stratton pro 13 remes papir spendabilis, 6 dossenis linthiaminum veterum, 300 alnis tele lini spenall. Precii £7 .... sb' 7s

De Johanne Malvern pro 18 gros glases, 15 dossenis rough hattys, 2000 ballys et diverso haberdashe. Precii £12 .... sb' 12s

De Thoma Osteryche pro 1 bundello brusches, 2 mandis forcers. Precii £3 20d .... sb' 3s 1d

De Thoma Berrard pro 8 dossenis rough hattys. Precii 53s 4d .... sb' 2s 8d

De James Beaugraunt pro 3 barellis sope, 1 bala mader, 83 skyve tasilles. Precii £5 13s 4d .... sb' 5s 8d

De Henrico Frowyk pro 415 alnis tele Westfale, 650 alnis tele crude, 474 alnis tele Henaud, 376 alnis tele lini Flandrie albe. Precii £24 .... sb' 24s

De Johanne Lok pro 7½ peciis bultelli, 600 alnis tele werkyn et diversis mercandisis. Precii £8 13s 4d .... sb' 8s 8d

De Johanne Penne pro 32 remes papir spendabilis, 200 alnis tele Niperfeld. Precii £3 6s 8d .... sb' 3s 4d

De Willelmo Hatter pro 300 alnis tele werkyn, 308 alnis tele lini crude. Precii £5 8s 4d .... sb' 5s 5d

De Willelmo Salkeld pro 1650 alnis [a]Pruse[a] canvas, 800 lb. pakfili. Precii £18 .... sb' 18s
De Johanne Stokdon pro 300 alnis tele lini werkyn, 2 dossenis bankers, 200 alnis tele lini Sultwyche et diversis mercandisis. Precii £8 20d.......... sb' 8s 1d
De Willelmo Gronde pro 6 peciis bokerams curtorum, 60 lb. bedys de ossibus et diverso haberdasche. Precii £4 16s 8d .... sb' 4s 10d
De Johanne Bastewyke pro 1 fedirbed, 1 bolster, 2 pelowes, 2 doseyn quysson clothes. Precii 40s .... sb' 2s
De Petro Piersson pro 3 doseyn felt hattys. Precii 20s .... sb' 12d
De Thoma Niche pro 350 alnis tele Niperfeld, 17 dossenis quysson clothes, 17 peciis bultelli et diversis mercandisis. Precii £12 10s.......... sb' 12s 6d
De Alberto Wynter pro 1 barello bristilles. Precii 53s 4d .... sb' 2s 8d

<aa>Totalis valor mercandisarum, unde 12d — [b]£143 18s 4d sb' — £7 3s 11d[b]•<aa>

f. 6[v]

De eodem magistro pro 1000 pavyngtile magnis, 25 skyve tasylles, 100 werpes ollarum et patellarum terre. Precii 33s 4d .... sb' 20d
De Johanne Olney pro 1000 alnis tele lini crude, 715 alnis tele Henaud, 2 peciis umple. Precii £33 6s 8d .... sb' 33s 4d
De Roberto Stowe pro 1000 pavingstone magnis. Precii 13s 4d.......... sb' 8d
De Johanne Midelton pro 912 alnis tele lini Sultwyche, 422 alnis tele Busk. Precii £13 6s 8d .... sb' 13s 4d
De Johanne Sencle pro 3015 gros glases, 300 boxes, 6 dossenis forcers. Precii £5 .... sb' 5s
De Arnoldo Henriksson pro [c]40 dossenis glasis, 12 grose sholasis, 12 dossenis hamers, 3 dossenis felt hattes et diverso haberdashe. Precii £6 .... sb' 6s[c]

[a-a] *Interlined L.* [b-b] *Interlined above* £143 18s 4d — sb' £4 3s 11d, *written over erasure and struck through L..* [c-c] *Entered by a different hand in darker ink L.*

[42] De navi Petri Piersson eodem die *[3 Nov. 1445]*

De eodem magistro pro 200 barellis ceparum, 200 caboges, 1½ lastis allecis albi, 60 lb. lini. Precii £11 10s .... sb' 11s 6d

[43] De navi Johannis Cole eodem die *[3 Nov. 1445]*

De eodem magistro pro 2000 pavyngtile, 1 barello salmonis salsi. Precii 33s 4d .... sb' 20d
De Willelmo Rooke pro 1 barello, 2 kilderkyns allecis albi, 2 dimidiis barellis, 4 ferdkyns, 2 eytyndelles anguillarum salsarum. Precii 53s 4d .... sb' 2s 8d
De Lambe van Passe pro 80 pontellis wolde. Precii 40s .... sb' 2s
De Leonardo van Brussell pro 12 dossenis throme hattys et felt, 200 cruses, 30 fase vitri. Precii £6 3s 4d .... sb' 6s 2d

<aa>-<aa> *Auditor's marginated entry: Sum of the issues on the page L.*

De Willelmo Halle pro 6 barellis olei, 500 lb. canebis, 35 skyve tasilles. Precii £8 6s 8d........ sb' 8s 4d

De Henrico van Ofstade pro 4 dossenis parvarum ymaginum, 3 mark sherys, 2 dossenis salettes, 20 alnis tele lini, 3 dossenis parvorum pannorum depictorum. Precii £5........ sb' 5s

De Matys van Arnebury pro 10 dossenis shepys bellys, 24 lb. countours, 1 gros sporis et diverso haberdasche. Precii £4........ sb' 4s

De Ricardo Williamson pro 100 lb. hattheer, 6 lb. jete bedys, 3 gros lokkes, 18 dossenis cultellorum et diverso haberdashe. Precii £3 10s........ sb' 3s 6d

De Otte van Dorne pro 1 gros compas, 3 gros sholacys, 2 gros sporis, 300 pectinibus ligni et diverso haberdashe. Precii £3........ sb' 3s

De Johanne Wynter pro 80 alnis tele lini, 2 fedirbeddes. Precii 40s........ sb' 2s

<aa>Totalis valor mercandisarum, unde 12d — £109 16s 8d sb' — 109s 10d[a]•<aa>

f. 7r

De Reynoldo Crokbaker pro 4 baskettes cum crusis terre, 4 dossenis parvorum felt hattys, 100 lb. plumarum, 3 ketilles. Precii 53s 4d........ sb' 2s 8d

De predicto magistro pro 6 barellis calcis nigre. Precii 6s 8d........ sb' 4d

[a] 109s 10d *entered a second time at the bottom of the page by a different hand L.*

[44] De navi Lambe van Passe eodem die *[3 Nov. 1445]*

De eodem magistro pro 1000 pavingtile magnis. Precii 13s 4d........ sb' 8d

De Thoma Catesby pro 1100 alnis canvas debilis. Precii £9 6s 8d........ sb' 9s 4d

De Bartholomeo Leyke pro 400 hoppes, 9 dossenis baskettorum vacuorum, 1000 patyntrees, 9 Yperlinges debilibus. Precii 33s 4d........ sb' 20d

De Petro Piersson pro 200 lb. hatteheer. Precii 13s 4d........ sb' 8d

De Johanne Henryksson pro 1 almery, 1 longe setyll, 3 dossenis shovylles, 3 polaxes. Precii 26s 8d........ sb' 16d

De Leonardo van Brussell pro 18 dossenis thrommes et felt hattys. Precii £5........ sb' 5s

De Dankard Johanssone pro 4 hodes hoppes, 600 lb. canebis, 300 alnis tele lini crude, 46 dossenis zonarum de coreo, 29 gros lasyng poyntes, 2000 pynnys et diverso haberdasche. Precii £14 16s 8d........ sb' 14s 10d

De Willelmo Halle pro ½ lasto olei, 500 lb. canebis. Precii £7 6s 8d........ sb' 7s 4d

De Giles Brayneford pro 2 dossenis sarrarum, 15 skyve tasylles, 100 lb. plumarum, 100 alnis canvas, 3 dossenis gyrdylles de coreo, 5 lb. pakfili, 1 dossena felt hattys. Precii £3 10s........ sb' 3s 6d

De Otte van Dorne pro 1 gros gymelottys, 600 floytys, 1 gros perser yrenes, 1 gros file yrenes et diverso haberdashe. Precii £3........ sb' 3s

De Ricardo Williamson pro 1 reme paper depicti, 100 heer brusshes, 6 papir poyntes, 16 gros lasyng poyntes et diverso haberdashe. Precii £3 .... sb' 3s
De Matys van Arnebury pro[a] 80 mark sherys, 6 lb. jete bedys, 10 dossenis lokkes et diverso haberdashe. Precii £5 .... sb' 5s
De Johanne de Pyna pro 1 parvo fatte vini de Reyna .... sb' 18d
De Thoma Pynde pro 6 barellis sope, 400 lb. canebis, 300 pottes terre. Precii £7 3s 4d .... sb' 7s 2d
De Willelmo Segard pro 12 dossenis rough hattys. Precii £3 6s 8d .... sb' 3s 4d

[a] cum *L, in error.*

[45] De navi Johannis Parker 4[to] die Novembris *[4 Nov. 1445]*

De Johanne Bocher pro 5 lastis allecis albi. Precii £20 .... sb' 20s

<aa>Totalis valor mercandisarum, unde 12d — £88 16s 8d sb' — £4 8s 10d
Vinum — 1 fatte vini de Reyna sb' — 18d
[Totalis] £4 10s 4d<aa>

f. 7[v]

[46] De navi Willelmi Osey eodem die *[4 Nov. 1445]*

De Johanne Wellys pro 30 barellis allecis albi. Precii £10 .... sb' 10s
De Johanne Malvern pro 3 lastis allecis albi. Precii £12 .... sb' 12s

[47] De navi Gerrardi Masson eodem die *[4 Nov. 1445]*

De eodem magistro pro 800 beer cruses, 2 quernestones, 2 barellis samonis debilis, 2 hodes hoppes. Precii 46s 8d .... sb' 2s 4d
Et pro 500 parvis crusis. Precii 13s 4d .... sb' 8d

[48] De navi Petri Bischopp eodem die *[4 Nov. 1445]*

De Nicholao Heyman pro 1 lasto allecis albi. Precii £4 .... sb' 4s
De Edmundo Mellysson pro 48 alnis tele lini. Precii 16s 8d .... sb' 10d
De Matheo Fowcher pro 50 skyve tasylles. Precii 25s .... sb' 15d
De Roberto Stone pro 5 laste allecis albi. Precii £20 .... sb' 20s
De Thoma Dey pro 2 lastis allecis. Precii £8 .... sb' 8s
De Johanne Dey pro 2 balis cours mader. Precii £4 .... sb' 4s
De Johanne Brodde pro 2 balis mader. Precii £4 .... sb' 4s

[49] De navi Johannis Wattys eodem die *[4 Nov. 1445]*

De Johanne Boccher pro [a]5[a] lastis, 2 barellis [allecis albi]. Precii £20 ...... sb' 20s

[a-a] *Interlined above* 4, *struck through L.*

<aa>-<aa> *Auditor's marginated entry: Sum of the issues on the page L.*

[50] De navi Johannis Gerrardesson 8° die Novembris *[8 Nov. 1445]*

De Henrico Williamsson pro 100 barellis ceparum, 32 skyve tasylles, 2000 bunchis allei, 3 barellis olei. Precii £10 6s 8d................................sb' 10s 4d

[51] De navi Petri Hughsson eodem die *[8 Nov. 1445]*

De Willelmo Salkeld pro 2000 pavyngtile, 250 pontellis wolde, 8 barellis salmonis salsi parve bonde. Precii £10 6s 8d....................................sb' 10s 4d

<aa>Totalis valor mercandisarum, unde 12d — £107 15s sb' — 107s 9d<aa>

f. 8r

[52] De navi Coppyn Puryman 8° die Novembris *[8 Nov. 1445]*

De Simone Marschall pro 275 [a]lb.[a] cotoni, 100 lb. aunes. Precii £6 13s 4d sb' 6s 8d

De Willelmo Salkeld pro 2 barellis samonis salsi parve bonde, 1600 lb. rosyn, 1400 alnis tele lini, 120 alnis tele Holandie, 5 mantellis boge. Precii £21 13s 4d..sb' 21s 8d

De Johanne Adams pro 2750 ballys et 1 Yperling. Precii 40s...................sb' 2s

De Johanne Brodde pro 2 balis cours mader. Precii £4.............................sb' 4s

De Rogero Midelmore pro 850 alnis tele crude, 400 alnis tele Henaud et diversis mercandisis. Precii £18...sb' 18s

De Roberto Damyan pro 6 peciis Burgoyne canvas, 4 peciis ravelli, 6 peciis tele lini werkyn et diverso haberdashe. Precii £6 13s 4d...................sb' 6s 8d

De Waryn Turpyn pro 1 barello clavorum, 4 dossenis hattys. Precii £3 13s 4d ....sb' 3s 8d

De Ricardo Stowe pro 100 skyve tasylles, 1000 pavyngtile. Precii 53s 4d. sb' 2s 8d

De Willelmo Milrede pro 350 alnis tele lini Sultwyche, 850 alnis tele Busk. Precii £11 13s 4d...sb' 11s 8d

De Johanne Harough pro 850 alnis tele lini Busk. Precii £7 10s...........sb' 7s 6d

De James Beaugraunt pro 1 casa pectinum ligni, 4 dossenis quysson clothes et diverso haberdasche. Precii £3 15s..sb' 3s 9d

De Willelmo Haxey pro 300 alnis tele Niperfeld, 300 lb. canebis, 4 dossenis lb. fili spenall. Precii £6 13s 4d...sb' 6s 8d

De Johanne Smyth pro 6 dossenis quysson clothes, 4 dossenis pannorum depictorum. Precii 40s...sb' 2s

De Austyn Stratton pro 250 alnis tele werkyn, 300 alnis tele lini Flandrie crude et diversis mercandisis. Precii £8 10s..sb' 8s 6d

De Hugone Wyche pro 227 alnis tele Brounswyke, 305 alnis tele lini Westfale. Precii £4 20d .... sb' 4s 1d
De Alexandro Orabill pro 250 alnis tele Guttynges, 1900 alnis tele Brounswyke. Precii £18 10s .... sb' 18s 6d
De Thoma Nyche pro 375 alnis tele lini Henaud, 731 alnis tele lini bolte, 450 alnis tele lini Busk stricte. Precii £15 15s .... sb' 15s 9d
De Johanne Litilton pro 450 alnis tele lini Sultwyche, 12 peciis bokerams curtorum et diversis mercandisis. Precii £9 .... sb' 9s
De Willelmo Hatter pro 27,000 swannes fedirs, 500 lb. canebis, 4 dossenis throme hattys. Precii £8 10s .... sb' 8s 6d
De Johanne Midelton pro 125 alnis tele Sultwyche, 12 doseynes sporys, 2 peciis bultelli. Precii £3 10s .... sb' 3s 6d
De Thoma Steele pro 950 alnis tele lini Guttynges, 630 alnis tele lini Busk, 700 alnis tele Niperfeld et diversis mercandisis. Precii £28 10s .... sb' 28s 6d
De Johanne Malvern pro 2 gros sporis, 6 dossenis stoklokkes, 6 gros cultellorum et diverso haberdasche. Precii £10 .... sb' 10s

<aa>Totalis valor mercandisarum, unde 12d — £203 5s sb' — £10 3s 3d<aa>

f. 8^{v}

De Ricardo Ryche pro 3 peciis bustian, 6 papers laune, 3 peciis umple et diversis mercandisis. Precii £18 10s .... sb' 18s 6d
De Willelmo Stevenes pro 54 remes papir, 100 lb. canebis, 700,000 alle yrenes et diverso haberdashe. Precii £7 6s 8d .... sb' 7s 4d
De Thoma Dugmanton pro 1120 alnis tele lini Busk. Precii £12 3s 4d .... sb' 12s 2d
De Roberto Drop pro [a]3[a] fedirbeddes, 3 bolsters veteribus. Precii 40s .... sb' 2s
De Radulpho Verney pro 250 alnis tele lini Brissyll, 46 alnis tele lini Holandie, 8 Iperlinges. Precii £4 8s 4d .... sb' 4s 5d
De Johanne Norlonge pro 16 remes paper spendabilis, 650 alnis tele lini Brounswyke, 2 dossenis hattys et diversis mercandisis. Precii £13 6s 8d .... sb' 13s 4d
De Thoma Berrade pro 60 lb. fili Burgoyn, 3 remes papir, 4 peciis ravelli. Precii 46s 8d .... sb' 2s 4d
De Willelmo Fynche pro 30 lb. jete [a]bedes[a], 3000 spangelles et diverso haberdashe. Precii £6 13s 4d .... sb' 6s 8d
De Henrico Massyngham pro 10 dimidiis peciis fustian, 1 dossena lb. fili Outenard. Precii £3 .... sb' 3s
De Thoma Dey pro 3 lastis allecis albi. Precii £12 .... sb' 12s
De Henrico Hode pro 1 parvo fardello cum 4 dossenis felt hattys. Precii 26s 8d .... sb' 16d

[a-a] *Interlined L.*

<aa>-<aa> *Auditor's marginated entry: Sum of the issues on the page L.*

[53] De navi Johannis Colwyll eodem die *[8 Nov. 1445]*

De Willelmo Haxey pro 450 alnis tele casedoke, 426 alnis tele lini Henaud, 12 remes papir spendabilis, 8 dossenis quysson clothes. Precii £8 6s 8d sb' 8s 4d

De Johanne Adams pro 280 alnis tele lini Flandrie crude, 450 alnis tele lini Sultwyche, 2 dossenis pannorum depictorum et diversis mercandisis. Precii £13 19s 2d........ sb' 14s

De Hugone Wyche pro 2 dossenis, 9 lb. fili, 350 alnis tele Brounswyke, 402 alnis tele lini Westfale stricte. Precii £8 15s........ sb' 8s 9d

De Roberto Baron pro 360 alnis tele lini Sultwyche, 8 coverlites Flandrie et diversis mercandisis. Precii £9 10s........ sb' 9s 6d

De Johanne Grene pro 6 dossenis hattys, 10 remes papir, 40 alnis tele lini werkyn. Precii £3 6s 8d........ sb' 3s 4d

De Johanne Litilton pro 170 alnis tele Sultwyche, 500 alnis tele Flandrie albe, 10 dossenis bankers, 9 parvis coverlites. Precii £13 6s 8d........ sb' 13s 4d

De Thoma Nyche pro 96 remes papir spendabilis, 124 alnis tele Westfale crude. Precii £5 8s 4d........ sb' 5s 5d

De Johanne Okehirste pro 3 balis cours mader. Precii £6........ sb' 6s

De Thoma Hawkyns pro 8 balettis almundes, 3 balettis aunes, 1 balet comyn, 600 lb. canebis. Precii £20........ sb' 20s

<aa>Totalis valor mercandisarum, unde 12d — £171 14s 2d sb' — £8 11s 9d<aa>

f. 9r

De Johanne Roo pro 500 alnis tele Niperfeld, 450 alnis tele lini Busk crude, 200 alnis tele lini Shoton'. Precii £12........ sb' 12s

De Thoma Steele pro 450 alnis tele lini Henaud, 12 peciis bokerams longe, 6 peciis borde alisaundre et diversis mercandisis. Precii £18 16s 8d. sb' 18s 10d

De Agnete Rooke pro 4 beddys, 13 peciis ravelli, 12 dossenis quysson clothes et diverso haberdasche. Precii £10 10s........ sb' 10s 6d

De Willelmo Stevenes pro 22 dossenis sporis, 36 lb. canebis. Precii £3 13s 4d........ sb' 3s 8d[a]

De Thoma Dugmanton pro 300 alnis tele Niperfeld, 600 alnis tele lini Flandrie crude, 500 alnis tele Henaud et diversis mercandisis. Precii £16 18s 4d........ sb' 16s 11d

De Austyn Stratton pro 100 remes papir spendabilis, 600 alnis tele lini Sultwyche et diversis mercandisis. Precii £11 3s 4d........ sb' 11s 2d

De Thoma Filer pro 700 alnis tele lini stricte, 200 alnis tele lini Henaud. Precii £16 6s 8d........ sb' 16s 4d

De Johanne Stokdon pro 8 dimidiis peciis bultelli, 500 alnis tele lini Sultwyche, 211 alnis tele lini Henaud, 15 remes papir, 300 alnis canvas albi. Precii £13 8s 4d........ sb' 13s 5d

De Raufe Verney pro 800 alnis canvas Barras, 200 alnis tele Niperfeld, 2 lb. fili albi. Precii £7 3s 4d........ sb' 7s 2d

De Johanne Harough pro 6 barellis sope. Precii £4.................................... sb' 4s

[a] *Corrected in L from* 7d.

[54] De navi Johannis Hayburne eodem die *[8 Nov. 1445]*

De Willelmo Milrede pro 250 alnis tele lini Sultwyche, 280 alnis tele lini Flandrie crude, 550 alnis tele lini Busk. Precii £12 6s 8d................. sb' 12s 4d

De Johanne Harough pro 450 alnis tele lini Guttynges, 1250 alnis tele Flandrie crude, 12 peciis bulter et diversis mercandisis. Precii £23 10s......... sb' 23s 6d

De Edmundo Redeknap pro 32 remes papir spendabilis, 806 alnis tele lini bolte, 4 peciis fustian, 650 alnis tele lini Henaud et diversis mercandisis. Precii £17 10s .... sb' 17s 6d

De Johanne Adams pro 20½ doseyns throme hattes, 1 Yperlinge. Precii £7 .... sb' 7s

De Henrico Frowyk pro 1100 alnis tele lini Busk, 1250 alnis tele lini spenall. Precii £24.. sb' 24s

De Raufe Kemp pro 366 alnis tele Niperfeld, 400 alnis tele lini Westfale, 435 alnis tele lini crude et diversis mercandisis. Precii £26 13s 4d......... sb' 26s 8d

De Johanne Brodde pro 49 dossenis rough hattys, 400 alnis tele lini Brounswyke, 28 remes papir, 24 dossenis quysson clothes et diversis marcandisis. Precii £25 10s .... sb' 25s 6d

<aa>Totalis valor mercandisarum, unde 12d — £250 10s sb' — £12 10s 6d<aa>

f. 9[v]

De Johanne Litilton pro 423 alnis tele lini Sultwyche, 672 alnis tele[a] lini crude, 232 alnis tele lini Flandrie albe et diversis mercandisis. Precii £18 6s 8d .... sb' 18s 4d

De Thoma Hawkyn pro 12 balettis almundes, 1 bala wolle cottone. Precii £16 .... sb' 16s

De Willelmo Hatter pro 300 alnis canvas, 16 dossenis quysson clothes, 2 dossenis pellium boge et diversis mercandisis. Precii £12 10s................ sb' 12s 6d

De Johanne Midelton pro 330 alnis tele lini stricte, 617 alnis tele lini Henaud, 12 remes papir. Precii £12 10s... sb' 12s 6d

De Thoma Steele pro 800 alnis tele Guttynges, 1900 alnis tele lini stricte, 400 alnis tele lini albe et diversis mercandisis. Precii £40........................... sb' 40s

De Agnete Rooke pro 16 dossenis sporis, 24 papir poyntes, 1000 ballys et diverso haberdashe. Precii £7 10s... sb' 7s 6d

De Alexandro Orabill pro 331 alnis tele Guttynges, 900 alnis tele lini Flandrie, 650 alnis tele lini Guttynges et diversis mercandisis. Precii £21 10ssb' 21s 6d

De Thoma Dugmanton pro 250 alnis tele lini Sultwyche, 200 alnis tele stricte, 309 alnis tele Niperfeld, 1000 alnis tele Flandrie crude et albe, 200 alnis tele Henaud. Precii £18 15s.. sb' 18s 9d

<aa>-<aa> *Auditor's marginated entry: Sum of the issues on the page L.*

De Thoma Onehande pro 400 alnis tele Guttynges, 2200 alnis tele Flandrie, 500 alnis tele Busk. Precii £46... sb' 46s

De Thoma Nyche pro 933 alnis tele lini stricte, 750 alnis tele lini spenall et diversis mercandisis. Precii £20... sb' 20s

De Austyn Stratton pro 1600 alnis tele lini bolte. Precii £15 3s 4d ... sb' 15s 2d

De Roberto Baron pro 500 alnis tele Sultwyche, 680 alnis tele lini Flandrie crude et diversis mercandisis. Precii £18 10s ... sb' 18s 6d

De Johanne Jacombe pro 350 alnis tele Flandrie albe, 560 alnis tele lini Flandrie crude, 300 alnis tele lini Henaud et diversis mercandisis. Precii £15 16s 8d... sb' 15s 10d

De Raufe Verney pro 20 remes papir. Precii £3 6s 8d... sb' 3s 4d

De Johanne Crowe pro 14 gros bolions, 6 petris wire et diverso haberdashe. Precii £6 13s 4d ... sb' 6s 8d

De Waryn Turpyn pro 6 gros glases, 11 paper poyntes, 6 hattys. Precii 26s 8d ... sb' 16d

De Willelmo Gronde pro 100 alnis tele lini werkyn, 400 alnis tele lini stricte, 3 dossenis throme hattys et diversis mercandisis. Precii £7 3s 4d... sb' 7s 2d

De Johanne Norlonge pro 950 alnis tele lini Brounswyke, 8 peciis ravelli, 2 balis papir, 10 dossenis quysson clothes. Precii £13 6s 8d... sb' 13s 4d

<aa>Valor mercandisarum, unde 12d — £294 8s 4d sb' — £14 14s 5d<aa>

f. 10r

De Johanne Asshe pro 1500 alnis tele spenall stricte et large, 300 alnis tele lini Niperfeld, 200 alnis tele Hustre, 150 alnis tele lini Henaud et diversis mercandisis. Precii £23 6s 8d... sb' 23s 4d

De Ricardo Everley pro 380 alnis canvas, 400 alnis tele lini Henaud, 350 alnis tele lini Flandrie albe et diversis mercandisis. Precii £33 6s 8d ... sb' 33s 4d

De Hugone Wycche pro 40 rem papir spendabilis, 350 alnis tele Flandrie crude, 425 alnis tele lini Flandrie albe et diversis mercandisis. Precii £16 10s ... sb' 16s 6d

De Johanne Grene pro 600 alnis tele lini Busk, 250 alnis tele lini Flandrie crude, 15 remes papir et diversis mercandisis. Precii £20 ... sb' 20s

De Ricardo Ryche pro 900 alnis tele Busk, 600 alnis tele Flandrie crude, 200 alnis tele Champeyn et diversis mercandisis. Precii £34 16s 8d... sb' 34s 10d

De Roberto Stroder pro 226 alnis tele Sultwyche, 250 alnis tele pikeling, 300 alnis tele Henaud, 2 dossenis [et] 6 hattys. Precii £8 10s ... sb' 8s 6d

De Johanne Penne pro 300 alnis tele lini Busk crude, 400 alnis tele lini Flandrie, 200 alnis tele Henaud. Precii £8 10s... sb' 8s 6d

De Johanne Artour pro 12 coverlites Flandrie, 4 dossenis felt hattys. Precii £4 10s... sb' 4s 6d

De Johanne Berkley pro 150 alnis tele werkyn, 320 alnis tele lini Sultwyche, 350 alnis tele Flandrie crude, 400 alnis tele lini Henaud et diversis mercandisis. Precii £16 13s 4d .... sb' 16s 8d

De Johanne Donne pro 300 alnis tele lini Niperfeld, 200 alnis tele lini Henaud, 10 remes papir. Precii £8 6s 8d .... sb' 8s 4d

De Johanne Lok pro 10 remes papir, 1 casa pectinum ligni, 100 lb. canebis, 250[b] alnis tele lini Henaud. Precii £10 5s .... sb' 10s 3d

De Thoma Boston pro 600 alnis tele lini Busk, 415 alnis tele Niperfeld, 322 alnis tele lini Sultwyche et diversis mercandisis. Precii £20 10s ...... sb' 20s 6d

De Johanne Swetelove pro 1000 alnis tele lini crude. Precii £13 6s 8d .... sb' 13s 4d

De Johanne Sturgeon pro 800 alnis tele Flandrie crude, 200 alnis tele lini Henaud, 400 alnis tele lini Busk et diversis mercandisis. Precii £13 6s 8d sb' 13s 4d

De Johanne Stokdon pro 1021 alnis tele bolte, 800 alnis tele lini Flandrie crude et diversis mercandisis. Precii £23 10s .... sb' 23s 6d

De Willelmo Hertewell pro 400 alnis tele lini Guttynges, 3 peciis bultelli, 200 alnis canvas albi. Precii £7 10s .... sb' 7s 6d

De Johanne Reynekyn pro 410 alnis tele lini Niperfeld, 10 dossenis pannorum depictorum, 600 alnis Barras canvas, 12 remes paper spendabilis. Precii £16 13s 4d .... sb' 16s 8d

<aa>Totalis valor mercandisarum, unde 12d — £279 11s 8d sb' — £13 19d 7d<aa>

f. 10v

De Thoma Hurste pro 12 dossenis pannorum depictorum, 100 lb. canebis, 2 doseyns felt hattys. Precii £3 6s 8d .... sb' 3s 4d

De Johanne Lambard pro 250 alnis tele lini pykelinge, 200 alnis tele lini Henaud, 110 lb. fili spenall. Precii £4 20d .... sb' 4s 1d

[a] tele *repeated L, in error.* [b] *Corrected in L from* 200.

[55] De navi Willelmi Vykary eodem die *[8 Nov. 1445]*

De Ada[a] Turkyll pro 1 lasto allecis albi, 6 barellis olei, 200 bunchis ceparum. Precii £8 3s 4d .... sb' 8s 2d

[a] Adam *L, in error.*

[56] De navi Peronettys de Menye eodem die *[8 Nov. 1445]*

De Johanne Walsch et Johanne Blundell pro 46 doliis pomorum. Precii £23 .... sb' 23s

<aa>-<aa> *Auditor's marginated entry: Sum of the issues on the page L.*

[57] De navi Johannis Clynke eodem die *[8 Nov. 1445]*

De Johanne Levynge pro 2 lastis, 6 barellis allecis albi. Precii £10.......... sb' 10s

De Boytes Turne pro 2 lastis allecis albi, 2 lastis olei, 6 hodes hoppes, 375 bunchis ceparum. Precii £26 .... sb' 26s

[58] De navi Thome Hawkyn eodem die *[8 Nov. 1445]*

De Amory Mateney pro 2½ lastis allecis albi, 2 doliis wode. Precii £15.. sb' 15s

De Cassyn Torridas pro 5 pipis cum varres vitri et 150 botellis vitri. Precii £4 .... sb' 4s

[59] De navi Johannis Clerk eodem die *[8 Nov. 1445]*

De Baudewyn Boteler pro 3 lastis fungearum to gilles, 9 barellis olei, 8 shipp poundes whestones. Precii £18 6s 8d.......... sb' 18s 4d

De Thoma Twig pro 2 lastis fungearum to gilles, 2½ lastis olei, 10 dosenys shep skynnes, 60 fathome russheware, 1 barello litmose. Precii £23 6s 8d .... sb' 23s 4d

De Willelmo Maihew et Thoma Norwode pro 400 funger[b] to gilles, 6 barellis olei. Precii £5.......... sb' 5s

De Johanne Benett pro 2 lastis fungearum to gilles. Precii £8 .... sb' 8s

De Ricardo Gardener pro 1 lasto fungearum to gilles. Precii £4.......... sb' 4s[a]

[a] 5s *L, in error.* [b] *Sic L.*

<aa>Totalis valor mercandisarum, unde 12d — £152 5s sb' — £7 13s[a] 3d<aa>

[a] *Corrected in L from* 12s.

f. 11r

[60] De navi Thome Hawker 11° die Novembris *[11 Nov. 1445]*

De Johanne Felde pro 2 lastis allecis albi. Precii £8 .... sb' 8s

[61] De navi Laurencii Covente eodem die *[11 Nov. 1445]*

De eodem magistro pro 200 caboges, 200 bunchis ceparum. Precii 13s 4dsb' 8d

[62] De navi Johannis Newman 16° die Novembris *[16 Nov. 1445]*

De Thoma Gray pro 2 doliis, 2 hoggeshedes vini .... sb' 7s 6d

De Waltero Gilberd pro 2 doliis vini.......... sb' 6s

De eodem magistro et sociis suis pro 6 doliis vini .... sb' 18s

Et pro 300 lb. rosyn. Precii 6s 8d .... sb' 4d

De Roberto Kyngesson pro 2 doliis, 2 hoggeshedes vini.......... sb' 7s 6d

De Johanne Parys pro 1 dolio vini .... sb' 3s

De David Selly pro 2 doliis, 1 pipa vini .... sb' 7s 6d
De Willelmo de Lunys pro 24 doliis vini .... sb' £3 12s
De Edmundo Sheffeld pro 4 doliis, 1 pipa vini .... sb' 13s 6d
De Johanne Flexmer pro 3 doliis vini .... sb' 9s
De Ricardo Stapill pro 4 doliis vini .... sb' 12s
De Johanne Aleyn pro 12 doliis vini .... sb' 36s
De Johanne Styward pro 1 pipa, 2 hoggeshedes vini .... sb' 3s
De Willelmo Benteley pro 4 doliis, 1 pipa vini .... sb' 13s 6d
De Thoma Byggynge pro 3 doliis vini .... sb' 9s
De Henrico Cherchesey pro 3 doliis vini .... sb' 9s
De Rogero Eston pro 3 doliis vini .... sb' 9s
De Johanne Gegge pro 4 doliis, 2 hoggeshedes vini .... sb' 13s 6d
De Johanne Tregeran pro 5 doliis vini .... sb' 15s
De Willelmo Hideman pro 1 dolio vini .... sb' 3s

<aa>Valor mercandisarum, unde 12d — £9 sb' — 9s
Vinum — 89 dolia sb' — £13 7s
[Totalis] £13 16s<aa>

f. 11[v]

[63] De navi Johannis Sopp eodem die *[16 Nov. 1445]*

De Johanne Stokker pro 98 chargiis salis de Bay. Precii £26 .... sb' 26s
De Johanne Normasters pro 98 chargiis salis de Bay. Precii £26 .... sb' 26s
De Johanne atte Celly pro 20 chargiis salis de Bay. Precii £6 13s 4d.... sb' 6s 8d
De Roberto Stokker pro 12 chargiis salis de Bay. Precii £4........ sb' 4s
De Henrico Mason et sociis suis pro 8 chargiis salis de Bay. Precii 53s 4d .... sb' 2s 8d
[a]De Hans Camerowe pro 4 chargiis salis. Precii 26s 8d........ sb' 16d[a]

[a-a] *Entered by a different hand in grey ink L.*

[64] De navi Johannis Meux 18° die Novembris *[18 Nov. 1445]*

De Johanne Levynge pro 1 lasto allecis albi. Precii £4........ sb' 4s
De Johanne Feld pro 2½ lastis allecis albi. Precii £10 .... sb' 10s
De Alano Johnsson pro 10 barellis allecis albi. Precii £3 6s 8d........ sb' 3s 4d

[65] De navi Alffons Vascus 20° die Novembris *[20 Nov. 1445]*

De Alexandro Heysaund pro 1 dolio olei, 300 peciis fructus. Precii £24 . sb' 24s
De eodem magistro pro 30 peciis fructus. Precii 40s .... sb' 2s
De Willelmo Pychard pro 280 peciis fructus, 1 dolio olei, [a]700 orenges[a]. Precii £22 13s 4d........ sb' 22s 8d

<aa>-<aa> *Auditor's marginated entry: Sum of the issues on the page L.*

De Petro Alberus pro 37 peciis fructus, 2000 orenges. Precii 56s 8d .. sb' 2s 10d
De Alffons Yanus pro 37 peciis fructus. Precii 50s .... sb' 2s 6d
De Gonsalvo Trigus pro 54 peciis fructus. Precii £3 12s .... sb' 3s 7¼d
De Willelmo Walden pro 120 peciis fructus. Precii £8 .... sb' 8s
De Henrico Logan pro 50 sorte fructus. Precii £10 .... sb' 10s
De Willelmo Haydok pro 80 peciis fructus. Precii £5 6s 8d .... sb' 5s 4d
De Willelmo Swan pro 90 peciis fructus. Precii £6 .... sb' 6s
De Bartholomeo James pro 90 peciis fructus. Precii £6............................. sb' 6s
De Roberto Broke pro 3 doliis fructus. Precii £6 .... sb' 6s
De Willelmo Wodehouse et Thoma Shrubbe pro 6 doliis fructus. Precii £12 .... sb' 12s

[a-a] *Interlined L.*

[66] De navi Johannis Troyloyn eodem die *[20 Nov. 1445]*

De eodem magistro et Johanne Bylliok pro 5 doliis, 1 pipa vini.......... sb' 16s 6d

<aa>Valor mercandisarum, unde 12d — £194 18s 8d sb' — £9 14s 11¼d
Vinum — 5 dolia [1] pipa sb' — 16s 6d
[Totalis] £10 11s 5¼d<aa>

f. 12r

De Johanne Heron pro 1 dolio, 1 pipa vini... sb' 4s 6d
De Johanne Mayak pro 6 doliis vini.. sb' 18s
De Pey de Mawepertes pro 4 doliis, 1 hoggeshede vini .... sb' 12s 9d
De Berteram de la Grayr pro 3 doliis vini .... sb' 9s
De Johanne Levyng pro 13 doliis, 1 pipa vini.................................... sb' 40s 6d
De Remonet Russewe pro 2 doliis vini .... sb' 6s
De Henrico Ryewen pro 2 peciis rosyn. Precii 5s .... sb' 3d

[67] De galea Johannis Cappelle patroni 22° die Novembris *[22 Nov. 1445]*

De Remond Vidale et Francisco Penell pro 1000 lb. grani paradisi £66 13s 4d, 300 lb. serici Messyn £90, 30 lb. corall £20. Summa £176 13s 4d .... sb' £8 16s 8d
De Nicholao Gelio pro 3 barellis cum pyones. Precii 20s........................ sb' 12d
De Anthonio Centurioun pro 20 lb. serici de Malik. Precii £10................ sb' 10s
De Rambell Spynola pro 40 lb. serici de Malik £20, 200 lb. grani de Hispania pro pannis £15. Summa £35 .... sb' 35s
De Galeaceo de Negro pro 100 lb. grani de Hispania pro pannis. Precii £7 10s .... sb' 7s 6d
De Thoma Rytsoo pro 800 lb. grani Hispanie pro pannis. Precii £60 .... sb' £3
De Christoforo Cataneo pro 300 lb. grani Hispanie pro pannis £22 10s, 13 parvis mantellis boge 40s. Summa £24 10s .... sb' 24s 6d

De Johanne Capelle pro 40 lb. serici de Malik. Precii £20 .... sb' 20s
De Frederico Centurion pro 100 lb. grani de Hispania pro pannis. Precii £7 10s .... sb' 7s 6d
De Augustyno Cassan et Simone Sygall pro 100 lb. grani de Hispania pro pannis. Precii £7 10s .... sb' 7s 6d
De Franco Salvator pro 400 lb. grani Hispanie pro pannis. Precii £30 ..... sb' 30s
De Clement Danyell pro 200 bowestaves 20s, 1000 lb. piperis £16 13s 4d, 24 lb. sugre de 2 cote 12s. Summa £18 5s 4d .... sb' 18s 3¼d
Et pro 20 barellis vini dulcis .... sb' 10s

<aa>Valor mercandisarum, unde 12d — £398 3s 8d sb' — £19 18s 2¼d
Vinum — 30 dolia, 1 hoggeshede sb' — £4 10s 9d
Vinum dulce — 20 barelli sb' — 10s
[Totalis] £24 18s 11¼d<aa>

f. 12[v]

De Jacomo Rytsoo pro 200 lb. piperis £3 6s 8d, 100 bowestaves debilibus 13s 4d, 24 lb. sugre de 2 cote 12s, 100 lb. piperis 33s 4d. Summa £6 5s 4d .... sb' 6s 3¼d
Et pro 7 barellis vini dulcis .... sb' 3s 6d
De Bertuse Dedo pro 50 lb. sugre de 3 cote 33s 4d, 40 lb. pectinum de yvore £10. Summa £11 13s 4d .... sb' 11s 8d
De Jacomo Centoro Chalaphado pro 180 bowestaves. Precii 26s 8d .... sb' 16d
De Marco de Dulcenio pro 1 dossena ollarum de Malik et 3 dossenis disshes 5s, 1 lb. pectinum de yvore 5s, 2½ dossenis fili rames 2s 6d. Summa 12s 6d .... sb' 7½d
De Nicholao de Hungaro pro 30 lb. treacle 10s, 25 ollis de Malik 4s. Summa 14s .... sb' 8½d
De Meladyn Cursula pro 20 lb. treacle 6s 8d, 17 ollis zinziberis viridis 13s 4d. Summa 20s .... sb' 12d
De Rigo de Frauncisco [a]pro[a] 160 boxis citrinade 13s 4d, 150 lb. resouns Coraunce 18s 9d. Summa 32s 1d .... sb' 19¼d
De Margeot de Napoly pro 150 lb. datys. Precii 12s 6d .... sb' 7½d
De Michaele de Spalato pro 150 lb. resouns Coraunce 18s 9d, 30 ollis de Malik 5s. Summa 23s 9d .... sb' 14¼d
De Johanne Beanque pro 100 lb. resouns Coraunce. Precii 12s 6d .... sb' 7½d
De Polo de Squitery pro 800 [lb.] resouns Coraunce. Precii £5 .... sb' 5s
De Beaceo de Lago pro 100 lb. resouns Coraunce. Precii 12s 6d .... sb' 7½d
De Polo de Squytery quondam Jane pro 100 lb. piperis 33s 4d, 300 lb. resouns Coraunce 37s 6d. Summa £3 10s 10d .... sb' 3s 6½d
De George de Bolege pro 300 lb. resouns Coraunce. Precii 37s 6d...... sb' 22½d
De Todero de Alleceo pro 100 lb. resouns Coraunce. Precii 12s 6d .... sb' 7½d

<aa>-<aa> *Auditor's marginated entry: Sum of the issues on the page L.*

De Andrea de Cursula pro 150 lb. resouns Coraunce 18s 9d, 20 lb. treacle 6s 8d, 100 boxis citrinade 8s 4d, 2 ollis confeccionis 2s, 50 pellibus boge 6s 8d, 2 lb. pectinum de yvore 10s, 20 ollis de Malik 2s, ½ lb. borace paste 8d. Summa 55s 1d .... sb' 2s 9¼d
De George de Drivesto pro 100 lb. resouns Coraunce. Precii 12s 6d ..... sb' 7½d
De Johanne de Sophia pro 1 barello cum 100 lb. resouns Coraunce. Precii 12s 6s........ sb' 7½d
De Stephano de Candea pro 1 barello vini albi .... sb' 3d
De George de Nicosia pro 150 lb. resouns Coraunce. Precii 18s [b]9d[b]... sb' 11¼d
Et pro 1 barello vini albi .... sb' 3d

<aa>Valor mercandisarum, unde 12d — £42 4s 10d sb' — 42s 3¼d
Vinum — 2 barelli sb' — 6d
Vinum dulce — 7 barelli sb' — 3s 6d
Totalis — 46s 3¼d<aa>

f. 13r
De George de Romenya pro 1 barello vini albi .... sb' 3d
De Andrea Russe pro 5 barellis vini dulcis .... sb' 2s 6d
De Adronico de Loro pro 10 barellis vini dulcis .... sb' 5s
De Francisco dAragose pro 6 barellis vini dulcis .... sb' 3s
De Polo dAragose pro 2 barellis vini dulcis .... sb' 12d
De George de Cipro pro 120 lb. resouns Coraunce. Precii 15s .... sb' 9d
De Lazaro de Boyano pro 50 lb. treacle 16s 8d, 100 lb. resouns Coraunce 12s 6d, 15 ollis socate 13s 4d, 1 lb. pectinum de yvore 5s, 1 lb. fili de rame 12d, 2 dossenis musk ballys 2s. Summa 50s 6d .... sb' 2s 6½d
De Nicholao de Dulcenio pro 150 lb. resouns Coraunce 18s 9d, 15 ollis socate 13s 4d, 2 dossenis files 2s, 2 lb. fili de rame 2s. Summa 36s 2d .... sb' 21¾d
De George de Dulcenio pro 100 lb. resouns Coraunce. Precii 12s 6d..... sb' 7½d
De Martyn de Squytery pro 300 lb. resouns Coraunce. Precii 37 6d .... sb' 22½d
De George de Squytery pro 150 lb. resouns Coraunce. Precii 18 9d .... sb' 11¼d
De Blaseo de Nicholo pro 150 lb. resouns Coraunce 18s 9d, 2 lb. pectinum [de] yvore 10s, 50 sponges 3s 4d, 50 [lb.] resouns Coraunce 6s 3d. Summa 38s 4d........ sb' 23¼d
De Pero de Denya pro 150 lb. resyns Coraunce. Precii 18s 9d .... sb' 11¼d
De Casperyn de Squtery pro 300 lb. resouns Coraunce 37s 6d, 11 ollis socate 10s. Summa 47s 6d .... sb' 2s 4½d
De George de Dryvesto pro 100 lb. resouns Coraunce. Precii 12s 6d..... sb' 7½d
De Mitre de Squytery pro 100 lb. reysouns Coraunce. Precii 12s 6d...... sb' 7½d
De Pero dAntyvor pro 40 lb. treacle. Precii 13s 4d........ sb' 8d
De Johanne dAragose pro 100 lb. resouns Coraunce debilium 8s 4d, 8 ollis socate 10s, 20 lb. treacle 6s 8d. Summa 25s .... sb' 15d
Et pro 2 barellis vini [c]dulcis[c] .... sb' 12d

De George de Constantinopole pro 3 barellis vini [c]dulcis[c] .... sb' 18d
De Johanne de Dulcenio pro 80 lb. zinziberis viridis £4, 100 lb. clowes £7 10s, 24 lb. borace paste 32s, 150 lb. sugre de 2 cote £3 15s, 130 lb. piperis 43s 4d. Summa £19 4d .... sb' 19s ¼d

<aa>Valor mercandisarum, unde 12d — £35 19s 1d sb' — 35s 11¾d
Vinum — 1 barellus sb' — 3d
Vinum dulce — 2 dolia, 4 barelli sb' — 14s
Totalis — 50s 2¾d<aa>

f. 13[v]

De Allegreto de Bodna pro 500 lb. resouns Corance. Precii £3 2s 6d sb' 3s 1½d
De Johanne de Nicholao pro 4 lb. galbanum 20d, 6 lb. sal armonyak 4s. Summa 5s 8d .... sb' 3½d
De Alegreto de Montana pro 3 barellis vini dulcis .... sb' 18d
De Johanne de Mounbello pro 8 lb. croci 53s 4d, 12 lb. poppyng 10s, 300 lb. piperis £5. Summa £8 3s 4d .... sb' 8s 2d
De Jacomo de Aveman pro 3 barellis vini dulcis .... sb' 18d
De Beaceo de Venesia pro 3 barellis vini dulcis .... sb' 18d
De George de Larta pro 100 lb. resouns Coraunce. Precii 12s 6d .... sb' 7½d
Et pro 12 barellis vini dulcis .... sb' 6s
De Luca dAragose pro 5 ollis socate. Precii 8s 4d .... sb' 5d
De George de Squytery pro 100 lb. resouns Coraunce. Precii 12s 6d..... sb' 7½d
De Johanne de Cera pro 400 lb. grani de Hispania pro pannis. Precii £30sb' 30s
De George dAntyvor pro 100 lb. resins Coraunce. Precii 12s 6d .... sb' 7½d
De Pero dAntyvor pro 100 lb. resouns Coraunce. Precii 12s 6d .... sb' 7½d
De Pero Sasento pro 2 barellis vini dulcis .... sb' 12d
De Nicholao de Napoly pro 1 carpett 26s 8d, 150 lb. resouns Coraunce 18s 9d, 150 pellibus boge 20s, 150 lb. piperis 50s, 70 botellis aque rosarum 20s, 40 lb. sugre candy 40s, 1 tabille 33s 4d. Summa £10 8s 9d................ sb' 10s 5¼d
De Polo de Bodna pro 150 lb. resins Coraunce. Precii 18s 9d .... sb' 11¼d
De Polo de Squytery pro 300 lb. resouns Coraunce 37s 6d, 100 lb. datys debilium 10s, 36 ollis aque rosarum, 8 ollis socate, 2 dossenis hoke yrenes pro scissoribus 20s. Summa £3 7s 6d.. sb' 3s 4½d
De Dominico de Swaso pro 400 lb. resouns Coraunce 50s, 100 lb. treacle 33s 4d, 3 lb. serici Messyn 18s, 1 barello millacy 6s 8d. Summa £5 8s.... sb' 5s 5d
Et pro 1 barello vini dulcis .... sb' 6d
De Tamiso de Dulcenio pro 160 lb. sugre de 3 cote £5 6s 8d[d], 4 lb. fili de rame 3s 4d, 6 lb. fili de cotono 3s. Summa £5 13s .... sb' 5s 8d

<aa>Valor mercandisarum, unde 12d — £70 5s 10d sb' — 70s 4d[e]
Vinum dulce — 2 dolia sb' — 12s
[Totalis] £4 2s 4d<aa>

<aa>-<aa> *Auditor's marginated entry: Sum of the issues on the page L.*

*f. 14*r

De Nicholao de Veloo pro 400 lb. resouns Coraunce. Precii 50s ... sb' 2s 6d
De Lazaro de Liege pro 140 lb. arsenek. Precii 17s 6d ... sb' 10½d
De George Scandy pro 1½ lb. croci 10s, 4 lb. serici Mesane 24s, 6 ollis socate 6s 8d, 2 fraillis resouns grosse debilium 3s 4d, 60 pellibus boge 8s 4d. Summa 52s 4d ... sb' 2s 7½d
De Bevino Germany pro 16 lb. treacle 5s 4d, 300 lb. resouns Coraunce 37s 6d, 80 lb. resalgar 26s 8d, 16 ollis socate 13s 4d. Summa £4 2s 10d ... sb' 4s 1¾d
De Johanne de Jalina pro 4 lb. fili de rame 4s, 80 lb. sugre de 2 cote 40s. Summa 44s ... sb' 2s 2½d
Et pro 10 barellis vini dulcis ... sb' 5s
De Anthonio Remer pro 100 lb. resouns Coraunce. Precii 12s 6d ... sb' 7½d
Et pro 2 barellis vini dulcis ... sb' 12d
De Michaele de Curfewe pro 6 barellis vini dulcis ... sb' 3s
De Ricardo de Mortato pro 8 lb. serici Talani. Precii 48s ... sb' 2s 5d
De Frauncisco dAcateroo pro 6 barellis vini dulcis ... sb' 3s
De Anthonio Castellan pro 5 barellis vini dulcis ... sb' 2s 6d
De Petro de Cursula pro 12 ollis de Malik, 12 ollis confeccionis. Precii 15s ... sb' 9d
De Pero de Jara pro 200 lb. resins Coraunce. Precii 25s ... sb' 15d
De Michaele de Candea pro 8 barellis vini dulcis ... sb' 4s
De Mathea de Sabay pro 2 barellis vini dulcis ... sb' 12d
De Luca de Beneto pro 6 barellis vini dulcis ... sb' 3s
De Andrea Curfewe pro 40 lb. resouns Coraunce putred. Precii 3s 4d ... sb' 2d
De Johanne de Curfewe pro 4 lb. pectinum de yvore[f] 20s, 80 lb. sugre de 2 cote 40s. Summa £3 ... sb' 3s
De Nicholao de Napoly pro 6 lb. reopantico. Precii £3 ... sb' 3s
De Andrea dAndrea pro 3 lb. pectinum de yvore 15s, 44 ollis zinziberis viridis 40s, 100 lb. resouns Coraunce 12s 6d. Summa £3 7s 6d ... sb' 3s 4½d
De Michaele de Patrase pro 8 barellis vini dulcis ... sb' 4s

<aa>Valor mercandisarum, unde 12d — £26 18s sb' — 26s 11¼d
Vinum dulce — 4 dolia, 5 barelli sb' — 26s 6d
[Totalis] 53s 5¼d<aa>

*f. 14*v

De Andronico de Constantinopolin pro 1 parvo barello zinziberis viridis. Precii 53s 4d ... sb' 2s 8d
Et pro 4 barellis vini albi ... sb' 12d
De Johanne de Maryn pro 1 simea 20s, 200 lb. resins Coraunce 25s. Summa 45s ... sb' 2s 3d
Et pro 4 barellis vini albi ... sb' 12d
De Francisco Justinean pro 800 lb. sugre de [a]1[a] cote. Precii £13 6s 8d sb' 13s 4d

De Luca de Boyana pro 60 ollis Malik 5s, [c]4 carpettes 20s[c], 4 dossenis sportelles 2s, 30 ollis zinziberis viridis 30s, 100 lb. prunys 10s, 60 lb. citrinade 6s 8d. Summa 73s[g] 8d .... sb' 3s 8¼d
De George dAntyvor pro 125 [lb.] resouns Coraunce 15s 7½d, 4 carpettes 20s, 2 dossenis sportelles 12d. Summa 36s 7½d .... sb' 22d
De Andrea de Fontana pro 100 lb. resins Coraunce. Precii 12s 6d .... sb' 7½d
De Roderigo de Almania pro 10 mantellis boge 33s 4d, 800 pellibus boge crude £5 6s 8d, 100 pellibus boge crude debilibus 6s 8d. Summa £7 6s 8d .... sb' 7s 4d
De Nicholao de Beanco pro 500 lb. resouns Coraunce £3 2s 6d, 5 fraiellis resins grosse 8s 4d. Summa £3 10s 10d .... sb' 3s 6½d
De Nicholao de Stella pro 400 lb. resins Coraunce. Precii 50s .... sb' 2s 6d
De George Caraldo pro 1 barello ynde debilis. Precii 20s .... sb' 12d
De Anthonio de Dominico pro 300 lb. resins Coraunce 37s 6d, 4 frayellis et 300 lb. resins grosse debilium 20s. Summa 57s 6d .... sb' 2s 10½d
Et pro 4 barellis vini dulcis .... sb' 2s
De Thoma Couper pro 1540 lb. sugre de 1 cote £25 13s 4d, 600 parvis pellibus deauratis £6, 8 lb. croci 53s 4d, 1 lb. serici Liege 8s, 60 lb. grani paradisi £4, 16 virgis damaske £5 6s 8d. Summa £44 [h]16d[h] .... sb' 44s [h]1d[h]
De Benedicto de Marconovo pro 200 lb. resins Coraunce. Precii 25s .... sb' 15d
Et pro 3 barellis vini dulcis .... sb' 18d
De Paulo de Vasco pro 100 ollis de Malik. Precii 10s .... sb' 6d
De Francisco Queryne pro 400 lb. cere. Precii £6 13s 4d .... sb' 6s 8d
Et pro 12 barellis vini dulcis .... sb' 6s
De Costa dAgapha pro 200 lb. salpetre. Precii 25s .... sb' 15d
De George de Dominico pro 200 lb. resins Coraunce. Precii 25s .... sb' 15d
De Marco Malipero pro 80 lb. sugre de 1 cote 26s 8d, 300 lb. cere £5. Summa £6 6s 8d .... sb' 6s 4d
De dicto George Caraldo pro 15 barellis vini dulcis .... sb' 7s 6d
De dicto Costa dAgafa pro 4 barellis vini dulcis .... sb' 2s

<aa>Valor mercandisarum, unde 12d — £102 19s 1½d sb' — 102s 11¾d
Vinum dulce — 3 dolia, 2 barelli sb' — 19s
Vinum — 1 pipa, 2 barelli sb' — 2s
[Totalis] £6 3s 11¾d<aa>

f. 15r

De Johanne de Posago pro 300 pellibus boge 40s, 4 dossenis disshes de Malik 3s 4d. Summa 43s 4d .... sb' 2s 2d
De Blaseo de Drivesto pro 40 lb. treacle. Precii 13s 4d .... sb' 8d
De Bernardo Barber pro 6 parvis forcers de yvore 20s, 2 corses auri Venesie 26s 8d, 3 paternosters de jete 3s 4d, 45 ollis terre 3s 4d, 300 pellibus boge

<aa>-<aa> *Auditor's marginated entry: Sum of the issues on the page L.*

40s, 60 parvis ollis zinziberis viridis 40s, 30 lb. treacle 10s. [Summa] £7 3s 4d .... sb' 7s 2d

De Johanne Creke pro 8[i] lb. macez 8s, 34 lb. spykenard 22s 8d, 1 gowne, 1 huke de velvet vetere £5 6s 8d, 6900 pellibus boge crude £34 10s, 48 lb. garbeloure de spykenard 16s, 160 lb. mastik £6, 60 pellibus foynes stage 40s, 100 lb. serici crude Talani £33 6s 8d, 100 parvis mantellis boge £10, 386 pellibus martrons £19 6s 8d. Summa £112 16s 8d........ sb' £5 12s 10d

Mercatores ejusdem Galee

De Marco Pryole pro 52 saccis cottoni £138 13s 4d, 1800 lb. piperis £30, 800 lb. [a]cas'[a] zinziberis £40, 900 lb. zinziberis [a]belandyn[a] £33 15s. Summa £242 8s 4d........ sb' £12 2s 5d

De Marco Barbarigo pro 22 saccis cottoni £58 13s 4d, 400 lb. clowes £30, 9600 lb. piperis £160. Summa £248 13s 4d........ sb' £12 8s 8d

De Benasdo Pascalego pro 1200 lb. zinziberis £45, 4 lb. auri Ven[i]sie £6 13s 4d. Summa £51 13s 4d........ sb' 51s 8d

De Johanne Maunche pro 300 lb. zinziberis £11 5s, 5 barellis zinziberis viridis £25. Summa £36 5s........ sb' 36s 3d

De Andrea Musshlyn pro 6 casis canelle. Precii £24........ sb' 24s

De Andrea et Frederigo Corner pro 4800 [lb.] piperis £80, 650 lb. zinziberis belandyn £24 7s 6d, 500 lb. clowes £37 10s, 8 casis canelle £32, 2500 lb. brasylle £20 16d 8d, 350 lb. saundres £8 15s, 15 balis papir £20. [Summa] £223 9s 2d........ sb' £11 3s 5½d

De Willelmo Estefeld et Ricardo Quatermayns pro 6000 lb. piperis £100, 600 lb. clowes £45. Summa £145........ sb' £7 5s

<aa>Totalis valor mercandisarum, unde 12d — £1094 5s 10d sb' — £54 14s 3½d<aa>

f. 15^{v}

De Johanne de Negro pro 4 barellis zinziberis viridis. Precii £20........ sb' 20s

De Michaele Morosyn pro 3000 lb. piperis. Precii £50........ sb' 50s

De Johanne de George de Dulcenio pro 900 lb. piperis. Precii £15........ sb' 15s

De Andrea Morosyn pro 1800 lb. piperis. Precii £30........ sb' 30s

De Nicholao de Napoly pro 600 lb. piperis. Precii £10........ sb' 10s

De Lowes Bernard pro 3800 lb. piperis. Precii £80........ sb' £4

De Johanne de Pounte pro 300 lb. brasylle. Precii 50s........ sb' 2s 6d

De Jacomo Dodo pro 2400 lb. piperis. Precii £40........ sb' 40s

De Carlo Conteryn pro 600 lb. brasilli £5, 150 lb. seminis pro vermibus £3 15s. Summa £8 15s........ sb' 8s 9d

De Thoma Couper pro 3 casis canelle. Precii £12........ sb' 12s

De Johanne Cappelle pro 45 saccis cottoni £120, 8 buttes resouns Coraunce £33, 10,200 lb. piperis £170, 100 lb. zinziberis belandyn £3 15s, 12 casis canelle £48, 20 balis papir debilis £20, 1800 lb. brasylle £15, 350 lb. saundres £8 15s, 500 bowestaves £3 6s 8d, 90 lb. serici crude horstaille £27, 400 lb. seminis pro vermibus £10, 460 lb. clowes £34 10s, 280 lb. nucum muscatarum £9 6s 8d, 80 lb. ynde £3 6s 8d, 660 lb. galingale £13 15s. Summa £519 15s .... sb' £25 19s 9d

Et pro 36 buttes vini dulcis .... sb' £5 8s

[a-a] *Interlined L.* [b-b] *Interlined above* 4[d], *struck through L.* [c-c] *Interlined by a different hand (probably the auditor's) in lighter ink L.* [d] 6d *L, in error.* + *[cross] entered above this number L.* [e] ½d *follows, struck through L.* [f] yovore *L, apparently in error.* [g] *Written by a different hand (probably the auditor's) in lighter ink over* 53s, *expunged.* [h-h] *Written over erasure L.* [i] *Corrected in L from* 6.

[68] De galea Marco de Pryole patrone eodem die *[22 Nov. 1445]*

De Jacomo de Jacomo pro 20 ollis socate 33s 4d, 8 lb. amelle 10s. Summa 43s 4d .... sb' 2s 2d

Et pro 3 barellis vini dulcis .... sb' 18d

De Pero dAntyvor pro 100 lb. resins Coraunce. Precii 12s 6d .... sb' 7½d

Et pro 1 barello vini albi .... sb' 3d

[<aa>]Totalis valor mercandisarum, unde 12d — £790 15s 10d sb' — £39 10s 9½d

Vinum — 1 barellus sb' — 3d

Vinum dulce — 36 buttes, 3 barelli sb' — 109s 6d

[Totalis] £45 6½d[<aa>]

f. 16r

De Stephano Dyamant pro 260 lb. resins Coraunce. Precii 32s 6d .... sb' 19½d

Et pro 1 barello vini dulcis .... sb' 6d

De George [a]de[a] Vernay pro 128 lb. piperis 42s 8d, 350 lb. resins Coraunce 43s 9d, 4 lb. pectinum de yvore 20s, 23 peciis relesaunce 23s, 60 boxis sitrinade 5s. Summa £6 14s 5d .... sb' 6s 8¾d

De Stephano Disdrema pro 150 lb. resins Coraunce. Precii 18s 9d .... sb' 11¼d

De Stephano de Dulcenio pro 150 lb. resins Coraunce. Precii 18s 9d .. sb' 11¼d

Et pro 1 barello vini dulcis .... sb' 6d

De Clement de Posago pro 4 carpettes 40s, 200 box citrinade 16s 8d. Summa 56s 8d .... sb' 2s 10d

De George de Seint George pro 90 lb. sugre de 3 cote. Precii 46s 8d.... sb' 2s 4d

Et pro 1 barello vini albi .... sb' 3d

De George Caverysan pro 5 barellis vini [b]dulcis[b] .... sb' 2s 6d

De Pero Compostell pro 5 barellis vini [b]dulcis[b] .... sb' 2s 6d

De Polo de Petua pro 200 box citrinade. Precii 16s 8d .... sb' 10d

[<aa>-<aa>] *Auditor's marginated entry: Sum of the issues on the page L.*

De Polo de Posago pro 3 barellis vini [b]dulcis[b] .... sb' 18d
De Johanne dAragose pro 36 lb. cottoni 12s, 280 pellibus boge crude 36s 8d, 1000 lymyns 6s 8d, 30 lb. resins Coraunce 3s 9d. Summa 59s 1d sb' 2s 11½d
De Michaele de George pro 300 lb. resins Coraunce 37s 6d, 7 dossenis ollarum de Malik 10s. Summa 47s 6d .... sb' 2s 4½d
Et pro 1 barello vini dulcis .... sb' 6d
De George de Dryvesto pro 300 lb. resins Coraunce 37s 6d, 50 lb. zinziberis viridis 50s, 100 pellibus boge 13s 4d, 40 lb. resins grosse 3s 4d, 1 lb. pectinum de yvore 5s. Summa £5 9s 2d .... sb' 5s 5½d
De Anthonio de Traho pro 110 lb. sugre de 3 cote £3 13s 4d, 16 ollis socate 30s, 80 lb. triacle 26s 8d, 200 pellibus boge 26s 8d, 300 lb. resins Coraunce 37s 6d. Summa £9 14s 2d .... sb' 9s 8½d
Et pro 1 barello vini albi .... sub' 3d
De Allegreto de Cursula pro 80 lb. sugre de 3 cote 53s 4d, 150 lb. resins Coraunce 18s 9d, 200 lb. dates 16s 8d. Summa £4 8s 9d .... sb' 4s 5¼d
Et pro 1 barello vini dulcis .... sb' 6d
De Andronico de Constantinopolin pro 150 lb. resins Coraunce. Precii 18s 9d .... sb' 11¼d
Et pro 10 barellis vini dulcis .... sb' 5s

<aa>Totalis valor mercandisarum, unde 12d — £42 20d sb' — 42s 1¼d
Vinum dulce — 27 barelli sb' — 13s 6d [Totalis] 56s 1¼d
Vinum — 2 barelli sb' — 6d<aa>

f. 16v

De Johanne de Faucon pro 11 ollis socate. Precii 16s 8d .... sb' 10d
Et pro 3 barellis vini dulcis .... sb' 18d
De Andrea Russo pro 2 barellis vini albi .... sb' 6d
De Phelippo de Jane pro 2 barellis vini dulcis .... sb' 12d
De George de Andrea pro 300 lb. resins Coraunce. Precii 37s 6d .... sb' 22½d
De George de Squytery pro 60 cavellis fili de rame 2s 6d, 2 lb. pectinum de yvore 10s. Summa 12s 6d .... sb' 7½d
De Johanne de Dryvesto pro 500 lb. resins Coraunce £3 2s 6d, 30 cavellis fili de rame 16d, 1 carpetto 10s. Summa £3 13s 10d .... sb' 3s 8½d
De Marco de Cursola pro 300 pellibus boge. Precii 40s .... sb' 2s
De Johanne dAragose pro 400 lb. resins Coraunce. Precii 50s .... sb' 2s 6d
De Andrea dAragose pro 180 lb. piperis. Precii £3 .... sb' 3s
De Francisco de Narenta pro 40 lb. treacle. Precii 13s 4d .... sb' 8d
De Damyan de Lastna pro 150 lb. resins Coraunce 18s 9d, 50 lb. triacle 16s 8d. Summa 35s 5d .... sb' 21¼d
De Novello dAntyvor pro 250 lb. resins Coraunce. Precii 31s 3d .... sb' 18¾d
De Mitre de Catero pro 50 lb. treacle 16s 8d, 114 boxes sitrinad 9s 6d, 76 lb. sugre de 3 cote 50s 8d. Summa £3 16s 10d .... sb' 3s 10¼d

De Johanne de Senia pro 40 lb. sugre de 3 cote 26s 8d, 120 boxes citrinad 10s. Summa 36s 8d .... sb' 22d
Et pro 1 barello vini dulcis .... sb' 6d
De Luca de Michaele pro 600 [a]lb.[a] resins Coraunce £3 15s, 120 boxes citrinad 10s. Summa £4 5s .... sb' 4s 3d
De Leo Tonson pro 5 barellis vini dulcis .... sb' 2s 6d
De Lowes Gyse pro 5 barellis vini dulcis .... sb' 2s 6d
De George de Traho et Nadale de Pero pro 1 parva casa canelle £3, 400 lb. sugre de 2 cote £10, 120 lb. piperis 40s. Summa £15 .... sb' 15s
De Nicholao Longo pro 3 parvis verres aque rosarum 13s 4d, 30 lb. treacle 10s. Summa 23s 4d .... sb' 14d
De Johanne de Romanya pro 400 lb. resins Coraunce. Precii 50s .... sb' 2s 6d
Et pro 1 barello vini albi .... sb' 3d

<aa>Totalis valor mercandisarum, unde 12d — £47 2s 4d sb' — 47s 1¾d
Vinum dulce — 1 dolium, 4 barelli sb' — 8s [Totalis] 55s 10¾d
Vinum — 3 barelli sb' — 9d<aa>

f. 17r

De Bartholomeo Maragon pro 12 barellis vini dulcis .... sb' 6s
De Luca de la Turr pro 60 ollis de Malik, 14 grype ovis 26s 8d, 200 lb. resins Coraunce 25s. Summa 51s 8d .... sb' 2s [7d]
De Pero Ruscolo pro 5 barellis vini dulcis .... sb' [2s] 6d
De Polo Soma pro 450 lb. resins Coraunce. Precii 56s 8d .... sb' 2s 10d
De Nicholao Turre pro 2 barellis milase 10s, 160 lb. sugre de 3 cote £5 6s 8d. Summa £5 16s 8d .... sb' 5s 10d
Et pro 6 barellis vini dulcis .... sb' 3s
De Pero Soma pro 250 lb. resins Coraunce 31s 3d, 400 lb. piperis £6 13s 4d, 2 ollis socate 3s 4d. Summa £8 7s 11d .... sb' 8s 4¾d
De Marco dAntyvor pro 40 ollis damask, 36 parvis ollis. Precii 5s .... sb' 3d
Et pro 2 barellis vini albi[c] .... sb' 6d
De George Sprover pro 300 lb. resins Coraunce 37s 6d, 8 lb. yreos 12d, 40 lb. galingalc 16s 8d, 100 lb. rcsins Corauncc 12s 6d. Summa £3 7s 8d sb' 3s 4¾d
De Allegreto de Denya pro 150 lb. resins Coraunce 18s 9d, 3 ollis socate 5s. Summa 23s 9d .... sb' 14¼d
De Johanne Soma pro 300 lb. resins Coraunce. Precii 37s 6d .... sb' 22½d
De Andrea Boyana pro 150 lb. resins Coraunce. Precii 18s 9d .... sb' 11¼d
De Nicholao de Dulcenio pro 250 lb. resins Coraunce. Precii 31s 3d... sb' 18¾d
De George de Lago pro 150 lb. resins Coraunce 18s 9d, 1 carpetto 40s. Summa 58s 9d .... sb' 2s 11¼d
Et pro 2 barellis vini dulcis .... sb' 12d
De George Lucian pro 400 cavellis fili de rame. Precii 33s 4d .... sb' 20d

<aa>-<aa> *Auditor's marginated entry: Sum of the issues on the page L.*

De Pero de Chappa pro 60 lb. sugre de 1 cote 20s, 200 lb. piperis £3 6s 8d, 200 lb. sugre de 1 cote £3 6s 8d, 10 lb. piperis 3s 4d. Summa £7 16s 8d sb' 7s 10d
De Thomaso de Duraso pro 300 lb. resins Coraunce 37s 6d, 50 lb. clowes £3 15s, 400 lb. resins Coraunce 50s. Summa £8 2s 6d .... sb' 8s 1[½]d
De Pero de Catero pro 100 lb. resins Coraunce. Precii 12s 6d .... sb' 7½d
De Damyo de Catero pro 140 lb. resins Coraunce. Precii 17s 6d ....sb' 10[½d]

<aa>Totalis valor mercandisarum, unde 12d — £50 18s 1d sb' — 50s 11d
Vinum dulce — 2 dolia, 1 barellus sb' — 12s 6d [Totalis] 63s 11d
Vinum — 2 barelli sb' — 6d<aa>

f. 17v

De Alleceo de Meda pro 12 ollis de Malik 20d, 200 lb. resins Coraunce 25s, 5 ollis socate 10s. Summa 36s 8d .... [sb' 22d]
De Allegreto dAntyvor pro 350 lb. resins Coraunce 43s 9d, 20 ollis de Malik 3s 4d. Summa 47s 1d .... sb' 2s 4d
De George de Metlyn pro 150 lb. resins Coraunce 18s 9d, 20 ollis vacuis 12d, 100 lb. resins Coraunce 12s 6d. Summa 32s 3d .... sb' 19½d
De Andrea de Catepesero pro 100 lb. resins Coraunce 12s 6d, 80 boxes sitrinad 6s 8d, 1 carpetto 5s. Summa 24s 2d .... sb' 14½d
Et pro 1 barello vini dulcis .... sb' 6d
De Martyno Ursoo pro 400 lb. resins Coraunce 50s, 1 barello sitrinad 5s. Summa 55s .... sb' 2s 9d
De Stephano de Dulcenio pro 24 ollis de Malik 2s, 14 parvis ollis zinziberis viridis 13s 4d, 10 lb. boras paste 13s 4d, 1 barello zinziberis viridis £5, 100 lb. resins Coraunce 12s 6d. Summa £7 14d .... sb' 7s ¾d
De Allegreto de Squitery pro 200 lb. resins Coraunce. Precii 25s .... sb' 15d
De Nicholao de Boyana pro 500 lb. resins Coraunce. Precii £3 2s 6d sb' 3s 1½d
De Nicholao[d] dAragose pro 200 salte saleres vitri. Precii 16s 8d .... sb' 10d
De Alowes Sancto Ouro pro 8 barellis vini dulcis .... sb' 4s
De Johanne de Pero pro 20 lb. zinziberis viridis 20s, 50 lb. treacle 16s 8d. Summa 36s 8d .... sb' 22d
De Andrea de Laboyand pro 3 barellis vini dulcis .... sb' 18d
De Andrea Speron pro 150 pellibus boge 20s, 300 lb. resins Coraunce 37s 6d. Summa 57s 6d .... sb' 2s 10½d
De Maryn de Jane pro 30 lb. treacle 10s, 350 lb. resins Coraunce 43s 9d, 4 lb. nucum muscatarum 20d, 4 lb. zinziberis belandyn 3s 4d, 4 dossenis ollarum de Malik 4s, 12 peciis relesaunce 12s, 40 boxes sitrinad 3s 4d, 2 carpettis veteribus, 1 bagge cum sponges 10s. Summa £4 8s 1d .... sb' 4s 5d
De Novello de Catero pro 450 lb. resins Coraunce. Precii 56s 3d ...... sb' 2s 9¾d

De Andrea de Andrea pro[e] lb. zinziberis viridis 26s 8d,[2] 800 lb. resins Coraunce £5. Summa £6 6s 8d .... sb' 6s 4d
De George de la Canena pro 100 lb. resins grosse. Precii 8s[f] 4d .... sb' 5d
De Damyan de Bodna pro 200 box citrinad 8s 4d, 300 lb. resins Coraunce 37s 6d. Summa 45s 10d .... sb' 2s 3½d
De Bartholomeo de Pero pro 1 barello vini albi .... sb' 3d
[g]De Andrea de Cromena pro 12 ollis de Malik. Precii 13s 4d .... sb' 8d[g]

<aa>Valor mercandisarum, unde 12d — £43 13s 2d sb' — 43s 8¼d
Vinum dulce — 1 dolium sb' — 6s [Totalis] 49s 11¼d
Vinum — 1 barellus sb' — 3d<aa>

f. 18r

De Pero de Curfewe pro 2500 lb. resins Coraunce £15 12s 6d, 60 lb. yvore refutz 20s, 100 lb. prunys 8s 4d. [Summa] £17 10d .... sb' 17s ½d
De Rigo de Almania pro 2000 pellibus boge crude. Precii £13 6s 8d.. sb' 13s 4d
De Nicholao de Sancto Mauro pro 300 lb. resins Coraunce. Precii 37s 6d .... sb' 22½d
De Francisco Pascalego pro 1 lb. storax calamite 10d, 300 lb. sugre de 3 cote £10, 20 ollis confeccionis 40s. Summa £12 10d .... sb' 12s ½d
Et pro 10 barellis vini dulcis .... sb' 5s
De Andrea Soro pro 24 ollis confeccionis 40s, 2900 pellibus boge crude debilibus £14 10s, 360 arcubus 40s, 2 peciis balsami 13s 4d, 50 lb. serici Liege £16 13s 4d, 20 lb. serici Messyn £6, 100 lb. brasilli 16s 8d. Summa £42 13s 4d .... sb' 42s 8d
Et pro 1 barello vini dulcis .... sb' 6d
De Johanne de Pounte pro 40 barellis vini dulcis .... sb' 20s
De Anthonio de Liege pro 40 lb. sugre de 3 cote. Precii 26s 8d .... sb' 16d
De Jerolimo Badner pro 120 lb. sugre de 3 cote. Precii £4 .... sb' 4s
De Michaele de Liege pro 120 ollis de Malik 10s, 4 bundellis sportelles 5s. Summa 15s .... sb' 9d
De Jacomo de Napoly pro 650 lb. resins Coraunce. Precii £4 15d .... sb' 4s ¾d
De Johanne dAndrea pro 1000 lb. resins Coraunce £6 5s, 100 lb. zinziberis viridis £5, 6 carpettis £6, 2 lb. grani Hispanie pro pannis 3s, 8 lb. serici 48s, 100 pellibus martrons 53s 4d, 300 lb. cere £5, 100 lb. zinziberis belandyn £3 15s, 6 lb. clowes 9s, 20 lb. armoniak 3s 4d. Summa £31 16s 8d.... sb' 31s 10d
Et pro 10 barellis vini dulcis .... sb' 5s
De Augustin de Priole pro 26 lb. sugre de 2 cote 13s, 20 lb. garbellure de macez 20s, 17 ollis socate 16s 8d, 8 lb. clowes 12s, 6 lb. ynde 5s. Precii £3 6s 8d .... sb' 3s 4d

---

[2] *In all other entries in L, green ginger* (zinziber viridis) *cost exactly 1s/lb. Hence, 26s 8d must have corresponded to 26⅔ lb. of ginger.*

<aa>-<aa> *Auditor's marginated entry: Sum of the issues on the page L.*

De Alleceo de Drivesto pro 500 lb. resins Coraunce. Precii £3 2s 6d. sb' 3s 1½d
De Dominico de Squytery pro 100 lb. resins Coraunce. Precii 12s 6d ... sb' 7½d
De Thomazo de Jara pro 250 lb. resins Coraunce. Precii 31s 3d .... sb' 18¾d

<aa>Valor mercandisarum, unde 12d — £137 11s 8d sb' — £6 17s 7d
Vinum dulce: 5 dolia, 1 barellus sb' — 30s 6d
[Totalis] £8 8s 1d<aa>

f. 18v

De George de Traho pro 30 ollis zinziberis viridis £5, 2 dossenis ollarum de Malik 6s 8d. Summa £5 6s 8d .... sb' [5s 4d]
Et pro 3 barellis vini dulcis .... sb' 18d
De Tamiso de Dulceno pro 600 lb. resins Coraunce £3 15s, 60 lb. zinziberis viridis £3, 3 lb. borace roche 10s, 8 lb. vermilon 4s, 20 ollis socate 20s. Summa £8 9s .... sb' 8s 5½d
De Damyan de Bodna pro 250 lb. [resins Coraunce][3] 31s 3d, 1 parvo barello olei 20d. Summa 32s 11d .... sb' 19¾d
De Nicholao de Squytery pro 6 lb. pectinum de yvore. Precii 35s........... sb' 21d
De Johanne de Spalato pro 1 barello vini albi .... sb' 3d
De Nicholao de Posago pro 200 pellibus boge 26s 8d, 11 ollis socate 18s, 5 box citrinad 4d. Summa 45s .... sb' 2s 3d
De Andrea de Boyan pro 150 lb. resins Coraunce. Precii 18s 9d.......... sb' 11¼d
De Remond Vidale pro 100 lb. grani Hispanie pro pannis. Precii £7 10s .... sb' 7s 6d
De Raphaelle de Aurea pro 800 lb. grani Hispanie pro pannis. Precii £60 sb' £3
De Francisco Queryn pro 60 lb. cere 20s, 4 lb. storax calamite 13s 4d, 200 lb. grani paradisi £13 6s 8d. Summa £15 .... sb' 15s
Et pro 16 barellis vini dulcis .... sb' 8s
De Nicholao de Anthonio pro 20 lb. clowes 30s, 260 lb. sugre de 1 cote £4 6s 8d, 28 ollis socate 28s, 25 lb. seduale 8s 4d, 6 corffes serici 20s. Summa £8 13s .... sb' 8s 8d
Et pro 10 barellis vini dulcis .... sb' 5s
De Pero de Grandulpho pro 450 lb. resins Coraunce. Precii 56s 3d ... sb' 2s 9¾d
De Maryn de Dulcenio pro 200 lb. resins Coraunce. Precii 25s .... sb' 15d
De Jacomo de Portingal pro 200 lb. sugre de 3 cote. Precii £6 13s 4d... sb' 6s 8d
De George de Seint Martyn pro 150 lb. resins Coraunce. Precii 18s 9d sb' 11¼d
De Matheo de Sagabrea pro 40 disshes de Malik, 100 roses beate Marie 6s 8d, 10 ollis socate 20s, 300 box citrinad 25s, 8 lb. confeccionis 4s. Summa 55s 8d .... sb' 2s 9½d
De Matheo de Senio pro 11 ollis socate 22s, 14 lb. sugre de 3 cote 9s 4d. Summa 31s 4d .... sb' 19d

---

[3] *L does not specify the product, but the price permits an unambigious identification.*

De Pero de Staneo pro 100 lb. resins Coraunce 12s 6d, 7 ollis socate 10s. [Summa] 22s 6d .... sb' 13½d

<aa>Valor mercandisarum, unde 12d — £128 13s 2d sb' — £6 8s 8½d
Vinum dulce — 2 dolia, 5 barelli sb' — 14s 6d [Totalis] £7 3s 5½d
Vinum — 1 barellus sb' — 3d<aa>

f. 19r

De Anthonio de Jare pro 200 [a]lb.[a] resins Coraunce 25s, 60 disshes de Malik 5s. Summa 30s .... sb' 18d
De Nicholao de George pro 160 lb. resins Coraunce. Precii 20s .... sb' 12d
De George de Bodna pro 50 lb. treacle. Precii 16s 8d .... sb' 10d
De Johanne de Meda pro 150 lb. resins Coraunce. Precii 18s 9d .... sb' 11¼d
De Francisco Reymer pro 140 lb. resins Coraunce. Precii 17s 6d .... sb' 10½d
Et pro 2 barellis vini dulcis .... sb' 12d
De Alleceo dAndrea pro 100 lb. resins Coraunce. Precii 12s 6d .... sb' 7½d
De Matheo de Cursula pro 150 lb. resins Coraunce. Precii 18s 9d .... sb' 11¼d
De Johanne Spurver pro 18 lb. treacle 6s, 7 carpettys 23s 4d. Summa 29s 4d .... sb' 17¾d
De Dimitre de Larta pro 2 fraillis resins grosse 3s 4d, 100 lb. resins Coraunce 12s 6d. Summa 15s 10d .... sb' 9½d
De Nicholao de Duraso pro 19 ollis socate 31s 8d, 12 parvis cofferes de boon 20s. Summa 51s 8d .... sb' 2s 7d
De Nicholao de Pero pro 500 lb. resins Coraunce. Precii £3 2s 6d .... sb' 3s 1½d
De Primo de Catero pro 38 ollis sucate. Precii 26s 8d .... sb' 16d
De George de Jane pro 500 lb. resins Coraunce £3 2s 6d, 200 parvis pottys pro treacle 3s 4d. Summa £3 5s 10d .... sb' 3s 3½d
De Gaspero Furian pro 200 lb. sugre de 3 cote £6 13s 4d, 400 lb. piperis £6 13s 4d. Summa £13 6s 8d .... sb' 13s 4d
Et pro 3 barellis vini dulcis .... sb' 18d

Mercatores ejusdem galee

De Johanne de George pro 1800 lb. piperis. Precii £30 .... sb' 30s
De Bernardo Pascalego pro 1500 lb. zinziberis belandyn. Precii £56 5s .... sb' 56s 3d
De Lowes Bernard pro 12,000 lb. piperis. Precii £200 .... sb' £10

<aa>Valor mercandisarum, unde 12d — £318 17s 8d sb' — £15 18s 10¾d
Vinum dulce — 5 barelli sb' — 2s 6d
[Totalis] £16 [h]16¾d[h]•<aa>

f. 19v

De Johanne Capelle pro 14 buttes resins Corance £57, 900 lb. zinziberis belandyn £33 15s, 22,800 lb. piperis £360, 700 lb. seminis pro vermibus £17 10s, 3 casis canelle £12, 350 lb. saundres £8 15s, 130 lb. grani paradisi £8

<aa>-<aa> *Auditor's marginated entry: Sum of the issues on the page L.*

13s 4d, 600 lb. piperis longi £12 10s, 180 lb. macez £12. Precii £522 3s 4d .... sb' £26 2s 2d

De Nicholao Anthonio pro 20 saccis wod £13 6s 8d, 1500 lb. piperis £25, 1 pecia velvet s[erici] sateyn £8, 2½ peciis damask ynde broched cum auro £10, 6 peciis imperiall £6, 6 peciis siclaton £4. Summa £66 6s 8d sb' £3 6s 4d

De Andrea Morosyn pro 1800 lb. piperis £30, 29 carpettis £18. Summa £48 .... sb' 48s

De Johanne Maunche pro 11 barellis zinziberis viridis £55, 300 lb. zinziberis belandyn £11 5s, 60 lb. serici Liege £24. Summa £90 5s .... sb' £4 10s 3d

De Jacomo Dodo pro 7800 lb. piperis £130, 250 lb. brasylle 41s 8d, 80 lb. galbanum 33s 4d, 2 lb. auri Venesie £3 6s 8d. Summa £137 20d .... sb' £6 17s 1d

De Andrea Musshelyn pro 11 casis canelle £44, 200 lb. piperis longi £4 3s 4d, 40 lb. serici Liege £16. Summa £64 3s 4d .... sb' £3 4s 2d

De Johanne de Negro pro 6 barellis zinziberis viridis. Precii £30 .... sb' 30s

De Marco Barbarigo pro 13,800 lb. piperis £230, 2 casis canelle £8, 200 lb. zinziberis cas' £10, 450 lb. clowes £33 15s, 1 toga vetere de panno auri £16. Summa £297 15s .... sb' £14 17s 9d

De Johanne de Dulcenio pro 400 lb. piperis. Precii £6 13s 4d .... sb' 6s 8d

De Nadale de Pero pro 1200 lb. piperis. Precii £20 .... sb' 20s

De Felys Favean pro 3600 lb. piperis. Precii £60 .... sb' £3

De Augustino Pryole pro 600 lb. piperis. Precii £10 .... sb' 10s

De Thoma Couper pro 4 casis canelle. Precii £16 .... sb' 16s

<aa>Totalis valor mercandisarum, unde 12d — £1368 8s 4d sb' — £68 8s 5d<aa>

f. 20r

De Andrea et Frederigo Coroner pro 15 cassis canelle £60, 4800 lb. piperis £80, 350 lb. zinziberis belandyn £13 2s 6d, 2200 lb. saundres £56 5s, 200 lb. piperis longi £4 3s 4d, 200 lb. seminis pro vermibus £5, 33 lb. serici fyn £19 16s, 130 lb. serici Liege £52, 24 lb. serici Mesane £7 4s, 210 peciis tarterne £105, 1500 lb. brasylle £12 10s. Summa £415 10d .... sb' £20 15s ½d

De Marco Malipero pro 3 buttes vini dulcis .... sb' 9s

De Johanne dAndrea pro 600 lb. piperis. Precii £10 .... sb' 10s

De Francisco Pascalego pro 250 lb. zinziberis belandyn. Precii £9 7s 6d .... sb' 9s 4½d

De Alexandro Boromey pro 200 lb. serici Liege £80, 100 peciis tarterne £50. Summa £130 .... sb' £6 10s

De Ambrosio de Tavernis pro 200 peciis tarterne sengle. Precii £100 ...... sb' £5

De Marco de Priole pro 2100 lb. zinziberis belandyn £78 15s, 3000 lb. piperis £50, 1800 lb. zinziberis cas' £90, 1600 lb. sugre £26 13s 4d, 300 lb. sugre de 1 cote £5, 600 bowestaves debilibus £4, 150 lb. lake 25s, 800 lb. resins Coraunce £5, 22 lb. storax calamite 36s 8d, 200 lb. galbanum £4 3s 4d, 1 toga crymsyn vetere de auro £15. Summa £281 13s 4d .... sb' £14 20d

De Willelmo Estefeld et Ricardo Quatermayns pro 18,000 lb. piperis £300, 60 lb. ynde 50s, 200 lb. sugre candy £10, 20 lb. serici Liege £6 13s 4d. Summa £319 3s 4d..sb' £15 19s 2d
De Forest de Rabatta pro 2 barellis vini dulcis .... sb' 12d
De Francisco Justinean pro 800 lb. sugre de 1 cote. Precii £13 6s 8d..sb' 13s 4d
De Felyze Cokero pro 1000 lb. grani Hispanie pro pannis. Precii £75 sb' £3 15s
De dicto Marco de Priole pro 60 buttes, 60 barellis vini dulcis ....sb' £10 10s

[a-a] *Interlined L.* [b-b] *Interlined by the auditor in darker ink L.* [c] precii *follows, struck through L.* [d] de *follows L, in error.* [e] *1 cm room left for completion of the entry (cf. note 2).* [f] 1 *follows, struck through L.* [g-g] *Entered subsequently by the auditor in darker ink L.* [g-g] *Interlined above* 4¾d, *struck through L.*

<aa>Valor mercandisarum, unde 12d — £1353 11s 8d sb' — £67 13s 7d
Vinum dulce — 36 dolia, [1] pipa, 2 barelli sb' — £11
[Totalis] £78 13s 7d<aa>

f. 20v

[69] De navi Sabaott de Larre 23° die Novembris *[23 Nov. 1445]*

De eodem magistro pro 16 doliis ponderis ferri et pro 1 dolio ponderis rosine. [Precii] £41 3s 4d..sb' 41s 2d
Et pro 16 doliis, 80 hoggeshedes vini..sb' £4 13s
De Johanne Tregeran pro 12[a] doliis vini ....sb' 36s
De Bonefacio Burnell pro 1 dolio, 1 pipa, 2 hoggeshedes vini ....sb' 6s
De Arnaud de Verges pro 1 dolio ponderis ferri. Precii 50s ....sb' 2s 6d
Et pro 7 doliis, 20 hoggeshedes vini..sb' 36s
De Willelmo Abraham pro 1 cargia bevere. Precii £3 ....sb' 3s
De Johanne Reynekyn pro 10 hoggeshedes vini ....sb' 7s 6d
De Arnoldo Saunze pro 5 doliis, 40 hoggeshedes vini.............................sb' 45s
De Perrott de Rottey pro 4 doliis, 1 pipa, 12 hoggeshedes vini ....sb' 22s 6d
De predicto Arnoldo Saunze pro 3 hoggeshedes ponderis rosyn. Precii 20s .... sb' 12d
De Pernawton de Gay pro 2 doliis, 24 hoggeshedes vini ....sb' 24s
De Janycot de Vakne pro 1 pipa, 10 hoggeshedes vini ....sb' 9s
Et pro 1000 pectinibus ligni. Precii 6s 8d.. sb' 4d
De Perynyn de Seint John pro 5 doliis, 22 hoggeshedes vini..............sb' 31s 6d
De Willelmo Fraunceys pro 10 hoggeshedes vini ....sb' 7s 6d
Et pro 1 cargia bevere. Precii £3 ....sb' 3s
De Stephano Forster pro 8 doliis, 1 pipa ponderis ferri[b]. Precii £21 5s sb' 21s 3d
De Pernauton de Pedaitz pro 4 doliis, 12 hoggeshedes vini ....sb' 21s
De Willelmo Kerver pro 1 cargia bevere. Precii £3 ....sb' 3s
De Johanne dArtosapalo pro 4 cargiis bevere. Precii £12........................sb' 12s

<aa>-<aa> *Auditor's marginated entry: Sum of the issues on the page L.*

De Johannis Coo pro 3 barellis vini [c]dulcis[c] .... sb' 18d

[a] *Corrected in L from* 13. [b] ferre *L, in error.* [c-c] *Entered subsequently by the auditor in darker ink L.*

[70] De navi Bowden Henrykesson 24° die Novembris *[24 Nov. 1445]*

De Roberto Newerk pro 12 barellis allecis albi. Precii £4 .... sb' 4s
De Johanne Bolle pro 2 lastis allecis albi. Precii £8................................ sb' 8s
De Johanne Feld pro 1 lasto allecis albi, 1 lasto allecis shotyn. Precii £6... sb' 6s
De Alano Johansson pro 5 lastis allecis albi. Precii £20 .... sb' 20s
De Johanne Wellys pro 1 lasto allecis albi. Precii £4............................... sb' 4s

<aa>Valor mercandisarum, unde 12d — £129 5s sb' — £6 9s 3d
Vinum [a]dulce[a] — 3 barelli sb' — 18d [Totalis] [b]£23 9s 9d[b]
Vinum — 113 dolia sb' — £16 [c]19s[c]<aa>

[a-a] *Interlined L.* [b-b] *Entered a second time at the bottom of the page L.* [c-c] *Interlined above* 18s, *struck through L.*

f. 21r

[71] De navi Johannis Alffouns 26° die Novembris *[26 Nov. 1445]*

De eodem magistro et sociis suis pro 1 pipa vini .... sb' 18d
Et pro 21 peciis frute. Precii 28s .... sb' 17d
De Johanne de Meng et Thoma Alffouns pro 8 pipis vini .... sb' 12s
De Raphael dOreo pro 2664 peciis frute. Precii £177......................... sb' £8 17s
Et pro 9 doliis vini dulcis .... sb' 54s
De dictis Johanne Meng et Thoma Alffons pro 407 peciis frute, 1000 orenges, 200 pomegarnettes. Precii £27 13s 4d .... sb' 27s 8d
Et pro 50 lb. grani pro pannis, 100 lb. cere. Precii £5 8s 4d........... sb' 5s 5d

[72] De navi Lupo Janus eodem die *[26 Nov. 1445]*

De eodem magistro et sociis suis pro 120 peciis frute. Precii £8 .... sb' 8s
De Johanne Alffons pro 260 sorte frute. Precii £52 .... sb' 52s
De Petro Alffolde pro 300 sorte frute. Precii £60 .... sb' £3
De Ochea Spanell pro 900 pomegarnettes. Precii 20s............................. sb' 12d

[73] De navi Sogar Petirsson 4° die Decembris *[4 Dec. 1445]*

De eodem magistro pro 4 millestones. Precii 40s .... sb' 2s
De Adrean Petirsson pro 1 lasto dogstones, 1½ barellis olei, 2 barellis salmonis salsi, 1 vaga vitri, 200 parvis crusis, 2 parvis baskettis cum cruses pro vino, 30 caboges. Precii £5 .... sb' 5s

[74] De navi Gerrardi Johansson 7° die Decembris *[7 Dec. 1445]*

De Gerrardo de Bed pro 1 rothe vini de Ryna .... sb' 6s
De eodem magistro pro 4000 pavingtile, 40 skyve tasilles, 80 pontellis wold. Precii £5 13s 4d .... sb' 5s 8d

[75] De navi Johannis Osegard 10° die Decembris *[10 Dec. 1445]*

De eodem magistro pro 250 caboges. Precii 6s 8d .... sb' 4d
De Johanne Wellys pro 1 lasto allecis albi. Precii £4 .... sb' 4s
De Thoma Edmound pro 1 lasto allecis albi. Precii £4 .... sb' 4s
De Thoma Segryme pro 4 barellis olei. Precii 53s 4d .... sb' 2s 8d
De Henrico Chapman pro 2 barellis allecis albi. Precii 13s 4d .... sb' 8d

<aa>Valor mercandisarum, unde 12d — £356 16s 4d sb' — £17 16s 10d
Vinum dulce — 9 dolia sb' — 54s [Totalis] £21 10s 4d
Vinum — 6 dolia, [1] pipa sb' — 19s 6d<aa>

f. 21v

[76] De navi Willelmi Danyell 13° die Decembris *[13 Dec. 1445]*

De Roberto Newerk pro 4 lastis allecis albi. Precii £16 .... sb' 16s
De Alano Johnsson pro 2 lastis allecis albi. Precii £8 .... sb' 8s
De Johanne Wellys pro 1 lasto allecis albi. Precii £4 .... sb' 4s
De Johanne Bolle pro 1 lasto olei, 6 barellis allecis albi. Precii £10 .... sb' 10s

[77] De navi Ricardi Petite eodem die *[13 Dec. 1445]*

De Johanne Levynge pro 4½ lastis allecis albi. Precii £18 .... sb' 18s
De Perys Bate pro 4½ lastis allecis albi. Precii £18 .... sb' 18s
De Johanne Litilton pro 4 lastis allecis albi. Precii £16 .... sb' 16s

[78] De navi Johannis Paye eodem die *[13 Dec. 1445]*

De Aleyn Johnsson pro 2 lastis allecis albi. Precii £8 .... sb' 8s
De Johanne Levyng pro 2 lastis allecis albi. Precii £8 .... sb' 8s
De Johanne Feld pro 2 lastis allecis albi. Precii £8 .... sb' 8s
De eodem magistro pro 3 lastis allecis albi. Precii £12 .... sb' 12s
De Johanne Bolle pro 2 lastis allecis albi. Precii £8 .... sb' 8s

[79] De navi Johannis Castellyn eodem die *[13 Dec. 1445]*

De Johanne Roo pro 6 barellis allecis albi. Precii 40s .... sb' 2s
De Johanne Thomsson pro 1 lasto allecis albi. Precii £4 .... sb' 4s

<aa>-<aa> *Auditor's marginated entry: Sum of the issues on the page L.*

De Nicholao Childe pro 1 lasto allecis albi. Precii £4................................sb' 4s
De Johanne Passelewe pro 6 dimidiis barellis allecis albi. Precii 20s...... sb' 12d
De Alano Johansson pro 1 lasto allecis albi. Precii £4...............................sb' 4s
De Edmondo Arnalde pro 1 lasto allecis albi. Precii £4.............................sb' 4s
De domina Margeria Lyle pro 1 barello heryng. Precii 6s 8d.................. sb' 4d

<aa>Valor mercandisarum, unde 12d — £153 6s 8d sb' — £7 13s 4d<aa>

f. 22r

[80] De navi Roberti Coyse eodem die *[13 Dec. 1445]*

De Thoma Piersson pro 1½ lastis allecis albi. Precii £6 ....sb' 6s
De Johanne Wellys pro 1 lasto allecis albi. Precii £4................................sb' 4s

[81] De navi Arnolde Mounche eodem die *[13 Dec. 1445]*

De eodem magistro pro 500 caboges, 300 bunchis ceparum, 14 patellis terre. Precii 23s 4d .... sb' 14d

[82] De navi Thome Hawkyn eodem die *[13 Dec. 1445]*

De Gerrardo Goldsmyth pro 2 lastis olei, 5 lastis allecis albi, 100 bunchis ceparum. Precii £36...sb' 36s

[83] De navi Michaelis Henrykesson eodem die *[13 Dec. 1445]*

De eodem magistro pro 140 barellis ceparum, 100 lb. lini, 300 caboges. Precii £4 ....sb' 4s
De Adreano Hughsson pro 1½ lastis allecis albi, 3 barellis liversmolte. Precii £7 ....sb' 7s
De Derik Reynersson pro 2 lastis allecis albi. Precii £8.............................sb' 8s

[84] De navi Petri Piersson eodem die *[13 Dec. 1445]*

De eodem magistro pro 200 barellis ceparum, 1½ lastis allecis albi, 100 lb. lini. Precii £11 6s 8d...sb' 11s 4d

[85] De navi Thome Shippeman eodem die *[13 Dec. 1445]*

De Roberto Cliderowe pro 2½ lastis allecis albi. Precii £10.....................sb' 10s
De Willelmo Wyder pro 1 lasto allecis albi, 100 piscibus salsis. Precii £5 6s 8d ....sb' 5s 4d
De Willelmo Fraunceys pro 7 barellis allecis albi, 1 pipa cum piscibus salsis, 1 maunde cum capitibus piscium salsorum. Precii £3 ....sb' 3s
De Johanne Cantelewe pro 2 lastis olei. Precii £16.................................sb' 16s
De Willelmo Croucher pro 3 lastis allecis albi. Precii £12 ....sb' 12s

<aa>Valor mercandisarum, unde 12d — £123 16s 8d sb' — £6 3s 10d<aa>

f. 22v

[86] De navi Willelmi Brode eodem die *[13 Dec. 1445]*

De Johanne Levynge pro 3 lastis allecis albi. Precii £12 .... sb' 12s
De Johanne Bussh pro 4 lastis allecis albi. Precii £16 .... sb' 16s
De Ricardo Whiαte pro 1 lasto allecis albi. Precii £4 .... sb' 4s
De eodem magistro pro 2 barellis olei. Precii 26s 8d .... sb' 16d
De Willelmo Haller pro 20 barellis allecis albi. Precii £6 13s 4d .... sb' 6s 8d

[87] De [a]navi[a] Johannis Edward eodem die *[13 Dec. 1445]*

De Johanne Tomson pro 5 lastis allecis albi. Precii £20 .... sb' 20s
De Willelmo Croucher pro 1 lasto allecis albi. Precii £4 .... sb' 4s
De Johanne Walden pro 2 lastis allecis albi. Precii £8 .... sb' 8s

[a-a] *Interlined L.*

[88] De navi Johannis Alisaundre eodem die *[13 Dec. 1445]*

De Ricardo Froste pro 40 pipis pomorum. Precii £10 13s 4d .... sb' 10s 8d
De Johanne Harpour pro 1 parvo barello byrdelyme, 12 axes, 3 fedirbeddys, 40 alnis tele lini, 6 palettes, 3 dossenis dagers et diverso haberdashe. Precii £9 .... sb' 9s
Et pro 2 doliis vini .... sb' 6s

[89] De navi Johannis Gillott eodem die *[13 Dec. 1445]*

De Rogero Amery pro 31 pipis pomorum, 5 pipis nucum, 3 pipis seminis cenapii, 8 quarteriis frumenti, 2 millestones, 90 alnis tele lini. Precii £21 sb' 21s
De Willelmo Minor pro 1 pipa pomorum. Precii 6s 8d .... sb' 4d
De Willelmo Corbett pro 2 pipis pomorum. Precii 13s 4d .... sb' 8d
De Rogero Berlawe pro 1 pipa vini .... sb' 18d

[90] De navi Petri Clerk eodem die *[13 Dec. 1445]*

De eodem magistro pro 200 bunchis ceparum, 400 caboges, 2000 bakstone. Precii 26s 8d .... sb' 16d

[<aa>]Valor mercandisarum, unde 12d — £115 sb' — 115s
Vinum — 2 dolia, [1] pipa sb' — 7s 6d Totalis — £6 2s 6d[<aa>]

f. 23r

[91] De navi Johannis Bilter eodem die *[13 Dec. 1445]*

De Willelmo Beer pro 1 lasto allecis albi, 6 barellis olei. Precii £8 .... sb' 8s
De Willelmo Holand pro 15 barellis olei. Precii £10 .... sb' 10s
De Rogero Androwe pro 2 lastis allecis albi. Precii £8 .... sb' 8s

[<aa>-<aa>] *Auditor's marginated entry: Sum of the issues on the page L.*

De Thoma Charles pro 1400 caboges. Precii 30s.......... sb' 18d
De Johanne Levynge pro 4 barellis allecis albi. Precii 26s 8d.......... sb' 16d
De Watkyn Brewes pro 3 barellis allecis albi. Precii 20s.......... sb' 12d

[92] De navi Willelmi Warrott 14° die Decembris *[14 Dec. 1445]*

De eodem magistro pro 2 doliis, 2 hoggeshedes vini dulcis.......... sb' 15s
De Matheo Borde pro 41 doliis vini dulcis.......... sb' £12 6s

[93] De navi Johannis Amtyll eodem die *[14 Dec. 1445]*

De Colyn Ingelisch pro 6 doliis vini.......... sb' 18s
De Willelmo Berkynge pro 1 dolio vini.......... sb' 3s
De Thoma Weste pro 12 salettys. Precii 16s 8d.......... sb' 10d
[a]De monseignur Dorset pro 6 doliis vini[a]

[a-a] *Entered subsequently by the auditor, then struck through, with the subsidy entry being erased. Auditor's entry* nichil *marginated against the entry L.*

[94] De navi Willelmi Cruse eodem die *[14 Dec. 1445]*

De Stephano Forster pro 3 doliis vini.......... sb' 9s
Et pro 6 doliis ponderis ferri. Precii £15.......... sb' 15s
De Willelmo de Lunys pro 15 doliis, 8 hoggeshedes vini.......... sb' 51s
De Thoma Acton pro 3 doliis, 1 pipa vini.......... sb' 10s 6d
De Johanne Flexmer pro 3 doliis, 1 pipa vini.......... sb' 10s 6d
De Edmoundo Sheffelde pro 11 doliis, 1 pipa vini.......... sb' 34s 6d
De Johannes Blakburne pro 4 doliis, 4 hoggeshedes vini.......... sb'[a] 15s
De Thoma Cave pro 1 dolio, 3 hoggeshedes vini.......... sb' 5s 3d
De Thoma Gray pro 3 doliis, 1 pipa vini.......... sb' 10s 6d

<aa>Valor mercandisarum, unde 12d — £45 13s 4d sb' — 45s 8d
Vinum dulce — 43 dolia, [1] pipa sb' — £13 12d
Vinum — 55 dolia, [1] pipa, [1] hoggeshede sb' — £8 7s 3d
[Totalis] £23 13s 11d<aa>

f. 23ᵛ

De Roberto Stowell pro 3 doliis, 1 pipa vini.......... sb' 10s 6d
De Willelmo Abraham pro 7 doliis vini.......... sb' 21s
De Johanne Melburne pro 4 doliis vini.......... sb' 12s
De Johanne Maynewe pro 3 doliis, 1 pipa vini.......... sb' 10s 6d
De Ricardo Appilton pro 4 doliis, 1 pipa vini.......... sb' 13s 6d
De Ricardo Rough pro 1 dolio, 1 pipa vini.......... sb' 4s 6d
De Andrea Body pro 3 doliis, 1 pipa vini.......... sb' 10s 6d
De Johanne Gegge pro 2 doliis vini.......... sb' 6s
De Willelmo Stafford pro 1 dolio, 1 pipa vini.......... sb' 4s 6d

De Petro Johnsson pro 1 dolio vini .... sb' 3s
De Roberto Wolverton pro 1 dolio vini .... sb' 3s
De Johanne Doland pro 7 doliis vini .... sb' 21s
De Johanne Aleyn pro 5 doliis vini .... sb' 15s
De Willelmo Swanne pro 7 doliis vini .... sb' 21s
De Henrico Logan pro 1 dolio vini .... sb' 3s
De Stephano Morys pro 1 dolio vini .... sb' 3s
De Johanne Johanesson pro 4 doliis, 1 pipa vini .... sb' 13s 6d
De Johanne Copyndale pro 1 dolio vini .... sb' 3s
De Thoma Dey pro 1 dolio vini .... sb' 3s
De Willelmo Clerke pro 1 dolio vini .... sb' 3s
De Johanne Tregeran pro 9 doliis vini .... sb' 27s
De Roberto Kyngesson pro 2 doliis vini .... sb' 6s
De Willelmo Bodvyle pro 10 doliis, 1 pipa vini .... sb' 31s 6d
De Willelmo Downe pro 1 dolio, 1 pipa vini .... sb' 4s 6d
De Agerott Seint Pier pro 5 doliis ponderis ferri. Precii £12 10s .... sb' 12s 6d
De Willelmo Salvayn pro 1 hoggeshede vini .... sb' 9d
[b]De monseigneur de Dangladase[c] pro 7 doliis vini .... sb'[b]

[b]Nichil per breve regis[d] nunc Henrici Sexti de magno sigillo suo datum 8° die Januarii anno regni sui 24to *[8 Jan. 1446]* prefatis collectoribus inde directum *[untraceable]* et eidem [folio] consutum[b]

[b]De Johanne Bukelande pro 3 hoggeshedes vini .... sb' 2s 3d[b]

<aa>Valor mercandisarum, unde 12d de £ — £12 10s sb' — 12s 6d
Vinum — 85[e] dolia, 1 pipa sb' — £12 16s 6d [Totalis] [f]£13 9s[f]<aa>

[a] 12s *follows, struck through L..* [b-b] *Entered subsequently by the auditor L.* [c] *Corrected in L from* Angladase *in darker ink.* [d] *The writ, which was originally sewn onto the left-hand side of the page, has gone astry, but the sewing holes are visible L.* [e] *Corrected in L from* 80. [f-f] *Sum entered a second time at the bottom of the page L.*

f. 24r

[95] De navi Johannis Hadham eodem die *[14 Dec. 1445]*

De Aleyn Johnsson pro 10 doliis vini .... sb' 30s
De Thoma Gray pro 3 doliis vini .... sb' 9s
De Willelmo Halhed pro 11 doliis vini .... sb' 33s
De Johanne Gege pro 1 dolio, 1 hoggeshede vini .... sb' 3s 9d
De Edmoundo Sheffeld pro 3 doliis vini .... sb' 9s
De Willelmo Hawkesworth pro 3 doliis vini .... sb' 9s
De David Selly pro 5 doliis vini .... sb' 15s
De Willelmo Stafford pro 2 doliis, 6 hoggeshedes vini .... sb' 10s 6d
De Johanne Aleyn pro 6 doliis vini .... sb' 18s
De Willelmo Abraham pro 6 doliis, 8 hoggeshedes vini .... sb' 24s

<aa>-<aa> *Auditor's marginated entry: Sum of the issues on the page L.*

De eodem magistro pro 6 doliis vini … sb' 18s
De Waltero Gilberd pro 9 doliis vini … sb' 27s
De Awgey [a]Marshall[a] pro 4 doliis, 1 pipa vini … sb' 13s 6d
De Ricardo Appilton pro 4 doliis, 1 pipa vini … sb' 13s 6d
De Henrico Logan pro 1 pipa, 2 hoggeshedes vini … sb' 3s
De Willelmo Chattok pro 25 doliis vini … sb' £3 15s
De Johanne Melburne pro 7 doliis vini … sb' 21s
De Willelmo Clerke pro 3 doliis, 1 pipa vini … sb' 10s 6d
De Thoma Danyell pro 1 dolio, 3 hoggeshedes vini … sb' 5s 3d
De Roberto Johnsson pro 4 doliis vini … sb' 12s
De Johanne Maynew pro 4 doliis, 1 pipa vini … sb' 13s 6d
De Johanna Buklond pro 8 hoggeshedes vini … sb' 6s
De Ricardo Rough pro 2 doliis, 1 pipa vini … sb' 7s 6d
De Stephano Morys pro 4 doliis, 1 pipa vini … sb' 13s 6d
De Ricardo Fyps pro 2 doliis vini … sb' 6s
De Alexandro Heysaunt pro 7 doliis vini … sb' 21s
De Johanne de Vacche pro 3 doliis, 1 pipa vini … sb' 10s 6d
De Willelmo Turke pro 10 doliis vini … sb' 30s
[b]De Roberto Reese, milite, pro 4 doliis vini[b]

Non respondent per breve regis[c] nunc Henrici Sexti de magno sigillo suo datum 16mo die Decembris anno regni sui 24to *[16 Dec. 1445]* prefatis collectoribus inde directum *[mandate untraceable]* et eidem [folio] consutum

[<aa>]Valor mercandisarum, unde 12d — nullum
Vinum — 156 dolia sb' — £23 8s[<aa>]

f. 24^{v}

De Johanne Defford pro 1 pipa, 2 hoggeshedes vini … sb' 3s
De Willelmo Hydeman pro 1 dolio vini … sb' 3s
De Johanne Flexmere pro 6 doliis vini … sb' 18s
De Willelmo de Lunys pro 4 doliis [d]vini … sb' 12s[d]
De Roberto Kyngesson pro 2 doliis vini … sb' 6s
De Willelmo Corbett pro 1 dolio vini … sb' 3s
De Willelmo Haydok pro 3 doliis vini … sb' 9s
De Henrico Kente pro 1 dolio, 1 pipa vini … sb' 4s 6d
De Ricardo Stapill pro 3 doliis, 2 hoggeshedes vini … sb' 10s 6d
De Ricardo Smyth pro 2 doliis vini … sb' 6s
De Willelmo Downe pro 1 hoggeshede vini … sb' 9d
[e]De [d]Ricardo[d] Sturgeon pro 2 doliis vini

Non respondent per breve regis[c] nunc Henrici Sexti de magno sigillo suo datum 20° die Januarii anno regni sui 24to *[20 Jan. 1446]* prefatis collectoribus inde directum *[mandate untraceable]* et huic folio consutum

[e]De Johanne Tiptofte pro 1 pipa vini

Non respondent per breve regis[c] nunc Henrici Sexti de magno sigillo suo datum 8° die Decembris anno regni sui 24[to] *[8 Dec. 1445]* prefatis collectoribus inde directum *[mandate untraceable]* et huic folio consutum

[a-a] *Interlined subsequently by the auditor L.* [b-b] *Entered subsequently by the auditor, with the subsidy entry being erased L. Auditor's entry* per breve *marginated against the entry.* [c] *The writ, which was originally sewn onto the left-hand side of the page, has gone astray, but the sewing holes are visible L.* [d-d] *Entered subsequently by the auditor L.* [e] breve *marginated against this entry L.*

[96] De navi Johannis Rycchefford eodem die *[14 Dec. 1445]*

De eodem magistro pro 1 [dolio] vini	sb' 3s
Et pro 600 lb. rosyn. Precii 13s 4d	sb' 8d
De Johanne Steele pro 23 doliis vini	sb' £3 9s
De Johanne Mayak pro 5 doliis vini	sb' 15s
De Ricardo Forster et Johanne Hawkyn pro 2 doliis, 1 pipa vini	sb' 7s 6d
De Willelmo Laurence pro 6 doliis vini	sb' 18s
De Willelmo Kynge pro 1 pipa, 4 hoggeshedes vini	sb' 4s 6d
De Willelmo Falham et Johanne Johnsson pro 2 doliis, 1 pipa vini	[a]sb' 7s 6d[a]

[a-a] *Entered subsequently by the auditor L.*

[97] De navi Henrici Neyndanke eodem die *[14 Dec. 1445]*

De eodem magistro pro 1 pipa vini	sb' 18d
De Johanne Peverell pro 9 doliis vini	sb' 27s
De Eliott Bedawe pro 10 doliis vini	sb' 30s
De Roberto Reef pro 9 doliis vini	sb' 27s
De Jacobo Shippman pro 1 hoggeshede vini	sb' 9d

<aa>Valor mercandisarum, unde 12d — 13s 4d sb' — 8d

Vinum — 95 dolia, [a]1 pipa[a] sb' — £14 6s 6d [Totalis] £14 7s 2d<aa>

[a-a] *Interlined L.*

<aa>-<aa> *Auditor's marginated entry: Sum of the issues on the page L.*

PARCELLE COMPOTI

[P 1] *John, earl of Shrewsbury* (comes Salop'), *lord Talbot and* de Furnyvale *acknowledges the receipt from the collectors of tunnage and poundage in London of 300 marks (sterling) for Easter term 1446 and Michaelmas term 1446* (pro terminis Pasche anno regni domini regis nunc vicesimo quarto et sancti Michaelis anno regni ejusdem regis vicesimo quinto) *of the 300 marks (sterling) which Henry VI had granted him from the issues of tunnage and poundage in London until such time as his loan to the crown of £10,426 4¼d be paid off, as may be seen more clearly from the king's patent.*[1] — *1446 Dec. 2* (Per presentes sigillo nostro signatas. Datum secundo die mensis Decembris anno regni regis Henrici Sexti predicti post conquestum vicesimo quinto). *[London].*

L TNA: PRO, E122/70/26/58. Original. Parchment. Remains of seal on tongue. On the dorse: Allocatur; *(beneath that)* Pro Ricardo Quatermayns et Thoma Walsyngham; *(beneath that)* Allocatur in compoto Ricardi Quatremayns et Thome Walsyngham collectorum subsidii 3s de dolio et 12d de libra in portu civitatis London' computancium a festo sancti Michaelis anno 24to regis Henrici vj^{ti} usque idem festum proxime sequens. *[No. A 3 § 27]*

---

[1] *CPR 1441-6, p. 227-8.*

ACCOUNTING DOCUMENTS

[A 1] Richard Quatermayns *names his colleague Thomas* Walsyngham *as his attorney for the purpose of accounting before the Exchequer for the issues of tunnage and poundage in London for the period when they were both customers [29 Sept. 1445 to 29 Sept. 1446]*

L TNA: PRO, E159/223 Communia: Adhuc fines, manucapciones, dies datus, attornati, respectus et visus Michaelmas m 2d. Contemporaneous official fair copy of the Exchequer proceedings. Parchment. Unsealed.

[Marginated] London'; De die dato

Ricardus Quatermayns unus collectorum subsidiorum tonagii et pondagii in portu civitatis London' ponit loco suo Thomam Walsyngham alterum collectorem eorundem subsidiorum ibidem ad reddendum pro eo domino regi compotum de subsidiis predictis de tempore, quo inde fuerunt collectores et non computarunt, et ad omnia alia dictum compotum tangencia facienda, prout idem Ricardus faceret, si personaliter interesset.

Per J. Holme

[A 2] Richard Quatremayns *and Thomas* Walsyngham *appear before the Exchequer in Michaelmas term 1446 to account for the issues of tunnage and poundage in London in the period from 29 Sept. 1445 to 29 Sept. 1446. Since they and the controller William* Beaufitz *continue in office, the London sheriffs are ordered to distrain them to appear on 17 Apr. 1447.*

L PRO, E159/223 Recorda Michaelmas m 2d. Contemporaneous official fair copy of the Exchequer proceedings. Parchment. Unsealed.

[Marginated] London'

Memorandum, quod Ricardus Quatremayns et Thomas Walsyngham collectores subsidiorum tonagii et pondagii, videlicet trium solidorum de dolio vini et duodecim denariorum de libra, in portu civitatis London' venerunt et computarunt de eisdem subsidiis ibidem videlicet a festo sancti Michaelis anno 24[to] regis hujus *[29 Sept. 1445]* usque idem festum proxime sequens *[29 Sept. 1446]*, a quo quidem festo iidem collectores per visum et testimonium Willelmi Beaufitz contrarotulatoris eorundem subsidiorum ibidem sunt alias inde computaturi. [a]Ideo preceptum sit vicecomitibus, quod ipsos collectores et contrarotulatorem distringant per terras etc., ita etc. in crastino Clausi Pasche *[17 Apr. 1447]*, dictos videlicet collectores ad computandum et dictum contrarotulatorem ad testificandum in premissis.

[a] *The remainder of the document was written by a different hand L.* r' *written over* s' *marginated against this line.*

[A 3] Richard Quatermayns *and Thomas* Walsyngham *appear before the Exchequer in Michaelmas term 1446 and account for the issues of tunnage and poundage in London in the period from 29 Sept. 1445 and 29 Sept. 1446.*

L TNA: PRO, E356/16 m 27. Contemporaneous official fair copy of the Exchequer proceedings. Parchment. Unsealed. In the margina: s'; Termino sancti Michaelis anno 25to regis Henrici Sexti. *In the 5 cm left free by the indentation of the first line: Auditores:* J. Holme baro, J. Somer clericus.

[Marginated] London'

[1] Compotus Ricardi Quatermayns et Thome Walsyngham collectorum subsidiorum tonagii et pondagii tam de mercatoribus Anglicanis quam de alienigenis in portu civitatis London' et in singulis portubus et locis eidem portui adjacentibus per breve regis nunc Henrici Sexti de magno sigillo suo datum 21mo die Septembris anno regni sui 24to *[21 Sept. 1445]* prefatis collectoribus inde directum et penes ipsos collectores remanens aliasque in compoto suo de eodem anno *[TNA: PRO, E356/16 m 27]*[1] plenius annotatum, videlicet de hujusmodi subsidiis regis ibidem a festo sancti Michaelis anno 24to regis predicti *[29 Sept. 1445]*, ante quod festum prefati collectores inde computarunt rotulo compotorum de subsidio *[TNA: PRO, E356/16 m 27]*[1], usque festum sancti Michaelis extunc proxime sequens *[29 Sept. 1446]*, scilicet per unum annum integrum, per visum et testimonium Willelmi Beaufitz contrarotulatoris hujusmodi subs[idiorum] regis ibidem per idem tempus, a quo quidem festo sancti Michaelis anno 25to regis predicti prefati Ricardus et Thomas collectores ibidem per visum et testimonium predicti Willelmi Beaufitz contrarotulatoris subs[idiorum] regis predicti sunt alias inde computaturi.

[Marginated] Recepta denariorum

[2] Iidem reddunt compotum de £485 6s 6d de subsidio tonagii contingente tam 2922 dolia, 1 hoggeshede, 3 barellos vini Vasconiensis quam 156 dolia, [1] pipam vini dulcis diversorum mercatorum tam indigenarum quam alienigenarum ad portum et loca predicta adducta per predictum tempus hujus compoti, videlicet de quolibet hujusmodi dolio vini Vasconiensis 3s et de quolibet hujusmodi dolio vini dulcis 6s, per breve regis predictum supra in titulo hujus compoti annotatum, sicut continetur tam in quodam libro ipsorum collectorum de particulis sub sigillo hujus scaccarii quam in 31 rotulis prefati contrarotulatoris de particulis inde hic in thesauro liberatis.

[3] De aliquo hujusmodi subsidio tonagii 9 doliorum vini Vasconiensis le seignur de Dangladase, unde 7 dolia in navi Willelmi Cruse intrante 14mo die Decembris anno 24to *[14 Dec. 1445; Ship No. 94]* et 2 dolia in navi Henrici

---

[1] *Stuart Jenks (ed.), The Enrolled Customs Accounts (PRO, E356, E372, E364) 1279/80-1508/09 (1523/24) Volume 6: E356/15, E356/16 (List and Index Society) [in press], E356/16, No. 245.*

Lancassak intrante 6to die Januarii eodem anno *[6 Jan. 1446]*, aut 2 doliorum vini Vasconiensis Johannis Copyn intrante in eadem navi eodem 6to die Januarii *[6 Jan. 1446]* vel 5 doliorum, [1] pipe vini Vasconiensis Francissi de Lunes in eadem navi intrante eisdem die et anno infra dictum tempus hujus compoti adductorum non respondent per breve regis predicti datum 8° die Januarii anno regni sui 24to *[8 Jan. 1446]* prefatis collectoribus inde directum et super hunc compotum liberatum *[cf. Ship No. 94, variant c]*, per quod breve rex mandavit prefatis collectoribus, quod prefato [a]le[a] seignur de Dangladase per nomen Johannis Danglades militis predicta novem dolia vini, Francisco de Lunes sex dolia vini et Johanni Copyn duo dolia vini, que ipsi a partibus Vasconie usque portum predictum pro expensis suis et non vendicioni aliqualiter exponendo adduci fecerunt, prout coram rege in cancellaria sua sufficienter est testificatum, absque subsidio inde ad opus regis capiendo liberent indilate, voluit enim rex prefatos collectores inde erga se exonerari, sicut continetur ibidem.

[4] Nec respondent de aliquo hujusmodi subsidio tonagii 8 doliorum vini Vasconiensis Roberti Roos militis, unde 4 dolia in navi Johannis Hadham intrante 14mo die Decembris predicto anno 24to *[14 Dec. 1445]* et 4 dolia in navi Samsonis Chevals intrante eisdem die et anno infra tempus supradictum, adductorum per breve regis supradicti datum 16° die Decembris predicto anno 24to *[16 Dec. 1445]* prefatis collectoribus inde directum et super hunc compotum liberatum *[cf. Ship No. 95 variant c]*, per quod breve rex mandavit prefatis collectoribus, quod predicta 8 dolia vini, que dilectus et fidelis miles suus Robertus Roos a partibus Vasconie usque portum predictum pro expensis hospicii sui adduci fecit et non vendicioni exponendo, prout idem Robertus coram rege in cancellaria sua sufficienter est testificatus, eidem Roberto absque subsidio inde ad opus regis capiendo liberent indilate, voluit enim rex prefatos collectores inde erga se exonerari, sicut continetur ibidem.

[5] Nec respondent de aliquo hujusmodi subsidio tonagii duorum doliorum vini Vasconiensis Ricardi Sturgeon in navi prefati Johannis Hadham intrante predicto 14mo die Decembris dicto anno 24to *[14 Dec. 1445]* infra tempus supradictum adductorum per breve regis predicti datum 20mo die Januarii anno regni sui 24to *[20 Jan. 1446]* prefatis collectoribus inde directum et super hunc compotum liberatum *[cf. Ship No. 95 variant e]*, per quod breve rex mandavit prefatis collectoribus, quod predicto Ricardo Sturgeon predicta duo dolia vini sibi a partibus Vasconie pro expensis hospicii sui et non vendicioni aliqualiter exponendo missa, prout satis sufficienter regi informatur, absque subsidio inde ad opus regis capiendo liberent, voluit enim rex prefatos collectores inde erga se exonerari, sicut continetur ibidem.

[6] Nec respondent de aliquo hujusmodi subsidio tonagii 1 pipe vini Vasconiensis in eadem navi eisdem die et anno intrante infra tempus supradictum adducte per breve regis supradicti datum 8vo die Decembris predicto anno 24to *[8 Dec. 1445]* prefatis collectoribus inde directum et super hunc compotum liberatum *[cf. Ship No. 95 variant e]*, per quod breve rex mandavit prefatis

collectoribus, quod unam pipam vini a partibus transmarinis ad opus dilecti et fidelis regis Johannis Tiptoft emptam et provisam et ad portum predictum in navi adductam, prout ex parte ipsius Johannis coram rege in cancellaria sua sufficienter est testificatum, eidem Johanni vel ejus in hac parte attornato seu deputato absque custuma et subsidio et aliis deveriis ad opus regis capiendis seu solvendis liberent indilate, sicut continetur ibidem.

[7] Nec respondent de aliquo hujusmodi subsidio tonagii 16 doliorum vini Vasconiensis Gallardi domini de Duras in navi Samsonis Chavals intrante predicto 14mo die Decembris predicto anno 24to *[14 Dec. 1445]* infra tempus predictum adductorum per breve regis supradicti datum 15mo die Decembris predicto anno 24to *[15 Dec. 1445]* prefatis collectoribus inde directum et super hunc compotum liberatum *[untraceable]*, per quod breve rex mandavit prefatis collectoribus, quod predicta 16 dolia vini, que dilectus regis prefatus Gallardus de Durafford dominus de Duras a partibus transmarinis in regnum regis Anglie tam pro expensis hospicii sui quam aliorum, quibus ipse magnam partem vinorum illorum protulit, transmisit et quicquam vendicioni inde non exposuit, sicut idem Gallardus coram rege in cancellaria sua sufficienter est testificatus, eidem Gallardo aut ejus in hac parte deputato absque subsidio inde ad opus regis solvendo liberent, voluit enim rex prefatos collectores inde erga se exonerari, sicut continetur ibidem.

[8] Nec respondent de aliquo hujusmodi subsidio tonagii 4 doliorum vini Vasconiensis Willelmi[2] Brewster in navi Johannis Blakeman predicto 14mo die Decembris eodem anno 24to *[14 Dec. 1445]* infra tempus predictum adductorum per breve regis supradicti de magno sigillo suo datum 18vo die Marcii predicto anno 24to *[18 Mar. 1446]* prefatis collectoribus inde directum et super hunc compotum liberatum *[untraceable]*, per quod breve rex mandavit prefatis collectoribus, quod dilecto clerico suo prefato Johanni[2] Brewster vel ejus deputato predicta 4^{or} dolia vini per ipsum deputatum in partibus transmarinis pro expensis hospicii ipsius Johannis empta et provisa et ad portum predictum adducta, sicut idem Johannes coram rege in cancellaria sua personaliter constitutus sacramentum prestitit corporale, absque custuma sive subsidio inde ad opus regis capiendo liberent seu deliberari faciant, sicut continetur ibidem.

[9] Nec respondent de aliquo hujusmodi subsidio tonagii 4^{or} doliorum, [1] pipe vini Vasconiensis Georgii Swelington in eadem navi eisdem die et anno infra tempus supradictum adductorum per breve regis nunc Henrici Sexti de magno sigillo suo datum 9no die Februarii predicto anno 24to *[9 Feb. 1446]* prefatis collectoribus inde directum et super hunc compotum liberatum *[untraceable]*, per quod breve rex mandavit prefatis collectoribus, quod dilecto regis prefato Georgio Swelyngton vel ejus deputato predicta 4 dolia et unam pipam vini per ipsum in partibus transmarinis pro expensis hospicii ipsius Georgii empta et provisa et ad portum predictum adducta, sicut idem Georgius coram rege in cancellaria regis personaliter constitutus sacramentum prestitit

[2] *Clearly, William Brewster was acting as John Brewster's deputy.*

corporale, absque custuma sive subsidio inde ad opus regis capiendo liberent seu liberari faciant, sicut continetur ibidem.

[10] Nec respondent de aliquo hujusmodi subsidio tonagii 125 doliorum, [1] pipe, [a]2 barellorum[a] vini Vasconiensis Johannis ducis Exonie, unde 10 dolia, [1] pipa in navi Rogeri Amys vocata Cristofer Afych intrante predicto 14mo die Decembris predicto anno 24to *[14 Dec. 1445]*, 26 dolia, [1] pipa, 1 barellus in navi Laurencii Houchoun intrante eodem 14mo die Decembris *[14 Dec. 1445]*, 42 dolia in navi Johannis Hegowe vocata le Jamys de Fowey intrante eodem 14mo die Decembris *[14 Dec. 1445]*, 46 dolia, [1] pipa, 1 barellus in navi Henrici Lansak intrante 6to die Januarii eodem anno 24to *[6 Jan. 1446]* infra tempus supradictum adducta, per breve regis supradicti de magno sigillo suo datum 7mo die Februarii anno regni sui 24to *[7 Feb. 1446]* prefatis collectoribus inde directum et super hunc compotum liberatum *[untraceable]*, per quod breve rex mandavit prefatis collectoribus, quod carissimo consanguineo suo Johanni duci Exonie sive ejus in hac parte deputato centum, viginti et quinque dolia, unam pipam et duos barellos vini de Vasconia [a]in partibus Vasconie[a] pro expensis hospicii ipsius ducis empta et provisa et ad portum predictum in diversis navibus adducta, sicut Johannes Hoggeseson unus servientum ejusdem ducis coram rege in cancellaria sua personaliter constitutus sacramentum prestitit corporale, absque subsidio seu aliis deveriis ad opus regis in hac parte capiendo seu solvendo liberent indilate, et rex prefatos collectores inde in compoto suo ad scaccarium suum debitam allocacionem habere faciat, sicut continetur ibidem.

[11] Nec respondent de 26 doliis, [1] pipa vini Vasconiensis domini Johannis ducis Norffolcie in navi Johannis Blakeman intrante supradicto 14mo die Decembris infra tempus supradictum *[14 Dec. 1445]* adductis per breve regis supradicti de magno sigillo suo [a]datum[a] 12mo die Julii predicto anno 24to *[24 July 1446]* prefatis collectoribus inde directum et super hunc compotum liberatum *[untraceable]*, per quod breve rex precepit prefatis collectoribus, quod predicta 26 dolia, [1] pipam vini in partibus exteris pro expensis hospicii supradicti ducis provisa [et] in supradicta navi Johannis Blakeman ad portum predictum ex causa predicta adducta, sicut Robertus Wynkefeld miles et Ricardus Quatremayns coram rege in cancellaria sua sacramenta prestiterunt corporalia, eidem duci vel ejus in hac parte deputatis absque custuma, subsidio et aliis deveriis regi in hac parte debitis liberent indilate, voluit enim rex prefatos collectores inde erga se exonerari, sicut continetur ibidem.

[12] Nec respondent de aliquo hujusmodi subsidio tonagii 7 doliorum vini Vasconiensis Galiardi domini de Duras in navi Johannis Bratker intrante supradicto 14mo die Decembris infra tempus supradictum *[14 Dec. 1445]* adductorum per breve regis supradicti de magno sigillo suo datum quinto die Julii dicto anno 24to *[5 July 1446]* prefatis collectoribus inde directum et super hunc compotum liberatum *[untraceable]*, per quod breve rex mandavit prefatis collectoribus, quod dilecto suo Galiardo de Dureford domino de Duras et de Blankford per Johannem Mayac deputatum suum 7 dolia vini in partibus

transmarinis pro expensis hospicii sui empta et provisa et ad portum predictum adducta, sicut idem deputatus coram rege in cancellaria sua personaliter constitutus sacramentum prestitit corporale, absque custuma sive subsidio inde ad opus nostrum capiendo liberent, aliquo mandato prefatis collectoribus prius incontrarium directo non obstante, sicut continetur ibidem.

[13] Nec respondent de aliquo hujusmodi subsidio tonagii 52 doliorum vini domini de Capetowe, unde 6 dolia, [1] pipa, 16 hoggeshedes vini in navi Willelmi Dawe intrante supradicto 6to die Januarii predicto anno 24to *[6 Jan. 1446]*, 21 dolia, 40 hoggeshedes vini in navi Thome Lambton intrante eisdem die et anno et 8 dolia, [1] pipa, 8 hoggeshedes vini in navi Willelmi Ryby intrante eisdem die et anno infra tempus supradictum adducta, per breve regis supradicti de magno sigillo suo datum 30mo die Marcii predicto anno 24to *[30 Mar. 1446]* prefatis collectoribus inde directum et super hunc compotum liberatum *[untraceable]*, per quod breve rex mandavit prefatis collectoribus, quod sexaginta et unum dolia vini, que dictus dominus de Captan' a partibus Vasconie usque portum predictum tam pro expensis suis quam ceteris dominis et amicicis suis dando et non vendicioni aliqualiter exponendo adduci fecit, prout Nando Brange coram rege in cancellaria sua sacramentum prestitit corporale, eidem domino seu ejus in hac parte attornato absque subsidio inde ad opus regis capiendo liberent indilate, voluit enim rex prefatos collectores inde erga se exonerari, sicut continetur ibidem.

[14] Nec respondent de aliquo hujusmodi subsidio tonagii 5 doliorum vini Vasconiensis Amaynewe seignur de Seint Creke in navi Francisci de Berkus intrante tercio die Januarii eodem anno 24to *[3 Jan. 1446]* infra tempus supradictum adductorum per breve regis supradicti de magno sigillo suo datum primo die Junii eodem anno 24to *[1 June 1446]* prefatis collectoribus inde directum et super hunc compotum liberatum *[untraceable]*, per quod breve rex mandavit prefatis collectoribus, quod predicta quinque dolia vini, que dictus dominus de Seint Crike ad portum predictum adduci fecit et certis amicis et benevolis suis dare intendit et que vendicioni minime exponet, sicut coram rege in cancellaria sua sufficienter est testificatum, eidem domino seu ejus in hac parte deputato absque subsidio inde ad opus regis capiendo liberent indilate, voluit enim rex prefatos collectores inde in compoto suo erga se exonerari, sicut continetur ibidem.

[15] Nec respondent de aliquo hujusmodi subsidio tonagii 8 doliorum, [1] pipe vini Vasconiensis Willelmi marchionis et comitis Suffolcie in navi Gylmyn Bassyn intrante tercio die Marcii predicto anno 24to *[3 Mar. 1446]* infra tempus supradictum adductorum per breve regis supradicti de magno sigillo suo datum 14mo die Maii eodem anno 24to *[14 May 1446]* prefatis collectoribus inde directum et super hunc compotum liberatum *[untraceable]*, per quod breve rex precepit prefatis collectoribus, quod carissimo consanguineo suo prefato Willelmo marchioni et comiti Suffolcie dicta octo dolia et 1 pipam vini eidem marchioni a partibus transmarinis pro expensis hospicii sui et non in alios usus ponenda transmissa absque custuma seu subsidio inde ad opus regis

capiendo liberent, voluit enim rex prefatos collectores inde erga se exonerari, sicut continetur ibidem.

[16] Nec respondent de aliquo hujusmodi subsidio tonagii unius dolii vini Marticot Derm in navi sua intrante 7mo die Maii eodem anno 24to *[7 May 1446]* ad portum predictum infra tempus supradictum adducti per breve regis supradicti de magno sigillo suo datum 24to die Maii eodem anno 24to *[24 May 1446]* prefatis collectoribus inde directum et super hunc compotum liberatum *[untraceable]*, per quod breve rex mandavit prefatis collectoribus, quod dicto Marticot Derm vel ejus deputato unum dolium vini per ipsum Marticot in partibus transmarinis pro expensis hospicii sui emptum et provisum et ad portum predictum adductum, sicut idem Marticot coram rege in cancellaria sua personaliter constitutus sacramentum prestitit corporale, absque custuma sive subsidio inde ad opus regis capiendo liberent seu liberari faciant, sicut continetur ibidem.

[17] Nec respondent de 129 pipis vini albi Margarete regine Anglie in navi Johannis Carrys intrante 16mo die Maii eodem anno 24to *[16 May 1446]* ad portum predictum infra tempus supradictum adductis per breve regis predicti de magno sigillo suo datum 17mo die Maii eodem anno 24to *[17 May 1446]* prefatis collectoribus inde directum et super hunc compotum liberatum *[untraceable]*, per quod breve rex mandavit prefatis collectoribus, quod dictas centum et viginti et novem pipas vini albi carissime consorti regis prefate Margarete regine Anglie per regem Cecilie patrem ejusdem regine in regnum regis Anglie pro expensis hospicii sui missas et in portu civitatis predicte in navi vocata le Trinite de Nawntes, unde predictus Johannes de Carrys est magister, existentes eidem regine aut ejus in hac parte attornato seu deputato absque subsidio, custuma aut aliis deveriis regi inde solvendo liberent indilate et hoc nullatenus omittant.

[18] Nec respondent de aliquo hujusmodi subsidio tonagii 6 doliorum vini Vasconiensis in navi Willelmi Baudewyn intrante 23^{cio} die Maii eodem anno 24to *[23 May 1446]* ad portum predictum infra tempus supradictum adductorum per breve regis supradicti de magno sigillo suo datum 10mo die Maii eodem anno 24to *[10 May 1446]* prefatis collectoribus inde directum et super hunc compotum liberatum *[untraceable]*, per quod breve rex mandavit prefatis collectoribus, quod eidem venerabili patri Johanni episcopo Bathoniensis et Wellensis dicta 6 dolia vini rubei de Vasconia pro usu et expensis hospicii sui in partibus Burdegale empta et provisa et usque portum predictum adducta, prout coram rege in cancellaria sua sufficienter est testificatum, absque hujusmodi subsidio liberent, sicut continetur ibidem.

[19] Nec respondent de aliquo hujusmodi subsidio tonagii 10 doliorum vini Vasconiensis in navi Fraunson Capetane intrante eodem 23^{cio} die Maii eodem anno 24to *[23 May 1446]* ad portum predictum infra tempus supradictum adductorum per breve regis supradicti de magno sigillo suo datum primo die Junii anno supradicto *[1 June 1446]* prefatis collectoribus inde directum et super hunc compotum liberatum *[untraceable]*, per quod breve rex mandavit

prefatis collectoribus, quod eadem 10^{cem} dolia vini, que Archambandus [a]de[a] Lescoigne ad portum predictum pro expensis hospicii sui infra regnum regis Anglie adduci fecit et que vendicioni minime exponentur, sicut coram rege in cancellaria sua sufficienter est testificatum, eidem Archambando seu ejus in hac parte deputato absque subsidio inde ad opus regis capiendo liberent indilate, voluit enim rex prefatos collectores erga se in compoto suo exonerari, sicut continetur ibidem.

[20] Nec respondent de aliquo hujusmodi subsidio tonagii 6 doliorum vini Vasconiensis monseignur Dorset in navi Johannis Hamtyll 14mo die Decembris infra tempus supradictum *[14 Dec. 1445]* adductorum per breve regis supradicti de magno sigillo suo datum 18vo die Januarii eodem anno 24to *[18 Jan. 1446]* prefatis collectoribus inde directum et super hunc compotum liberatum *[cf. Ship No. 93, variant a]*, per quod breve rex mandavit prefatis collectoribus, quod dicta sex dolia vini in partibus exteris pro expensis hospicii prefati monseignur Dorset per nomen Edmundi marchionis Dorset in navi prefati Johannis Hamptill ad portum predictum ex causa predicta adducta, sicut Thomas Walsyngham coram rege in cancellaria sua sacramentum prestitit corporale, eidem marchioni vel ejus in hac parte deputatis absque custuma, subsidio et aliis deveriis regi inde solvendo liberari faciant indilate, voluit enim rex prefatos collectores inde erga se totaliter exonerari, sicut continetur ibidem.

[21] Nec respondent de aliquo hujusmodi subsidio tonagii 11 doliorum, [1] pipe vini Thome Gray militis, unde 4 dolia, [1] pipa in navi Samsonis Chevals vocata le Elyn de London' intrante predicto 14mo die Decembris predicto anno 24to *[14 Dec. 1445]* et 5 dolia, 8 hoggeshedes vini in navi Henrici Lancassak vocata Marie de Cherburgh intrante 6to die Januarii eodem anno 24to *[6 Jan. 1446]*, per breve regis predicti de magno sigillo suo datum 4to die Februarii anno regni sui 24to *[4 Feb. 1446]* prefatis collectoribus inde directum et super hunc compotum liberatum,[3] per quod breve rex mandavit prefatis collectoribus, quod dilecto et fideli suo prefato Thome Gray militi sive ejus in hac parte deputato predicta 11 dolia et 1 pipam vini de Vasconia in partibus regis Vasconie pro expensis domisilii ipsius Thome empta et provisa et ad portum predictum in navibus predictis adducta, sicut Johannes de Chamber coram rege in cancellaria sua personaliter constitutus sacramentum prestitit corporale, absque subsidio seu aliis deveriis ad opus regis in hac parte capiendo seu solvendo liberent indilate, et rex prefatos collectores inde in compoto suo ad scaccarium regis debitam allocacionem habere faciat, sicut continetur ibidem.

[22] Sed respondent de £1593 4s ½d de subsidio pondagii diversarum rerum et mercandisarum diversorum mercatorum indigenarum et alienigenarum in portu et locis predictis tam adductarum quam eductarum et ibidem custumatarum infra tempus predictum, que quidem res et mercandise ad £31,861 10s 7d estimabantur juxta verum valorem earundem, videlicet de qualibet hujusmodi libra 12d, per breve predictum supra in titulo hujus compoti annotatum, sicut

---

[3] *CCR 1441-7, p. 331.*

continetur ibidem.

[23] De aliquo hujusmodi subsidio pondagii 1 fardelli cum uno lecto de Arras continente 7 pecias, 3 peciis panni linei Holandie continentibus 203 virgas, 1 pecia panni linei pro mappis continente 40 virgas et una pecia pro mappalibus continente 20 virgas duplicata magistri Vincencii Clement in navi Petri George 25to die Januarii predicto anno 24to *[25 Jan. 1446]* intrante infra tempus supradictum adducti per breve regis supradicti de magno sigillo suo datum tercio die Februarii anno regni sui 24to *[3 Feb. 1446]* prefatis collectoribus inde directum et super hunc compotum liberatum *[untraceable]*, per quod breve rex mandavit prefatis collectoribus, quod dictum fardellum, in quo[b] continetur quidam lectus de Arras habens septem pecias, tres pecias panni linei de Holandia continentes ducentas et tres virgas, una pecia panni linei pro mappis continens 40 virgas et una pecia pro mappalibus continens 20^{ti} virgas duplicata ad usum dilecti regis magistri Vincencii Clement in partibus Flandrie empta et provisa et in portu predicto ad presens existencia et que vendicioni minime exponentur, prout sufficienter regi informatur, eidem Vincencio seu ejus in hac parte deputato absque subsidio inde ad opus regis capiendo liberent indilate, voluit enim rex prefatos collectores inde erga se exonerari, sicut continetur ibidem.

[Marginated] Examinatur

Summa totalis recepte: £2078 10s 6½d, unde subsidium tonagii £485 6s 6d, subsidium pondagii £1593 4s ½d.

[24] In thesauro £862 12s 9½d in 15 talliis.

[25] Et in thesauro £87 27° die Junii anno 24to *[27 June 1446]*.

[26] Et in parte superplusagii, quod iidem Ricardus et Thomas habent in rotulo 24to regis hujus in Item London' *[No. S 2]* de hujusmodi subsidiis £928 17s 9d

[27] Et Johanni comiti Salopie domino[c] Talbot et de Furnyvale, cui rex tercio die Decembris anno 22do *[3 Dec. 1443]* inter alia concessit[4] 300 marcas per annum de subs[idio] 3s de dolio vini et 12d de libra in portu London' percipiendas per manus custumariorum sive collectorum ejusdem subsidii in portu predicto pro tempore existencium ad terminos Pasche et sancti Michaelis per equales porciones, quousque eidem comiti de summa £10,426[d] 4¼d plenarie solutum fuerit et contentatum, in portu predicto et in aliis diversis locis £200, videlicet de hujusmodi subs[idio] in eodem portu de termino Pasche anno 24to et termino sancti Michaelis anno 25to ultra £1433 6s 8d prius allocata de summa predicta, sicut continetur in compoto Willelmi Soper et Willelmi Marys nuper collectorum custumarum et subsidiorum in portu ville Suthamptonie computantium a festo sancti Michaelis anno 24to regis hujus *[29 Sept. 1445]* usque 28^{m} diem Septembris tunc proxime sequentem *[28 Sept. 1446]*

---

[4] *CPR 1441-6, p. 227-8.*

rotulo compotorum de custumis *[TNA: PRO, E356/19 m 20-20d]*,[5] per breve regis irrotulatum in memorandis[6] de anno 23[cio] regis hujus termino Pasche rotulo 11[mo] *[No. S 1]* et litteras acquietancie ipsius comitis de recepta *[No. P 1]* et sicut allocatum est prefatis collectoribus in rotulo[e] 23[cio] regis hujus *[TNA: PRO, E372/290]* in Adhuc Res' London' *[No. S 3]*.

[28] Et quieti sunt.

[a–a] *Interlined L.* [b] qua *L, in error.* [c] de *follows, underlined for the purpose of cancellation L.* [d] *Corrected in L from* £10,526. [e] in rotulo *follows, underlined for the purpose of cancellation L.*

[A 4] Audit [in Michaelmas term 1446] of the account of Richard Quatermayns *and Thomas* Walsyngham *for the issues of tunnage and poundage in London in the period from 29 Sept. 1445 and 29 Sept. 1446.*

L TNA: PRO, E368/219 Visus et status compotorum Michaelmas m 9 (m 276 stamped). Contemporaneous official fair copy of the Exchequer proceedings. Parchment. Unsealed.

[Marginated] London'

[1] Audito compoto Ricardi Quatermayns et Thome Walsyngham collectorum subsidii tonagii et pondagii tam de mercatoribus Anglicanis quam de alienigenis in portu civitatis London' et in singulis portubus et locis eidem portui adjacentibus, videlicet de hujusmodi subsidio regis ibidem a festo sancti Michaelis anno 24[to] regis nunc *[29 Sept. 1445]* usque festum sancti Michaelis tunc proxime sequens *[29 Sept. 1446]*, per visum et testimonium Willelmi Beaufitz contrarotulatoris hujusmodi subsidii regis ibidem per idem tempus.

[2] Debent £2078 10s 6½d.

[3] Et factis allocacionibus in dicto compoto ingrossato *[No. A 3 § 24-28]* quieti sunt ibidem. *[The 'finished' sign follows]*.

---

[5] *Stuart Jenks (ed.), The Enrolled Customs Accounts (PRO, E356, E372, E364) 1279/80-1508/09 (1523/24) Volume 8: E356/19, E356/20 (List and Index Society) [in press], E356/19, No. 81.*

[6] *This would have to be a reference to TNA: PRO, E159/221 Brevia directa baronibus Easter m 11. Compare the cross-reference in the audit of the previous tunnage and poundage account of* Quatermayns *and* Walsyngham *for the period from 29 Sept. 1444 to 29 Sept. 1445 (TNA: PRO, E368/218 Visus et status compotorum Easter m 15 (m 223 stamped), where the location of the order to the Exchequer is given as* irrotulatum inter brevia directa baronibus de termino Pasche anno 23[cio] regis nunc rotulo 11[mo] ex parte alterius rememoratoris. *However, no corresponding document was enrolled in E159/221 Brevia directa baronibus Easter m 11 or in the corresponding place in the Lord Treasurer's memoranda roll (TNA: PRO, E368/217 Recorda Pasche m 11). However, it was enrolled (together with the corresponding order to the collectors of tunnage and poundage in London) in the following year: TNA: PRO, E368/218 Visus et status compotorum Easter m 15 (No. S 1).*

SUBSIDIARY DOCUMENTS

[S 1] *Henry VI to the treasurer and barons of the Exchequer: since the king wishes to repay the £10,426 4¼d which John, earl of Shrewsbury* (Salopie), *lord Talbot and* de Furnyvale *loaned to the crown, he has – by patent*[1] *issued on 3 Dec. 1443* (tercio die Decembris anno regni nostri vicesimo secundo) – *granted him 300 marks sterling yearly, payable in equal portions at Easter and Michaelmas from the issues of tunnage and poundage in London, until the debt is repaid. This grant is, however, only valid once the king's debt of £21,000 owing to his uncle, Henry, cardinal of England and bishop of Winchester, has been repaid. Since the king has now learned that this latter debt has indeed been repaid and has accordingly directed the collectors of tunnage and poundage in London to pay the earl of Shrewsbury all sums owing from Michaelmas term last* (pro termino sancti Michaelis ultimo preterito), *he orders the Exchequer to allocate* (debite allocetis) *any payments these customers might have made in this regard when the customers come to account, providing they produce this writ of payment and Shrewsbury's receipts* (litteras acquietancie). — *1445 Feb. 12* (Teste me ipso apud Westmonasterium, 12mo die Februarii anno regni nostri vicesimo tercio). *Westminster.*

L TNA: PRO, E368/218 Visus et status compotorum Easter m 15 (m 223 stamped). Contemporaneous official copy. Parchment. Unsealed. Inserted in the audit of the account of Richard Quatermayns *and Thomas* Walsyngham *for the issues of tunnage and poundage in London in the period from 29 Sept. 1444 to 29 Sept. 1445* (a festo sancti Michaelis anno 23^{cio} regis nunc usque festum sancti Michaelis extunc proxime sequens).

[S 2] *Extract from the account of Richard* Quatermayns *and Thomas* Walsyngham *for the issues of tunnage and poundage in London in the period from 29 Sept. 1444 to 29 Sept. 1445* (a festo sancti Michaelis anno 23^{cio} regis hujus usque festum sancti Michaelis tunc proxime sequens).

L TNA: PRO, E372/291 Item London' (dorse). Contemporaneous official fair copy of the Exchequer proceedings. Parchment. Unsealed.

---

[1] *CPR 1441-6, p. 227-8.*

In the margin. Allocantur per preceptum baronum et ex assensu Radulphi Boteler thesaurarii Anglie.

Et habent superplusagium £946 2s 10d. De quibus allocantur eisdem collectoribus in compoto suo de hujusmodi subsidiis in portu predicto a festo sancti Michaelis anno 24to *[29 Sept. 1445]* usque festum sancti Michaelis tunc proxime sequens anno 25to *[29 Sept. 1446]* rotulo compotorum de hujusmodi subsidio *[No. A 3 § 26]*: £928 17s 9d. Et remanent £17 5s 1d.

[S 3] *Extract from the continuation of the account of John* Melborne *and William* de Lwnes *for the issues of the petty customs in London in the period from 29 Sept. 1444 to 29 Sept. 1445* (a festo sancti Michaelis anno 23^{cio} regis hujus usque idem festum tunc proxime sequens).

L TNA: PRO, E372/290 Adhuc Res' London'. Contemporaneous official fair copy of the Exchequer proceedings. Parchment. Unsealed.

Et eisdem collectoribus pro denariis per ipsos solutis Johanni comiti Salopie domino de Talbot et de Furnevalle, cui rex tercio die Decembris anno 22do *[3 Dec. 1443]* inter alia concessit[2] £200 de parva custuma regis in portu London' per manus custumariorum sive collectorum ejusdem custume in portu illo pro tempore existencium ad terminos Pasche et sancti Michaelis per equales porciones, quousque eidem comiti de dicta summa decem milium, quadringentarum, viginti et sex librarum, quatuor denariorum et unius quadrantis plenarie solutum fuerit et contentatum, in portu predicto et in aliis diversis locis: £200 de termino Pasche anno 23^{cio} et termino sancti Michaelis anno 24to ultra £533 6s 8d prius allocata de summa predicta, sicut continetur alibi in hoc rotulo *[TNA: PRO, E372/290]* in Item Adhuc Item London' in debito Johannis Poutrell et Thome Pounde collectorum custumarum et subsidiorum lanarum et pellium lanutarum ac custume coriorum in portu civitatis London' per processum inde habitum et consideracionem baronum annotata in memorandis ex parte remembratoris thesaurarii de anno 24to regis hujus, videlicet inter status et visus compotorum de termino Pasche rotulo [15] *[TNA: PRO, E368/218 Visus et status compotorum Easter m 15]*.

---

[2] *CPR 1441-6, p. 227-8.*

APPENDIX I
HOW DID THE CROWN PAY?

It is one of the many conundra which bedevil studies of the medieval Exchequer that no one has systematically investigated such a seemingly simple question as the administrative mechanics of how the crown paid out money to its creditors. The best study is still Willard's analysis of the period 1290 to 1334 with regard to the collectors of parliamentary subsidies,[1] which draws together the conclusions of a number of his articles.

Willard distinguishes two methods of payment, the Writ and Letter system and the Writ and Tally system. The first came into effect once the Exchequer gained control over disbursements in 1294 and the second in the early fourteenth century. In both cases, payment was initiated by some form of crown warrant for issue – whether by order under the Great or Privy Seal or wardrobe bill – which constituted proof of crown indebtedness and communicated this state of affairs to the Exchequer. This posed the question to the Exchequer of whether it was prepared to pay cash. If not – as was usually the case, since the government was chronically short of liquid funds – the debt was assigned.[2]

In the Writ and Letter system, the crown warrant generated an Exchequer writ[3] directed to some official responsible for collecting crown revenue who was informed of the reason for payment, ordered to pay a beneficiary named in the writ and to obtain some form of receipt, usually specified as a patent letter

---

[1] James F. Willard, *Parliamentary Taxes on Personal Property 1290 to 1334. A Study in Mediaeval English Financial Administration* (Publications of the Mediaeval Academy of America 9), Cambridge/Mass. 1934 repr. 1970, p. 230-49.

[2] Administratively, it made no difference whether funds were disbursed in cash to the payee at the Exchequer in Westminster or paid directly to him in the field in return for his receipt, which was subsequently presented to the Exchequer. In the first case (from 1332/33 onwards), the issue roll distinguished between cash payments and assignments by marginating *sol'* or *soluc'* against the entry as opposed to *assign'*: Anthony Steel, *The Receipt of the Exchequer 1377-1485*, Cambridge/Engl. 1954, p. xxxi. Between 1336 and 1349, the receipt rolls began to make the same distinction, marginating *sol'* for cash payments into the Exchequer and a *pro* entry for proof of payment on an assignment: *ibid.*

[3] Although originally both Remembrancers enrolled Exchequer writs in their Memoranda Rolls, the task was delegated more or less completely to the King's Remembrancer by the Exchequer reforms of 1323, who copied them in the *Brevia irretornabilia* section of his Memoranda Roll: Willard, *Parliamentary Taxes*, p. 238.

sealed by the payee. In addition, the official was assured that the sum in question would be allowed in his account at the Exchequer. Around the beginning of the fourteenth century – Willard's first example dates from 8 Edward II (1314/15) – the wording of the allowment clause became more specific: The official was now assured that upon presentation of the Exchequer's writ of assignment and the patent letter of the payee at the Exchequer a tally would be levied which would suffice for allowance at accounting. This change of wording, Willard emphasizes, did not indicate any substantial change in procedure. Not stated as such in the writ, but demonstrable from practice was the fact that the issuance of the tally generated an entry in the receipt rolls crediting the official with the amount named in the tally and the writ.[4] Note that in the Writ and Letter system the Exchequer's writ of assignment would be dated well before the time the tally was struck and the entry in the receipt rolls effected.

In the early fourteenth century (between 1306 and 1319), a second system of effecting payments came into use: the Writ and Tally system. As in the Writ and Letter system, the crown warrant generated an Exchequer writ directed to some official who was ordered to pay the beneficiary and receive from him the Exchequer writ and – this was new – a tally levied by the Exchequer in the official's name for the stated amount. This tally, the writ stated, would be sufficient for allowance of the sum in question. Finally, the warranty clause – which specified the authority on which the Exchequer writ was issued – included one of a number of variations mentioning tallies – 'by the treasurer and a tally of the Exchequer', 'by a writ of liberate and a tally', 'by the treasurer and the issue roll', 'by a tally and the issue roll at the receipt' and so forth.[5] Here (as before) the Exchequer writ generated an entry in the receipt rolls of even date (or, if the Exchequer was very busy, of a slightly later date) crediting the official with payment. What was new was that the writ of assignment also generated an entry in the issue roll showing payment by the official to the beneficiary. Note that under the Writ and Tally system the dates of issuance of the Exchequer writ, of the striking of the tally (as recorded in the receipt rolls) and of the corresponding entry in the issue rolls were very close to one another, whereas in the Writ and Letter System the date of the striking of the tally (and the receipt roll entry) was considerably later than the date of issuance of the Exchequer writ (and the issue roll entry), the former only being effected when the official came into Westminster to account. Digramm 1 illustrates the two systems.

---

[4] Willard, *Parliamentary Taxes*, p. 230-35.

[5] Willard, *Parliamentary Taxes*, p. 237-38, 273-74. The warranty clause in the Writ and Letter system mentioned writs under the great or privy seal, a writ of liberate or the treasurer himself, but never a tally.

Diagramm 1: Systems of assignment	
Writ and Letter system	**Writ and Tally system**
crown warrant for issue	crown warrant for issue
generates	generates
	(1) levying of a tally (entry on receipt roll)
Exchequer writ of assignment (entry on issue roll)	(2) Exchequer writ of assignment (entry on issue roll)
payment (writ handed to official) (payment receipted by patent letter)	payment (writ and tally handed to official)
official at Exchequer for accounting (writ and patent handed over)	official at Exchequer for accounting
generates	
levying of a tally (entry on receipt roll)	
official accounts (writ and tally proferred for allowance)	official accounts (writ and tally proferred for allowance)

It will be seen that the only difference between the two systems was that in the Writ and Tally system the tally was levied *prior* to payment of the beneficiary, whereas in the Writ and Letter system it was not struck until the official came into Westminster to account, in other words long *after* payment had been made. In both instances, the tally served the Upper Exchequer as proof of payment. In the Writ and Tally system it also served as the receipt of the payee acknowledging payment, since it was not handed over to the official until payment had been effected. According to Willard, this simplified accounting procedure: The official did not have to visit the Exchequer of Receipt, but could proceed directly to the Upper Exchequer to account.

For the period he investigates, Willard's conclusions may be readily confirmed. Since he largely, if not wholly, translates from the Latin, it is instructive to take a closer look at the original text of two typical Exchequer writs, one of each type. The mandate to pay Thomas de Bradeston[6] dated 4 October 1340 is a good example of the Writ and Letter system.

[Marginated] *Devon'; De denariis solvendis Thome de Bradestan*

[1] Rex dilecto clerico suo Waltero de Meryet cancellario Exonie receptori denariorum proveniencium de subsidio none nobis a laicis concesso in

[6] TNA: PRO, E159/117 Brevia irretornabilia Michaelmas m 1 (m 400 in pencil); http://aalt.law.uh.edu/AALT2/E3/E159no117/aE159no117fronts/IMG_0656.htm.

domitatu Devonie salutem. [2] Cum teneamur dilecto et fideli nostro Thome de Bradestan in trescentis marcis, videlicet in ducentis et quinquaginta marcis de illis quingentis marcis, quas ei nuper per litteras nostras patentes[7] *concessimus, percipiendas sibi et heredibus suis singulis annis ad scaccarium nostrum et heredum nostrorum de termino Pasche proximo preterito, et in quinquaginta marcis, quas idem Thomas nobis in partibus transmarinis pro expedicione negociorum nostrorum mutuavit, velimusque eidem Thome de dictis trescentis marcis cum omni celeritate satisfieri, prout decet, [3] vobis mandamus, quod de denariis provenientibus de dicto subsidio in civitate Exonie et burgis in comitatu predicto solvi et habere facias prefato Thome* [a]*vel Thome de Chiltenham attornato suo*[a] *summam trescentarum marcarum supradictam, [4] recipientes ab eodem* [a]*Thoma vel dicto attornato suo*[a] *litteras suas patentes etc., [5] per quas et hujus brevis pretextu tallias de scaccario nostro sub nomine vestro levari et vobis in compoto vestro ad idem scaccarium nostrum de subsidio predicto allocari faciemus. Teste R[ogero] Coventre et Lich' episcopo thesaurario nostro ac quarto die Octobris — [6] per breve de magno sigillo adhuc inter communia de hoc anno et per ipsum thesaurarium quoad solucionem et rotulum memorandorum de eodem anno 15° Michaelis [et] commissionem quoad attornatum.*

[a-a] Interlined.

We note that here, as Willard states, a royal writ under the great seal (6) actuated the treasurer, Roger Northburgh,[8] to send an Exchequer writ to Walter de Meryet, receiver of the Ninth in Exeter (1), who is given the reason for payment to Thomas de Bradeston (2), ordered to pay Thomas or his attorney (3) and receive his patent letter of receipt (4), upon presentation of which – and by reason of the present Exchequer writ – tallies will be levied at the Exchequer in Walter's name (5) which will suffice for allowance when he accounted.

The Writ and Tally system is illustrated by the following example, in which the collectors of the clerical Tenth were ordered to pay the Nottingham merchant William de Amyas £150.[9]

[Marginated] *Not'; De denariis solvendis Willelmo Amyas de Notyngham mercatori*

[1] Rex dilectis sibi collectoribus decime biennalis nobis a clero concesse in instanti anno quartodecimo in archidiaconatu Not' salutem. [2] Manda-

---

[7] CPR 1338-40, p. 471 dated 26 Apr. 1340.

[8] Roger Northburgh was treasurer from 26 June to 1 Dec. 1340: E.B. Fryde et al. (eds.), *Handbook of British Chronology* (RHS Guides and Handbooks 12), 3rd ed., London 1986, p. 105.

[9] TNA, PRO, E368/112 Brevia irretornabilia Easter [14 Edw III] m 1: http://aalt.law.uh.edu/AALT2/E3/E368no112/aE368no112fronts/IMG_0249.htm. The King's Remembrancer enrolled an abbreviated copy of the same writ: TNA: PRO, E159/116 Brevia irretornabilia Easter [14 Edw. III] m 1: http://aalt.law.uh.edu/AALT2/E3/E159no116/aE159no116fronts/IMG_0637.htm.

mus vobis, quod de denariis provenientibus de decima predicta de primo termino solucionis ejusdem solvi et habere faciatis dilecto mercatori nostro Willelmo de Amyas de Notyngham £150 de quadam summa £300, [3] in quibus ei tenemur pro tot denariis per ipsum Willelmum nobis mutuatis pro expensis guerre nostre Francie. Nolumus enim, quod per aliquod mandatum tempore futuro vobis dirigendum assignacio predicta ullo modo infringatur, quin se teneat juxta vim et effectum ejusdem, [4] recipientes a prefato Willelmo vel ejus in hac parte attornato unam talliam de scaccario nostro sub nominibus vestris levatam predictam summam £150 continentem [5] vobis ad scaccarium nostrum, prout moris est, allocandam. Teste R[oberto] de Sadyngton[10] *apud Westmonasterium, tercio die Maii anno regni nostri Anglie quartodecimo, regni vero nostro Francie primo* [3 May 1340]. — *[6] per breve de privato sigillo residens ad receptam scaccarii inter brevia de termino Pasche eodem anno 14*^mo^ *de assignacione predicta facienda in forma predicta et pellem memorandorum de eodem termino et talliam predictam.*

We note that here, again as Willard states, a royal writ under the privy seal (6) actuated the treasurer, Robert de Sadyngton, to send an Exchequer writ to the collectors of the clerical tenth in the archdeaconry of Nottingham (1), who were ordered to pay William Amyas (2) and given the reason for payment (3), receiving the Exchequer tally struck in their names for the sum in question in advance of payment (4), which will be allocated to them when they account (5).

Needless to say, numerous examples of each system of payment can be found in the King's Remembrancer's Memoranda Rolls, and nothing I or other scholars have found vitiates Willard's conclusions for the period 1290 to 1334. However, Willard did not pursue the subject beyond the year of the last direct assessment of parliamentary subsidies, and developments in later years escaped his cognizance. Two of these are relevant for our question. First, Willard's statement that 'many, if not most, of the collectors within our period came to Westminster with writs and letters patent of receipt' is only correct for his period of investigation.[11] As Larson shows,[12] the preponderance of the Writ and Letter system characteristic of the years up to 1333/34 was reversed during the ensuing five years and made a comeback in the next five years (Graph 1). Second, enrolments of Exchequer writs became rare from 1348/49 and disappeared altogether from 1353/54 onwards,[13] in the same year that the *brevia irretornabilia* section of the King's Remembrancer's Memoranda Roll was

[10] According to the *Handbook of British Chronology*, p. 105, Robert Sadington kt. was treasurer from 5 May to 26 June 1340. Clearly, as the writ indicates, his appointment must have taken effect a bit earlier.

[11] Willard, *Parliamentary Taxes*, p. 238.

[12] A.T. Larson, 'Some Aspects of the Mediaeval Exchequer Memoranda Rolls', *BIHR* 16, 1938-39, p. 12-18, here p. 17.

[13] Larson, 'Some Aspects', p. 18.

dropped. Although it was revived in a fashion at the beginning of Richard II's reign – when the *brevia retornabilia* section was styled *brevia retornabilia et irretornabilia* –, the newly entitled section did not include any Exchequer writs of assignment,[14] and they do not seem to have been enrolled anywhere else in either Memoranda Roll.

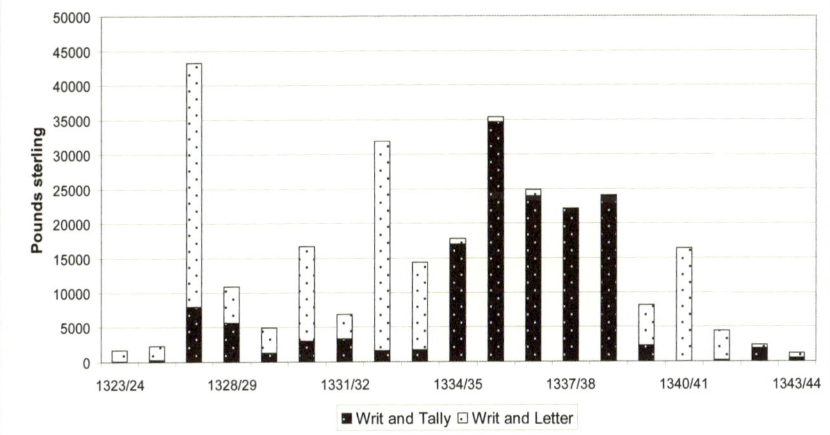

Graph 1: Systems of assignment, 1323/24-1343/44[15]

This poses a serious problem for the investigation of the administrative mechanics of how the crown paid out money to its creditors in the period from 1392/93 to 1462/63. Are we to conclude that the Exchequer no longer ordered payment by royal officials? If so, who did: the chancellor, the keeper of the privy seal or the king himself? Was the Exchequer informed, or did the king and various departments simply order payment by assignment without overall control?

In order to solve the conundrum, it seems best to examine the various types of accounting documents one by one and see what light they throw upon the problem. The Enrolled Customs Accounts (and the Pipe Rolls) do contribute to our knowledge, but do not resolve all difficulties. Clearly, they show that there were two methods by which payments were effected. The first, which always follows immediately upon the *summa recepte*, was by tally. The following entry, taken from the wool customs and subsidy account of John Poutrell and Thomas Pound for 24 Henry VI, shows just how frustratingly brief these entries are:

[14] Larson, 'Some Aspects', p. 15. My own researches confirm this conclusion.

[15] Source: Larson, 'Some Aspects', p. 16-17, supplemented for 1342/43 from TNA: PRO, E159/119 *Brevia irretornabilia*: http://aalt.law.uh.edu/AALT2/E3/E159no119/aE159no119fronts/IMG_0677 to IMG_0688.htm and http://aalt.law.uh.edu/AALT2/E3/E159no119/bE159no119dorses/IMG_1266.htm to IMG_1272.htm

> *In thesauro £973 14s 6½d in 21 talliis de cust[uma] et subs[idio]. Et in thesauro £3681 5s 3d in 64 talliis de subs[idio] lanarum. Et in thesauro £5471 10s 8d in 6 talliis de subs[idio] lanarum. Et in thesauro £67 10s in 2 talliis de cust[uma] et subs[idio] lanarum.*[16]

The second method of effecting payment – which follows immediately upon the tally entry – consistently names a royal patent letter as warrant, includes a cross-reference to a *breve de allocate* produced in the chancery[17] addressed to the treasurer and barons (and copied in the *brevia directa baronibus* section of the King's Remembrancer's Memoranda Roll) and cites one or more receipts from the beneficiary as proof of payment. When the *parcelle compoti* are transmitted, we also find a *breve de liberate* directed to the customers themselves ordering them to pay the beneficiary a specific sum.[18] If the *parcelle compoti* bundle has survived intact, all documents are found sewn together in the order *breve de allocate*, *breve de liberate*, receipt(s).

On the face of it, then, it would seem that the Writ and Tally system had survived, but that the Writ and Letter system had been modified. Instead of an Exchequer writ directed to the royal official – attested by the treasurer and sealed with the Exchequer seal –, we now have a mandate for payment (*breve de liberate*) directed to the official, attested by the king himself and sealed with the great seal, which was communicated in substance to the Exchequer (*breve de allocate*) and ordered it to allow the customers any payments demonstrably made by authority of the *breve de liberate*. Proof of payment was one or more receipts sealed by the beneficiary.

THE TALLY SYSTEM

The entries in the Enrolled Customs Accounts (and the Pipe Rolls) are, as seen above, maddeningly brief. More detailed information about the tallies presented by the customers is contained in some, if not all of the *visus compoti*. Let us take as an example the *visus* of the Lynn customers John Bukworth and John Bokenham for the period Michaelmas 4 Henry V (1416) to 14 January 1417.[19] The customers had been distrained to appear at the beginning of Hilary term, on 14 Jan. of 4 Henry V (1417),[20] and the *visus* was taken in that term.

---

[16] Wool account for 24 Henry VI, No. A 3 § 12.

[17] The clerks who signed the original writs (and whose names were not included in the copy in the *brevia directa baronibus*) are all chancery clerks: 'Mouter' (P 31) is, for instance, the chancery clerk Ralph Mouter (CCR 1441-47, p. 384 et passim).

[18] See the payment to Robert Roos kt. in the wool account for 24 Henry VI: No. A 3 § 18 and P 30 (*breve de allocate*), P 31 (*breve de liberate*) and P 17 (receipt).

[19] TNA: PRO, E159/193 Fines ... visus Hilary m [11]: http://aalt.law.uh.edu/H5/E159no193/aE159no193fronts/IMG_0499.htm: *a quo quidem festo* [Michaelmas 4 Henry V] *iidem collectores sunt alias inde cumputuri. Ideo preceptum sit vicecomitibus London', quod ipsos distringant per terras etc. ita etc. in crastino sancti Hillarii* [14 Jan. 1417].

[20] TNA: PRO, E159/193 Recorda Michaelmas m 3: http://aalt.law.uh.edu/H5/E159no193/aE159no193fronts/IMG_0282.htm.

The customers charged themselves with a total of £999 23d. Against this, they reckoned the following tallies:

[1] *1 talliam levatam 20 die Decembris anno tercio* [20 Dec. 1415] *pro hospicio domini regis de custuma lanarum* *£66 13s 4d*

[2] *1 aliam talliam levatam 23 die Januarii dicto anno tercio* [23 Jan. 1416] *pro eodem hospicio de eadem custuma* *£48 9s 6½d*

[3-4] *2 tallias levatas 21 die Junii dicto anno tercio* [21 June 1415] *pro villa regis Calesie de subsidio lanarum* *£670 4s 3½d*

[5] *1 aliam talliam levatam 10mo die Augusti anno quarto* [10 Aug. 1416] *pro dicto hospicio continentem £100 de subsidio 12d de £* *£40*

[6] *1 aliam talliam [levatam] 23 die Januarii dicto anno tercio* [23 Jan. 1416] *pro dicto hospicio* *£43 10s 6d*

[7] *1 talliam levatam tercio die Februarii dicto anno quarto* [3 Feb. 1417] *ad receptam scaccarii de custuma lanarum* *3s 10d*

[8] *1 aliam talliam levatam eisdem die et anno* [3 Feb. 1417] *ibidem de parva custuma* *20s 1½d*

[9] *1 aliam talliam levatam eisdem die et anno* [3 Feb. 1417] *ibidem de subsidio 12d de libra* *2s*

Now, quite clearly, the tallies Bukworth and Bokenham presented in Hilary term of 1417 fall into two groups: old tallies (No. 1-6) which had been levied five to eighteen months prior to the beginning of Hilary term in 1417 and very recent tallies (No. 7-9) which had all been levied during Hilary term 1417 itself (on 3 February), and indeed, as the *visus* notes, at the Exchequer of Receipt. The conclusion is inescapable that the recent tallies represent cash payments at the Exchequer of Receipt upon arrival of the customers for the *visus*. It seems equally clear that the old tallies had been handed over to the customers in receipt of payment. However, no further information is given. In particular, we have no indication of how – and by whom and in what form – the customers were ordered to pay. Consequently, we also have no idea of what the customers brought into the Exchequer when they appeared for a *visus* or final accounting. This is particularly worrying, because it would have been highly uncharacteristic of the Exchequer not to enroll – or at least file – accounting documents.

The solution to the puzzle is deceptively simple: The tally alone was perfectly adequate as a mandate for the customers to pay a beneficiary, whose possession of the tally struck in the Exchequer was sufficient proof of his right to receive payment. Since the tally was by its nature a receipt made out to a particular person (or persons) for a specific amount of money, there was no need for the customers to profer any further documents in proof of payment when they came to Westminster for accounting, since the tally had been made out in their names at the outset.

It would seem, therefore, that the old Writ and Tally system had been simplified by dropping the writ, leaving only the tally. As was the case before

1353/54, a royal warrant for issue, directed to the treasurer and chamberlains, initiated the process of payment. Once it arrived in the Exchequer of Receipt, the warrant generated an entry on the issue roll recording disbursement of funds to the payee and – if the Exchequer was unable or unwilling to pay cash – the levying of a tally in assignment and a corresponding entry on the receipt roll recording payment by the official.[21] The tally was then handed over to the payee, who presented it in due course to the royal official whose name was enscribed on the tally and entered in the receipt roll. Once the official had paid the sum in question, the beneficiary handed over the tally[22] which the official then presented to the Exchequer of Receipt when he came in to account. If both halves of the tally matched up, proof of payment was complete and the corresponding sum was allowed to the official, the tallies being filed.

This procedure is illustrated by a rather famous warrant for issue, by which Henry VII ordered payment of John Cabot's annuity of £20 per annum on 22 February 1498. Even if the warrant has been published repeatedly, it is useful to reproduce the text here.[23]

> *Henry by the grace of God king of England and of Fraunce and lord of Irland to the tresourer and chambrelains of oure eschequier greting. Whereas we by oure warrant under oure signet for certain consideracions have yeven and graunted unto John Caboote £20 yerely during oure pleasur to be had and perceyved by the handes of oure custumers in oure poorte of Bristowe,*[24] *and as we be enfourmed the said John Caboote is dilaied of his payement bicause the said custumers have no sufficient matier*

---

[21] For the generation of issue roll entries by warrants for issue and of receipt roll entries by the counter-tallies, see W.M. Ormrod, 'The Protecolla Rolls and English Government Finance, 1353-1364', *EHR* 102, 1987, p. 622-32, here p. 622.

[22] One should note that partial payments of tallies do occur, although they are by the logic of the system impossible: The *visus* of John Bukworth and John Bukenham for the issues of tunnage and poundage in Lynn in the period from 14 Jan. to 1 May 1417 – taken in Easter term 1417 – contains two: *De quibus* [£119 7s 2½d] *iidem collectores computant in denariis solutis ad receptam hujus scaccarii in partem solucionis unius tallie continentis £100 nuper assignate thesaurario hospicii regis super expensis ejusdem hospicii ultra £40 per ipsos collectores alias eidem thesaurario solutas, prout in visu compoti eorundem collectorum in custodia remembratoris regis remanente plenius apparet — £40; Et in denariis solutis ad eandem receptam in partem solucionis alterius tallie levate 24to die Januarii anno tercio* [24 Jan. 1416] *continentis £79 16s 2d nuper assignate Thome Chaucer capitali pincerne regis super expensis officii sui per acquietanciam ipius Thome super hunc visum ostensam et penes ipsos collectores remanentem — £64*: TNA: PRO, E159/193 fines ... visus Easter m [1d]: http://aalt.law.uh.edu/H5/E159no193/bE159no193dorses/IMG_1150.htm.

[23] Reproduced from James A. Williamson, *The Cabot Voyages and Bristol Discovery under Henry VII*, Cambridge/Engl. 1962, No. 18, p. 217-18.

[24] The privy seal writ directing the chancellor to issue a patent under the great seal was dated 13 Dec. 1497, the patent having been issued on 28 Jan. 1498: Williamson, *Cabot Voyages*, No. 27, p. 217.

of discharge for their indempnitie to be yolden at their accomptes before the barons of oure eschequier, wherefore we wol and charge you that ye oure said treasourer and chambrelains that now be and hereafter shall be, that ye, unto suche tyme as ye shall have from us otherwise in commaundement, do to be levied in due fourme 2 severall talles, every of theim conteignying £10 upon the customers of the revenues in our said poort of Bristowe at two usuell terms of the yere, whereof oon taill to be levied at this tyme conteignying £10 of the revenues of oure said poort upon Richard Meryk and Arthure Kemys, late custumers of the same, and the same taill or tailles in due and sufficient fourme levied ye delyver unto the said John Caboote to be had of oure gift by way of rewarde without prest or eny other charge to be sette upon hym or any of theim for the same. And thies oure letters shal be youre sufficient warrant in that behalf. Yeven undre oure prive seal at our manour of Chene the 22th *day of February the 13*th *yere of oure reigne.*

Note that, in this warrant for issue under the privy seal, the king orders the treasurer and chamberlains to cause a tally for £10 – bearing the names of the Bristol customers Richard Meryk and Arthur Kemys[25] – to be struck and handed over to Cabot to cover the arrears of his annuity – which the customers had refused to disburse – and further tallies to be struck in due course for each half-yearly payment as it should fall due. No other form of documentation was mentioned. Nor was any necessary: As the king states, the privy seal warrant itself *shal be youre sufficient warrant in that behalf.* The Enrolled Account of the Bristol customers for the period 29 September 1497 to 29 September 1498 records payment by tally in the same – maddeningly brief – form as that of Poutrell and Pound for the wool customs and subsidy in 24 Henry VI had done:

Et in thesauro £20 10mo *die Maii anno 14*^{mo} [10 May 1499] *per dictos nuper collectores de eisdem custumis et subsidiis pro Johanne Caboot*[26]

Now, it might be objected that it is all well and good to demonstrate that the Tally system – as I shall designate it for lack of a better term – was in force at the end of the fifteenth century, but what of the intervening 150 years? Is there sufficient evidence to prove – or at least plausibly suggest – that it was in operation between 1392/93 and 1462/63? Needless to say, I am persuaded that this was the case, but the reader should be aware that I have not conducted an exhaustive investigation of the warrants for issue, examining their dorsal entries and matching them to the entries in the issue and receipt rolls. That – and only that – would constitute incontrovertible proof that the Tally system was in

[25] Arthur Kemys and Richard a Meryk were customers in Bristol between 29 Sept. 1493 and 17 Dec. 1502. The account in question ran from 29 Sept. 1497 to 29 Sept. 1498: TNA: PRO, E356/23 m 3d, calendared Stuart Jenks (ed.), *The Enrolled Customs Accounts (PRO, E356, E372, E364) 1279/80-1508/09 (1523/24) vol. 11: E356/23* (List and Index Society 345), London 2012, No. 13.

[26] TNA: PRO, E356/23 m 3d.

operation. Therefore, the reader should bear in mind that my results are preliminary.

There can be no doubt that the crown issued large numbers of warrants for issue during our period, ordering the treasurer and chamberlains to make payments of one sort or another.[27] Whether the Exchequer paid cash or assigned the sum can be determined by examining the dorse of the warrant for issue. Henry VI's privy seal warrant dated 11 July 1444,[28] directing the treasurer and chamberlains to pay 100 marks to the envoys of the Rhenish palgrave Louis III demonstrates this clearly:

> *Henri par la grace de Dieu roy dEngleterre et de France et seignur dIrlande as tresorer et chamberlains de nostre eschequier salutz. Nous volons de ladvis de nostre counsail et vous mandons, qe a noz bien amez maistre Nicholas de Wachenhem docteur en divinitee et a Herman de Rubeto ambassadeurs de nostre trescher et tresame cousin le duc de Bayer, lesquelx sount par luy a nous envoiez pour avoir receuz de nous certaines sommes de monnoie, qi sont par nous a luy duez, vous facez delivere en partie de paiement de lesdictes sommes cent marcs. Doun soubz nostre prive seal a Westminstre, le 11 jour de Juyl lan de nostre regne vynt secounde.* *Benet*

While the king only ordered the treasurer and chamberlains to pay, leaving to them the decision of how to do so, the entry of the words *Persolutum in denariis hoc termino* on the dorse of the warrant permits no doubt that payment was made in cash.

On the other hand, the Exchequer might, and usually did decide to pay by assignment, and here, too, the dorsal entry must be consulted. Henry VI's order dated 2 July 1440, ordering the treasurer and chamberlains to pay the Hanseatic merchants Henry Overbagh and Johan Bernefrois £20 for 400 spear shafts purchased on 14 October 1435 by the king's sergeant of artillery John Stanley,[29] bears the dorsal entry *Persolutum per assignacionem hoc termino.* Maddeningly, many warrants for issue have only *Persolutum* on the dorse, which does indicate any particular form of payment. In order to find out just how the sum in question was paid, one would have to consult the issue and receipt rolls. The issue rolls generally differentiate between payment in cash (*in denariis sibi liberatis*) and by assignment (*in denariis sibi liberatis per assignacionem*) in the text of the entry.[30] The receipt rolls are more informa-

---

[27] The PRO catalogue lists 622 bundles for document class E404, most of which date from the period 1399-1485: http://www.nationalarchives.gov.uk/catalogue/displaycataloguedetails.asp?CATID=5395&CATLN=3&Highlight=&FullDetails=True.

[28] TNA: PRO, E404/60/231.

[29] TNA: PRO, E404/59/256.

[30] Occasionally, the issue rolls record a mixture of payments, as shown in the payment to the Keeper of the Wardrobe John Rothenale on 20 June 1418: *Johanni Rothenale militi custodi garderobe domini regis in denariis sibi liberatis, videlicet per assignacionem factam isto die per manus Thome Burcestre pro frumento empto de constabulario de Newebo £4 14s 7d, et pro frumento empto de constabulario de Denton*

tive, since there the right-hand margin contains one of two annotations: *sol'* (for cash payments into the Receipt) and *pro* followed by the name of a payee and a reason for payment (in the case of assignments), while a dot marginated to the left of the entry indicates that a tally had been struck. Although I have not conducted a systematic investigation of all payments by tally effected by the customers who accounted in my ten year steps, as recorded in the Enrolled Customs Accounts, I think it is reasonable to record a Nihil obstat as a preliminary conclusion: Nothing I have found so far prohibits us from concluding that the Writ and Tally system had been supplanted by the Tally system.

This conclusion is supported by a number of literary complaints about royal purveyors paying for goods with sticks rather than money.[31] However, the argument which, to my mind, clinches the case is the dishonoured tally which was allegedly levied on 14 Nov. 1452, which directed payment of £46 13s 3d out of the London wool customs and subsidy to the royal household.[32] The record in the King's Remembrancer's Memoranda Roll states that the tally was examined by the barons and found to be counterfeit, presumably because the counterfoil could not be found, although this is not stated explicitly. At no point in the case was reference made to any other document for which a fruitless search was conducted, although one would expect such a statement if, in fact, the Writ and Tally system were still in operation. After all, counterfoils could, theoretically, be misfiled or lost, and if an Exchequer writ directing the London customers to pay £46 13s 3d to the household was in fact in existence – whether on file or in copy –, then one would have expected that the barons would have ordered a search to be made and that the record would state that no such writ was found. Since the record in the King's Remembrancer's Memoranda Roll is silent on this point, I feel emboldened to conclude that the Writ and Tally system had in fact been replaced by the Tally system.

THE WRIT AND LETTER SYSTEM IN THE FIFTEENTH CENTURY

The second method of payment employed by the crown is much better documented, and there can be no doubt as to the procedure which was followed. If we again consult the wool customs and subsidy account for 24 Henry VI, we find – immediately following the tally entry – a number of entries which (1) consistently name a royal patent letter as warrant, (2) include a cross-reference to a *breve de allocate* produced in the chancery and addressed to the treasurer and barons (and copied in the *brevia directa baronibus* section of the King's

---

20s, et in obligacionibus per manus Roberti Ottley £77 19s 2d, et in pecunia numerata per manus ejusdem Roberti pro speciebus ab eo emptis 43s 1d, per manus Stephani Rought unius oratorum regis 20s, per manus Thome Chaucers nuper capitalis pincerne regis pro vinis emptis de Hans Dasse £47 8s 8d, et per manus Johannis Water pro expensis regis Scotorum; de prestito super expensis hospicii regis ut supra — £140 18s 10d, unde respondebit: TNA: PRO, E403/636 m 8.

[31] Steel, *Receipt*, p. xxxiv-xxxv.

[32] TNA: PRO, E159/229 Recorda Easter m 6. The case is transcribed in Appendix III.

Remembrancer's Memoranda Roll) and (3) cite one or more receipts from the beneficiary as proof of payment. Whenever the *parcelle compoti* are transmitted without loss, we also find a *breve de liberate* directed to the customers ordering them to pay the beneficiary a certain sum of money.[33] If the *parcelle compoti* bundle has survived intact, all documents are found sewn together in the order *breve de allocate*, *breve de liberate*, receipt(s).

Let us take a specific example to illustrate this. The Enrolled Account of the collectors of the petty customs in London William de Lunes and Thomas Chynnore for the period from 10 May to 29 Sept. 1440 records the disbursement of £20 to Simon Camp, esq., for Michaelmas term 19 Henry VI (1440/41) in part payment of his annuity of £40.[34]

> [1] *Et Simoni Camp armigero,* [2] *cui dominus Henricus nuper rex Anglie Quartus per litteras suas patentes, quas rex nunc 14mo die Decembris anno primo* [14 Dec. 1422] *confirmavit,*[35] *concessit quadraginta libras percipiendas annuatim durante vita sua de parva custuma regis trium denariorum de libra in portu predicto per manus collectorum ejusdem custume pro tempore existencium ad terminos sancti Michaelis et Pasche per equales porciones,* [3] *£20 de termino Michaelis anno 19no* [4] *per breve regis irrotulatum in memorandis de anno 19no regis hujus termino sancti Michaelis rotulo 38°* [TNA: PRO, E159/217 Brevia directa baronibus Michaelmas m 38] *et* [5] *litteras patentes ipsius Simonis de recepta.*

Note that the entry begins by naming the payee (1) and citing Henry VI's confirmation (on 14 Dec. 1422) of Henry IV's patent granting Camp £40 per annum for life, payable from the petty customs in London at Michaelmas and Easter in equal portions, as warrant for all such payments (2). It then notes how much was paid in Michaelmas term 19 Henry VI (3), refers to the king's writ enrolled in the King's Remembrancer's Memoranda Roll in the *Brevia directa baronibus* section for Michaelmas 19 Henry VI as warrant for this particular payment (4) and cites Camp's sealed receipt as proof of payment (5).

Now, the *parcelle compoti* for this account have survived as an original bundle.[36] Here we find the *breve de allocate* (Illustration 1a) dated 2 October 1440 and attested by the chancery clerk Richard Selby[37] and Camp's receipt (Illustration 1c) dated 10 November 1440, which we would have expected from the entry in the Enrolled Customs Accounts. We also find the *breve de liberate* (Illustration 1b) dated 1 October 1440 and also attested by Selby, which the Enrolled Account did not mention. In addition, we note that the

[33] See the payment to Robert Roos kt. in the wool account for 24 Henry VI: No. A 3 § 18 and P 30 (*breve de allocate*), P 31 (*breve de liberate*) and P 17 (receipt).

[34] TNA: PRO, E356/19 m 8d.

[35] Henry IV's patent was issued on 3 Sept. 1401 (CPR 1399-1401, p. 535) and Henry VI's confirmation on 14 Dec. 1422 (CPR 1422-29, p. 10-11). In the meantime, Henry V had confirmed the patent on 14 Apr. 1414 (CPR 1413-16, p. 193).

[36] TNA: PRO, E122/75/33.

[37] For Richard Selby as chancery clerk see CCR 1441-47, p. 384.

breve de allocate has a hole between the second and third lines, clearly indicating that it was spindled in the Exchequer awaiting the customers' presentation of the *breve de liberate* and the receipt after payment had been completed. Finally, we note that all three documents are sewn together in the bundle in the order *breve de allocate, breve de liberate* and receipt.[38]

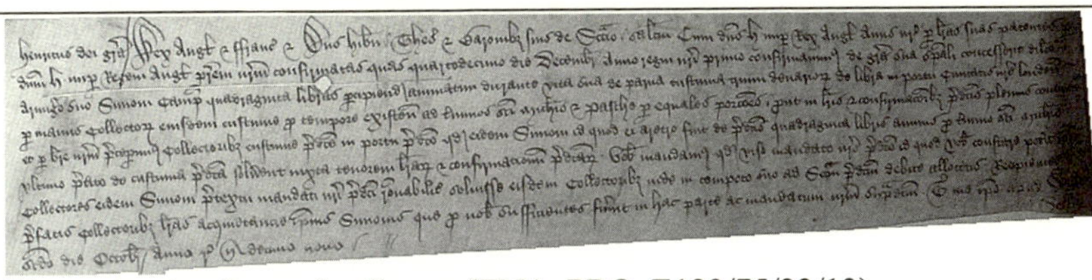

Illustration 1a: *Breve de allocate* (TNA: PRO, E122/75/33/13)

Henricus Dei gracia rex Anglie et Francie et dominus Hibernie thesaurario et baronibus suis de scaccario salutem. Cum dominus H[enricus] nuper rex Anglie avus noster per litteras suas patentes per dominum H[enricum] nuper regem Anglie patrem nostrum confirmatas, quas quartodecimo die Decembris anno regni nostro primo [14 Dec. 1422] *confirmavimus, de gracia sua speciali concesserit dilecto armigero suo Simoni Campe quadraginta libras percipiendas annuatim durante vita sua de parva custuma trium denariorum de libra in portu civitatis nostre London' per manus collectorum ejusdem custume pro tempore existencium ad terminos sancti Michaelis et Pasche per equales porciones, prout in litteris et confirmacionibus predictis plenius continetur, et per breve nostrum precepierimus collectoribus custume predicte in portu predicto, quod eidem Simoni id, quod ei aretro fuit de predictis quadraginta libris annuis pro termino sancti Michaelis ultimo preterito de custuma predicta solverent juxta tenorem litterarum et confirmacionum predictarum, vobis mandamus, quod viso mandato nostro predicto id, quod vobis constare poterit ipsos collectores eidem Simoni pretextu mandati nostri predicti racionabiliter solvisse, eisdem collectoribus inde in compoto suo ad scaccarium predictum debite allocetis, recipientes a prefatis collectoribus litteras acquietancie ipsius Simonis, que pro nobis sufficientes fuerint in hac parte, ac mandatum nostrum supradictum. Teste me ipso apud Westmonasterium, secundo die Octobris anno regni nostri decimo nono* [2 Oct. 1440] *Selby*

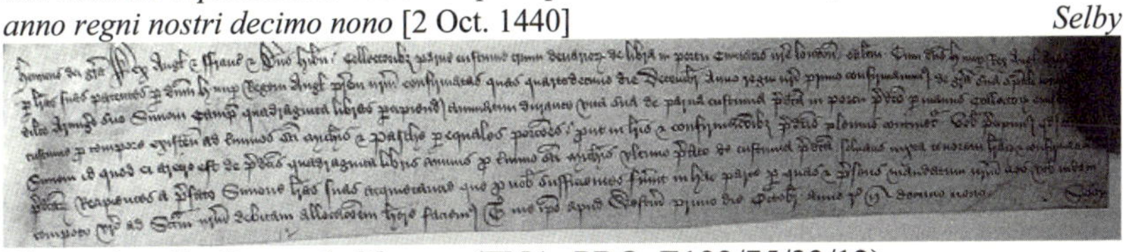

Illustration 1b: *Breve de liberate* (TNA: PRO, E122/75/33/12)

Henricus Dei gracia rex Anglie et Francie et dominus Hibernie collectoribus parve custume trium denariorum de libra in portu civitatis nostre London' salutem. Cum dominus H[enricus] nuper rex Anglie avus noster per litteras suas patentes per dominum H[enricum] nuper regem Anglie patrem nostrum confirmatas, quas quartodecimo die Decembris anno regni nostro primo [14 Dec. 1422] *confirmavimus, de gracia sua speciali concesserit dilecto armigero suo Simoni Campe quadraginta libras percipien-*

[38] The numbers recorded on the front of the documents in Illustrations 1a to 1c – 11, 12 and 13 – are erroneous. The correct numbers (13, 12 and 11) are on the dorse.

das annuatim durante vita sua de parva custuma predicta in portu predicto per manus collectorum ejusdem custume pro tempore existentes ad terminos sancti Michaelis et Pasche per equales porciones, prout in litteris et confirmacionibus predictis plenius continetur, vobis precipimus, quod eidem Simoni id, quod ei aretro est de predictis quadraginta libris annuis pro termino sancti Michaelis ultimo preterito de custuma predicta solvatis juxta tenorem litterarum et confirmacionum predictarum, recipientes a prefato Simone litteras suas acquietancie, que pro nobis sufficientes fuerint in hac parte, per quas et presens mandatum nostrum nos vobis inde in compoto vestro ad scaccarium nostrum debitam allocacionem habere faciemus. Teste me ipso apud Westmonasterium, primo die Octobris anno regni nostri decimo nono [1 Oct. 1440] *Selby*

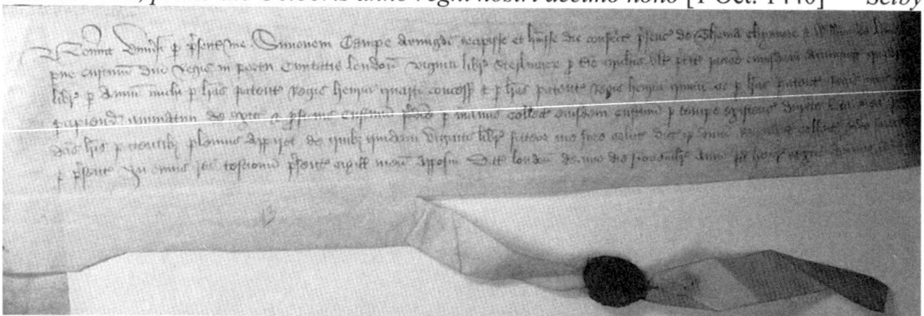

Illustration 1c: Receipt under the seal of the beneficiary (TNA: PRO, E122/75/33/11)

Noverint universi per presentes me Simonem Campe armigerum recipisse et habuisse die confeccionis presencium de Thoma Chynnore et Willelmo de Lunys collectoribus parve custume domini regis in portu civitatis London' viginti libras sterlingorum pro termino Michaelis ultimo preterito racione cujusdam annuitatis quadraginta librarum per annum michi per litteras patentes regis Henrici Quarti concesse et per litteras patentes regis Henrici Quinti ac per litteras patentes regis nunc confirmate percipiendarum annuatim de exitibus et proficuis custume predicte per manus collectorum ejusdem custume pro tempore existencium durante vita mea, prout in dictis litteris patentibus plenius apparet. De quibus quidem viginti libris fateor me fore solutum dictosque dominum regem et collectores inde fore quietos per presentes. In cujus rei testimonium presentibus sigillum meum apposui. Datum London', decimo die Novembris anno regni regis Henrici Sexti decimo nono [10 Nov. 1440].

Now, these three documents illustrate the procedure with perfect clarity. Ultimately, a royal patent – originally issued by Henry IV on 3 September 1401[39] and confirmed by Henry V on 14 April 1414[40] and Henry VI on 14 December 1422[41] – was the warrant for payment of each half-yearly instalment of Simon Camp's annuity. At the beginning of each half year, the chancery produced first a *breve de liberate* under the great seal[42] (here on 1 October 1440) di-

---

[39] CPR 1399-1401, p. 535.

[40] CPR 1413-16, p. 193.

[41] CPR 1422-29, p. 10-11.

[42] These *brevia* must have been issued under the great seal, since they are not folded like privy seal writs. After the customers handed the writ in at the Exchequer, the tongue was torn away and the wax re-used. The tear is obvious on a number of writs.

rected to the customers and attested by a chancery clerk, ordering them to pay Camp his half-yearly instalment, and handed it over to Camp, who was then free to seek out the customers and try to obtain payment. More or less simultaneously (here on 2 October 1440), the chancery directed a *breve de allocate* to the treasurer and barons under the great seal[43] also attested by the same chancery clerk, ordering them to allow the customers any payments they had made in consequence of the *breve de liberate*, provided they produce that writ and the payee's receipt(s). This writ was enrolled in the *brevia directa baronibus* section of the King's Remembrancer's Memoranda Roll for 19 Henry VI on m 38 of Michaelmas term, as the entry on the dorse of the *breve de allocate* (Illustration 1d, top entry) indicates (*Irrotulatur termino sancti Michaelis anno 19no rotulo 38°*). The writ was then spindled until the customers came in to account. Meanwhile, Camp had obtained payment of the £20 due to him for Michaelmas term on 10 November 1440, and had consequently handed over the *breve de liberate* and produced a receipt, acknowledging payment (Illustration 1b). When the customers arrived in Westminster to account, they proferred the *breve de liberate* and Camp's receipt, which were joined up with the spindled *breve de allocate*. Once the sum had been allowed, a corresponding entry (Illustration 1d, bottom entry) was made on the dorse of the *breve de allocate* (*Allocatur in compoto Willelmi de Lwnys et Thome Chynnor collectorum parve custume regis in portu civitatis London computancium a 10° die Maii anno 18mo regis Henrici vj^ti^ usque festum sancti [Michaelis] tunc proxime sequens*). All three documents were then sewn together and filed.

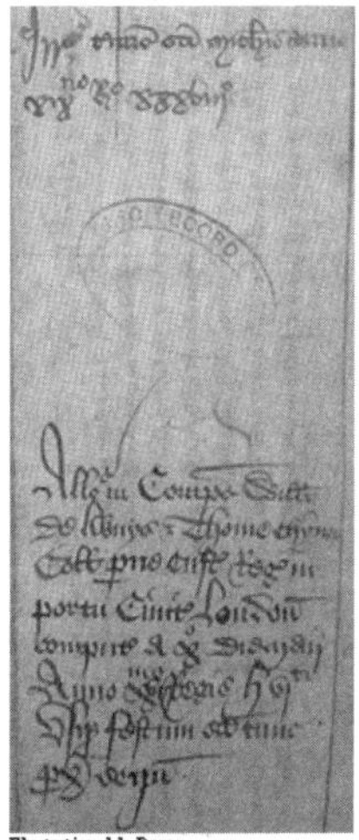
Illustration 1d: Dorse of the *breve de allocate* (TNA: PRO, E122/75/33/13)

Thus we can see that the Writ and Letter system had evolved. In the old system of assignment, a crown warrant had generated an Exchequer writ, issued under the Exchequer seal and attested by the treasurer, ordering an official to pay a named beneficiary and obtain a receipt, normally under the seal of the payee, which would suffice for allocation when the official accounted. Now, the chancery directed the official to pay directly, without making a detour via the treasurer and chamberlains, by issuing a *breve de liberate* and handing it over to the beneficiary. Simultaneously, it directed the Upper Exchequer to allow the official any funds he had disbursed to the payee by reason of the *breve de liberate*, by issuing a *breve de allocate* under the great seal directed to the treasurer and barons which named the patent which was the ultimate warrant for all payments. Once payment was made, the payee handed over the *breve de liberate* to the official and produced a receipt under his own

[43] Here, too, the tongue was torn away and the wax re-used.

seal, just as he had done with the Exchequer's writ in the old Writ and Letter system.

Finally, it is to be noted that the use of the Writ and Letter system was not restricted to annuities and other periodic payments, but was utilized whenever a patent letter was the immediate or ultimate warrant for payment. The payment to the Cologne merchant Johan Rosencrans is a case in point. On 28 August 1442, the king's council decided to pay Rosencrans 250 marks for his diplomatic services to the crown, for which he had not yet received anything for the costs he had incurred, much less in the way of remuneration.[44] On the following day, the chancery issued a corresponding patent letter, which foresaw payment from the customs paid in London by Hanseatic merchants.[45] On 8 February 1443, a further patent to the same effect had to be issued, since the first had not named a date from which Rosencrans was to be repaid.[46] On the same day, the chancery issued a *breve de liberate* to the collectors of the petty customs in London,[47] and a *breve de allocate dormant* to the Exchequer.[48] On 2 April 1443, Rosencrans acknowledged receipt of an initial 100 marks and on 1 May 1443 of a further £100.[49] With that, the crown's debt was discharged. Thus, a one-time payment was effected by the new Writ and Letter system – because payment was mandated by a patent letter – and not by the Tally system.

[44] Nicholas Harris Nicolas (ed.), *Proceedings and Ordinances of the Privy Council of England (1386-1542),* 7 vols., London 1834-7, vol. 5, p. 206.

[45] CPR 1441-46, p. 92.

[46] CPR 1441-46, p. 144, naming the day as 3 Sept. 1442.

[47] TNA: PRO, E368/216 Status et visus compotorum Michaelmas m 14d.

[48] TNA: PRO, E368/216 Status et visus compotorum Michaelmas m 14d and E159/219 Brevia directa baronibus Hilary m 12d.

[49] TNA: PRO, E368/216 Status et visus compotorum Michaelmas m 14d.

APPENDIX II
TALLIES

A.1 *A dishonoured tally. — 1453 May 3.*

L TNA: PRO, E159/229 Recorda Easter m 6. Contemporaneous official fair copy of the Exchequer proceeding. Parchment. Unsealed. http://aalt.law.uh.edu/AALT2/H6/E159no229/aE159no229fronts/IMG_0396.htm to IMG_0397.htm

[Marginated] Anglia; Midd'; De Thoma Dollyng et Johanne Radeford commissis prisone domini regis pro contrafaccione cujusdam tallie per ipsos fabricate et contrafacte etc.

Memorandum, quod Johannes, comes Wygorn', thesaurarius Anglie presenis hic in curia in propria persona sua tercio die Maii hoc termino *[3 May 1453]* liberavit quandam talliam quadraginta sex librarum, tresdecim dolidorum et trium denariorum continentem modo et forma subsequentibus literaliter inscriptam

London' De Johanne Poutrelle et Thoma Pounde collectoribus custumarum et subsidiorum lanarum in portu London' de eisdem custumarum et subsidiorum Michaelis 14 die Novembris anno tricesimo primo regis Henrici Sexti pro hospicio regis

asserens Thomam Dollyng et Johannem Radeford talliam predictam falso, subtiliter et deceptive in dampnum et prejudicium domini regis ac presentis curie et populi ejusdem domini regis decepcionem manifestam decimo die Decembris anno tricesimo primo supradicto in parochia Sancte Katerine juxta Turrim London', videlicet in comitatu Midd', fabriacatam et controfactam fuisse, petens idem Johannes comes Wygorn' pro domino regis avisamentum curie in premissis, que quidem tallia remanet in custodia remembratoris regis. Et predictus thesaurarius dicit, quod predicti Thomas Dollyng et Johannes Radeford in prisona dicti domini regis sub custodia vicecomitum London' ad presens existunt.

Super quo visa tallia predicta per barones, quia evidenter eis apparet talliam illam controfactam et fabricatam fuisse, prout superius declaratur, preceptam fuit vicecomitibus London' per separalia brevia sub sigillo hujus scaccarii, quod corpora predictorum Thome Dollyng et Johannis Radeford in prisona regis sub custodia sua detentorum tabeant hic etc. – una cum causa et die capcionis et detencionis eorundem in eadem – ad respondendum certis articulis etc. Et preceptum suit separatim vicecomitibus in forma predicta, ita etc. die Martis octavo die Maii hoc termino *[8 May 1453]*.

Ad quem [diem] [a]vicecomites, videlicet Ricardus Alley[a] [b]et Ricardus[b] Lee, retornarunt brevia eis in premissis separatim directa indorsata sic, videlicet verus predictum Thomam Dollyng in hec verba

Ante adventum istius brevis, videlicet vicesimo primo die Decembris anno tricecimo primo infrascripto *[21 Dec. 1453],* Thomam Dollyng infranominatum de custode prisone domini regis de Flete pretextu cujusdam alterius brevis domini regis, cujus transcriptum vobis mittimus huis brevi consutum, recepimus et ipsum in prisona domini regis de Neugate salvo custodiri fecimus.

Et idem Thomas Dollyng detentus est eciam in prisona predicta per nomen Thome Dollyng de villa Westmonasterii in comitatu Midd' pro 45s 4d, quod Henrico Dene de civitate London' scissor et custos gaole de Ludgate versus ipsum recuperavit in placito debiti in curia domini regis coram me Ricardo Lee uno vicecomitum London'.

Item Thomas Dollyng detentus est eciam in prisona predicta per nomen Thome Dollyng ad sectam Thome Wyg caryour in placito compoti super recepcione bonorum et catallorum ad valenciam quatuor librarum in curia domini regis coram me prefato vicecomite levate, super qua quidem querela ante adventum istius brevis, videlicet ad curiam domini regis tentam in guihalda civitatis London coram me predicto vicecomite die Mercurii proximo post festum sancti Gregorii Pape anno tricesimo primo infrascripto *[14 Mar. 1453],* consideratum fuit, quod dictus Thomas computet. Et super hoc adtunc et ibidem assignantur auditores per curiam predictam, videlicet Ricardus Lovelle et Robertus Chapmansford, ad audiendum compotum predictum.

Corpus tamen prefati Thome Dollyng coram baronibus interius specificatis ad diem et locum infracontentes habemus, prout nobis interius precipitur.

Ac dictum breve versus predictum Johannem Radevord in hec verba:

Ante adventum istius brevis, videlicet vicesimo tercio die Decembris anno infrascripto *[23 Dec. 1452],* Johannem Radeford infrascriptum a custode prisone domini regis de Flete pretextu cujusdam alterius brevis dicti domini regis nobis directi, cujus transcriptum vobis mittimus huic brevi consutum recepimus et ipsum in prisona ejusdem domini regis de Neugate pretextu dicti alterius brevis salvo custodiri fecimus.

Corpus tamen prefati Johannis coram baronibus interius specificatis ad diem et locum infracontentos habemus, prout interius nobis precipitur.

Et tenor transcripti predicti sequitur – [a]in dictis brevibus separatim contenti[a] – in hec verba:

Henricus Dei gracia rex Anglie et Francie et dominus Hibernie vicecomitibus London' salutem. Precipimus vobis, quod Johannem Radeford et Thomam Dollyng a custode prisone nostre de Flete per indenturas inde inter vos et prefatum custodem debite conficiendas recipiatis et ipsos in gaola nostra de Neugate salvo et secure, quousque pro eorum deliberacione aliud a nobis habueritis in mandatis, custodiri faciatis, mandavimus enim eidem custodi, quod ipsos Johannem et Thomam vobis in forma predicta deliberet. Teste me ipso apud Westmonasterium, 21 die Decembris anno regni nostri tricesimo primo *[21 Dec. 1452]*.

Et predicti Thomas Dollyng et Johannes Radeford – per predictos vicecomites huc ducti – veniunt in propriis personis suis. Et dicunt, quod ipsi de premissis seu aliquo premissorum in nullo sunt inde culpabiles nec eorum alter est inde culpabilis. Et hoc parati sunt et uterque eorum paratus est verificare, qualitercumque curia etc. [c]Ac iidem Thomas Dollyng et Johannes Radeford pro decepcione et falsicate predictis committuntur prisone domini regis de Flete ibidem moraturi, quousque etc. Predictus tamen Johannes Radeford traditur in ballium Galfrido Downes de London' yoman et Thome Wagewyk de eadem yoman usque diem Mercurii nonum diem Maii proximum futurum *[9 May 1453]*, [a]cujus ballii pretextu idem Johannes Radeford deliberatur a prisona predicta[a].

Ad quem diem predictus Johannes Radeford venit in propria persona sua. Et ut parcatur misis et expensis circa capcionem inquisicionis inter dominum regem et prefatum Johannem Radeford in premissis capiende, idem Johannes petit se ad racinabilem finem cum domino rege in premissis faciendum admitti. Et admissus est. Et predictus Johannes Radeford fecit finem in premissis, sicut continetur alibi in hiis memorandis, videlicet inter fines de hoc termino *[TNA: PRO, E159/229 Fines Easter m 3d; No. A.2]*. Ideo consideratum est per barones, quod versus predictum Johannem Radeford in premissis non fiat hic ulterius execucio.

Et dictum est pro domino regis, quod predictus Thomas Dollyng de premissis est culpabilis modo et forma, quibus superius per informacionem predictam pro domino rege supponitur. Et hec omnia et singula petitur pro eodem domino rege, quod inquirantur etc. Et quod predictus Thomas Dollyng dicit, ut prius, et petit similiter. Ideo fiat inde inquisicio.

Postea tamen, videlicet ad octabas sancte Trinitatis dicto anno tricesimo primo *[4 June 1453]*, predictus Thomas Dollyng per custodem prisone regis de Flete huc ductus, ut parcatus misis et expensis circa capcionem inquisicione predicte et ne idem Thomas de cetero vexetur in premissis, petit se de gracia curie ad racionabilem finem cum domino rege in premissis faciendum admitti. Et admissus est. Et super hoc idem Thomas fecit finem cum domino rege in premissis, sicut continetur alibi in hiis memorandis, videlicet inter fines de termino sancte Trinitatis *[TNA: PRO, E159/229 Fines Trinity m 1; No. A.3]*. Ideo consideratum est per barones, quod versus eundem Thomam Dollyng in premissis non fiat hic ulterius execucio. *[The 'finished' sign follows thrice, filling up the line]*.

[a-a] *Interlined L.* [b-b] *Written over* diem, *erased L.* [c] Flete *marginated against this line and subsequently struck through L.*

A.2 John Radford's fine. — 1453 May 9.

L PRO, E159/229 Fines ... visus Easter m 3d. Contemporaneous official copy. Parchment. Unsealed.
http://aalt.law.uh.edu/AALT2/H6/E159no229/aE159no229fronts/IMG_0565.htm

[Marginated] London'; De fine; In rotulo 31mo; finis 20s.

Johannes Radeford venit coram baronibus nono die Maii hoc termino *[9 May 1453]* et fecit finem cum domino rege, ut parcatur misis et expensis circa capcionem cujusdam inquisicionis inter dominum regem et prefatum Johannem capiende pro diversis transgressionibus et offensis per ipsum, ut dicitur, factis et annotatis alibi in hiis memorandis, videlicet inter recorda de hoc termino rotulo [6] in quodam processu tangente eundem Johannem per 20s

A.3 Thomas Dollyng's fine. — 1453 June 12.

L PRO, E159/229 Fines ... Trinity m 1. Contemporaneous official copy. Parchment. Unsealed.
http://aalt.law.uh.edu/AALT2/H6/E159no229/aE159no229fronts/IMG_0598.htm

[Marginated] London'; De fine; In rotulo 31mo; finis 20s.

Thomas Dollyng venit coram baronibus duodecimo die Junii hoc termino *[12 June 1453]* et fecit finem cum domino rege ut parcatur misis et expensis circa capcionem cujusdam inquisicionis inter dominum regem et prefatum Thomam capiende pro diversis transgressionibus et offensis per ipsum, ut dicitur, factis et annotatis alibi in hiis memorandis, videlicet inter recorda de termino sancte Trinitatis rotulo [recte termino Pasche m 6] in quodam processu tangente eundem Thomam per 20s

B. A queried tally (1453)

L TNA: PRO, E159/229 Recorda Trinity m 8. Contemporaneous official copy. Parchment. Unsealed.
http://aalt.law.uh.edu/AALT2/H6/E159no229/aE159no229fronts/IMG_0427.htm

[Marginated] Anglia; De Thoma Blythe[1] nuper clerico Radulphi domini de Cromwelle unius camerariorum [a]scaccarii[a] regis allocuto ad ostendendum, quare ipse finem cum domino rege pro quodam offenso per ipsum facto facere non debet etc.

Memorandum, quod Willelmus Lynde[2] presens hic in curia in propria per-

---

[1] Thomas Blythe was a deputy chamberlain of the Exchequer of Account: Sainty, *Officers*, p. 24.

[2] William Lynde was designated variously as king's servant (CPR 1446-52, p. 34 dated 20 Feb. 1447) and gentleman of the king's household (CCR 1441-47, p. 402). He was instrumental in helping Henry VI to found Eton College (CPR 1441-46, p. 32-3, 35, 38). For his labours he was named controller of the petty customs in London (CPR 1441-46, p. 350 dated 1 Aug. 1445) and, in lieu of that grant, collector of tunnage and poundage in London (CPR 1441-46, p. 372 dated 11 Sept. 1445). Neither grant took

sona sua quinto die Julii hoc termino *[5 July 1453]* et detulit hic duas tallias levatas decimo octavo die Julii anno vicesimo quinto regis hujus *[18 July 1447]*, videlicet unam earundem summam £100 continentem levatam De Ricardo Quatermayns et Johanne Melbourne collectoribus subsidii trium solidorum de dolio et duodecim denariorum et libra in portu London' et alteram talliam summam £100 continentem levatam De Johanne Poutrelle et Willelmo Beaufitz collectoribus subsidii lanarum in portu London' assignatas pro Johanne Seyntlo[3] pro denariis mutuatis, petens idem Willelmus tallias predictas contratalliis earundem per camerarios hujus scaccarii jungi. Super quod facto scrutinio per prefatos camerarios hujus scaccarii non est inventa aliqua contratallia in custodia camerariorum predictorum concordans talliis predictis nec alicui earundem. Postea tamen, scilicet sexto die Julii hoc termino *[6 July 1453]*, venit coram prefatis baronibus quidam Ricardus Symson[4] nuper serviens Thome Blythe nuper clerici Radulphi domini de Cromwelle unius camerariorum hujus scaccarii et deliberavit hic in curia contratallias talliarum predictarum asserens et informans prefatis baronibus, quod predictus Thomas Blythe contratallias illas tempore, quo ipse officium camerarii predicti sub prefato domino de Cromwelle occupavit, extra filacium contratalliarum comitatus London' sub custodia ipsius Thome tunc existentes abstulerat easdem contratallias apud London' in parochia Sancte Margarete in Fridaystrete in warda de Quenehithe in quadam cameraria sua[5] ibidem per tres annos jam elapsos et amplius penes se detinendo et quod dictus Thomas contratallias illas dicto sexto die Julii prefato Ricardo liberavit ad illas huic curie restituendas. Et quia barones hujus scaccarii, utrum tallie et contratallie predicte vere sint aut ficte vel si aliqua discrepancia inter tallias et contratallias predictas et pellem memorandorum de recepta de termino Pasche dicto anno vicesimo quinto ad receptam hujus scaccarii remanentem in summa vel aliter habeatur, pro commodo regis certitudinaliter volunt informari, antequam ulterius procedantur in premissis, preceptum est per barones Johanni Iwardeby[6] et Roberto Burton[7]

---

effect (cf. CPR 1446-52, p. 205 dated 30 Nov. 1448). At least once previously, he had renewed tallies: CCR 1447-54, p. 311 dated 1 Sept. 1451.

[3] TNA: PRO, E404/63/119 dated 12 July 1447. Seyntlo was designated as esquire (CPR 1446-52, p. 61 dated 17 May 1447) and – already deceased – as 'esquire about the king's person' (CCR 1447-54, p. 73 dated 13 Apr. 1448; CPR 1446-52, p. 242 dated 25 Mar. 1449; CPR 1452-61, p. 247).

[4] Richard Sympson was later (from 15 July 1455) Warwick deputy chamberlain of the Exchequer of Account: Sainty, *Officers*, p. 28.

[5] This was not as unusual as might be thought. A number of Elizabethan Exchequer officers also conducted their official business from their homes: J.D. Alsop, 'Government, Finance and the Community of the Exchequer', Christopher Haigh (ed.), *The Reign of Elizabeth I*, London 1987, p. 113.

[6] John Iwardby was *scriptor talliarum* in the Exchequer of Receipt: Sainty, *Officers*, p. 205.

[7] Robert Burton was clerk of the pells in the Exchequer of Receipt: Sainty, *Officers*, p. 214.

clericis inferioris scaccarii – recepte scaccarii vulgariter nuncupate – nono die Julii hoc termino *[9 July 1453]* coram prefatis baronibus hic personaliter existentes, sub quorum custodia pellis predicta residet, quod deferant hic coram baronibus pellem predictam decimo die Julii proximo futuro *[10 July 1453]* et hoc sub pena £100 etc., ut iidem barones superinde tam pro domino rege quam pro prefato Johanne Seyntlo facere valeant, quod in premissis justum fuerit faciendum. Qui quidem Johannes Iwardeby, Robertus Burton postea, scilicet duodecimo die Julii tunc proximo sequenti *[12 July 1453]*, detulerunt hic coram baronibus pellem predictam extra receptam predictam. Super quo – visis pelle predicta per barones predictos ac taliis et contratalliis predictis per eandem pellem coram prefatis baronibus diligenter examinatis – non est inventa aliqua discrepancia inter pellem predictam et tallias ac contratallias predictas, set concordant in omnibus. Et super hoc folia predicta deliberantur Johanni Broune[8] uni camerariorum hujus scaccarii custodienda, prout officio suo incumbit etc. Et concordatum est inter barones, quod mandetur [a]predicto[a] Thome Blythe de Chesthunt in comitatu Hertford breve de sub pena essendi hic etc. in crastino sancti Michaelis *[30 Sept. 1453]* sub pena £200 etc. ad ostendendum domino regi, quare ipse finem in premissis cum eodem domino rege facere non debet. [b]Ad quem diem idem Thomas venit in propria persona sua[b] *[case breaks off]*.

[a-a] *Interlined L.* [b-b] *Entered by a different hand L.*

C. The whereabouts of the tallies

The whereabouts of the tallies is a murky subject. What is clear is that – once the tally had been struck in the receipt of the Exchequer – one half was handed over to the payee and the counter-tally given to the deputy chamberlains of the Exchequer of Receipt to be put in their chest until picked up by the deputy chamberlains of the Exchequer of Account for comparison with the tally, which – the corresponding sum having been paid – would be returned into the Exchequer by the accountant.[9]

What happened then is, given the taciturn nature of the records, maddeningly difficult to determine with confidence. While Willard[10] thinks that the auditor matched tallies and counter-tallies and the plenary session of the Exchequer accepted unquestioningly his report of which tallies were 'in the treasury', Broome presents two cases from 30 Edw. III[11] and 19-20 Edw. III[12] which point in a very different direction. Both cases turn on the fact that the Warwick chamberlain failed to turn up when called before a plenary session of the Exchequer in order to open the chest where the counter-tallies were stored, so that accounting was delayed. It is clear in the case from 20 Edw. III that during a

---

[8] John Brown was Warwick chamberlain: Sainty, *Officers*, p. 16.

[9] Steel, *Receipt*, p. 6.

[10] Willard, *Parliamentary Taxes*, p. 328-9.

[11] Broome, *Exchequer*, Appendix III, No. XXII, p. cxvii-cxix.

[12] Broome, *Exchequer*, Appendix III, No. XXVII, p. cxxvi-cxxvii.

full session of the Exchequer (*sedentibus ... thesaurario et baronibus et omnibus aliis ministris hujus scaccarii*) the accountant, the sheriff of Norfolk and Suffolk, was presenting for allocation not merely tallies struck in the Lower Exchequer in receipt of cash paid in, but also tallies accepted from payees (*petente allocacionem de diversis pecuniarum summis per ipsum solutis ad receptam scaccarii et a l i u n d e per diversas tallias, quas tunc exhibuit, allocandas*).[13] The case from 30 Edw. III makes it clear that it was the chamberlains' task to take custody of the counter-tallies or appoint an attorney to do so (*cum ex antiqua consuetudine hujus scaccarii statutum sit, quod custodia talliarum hic in scaccario fiat per duos camerarios vel eorum attornatos*) and to produce them to be matched with the tallies proferred by accountants (*vocati sunt duos camerarios hujus scaccarii ad proponendum folia talliarum predictarum jungenda stipitibus earumdem et allocanda, ut est moris*).[14] What is confusing is the fact that, in the case from 20 Edw. III, it was the deputy chamberlain of the Exchequer of Account, Henry Eccleshale,[15] who was at fault, and in the case from 30 Edw. III, the Warwick chamberlain, Richard Piriton.[16] In any event, it is clear that tally and counter-tally were matched – not by the auditor, as Willard thought – but by the (deputy) chamberlains of the Upper Exchequer in the course of final accounting before the treasurer and all the barons.

However, in view of the momentous changes which took place regarding the chamberlains and their various deputies in the Exchequer of Account and the Exchequer of Receipt in the fourteenth century,[17] it might be objected that evidence from 1346/47 and 1356/57 is of doubtful relevance to our period. However, the deputy chamberlains of the Exchequer of Account are regularly described in the issue rolls from 1413 onwards as the *clerici camerariorum ad folia talliarum custodiendum*,[18] and the case transcribed above in II.B demonstrates beyond doubt that the Exchequer of Account expected that the chamberlains would be in a position to produce counter-tallies when required by a plenary session and would take charge of them thereafter, *prout officio suo incumbit*. It is clear, therefore, that the counter-tallies were no longer in the Exchequer of Receipt, whose officials (John Inwardby and Robert Burton) were only called on to verify that the tallies in question had in fact been levied six years earlier. Finally, Lawrence Squibb, writing in 1642 on the duties of Exchequer officials, states that the counter-tallies were kept in the chest of the deputy chamberlains of the Receipt until such time as the deputy chamberlains of the Exchequer of Account came to fetch them. They were then kept in a

---

13 Broome, *Exchequer*, p. cxxvi.

14 Broome, *Exchequer*, p. cxvii-cxviii.

15 On Eccleshale see Sainty, *Officers*, p. 27.

16 On Piriton see Sainty, *Officers*, p. 15.

17 Sainty, *Officers*, p. 2-3, 20, 164.

18 TNA: PRO, E403/619 m 18 et passim.

room under the Exchequer court until the accountants brought in their tallies, at which point the deputy chamberlains of the Exchequer of Account were required to search out the counter-tallies and join them to the accountants' tallies.[19] It seems reasonable to conclude that Exchequer procedure remained substantially the same between the mid-fourteenth and the mid-seventeenth century.

---

[19] Lawrence Squibb, *A book of all the several officers of the court of Exchequer* ..., ed. W. Hamilton Bryson, Camden Miscellany vol. 26 (Camden Fourth Series 14), London 1975, p. 77-136, here p. 130, 113-4.

SCHEDULE OF EXCHEQUER FEES

Although this schedule has been published – in very abbreviated form and in translation into modern English – the entire text has not – to my knowledge – been edited in full.

L TNA: PRO, E159/234 Recorda Michaelmas m 56. Contemporary copy. Parchment. Unsealed.

Published (without the text of the privy seal writ or of the act in council) This is a true copy of the ordinaunce made in the tyme of the reygne of kynge Henry the .vi. to be obserued in the kynges Eschequier, by the offycers and clerkes of the same, for takyng of fees of the kynges accomptis in the same courte, *London: Robert Redman [1533?] – A.W. Pollard, G.R. Redgrave (eds.), A Short-Title Catalogue of Books printed in England, Scotland, & Ireland and of English Books printed abroad 1475-1640, 2nd ed. revised by W.A. Jackson, F.S. Ferguson and Katharine F. Pantzer, 3 vols., London 1976-91, vol. 1, No. 7696, p. 349 – and reprinted numerous times in the 16th century: STC 7695-7698.*

Published in part (in modern English): A.R. Myers (ed.), English Historical Documents 1327-1485, London 1969, No. 327, p. 522-4.

[Marginated] Anglia; Ordinacio facta per dominos de consilio pro feodis capiendis in scaccario.

Dominus rex mandavit hic breve suum de privato sigillo suo thesaurario et baronibus hujus scaccarii directum in hec verba:

Henry by the grace of God kyng of England and of Fraunce and lorde of Irlande to the tresorer and barons of oure eschequier that now be and that for the tyme shall be gretyng. For asmuche as in oure parlement comenced at Westminster the 9^the^ day of Juylle of the 33 yere of oure regne *[9 July 1455]* we by thassent of the lordys spirituelle and temperelle and the comunes of this oure reaume assembled in the same yave oure assent to a comune peticioun made unto us by oure seide comunes[1] that the lordes of oure counselle shoulde take direccioun in that behalf suche as should be thought resonable afore the fest of seint Michelle the yere of oure regne 35 *[29 Sept. 1456]* or ellys the seide peticioun to stande in his strenght. And the seide lordys the 28 day of Juylle next before the seide fest of seint Michelle *[28 July 1456]* have in that bchalf take direccioun suche as is conteigned in an act of oure counsaille made by the seide lordys. We sende unto you the seide acte, ordenaunce and direccioun made and taken by the seide lordys, willyng and chargyng you straitely that ye observe and make to be observed in oure seide eschequier the seide ordenaunce and direc-

[1] *Cf. 33 Hen. VI, St. 1 c. 3 (= Statutes of the Realm, vol. 2, p. 372-4).*

cioun so that hereafter all grucchinges and complayntes may ceesse and be leyde apart ayenst the officers and clerkys of oure seide eschequier and that ye do the seide direccioun and ordenaunce to be opened and knowe to oure people, and that they be redde openly in the same oure eschequier at the receyvyng of these oure lettres and afterward as ofte as it shall be thought unto you necessarie. Yeven under oure prive seal at Westminster, the 11 day of Novembre the yere of oure regne 36[ti] *[11 Nov. 1457]*.

Et tenor actus, ordinacionis [a]et direccionis[a] predicti sequitur in hec verba:

The 28 day of Juille the yere of our soverein lord king Henry the Sext 34[ti] *[28 July 1455]* the lordys of the kinges counsail assembled at Westminster in the sterred chambre considering the answer made by the kinges highnesse to a commune peticioune made unto his said highness by the comunes of this his reame wherof the copie is annexed herto ordeigned, advised and toke direccioun such as foloweth to be kepte and observed in the said eschequier in such thinges and by such officers and their clerkys as ben remembred and specified in the said commune peticioun and by them that herafter shall occupie in their places, willing and ordeignyng that if any of the said officers and clerkys do contrary to this present ordinaunce made by the said lordes that thenne he renne in to the payn conteyned in the said peticioun, and that alle thinges conteyned in the same remaigne and abide in his strengthe with the ordinaunce modifieng and direction as foloweth.

[Marginated against the following line] R[emembrator] R[egis]

IN THOFFICE OF THE KYNGES REMEMBRAUNCER

Furst for thentre of a custumers vewe or accountes in the portes of Briggewater, Chichestre, Newe Castell, Plymmouth, Fowey, Pole and Berwyk... 3s 4d
Item for the entre of a custumers vewe or accompt of every othir port....... 6s 8d
Item to the secundary clerk of the said every othir port................................20d
Item for thentre of processes or plees of accountantz conteyneng half a rolle 3s 4d
Item yf it conteyne an hole rolle.. 6s 8d
And so aftre thafferant yf it conteyne more
Item for thentre of lettres patentes, escriptes, confessed or othre recordes conteygnyng lasse than half a rolle... 2s
And yf if conteyne half a rolle 3s 4d
And so aftre thafferant
Item for entre of dayes of contynuance of accountantes 20d
Item for makyng of every vewe or account of collectours of dismes graunted by the clergye of the archideconries of Rouchestre, Surrey, Cornewaille, Seynt Albons, Stafford, Chestre, Lancastre, Saint David, Saint Assaphe, Landaff, Cardigan, Brecon, Shrovesbury in the diocese of Coventre, Clyfland, Rychemond and diocese of Duresme everich of theym 3s 4d
Item of every other archideconry and countee 6s 8d
Item for makyng of writtes of privelege.. 2s

Item of the collectours and accountantes of the 15th peny .... nichil

Item for entre of writtys undre the grete or prive seall direct to the tresourer and barons for accountantes yf it conteigne half a rolle 2s

And yf it conteyn [a]half[a] a side of a rolle 12d

And yf it conteyne lasse 4d

And yf it conteyne more thanne half a rolle aftir thafferant the whiche shall remayne to the clerkys except 'mittimus' and other writtys which have ben used of olde tyme to be entred amonge records

Item to the clerkys for their peticions yf they conteyne half a skynne of parchemyn prestwyse 2s

And so aftir thafferant yf they conteyne more

Item to the clerkys for thentre of foreyn accountys of Scottysh money etc. ..20d

Item to the clerkys for thentre of warrantis of attourney 4d

Item to the clerkys for makyng of 'sistas in auxilium', 'constat', 'nisi prius' and commissions of 'nisi prius' at the seute of partys conteynyng lasse than half a rolle of parchemyne prestwyse 2s

And so aftir thafferant yf it conteigne more

[Marginated against the following line] R[emembrator] T[hesaurarii]

IN THOFFICE OF THE TRESORERS REMEMBRAUNCER

Furste to the mayster for makyng, provyng, castyng, dischargyng and allowance of the viewes of the shires of Cornewaille, Worcestre, Rotland and Westmorland and eche of theym 5s

And citees and borghes made shires 3s 4d

And of other double and grete shires 6s 8d

Item to the clerkys laboryng, wrytyng and charging of the said viewes 2s

Excepte the said citees and bourghes made shires of everych of the whiche the clerkys abovesaid shall take for the said viewes but only 20d

Item to the mayster for laboure of redyng, endosyng and tryeng of peticiouns and fynes for contempt yf eny bee of the shirefes of London' and Midd', Surrey and Sussex', Somerset and Dorset, Warr' and Leyc', Oxon' and Berk', Bedford and Buk', Essex' and Hertford, Norff' and Suff', York and Lincoln, of everyche of the shirefes 10s

And of the shirefes of Kent, *[m 56d]* Hampshire, Wilteshire, Gloucestershire, Notynghamshire and Derbyshire, Herfordshire, Salop', Cumbreland, Cambrige and Huntyngdonshires, Devonshire, Cornewaille, Stafford, Northumbria, Worcestre and Rotland everych of the shirefes 6s 8d

And of the shirefes of Westmorland and of eche other of citees and bourghes made shires 3s 4d

Item to the mayster for thentre of peticions of custumers, eschetours and other foreyn accounttantes conteynyng half a rolle 3s 4d

And yf it conteyne more or lasse aftir thafferant

Item to the mayster for thentre of shirefes dayes, eschetours and othre accountauntes except dismes and quinzismes 20d

Item to the mayster for entre of clayme of franchises, of issues, fines and

amercimentis conteynyng half a rolle 3s 4d
And yf it conteyne[b] more either lasse after thafferant
Item to the mayster for makyng of writtes of privelege 2s
Item to the mayster for makyng, provyng and dischargyng of every viewe of baillief of fraunchises 20d
Item to the clerkys laboryng, writyng and chargyng of every suche viewe ... 12d
Item of collectours of dismes and quinzismes.. nichil
Item to the clerkys for makyng of the tenour of the recorde and writte of every 'nisi prius' conteynyng lasse than half a rolle 2s
And for more after thafferant
Item to the clerkys for the commissioun of the same 2s
Item to the clerkys for thentre of the verdit of every suche 'nisi prius' retourned 2s
Item to the clerkys for makyng of 'sistas in auxilium', 'constat', 'supersedeas' of land and 'utrelemain' 2s
Item to the clerkys for 'fieri facias' upon tailles and othir writtes 6d
Item to the clerkys for entre of warantes of attourney and of mainprice 4d
[Marginated against the following line] Pipa

IN THE OFFICE OF THENGROSSER

Furste to the mayster for his fee makyng of allowance and discharge of the shirefes of Cornewail, Worcestre, Rotland and Westmorland of eche of theym 5s
Item to the mayster of citees and bourghes made shires of eche of theym.. 3s 4d
And of every double shire and eche othre grete shire 10s
Item to the clerkys for allouaunce of tailles in the said double and grete shires 2s
Item to the clerkys for tottes and parcelles and discharge and allouaunces of the said double and grete shires.. 6s 8d
Item to the clerkys in the shires of Cornewail, Worcestre, Rotland and Westmorland for allouaunce of tailles.. 20d
Item to the clerkys for tottes and parcelles, discharge and allouaunces of the same 3s 4d
Item to the clerkys of citees and bourghes made shires for allouaunce of tailles 12d
Item to the clerkys for tottes and parcelles, discharge and allouaunce of the same 2s
Item to the mayster for allouaunces and discharges of baillieffes of franchises 20d
Item to the mayster of every eschetour of the shires of London', Stafford, Worcestre, Shrovesbury and Hereford 3s 4d
Item to the mayster of every other eschetour yf he have any peticions............ 5s
And yf he have no peticions oonly 3s 4d
Item of citees and bourghes made shires... nichil
Item to the clerkys for allouaunce of tailles of every eschetour of London',

Stafford, Worcestre, Salop', Hereford and citees and bourghes made shires. 12d
Item to the clerkys for semble allouaunces of every othir eschetour 20d
Item to the clerkys for allouaunce of tailles of bailliefes of franchises.......... 12d
Item to the clerkys for discharge of bailliefes of franchises.............................8d
Item to the mayster of every custumer in the portes of Briggewater, Chichester, Newcastell, Plymmouth, Fowy, Pole and Berwyk..................................... 3s 4d
Item to the clerkys of the said portes for allouaunce of tailles 12d
And for discharge of them..20d
Item to the mayster of every custumer in other portes 6s 8d
Item to the clerkys in the same other portes for thallouaunce of taillis..........20d
And for discharge of theym... 3s 4d
Item to the mayster of collectours of dismes in smale archidecanries, that is to say Rouchestre, Cornewaille, Seint Albons, Stafford, Chester, Lancastre, Seint David, Seint Assaph, Landaff, Cardigan, Brechon, Salop' in the diocise of Coventre, Duresme, Clyfland and Richemond for the allouaunce of everych of them 3s 4d
Item to the mayster of collectours of dismes in every othre archideconry for the allouaunces of theym 6s 8d
Item of collectours of quinzismes ....nichil
Item for thengrossyng of grete accountes with sette hand, that is to say of the tresourer of the kynges houshold 26s 8d
Of the kynges warderober.. 26s 8d
Of the tresourer of Caleys 26s 8d
Of the vitailler of Caleis... 13s 4d
Of the clerk of the kynges werkes.. 13s 4d
And of the duchie of Cornewail..20s
And thees sommes of the said grete accountantes to be devided betuyx the said maister and the clerkys, that is to say tuo partes to the maister and the third to the clerkys
Item of other smale accountes that conteyne half a rolle of parchemyn of the pipe to the clerkys that come late in to the said office excepte of shireffes and benefices not taxed, wherof nothing shalbe taken.. 2s

[c]IN THOFFICE OF THE COUNTROLLERSHIP

Furst to the mayster for his fees and rewardes of the shirrefes of Cornewaille, Worcestre, Rotteland and Westmorland of eche of theym.......................... 3s 4d
Item of citees *[m 56A]* and bourghes made shires of eche of theym...........nichil
Item to the mayster of every double shire and eche other grete shire 6s 8d
[Marginated against the next line] Placita

IN OFFICIO CLERICI PLACITORUM DE SCACCARIO DOMINI REGIS

In primis pro brevi originali ad sectam alicujus computantis in scaccario predicto prosecutantis versus aliquam aliam personam 2s
Item pro brevi judiciali etc. 6d
Item [pro] intracione declaracionis superinde facta in rotulo.......................... 2s

Item pro intracione de 'nichil dicit' facta super aliquo computante etc. 2s
Item pro intracione judicii redditi etc. 2s
Item pro brevi de constat ad sectam alicujus computantis etc. 2s
Item pro commissione facta pro aliquo computante, quorum nomina 3s 4d
Item pro irrotulacione ejusdem commissionis.. 12d
Item pro brevi de fieri facias super aliqua assignacione facta pro aliquo computante vel aliqua alia persona per aliam assignacionem sive concessionem etc. 2s
Set super fieri facias per talliam .... 6d tantum
Item pro brevi de scire facias super allocacione habita in eodem scaccario etc. 2s
Item pro intracione placiti sive responsionis pro aliquo computante etc. 2s
Item pro intracione facta in rotulo pro innovacione tallie perdite per aliquem computantem etc. 2s
Item pro exemplificacione recordi habiti pro aliquo computante etc. 6s 8d
[Marginated against the next line] Auditores

PRO AUDITORIBUS ET CLERICIS SUIS

Furst for makyng and writyng of every viewe of an eschetour 5s
Item for thexamynyng, makyng and writyng of thaccountes of eschetours for every prest of the assise of the pipe writen on bothe sides 6s 8d
And if it be lesse thanne a prest, than lasse aftre thafferant
Item for thexaminyng, prevyng, devidyng, castyng and writyng of every accounte of custumers in the portes of London' (the grete custume), Sandewich, Southampton, Hull, Boston and Yeppeswich yf ther be shippyng of wolles and no reteigners nor licences, for every such accounte of a yere or more...... 26s 8d
And yf it be lasse than a yere after thafferant of 26s 8d by the yere
Item yf ther be reteigners or licences, for every suche account of a yere or more 40s
And yf it be lasse than a yere after thafferant of 40s by the yere
Item for every accounte of the said custumers in the said portes, yf ther be no shippyng of wolles, for a yere or more 13s 4d
And yf it be lasse than a yere, after thafferent of 13s 4d by the yere
Item for every accounte of the custumers of the tonnage and poundage of London', of pety custume of London' and of the custumers of Bristowe for every suche accounte of a yere or more 26s 8d
And yf it be lasse than a yere after thafferant of 26s 8d by the yere
Item for every accounte of the custumers in the portes of Pole, Excestre, Dertmouth, Plymmouth, Fowy, Yernemouth, Lynne and Newcastell for every suche account of a yere or more 13s 4d
And if it be lasse than a yere, after thafferant of 13s 4d by the yere
Item for every accounte of the custumers in the portes of Chichestre and Briggewater for a yere or more 10s
And if it be lasse than a yere, after the afferant of 10s by [the] yere
Item for every viewe of custumers in the said portes of London' (the grete

custume), Sandewiche, Southampton, Hull, Boston and Yppeswich, yf ther be shippyng of wolles 10s
Item if ther be no shippyng of wolles, for every suche viewe 6s 8d
Item for every viewe of custumers of tonnage and poundage and pety custume of London' and Bristowe 10s
Item for every viewe of custumers in the portes of Pole, Excestre, Dertmouth, Plymmouth, Fowy, Yernemouth and Lynne 6s 8d
Item for every viewe of custumers in the portes of Chichestre, Newcastell and Briggewater 5s
Item for thexaminacioun, preving, casting and makyng of thaccountes of the tresorer of houshold 40s
Item for the kynges warderober 26s 8d
Item for the clerk of the werkes 26s 8d
Item for the tresorer of Caleis 40s
Item for the viteller of Caleis 33s 4d
Item for the duchie of Cornewaille 40s
Item for thaccountes of the constable of the castell of Wyndesore 26s 8d
Item for thaccountes of the tresorer of Irland 20s
Item for thaccountes of the constable of the castell of Burdeux 66s 8d
Item for thaccountes of the chambirleyn of Berwik 20s
Item for thaccountes of the chambirlein of South Wales 26s 8d
Item for thaccountes of the chambirlein of North Wales 26s 8d
Item for thaccountes of the chamberlein of Chestre 26s 8d
Item for thaccountes of the clerk of the hanaper 20s
Item for thaccountes of the baillif of Sandewich 10s
Item for thaccountes of the maister of the kynges hors 13s 4d
Item for every accounte of every fermour of the subsidie of alienes, sercheurs and gaugiers in the portes 3s 4d
Item for every forein accounte of shirriffes and ulnage 12d
Item if it be a newe seiser 2s
Item for every account of prestes or any other forein accounte, so it conteigne the lengthe of an hole prest withinforth 3s 4d
And so more or lasse after the afferant
Item for every viewe of collectours of benefices not taxed 20d
Item for thaccounte therof 3s 4d
Item for every accounte *[m 56Ad]* of the resumpcioun in the last parlement graunted[2] yf it drawe to any extent 10s
Item of nichil inde venit .... nichil
Furthermore the seid auditours shall take nothing of collectours of quinzismes for any viewe or accounte makyng
[Marginated against the next line] Oppositor forinsecum

IN THOFFICE OF THE FOREIN OPPOSER

---

[2] *Rotuli Parliamentorum, vol. 5, p. 300-320.*

Furst of the shirreffes of London' and Midd', Surrey and Sussex', Somerset and Dorset, Warr' and Leic', Oxon' and Berk', Bedd' and Buk', Cant' and Hunt', Essex' and Hertford, Norff' and Suff', Not' and Derby, Kent, Hampshire, Wilteshire, Devon, Cornewaille, Gloucestre, Northumbria, Lincoln and York of every shirreff of thees shires thopposer 6s 8d
And his clerkes 40d
Item for billes of allouaunce of justices of the pees, fees of everiche of the seid shirreffes 3s 4d
Item of baillifes of fraunchises for their claymes within thees shires aforeseid 20d
Item of the shirrieffes of the citee of Norwiche, citee of York, citee of Lincoln', Kyngeston' upon Hull, Herford, Worcestre, Salop', Stafford, Rotland, Northumbria, Cumbreland, Westmorland, Newcastell, Bristowe, Coventre and Notingham of everich of thees shirreffes the forein opposer etc. 3s 4d
And his clerkes 20d
Item for billes of allouaunce of justices of the pees, wages of everiche of the seid shirreffes 20d
Item of bailliffes of fraunchises of thees shires for theire claymes 12d
[Marginated against the next line] Camerarii

IN THOFFICE OF CHAMBERLEINS ETC.

Furste of every shirreff of the shires of London' and Midd', Surrey and Sussex', Somerset and Dorset, Warr' and Leic', Oxon' and Berk', Bedd' and Buk', Essex' and Hertford, Norff' and Suff', York, Lincoln for jo[y]nyng of tailles of everech of the seid shirreffes 3s 4d
Item for jo[y]nyng of tailles of every eschetour of the said shires except[d] Midd' 20d
Item of the shirreffes of Kent, Suthampton', Wiltes', Gloucestre, Not' and Derby, Herford, Salop', Cant' and Hunt' and Cumbreland for joynyng of tailles of everich of the said shirreffes 2s
Item for jo[y]nyng of tailles of every eschctour in the same shires except Kent and Cumbreland 20d
Item of the shirreffes of Devon, Cornewaille, Stafford, Northumbria, Worcestre, Rotland, Westmorland and of eche other citee and burgh made shires for joynyng of tailles of yche of the seid shirreffes 20d
Item for joynyng of tailles of every eschetour of the seid shires except Devonshire, Cornewaille, Northumbria, Rotland and Westmorland 12d
Item of every eschetour of the shires of Kent and Midd', Devonshire, Cornewaille, Northumbria, Rotland, Cumbreland and Westmorland for joynyng of tailles 2s
Item of every baillif of franchises for joynyng of tailles of the somme of 20s or above 12d
Item of every baillif of franchises for joynyng of tailles byneth 20s 4d
Item of custumers in every of the portes of London', Sandewich, Southampton, Hull, Boston and Yppeswich for joynyng of tailles 5s

Item of the custumers in everiche of the portes of Pole, Excestre, Dertmouth, Plymmouth, Fowy, Yernemouth, Lynne and Newcastell............................ 3s 4d
Item of the custumers in every of the portes of Chichestre and Briggewater. 20d
Item of every fermour or dettour not accountaunt for joynyng of every taille to be allowed to the seid fermour or dettour and not allowed to any shirreff or baillif, yf the seid taille be byneth £20 .... 4d
And if the seid taille be of £20 or more, undre £40.. 6d
Item yf the seid taille be of £40 or above 12d
Item of every collectour of dismes graunted by the clergie 12d
Item of collectours of quinzismes .... nichil
[Marginated against the next line] Extractor

IN THOFFICE OF THE CLERK OF THEXTRETES

Onely his fees and rewardes of the kynge

a-a *Interlined L.* b conceyne *L, in error.* c *Margination illegible L.* d except *repeated in error L.*

APPENDIX IV
EXCHEQUER TERMS 1392/93–1462/63

Since various officials of the Exchequer were paid less per diem during vacations than during term, the issue rolls distinguish between the two when recording per diem payments to officials at the end of term.[1] The Exchequer terms ermerge from these *liberaciones*, but they never note a break between Easter and Trinity terms.

	Michaelmas	Hilary	Easter/Trinity	TNA: PRO, E403
1392/93	30/9-26/11	14/1-1/3	14/4-19/7	541 m 7, m 19; 543 m 17
1393/94	30/9-3/12	14/1-9/3	27/4-21/7	546 m 13, m 23; 548 m 17
1394/95	30/9-5/12	14/1-27/2	19/4-17/7	549 m 5, m 13; 551 m 15
1395/96	30/9-14/12	14/1-19/2	–	554 m 13, m 18
1396/97	–	–	30/4-21/7	555 m 20
1397/98	1/10-4/12	14/1-23/2	15/4-13/7	556 m 17, m 28; 559 m 12
1398/99	30/9-9/12	15/1-21/2	7/4-12/7	561 m 8, m 15; 562 m 18
1399/00	30/9-10/12	7/1-21/2	26/4-13/7	564 m 5, m 11; 567 m 13
1400/01	1/10-11/12	15/1-25/2	–	569 m 10, m 19
1401/02	30/9-14/12	13/1-27/2	3/4-15/7	571 m 17, m 24; 573 m 21
1402/03	30/9-7/12	15/1-23/2	23/4-17/7	574 m 7, m 16; 576 m 18
1403/04	30/9-10/12	13/1-27/2	7/4-15/7	578 m 12, m 20; 579 m 4
1404/05	30/9-13/12	13/1-2/3	–	581 m 5, m 12
1405/06	–	–	–	

[1] J.C. Sainty, *Officers of the Exchequer* (List and Index Society Special Series 18), London 1983. Per diem rates were paid to the chamberlains (8d per diem in and out of term: ibid., p. 4), treasurer's clerk (8d in vacation, 5d in term: ibid., p. 191), clerk of the pipe and controller of the pipe (5d each in term, nothing in vacation: ibid., p. 59, 69), tellers (3d per diem in term and in vacation: ibid., p. 218), usher of the Upper Exchequer (5d per diem in term and in vacation: ibid., p. 140, ushers of the Exchequer of Receipt (2d per diem in vacation, 1½d per diem in term: ibid., p. 247).

	Michaelmas	Hilary	Easter/Trinity	TNA: PRO, E403
1406/07	–	[14/1-4/3]	4/4-15/7	591 m 11
1407/08	30/9-28/11	14/1-20/3	23/4-19/7	593 m 6; 594 m 19; 595 m 19
1408/09	30/9-4/12	14/1-9/3	15/4-16/7	596 m 8, m 13; 599 m 11
1409/10	30/9-4/12	14/1-1/3	31/3-17/7	602 m 11, m 15; 605 m 8
1410/11	29/9-9/12	14/1-23/2	20/4-23/7	607 m 9, m 11; 608 m 11
1411/12	30/9-16/12	14/1-27/2	[11/4-17/7]	609 m 5, m 13
1412/13	30/9-10/12	14/1-2/3	1/5-14/7	611 m 12; 610 m 6; 612 m 5
1413/14	30/9-11/12	[14/1-22/2]	[16/4-19/7]	614 m 9, m 19; 617 m 15
1414/15	[30/9-7/12]	[14/1-16/3]	–	619 m 9, m 18
1415/16	30/9-23/12	[14/1-2/3]	27/4-24/7	622 m 7, m 12; 624 m 12
1416/17	30/9-19/12	14/1-13/3	19/4-17/7	627 m 22, m 30; 630 m 10
1417/18	30/9-15/12	14/1-5/3	4/4-16/7	633 m 8, m 17; 636 m 12
1418/19	30/9-10/12	14/1-11/3	24/4-15/7	638 m 11, m 16; 640 m 12
1419/20	30/9-5/12	14/1-12/3	15/4-12/7	643 m 11; 644 m 23; 645 m 13
1420/21	30/9-14/12	14/1-20/2	31/3-16/7	646 m 10, m 14; 649 m 16
1421/22	30/9-13/12	14/1-28/3	20/4-17/7	652 m 13, m 21; 655 m 14
1422/23	30/9-21/12	14/1-27/2	12/4-17/7	658 m 5, m 11; 660 m 14
1423/24	30/9-15/12	14/1-23/2	1/5-21/7	663 m 12; 664 m 19; 666 m 13
1424/25	30/9-13/12	14/1-28/2	16/4-20/7	669 m 10, m 16; 671 m 14
1425/26	30/9-13/12	14/1-21/2	8/4-17/7	673 m 8, m 14; 675 m 10
1426/27	30/9-5/12	14/1-1/3	28/4-18/7	677 m 9, m 16; 680 m 12
1427/28	30/9-5/12	14/1-21/2	12/4-19/7	683 m 10, m 15; 686 m 11
1428/29	1/10-4/12	14/1-25/2	4/4-14/7	688 m 9, m 14; 689 m 15
1429/30	30/9-23/12	14/1-8/4	24/4-19/7	692 m 12; 693 m 12; 694 m 14
1430/31	30/9-16/12	14/1-28/2	9/4-18/7	697 m 12, m 17; 698 m 10

	Michaelmas	Hilary	Easter/Trinity	TNA: PRO, E403
1431/32	30/9-13/12	14/1-27/2	28/4-15/7	700 m 9, m 16; 703 m 12
1432/33	30/9-4/12	14/1-2/3	20/4-18/7	706 m 10, m 18; 709 m 11
1433/34	30/9-19/12	14/1-25/2	5/4-14/7	712 m 6, m 12; 716 m 16
1434/35	30/9-30/11	14/1-21/2	25/4-21/7	718 m 7, m 13; 720 m 13
1435/36	30/9-16/12	14/1-4/4	16/4-25/9	721 m 12, m 17; 723 m 14
1436/37	30/9-7/12	14/1-4/3	8/4-19/7	726 m 10, m 15; 728 m 11
1437/38	30/9-10/12	14/1-24/2	21/4-16/7	729 m 9, m 13; 731 m 14
1438/39	30/9-4/12	14/1-2/3	13/4-23/7	733 m 8, m 13; 734 m 13-4
1439/40	30/9-11/12	14/1-28/2	4/4-18/7	736 m 11, m 18; 738 m 15
1440/41	30/9-3/12	14/1-25/2	24/4-21/7	740 m 9, m 16; 742 m 11
1441/42	30/9-11/12	14/1-26/2	9/4-18/7	743 m 8, m 13; 746 m 12
1442/43	1/10-10/12	14/1-6/4	29/4-20/7	747 m 9, m 16; 749 m 19
1443/44	30/9-7/12	14/1-22/2	20/4-17/7	752 m 4, m 7-8; 754 m 7
1444/45	30/9-28/11	14/1-23/2	5/4-16/7	756 m 8, m 12; 757 m 10
1445/46	30/9-4/12	14/1-25/2	25/4-16/7	759 m 10, m 15; 762 m 12
1446/47	30/9-7/12	14/1-18/2	17/4-18/7	765 m 12-3, m 15; 768 m 13
1447/48	30/9-7/12	14/1-21/2	1/4-17/7	769 m 9, m 14; 771 m 11
1448/49	30/9-5/12	14/1-24/2	21/4-21/7	774 m 9, m 16; 776 m 8
1449/50	30/9-13/12	14/1-25/2	13/4-4/7	778 m 7, m 11; 779 m 10
1450/51	30/9-5/12	14/1-3/4	3/5-21/7	781 m 4, m 8; 785 m 9
1451/52	29/9-11/12	14/1-19/2	17/4-4/8	786 m 7, m 11; 790 m 7
1452/53	30/9-5/12	14/1-28/2	9/4-16/7	791 m 6, m 13; 793 m 11
1453/54	30/9-7/12	14/1-2/3	29/4-13/7	795 m 8; 796 m 14; 798 m 8
1454/55	30/9-7/12	14/1-22/2	14/4-15/7	800 m 6, m 12; 801 m 6
1455/56	–	–	[5/4-17/7]	
1456/57	30/9-4/12	[14/1-19/2]	25/4-15/7	809 m 4; 810 m 10
1457/58	–	[14/1-20/2]	10/4-15/7	816 m 4
1458/59	30/9-5/12	14/1-28/2	–	818 m 3, m 7
1459/60	–	–	–	

	Michaelmas	Hilary	Easter/Trinity	TNA: PRO, E403
1460/61	–	[14/1-13/2]	13/4-17/7	822 m 4
1461/62	30/9-11/12	[14/1-1/4]	26/4-21/7	824 m 5, m 10
1462/63	30/9-15/11	14/1-5/3	–	827 m 4, m 12

INDEX TO THE INTRODUCTION

Personal names are in normal type, places in small caps and subjects in italics.

INDEX OF PEOPLE AND PLACES

Italian and Spanish names are given in the 'ablative', if this seems to be a reproduction of the Italian or Spanish spelling (Andrea, Beaceo, Roderigo rather than Andreas, Beaceus, Roderigus). The order of the names is phonological, so that, for instance, 'y' is alphabetized as 'i'. I have enclosed information on the origins of Italian and Hansetic merchants (e.g. 'of Cologne', 'Venetian merchant') which is not in the accounts themselves in square brackets.
Place names are in small capitals.

– A –

– B –

– E –

– H –

– I –

– T –

INDEX OF SUBJECTS

The index is structured so as to serve as a glossary. Hence, the main entry is under the word as it appears in the sources (*zinziber*), and a cross-reference leads the reader from the modern English term to the main entry (ginger see *zinziber*). If a term is in Middle English, the plural form is given; if in Latin, the genitive.

More than one reference per page is not noted.

Brief references to the scholarly literature:

Cobb: H.S. Cobb (ed.), *The Overseas Trade of London. Exchequer Customs Accounts 1480-1* (London Record Society Publications 27), London 1990

Day: John Day, *Les douanes de Gênes 1376-1377* (École Pratique des Hautes Études – VIe Section Centre des Recherches Historiques: Ports, Routes, Trafics 17), 2 vols., Paris 1963

Gras: Norman Scott Brien Gras, *The Early English Customs System. A Documentary Study of the Institutional and Economic History of the Customs from the Thirteenth to the Sixteenth Century*, Cambridge/Mass. 1918

Hanham: Alison Hanham (ed.), *The Cely Letters, 1472-1488* (Early English Text Society 273), London 1975

Heyd: Wilhelm Heyd, *Geschichte des Levanthandels im Mittelalter*, 2 vols., Stuttgart 1879, repr. Hildesheim 1984

Latham, Dictionary: R.E. Latham, D.R. Howlett (eds.), *Dictionary of Medieval Latin from British Sources*, Oxford 1975-

Latham, Word-List: R.E. Latham (ed.), *Revised Medieval Latin Word-List from British and Irish Sources*, revised ed., Oxford 1973

MED: *Middle English Dictionary*, Ann Arbor 1954-99

Melis: Federigo Melis, *Documenti per la storia economica dei secoli XIII-XVI* (Istituto Internazionale di Storia Economica "F. Datini" Pubblicazioni – Serie I, Documenti 1), Florence 1972

OED: *Oxford English Dictionary*, 2nd ed., Oxford 1989

Pegolotti: Francesco Balducci Pegolotti, *La pratica della mercatura*, ed. allan Evans (Mediaeval Academy of America Publications 24), Cambridge/Mass. 1936

Smit: Homme Jakob Smit (ed.) *Bronnen tot de geschiedenis van den handel met Engeland, Schotland en Ierland* (Rijks Geschiedkundige Publicatiën 65, 66, 86, 91), 4 vols., The Hague 1928-50

Stieda: Wilhelm Stieda, *Hansisch-venetianische Handelsbeziehungen im 15. Jahrhundert*, Rostock 1894

Veale: Elspeth M. Veale, *The English Fur Trade in the Later Middle Ages*, 2nd ed. (London Record Society Publications 38), London 2003

Zupko: Ronald Zupko, *A Dictionary of Weights and Measures for the British Isles: The Middle Ages to the Twentieth Century* (Memoirs of the American Philosophical Society 168), Philadelphia 1985

– D –

– F –

– G –

– H –

– N –

– O –

– U –

– V –

INDEX OF SHIPS BY NAME

INDEX OF SHIPS BY HOME PORT

For the location of the home ports, see the maps at the end of the index. Needless to say, some home ports are difficult to identify with any confidence (Castelond, Cosyche/Cosive, Harlow, Stanby). In these cases, I decided to err on the side of caution, feeling that it was preferable to leave a home port unlocalized rather than grasp at straws and – most probably – introduce an erroneous place identification into the scholarly literature.

[1] 'Bury' is a scribal error for *Barowe* or some other variant of the medieval name for Bergen op Zoom. The correct identification emerges from the fact that the *Christofor de Barewe del Sam* (skipper *Henricus Dancart*, 40 tonnes) was taken into royal service between 24 Feb. 1441

and 14 June 1442 in order to transport John, lord Talbot, and his retinue from Winchelsea to France: TNA: PRO E101/53/39 m 6 and E403/745 m 7).

[2] This is obviously an English ship, but its home port is entirely obscure. It is just barely conceivable that it is to be identified with Castle Hill in Norwich: Karl Inge Sandred, Bengt Lindström, *The Place-Names of Norfolk. Part I: The Place-Names of the City of Norfolk* (English Place-Name Society 61), 1989, p. 23, but no further evidence can be adduced.

[3] Since the skipper of this vessel is clearly Dutch, one must suspect that 'Harlow' is a scribal error, possibly for 'Harlem'. However, no such variant spelling for Harlem can be found in the published Dutch records. Nonetheless, one can firmly reject an identification with Harlow (Essex) and Harlow (part of Harrogate, West Yorkshire).

[4] Here, again, the obvious fact that the skipper is Dutch suggests scribale error for some town in the Netherlands and precludes an identification with Stainby or Little Stanesby (both Lincolnshire).

[5] Thorphith is reasonably well-attested as a place in Suffolk (CPR 1408-13, p. 271; CPR 1452-61, p. 269) and probably lay in Samford hundred (CCR 1422-9, p. 291). Three aliens were dwelling there in 1436 (CPR1429-36, p. 576), and it was the home port of the *Kateryn de Thorpehight*, skipper William Galkehorne (TNA: PRO, E122/73/26 f. 25^{v}). However, while Suffolk had a number of localities with the place-name element 'Thorp' (the parish of Thorpe TM 201623, Thorpe Morieux TL 943533; the manor of Goodrich Thorp TM 130690, Ixworth Thorpe TL 918725, Thorpness TM 474598 and Westhorpe TM 044692), none of them lie in Samford hundred. Consequently, it would be foolhardy to press the meagre evidence for the exact location of Thorphith too far.

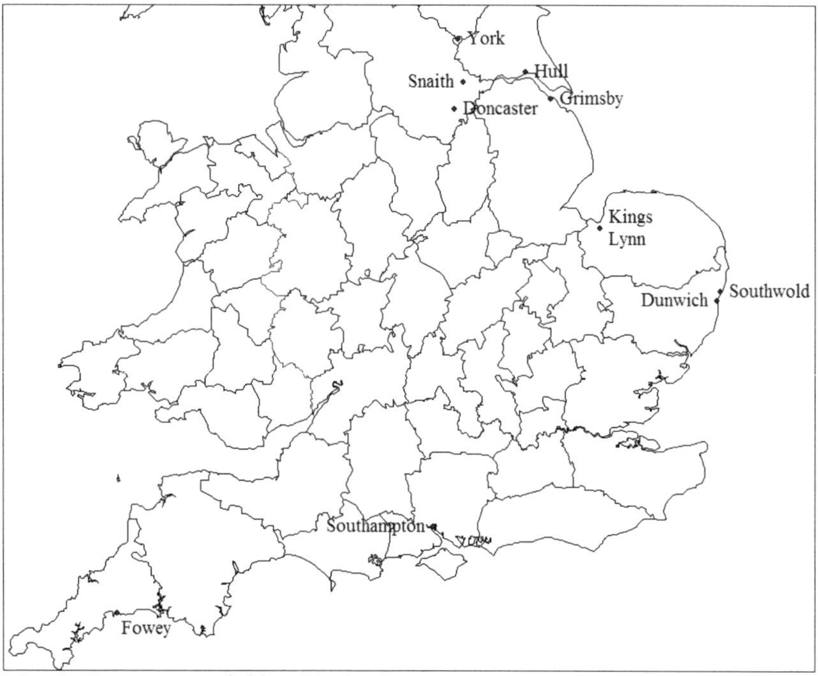

Map 2: Home ports of ships: England

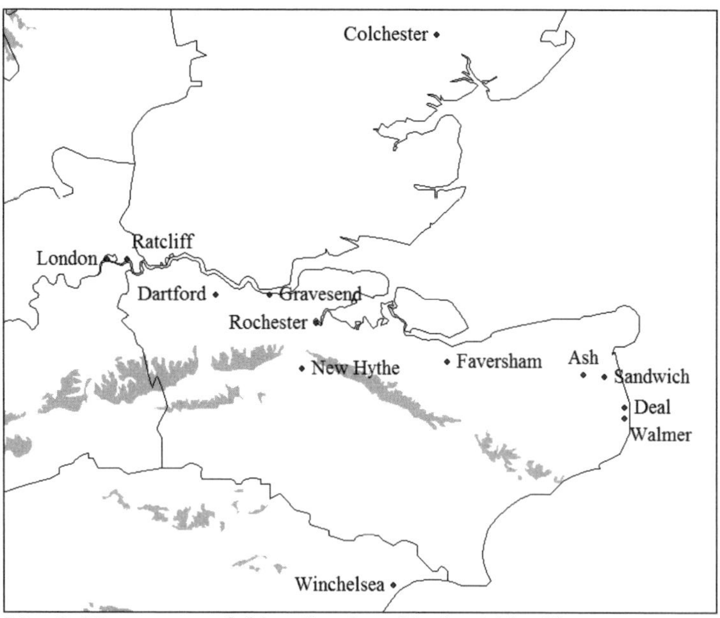

Map 3: Home ports of ships: Southern England (detail)

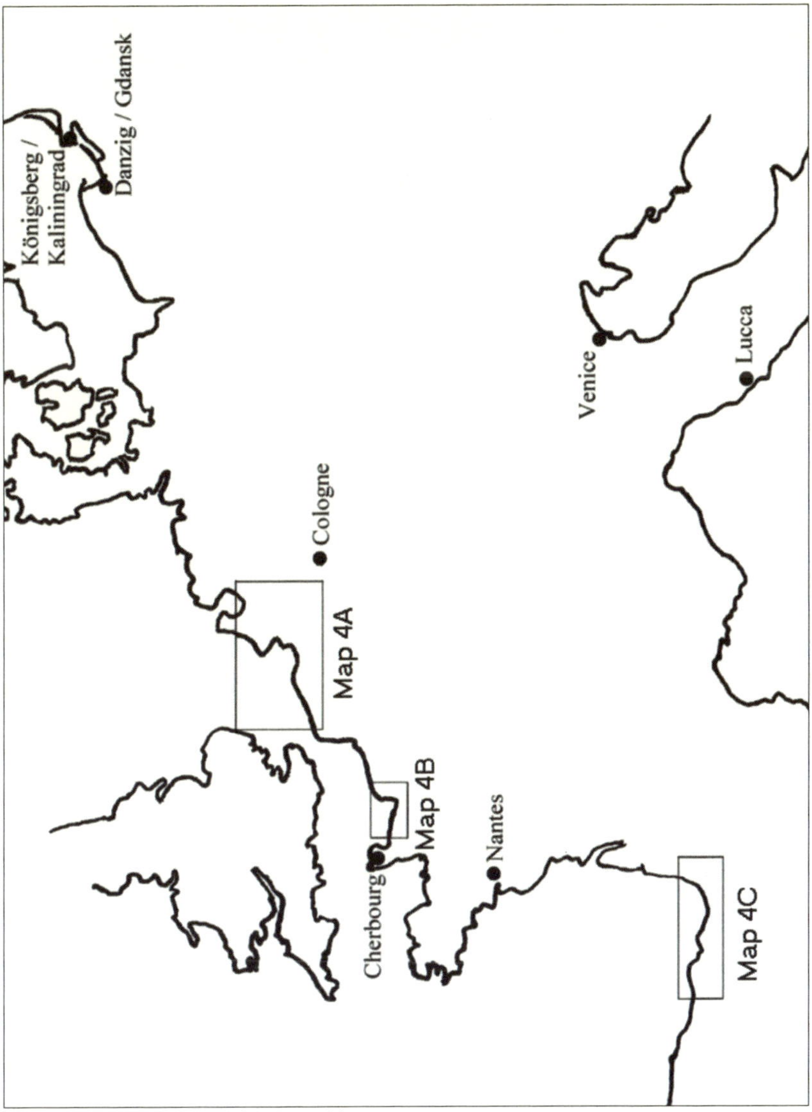

Map 4: Home ports of foreign ships

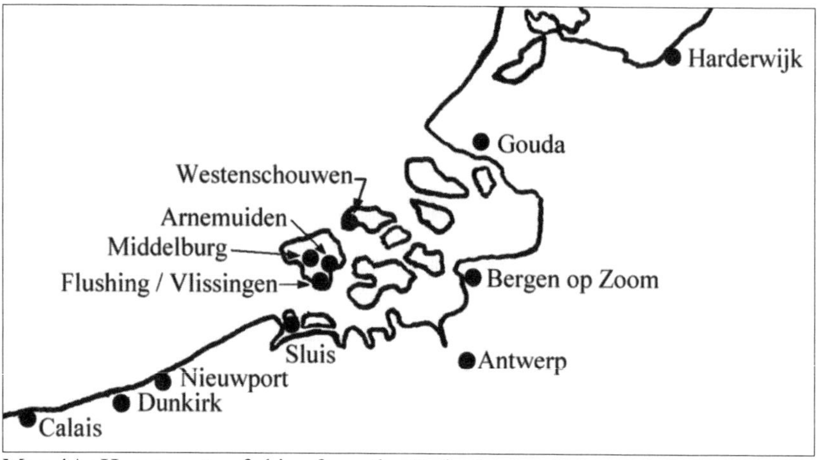

Map 4A: Home ports of ships from the Netherlands

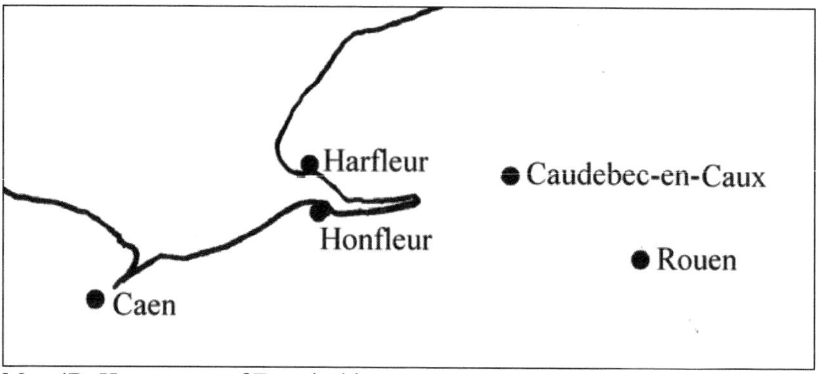

Map 4B: Home ports of French ships

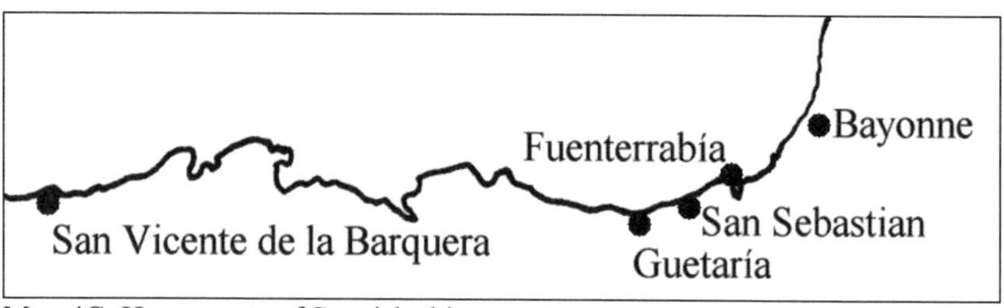

Map 4C: Home ports of Spanish ships

The words "masterly" and "seminal" are much over-used: in this instance they barely do justice to Stuart Jenks's work on the London customs. This edition is likely to become the gold standard by which others are measured. It includes not just details of merchants shipping and commodities traded, but also the auditors' notes that help explain process, and the textual variants that are so useful to linguists. But Jenks provides far more than an edition of all surviving customs accounts for one year for the most important port in the realm. He uses this as a foundation for a ground-breaking study of the operation of the late medieval Exchequer, and of an important source of Crown finance. His painstaking explanations of the details of process, and of the interrelationships of Exchequer officers and discrete record series, can be extended to studies of other aspects of the operation of the English state. Above this, Jenks' transcriptions provide a formulary of administrative texts, plugging a gap in that genre, which is so often weighted to the fourteenth century and earlier. To produce a text of these documents is an achievement in itself. To ask "How did the Crown Pay?" (and to show how the Crown was paid) is courageous. But to demonstrate so convincingly just why these documents matter is the work of a master.

Margaret Condon, formerly an assistant keeper, Public Record Office